CONNECTICUT'S MILITARY HEROES

MEDAL OF HONOR RECÍPIENTS

THE STORIES OF THE LIFE AND SERVICE OF

THOSE WITH A CONNECTION TO CONNECTICUT

WHO WERE AWARDED THE MEDAL OF HONOR

CONNECTICUT'S MILITARY HEROES

MEDAL OF HONOR RECIPIENTS

THE STORIES OF THE LIFE AND SERVICE OF

THOSE WITH A CONNECTION TO CONNECTICUT

WHO WERE AWARDED THE MEDAL OF HONOR

FIRST EDITION

"To Know Them, So We Don't Forget Them"

Connecticut's Military Heroes: Medal of Honor Recipients
First Edition

ISBN: 9798853370173
Imprint: Independently Published
MHID: None

OTHER BOOKS IN THE SERIES
Connecticut: Pearl Harbor Heroes
Connecticut: Battle of Iwo Jima
Norwalk: World War I
Norwalk: World War I Women
Norwalk: World War II
Norwalk: Korean War
Norwalk: Vietnam War

If any city, town, or municipality is interested in similar books to honor their war dead or a military-related event, please contact the author at jeffrey.r.dewitt@gmail.com.

About the Author

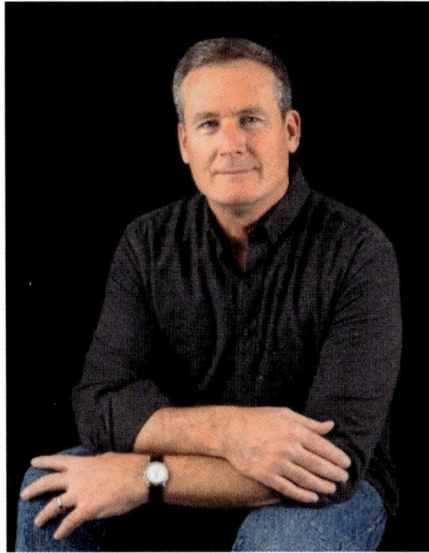

Jeffrey DeWitt is a 26-year United States Air Force veteran who retired in the rank of Chief Master Sergeant, the top 1% of all enlisted grades. His medals include the Meritorious Service Medal with 4 oak leaf clusters, Air Force Commendation Medal with 3 oak leaf clusters, Air Force Outstanding Unit Award with 6 oak leaf clusters, Air Force Good Conduct Medal with 7 oak leaf clusters, National Defense Service Medal with 1 star, Iraq Campaign Medal, Global War on Terrorism Service Medal, Korean Defense Service Medal, Humanitarian Service Medal, and the Air Force Expeditionary Service Ribbon with Gold Border.

He is a member of the Board of Directors and Historian for the Iwo Jima Memorial Historical Foundation based in Connecticut. For his work for the foundation, he was selected for the 2022 Veterans Public Service Award For Excellence from Central Connecticut State University. Born and raised in Norwalk, Connecticut, he has researched countless veterans and their stories, focusing on those who died during wartime service.

He is a life member of the American Legion. He has served in various roles for Frank C. Godfrey American Legion Post 12 in Norwalk. He is also a legacy life member of the Veterans of Foreign Wars. He has been the Quartermaster for Mulvoy - Tarlov - Aquino VFW Post 603 in Norwalk since 2018. He has served in various VFW positions in two states at the post and district levels.

"THERE IS NO GREATER HONOR THAN THE OPPORTUNITY TO SERVE AND HELP PRESERVE OUR FREEDOM – IT'S THE ESSENCE OF HUMANITY."

-- JAMES LIVINGSTON, MARINE CORPS, VIETNAM

TABLE OF CONTENTS

FOREWORD

I began thinking about writing this book in 2018. Since then, my priorities were constantly reshuffled by life and deadlines until early 2023, when I finally could sink my teeth into the project. The subjects on the pages of this book are exceptional. Roughly forty million people have served in the Armed Forces, and the medal has been awarded to only 3,517 people or 0.00009 percent. Their heroism in the face of what the average citizen may have seen as impossible circumstances was enough to warrant the unique distinction as a recipient.

In researching the heroes in this book, I came across many instances of newspaper reporters writing about how a recipient "won" the Medal of Honor. I have a hunch that if you ask a recipient if they feel like they _won_ anything, the answer would be an emphatic "no." Many of them were ordinary people who displayed extraordinary bravery and heroism. If you drilled down into each recipient's journey, they likely had that 'something' that can't be taught. "Doing the right thing" is too simplistic. These soldiers, sailors, airmen, and marines were well-trained instruments of national defense of the United States and performed heroic deeds.

Regrettably, some recipients were awarded the medal posthumously. While many have made the ultimate sacrifice and later were awarded the Medal of Honor for their heroism and sacrifice, posthumous awards make up less than 20% of the medals. There weren't any parades or fanfare for their accomplishments. Instead, cities named streets, schools, veteran organizations, and more so their legacy would live forever. It's these recipients that I hold in the highest regard.

I could have scaled back this book and only included recipients whose medals were accredited to Connecticut. To have a full accounting of recipients, I wanted to include all of them who had a connection to Connecticut. Some were born in Connecticut and died elsewhere. Others were born elsewhere but died in Connecticut. Two recipients received the medal based on an event that happened in Connecticut. They all deserve a spot in the book.

This book is a tribute to those from Connecticut who received the highest military honor. The primary intent of the author is for schools throughout the state and beyond to use the book as a teaching tool so future generations of Connecticut residents can better understand what service and sacrifice look like. A secondary intent is to keep the heroes in these pages alive by telling their stories.

Many thanks to the Congressional Medal of Honor Society and Laura S. Jowdy, the Director of Archives, Collections & Museum. Also, historical societies, libraries, cemeteries, and families of some of the recipients. It's an honor to be able to bring the stories of these heroes to life. They are more than deserving of the public's gratitude and appreciation.

May the stories of these heroes resonate with you. I hope their service and sacrifice are shared in your homes and schools. As a nation, we all need to preserve their legacy in a meaningful way so future generations will continue to honor them.

Please forward any recommended edits to jeffrey.r.dewitt@gmail.com.

"THEY SAID WE WERE SOFT, THAT WE WOULD NOT FIGHT, THAT WE COULD NOT WIN. WE ARE NOT A WARLIKE NATION. WE DO NOT GO TO WAR FOR GAIN OR FOR TERRITORY; WE GO TO WAR FOR PRINCIPLES, AND WE PRODUCE YOUNG MEN LIKE THESE. I THINK I TOLD EVERY ONE OF THEM THAT I WOULD RATHER HAVE THAT MEDAL, THE CONGRESSIONAL MEDAL OF HONOR, THAN TO BE PRESIDENT OF THE UNITED STATES."

-- PRESIDENT HARRY S. TRUMAN

THE MEDAL

Significance

The Medal of Honor is the highest award for bravery for any individual serving in the Armed Forces of the United States of America. Since its inception in 1861, approximately 3,500 Medals have been authorized and bestowed.

The Medal of Honor is awarded for a deed of personal bravery or self-sacrifice above and beyond the call of duty while the person, as a member of the Armed Forces, is in action against an enemy of the United States or is engaged in military operations involving conflict with an opposing foreign force, or is serving with friendly foreign forces engaged in armed conflict against an opposing armed force in which the United States is not a belligerent party.

The deed must be proved by incontestable evidence of at least two eyewitnesses. It must be so outstanding that it clearly distinguishes gallantry beyond the call of duty from lesser forms of bravery. It must involve the risk of his life. Each Armed Force's service regulation permits no margin of doubt or error for judging whether a person is entitled to the Medal of Honor.

It is presented by the President or by a high official "in the name of the Congress of the United States." thus being referred to as the Congressional Medal of Honor. The Congressional Medal of Honor Society was chartered by the 85th Congress and signed into law by President Eisenhower in 1958.

The fate of nations often hangs in the balance during great battles. These battles themselves often turn upon the actions of great men or a single towering and heroic individual. A grateful nation recognizes, salutes, and memorializes the deeds of Medal of Honor recipients.

History

The first formal system for rewarding acts of individual gallantry by the nation's military was established by General George Washington on August 7, 1782. Designed to recognize "any singularly meritorious action," the award consisted of a purple cloth heart. Records show that only four people received the award. They are Sergeant Elijah Churchill (1755-1841), born in Florida, New York; Sergeant William Brown (1761-1804), born in Stamford, Connecticut; Sergeant Daniel Bissel, Jr. (1754-1824), born in Windsor, Connecticut; and * Corporal Samuel Jackson (1759-1843) born in Bethlehem, Connecticut.

* = Corporal Jackson was added at the advice of Michael H. Bird, Sons of the American Revolution (SAR).

The Badge of Military Merit, as it was called, fell into oblivion until 1932, when General Douglas MacArthur, then Army Chief of Staff, pressed for its revival. Officially reinstituted on February 22, 1932, the now familiar Purple Heart was at first an Army award given to those who had been wounded in World War I or who possessed a Meritorious Service Citation Certificate. In 1943, the order was amended to include Navy, Marine Corps, and Coast Guard personnel. Coverage was eventually extended to include all services and "any civilian national" wounded while serving with the Armed Forces.

Although the Badge of Military Merit fell into disuse after the Revolutionary War, the idea of a decoration for individual gallantry remained through the early 1800s. In 1847, after the outbreak of the Mexican-American War, a "certificate of merit" was established for any soldier who distinguished himself in action. No medal went with the honor. After the Mexican-American War, the award was discontinued, meaning there was no military award to recognize the nation's fighting men.

Early in the U.S. Civil War, a medal for individual valor was proposed to General-in-Chief of the Army Winfield Scott. But Scott felt medals were rooted in European affectation and pretense, so he killed the idea.

The medal found support in the Navy, however, where it was felt recognition of courage in strife was needed. Public Resolution 82, containing a provision for a Navy Medal of Valor, was signed into law by President Abraham Lincoln on December 21, 1861. The medal was "to be bestowed upon such petty officers, seamen, landsmen, and Marines as shall most distinguish themselves by their gallantry and other seamanlike qualities during the present war."

1886 US Navy Medal of Honor, courtesy of the US Naval History and Heritage Command

Shortly after this, a resolution similar in wording was introduced on behalf of the Army. Signed into law July 12, 1862, the measure provided for awarding a Medal of Honor "to such noncommissioned officers and privates as shall most distinguish themselves by their gallantry in action, and other soldierlike qualities, during the present insurrection." Although it was created for the Civil War, Congress made the Medal of Honor a permanent decoration in 1863. *(American Forces Information Service pamphlet)*

Since then, the medal has undergone numerous legislative, design, and presentation changes while still retaining what makes it truly special – its status as the United States' highest award for military valor in action.

In July 2021, the House of Representatives reached a united front by voting unanimously for the National Medal of Honor Monument Act. In December 2021, the Senate followed suit and unanimously authorized the National Medal of Honor Monument Act. Finally, on December 27, 2021, the President of the United States officially signed the National Medal of Honor Monument Act. In addition, the National Medal of Honor Institute, embedded in the National Medal of Honor Museum in Arlington, Texas, will open in the Fall/Winter of 2024.

Wearing the medal

Though it was not uncommon for Medals of Honor to continue to be pinned to a soldier's tunic during World War II, the practice of draping it around a recipient's neck became increasingly used. For this purpose, the modern Medal of Honor was suspended from an 8-sided "pad" bearing 13 white stars, to which the blue silk neck ribbon was attached. The Medal of Honor is the only United States Military Award that is worn around the neck rather than pinned to the uniform.

On May 2, 1895, Congress authorized "a rosette or knot to be worn in lieu of the medal and a ribbon to be worn with the medal." Today's Medal of Honor Ribbon is blue with five stars, two at the top and three at the bottom. One of the most common mistakes people make when displaying Medal of Honor graphics is to display the ribbon upside down. The six-sided blue silk rosette bears 13 stars and is worn on civilian attire. Medal of Honor recipients also wear the Medal itself around the neck of civilian attire for special occasions.

DETAILS

Recipients by Conflict

1,523 – Civil War *(43% of all medals)*
426 – Indian Campaigns
15 – Korean Campaign of 1871
110 – Spanish-American War
4 – Samoa Campaign
80 – Philippine Insurrection
6 – Action against outlaws in the Philippines in 1911
59 – China Relief Expedition (Boxer Rebellion)
56 – Mexican Campaign (Vera Cruz)
6 – Haitian Campaign of 1915
3 – Dominican Campaign
126 – World War I
2 – Haitian Campaign of 1919-1920
2 – Second Nicaraguan Campaign
472 – World War II
146 – Korean War
268 – Vietnam War
2 – Somalia (Operation Restore Hope)
20 – War on Terrorism (Afghanistan)
8 – War on Terrorism (Iraq)
193 – Non Combat
9 – Unknown
TOTAL: 3,536 to 3,517 recipients

Recipients by Branch Of Service

1 - U.S. Coast Guard
19 - U.S. Air Force
300 - U.S. Marine Corps
749 - U.S. Navy
2,452 - U.S. Army
TOTAL: 3,521

"MEDIOCRITY AND FAILURE RESULT FROM CHOICE, NOT CHANCE. SUCCESS IS BORN OF COURAGE ALONE AND GOD HAS MADE THIS MARVELOUS GIFT INFINITELY AVAILABLE TO ALL WHO ASK FOR IT."

-- PATRICK H. BRADY, ARMY, VIETNAM

MEDAL OF HONOR INTERESTING FACTS

Correct Title

The correct title for the award, often called the "Congressional Medal of Honor," is simply "Medal of Honor," and the people who have received it prefer to be called "Recipients" (of the award), not "winners." It is the only United States Military Award that is worn from a ribbon hung around the neck and the only award presented "By the President In the Name of the Congress."

Father and Son Recipients

1st Lieutenant Arthur MacArthur (Civil War) and General Douglas MacArthur (WWII) were the only father and sons in history to each receive a Medal of Honor until the January 16, 2000 presentation of the Medal of Honor to Theodore Roosevelt. The award has been presented to 5 sets of brothers.

A Female Award Recipient

Only one woman, Dr. Mary Edwards Walker (Civil War), has received the Medal of Honor. However, an additional woman's name is on the Roll of Honor. During the Vietnam War, Marine Captain Jay R. Vargas received the Medal of Honor. Before his award could be presented to him, his mother passed away at home in Arizona. Vargas requested that his mother's name be engraved on the back of his Medal of Honor instead of his own. President Nixon honored that loving request and the name of M. Sando Vargas...Jay Vargas' mother was added to the Honor Roll.

Mary Walker. Photo courtesy of the National Archives, photo no. LC-DIG-ppmsca-72705.

Mary Walker. Photo courtesy of the Library of Congress.

A President Receives the Award

Theodore Roosevelt was the only President to receive the Medal of Honor. The sons of two Presidents have received Medals of Honor: Webb Cook Hayes (Philippine Insurrection) and Theodore Roosevelt, Jr. (World War II).

AUTHOR NOTE: Although countless pages have documented the Rough Riders in Cuba, the Medal of Honor issue for Roosevelt has been largely ignored in print. Even two of Roosevelt's own publications, *The Rough Riders*, and *An Autobiography*, fail to mention in the narrative his desire for the award. Many War Department documents and Roosevelt's published letters clearly state his argument that "I am entitled to the Medal of Honor, and I want it." Theodore Roosevelt's Medal of Honor was presented on January 16, 2001, in The White House (Roosevelt Room). President William J. Clinton presented it to Tweed Roosevelt and his family. Theodore Roosevelt's son, Brigadier General Theodore Roosevelt, Jr., received the Medal of Honor posthumously for "gallantry and intrepidity at the risk of his life above and beyond the call of duty on 6 June 1944 [D-Day], in France. *(archives.org and cmohs.org)*

Andrew's Raiders

Secretary of War Edwin Stanton awarded the first Medal of Honor ever presented on March 25, 1863, to 19-year-old Ohio Army Private Jacob Parrott. Parrott was a member of Andrew's Raiders, immortalized in the movie "The Great Locomotive Chase." Eventually, Parrott's 18 fellow soldiers from that mission received Medals of Honor, 4 of them posthumously. All 19 of these heroes are from Ohio. As a civilian, James Andrews himself was not eligible for the Medal of Honor.

Youngest and Oldest Recipients

The youngest person to receive the Medal of Honor was probably William "Willie" Johnston, who earned the Medal during the Civil War just before his 12th birthday and received his award six weeks after his 13th.

General Douglas MacArthur was the oldest Medal of Honor recipient. He was 62 years old when he received the Medal.

World War II hero Jack Lucas became the youngest man in the 20th century to receive the award when he threw his body over two grenades at Iwo Jima just five days after his 17th birthday. At the time of his heroism, he had already been in the Marine Corps for three years.

Last Vietnam War Recipient

The Vietnam War's last Medal of Honor action occurred on Halloween night in 1972 when Navy SEAL Michael E. Thornton risked his own life to rescue his wounded team leader. His team leader, Navy Lieutenant Thomas R. Norris, had been submitted for the Medal of Honor for his own heroic actions just six months earlier. Thornton was the first person in more than a century to receive that honor for saving the life of another Medal of Honor recipient. Norris did not receive his award until March 6, 1976. The movie BAT 21 is based on the rescue mission that Halloween night in Vietnam.

A Strong Bond

The brotherhood of Medal recipients is strong and generates many long-lasting friendships. Private Jacob Parrott, the first person ever to be presented with the Medal of Honor, maintained such a close friendship with fellow "Raider" Wilson W. Brown (one of the two men who engineered The General in the "Great Locomotive Chase"), that their children became more than friends. Parrott's only son, John Marion Parrott, married Edith Gertrude Brown, one of Wilson Brown's eight children.

Is It Illegal to Wear Someone Else's Medal of Honor?

Yes, wearing someone else's Medal of Honor is illegal, but it is not illegal to pretend you have one. United States criminal law (Public Law No: 109-437) forbids the unauthorized wearing, manufacture, and sale of military decorations, and misuse of a Medal of Honor carries a particularly heavy penalty. The offender shall be fined under PL 109-437, imprisoned not more than one year, or both.

In 2006, President George W. Bush signed into law the Stolen Valor Act of 2005, which imposed a prison sentence of up to one year on anyone falsely claiming to have received a Medal of Honor. (Pretenders to other military decorations faced imprisonment for up to six months.) The Supreme Court struck down the act on June 28, 2012, ruling that it violated the right to free speech guaranteed by the First Amendment.

Congress passed an amendment in 2013 to make it a crime for a person intending to obtain money, property, or other tangible benefits to fraudulently hold oneself out to receive certain medals.

Courtesy of Home of Heroes; used with permission.

Double Medal of Honor Awards

1. Gunnery Sergeant Charles F. Hoffman
2. Sergeant Louis Cukela
3. Sergeant Matej Kocak
4. Private John Joseph Kelly
5. Corporal John Henry Pruitt
6. Second Lieutenant Thomas Ward Custer [General George Custer's brother]
7. Private Henry Hogan
8. Sergeant William Wilson
9. Ordinary Seaman Robert A. Sweeney
10. Captain/MT Albert Weisbogel
11. Captain H. Lewis William
12. Watertender John King
13. Franklin Dwight Baldwin
14. John Cooper
15. John Lafferty
16. Patrick Mullen
17. Daniel Joseph Daly
18. John McCloy
19. Smedley Darlington Butler

During World War I, a total of 8 Marines received Medals of Honor. Two were Marine aviators of the 1st Marine Aviation Force. The remaining six were members of the 5th and 6th Regiments of the 2nd Division, working closely with their Army counterparts. Five of the six received both the Army and Navy Medals of Honor for the same deed, with a separate citation from each branch of service. The eight recipients listed chronologically are:

1. GySgt Ernest A. Janson, for actions on June 6, 1918, near Château-Thierry, France
2. GySgt Fred W. Stockham, for actions on June 13 & 14, 1918, in Bois-de-Belleau, France [1]
3. Sgt Louis Cukela, for actions on July 18, 1918, near Villers-Cotterêts, France
4. Sgt Matej Kocak, for actions on July 18, 1918, south of Soissons, France [2]
5. Private John J. Kelly, for actions on October 3, 1918, near Blanc Mont Ridge, France
6. Corp John H. Pruitt, for actions on October 3, 1918, near Blanc Mont Ridge, France [3]
7. GySgt Robert G. Robinson, for actions on October 8 & 14, 1918, over Pittem, Belgium
8. 2nd Lieutenant Ralph Talbot, for actions on October 8 & 14, 1918, over Pittem, Belgium [4]

FOOTNOTES TO THE PREVIOUS LIST
1. GySgt Stockham was awarded the medal posthumously
2. Sgt Kocak was killed in action near Thiaucourt, France, on October 4, 1918
3. Corp Pruitt was awarded the medal posthumously
4. Lt Talbot died on October 25, 1918, when his DH-4 crashed on

The remaining 14 heroes received two awards for two separate actions. The military incidents were prior to World War I.

Since the reviews and changes of 1917, the laws governing the award of the Medal of Honor have ended all double awards of the Medal of Honor. A soldier may be nominated repeatedly for the Medal of Honor. During the Vietnam War, Special Forces hero Robert Lewis Howard was the most highly decorated officer of the Vietnam United States Army Special Forces. He was submitted for the Medal of Honor three times before he was finally awarded the Medal. He was nominated for the Medal of Honor three times over 13 months. Still, he received lesser medals for the first two nominations for actions performed in Cambodia, where the U.S. was fighting covertly. He was awarded the Medal of Honor for his actions on December 30, 1968, his third nomination.

The states and town with the most recipients

1. New York: 676
2. Pennsylvania: 380
3. Massachusetts: 264
4. Ohio: 253
5. Illinois: 208

Weymouth, Massachusetts, is home to five Congressional Medal of Honor recipients. It is the only town in the United States to hold that distinction. The recipients are:

1. Quartermaster, Thomas W. Hamilton (1833-1869); Navy, Civil War, 1863
2. Ordinary Seaman William Seach (1877-1978), Navy, China Relief, 1900
3. 2nd Lieutenant Ralph Talbot (1897-1918), World War I, 1918
4. Private Elden H. Johnson (1921-1944), Army, World War II, 1944
5. Private First Class, Frederick C. Murphy (1918-1945), Army, 1945

What can you do?

Each year, March 25th marks Medal of Honor Day, a date set aside to recognize those who have been awarded the United States' highest military decoration for valor in action against enemy forces. Citizens should honor these Medal of Honor recipients on this day and every day for their courageous acts of bravery and service.

CURRENT DESIGN

Since its creation during the American Civil War, the Medal of Honor has undergone several design changes. The U.S. Army and U.S. Navy have always had different designs for their personnel. Until the U.S. Air Force introduced its design in 1965, all airmen received the Army design. The U.S. Marine Corps and U.S. Coast Guard receive the U.S. Navy design.

What follows are images that illustrate the design of the three styles of the Medal of Honor representing the Army, Navy, and Air Force. The original designs were worn on the lapel of a recipient. Today, the Medal of Honor is the only U.S. Military medal that hangs around the neck.

"WHEN SOMETHING NEEDS TO BE DONE, PUSH AHEAD AND OVERCOME ALL OBSTACLES – THERE IS ALWAYS A WAY."

-- JAY ZEAMER, JR., ARMY, WORLD WAR II

Army

The current U.S. Army Medal of Honor is a five-pointed bronze star. Each point is tipped with trefoils, and a green laurel wreath surrounds the entire star to symbolize victory. The star and wreath are suspended from a gold bar with 'VALOR' inscribed and held by an eagle to symbolize the United States. The star's center features the head of Minerva, the Roman goddess of wisdom and war. Around Minerva's head are the words "United States of America," and each star ray has a green oak leaf, symbolizing strength. The circular wreath of laurel leaves, a symbol of victory, was added in 1904. On the opposite side, the medal is engraved 'The Congress to [Recipient's Name].' The medal is comprised of metal, red brass, and gold plating.

"MY MEDAL OF HONOR SHOULD BE SHARED
WITH ALL MY SHIPMATES."

-- RICHARD M. MCCOOL., NAVY, WORLD WAR II

Navy

The Navy version of the Medal of Honor is described as a five-pointed bronze star, each tipped with trefoils containing a crown of laurel and oak. The Roman Goddess of Wisdom and War is in the middle of the medal, Minerva. She is depicted warding off a man clutching snakes in his hand to symbolize wisdom and war and personify the United States. She stands with her left hand resting on the fasces, or a bundle of rods, and her right hand holding a shield with the coat of arms of the United States blazoned on it. The shield in Minerva's right hand is representative of the Union of our States, while the bundle of rods and axe blade in her left symbolizes authority. The owl perched on her helmet is a symbol of wisdom. Minerva repulses discord, which is represented by snakes and is appropriate in the context of the Civil War's discord. Clusters of laurel and oak leaves on each star's five points represent victory and strength. The 34 stars encircling the insignia equal the number of stars on the U.S. Flag in 1862. Each star represents a state from both Union and Confederate states. The Navy Medal of Honor is made of solid red brass.

"GO WITH HONOR, RETURN WITH HONOR. THAT IS AMERICA IN ACTION."

-- GEORGE E. "BUD" DAY, AIR FORCE, VIETNAM

Air Force

In 1965, the new Air Force Medal appeared. This medal is more distinct in its design when compared to the U.S. Army and U.S. Navy Medals of Honor. It is 50% larger than the other medals, and the current design includes a gold five-pointed star within a green laurel wreath. The wreath of laurel leaves, a symbol of victory, was carried over from the Army's Medal of Honor design. Each point of the star is tipped with trefoils and contains a crown of laurel and oak on a green background. In the center of the star and the medal is an annulet of 34 stars circling the head of the Statue of Liberty to represent the number of stars on the U.S. flag in 1862, as well as beauty, strength, and wisdom. This medal replaced Minerva with the Statue of Liberty, wearing a pointed crown instead of a helmet. While she stands for liberty, she is derived from the imagery of Semiramis, wife of Nimrod and Queen of Babylon. The mythical Semiramis, who may have been loosely based on a historical figure, was famed for beauty, strength, and wisdom and was said to have built the famous Hanging Gardens of Babylon and reigned for 42 years. The word VALOR is above an adaption of the thunderbolt from the Air Force Coat of Arms. This medal is made of metal, bronze, and gold plating.

For the State of Connecticut and beyond.

BRIGADIER GENERAL JOHN BRECKINRIDGE BABCOCK; ARMY

February 7, 1843 (New Orleans, LA) – April 26, 1909 (* at sea); 66 years old

Married Blandina P. Stanton (1850-1917) on May 18, 1875, in Stonington, Connecticut.

Three sons, Conrad S. [Brigadier General, Army] (1876-1950), John F. (1879-1911), and Franklin [Brigadier General, Army] (1885-1972).

Enlisted on May 29, 1862, in New York City.

Retired from the Army in 1903.

* General Babcock died of Bright's Disease while aboard the SS Prinz Friedrich Wilhelm. He was returning from a vacation in Europe with his wife and son.

Born to Giles Sr. (1808-1862) and Ann E. Denison Babcock (1814-1890). Five brothers, Giles (1834-1834), Samuel F.D. (1835-1836), Giles Jr. (1843-1931), Nathaniel P. (1851-1928), and Stephen T. (1854-1890). Three sisters, Anna D. Babcock Wood (1837-1907), Mary Babcock Williams (1846-1911), and Lucy B. Babcock Stanton (1849-1928).

Photo courtesy of Ancestry.com

MEDAL OF HONOR CITATION

AWARDED FOR ACTIONS DURING: Indian Campaigns
BRANCH OF SERVICE: Army
UNIT: 5th U.S. Cavalry
DATE OF ISSUE AND PRESENTATION: September 18, 1897 (28 years later)
AGE ON THE DAY OF THE EVENT: 26
CITATION:

The President of the United States of America, in the name of Congress, takes pleasure in presenting the Medal of Honor to First Lieutenant (Cavalry) John Breckinridge Babcock, United States Army, for extraordinary heroism on 16 May 1869, while serving with 5th U.S. Cavalry, in action at Spring Creek, Nebraska. While serving with a scouting column, First Lieutenant Babcock's troop was attacked by a vastly superior force of Indians. Advancing to high ground, he dismounted his men, remaining mounted himself to encourage them, and there fought the Indians until relieved, his horse being wounded.

From the Salina [Kansas] Sun April 10, 1909

WASHINGTON – For two consecutive sessions, a bill has been before Congress to give Brigadier General Frank D. Baldwin, United States Army (Retired), the rank of Major General. Someday, perhaps, the bill will become law, for it is worthy of passage, as Baldwin is worthy of honor. The home of this retired officer at present is in Colorado, though he comes to Washington occasionally to live over old days with comrade veterans, many of whom have chosen the nation's capital for their homes.

It is rare that one can get General Baldwin to speak of his services in the Army, but his friends are not slow in speaking for him, and every word that they say in praise is borne out by the records which are hidden away in the War Department.

Frank D. Baldwin has been in so many fights for his country that the counting of them assumes the proportion of a mathematical problem. For years upon years after the Civil War, in which he distinguished himself time and again, he fought nearly every form of Indian that the plains of the United States have produced. There was one fight in which Baldwin was engaged, which deserves a place in song and story if some song or story writer could be found equal to the occasion. In the days of the campaign of which this fight was a feature, there was only one bar on Baldwin's shoulder, for he was a junior First Lieutenant of infantry. The campaign was a long one, and the fights followed fast and followed faster.

While on detached service in Newport, Kentucky, in June 1874, Baldwin heard that his regiment was to be ordered, under Colonel Nelson A. Miles, to make an expedition into the Indian territory. The lieutenant went to the front as fast as a train and a horse could carry him. When he reported for duty, Miles, who knew Baldwin's record in the Civil War, put him in command of the scouts of the expedition, a command that was composed partly of whites and partly of Indians.

With his scouts in back of him, Lieutenant Baldwin had a dozen engagements, one after another, with the confederated bands of Cheyennes, Kiowas, Arapahoes, and the southern Comanches. The one fight, however, which for picturesqueness stands out most prominently in the battle list, did not take place until after Baldwin had been in the field for many months. It was the fight of his life, not in the engagement's size nor yet, perhaps, in its importance, but in what an officer who saw it declares to have been "its howlingly funny features."

It was picturesque, and it was funny all right, but it was dangerous as well, and Baldwin lost some of his men and took his own life in his hands 20 times before he won his splendid victory against tremendous odds. The daring of the thing was recognized by Colonel Miles, by the general commanding the department, and by the Congress of the United States, which gave Baldwin his second Medal of Honor for his work on that day.

By one of the military freaks of fortune, Baldwin, although only a lieutenant, found himself in November 1874 in command of D Company of the Fifth Infantry, D troop of the Sixth Cavalry, and of 12 of the scouts of the organization with which he had originally taken the field. He had about 100 men all told when he reached the banks of McClellan's Creek, Texas. There, he found in front of him fully 500 Indian warriors splendidly armed and apparently lusting for a fight. Every army officer who afterward learned the circumstances of the situation declared that Baldwin would have been justified in waiting for reinforcements, but Baldwin believed that he should strike at once and strike hard.

The Indians. a mixed command of the finest fighting savages on the plains, were led by Chief Gray Beard, a noted warrior. Baldwin learned that the Indians had with them two white girl captives, and his desire to rescue them reinforced his desire for a fight on general principles.

The lieutenant looked his men over and saw that they had a stomach for the coming scrimmage. With the command of four six-mule teams, Baldwin feared that a detachment of the reds might flank him when he was making his charge, kill his mules, and destroy his field necessities. He knew he could not leave a detachment to guard the wagons because it would weaken his force to a point which would make victory over the reds practically impossible.

Baldwin went to the teamsters and said: "I can't leave a force with you as a guard, and you've got to charge with us. I want you to put your teams in the center of the charging line and make those mules fly straight into the middle of things."

It probably was the first time in history that mule drivers, mules, and wagons had been ordered to participate as an offensive part of a cavalry charge. The infantry, on this occasion, was mounted. The mule drivers lost all sense of the danger in the fun of the thing. They told the lieutenant that with "good cussing" and with good lashing, they could lead the cavalry a mile.

The 500 Indians were on a plateau with sides shelving gradually down to the plains. Baldwin's plan was nothing less than the seemingly reckless one of crossing the open with his men and wagons, sweeping up the incline and driving the enemy, if he could, or fighting him hand to hand, if he must.

The horsemen rode up in line with the four mule teams abreast at the line's center. There was a word of command, a trumpet note or two, and the line swept across the plain with the mules on a keen jump, with black snake whips cracking and the drivers saying things that a mule understands.

The reds turned loose at the advancing hundred. Men and horses on the right and left went down here and there, but the mules in the center, with their huge wagons racking and clattering behind them, swept on with never a scratch. The reds on the plateau kept up their fusillade. Up, up, up the incline, the mules leading by yards all the way swept the blue detachment. The regulars were daring and fighting as American regulars always dare and fight.

One of the teamsters afterward swore that he could see Chief Gray Beard's eyes popping with fear at the sight of the charging mules. The level of the plateau was reached, and horses, men, mules, and wagons went hurtling forward. The teamsters were standing, cracking their whips, and howling. Infantrymen and cavalrymen caught the spirit of the thing and howled in unison.

Those four mule teams went straight through the heart of the big band of Gray Beard's Kiowas and Arapahoes. Meantime, every carbine, and every Long Tom was cracking, and with one last volley, the warriors of the allied tribes fled, leaving their dead and wounded and their white captives on the field.

Lieutenant Baldwin found that the two white girl prisoners were uninjured, and not long after the fight, they were restored to their parents. For this charge and for this victory, Lieutenant Baldwin was breveted a Captain and was given a Medal of Honor, but he always has maintained that the medal should have gone to the mules.

On the retired list of the army with General Baldwin is Brigadier General John B. Babcock, a close friend of the man who led the mule team charge and a frequent visitor to Washington. It is doubtful if General. Babcock's nearest neighbors in his little country home in Saratoga County, New York, suspect anything of the fire-eating possibilities that lie hidden in the person of this gray-haired, peaceful-looking, and reticent man.

Gen. Babcock left the service not long ago and at once departed for the little place in the foothills of the

Adirondack mountains where he might gratify his love of country life. If the general refuses to talk of his army achievements to his neighbors, and if they are curiously inclined, they might send for a government record, which, though only five lines long, contains in it the nub of the story of one of the most gallant feats ever performed by an officer of the United States Army.

The glory reaped from the achievement consists of a little bronze medal voted to the soldier by Congress, the consciousness of duty well done, and five lines in the war department record, which few people ever see. John B. Babcock went into the army at the outbreak of the Civil War as an enlisted man. He attracted attention by his gallantry as a volunteer, and the year 1868 found him a First Lieutenant of the Fifth Regular Cavalry.

In the spring of the fourth year of peace after the Civil War—that is to say, peace between white men – the Kiowas, the Arapahoes, and the Cheyennes made western Nebraska, western Kansas, and eastern Colorado a section of what John Hay might have called "gilt-edged hell." Lieutenant Babcock, in the absence of his captain, was ordered to the command of a troop of cavalry and to take the field.

With his trooper followers, Babcock was far in advance of the main command on the frontier of Nebraska. They reached the bank of Spring Creek on the morning of May 16, 1869. While there, a band of 250 of the best warriors of the plains appeared in front of the cavalry troops as though the savages had come from the ground. Lieutenant Babcock caught sight of the reds in time to give him a moment or two for preparation. He would not run, and he could not attack, for he was completely surrounded, and the savages outnumbered his force more than six to one.

Babcock gave a quick order and, with his men, dashed for a bit of high ground, a plateau-like formation with its flat surface occupying a little more than an acre. The instant he reached the place selected, he ordered his troopers to dismount and to entrench themselves as well as they could. The men lost no time in throwing up earth enough to give them some slight protection from the bullets which were pouring in.

Babcock would not get off his horse, although his men begged him to do so, and they were kept from dragging their commanding officer to the ground and to a place of partial safety only by instilled discipline and by Babcock's peremptory commands to leave him alone.

The Indians advanced within range and protected themselves in the hollows of the prairie. They sent volley after volley up the incline to the hilltop, and man after man behind the poor earthwork protection was stricken. Babcock continued his ride up and down the line. His blouse was cut twice by bullets, but his men did not know it.

"Boys, they can't hit a thing," said Babcock. They've been shooting at me, and no bullet has come nearer than the North Pole. Give it to 'em. Hold 'em off, and relief will be here in no time."

The shots from the Spencers and Henrys of the savages, or from most of them, ceased hitting the extemporized earthworks. The men lying prone knew that nearly all the projectiles were passing over their heads, and they knew also that every painted warrior antagonist was turning loose at the figure of the commanding officer riding back and forth on his horse as indifferently as if there were not an Indian on the frontier.

No one in that troop ever knew why Babcock was not killed. The Indians said afterward that he had some "big medicine" with him that turned away the bullets. Finally, a shot cut Babcock's boot and wounded his horse. He turned the animal about quickly so that its other flank was toward the men, to whom he serenely said: "Those fellows can't hit a barn door."

The commanding officer continued to ride up and down the line, and the bullets continued to cut the air all about him. Suddenly, every savage head showed at once. The troopers slammed in a volley that claimed some victims. The showing heads were followed by showing bodies, and in another instant, the warriors were erect and running to the far rear for their ponies. They made off, leaving their dead and wounded behind them. Far over the plains, Lieutenant Babcock, from his horse, saw the main column advancing. Relief was in sight.

The enlisted men told the story of Babcock's bravery, and Congress gave him a Medal of Honor. Later, the officer, who is now living in retirement, distinguished himself twice in action against the Apaches at Tonto Creek and at the Four Peaks in Arizona. There, he won the brevet rank of Lieutenant Colonel to add to the honor conferred by his Congressional medal of bronze.

From the New York Times April 28, 1909

GEN. JOHN B. BABCOCK IS DEAD
He Was a Gallant Indian Fighter and a Civil War Veteran

Brigadier General John Breckinridge Babcock, famous as an old Indian fighter and a veteran of the Civil War, died on Monday on the steamship Prinz Friederich Wilhelm, which arrived here from Bremen yesterday. Accompanied by Mrs. Babcock and their son Franklin, the General had been in Europe hoping that the trip might improve his health. He had long suffered from Brights's disease.

He was born in New Orleans, Louisiana, on February 7, 1847. At the age of 15, he became a Sergeant in the Thirty-seventh New York State Militia, rising in various New York regiments from that time to the end of the war. In 1865, he reached the rank of Major. He served under General Grant and General Sheridan and took part in the battles of Plain's Store, Port Hudson, Sabine Cross Roads, Pleasant Hill, Monnet's Bluff, Mansura Plains, and Yellow Bayou, all in Louisiana, and also in the siege of Petersburg and the campaign of General Sheridan in the Shenandoah Valley. For a number of years after the Civil War, he was almost constantly in the field against the Indians, fighting the Kiowas, Southern Cheyennes, Sioux, Apaches, and Utes.

For remarkable personal courage and daring, he received four brevets, those of First Lieutenant, Captain, Major, and Lieutenant Colonel. The last was for defeating a troop of Indians outnumbering his men six to one. In the Fall of 1879, in the famous Ute outbreak, Captain Babcock marched his troops 170 miles in sixty-five hours in time to relieve Major T.T. Thornburg's command and change the issue of the fight.

In 1885, he marched 600 miles to the protection of the Kansas border against the Indians. Several times, his horse was shot from under him, and once, he was shot in the breast with an arrow.

From the Norwich (Connecticut) Bulletin May 1, 1909

General John B. Babcock, who was buried in Stonington Thursday, had an excellent war record and was a Medal of Honor man. When a Major and assistant adjutant in charge of the military information bureau, he made an official visitation to the encampment of the Connecticut troops at Niantic and was the special guest of General George Haven, Brigade Commander and as Civil War veterans held campfires and recalled incidents of the dark days of the rebellion, together with Major George EL Albee of General Haven's staff. Major Albee, like General Babcock, was also an Indian fighter and Medal of Honor man and a commissioned officer of the regular army. Their recollections of the trials, hardships, perils, and pleasures of army life related in camp were vivid and interesting.

Being a Connecticut man, General Badcock was intensely interested in the state troops and, by reason of his careful inspection, came in contact with nearly all the commissioned officers and within the observation of the enlisted men. His soldiers' bearing and gentlemanly manners commanded the respect of every national guardsman in camp.

For nearly a quarter of a century, General Babcock was with the Fifth Cavalry, engaged with the Indians, and was an expert horseman. He tried almost every mount of the brigade staff and finally selected a New London horse as the best saddler in the outfit, not that the horse was really the best under saddle, but knock the deceit out of some officers who boasted of having "the best" and were eager as a matter of pride to have the regular army officer select their favorite animal as his mount. Although reserved, bordering on the austere, when not strictly on duty, he was decidedly companionable to the citizen soldiery of Connecticut fifteen years ago.

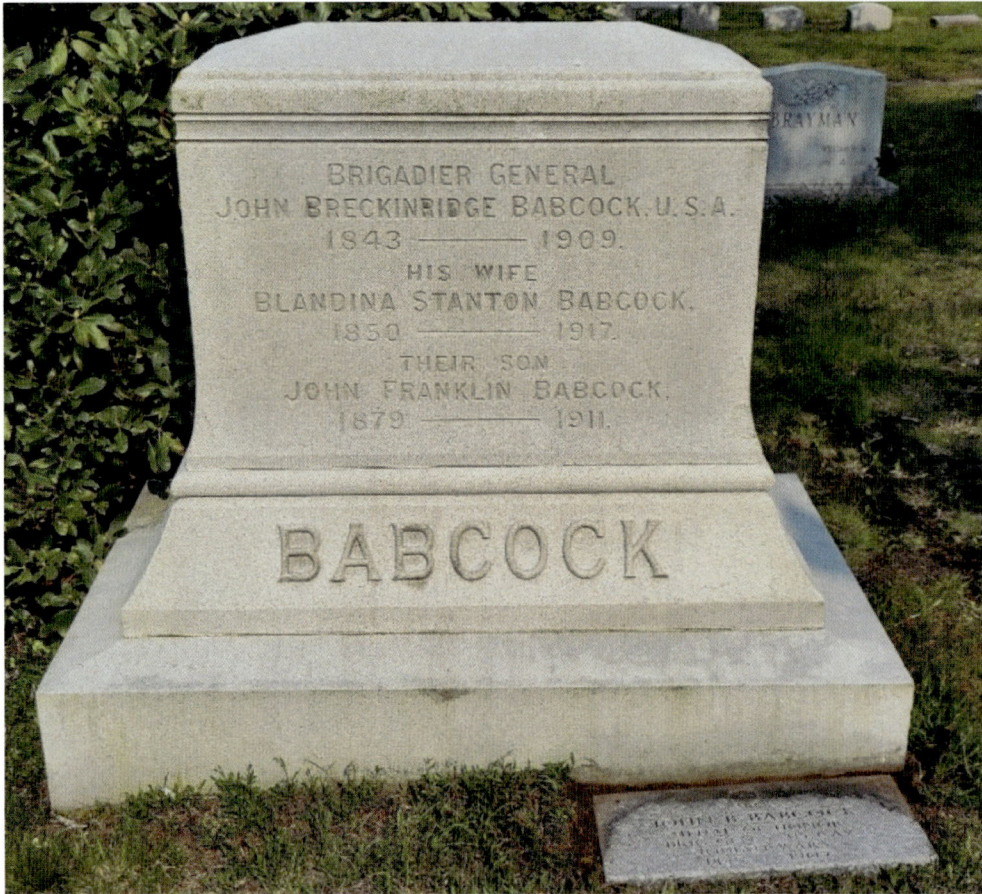

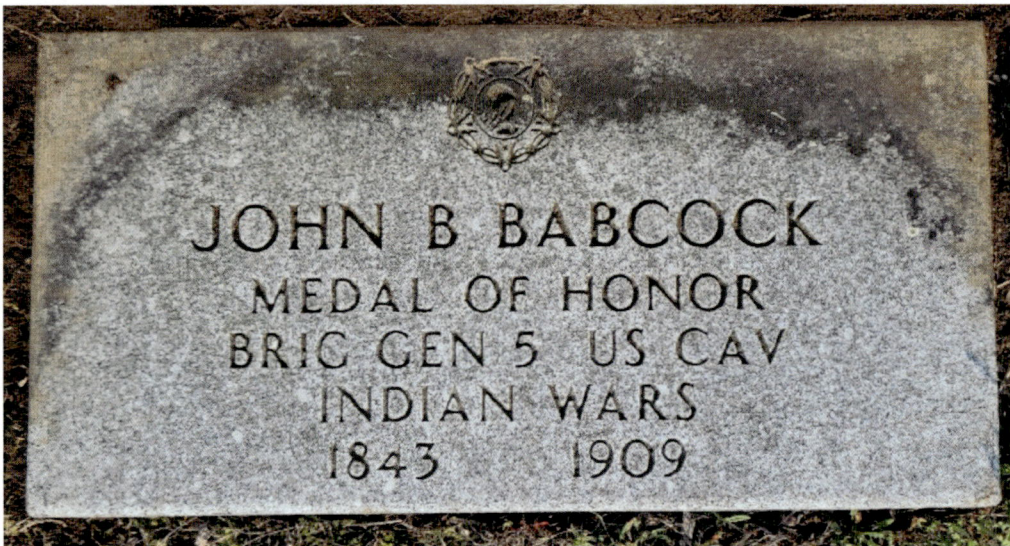

JOHN B BABCOCK
MEDAL OF HONOR
BRIG GEN 5 US CAV
INDIAN WARS
1843   1909

SERGEANT WILLIAM J. BABCOCK; ARMY

April 8, 1841 (Griswold, CT) – October 29, 1897 (South Kingstown, RI); 56 years old

Married to Phebe E. Gould (1845-1900).

Six sons, Alexander G. (1866-1869), William T. (1870-1956), James H. (1873-1919), John D. (1878-1903), Elmer E. (1880-1919), and Harry W. (1883-1912).

Two daughters, Abby L. (1868-1869) and Carrie A. (1875-1907).

Enlisted on June 5, 1861, in South Kingston, Rhode Island.

Mustered out on July 13, 1865, at Hall's Hill, Virginia.

Born to Gideon (1801-1877) and Caroline D. Carter Babcock (1803-1883). Five brothers, John (1825-1914), Alexander (1828-1873), Samuel G. (1835-1835), Charles H. (1836-1875), and Albert (1842-1898). Two sisters, Sarah C. Babcock Gallagher (1832-1907) and Abbie A. Babcock Barnes (1840-1865).

Photo courtesy of Ancestry.com

MEDAL OF HONOR CITATION

AWARDED FOR ACTIONS DURING: Civil War

BRANCH OF SERVICE: Army

UNIT: 2nd Rhode Island Infantry

DATE OF ISSUE AND PRESENTATION: March 2, 1895 (30 years later)

AGE ON THE DAY OF THE EVENT: 23

CITATION:

The President of the United States of America, in the name of Congress, takes pleasure in presenting the Medal of Honor to Sergeant William J. Babcock, United States Army, for extraordinary heroism on 2 April 1865, while serving with 2nd Rhode Island Infantry, in action at Petersburg, Virginia. Sergeant Babcock planted the flag upon the parapet while the enemy still occupied the line; was the first of his regiment to enter the works.

The Third Battle of Petersburg

With the Confederate defeat at Five Forks on April 1st, Lieutenant General Ulysses S. Grant and Major General George Meade ordered a general assault against the Petersburg lines by the Second, Ninth, Sixth, and Twenty-Fourth Corps on April 2nd. In the pre-dawn darkness, the Union infantry achieved a breakthrough when Major Gen. Horatio G. Wright's advancing Sixth Corps breached Confederate lines held by Lieutenant General A. P. Hill. Attempting to reach his men, Hill was killed in the ensuing. Confederate infantry pulled back to Forts Gregg and Whitworth as Major Gen. John Gibbon's Twenty Fourth Corps entered the fight, with Brigadier General William Birney's United States Colored Troops (USCT) division in reserve. The Confederates managed to delay Gibbon's advance at Fort Gregg and prevent the Federals from entering Petersburg that evening. Wright's breakthrough and the subsequent follow-up troops surged north and severed the South Side Railroad near Petersburg. The Union Army now had access to the Appomattox River and were free to cross the next day to threaten Lee's communications on the north side of the river. After dark, Lee informed President Jefferson Davis that he could "hold his position no longer" and that Petersburg and Richmond must be evacuated. Grant had finally achieved one of the major military objectives of the war: the capture of Petersburg, which led directly to the loss of the Confederate capital at Richmond, which finally fell on April 3rd. *(battelefields.org)*

Narrative of William Babcock's service contributed by Nathaniel Babcock, 5th cousin, five times removed, used with permission.

Prior to these heroic actions, he enlisted on June 5, 1861, as a private, where he would fight in the battles of First Bull Run, Yorktown, Williamsburg, Seven Pines, Oak Grove, White Oak Swamp, Malvern Hill, Antietam, Fredericksburg, Chancellorsville, Salem Heights, Gettysburg, Rappahannock Station, Wilderness Campaign (where he was shot just below the left knee and promoted for heroic actions to sergeant) then the siege of Petersburg. On April 2, 1864, Sergeant William J. Babcock and a small group of men from Company E rushed ahead of the main unit to a fortified battery position held by the 33rd North Carolina Infantry. Sergeant Babcock reached the enemy breastworks and, armed only with the American flag, planted the colors into the enemy parapet, confusing rebel defenders who soon retreated to another battery, and once his fellow troops from Company E arrived, he helped rush three more batteries and assisted in turning the batteries on other Confederate troops that had attempted to recapture the position.

From The Phoenix (Bristol, Rhode Island) on March 1, 1895

The gallant services of a Rhode Island man at Petersburg, Virginia, April 2nd, 1865, have been rewarded by a Medal of Honor presented by the President this week. William J. Babcock, late Sergeant of Company E, 2nd Rhode Island Volunteers, now residing in Wakefield, was "first in the enemy's works," but it has taken 30 years for the recognition to come.

From The Providence Evening Bulletin October 30, 1897

DISTINGUISHED VETERAN DEAD

Congress Awarded a Medal to William J. Babcock of Wakefield

William J. Babcock, who died in Wakefield, South Kingstown, Friday after a lingering illness, aged 56 years, was a veteran of the War and, by a vote of Congress, was awarded a medal for gallant conduct in front of Petersburg, Virginia, on April 2, 1865.

The deceased, who was a son of Gideon Babcock, was born in Griswold, Connecticut, in 1842, but when very young, he moved with his parents to South Kingstown, which town he had since made his home. Upon the breaking out of the Rebellion, Babcock, with three companions, Elisha Whitford,
E. Yoste and John G. Grinnell, the last of whom was killed in battle, enlisted June 6, 1861, in Company E, 2nd Rhode Island Volunteers, for three years, and on the 14th of November 1862, were promoted to Corporal. The deceased participated in all the battles in which his regiment was engaged and, on December 25, 1861, was discharged on account of the expiration of the term of his enlistment, but the next day, December 26th, Babcock re-enlisted for the war, and in the reformation of the old regiment was assigned to Company B and promoted to Color Sergeant. At the taking of the Confederate works at Petersburg, Babcock, bearing aloft the national colors and closely followed by Sergeant Thomas Parker, carrying the State flag and color guard, Private Maurice O'Hearne, was one of the first of the Union forces to mount the parapet of the enemy's works, and the first to plant Old Glory over the captured fort. For this gallant conduct, Babcock and his two companions were mentioned in the regimental dispatch to headquarters, and later Congress voted each a medal. The two other men received their memento many years ago, but Babcock, who, like many truly brave men, was of a retiring disposition, could not be induced to ask the War Department for his badge of bravery under fire until early in 1895, 30 years from the time he was discharged.

There is another act of possibly even greater heroism told of Sergeant Babcock by his comrades when, by the cool pluck of the deceased, the battle-worn flag of the 2nd Regiment closely engaged with the Confederates, was forced hastily to change its position, and during the confusion incident to such a maneuver it was not at first noticed that the Color Sergeant had disappeared from view. As nothing was seen of him upon the reformation of the line, it was feared that the faithful soldier had been seriously wounded or had, at last, met his fate, but as the old position was almost within the lines of the opposing troops, it was practically impossible to return in search of the missing color sergeant. Somewhat later, the entire command was made happy by seeing the color bearer walk in with the prized emblem of Liberty still in his possession. Although often questioned as to how he escaped capture, all that could be learned from him was that he was knocked down by a spent shot and, while lying on the ground, was seen by one or more of the Confederates who demanded that he upon pain of death, instantly surrender the flag, which he had still firmly grasped in his hands. This request Sergeant Babcock refused to accede to, and by strategy or other method, he succeeded in making his escape in safety with the flag that had first been Planted on the breastworks of Petersburg.

The deceased was married when at home on furlough to Miss Phebe Esther Gould of North Stonington, Connecticut, by Elder Joseph Taylor of the Christian Church of that borough. He had eight children, six of whom are now alive. His widow is an invalid, having sustained a paralytic stroke some months ago, which seriously affected her left side, rendering her limbs almost powerless. The deceased, besides being a brave soldier, was a citizen whom all his fellows loved and respected, and his loss will be much regretted.

The funeral will take place from G.A.R. Hall under the direction of the Sedgwick Post, of which the sergeant was a member, on Sunday at 2 p.m. The remains will be taken from his late residence to the hall at 1:20 p.m. under the escort of the Grand Army. The services will be after the form of the Episcopal Church, supplemented by the Grand Army ritual.

From an unknown newspaper or magazine. An article by Richard Katula and Charles Hathaway titled "Sergeant William J. Babcock; Civil War Hero from South Kingstown."

The Congressional Medal of Honor is awarded by the President, in the name of Congress, to an individual who has "distinguished himself conspicuously by gallantry and intrepidity at the risk of his life above and beyond the call of duty." There were 16 Medal of Honor recipients from Rhode Island in the Civil War. Only one of these men was from South Kingstown: SERGEANT WILLIAM J. BABCOCK. This is his story.

The Civil War became a reality for most Americans with the shock of the bombardment on Fort Sumter. Thousands of Rhode Islanders answered that call to arms. During the next four years, all would suffer, and many would die. June 6, 1861, 20-year-old Bill Babcock left his Pond Street address in South Kingstown to enlist in the Union Army. His reasons for taking arms are not recorded, and only one person is still alive who knew William personally: his daughter-in-law, Amy Babcock. Now in her 94th year, Mrs. Babcock is still adamant in her belief that William enlisted because he was, above all else, a patriot. In Amy's words: "He wanted to serve in the cause of the Union."

Traveling to Providence, William enlisted in Company E, 2nd Rhode Island Regiment, one of the most famous of all army corps. Not long after, the Regiment received its first assignment to Camp Sprague, near Washington, D.C. After being reviewed by President Lincoln, the troops were marched into the first battle of Bull Run on July 21, 1863.

At Bull Run, the regiment suffered heavy losses. Countless others were wounded and captured. Defeat often breeds determination, however, and so from March 1862 until April 1865, the now battle-wise troops fought like men possessed in some of the most memorable of Civil War engagements, including Antietam (which some say was the most sanguinary of all Civil War battles), Fredericksburg, Gettysburg, Wilderness, Winchester, Petersburg, and Sailor's Creed. General George Meade directed that the names of 19 major battles be inscribed on the Regiment's colors.

At the Battle of Wilderness, Virginia, in May 1864, the now Corporal Babcock was wounded in the left leg, below the knee. This injury, coupled with debilitating rheumatism he contracted from sleeping on cold, wet ground, was cause for great pain to the young infantryman. Nevertheless, he fought on.

Four months later, Babcock's wounds had somewhat healed. The 2nd Rhode Island was camped near Petersburg, Virginia, celebrating a day of acclamation given to them by the people of Rhode Island. A banner had been presented to the soldiers. Babcock's bravery led to promotion to Sergeant and being selected standard bearer for the ceremony. For three months, the soldiers of the 2nd Rhode Island languished near Petersburg. Diaries of the men record the grim, daily existence in the mud, hail, and rain of the Virginia winter. The majority could feel only the penetrating loneliness of war.

Preparation for a grand assault on the heavily fortified Confederate cities of Petersburg and Richmond had been in the works for some time. Daily rumors only added to the miseries. Petersburg was going to be Hell. April drew nearer, and the rumors of battle grew stronger.

Finally, at about 4:00 a.m. on April 2, 1865, the 2nd Rhode Island was brigaded with several other units in front of Fort Fisher, near Petersburg. The men knew that the time had come. Colonel Rhodes recorded in his diary the general feeling of the men at that moment; "Still packed up for the move, with orders to be ready to attack at a moment's notice. The enemy is evidently expecting some movement on our part, for their pickets are on alert and have already started the boys to the top of the hill to reload the pieces there and get them in position. Private Railton did not seem inclined to leave but went to work to load the piece, which he did, to the muzzle with stones, iron, etc., which were lying around. The enemy was advancing, closing en masse - so I said to him, "Come, the Johnnies are coming. Let's get up and keep the earthwork, anyway." The only reply was, "Be they? If they come here, I'll make them smell - well, brimstone." I stood and watched him, and then, when the enemy's line was not over thirty feet away, he touched off the gun, which blew into a thousand pieces, but such destruction of life I never saw, before or since. It broke their lines, and they were not reformed."

With the combined actions of men like Babcock and Railton, the Battle of Petersburg was over by the end of the day, and the Union Army was one giant but a bloody step closer to Appomattox. The 2nd Rhode Island again suffered heavy casualties. Their work was not yet complete. In fact, the regiment was not even permitted to visit Petersburg. Instead, they turned in pursuit of the Northern Army of Virginia, fighting off another vicious rebel stand at Sailor's Creek, finally ending up at Appomattox, where they were mustered out.

From The Evening Bulletin (Providence, Rhode Island) March 4, 1895

FOR BRAVERY IN THE WAR
Sergeant Babcock Receives a Medal for Gallant Conduct

FIRST INSIDE ENEMY'S WORKS AT PETERSBURG, VIRGINIA
Recommended for the Honor after the Close of the War, but Did Not Apply Until Recently – Sergeant Babcock is a Resident of Wakefield

William J. Babcock of Wakefield has just received from the War Department a Medal of Honor for conspicuous bravery at the storming of Petersburg, Virginia, on April 3, 1865, while color sergeant of Company B, 2nd Rhode Island Volunteers, under the command of Lieutenant Colonel Elisha H. Rhodes. Sergeant Babcock, who had been promoted from the ranks for his bravery at the Battle of Winchester on September 19, 1864, was the first man to plant a Union flag on the fortifications of Petersburg and one of the first in the works. He was recommended by Colonel Rhodes in dispatches after the battle for a Medal of Honor but did not apply for it until recently when it was at once sent to him.

Sergeant Babcock went to the front with the regiment in 1861, enlisting June 6th and being mustered on the same day, originally serving in Company E under the old organization. On November 14, 1862, he was promoted to Corporal, and on December 25, 1863, discharged, his term of enlistment having expired. He re-enlisted the next day, December 26, as a veteran volunteer. From February to April 1864, he was absent on furlough, this privilege being given to re-enlisted veteran volunteers. He was promoted to Sergeant in February 1865 and mustered out of the service on July 13, 1865.

Such is Sergeant Babcock's career, as given in the war records. As told by his old comrades of the 2nd Rhode Island Volunteers, it is another story. He made a name for himself as a conspicuously brave and daring soldier and was, for his bravery, given charge of the United States flag, always known as the colors, a distinction from the State flag, which was borne by Color Sergeant Thomas Parker, who afterward served in the regular army.

The 2nd Rhode Island Volunteers formed a part of the old Brigade, 1st Division of the 6th Army Corps, and was stationed about three miles from the city of Petersburg proper.

The Rhode Island troops were a part of that long blue line that, commencing near the mouth of the Appomattox River, stretched a distance of 45 miles around the rebel works to where Butler's army was located, at Bermuda Hundred, the morning of the 2nd of April, 1865, when the final and successful assault was made on the rebel defenses, was foggy. The dense mist settled down until it seemed as if it could be cut up into chunks, and men a few feet apart were hidden from each other by a dense, impenetrable curtain of fog. Preparations for the assault were made silently, and every precaution was taken to avoid alarming the enemy. The men packed their tin cups in their knapsacks to prevent any rattle, and orders were given to take the caps off the guns to prevent any premature discharge. The assault was to be made at the break of day, and the soldiers knew it would be a desperate one.

While the army was awaiting in silence the coming of the sun to give the signal for battle and alter all preparations had been made without alarming the rebel pickets, a mule loaded with camp equipage broke loose and ran straight for the rebel lines. The rebel picket line, thinking that they were being charged, fired at the animal and awakened the men in the forts, who prepared for an attack. At this moment, the signal for the charge was made, and the line of blue started forward. The Rhode Island men advanced from Fort Fisher and, more fortunate than the others, found an old cart path which led through the abattis into the rebel lines. On either side of the road stretched a line of trees, felled with the branches pointing out, and the other regiments were delayed until their pioneers could clear space with axes. In the road was very little obstruction, and the regiment, led by Lieutenant Colonel Rhodes, went through on the run. Beyond this was the glacis of a rebel fort, mounting four guns which, in the hands of the rebel gunners, were casting death broadcast on the slope.

On the regiment went with the flags and their commander in the lead, and up the incline, they climbed until suddenly the ground opened before them, and they poured down into a deep and wide ditch before the parapet. Those who led the charge were, for a moment, buried under the mass that followed, and one of the survivors said that it seemed as if a thousand men must have fallen on him before he could extricate himself from the pile and start for the rebel works. Quickly, the men got on their feet again and, always led by the flags, climbed the aides of the ditch and the steep parapet of the fort. The earth, usually hard and so firm as to afford little or no foothold, had been softened by the rains of the day before, and by digging their heels in, the soldiers were able to climb out of the ditch and up the parapet into the fort which they carried.

All through the advance, Sergeant Babcock, bearing the new colors presented to the regiment a short time before, had been at the head of the column, and he was one of the first men on the parapet of the rebel fort, where he planted the stars and stripes, the first Union flag in the works of Petersburg. With him were Color Sergeant Thomas Parker, with the flag of the State of Rhode Island, and Private Maurice O'Hearn. All three men were recommended in dispatches the next day, and Parker received his Medal of Honor some time ago. O'Hearn has been dead for a number of years. Lieutenant Colonel Rhodes, who was one of the first in the fort and who displayed great gallantry all through the assault, was for his conduct promoted to Colonel.

Lieutenant Colonel Rhodes's recommendation that these three men receive a Medal of Honor was endorsed by General Oliver Edwards, commanding the 3rd Brigade, and by General Frank Wheaton, commanding the 1st Division.

Sergeant Parker afterward applied for and received his medal, but Sergeant Babcock, who for his conduct was commissioned a Second Lieutenant but never mustered in because of the sudden ending of the war, did not ask for his and did not get it.

At the reunion of the 2nd Rhode Island Volunteer Veteran Association at Wakefield last summer, he spoke to his old comrades about the matter and was advised to write to Washington. This he did recently, and his letter was referred to General Rhodes, who returned it with the desired recommendation. As a result, Sergeant Babcock is now in possession of the medal, which he earned by his bravery 30 years ago.

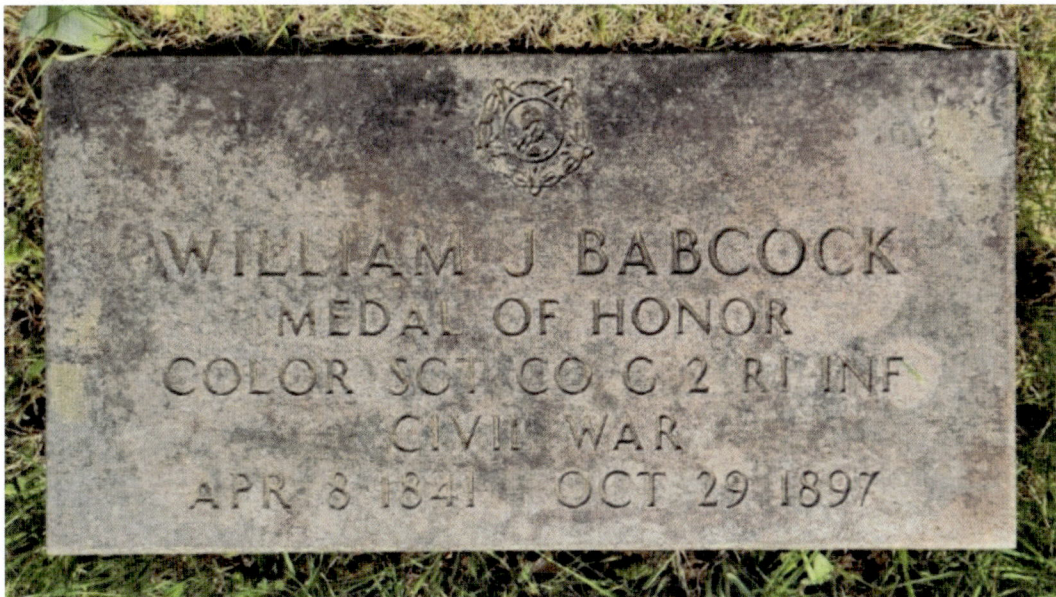

CORPORAL ELIJAH WILLIAM BACON; ARMY

1836 * (Burlington, CT) – May 6, 1864 (Wilderness, VA); 28 years old
Married Angeline E. Shelley (1838-1868) in 1855 in Madison, Connecticut.
Two daughters, Mary E. (1857-1937) and Jennie M. (1859-?).
Enlisted on July 28, 1862, in New Britain, Connecticut.
Mustered in August 25, 1862, in Hartford, Connecticut.

* The exact Date of Birth is unknown.

Born to Roswell J. (1810-1867) and Betsy E. Smith Bacon (1809-1898). Three brothers, Andrew J. [died of disease while a POW in Florence, South Carolina] (1833-1865), Oliver D. (1841-?), and Charles J. (1846-1846). One sister, Mary E. (1839-1845).

MEDAL OF HONOR CITATION

AWARDED FOR ACTIONS DURING: Civil War
BRANCH OF SERVICE: Army
UNIT: Company F, 14th Connecticut Infantry
DATE OF ISSUE: December 1, 1864 (Posthumous)
AGE ON THE DAY OF THE EVENT: 28
CITATION:

The President of the United States of America, in the name of Congress, takes pride in presenting the Medal of Honor (Posthumously) to Private Elijah William Bacon, United States Army, for extraordinary heroism on 3 July 1863, while serving with Company F, 14th Connecticut Infantry, in action at Gettysburg, Pennsylvania, for the capture of flag of 16th North Carolina regiment (Confederate States of America).

Presentation Date and Details: December 6, 1864, by Major General George G. Meade, at a review of the 2nd Army Corps Headquarters, Peebles' House, near Petersburg, Virginia. **AUTHOR NOTE**: This presentation event took place after Corporal Bacon was killed in the Battle of the Wilderness on May 6, 1864.

From CivilWarInTheEast.com

The 14th Connecticut Volunteer Infantry Regiment lost 17 officers, and 188 enlisted men killed and mortally wounded, and 1 officer and 191 enlisted men by disease during the Civil War. The 14th sustained the largest percentage of loss of any regiment from Connecticut. The regiment is honored by a monument at Gettysburg and another at Antietam. From the Gettysburg Monument:

"Lost in killed and died in the service, 366; wounded and disabled many hundreds. Original muster 1015; recruits 697, final muster of original members, present and absent, 234."

From the Antietam Monument:

Advanced to this point in a charge about 9:30 A.M., September 17th, 1862, then fell back eighty-eight yards to a cornfield fence and held position heavily engaged nearly two hours; then was sent to the support of the first brigade of its division at the Roulette Lane two hours; then was sent to the extreme left of the first division of this Corps to the support of Brooke's Brigade and at 5 P.M. was placed in support between the Brigades of Caldwell and Meagher of that Division, overlooking "Bloody Lane," holding position there until 10 A.M. of the 18th when relieved. The monument stands on the line of Companies B and G near the left of the Regiment. In this battle, the Regiment lost 38 killed and mortally wounded, 88 wounded, and 21 reported missing.

Antietam monument photo courtesy of CTMonuments.net

From The Journal (Meriden, CT) October 5, 1887

SOME TYPES OF SOLDIERS
AS THEY APPEARED TO COMRADE GOSS IN OLD WAR DAYS
Pen Pictures That Will be Promptly Recognized by the Men Who Went to the Front a Quarter of a Century Ago – A Tribute to Joe Pierce

I can recall, so vividly, so many types of soldiers that I will devote an article to that subject. As to the types of soldiers, there were so many that an article of a hundred pages, bound in calf, could be written if it would only pay to write it. Don't tempt me, or I may inflict untold misery upon The Journal readers.

I remember a circumstance that happened at Hatcher's Run. We had been supporting a battery almost all day on the crest of a sandy hill. Although it was in February, the day was warm, and no snow was on the ground. We had repulsed two determined attacks of the enemy, and they had finally retired beyond a piece of low woodland that sheltered them from our view. The want of water was seriously felt in the afternoon, and some of the men volunteered to take as many canteens as they could carry and try to get some water that we knew must be in the woods at the foot of the hill. Amongst the volunteers was myself. I slung about a dozen canteens around my neck and went down the slope, entered the woods, and found a fine spring of water and around it some dozen or so of Yanks. We soon found out that the enemy had retired further than at first thought and that we were in comparative safety. So, we sat, quaffing our fill of Nature's own remedy for thirst, when we were somewhat startled by the appearance of six stalwart Rebs, emerging from the underbrush without arms, holding up their hands in token of surrender, at the same time calling out "Don't shoot Yanks: we'es going to give up."

Of course, we told them to come on, and they did. Soon, we were chatting with them, giving them hard tack – as all old soldiers will do, and were having quite a confab, intending to go back soon, they, of course, going with us. Just then came down Lieutenant – to get water. He was close to us before catching sight of the Johnnies, but as soon as he espied us, he jerked out his toad sticker, threw himself into an attitude of "Come one, come all! These rocks shall fly from their firm base as soon as I!"

...and in thundering tones called out, "Surrender, you d----d scoundrels," – well, to have seen the situation would have been a scene for the greatest painter that ever held a brush, not even expecting "Brother Gardner" of the Lime Kiln club. The open-mouthed look, the wild bewilderment of the whole countenance of the Crackers was really amusing, and then the dozen or so of us who knew the situation and who looked at one another with that quizzical look that is habitual with old comrades and those little side scenes that go to make up a whole – take it all in all it was comical.

Lieutenant sternly bade them "Fall in, in single file" and boldly marched them up the sandy slope and turned them over to the provost as "armed prisoners, captured on the skirmish line." And he was really promoted to a captaincy for the brave act. Such is life.

"All is not gold that glitters." A few days afterward, I sent an account to a Hartford paper, detailing the brilliancy of the charge of our captain's cook who boldly captured five armed prisoners in the rear – miscreants who were trying to steal away from the Rebs and armed only with a frying pan, he actually coaxed them into camp and gave them their bellyful – which was most deserving of the two? Both of them are actual facts.

I knew another type of soldier, a man who enlisted and died in the service as a private, Elijah W. Bacon of Berlin, Connecticut, a man whose reputation for bravery was never, could never, be questioned: modest, kindly, loving his comrades as they loved him, and yet – the bravest of the brave – he died without shoulder straps when others less deserving got them. I saw him as he fell, facing the enemy, with a smile on his face – genial, kind, and worthy friends.

From The Berlin Herald, New Britain, Connecticut, May 27, 1989.

LOCAL MEDAL OF HONOR WINNER FROM CIVIL WAR REMEMBERED

BERLIN – It was just over a year ago that the Medal of Honor granite marker was placed alongside the grave of Corporal Elijah W. Bacon in Maple Cemetery on Worthington Ridge.

Flush with the ground, the marker was placed in Bacon's honor nearly 12 years after his death on May 6, 1864, at the Battle of the Wilderness in Virginia.

The battle was one of the Civil War's most lethal conflicts, according to Thomas F. Durning Jr., deputy secretary-treasurer of the Connecticut Department, Sons of Union Veterans of the Civil War.

The organization placed the marker at the Bacon gravesite in Maple Cemetery.

At the top of the marker is an engraving of the Medal of Honor as it now looks, followed by Bacon's name, the Medal of Honor designation, inscriptions of his unit, and the words "Civil War." And the date of his death.

Durning said Bacon was one of the 22 Union soldiers in Company F of the 14th Connecticut Volunteer Infantry Regiment who were awarded the Medal of Honor after fighting in the Battle of Gettysburg in Pennsylvania in 1863.

Although Bacon was born in Burlington, he enlisted for Union duty on July 28, 1862, in Berlin.

Durning said the 14th Connecticut mustered into U.S. service on August 23, 1862, and that the performance of the 14th was exceptional among Connecticut's infantry regiments.

Of the state's regiments, he said, the 14th was in the greatest number of battles (34) and in proportion to its size, lost the greatest number of men in combat.

Durning said that in addition to Gettysburg and the Wilderness, the 14th fought in such battles as Antietam, Fredericksburg, Chancellorsville, Spotsylvania, Cold Harbor, and Petersburg.

According to official records of the Union and Confederate Armies: Series 1, Volumes 27 and 42, Bacon was awarded the Medal of Honor on December 15, 1864, for capturing the flag of the 16th North Carolina and for "gallantry in action and other soldier-like qualities."

Although Bacon was reported killed at the Battle of the Wilderness, as were many of his fellow infantrymen, his remains are believed to never have been recovered, During said.

He explained that no one knows if Bacon is actually buried in the plot at Maple Cemetery because the remains of many soldiers killed in the Battle of the Wilderness were either consumed by fire or lost in the thick brush.

From The Hartford Courant July 29, 2013

BERLIN — It was a coming-out party Sunday for the solemn brownstone obelisk that for 150 years has stood largely unnoticed outside Kensington Congregational Church.

Following morning services, parishioners, neighborhood residents, assorted dignitaries, local veterans, and a color guard of Civil War re-enactors led by President Abraham Lincoln turned out in celebration of the 150th anniversary of the Kensington Soldier's Monument, which is now listed on the National Register of Historic Places as the country's oldest, permanent Civil War monument.

First dedicated on July 28, 1863, the 20-foot-tall memorial was created to honor the memory of six Kensington men who had died by that point in the war. Eleven more names were added as the war continued and the casualties grew.

Four female descendants of one of those named Private Elijah W. Bacon, who died May 6, 1864, and was awarded a posthumous Medal of Honor for heroism at Gettysburg, lay a ceremonial wreath at the monument.

"Now that it is on the National Register of Historic Places, perhaps it will receive more attention. The attention it deserves," Senator Richard Blumenthal said, speaking to a gathering of an estimated 150 participants and onlookers.

The very "simplicity and modesty" of the memorial, located at 312 Percival Ave., has caused it to be largely overlooked, Blumenthal said.

"I guess 99.9 percent of people who drive down this busy road have no idea that a monument of historical significance is here."

A campaign directed by Central Connecticut State University history professor Matthew Warshauer, co-chairman of the Connecticut Civil War Commemoration Commission, culminated on July 3 with the National Register listing. It had been placed on the State Register of Historic Places in April.

Among the approximately 150 Civil War memorials in Connecticut, the Kensington Soldier's Monument is the only one that was constructed during wartime, and it had a specific purpose, as reflected by its funereal design.

"This is not merely a monument to service. This is a monument specifically to honor those who died during the war," Warshauer said at the dedication.

Unlike later civic memorials, the Kensington Monument remains under the ownership and care of the church, which celebrated its 300th anniversary last year.

The Rev. Elias Brewster Hilliard, the congregation's patriotic wartime minister, proposed its construction in late 1862. It was designed by Nelson Augustus Moore, a noted landscape painter and church member, whose original sketch hangs inside the church meetinghouse. The brownstone used was quarried in Portland and brought by an oxen-pulled sled to an East Berlin stone yard where the monument was cut. The cost — $475 — was paid for by the congregation and community residents.

It remains in excellent condition despite being carved from vulnerable brownstone. "The care that has been taken has allowed it to survive these 150 years," Warshauer said.

To mark its sesquicentennial, a church committee was formed to push for federal recognition of the monument and plan its re-dedication. A landscape architect was retained to design a memorial garden enclosed by a new decorative, wrought iron fence. The iron fencing that Moore installed around the monument in 1873 was used in the fabrication.

Michael Cavaliere, chairman of the monument committee, said all the preparations were completed just last week. The fencing was installed four days ago, and the surrounding lawn was only just seeded and sprayed. "We're pretty pleased," he said.

Honored on the Soldier's Monument mentioned in the previous article. The monument is at 312 Percival Avenue, Berlin, Connecticut. Photos by the author.

Honored on a Civil War Monument, 291 Berlin Street, East Berlin, Connecticut. Photo by the author.

Buried in Maple Cemetery, 1166 Worthington Ridge, Berlin, Connecticut; Section A. Photos by the author.

ELIJAH W BACON
MEDAL OF HONOR
CORP CO F 14 CONN INF
CIVIL WAR
MAY 6 1864

BRIGADIER GENERAL GEORGE WILLIAM BAIRD; ARMY

December 13, 1839 (Milford, CT) – November 28, 1906 (Asheville, NC); 66 years old

Married Julia C. Rogers (1842-1926) on July 31, 1866, in Cheshire, Connecticut.

One son, [Colonel, U.S. Army] George H. (1876-1951).

Two daughters, Julia G.R. Baird Holmes (1868-1928) and Martha M. Baird Hall (1875-1966).

Enlisted as a Private on August 25, 1862, in Milford, Connecticut.

Commissioned on March 18, 1864.

Retired on February 20, 1903.

Born to Jonah Newton (1897-1853) and Minerva Gunn Baird (1799-1882). Three brothers, John G. (1826-1891), James W. (1833-1912), and Charles S. (1836-1911). Five sisters, Catherine N. (1828-1890), Martha M. Beard Hall (1830-1916), Anna A. Beard Andrew (1832-1892), and Emily J. (1842-1922).

He was the only soldier on record who was promoted from Private to Colonel during the Civil War. Colonel of the 32nd Regiment, United States Colored Infantry, in 1864.

Graduated from Yale University, Class of 1863.

Photos courtesy of the Library of Congress. Left photo pnp-ppmsca-73400-73448r, and right photo LC-DIG-bellcm-11159.

MEDAL OF HONOR CITATION

AWARDED FOR ACTIONS DURING: Indian Campaigns
BRANCH OF SERVICE: Army
UNIT: 5th U.S. Infantry
DATE OF ISSUE AND PRESENTATION: November 27, 1894 (17 years later)
AGE ON THE DAY OF THE EVENT: 37
CITATION:

The President of the United States of America, in the name of Congress, takes pleasure in presenting the Medal of Honor to First Lieutenant (Infantry) George William Baird, United States Army, for most distinguished gallantry in action with the Nez Perce Indians on 30 September 1877, while serving with 5th U.S. Infantry, in action at Bear Paw Mountain, Montana.

He was wounded on February 14, 1865, at James Island, South Carolina. He participated in several battles in South Carolina, Georgia, and Florida. The 1st Battery made an expedition to James Island and participated in operations against Charleston, South Carolina, from May 31 to June 28, 1862. The major part of the expedition was the Battle of Secessionville on June 16th, 1862. Later, he was made Colonel of the 32nd Regiment of the U.S. Colored Troops. The 32nd Regiment was ordered to Hilton Head S.C. in April 1864 and stood duty there until June. When the Civil War ended, he decided to make a career out of the military. He completed his engineering course at Sheffield Scientific school in 1866, and in May of that year, he was appointed Second Lieutenant in the regular army, and in 1871 he became the Adjutant General of his field command.

Indian Wars Medal of Honor Recipient. He rose from the rank of Private to Brigadier General. He was presented the Medal of Honor in 1894 for his actions at Bear Paw Mountain, Montana, on September 30, 1877, against Chief Joseph and the Nez Perce. He was at the time a 1st Lieutenant with the 5th Infantry. During the battle, he served in the 5th Infantry Regiment, nicknamed the "Bobcats." The 5th Infantry Regiment is the third-oldest infantry regiment of the United States Army, tracing its origins to 1808. It has participated in some way in most of the wars the United States has fought.

The 5th Infantry was pursuing Chief Joseph and his tribe of Nez Perce Indians. The battle started when the Nez Perce saw the 5th Infantry Regiment advancing on their position. The Indians didn't have time to flee, but they did have enough time to fortify their position. They made trenches on the side of the mountain to slow the advance of the attacking U.S. Army. Custer's outfit, the 7th Cavalry, charged in support of the 5th Infantry but was pushed back under a barrage of arrows shot by the Indian warriors. When the day was over, Colonel Nelson A. Miles, the commander of Baird's Regiment, tried to negotiate a peace treaty with Chief Joseph. While this was going on, each side removed their wounded from the field. On October 2, the United States 12-pound Napoleon artillery piece arrived at the battlefield. The Napoleon artillery fired on the Indian trenches, hoping to force the Nez Perce to surrender, which they did.

While he was giving orders and carrying notes across the battlefield, Baird was shot in the left forearm, and an arrow severed his ear. He recovered well from his injuries, and in 1878, Colonel Miles recommended that he receive the Medal of Honor for his duties at the Battle of Bear Paw Mountain. Baird was presented with the Medal of Honor in 1894.

From the Springfield Republican on November 30, 1906

Word was received in New York Wednesday night of the death Wednesday at Asheville, North Carolina, of Brigadier General George W. Baird, United States Army (retired). General Baird was born in Connecticut in

December 1839, entered the Union Army during the Civil War as a private, and rose to the colonelcy of a colored regiment. He served in operations in South Carolina, Georgia, and Florida and entered the regular army after the war. He served on the frontier and participated with great gallantry in several Indian campaigns, particularly against the Nez Perces. The latter years of his Army life were spent in the paymaster general's department. He retired two years ago and went to New York to make his home. His health had been failing for some months, and about a week ago, he was taken to Asheville. He is survived by a widow and a son who is a First Lieutenant in the army and is in the Philippines.

From The Boston Globe on December 2, 1906

The funeral of Brigadier General George W. Baird of Milford, Connecticut, was held in the Broadway Tabernacle in New York yesterday and was attended with military honors. A company of the 12th United States infantry formed the military escort, and the body was conveyed to the Tabernacle and to the railroad station on a gun caisson. The body will be sent to Milford for burial.

Buried in Milford Cemetery, 35 Gulf Street, Milford, Connecticut; Section G. Photos by the author.

GEORGE W BAIRD
MEDAL OF HONOR
BRIG GEN   US ARMY
INDIAN WARS
DEC 13 1839   NOV 28 1906

COLONEL HARVEY CURTISS "BARNEY" BARNUM JR.; MARINE CORPS

July 21, 1940 (Cheshire, CT) –
Married Martha E. Hill on June 27, 1992, at the Fort Myer Chapel, Arlington, Virginia
Commissioned in 1962.
Retired in August 1989.
Marine Corps Serial Numbers: E-1857459 and O-084262.

Born to Harvey C. Sr. (1914-1996) and Ann E. McGinty Barnum (1913-2003). One brother, Henry C. (1943-).

Member of the Connecticut Veterans Hall of Fame, Class of 2020.

Also the recipient of the Defense Superior Service Medal, the Legion of Merit, the Bronze Star Medal with "V" device for valor and gold star, the Purple Heart, the Meritorious Service Medal, the Navy Commendation Medal, the Navy Achievement Medal with "V" device, the Combat Action Ribbon, the Army Presidential Unit Citation, the Joint Meritorious Unit Award, the Navy Unit Commendation, two awards of the Navy Meritorious Unit Citation, National Defense Service Medal, the Vietnam Service Medal with 5 stars, the Sea Service Deployment Ribbon, the Vietnamese Cross of Gallantry (silver) and the Republic of Vietnam Campaign Medal with device.

Cheshire High School Class of '58 yearbook

HARVEY CURTISS BARNUM
"Barney"

Academic   Business Administration

"His good nature, truth, and good sense are the qualities that procure esteem and praise from all who know him."

"Smile!" . . . very friendly . . . thoughtful . . . reliable . . . hardworker . . . Ike and Mamie . . . pizza on Friday nights . . . hot relish . . . smiling Irishman . . . B.M.O.C. . . . pet peeve: Chemistry . . . ladies man . . . crew cut . . . "Of Mice and Men" . . . Loyal Boy Scout.

Football 2, 3, 4, Baseball 1, 2, 3, 4, Projectors 2, 3, Chess 2, Leaders 2, 3, Glee Club 2, 3, 4, Ramicabana 2, 3, 4, Hockey 3, Basketball Intramurals 2, 3, 4, Field Day, President 4, Prom Committee 3, 4, (Refreshments Chairman 3.)

BARNEY BARNUM
President

Photo courtesy of the Congressional Medal of Honor Society

MEDAL OF HONOR CITATION

AWARDED FOR ACTIONS DURING: Vietnam War
BRANCH OF SERVICE: Marine Corps
UNIT: Hotel Company, 2nd Battalion, 9th Marines, 3rd Marine Division (REIN)
AGE ON THE DAY OF THE EVENT: 24
CITATION:

The President of the United States of America, in the name of Congress, takes pleasure in presenting the Medal of Honor to Captain Harvey Curtiss "Barney" Barnum (MCSN: 0-84262), United States Marine Corps, for conspicuous gallantry and intrepidity at the risk of his life above and beyond the call of duty on 18 December 1965, while serving with the Company H, Second Battalion, Ninth Marines, THIRD Marine Division (Reinforced), Fleet Marine Force in action outside the village of Ky Phu, Quang Tin Province, Republic of Vietnam. When the company was suddenly pinned down by a hail of extremely accurate enemy fire and was quickly separated from the remainder of the battalion by over 500 meters of open and fire-swept ground, and casualties mounted rapidly. Lieutenant Barnum quickly made a hazardous reconnaissance of the area, seeking targets for his artillery. Finding the rifle company commander mortally wounded and the radio operator killed, he, with complete disregard for his safety, gave aid to the dying commander, then removed the radio from the dead operator and strapped it to himself. He immediately assumed command of the rifle company and, moving at once into the midst of the heavy fire, rallying and giving encouragement to all units, reorganized them to replace the loss of key personnel and led their attack on enemy positions from which deadly fire continued to come. His sound and swift decisions and his obvious calm served to stabilize the badly decimated units, and his gallant example, as he stood exposed repeatedly to point out targets, served as an inspiration to all. Provided with two armed helicopters, he moved fearlessly through enemy fire to control the air attack against the firmly entrenched enemy while skillfully directing one platoon in a successful counterattack on the key enemy positions. Having thus cleared a small area, he requested and directed the landing of two transport helicopters for the evacuation of the dead and wounded. He then assisted in the mopping up and final seizure of the battalion's objective. His gallant initiative and heroic conduct reflected great credit upon himself and were in keeping with the highest traditions of the Marine Corps and the United States Naval Service.

<u>Presentation Date and Details</u>: February 27, 1967, at the Marine Barracks, Washington, D.C., by Secretary of the Navy Paul H. Nitze.

Photo courtesy of the Congressional Medal of Honor Society. Then-Captain Barnum (l),
Secretary of the Navy Paul H. Nitze (r) and an unknown Marine (far right).

Attended Cheshire High School. Graduated from St. Anselm College in Manchester, New Hampshire, with a Bachelor of Arts in Economics. Commissioned a Second Lieutenant in the Marine Corps upon graduation in 1962.

His assignments include four tours as an artilleryman with the 3rd Marine Division, to include two tours in Vietnam, 2nd Marine Aircraft Wing; Guard Officer at Marine Barracks, Pearl Harbor and Operations Officer, Hawaiian Armed Forces Police; Weapons Instructor at the Basic School; 2nd Marine Division as an artillery battalion operations and executive officer and subsequently Division Staff Secretary; four years at Marine Corps Recruit Depot, Parris Island as Commanding Officer, Headquarters Company and 2nd Recruit Training Battalion of the Training Regiment; Chief of Current Operations, US Central Command where he planned and executed the first U.S./Jordanian joint exercise staff as the Commander of U.S. Forces and twice planned and executed operation BRIGHT STAR spread over four southwest Asian countries involving 26,000 personnel; attended The Basic School, U.S. Army Field Artillery School, Amphibious Warfare School, U.S. Army Command and General Staff College and the U.S. Naval War College; Headquarters Marine Corps tours included aide to the Assistant Commandant as a Captain and Deputy Director Public Affairs, Director Special Projects Directorate and Military Secretary to the Commandant as a Colonel.

After retirement from the USMC in 1989, he served as Principal Director of the Drug Enforcement Policy Office of the Secretary of Defense 1991-1993; Deputy Secretary of Defense (Reserve Affairs) 2001-2009; Acting Assistant

Secretary of the Navy (Manpower & Reserve Affairs) 2009.

In 2016, at a ceremony at Marine Barracks Washington, DC hosted by the Secretary of the Navy, an Arleigh Burke Class destroyer was named the U.S.S. HARVEY C BARNUM JR. (DDG 124). DDG 124 was built in Bath, Maine, christened on July 29, 2023, and will be commissioned in Norfolk, Virginia, in the spring of 2024.

Interview with Harvey C. Barnum, Jr., U.S. Marine Corps (ret), originally published in Vietnam Magazine, October 2006; Al Hemingway. Used with permission.

HARVEST MOON

In-country for just two weeks, artillery forward observer Harvey Barnum assumed command of Hotel Company, 2nd Battalion, 9th Marines, during a Viet Cong ambush.

As told by Colonel Harvey C. Barnum, Jr., U.S. Marine Corps (ret.)

As 1965 came to a close, the 1st Viet Cong (VC) Regiment, which had suffered a resounding defeat at the hands of the U.S. Marines during Operation Starlite in August, was back in the picture. In late November, the enemy unit attacked the Army of the Republic of Vietnam (ARVN) outpost at Hiep Duc, just 25 miles west of Tam Ky. By occupying this key position, the Communists had a clear road to the Nui Loc Son Basin, also called the Que Son Valley, in I Corps' Quang Tin province. Abundant in farms and heavily populated, the valley was considered an extremely important area, situated as it was between the major South Vietnamese cities of Da Nang and Chu Lai. The monsoon season provided excellent cover to the VC units attempting to occupy that vital region.

On November 22, after heavy fighting between enemy forces and the 2nd ARVN Division, 37th ARVN Ranger Battalion, and South Vietnamese Regional Forces, General William C. Westmoreland, head of Military Assistance Command, Vietnam (MACV), instructed Major General Lewis W.

Walt, commanding general of the 3rd Marine Division, to "conduct search and destroy operations...to drive the VC out." Walt was justifiably concerned about the rising Communist threat to Que Son, and the burly Marine commander conferred with ARVN Major General Nguyen Chanh Thi about the next course of action. The pair concluded that action must be taken to repulse the VC from this rich farming area. As a result, Operation Harvest Moon/ Lien Ket 18 was initiated.

Marine and ARVN units immediately went on the offensive to quell the enemy drive into the Que Son Valley. On December 18, Lieutenant Colonel Leon N. Utter's 2nd Battalion, 7th Marines (2/7), ran headlong into the 80th VC Battalion. As the Marines trudged through extremely rugged terrain, varying from flooded rice paddies to jungle-covered hills, the enemy hit the rear and flanks of the column.

At the rear of the column was Hotel Company, 2nd Battalion, 9th Marines (2/9), which had been attached to Colonel Utter's battalion for the operation. When both the company commander and his radio operator were killed, the artillery forward observer (FO), 1st Lieutenant Harvey C. Barnum, Jr., on temporary duty in Vietnam from the Marine Barracks at Pearl Harbor, took command. After hours of intense combat, Barnum and his Marines successfully broke contact and joined the remainder of their unit in the village of Ky Phu. For his heroic actions on that day, Barnum was awarded the Medal of Honor, becoming the fourth Marine to receive our nation's highest military decoration during the Vietnam conflict.

At the time of his retirement from the Marine Corps in 1989, Colonel Barnum was military secretary to the commandant. Barnum recently discussed his experiences during two Vietnam tours with Vietnam Magazine contributing editor Al Hemingway.

Vietnam: Why did you decide on the Marine Corps?

Barnum: Two reasons. My cousin was in the Marines during World War II, and my dad enlisted, but the age law was passed, and my dad didn't go, which was a good thing because everyone from his recruit platoon on Parris Island went to Iwo Jima. However, another thing that really turned the tide for me was Military Day during my senior year in high school. Every branch of the service had a representative come to the high school to try and recruit young men. Well, the Air Force recruiter got up to make a pitch, and there were a lot of catcalls. Then, the Army and Navy recruiters got the same treatment. A Marine gunnery sergeant was the last one to get up to speak in the auditorium. He said, "There isn't anybody in this room I would want in my Marine Corps." Then he tore into the faculty, accusing them of "jawjacking and scratching their butts while all this turmoil was going on" and saying, "This is embarrassing." He concluded by saying, "I'm wasting my time here," and he sat down.

Vietnam: Sounds like a typical Marine Corps "gunny" to me.

Barnum: Well, needless to say, there was a line at his table after the presentation. I joined the Platoon Leaders Course (PLC) in college and took my training at Quantico, Virginia, in 1959 and 1961. I was commissioned a second lieutenant upon graduation from college in 1962 and commenced my officer training at Quantico.

Vietnam: What was your military occupational specialty (MOS)?

Barnum: Artillery. After basic school, there was a month's artillery orientation course at Quantico. The school consisted mainly of gunnery basics. Some went to artillery school in Fort Sill, Oklahoma, but I went direct to Okinawa and joined Alpha Battery, 1st Battalion, 12th Marines, 3rd Marine Division. Later, I was assigned to the guard detachment at the Marine Barracks at Pearl Harbor.

Vietnam: How did you get to Vietnam?

Barnum: General Victor H. Krulak, commanding general of Fleet Marine Force, Pacific, had devised a program for company-grade officers and staff NCOs to go to Vietnam for 60 days to serve in their MOS. It was a morale booster, too. In the guard detachment in Hawaii, it got real old after a while, saluting generals and admirals all day. When I first arrived in Vietnam in December 1965, I was sent to Echo Battery, 2nd Battalion, 12th Marines (2/12), located in a stabilized position south of Da Nang, firing in support of 2/9. That's when I was assigned to Hotel Company 2/9 as their forward observer (FO).

Vietnam: Explain your duties as an FO.

Barnum: The job of an FO attached to a rifle company is to locate targets and call for and adjust artillery fire. At that time, an FO team consisted of an officer, a radio operator, and a wireman. An artillery battery is usually in direct support of an infantry battalion, and the FOs are attached to and travel with each rifle company. The FO's job is to look at the patrol route, recon it, and usually plan calls of fire, whether they be active targets or prep (preparatory) fires. The FO had to be aware of restricted areas of fire because of friendly villages, helicopter traffic, and a number of limiting factors. When the infantry set up a perimeter at night, the FO would register in defensive fires so that in the event we were probed or assaulted, defensive fires could be called for and delivered rapidly. It's a very active role in the company.

Vietnam: You mentioned restricted areas of fire. Did you have problems with getting clearance for a fire mission?

Barnum: During my first tour, in 1965-66, I was exposed to some of that. On my second tour, in 1968-69, I was up along the DMZ (Demilitarized Zone), and we didn't encounter many problems with getting clearance due to the very nature of the combat in that area. It was very isolated along the DMZ, and pretty much everything was a free-fire zone. Not many villages to worry about.

Vietnam: How did you become involved in Operation Harvest Moon?

Barnum: I was attached to Hotel Company 2/9, and we were on the Anderson Trail, south of Da Nang, on patrol. I really didn't know too many people in the unit; I had been in Vietnam only 14 days. We were attached to 2/7 and relieved Fox Company, 2/7, which had received several casualties and had Marines suffering from immersion foot. So, Hotel Company, 2/9, became part of 2/7. We participated in Harvest Moon for a couple of days; the operation was winding down. A radio message came in telling the company commander to report back to base camp immediately. We were traveling on the main north/south road when we got hit. The entire battalion march column was ambushed. We were maybe four miles from Highway 1.

Vietnam: From what I understand, when the VC ambushed the battalion, they were attempting to split the group in two. Is that the way it was?

Barnum: Yes. We were heading out of the mountains in a battalion march column. My company was the rear element. Now, a battalion march column is strung out quite a distance. In fact, the whole purpose is for rapid movement. The lead companies had already entered the village of Ky Phu, and we were about 200 yards back from the western limits of the village.

Vietnam: Ky Phu wasn't a very big village?

Barnum: No. It wasn't very big at all. We heard shooting toward the front of the column, and we heard RPGs (rocket-propelled grenades) going off. My company commander, Captain Paul Gormley, was just coming out into an exposed position, followed by his radio operator. The enemy zeroed in on them. I'm sure they saw the radio antenna and his .45-caliber pistol and thought that they were part of the command element. And they were exactly right. The initial round hit the skipper and his radio operator. The enemy soldiers were popping up out of spider holes and seemed to be everywhere.

Vietnam: The VC were really dug in.

Barnum: Absolutely. They were good at it. So, in essence, we had a battalion strung out over 500 yards, and everyone was engaged in a firefight. I remember, after hitting the deck and scanning the area, I heard someone holler that the skipper and his radio operator had been hit. They were about 50 or 60 yards ahead of me. I saw the corpsman, Doc West, get hit two or three times trying to reach Captain Gormley. Hotel Company had just come around a hill mass and were in the open when they hit us. When I saw Doc West get wounded the third time, I just got up and ran out to get him. Then I returned, picked up Captain Gormley, and carried him back to cover. When I went back out to grab Doc West, I saw that the radio operator was dead. It was then I realized that I was the highest-ranking officer present. Everybody was looking at me, and I could see in their eyes they were saying, "Hey, lieutenant, what do we do now?"

Vietnam: What a position to be in.

Barnum: The first thing I did was run out to where the radio operator was lying, take the radio off his back, strap it on mine, and hurry back to our defensive position. I assumed command of the company, analyzed the situation, and started giving orders.

Vietnam: Did you also continue as the FO?

Barnum: Yes. My FO team and I started calling in artillery on the enemy's positions. The fire was real close. The enemy was right on top of us. The artillery came in right over our heads. It was touch and go. We were right on the gun target line. The artillery fire helped reduce the odds, stunned the enemy, and gave me an opportunity to regroup and settle folks down.

Vietnam: Sounds like you were in a real fix.

Barnum: We were. I radioed battalion headquarters and told them that Captain Gormley was dead, and I was the FO and was assuming command of the company. The battalion commander asked lots of questions. I guess I convinced him I knew what the situation was and was taking appropriate action. He told me to make sure everyone knew I was now in command.

Vietnam: And you had been in-country only 14 days.

Barnum: Well, I was the boss, 14 days or not. Getting back to the radio, everybody was on the same net. The battalion commander, each company commander, the S-3 (operations officer), and even air support. So I could listen in to all transmissions, and I soon realized everyone was in a bad way. If you were worse off than somebody else who was transmitting, you cut in, and then everyone backed off and listened.

Vietnam: I would think that everyone being on the same net would lead to confusion.

Barnum: No, it worked well. I think that's the reason we were saved. We worked together as a team and overcame a numerically superior force. Also, Brig. Gen. Jonas M. Platt, the task force commander, was in a helicopter overhead. Being on the same net meant that I could make my decisions based on what was happening somewhere else.

Vietnam: So, communications wasn't your biggest problem?

Barnum: No, in fact, getting people to stop shooting and conserve ammunition was my biggest problem. We were calling in a lot of air support. I remember standing up on a knoll and firing 3.5-inch Willie Peter (white phosphorous) rockets to mark targets and for adjusting points. We did that until we ran out of 3.5 rounds. The enemy was moving in on us on our right flank. The VC knew we were low on ammo. God bless those helo pilots. They flew for about an hour after they were out of ammo to help keep the enemy off our backs. By then, it was getting dark. Battalion headquarters informed me that we had to get out on our own. They couldn't come and get us. Everyone else was in a fix as well. I finally got some choppers to come in and evacuate the dead and wounded. Then, I had everyone drop their packs and any inoperable weapons in a pile, and I told a couple of engineers to blow it in place. I requested the battalion commander and the rest of the unit to set up a base of fire, and in fire team rushes, we started out. It is the worst feeling in the world to charge across the fire-swept ground. You're right in the open. But I told everyone, "Once we start, guys, there's no stopping."

Vietnam: How far did you have to run?

Barnum: I'd say it was approximately 200 meters. And when it came to my turn, I never ran so damn fast in my life! We made it across, and once we reached the outer limits of Ky Phu, we established a defensive position tied in with the rest of 2/7.

Vietnam: What did your unit do next?

Barnum: Once we reached Highway 1, Hotel Company was released from 2/7, which was going back to Chu Lai. Hotel Company and the rest of 2/9 were heading back north to Da Nang. We were boarding trucks on Highway 1 when we got sniped at from this village. An Ontos (multi-barreled 106mm recoilless rifle gun system) was with us, and I directed its fire at the sniper. We leveled three huts. Needless to say, the sniper fire ceased. Later on that night, a second lieutenant, who had only been in-country for three or four days, turned me in for using excessive force.

Vietnam: Were there any ramifications from the incident?

Barnum: Back at FLSG (Force Logistics Support Group) Bravo, when we bivouacked en route back to Da Nang, I was questioned by a lieutenant colonel about the incident. Well, I told him that I only did what needed to be done. I also informed them that everyone on that convoy had just experienced some pretty heavy combat and that the sniper fire was interfering with our retrograde movement, not to mention hazardous to our health. I soon found out that I had been put in for the Medal of Honor, so I guess that sniper incident was forgotten. I still stand by my actions. We eliminated an enemy threat, and no Marines got injured.

Vietnam: How did you find out about the Medal of Honor nomination?

Barnum: A Lieutenant Colonel woke me up in the middle of the night at FLSG Bravo and questioned me about the battle. Not thinking that it was anything unusual, I went back to sleep. The next day, I was relieved of command of Hotel Company and rejoined my artillery battery south of Da Nang. I went to the corpsman upon arrival in my battery position and had my feet checked because I had contracted immersion foot. My battery commander then informed me that I was being put in for the Medal of Honor.

Vietnam: That must have been a shock.

Barnum: It was. I was lucky; I wasn't even wounded. My pack was all shot up. It just wasn't my turn to go. The good Lord was watching over me.

Vietnam: When did they finally award you the medal?

Barnum: Let's see, the Battle of Ky Phu was fought on December 18, 1965, and the Medal of Honor was presented to me on February 27, 1967, more than a year later. The award recommendation goes through channels, and that takes time. I was the fourth Marine to be the recipient of the Medal of Honor during the Vietnam War and the first living officer to receive it. Sergeant Bobby O'Malley was the first living enlisted man to get it.

Vietnam: Only a handful live to receive their medals. What happened next? Did you remain in-country?

Barnum: After Harvest Moon, I was ordered to Lima Battery, 4th Battalion, 12th Marines (4/12), which had towed and self-propelled guns. The gunline was strung out over an 11-mile area. I worked in the FDC (fire direction center) and on the guns. My battery gunny was Gunnery Sergeant Leland B. Crawford, who went on to become Sergeant Major of the Marine Corps. In February 1966, my 60 days was up, and I reported back to Marine Barracks, Pearl Harbor.

Vietnam: You went back for a second tour in Vietnam in 1968-69. Wasn't that unusual for a Medal of Honor recipient to be sent back to a combat zone?

Barnum: I was an aide to General Lew Walt, who, at that time, was assistant commandant of the Marine Corps. He said to me, "If you can last a year with me, I'll send you anywhere you want to go." When my year was up, I informed him I wanted to go back to Vietnam. He pulled some strings, and I was sent back as CO of Echo Battery, 2nd Battalion, 12th Marines, the battery I was with in 1965. My battalion was in support of the 9th Marines, and Colonel Robert H. Barrow, a future commandant of the Marine Corps, was their regimental commander. My battery saw a lot of action. We built 16 fire support bases throughout the northern I Corps and participated in Operation Dewey Canyon, supposedly the largest and most successful operation of the Vietnam War. I was very proud of my Marines. North Vietnamese Army forces tried to overrun my battery one night at Fire Support Base Cunningham. We won--they didn't. I was later wounded at FSB Spark when a bunker entryway I was standing in was struck by rockets and mortars and collapsed.

Vietnam: When did you retire?

Barnum: In 1989, after nearly 28 years of active service. And I must say it was an interesting 28 years. It was a great way of life.

Article from the Department of Defense website in a feature called "Medal of Honor Monday – Highlighting recipients of the nation's highest medal for valor." Written by Katie Lange, DOD News. Used with permission.

Marine Corps Colonel Harvey Curtiss Barnum Jr. barely had time to adjust to Vietnam as a young lieutenant before he found himself commanding a company in the middle of an enemy ambush. Barnum's calm demeanor and swift decisions helped stabilize his badly damaged unit, and they earned him the Medal of Honor.

Barnum was born July 21, 1940, in Cheshire, Connecticut, to parents Harvey and Ann Barnum. During an interview later in life, Barnum said he and his younger brother, Henry, were fortunate that their parents were both very involved in their upbringing, which is likely where his understanding and love of discipline began.

Barnum was a Boy Scout and played football and baseball at Cheshire High School. He was president of both his freshman and senior classes.

While Barnum's father was a Marine during World War II, he said he chose the service because of a Marine Corps recruiter who visited his school on a career day. Barnum said the recruiter had listened to the student's reactions to the other military recruiters and was appalled by their conduct. The recruiter told the crowd that none of them was worthy of the Marine Corps. Like many other students that day, Barnum immediately wanted to prove the man wrong.

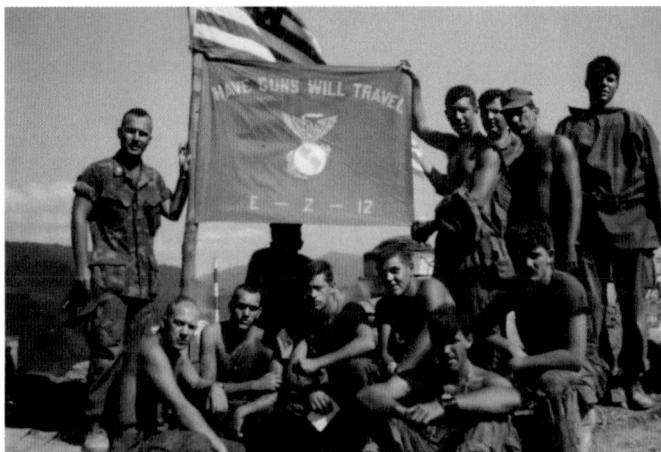

"[That recruiter] epitomized what I thought the military was all about — he stood up and took charge and made a big impression on this young 18-year-old," Barnum said in a Library of Congress Veterans History Project interview.

After graduating high school in 1958, Barnum went to St. Anselm College in New Hampshire, where he joined the Marine Corps Platoon Leaders Class, a summer program similar to ROTC. Four years later, he graduated with a degree in economics and was commissioned into the Marine Corps Reserve.

After training, Barnum was sent to serve with the 3rd Marine Division in Okinawa, Japan, before being stationed at Pearl Harbor, Hawaii, in early 1965. Later that year, his unit was ordered to go to Vietnam on a temporary deployment, and the first shipment of Marines was slated to leave prior to the holidays. Barnum said that because he was single and most of his fellow Marines weren't, he volunteered to go.

Barnum arrived in Vietnam in early December 1965 to serve with Company H, 2nd Battalion of the 9th Marines Regiment, 3rd Marine Division. Within two weeks, his unit would be enmeshed in a battle that earned him the nation's highest award for valor.

The Battle

In his Veterans History Project interview, Barnum said his unit was out on patrol when it was called back and flown to a mountain near the village of Ky Phu. They were told they would be replacing another company that had suffered several injuries during Operation Harvest Moon.

On December 18, then-1st Lt Barnum was the artillery forward observer for the company, which brought up the battalion's rear as it moved off the mountain to head back toward the village. Suddenly, they were pinned down by enemy fire from a large North Vietnamese force. The ambush separated his company from the rest of the battalion.

"It was the first time I'd been shot at," Barnum said. "So, I hit the deck."

Injuries mounted quickly for the company, but Barnum was OK. He quickly surveyed the scene and realized that the company's radio operator and its commander, Capt. Paul Gormley had fallen.

"When I ... looked around, I could see all these young Marines' eyes looking at me, and they're saying, 'OK, lieutenant, what the hell are we going to do?'" Barnum remembered. "At that point, I started doing what lieutenants do, and that's giving direction."

Barnum got up and immediately started calling in artillery, but he said he eventually called off the fire because some of the shrapnel was hitting his men. Without regard for his own safety, Barnum then ran into the open field to grab Gormley and bring him back to relative safety. He said they talked right before Gormley died in his arms.

Photo courtesy of the U.S. Navy

"The company commander just died, and the radio was still out there [on the field]," Barnum said. "So, I ran out, took the radio off the dead operator, carried it back, and strapped it to myself. I got on the phone, called the battalion commander, and told him what happened and that I was assuming command."

Barnum calmly reorganized and rallied the units around him before leading a counterattack on an enemy trench to their right. He said fixed-wing aircraft in the area couldn't come to their rescue due to bad weather, but leadership eventually provided them with two gunships to help. Barnum moved through intense enemy fire to get to a knoll where he could call in the air attacks, repeatedly exposing himself so he could physically point out the targets.

When Barnum eventually talked to the battalion commander in the village, the commander said help wouldn't be able to get them —that Barnum's company would have to fight its way out or be stuck by themselves overnight.

Photo courtesy of the U.S. Marine Corps

"I knew that was a nonstarter," Barnum said. "Casualties were mounting rapidly. Ammunition was getting low, and the ceiling was closing in on us. I didn't think our chances were going to be very good if we stayed."

So, Barnum had some Marines clear a small landing zone as he requested and directed the landing of two transport helicopters for the evacuation of the dead and wounded. The lieutenant said he and the remaining Marines then collected their packs and all the equipment that was no longer working and destroyed them "to make ourselves light." Their next move was to make it about 500 meters across open rice patties to the village without getting hit by enemy fire.

"Squad by squad, when I said 'go,' I said, 'Run as fast as you can. Don't even stop. The only time you stop is if someone gets shot and you pick them up,'" Barnum remembered.

He said it took about 45 minutes, but everyone managed to make it to the village, which the rest of the battalion was able to successfully evacuate.

Days later, Barnum learned that he was recommended for the Medal of Honor. He received it on February 27, 1967, from Navy Secretary Paul H. Nitze during a ceremony at Marine Barracks in Washington. His family, some friends, and several other Marines he fought with were able to attend.   Barnum, who was promoted to Captain in 1966, returned to Vietnam in October 1968 to command the same battery he'd served with during his first deployment. He remained in the Marines for a long time, retiring after 27 years of service in August 1989. A few years later, Barnum married a woman named Martha Hill.

During his Veterans History Project interview in the early 2000s, Barnum said that the medal can sometimes be a burden, but he's never forgotten what it stands for.

"I've worn this medal in honor of those great Marines and corpsmen who fought with me on the battlefield that day who didn't walk off or walked off seriously wounded," he said. "There were no superstars, but I happened to be the quarterback calling the plays."

Retired Marine Corps Col. Harvey Barnum, a Vietnam War veteran and Medal of Honor recipient, delivers remarks during a ceremony to name a ship in his honor at Marine Barracks Washington, D.C., July 28, 2016. The U.S.S. Harvey C. Barnum Jr. will be an Arleigh Burke-class guided-missile destroyer. DoD photo by Army Sgt. James K. McCann

Throughout his life, Barnum has continued to work with the military in an official capacity, as well as with veterans and service members through various organizations. He served as deputy assistant secretary of the Navy for reserve affairs from 2001-2009. He was also designated the acting assistant secretary of the Navy for manpower and reserve affairs in January 2009.

In 2016, it was announced that a new guided-missile destroyer would be named for him. Five years later, in April 2021, Barnum attended the keel-laying for that ship, the U.S.S. Harvey C. Barnum Jr.

Honored at the Town of Cheshire Memorial Plaza in front of Cheshire Town Hall, 84 South Main Street, Cheshire, Connecticut. Photo by the author.

Honored with a plaque and monument at the Medal of Honor Living Classroom, 554 South Main Street, Cheshire, Connecticut. Photos by the author.

Residents of Cheshire
Heroes of the United States

Medal of Honor Recipient
1st Lt. Harvey C. Barnum, Jr.
U.S. Marines
Vietnam

Medal of Honor
Recipient
Sgt. Eri D.
Woodbury
1st Vermont
Cavalry
Civil War

PRIVATE WALLACE A. BECKWITH; ARMY

February 28, 1843 (New London, CT) – November 22, 1929 (New London, CT); 86 years old
Married Josephine M. Dart (1844-1878).
Remarried Emma G. Douglas (1849-1925) in 1885.
Three sons, Richard S. (1870-1928), Lloyd P. (1873-1951), and Frederick H. (1875-1941).
Three daughters, Lucy M. Beckwith Farmer Forrest (1871-1940), Josephine M. (1878-1955), and Georgiana D.
    (1871-1879).
Stepdaughter Christine E. Hammell (1873-?).
Enlisted on August 14, 1862.
Mustered out June 16, 1865.

Born to Albert (1806-1879) and Lucy Harris Sprague Beckwith (1810-1888). Two brothers, Crandall S. (1835-1890) and Courtland A. (1839-1910).

Member of Masonic Brainard Lodge #102 in New London, Connecticut. One of five members of the 21st Connecticut to receive the Medal of Honor.

Photo courtesy of Ancestry.com

MEDAL OF HONOR CITATION

AWARDED FOR ACTIONS DURING: Civil War
BRANCH OF SERVICE: Army
UNIT: Company F, 21st Connecticut Infantry
DATE OF ISSUE AND PRESENTATION: February 15, 1897 (35 years later)
AGE ON THE DAY OF THE EVENT: 19
CITATION:

The President of the United States of America, in the name of Congress, takes pleasure in presenting the Medal of Honor to Private Wallace A. Beckwith, United States Army, for extraordinary heroism on 13 December 1862, while serving with Company F, 21st Connecticut Infantry, in action at Fredericksburg, Virginia. Private Beckwith gallantly responded to a call for volunteers to man a battery, serving with great heroism until the termination of the engagement.

The Medal of Honor was issued on February 15, 1897. Corporal John G. Palmer of Company F was also awarded the Medal of Honor for this deed. He was one of five 21st Connecticut soldiers to be awarded the Medal of Honor for bravery during the Civil War (the others being Corporal F. Clarence Buck, Sergeant Robert A. Gray, Captain William S. Hubbell, and Corporal John G. Palmer).

From Beyer, W. F., & Keydel, O. F. (2000). Deeds of valor: How America's Civil War Heroes won The Congressional Medal of Honor. Smithmark Publishers.

An example of dashing bravery and courage, which General Daniel E. Sickles designates "a heroic act," was furnished by Corporal John G. Palmer and Private Wallace A. Beckwith of Company F, Twenty-first Connecticut Infantry. The story is interestingly told by Corporal Palmer:

"At the time of Burnside's great battle of Fredericksburg, I was a boy seventeen years of age and a member of Company F, Twenty-first Connecticut Infantry. We were held in reserve in the streets of the city until the last afternoon of the desperate fight. At 4:30 p.m., we received a hurry order to go to the support of the Second Division. Away we went, glad to take an active part, as we had been under fire more or less for two or three days. As soon as we cleared the streets of the city, we were exposed to a perfect shower of bullets and exploding shells from a general attack which was now taking place all along the front. Amidst this terrible fire, we formed and moved rapidly towards the line of battle, our company marching for two or three blocks through the backyards of houses and dwellings. We had a most lively time pulling up and scaling numerous fences to keep up with that part of the line, which was meeting with less obstructions. We advanced to the scene of operations until the right of the regiment reached the railroad at the depot, the line extending to the left through some brick kilns. A light battery of four pieces, situated on a low ridge in front of the left of the regiment, was shelling the enemy, whose fronts were near, as fast as they could fire their guns.

"We were ordered to lie down, which we did in short order, and settled ourselves into the soft clay of the brickyard, which offered some degree of shelter from the iron and lead which were flying so furiously around and dangerously near our heads.

"After a time, the fire slackened. Our assault had met with a bloody repulse. Maneuvers were immediately ordered with a view of making one more grand final charge and ending the battle.

"As the attack ceased and the firing had become desultory, I raised up on my elbows; the colors of the regiment brushed my face. Pushing the flag aside, I glanced up and down the line. Our regiment appeared like two rows of dead men, everyone except the colonel, with his head face down in the mud as low as possible.

"Presently, the captain of a battery came running towards our regiment and hurriedly saluting the colonel, said: 'For God's sake, colonel, give me six men, quick, tho know something about firing a gun. I haven't men enough left to work my battery in the coming charge.'

"Our colonel faced the colors and repeated the call. Though I was the youngest member of the company, I had heard and seen enough for several days, and especially during the previous hour, to know the seriousness of the situation, to realize the probable consequences of the act, and to compare the exposure on the knoll with the safety of the shelter of the brick kilns.

"It took but a few moments for me to determine what to do. By the time the colonel had pronounced the word 'men,' I stepped from the ranks, closely followed by Comrade Beckwith and four others. We had but a few moments to look over the field and receive instructions from the Sergeant when the Captain, reading the signals from the church belfry, gave the order to stand by the guns, ready for action.

"The troops that were selected to make the final attack moved forward to the charge.

"Suddenly, the enemy opened with every gun and musket that could be brought to bear. As we occupied the only rise of ground on our side and were the only battery in action on our left, we found that several of the enemy's batteries were paying us particular attention and that we had to take their concentrated fire. The battle grew more fierce.

"Twilight came on; twilight passed to darkness. It was a grand and awe-inspiring spectacle - one mighty and thundering roar.

"Around us rained a perfect shower of bullets, which completely riddled a board fence in front of the knoll. They struck the guns and splintered the spokes of the wheels.

Shells exploded constantly over and around us and knocked down several of my comrades. Many officers and men were killed, and a great number, including several in my own regiment, were wounded in our immediate rear. We kept our little battery
barking. Our commander said that our shells were bursting squarely in the ranks of the enemy, but our army could not accomplish the impossible. The heights were too strong with earthworks, cannons, and men, and the assault ended the battle for the night.

"We lived through the entire attack uninjured. Sunday morning, the Captain of the battery thanked us heartily for our services and told us to return to our regiment. Our colonel said, as he received us: 'I am proud of my men.'"

Fredericksburg. - In December 1862, General Burnside, superseding McClellan as commander-in-chief of the Union Army, directed an attack against Fredericksburg, Virginia, on the southern bank of the Rappahannock. The town is situated on the steep slopes of one of the three wooded terraces in the narrow valley. The battle took place on the second terrace, while on the third, the enemy under Lee had gathered a force of 90,000 men.

Burnside, stationed at Falmouth, was occupied from December 11 to 13 in building bridges and throwing across the river the two divisions of Franklin and Sumner. On the 13th, assaults were made by these divisions, which were repulsed with great loss. Hooker, ordered across, had the same experience. The Union troops were gathered at Fredericksburg and withdrawn across the river.

Burnside's losses amounted to 13,000 men, while the Confederate loss was not more than a third of that number.

From The New York Times November 12, 1929

CIVIL WAR VETERAN, 86, WAS DECORATED FOR BRAVERY

NEW LONDON, Conn., November 22 – Wallace A. Beckwith, who received the Medal of Honor for Distinguished Service in the Civil War, died this morning at his home here. He was 86 years old.

He was born in this city on February 28, 1843. He was cited for gallantry under fire at Fredericksburg, Virginia.

In 1890, he was made an inspector in the Customs Service and continued in that office until 1894, when he left the service for five years. He returned to serve until 1923, when he was retired on a pension.

Mr. Beckwith made his home with his stepdaughter, Miss Christine Hammel. Besides Miss Hammel, he is survived by two daughters, Miss Josephine Beckwith and Mrs. Lucy Abels; two sons, Frederick Beckwith and Lloyd Beckwith; and a brother.

From The Day (New London, Connecticut) November 9, 1987

HERO OF 1862 BATTLE WILL HAVE A HEADSTONE

WATERFORD – Members of the Veterans of Foreign Wars will honor a Civil War veteran who received the Medal of Honor in 1897 but whose grave was unmarked for decades in a Veteran's Day ceremony in Jordan Cemetery.

The ceremony will take place at 11 a.m. Wednesday, thanks to the efforts of Thomas Durning, a veteran of the Vietnam War who has spent two years documenting Connecticut's Medal of Honor winners and making sure their graves are marked with a Veteran's Administration gravestone indicating that they had been awarded the medal.

During his research, Durning discovered the grave of Wallace A. Beckwith, a Private in Connecticut's regiment of volunteers who was honored for extraordinary heroism in the Battle of Fredericksburg, Virginia, in 1862. Beckwith did not receive the medal until 35 years later. He was one of five soldiers in his regiment to receive the medal, the nation's highest military award.

Durning, who is a firefighter in New Haven, began locating the state's Medal of Honor winners after the National Medal of Honor Historical Society contacted him through the Sons of Union Veterans of the Civil War, of which he is a member.

The Veteran's Administration supplies all veterans with a gravestone, Durning said, and the state will pay for the installation of the stones for veterans who served during wartime.

"Some people have no that they're entitled to a stone," Durning said.

Durning, who attends such ceremonies dressed as a Union soldier, has located more than 70 Medal of Honor winners in Connecticut so far, although Congress' record shows only 53. His explanation for the discrepancy is that many Connecticut residents who received the medal were incorrectly listed as residents of other states.

While looking for Beckwith's grave in Jordan Cemetery, Durning encountered John Rogers, a veteran himself, who is on the cemetery's board of supervisors.

"He was amazed there was a medal winner right in his own cemetery," Durning said.

Rogers, who is organizing Wednesday's ceremony with the Waterford VFW, is excited about the event.

"Harry Truman said he would rather receive the medal than be President of the United States," Rogers said.

From The Day (New London, CT) November 12, 1987

WATERFORD — Wallace A. Beckwith died more than a century ago, but his heroism in the Battle of Fredericksburg was extraordinary enough to bring more than 40 people out in Wednesday's frigid winds to honor his name.

Despite the rain and freezing temperatures, a crowd gathered at the Jordan Cemetery for a Veterans Day ceremony honoring the Civil War veteran who Received the Medal of Honor in 1897.

Beckwith, a Waterford resident and a private in Connecticut's 2ist Regiment of Volunteers, received the medal for his extraordinary heroism during the Virginia battle in 1862. He is buried in Jordan Cemetery.

Clad in a blue Union soldier's uniform, Thomas Durning, whose research turned up the information that Beckwith was a medal recipient, opened the 11 a.m. ceremony with a short speech on the life and service of the soldier.

"The people in Waterford are honoring Beckwith, and I'm proud to be here,' Durning said.

Many towns do nothing when they discover they have a Medal of Honor recipient, "but Waterford has given 100 percent," he said. "I'm pleased to let you know about the heroics of one of your town folk."

The Medal of Honor is the highest military honor awarded by the United States.

After his speech, members of the Veterans of Foreign Wars, American Legion, and Brainard, Lodge of Masons took turns standing by Beckwith's gravestone, speaking briefly about the soldier's and the ceremony's significance.

By remembering Beckwith, "we are honoring all veterans," said John Rogers, the Americanism Chairman of the American Legion and the VFW, who coordinated the ceremony.

Richard Faulker of Waterford, a World War II veteran, said, "Somebody who has given so much to their country should be recognized and not overlooked."

Jerry Brown of East Lyme, a member of the Norwich Vietnam Veterans Association, expressed the sentiment of most ceremony participants. "Having been in military combat, I know what he must have gone through and wanted to show my respect," Brown said.

The Brainard Lodge was invited Monday to the ceremony when Rogers discovered Beckwith had been affiliated with the organization.

More than a dozen Masons attended the ceremony.

"We came on such short notice because (Beckwith) is a brother and a proud part of our heritage," said Ralph Greene of Waterford, a Mason.

Christopher Wyld of Waterford, also a Mason, added, "He received the highest honor. The whole community should be here to honor him."

Beckwith is one of more than 70 medal recipients Durning has located, although Congress's record shows only 53.

Durning, a New Haven firefighter and a Vietnam War veteran, became involved in documenting Connecticut's Medal of Honor winners two years ago through his membership in the Sons of Union Veterans of the Civil War.

He began the project by getting a list of congressional veterans' names and matching them against records in the state library in Hartford. If there was a match, he traveled to the gravesite and had the cemetery verify the name. His search took him to three other states – Massachusetts, New York and Rhode Island.

Once winners are found, the Veterans Administration supplies the award-engraved gravestones, and the state pays for the installation, Durning said.

"One veteran said to me, 'It's a nice hobby.' But it's not a hobby. It's a duty," Durning said.

If the government is willing to recognize someone, we should be willing to go out and find them.

BECKWITH
WALLACE A. BECKWITH
1843 — 1929
Co. F. 21st REG. CONN. VOL.
MEMBER OF
MEDAL OF HONOR LEGION
HIS WIFE
EMMA G. DOUGLAS
1849 — 1925

LLOYD BECKWITH
1874 — 1951
ELIZABETH C. HAMMEL
1873 — 1967

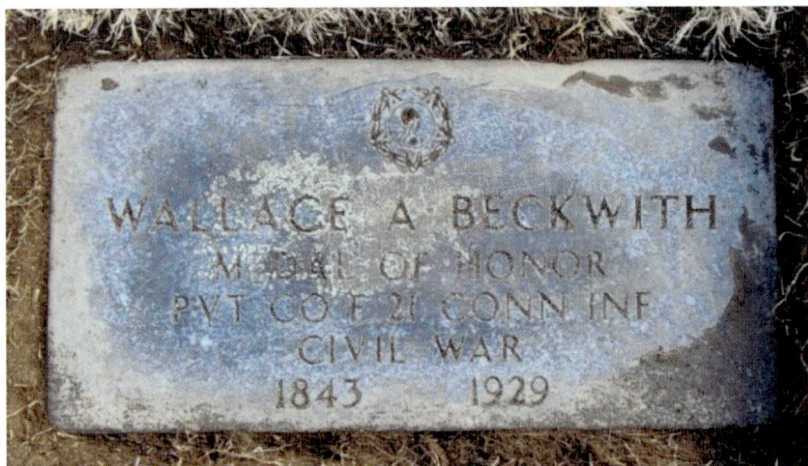

WALLACE A. BECKWITH
MEDAL OF HONOR
PVT CO F 21 CONN INF
CIVIL WAR
1843   1929

MAJOR * WILLIAM SULLIVAN "SULLY" BEEBE; ARMY

February 14, 1841 (Ithaca, NY) – October 12, 1898 (Havana, Cuba); 57 years old
Married to Sophi Sparks (1846-1914) on December 17, 1868.
Three daughters, Jessie L. (1873-1875), Frances (1878-1942), and Hannah C. (1882-1883).
Enlisted on April 23, 1864, in Thompson, Connecticut.

Born to Jeremiah S. (1790-1861) and Jessie Casey Beebe (1819-1875).

* Brevet promotion to Major. In many of the world's military establishments, a brevet was given to a commissioned officer with a higher rank title as a reward for gallantry or meritorious conduct but may not confer the authority, precedence, or pay of real rank.

   Graduated from the United States Military Academy at West Point, New York, in 1863 during the Civil War and was commissioned as a Regular Army First Lieutenant in the Ordnance Department. He remained in the Ordnance Department after the conclusion of the War, rising to Major. He died of yellow fever he contracted while serving in Cuba during the Spanish-American War.

Photo courtesy of FindAGrave.com

MEDAL OF HONOR CITATION

AWARDED FOR ACTIONS DURING: Civil War
BRANCH OF SERVICE: Army
UNIT: U.S. Army Ordnance
AGE ON THE DAY OF THE EVENT: 23
DATE OF ISSUE: June 30, 1897 (33 years later)
CITATION:

The President of the United States of America, in the name of Congress, takes pleasure in presenting the Medal of Honor to First Lieutenant William Sully Beebe, United States Army, for extraordinary heroism on 23 April 1864, while serving with U.S. Army Ordinance, in action at Cane River Crossing, Louisiana. First Lieutenant Beebe voluntarily led a successful assault on a fortified position. The President of the United States of America, in the name of Congress, takes pleasure in presenting the Medal of Honor to First Lieutenant William Sully Beebe, United States Army, for extraordinary heroism on 23 April 1864, while serving with U.S. Army Ordinance, in action at Cane River Crossing, Louisiana. First Lieutenant Beebe voluntarily led a successful assault on a fortified position.

From Beyer, W. F., & Keydel, O. F. (2000). Deeds of valor: How America's Civil War Heroes won The Congressional Medal of Honor. Smithmark Publishers.

A BATTLE BRIEF BUT BLOODY

Two hundred Union men were killed and wounded within a few minutes! This is the record of the engagement at Cane River Crossing, Louisiana, then which, considering its brief duration, there was no fiercer or more bloody struggle during the entire war. The Confederates were in a strongly fortified position; the Union forces had orders to drive them out. The two hostile bodies clashed on April 24, 1864.

First Lieutenant William S. Beebe of the Ordnance Department of the Army was the officer whose leadership won brilliant victory for the Federals on that memorable occasion. He led the one hundred and seventy-third New York Volunteers, commanded by Colonel Conrady, and so conspicuously distinguished himself that he was brevetted a Captain and awarded the Medal of Honor.

The details of the assault are told by Lieutenant Beebe himself as follows: "I was ordered by the Chief of Staff to join the assaulting column, to urge the necessity of instant attack, as I knew our rear guard was then engaged and we had to lay a pontoon bridge to cross Cane River. The division was deployed for an attack on Monett's Bluff; I stated the necessity of instant assault and offered to lead it. The offer was declined, but on its renewal, promptly accepted. I was the first man on the bluff. The color guard immediately behind me lost five men out of eight, and the killed and wounded in an affair of ten minutes were about two hundred."

From The St. John's (Arizona) Herald July 18, 1895

INTERESTING RUINS
An American's Discoveries in Peru and Bolivia
Though to Be the Most Ancient Remains of Lower Civilization to Be Found Upon the Western Hemisphere

Major William Sully Beebe, a retired Army officer living in Thompson, Connecticut, is about to send to the leading archeologists of this country and Europe what he considers proofs of some very remarkable discoveries that he has made during research that have cost him twenty years of study and a large sum of money expended in novel lines of investigation. He believes, says the New York Sun, that his findings will convince scientists that America is the seat of an older source of occidental civilization than either Assyria or Egypt. Major Beebe claims that the races that flourished around the Mediterranean – the Accadian, the Assyrian, the Egyptian, the Roman, and the Greek – prove themselves to have been the borrowers from an earlier people on this continent because, in the parallels that occur in the early traces of both civilizations, the greater purity is found in the American examples. Myths, symbols, and folklore tales that European students have not been able to make clear are simplified when read by the light of his American discoveries. In the journey to distant lands, they have been altered, copied blindly, or repeated ignorantly, he thinks, so that they have obtained altered or modified meanings on the other side. To give only one example, Major Beebe asserts that the zodiac sign of Sagittarius was at first an armadillo, the name of which in Peru meant an armored hare or rabbit. The sign and the name remained the same wherever the armadillo was known, but by the time the symbol reached northern Mexico and the region of our states, it became changed to an "armed rabbit" – a rabbit carrying a bow and arrow. It is the same sign, Major Beebe says, and stands for the same constellation in the heavens as the European symbol of a man with a bow and arrow, Sagittarius.

Major Beebe declares the most ancient remains of former civilizations on this continent to be those ruins of temples and cities that are found in the neighborhood of Lake Titicaca on the Bolivia-Peru border. These relics are scattered over a great extent of the country and reveal remarkable skill in stone cutting, in architecture, and in ornament. This region is fourteen thousand feet above the sea level and too cold to provide sustenance for more than a sparse population, but there is little doubt that its climate and its population were once very different. It once supported thousands of stonecutters who could neither live nor work there now. The Aymara tribe of Indians, the present inhabitants, have retained in great purity the language they spoke when the Spaniards conquered the country, and at that time, the Spaniards took down their fables and legends in great numbers. Major Beebe sent a capable man there to verify the old observations and make new ones, and after a study of eight other American tongues and people to the north of the Aymaras, he is convinced that they are the relics of the oldest American semi-civilization and that their influence spread over North America. Proofs of this he claims to have found as far away as Iowa and New Jersey. He asserts that there are in Egypt, and, for that matter, all around the Mediterranean, the most evident duplications of the work of these Aymaras in dials like that at Stonehenge, in Assyrian, and Egyptian buildings, in the folklore and in the languages of many peoples.

Of almost equal interest to Americans is Major Beebe's discovery with regard to the pictographic tablet found at Davenport, Iowa, and declared by Smithsonian experts to be spurious and worse than valueless. Major Beebe declares that he is able to read it. He says that it reproduces the symbols and myths of Aymara Indians and tells the same stories that are conveyed by means of the great dial temple at Tia Huanacu in their country – the same that Mr. Inwards, of London, found to correspond so nearly in appearance with a miniature temple left in Assyria. Major Beebe has reduced all his proofs to writing and arranged the vast number of analogies that he claims to have discovered between old and new world beginnings in such a manner that when all are collected and presented in print and sent out, the scholars of the world may, with the least possible trouble, examine his work and judge his claims. He is a man of leisure and of means, who, in taking up the study of Hebrew, had his attention directed to those similarities between the Israelites and our North American Indians, which have been often and generally discussed.

From The Hartford Courant October 13, 1898

DEATH OF MAJOR BEEBE
Member of Military Commission Dies of Yellow Fever at Havana

Major William S. Beebe, a member of the United States military commission to Cuba, died in Havana at 9 o'clock yesterday morning of yellow fever. A dispatch announcing his death was received by the war department from

General Wade yesterday.

Major Beebe was well known in the eastern part of the state, having been a resident of Thompson for about twelve years. He leaves a wife, Mrs. Susan Beebe, who was a Philadelphia woman, and a daughter, Miss Dorothy Beebe, both living in Thompson. Maior Beebe was a graduate of West Point and served during the War of the Rebellion in General Banks's expedition from New Orleans up the Red River. He was made a major in the ordnance bureau early in the war with Spain and was last at his home in Thompson early in September. He went to Havana with the military commission. Major Beebe was formerly the commander of H.E. Warner Post, No. 4, G. A. R., of Putnam. He was about 50 years old. Among all who knew him, especially Army officers with whom he enjoyed an extensive acquaintance, he was very highly spoken of.

Havana, Oct. 12. —General Wade has cabled to Washington, asking if the health authorities would permit Major Beebe's body to be taken to New York, enclosed in a metallic casket, by the first steamer available. He is waiting for an answer. If it is in the negative, the funeral may take place this afternoon, and the remains may be subsequently removed to the United States. The death of Major Beebe has been a great shock to all the members of the United States military commission, as his condition yesterday evening offered no reason to believe his death was approaching.

Buried in the National Cemetery at West Point, 329 Washington Road, West Point, New York; Section 20, Row A, Grave 11. Photos by the author.

The inscription on the large stone reads:

William Sullivan Beebe
Born in
Ithica, NY February 14, 1841
U.S.M.A. 1863
Brevet Captain
For intrepidity, daring and skill
in leading men in the face of the enemy.
Brevet Major
Apr 23, 1864 at the Siege of Fort Morgan, Ala.
Medal of Honor
For most distinguished gallantry in action
Cane River Crossing, Louisiana
Major, Chief Ordnance Officer
U.S.V. June 27, 1898.
Died at
Havana, Cuba. October 12, 1898.

Sophia Sparks
Born in
Philadelphia, Pa., February 4, 1846
Daughter of Thomas and Ann Eliza Sparks
Married
William Sullivan Beebe on Dec. 17, 1868
Died at
Thompson, Ct., July 19, 1914

TORPEDOMAN FIRST CLASS HENRY JOSEPH BREAULT; NAVY

October 14, 1900 (Putnam, CT) – December 5, 1941 (Newport, RI); 41 years old
Unmarried
Enlisted on July 14, 1920, after serving in the British Navy.
Serial number 2108003.
Assigned to the Submarine O-5, the U.S.S. Henley (DD-391) on February 23, 1937, and the U.S.S. Truxtun (DD-229) on September 15, 1939.

Born to Joseph J. (1874-1947) and Flora M. Alvina Breault (1877-1913). Two sisters, Diana Breault Drennan (1903-1941), Beatrice C. Breault Mylonas (1909-1999). One half-sister Estelle R. Breault Bickford (1916-1970). Henry was 12 or 13 years old when his mother passed in 1913.

Henry Breault has the distinction of being the only enlisted Navy submariner to receive the Medal of Honor. The submarine fleet would see seven more awarded during the Second World War, all submarine captains.

The Naval Submarine League Torpedoman Second Class Henry Breault Award for Submarine Professional Excellence recognizes E6 and below personnel for achievement, contribution, specific action, or consistent performance that best exemplifies the traditional spirit embodied in the Submarine Force.

Photo courtesy of Ancestry.com

Photo # NH 44551   USS O-5 off Provincetown, Massachusetts, during trials, 14 April 1918

Photo courtesy of the U.S. Naval Historical Center.

MEDAL OF HONOR CITATION

AWARDED FOR ACTIONS DURING: Peace Time Awards
BRANCH OF SERVICE: Navy
ASSIGNED TO: U.S. Submarine O-5
GENERAL ORDERS: War Department, General Orders No. 125, February 20, 1924
AGE ON THE DAY OF THE EVENT: 23
CITATION:

The President of the United States of America, in the name of Congress, takes pleasure in presenting the Medal of Honor to Torpedoman Second Class Henry Breault, United States Navy, for heroism and devotion to duty while serving on board the U.S. Submarine O-5 at the time of the sinking of that vessel at Limon Bay, Panama Canal Zone. On the morning of 28 October 1923, the 0-5 collided with the steamship Abangarez and sank in less than a minute. When the collision occurred, Torpedoman Second Class Breault was in the torpedo room. Upon reaching the hatch, he saw that the boat was rapidly sinking. Instead of jumping overboard to save his own life, he returned to the torpedo room to the rescue of a shipmate whom he knew was trapped in the boat, closing the torpedo room hatch on himself. Breault and Brown remained trapped in this compartment until rescued by the salvage party 31 hours later.

Presentation Date and Details: March 8, 1924, at the White House. Presented by President Calvin Coolidge.

Photo courtesy of the National Archives, photo no. LC-USZ62-131582.

Photo courtesy of Courtesy of the National Archives, photo no. LC-USZ62-131583.

Motor Machinist's Mate First Class Clyde E. Hughes, 22, of Easton, Illinois; Mess Attendant First Class Fred C. Smith, 37, of Barbados, West Indies; and Fireman First Class Thomas T. Metzler, 23, of Philadelphia, Pennsylvania, were the other missing sailors. Petty Officer Clyde E. Hughes' body was never found.

From The Idaho Statesman, November 1, 1923

TWO LOCKED IN WRECKED SUB
Survivors Tell of Experiences of Thirty Hours at Bottom of Sea

NEW YORK (AP) – Graphic stories of the experiences of two men locked for 30 hours in the wrecked American submarine O-5 on the bottom of the ocean are told in a dispatch from Balboa to the Evening World Wednesday.

The story was related by Lawrence T. Brown of Lowell, Massachusetts, Chief Electrician's Mate, one of the men rescued from the submarine, which was sunk in a collision with the steamship Abangarez off Panama Sunday.

"The first hour was the hardest," he said. "We didn't know just what had happened or what might pop next. After three hours, we knew they were working on the boat, and we quit worrying. But it wasn't very pleasant at that."

Henry Breault, 23, of White Plains, New York, a torpedo dispatcher, was the hero. Brown was warm in praise of the boy, and his sentiments were echoed by officers and others of the crew of the O-5. Breault was on the submarine deck and saw the looming bow of the Abangarez. Instead of jumping to safety in the sea, he hurled himself into a hatchway loading to the torpedo room because he thought "there might be others down there."

He awakened Brown, and they closed the door, but not until a foot of water had rushed in as the submarine started to sink.

"We went down in about 30 seconds," Brown said. "We settled in about 40 feet of water. Forty-five minutes after going down, the batteries in the after compartment exploded, and we spent five hot minutes in the hold.

"After we had been there about three hours, a diver came alongside. Breault and I separated, pounding on the boat's sides so that the rescuers would know there were two of us. Breault played a kind of tune with his hammer, indicating to them that we were in good shape and cheerful. We had no food and no water and only the light of a flashlight, but we were confident we could hold out for 48 hours.

"The air pressure gave violent headaches after 20 hours. We did very little talking or moving about; it excited our heart action too much."

The first hoist failed, he explained, after 12 hours.

"A long time afterward," Brown went on, "when we had forgotten time and didn't want to think about it, a second hoist started. We went up slowly. It seemed like an eternity. The last 20 minutes were terrible. Then, we heard our comrades walking on deck. We knew we were at the surface. Breault opened the hatch – and we were saved."

Charles R. Butler, Chief Machinist's Mate from New Haven, Connecticut, went down with the boat but fought his way to the surface through an open hatch.

From the New York Post March 15, 1924

HERO IN SEA CRASH TO "STICK WITH SHIP"

Congressional Medal of Honor Man Was In No Hurry For Decoration

LIKES LIFE ON SUBMARINE

Henry Breault, whose heroic conduct in the submarine O-5 disaster won him the Congressional Medal of Honor, sails this afternoon from New York on the General W.C. Gorgas after spending two days leave at the home of his parents, Mr. and Mrs. Joseph H. Breault of 15 Harrison Boulevard, Silver Lake Park, Harrison. He is bound for Panama, where the damaged submarine is undergoing repairs.

Breault, in an interview today, made it plain that he plans to spend the remainder of his life on the job, which made him one of the most famous young men in the country. He is twenty-three. His reply to the question as to whether he would stay in the service was, "I hope to tell you."

Breault was supposed to be in Washington a week ago Wednesday to receive the medal from President Coolidge, but he stayed in White Plains. He said he could see no reason to hurry.

Breault is modest. He was not wearing the blue button, which shows him to be one of the twenty-four men who have received the Congressional medal. He had both the medal and the button in his pocket. The medal is inscribed on the back:

"Henry Breault, Torpedoman Second Class, USN, U.S. Submarine O-5, for unusual heroism and devotion to duty in saving a life and government property. When in collision with the S.S. Abangarez, the U.S. submarine was sunk in forty feet of water on 28 October 1923."

This article was originally published in the U.S. Naval Institute's Proceedings magazine in the February 1972 edition. Copyright U.S. Naval Institute. Used with permission.

THE O-5 IS DOWN!

By Captain Julius Grigore, Jr., U.S. Naval Reserve

At 6:00 a.m. on Sunday, 28 October 1923, the U.S.S. O-5 (SS-66) had passed the luxurious Washington Hotel on Manzanillo Point, Colon, Panama, and was proceeding on a southerly course across Limon Bay en route to Gatun Locks. The 173-foot, 520-ton O-5, commanded by Lieutenant Harrison Avery, U. S. Navy, and attached to Commander, Submarine Force, Coco Solo, Canal Zone, was leading the *O-3, O-6,* and *O-8* in a routine transit of the Panama Canal to the Pacific.

Earlier, the United Fruit Company's 380-foot, 5,000-ton SS *Abangarez,* Captain W. A. Card, Master, had arrived from Havana and anchored in Limon Bay.

At 6:14 a.m., the *Abangarez* weighed anchor to proceed to Dock No. 6, Cristobal; at the same time, the O-5 received Panama Canal Pilot G. O. Kolle and was again underway at about 12 knots. The *Abangarez* was about 1,000 yards forward of the
O-5's starboard beam, swinging eastward to dock.

About two minutes after going ahead, the O-5 stopped to shift from direct diesel to electric motor drive to enable her to maneuver and use her propellers astern. The approximate speed, movements, and position of the two ships were as follows:

- o   The O-5's engines were stopped. She was unable to turn her propellers, drifting in a southerly direction and approaching the port bow of the *Abangarez.*
- o   The *Abangarez,* broad on the starboard bow of the O-5, was heading easterly with engines stopped, moving at about four knots across the main channel and across the course of the O-5.

One minute after the O-5's engines were stopped, the *Abangarez* and the O-5 converged, and obviously collision was unavoidable. Up to this time, no whistle or other signals were exchanged between either vessel.

At 6:22, Captain Card, seeing that the headings and speeds of the O-5 and *Abangarez* made collision imminent, sounded a danger signal of four short blasts. This was the first signal by either vessel. The *Abangarez* then backed emergency full speed and let go of her starboard anchor. Without acknowledgment of the *Abangarez's* danger signal, the O-5 held rudder amidships and continued on a southerly heading. Although unable to operate her propellers, the O-5 made no effort to check her headway by releasing anchors.

At 6:24, by the clocks of the *Abangarez* and Panama Canal Tug *U.S. Porto Bello,* the *Abangarez* hit the starboard side of the O-5, and stove in a hole about 10 feet long and 3 feet wide in the control room and No. 1 main ballast tank. The O-5, with 21 officers and men on board, rolled about 15 degrees to port and then righted. She then sank by the bow in seven fathoms of water within a minute. The *Abangarez* was undamaged.

Captain Card later reported to the Board of Inquiry investigating the collision that his ship was always dodging submarines in Limon Bay, and he went on to say: "Before we struck, I heard a call from the submarine's conning tower for everyone to come from below. When we struck, someone ordered the O-5 crew to jump overboard. We threw life rings and preservers overboard and dropped ends of mooring lines over the side. We picked up eight survivors, including Lieutenant Avery."

Eight minutes after the sinking, Chief Machinist's Mate C. R. Butler, U.S. Navy, was shot to the surface in an air pocket. He was rescued by the Panama Canal launch, *U. S. Rodman.* He did not know who was left in the submarine.

George W. Cadell, Master of the towboat *Porto Bello,* stated that his crew took six O-5 survivors on board and that the tug, *U. S. Tavernilla,* saved one man.

Captain Cadell witnessed the collision and reported to the Board:

> "I received orders to tug the Abangarez *to Dock No. 6. We were about to let lines go when I saw a line of submarines proceeding into the Canal channel and toward the port bow of the* Abangarez. *It looked as though there would be a collision. It is not customary, and against the Rules of the Road, to cross a ship's bow when you have her on your starboard side. I started for the scene at full speed. At first, it looked like the submarine might cross the bow of the* Abangarez. *When we were about halfway, the* Abangarez *rammed the* O-5. *The time was 6:24."*

Lieutenant Avery and the O-5 survivors were brought to Dock No. 6. Visibly shaken, Avery mustered his rescued officers and men. Sixteen were present. Five men were missing. They were Henry Breault, Torpedoman, Second Class; Lawrence T. Brown, Chief Electrician's Mate; C. E. Hughes, Motor Machinist's Mate, First Class; Thomas T. Metzler, Fireman, First Class; and Fred C. Smith, Mess Attendant, First Class.

Rescue efforts began immediately. Navy divers on a salvage tug stationed at Coco Solo arrived to inspect the O-5 on the bottom. Raps on her hull brought a response from within. Two men of the missing five, Breault and Brown, it would later be ascertained, were alive in the forward torpedo room. Hughes, Metzler, and Smith were not in the O-5. Metzler and Smith were found shortly after the collision and were buried with military honors at Mt. Hope Cemetery [sic], Canal Zone. The body of Hughes was never recovered.

Aside from reporting the extent and location of the damage and discovering that survivors were on board the O-5, Navy divers were helpless to rescue the trapped men. Therefore, a means to lift the submarine off the bottom had to be found if Breault and Brown were to be saved from suffocation.

Artificial lungs and rescue chambers had not been invented, and there were no salvage pontoons within 2,000 miles of the Canal Zone. By a stroke of luck, however, there were in the Canal Zone two 250-ton capacity crane barges, the *U.S. Ajax* and the *U.S. Hercules.* These leviathans had the mightiest lift in the world for floating equipment. They had been built in Germany, especially for handling the enormous lock gates of the Panama Canal. Captain Amos Bronson, Jr., U.S. Navy, Commander, Submarine Base, Coco Solo, and in charge of the O-5 salvage operation, requested the Panama Canal to furnish one of the floating cranes for service over the O-5.

To add to the rescuers' frustration, a slide had occurred in Gaillard Cut, the narrowest part of the Canal. Both cranes were opposite the slide, 50 miles from the O-5. Ironically, this was the first slide to block the Cut since 1916.

Working to remove the slide were two behemoth dipper dredges, the *U.S.S. Cascades* and *S.S. Paraiso.* Each of their bites could scoop 15 cubic yards of earth. They were the biggest in the world, built especially for enlarging and maintaining the Canal. Relentlessly, they cleared a narrow passage for the *Ajax,* and by 2:00 p.m. of the 28th, the *Ajax* squeezed through and was rushed by tow to the O-5. She appeared off Dock No. 6 at about 10:30 that night.

In advance of the arrival of the *Ajax,* Panama Canal salvage forces assembled over the luckless O-5. Among them was a 38-year-old Virginian, Sheppard J. Shreaves, who was dockmaster and foreman shipwright for the Panama

Canal Mechanical Division. Barrel-chested, tough, soft-spoken, and unassuming, Shep Shreaves was a qualified diver and supervisor of the Canal's highly proficient salvage and diving crew. Rather than risk the lives of his men on this treacherous underwater assignment, Shep himself went down. (Since Panama Canal forces and heavy equipment were being used to lift the bow of the O-5, it became the responsibility of the Canal organization to tunnel under the O-5, pass through the lifting cables, secure the cable to the hook of the *Ajax,* and otherwise prepare the O-5 for raising.) Shep Shreaves later recalled:

> "We spotted the O-5 on the bottom by the air bubbles exhausted from the compartment holding Breault and Brown. To survive, they were bleeding air from 3,000 lb. compressed air reserves in the forward torpedo room.
>
> "Since the Navy divers gave me a good briefing on the position of the O-5 and the location of the two trapped men, I went right in through the hole in her side. The light of my lamp was feeble against the black pitch. Inside, it was an awful mess. It was tight and slippery. I was constantly pushing away floating debris.
>
> "When I reached the forward bulkhead of the engine room, I rapped with my diving hammer. Faint taps were returned. Someone was still alive. I acknowledged with a feeling of hopelessness, as I could do no more at the time.
>
> "I emerged from O-5. By prearrangement, I signaled to lower the fire hose. The O-5 lay upright in several feet of soft mud. I began jetting a trench under her bow. Sluicing through the muck was easy—too easy, for it could cave in upon me. Swirling black engulfed me, and I worked by feel and instinct. I had to be careful not to dredge too much from under the bow, for the O-5 could crush down on me. Occasionally, I'd hit the hull to let the boys inside know someone was working to save them. Weak taps were returned each time."

Shep continued his desperate efforts to dredge out the mud, aware as he worked that he might well be digging his own grave.

Finally, the tunnel was through, and Shep passed a guideline under the O-5. It was attached to a 4-inch diameter steel cable. The cable was snaked under her bow, and both ends shackled to the lifting hook of the *Ajax.*

Three times, the cable broke from the weight of the O-5. Each time, a new cable was wrestled under the bow. Aside from the submarine's flooded weight, there was the problem of the powerful mud suction, which somehow had to be broken.

By the early morning of the 29th, round-the-clock efforts to raise the O-5 had failed miserably, and fears for Breault and Brown mounted.

Shep surfaced occasionally to report to Captain Bronson and to permit Navy doctors to examine him. They were concerned that his extreme exertion while working under pressure would put too great a strain on his heart. But, by now, Shep Shreaves had no thought of his own safety—paramount in his thoughts were those two entrapped men in the blackness below.

After being underwater and in his diving suit for almost 24 hours, Shep surfaced and seemed to be functioning on willpower alone. His job below was done, and the O-5 was ready for a fourth attempt to lift her. At 12:30 p.m. on the 29th, from topside, Shep released compressed air into the engine room of the O-5 to unflood that compartment and lighten the boat. Water and mud bubbled to the surface as from a boiling cauldron. The *Ajax* took a strain on the cable. When Shep sensed that the moment was right, he signaled the *Ajax* to commence lifting. The silence that followed was almost unbearable. The bay was as calm as glass, for which all were grateful. Usually, there was a two to four-foot chop, which was disruptive to diving operations. The *Ajax* continued to haul, and the bow of the O-5 inched upward. After what seemed an eternity, the bow broke the surface, and a roaring cheer was heard even in Cristobal. When the hatch leading to the men became accessible, a score of rescuers tried to jump onto the O-5 to open it.

The two imprisoned men crawled from the O-5. Topside, Brown fainted from prostration. The moment was charged with emotion, and many wept unashamedly in relief and thanksgiving.

Breault and Brown, while on the deck of the *Rodman,* hugged each other with joy at being alive and among their fellow men again. Rushed into a decompression chamber at Coco Solo Hospital, they were later taken to Colon Hospital to determine what ill effects they might have suffered from 31 hours of torturous confinement.

"I was a big hero for a while," Shreaves later recalled. "The boys carried me around on their shoulders. Everybody rushed down to the Stranger's Club in Colon for a big celebration and to relieve their tension. But me, I went to sleep at the party."

The O-5 incident established a world record for Shep. His [dives] were the longest duration dives up to that time.

There was now time to obtain the answers to the important question. How did Breault and Brown become confined in the O-5?

When the collision occurred, the 23-year-old Breault had been in the forward torpedo room. Upon hearing the order to abandon the O-5, he escaped to the main deck, but he quickly realized that his friend, Chief Lawrence T. Brown, was asleep in the forward battery room. Breault, with more concern for warning Brown than for saving his own life, dropped into the O-5 as she was sinking, securing the hatch cover. Brown was awake but had not heard the order to abandon the O-5. Until Breault appeared, he remained unaware of what had happened. With water engulfing them, they attempted an escape through the conning tower, but the deluge blocked that route. They struggled back into the forward torpedo room and forced shut its watertight door.

Immediately thereafter, the forward battery room, where Brown had been sleeping, filled with seawater. The batteries shorted, an incandescent arc ignited the chlorine gas, and a violent explosion erupted. Miraculously, the door to their steel tomb held. (This was the second battery explosion during the O-5's short life. On 5 October 1918, someone had accidentally left the ventilator to the battery room closed, causing gas to accumulate and explode. Two lives were lost, and two men were injured.)

About three hours after Breault and Brown became trapped, a Navy diver hammered the hull. Brown recalled:

> "Breault and I separated to pound on each of the boat's sides. In this way, the rescuers would know there were two of us. Breault played a kind of tune with his hammer, indicating to the diver that we were in good shape and cheerful. Neither of us knew Morse code. We had no food or water and only a flashlight. We were confident we could stay alive for forty-eight hours.
> "The high pressure and foul air gave us severe headaches. We did very little moving or talking; it excited our hearts too much.
> "We heard scraping on the hull for hours. A couple of times, we felt the O-5 being lifted, and then we got tossed roughly when the slings broke. We knew they were hard after us. This buoyed our hopes for rescue tremendously.
> "Finally, the sub began to be tilted upward slowly. We felt we would escape this time, but it seemed like forever. The last 20 minutes were unbearable. We heard our comrades walking on deck. Breault opened the hatch, and we could see daylight. We were saved!!!"

It was for Breault's act of selflessness and valor, by going to the assistance of his shipmate in the face of almost certain death, that he was awarded the Congressional Medal of Honor by President Calvin A. Coolidge on 4 April 1924.

Shep also was honored for his heroic O-5 exploit. The Acting Governor of the Canal Zone, H. Burgess, recommended Shep for a Congressional Life Saving Medal. He also received a 14-karat gold watch from 800 grateful members of the Coco Solo Submarine Base. The presentation was made at a Navy night banquet to inaugurate the opening of the Y.M.C.A. Army-Navy Club, Cristobal. The watch was inscribed, "To S. J. Shreaves, from Submarine Force, Coco Solo, C.Z., for his heroism in raising the O-5." Breault and Brown presented it to Shep.

Shep's performance on the O-5 was not the end of his heroic deeds. On 16 July 1924, four laborers were trapped in the hold of the SS Columbia. Shep went down after them, but he was too late. The laborers were dead from poisonous fumes, and Shep was hauled up unconscious.

For this rescue attempt, he received recognition from John Barton Payne, Chairman of the American Red Cross. Payne's commendation, which applied equally to his O-5 exploits, read:

> "Your extraordinary heroism has aroused my admiration. It is one thing to calmly perform a heroic act under the stimulation of a great wave of excitement, without having time to think much of danger, and quite another to calmly face death without excitement and inspiration of dramatic circumstances."

With more than 1,000 dives behind him, Shep retired to St. Petersburg, Florida, on December 31, 1945, after 32 years of Panama Canal service. He died in January 1968.

Other lives were touched by the O-5 sinking. R. G. Lewis, a photographer for Fox Movietone News, who now resides in retirement in the Republic of Panama, was awarded a five-dollar bonus by his company for the best subject of the current week. His extraordinary film documented the full pictorial sequence of the O-5 rescue and salvage operation.

W. H. Stone received a commendation for efficient and valuable services rendered in connection with the final raising of the O-5. It was Stone who suggested a plan for fitting a wooden cofferdam around the gash in the O-5. It permitted the O-5 to be pumped out sufficiently to raise and tow her to the U.S. Submarine Base, Coco Solo.

On 26 November 1923, Lieutenant Avery was found to be responsible for the collision, but a Court of Naval Inquiry later cleared the O-5 of blame for the collision. At the time of his death, in October 1934, Lieutenant Commander Avery commanded the *U.S.S. Isabel* (PY-10) of the Asiatic Fleet.

The ordeal suffered by them made her valueless for future naval service. She was stripped of valuable fittings and equipment and sold to a private individual for $3,125 on 12 December 1924. Her original cost had been $638,000.

This did not end the O-5 incident. On 14 August 1927, the SS *Abangarez* was seized by U.S. marshals on her arrival in New Orleans from Havana. Libels exceeding $336,000 were brought against the vessel. The government charged negligence among the reasons for the seizure. United States vs. United Fruit Company (Submarine O-5 — SS *Abangarez*) continued in the courts until 20 August 1932, when Federal Judge Wayne G. Borah, New Orleans, ruled the O-5 was at fault in the collision.

At a time when modern rescue and safety devices did not exist, and while submarines were still in their infancy, it remains a remarkable feat that the two men trapped in the O-5 were not only rescued but that their submarine was raised quickly thereafter. Rescue of personnel from within a disabled submarine was not duplicated until 16 years later, in 1939, when 33 men were saved from the U.S.S. *Squalus* (SS-192) through the use of a submarine rescue chamber.

Had the *Abangarez* and the O-5 collision occurred elsewhere, Breault and Brown would have perished for want of the rare combination of humanity and technology that was required to affect their rescue and which made the O-5 incident unique in the annals of submarine rescues.

From the Worcester Observer November 19, 1988

LOCAL HERO RECEIVES BELATED TRIBUTE

There are few people alive in Putnam today who knew Henry Breault, but a few do know of the heroic action that earned him the Congressional Medal of Honor, and they are determined that it not be forgotten.

Last week, members of the Putnam Veterans of Foreign Wars post unveiled a plaque at Breault's grave in St. Mary's Cemetery. The inscription commemorates how Breault saved the lives of two shipmates on a submarine after it had collided with a steamship off the coast of Panama on the morning of October 28, 1924. Breault was an experienced Navy man, having served aboard 2 British ships homeported in Halifax, Canada, during World War I. One living person who did know Breault well is 82-year-old Fred St. Onge of Providence Street, his first cousin.

St. Onge said Breault was born near Grand Isle, Vermont, on October 14, 1900. Breault moved as a child to Canada and joined the British Navy in 1916 at age 16, two years after the war broke out in Europe.

St. Onge said the sinking of the submarine wasn't the first rescue operation Breault was involved in. He explained that when his cousin was stationed in Halifax on the cruiser H.M.S. Niobe, the harbor was devasted by an explosion, and Breault was involved in searching for survivors.

After the war, Breault moved to Pumam to live with St. Onge's family, St. Onge said Breault found a job with the New Departure company in Bristol, making coaster brakes for bicycles.

But Breault only stayed with the job for a year. "He said he never felt well unless he was on the water," St Onge recalled. He always had a yen for salt water. It was in his blood because his father was a sailor in the Spanish-

American War.

"Henry said the ocean air was fresh and always made him feel good," St. Onge explained.

After he left New Departure, Breault joined the U.S. Navy's submarine service and worked on board the O-5 in the torpedo room. It was just outside the Panama Canal that the Abangarez, a United States Fruit Company ship, collided with the submarine.

St. Onge said several men died in the collision, but many escaped. Breault was just emerging from the hatch of the submarine as it was sinking, but he turned back because he knew two of his friends wouldn't make it out in time.

The O-5 sank to the bottom of the bay with the three men aboard. Because it went down in fairly shallow water, Breault was able to communicate with rescue personnel by tapping out Morse Code on the hull of the submarine.

The men remained submerged for 31 hours before being rescued.

On March 8, 1924, Breault received the Congressional Medal of Honor, the nation's highest military honor, at the White House from President Calvin Coolidge.

St. Onge said the submarine O-5 was raised from the bay and recommissioned. Breault went back to the boat and served on it until he died in the Newport Naval Hospital on December 5, 1941, just two days before the Japanese bombed Pearl Harbor.

St. Onge said Breault died from lung problems contracted as a result of being trapped in the sunk submarine.

Breault's body was taken from Newport to the Gilman Funeral Home in Putnam and buried in St. Mary's Cemetery.

Without the efforts of one man, only St. Onge and perhaps a few others would be aware that a Medal of Honor winner is buried in Putnam.

Earlier this year, Thomas F. Duming Jr., the secretary and treasurer for a group called the Connecticut Department Sons of Union Veterans of the Civil War, notified members of the Putnam Veterans of Foreign Wars that a Congressional Medal of Honor recipient was buried in town. Ironically, the Putnam VFW post is named in memory of Breault's uncle, Albert J. Breault.

Finding the graves of Medal of Honor winners is not normally a function of his job with the organization, Durning explained. However, a group called the Medal of Honor Historical Society had asked him to locate and obtain government grave markers specifically designed for Medal of Honor winners.

I took on this task and found that not only Civil War recipient's graves were not marked, but almost none were, up to and including Vietnam veterans' graves," he said.

To date, Durning has located and ordered 33 Medal of Honor grave markers in several cemeteries around the country. The markers are provided free of charge by the Veterans Administration, and in Connecticut, they are placed by the Veterans Home and Hospital for a small fee.

Durning explained that the Department of the Navy stopped issuing Medals of Honor during peacetime in 1963. Medals of Honor were first issued to Union troops during the Civil War. Legislation adopted in 1861 stipulated that the medals would be awarded in the Navy for "gallantry in action and other seaman-like qualities." Later, the wording was added stating the Congressional Medal of Honor would be awarded to seamen for "deeds of gallantry and heroism during times of war and of peace."

Durning said a photo of Breault will be displayed on the hangar deck of the U.S.S. Intrepid, which is permanently anchored in New York Harbor. The vessel is the headquarters for the Medal of Honor Historical Society.

Breault will be among other heroes represented there, including aviator Charles A. Lindbergh, Arctic explorer Adolphus Washington Greely, and U.S. Admiral and polar explorer Richard E. Byrd.

From 1865 to 1940, the Navy awarded 189 peacetime Medals of Honor, including 184 to sailors (five posthumously) and five to U.S. Marines.

St. Onge described his cousin Henry as "an average fellow, good-natured, very sociable, and a person with an open mind."

"I can still see him when he used to live with us. I remember clearly he used to smoke English Ovals and Turkish Trophies," St. Onge said.

From the Congressional Medal of Honor Society archives, an obituary in a Putnam, Connecticut newspaper dated December 10, 1941.

LOCAL MAN DIES AT NAVAL HOSPITAL

Seaman Henry Breault has Distinguished Record During 20 Years in the U.S. Navy
Was Decorated For Heroism When Submarine Sank in Panama Canal

Henry Breault, the nephew of Albert J. Breault, in whose honor the local VFW post was named, died last Thursday in the United States Naval Hospital in Newport at the age of 41. Breault had served for 20 years with the United States Navy and four years with the British Navy and distinguished himself as a hero at the time of the sinking of the Submarine O-S in the Panama Canal in 1923.

Breault had been suffering from a heart ailment for over a year. Although the Naval Department planned to retire him because of his health, at the Putnam man's request, he was allowed to continue on active service until he became seriously ill and was admitted to the Newport Hospital.

Born in Putnam on October 14th, 1900, he was the son of Joseph and Flora Breault. When he was 16 years old, he joined the British Navy and, served a term of four years, and later enlisted in the US. Navy and served for 20 years.

When the Submarine O-5 was rammed in the Panama Canal and sank, quick action on the part of Breault in clamping shut the hatch as the boat began to submerge saved the lives of all but three of the members of the crew.

The vessel was brought to the surface 36 hours after the accident. Breault was decorated for his valor by President Coolidge.

Besides his father, Joseph Breault of White Plains, NY, he is survived by two sisters, Mrs. Estelle Bickford of Riverhead, Long Island, and Beatrice Breault of Yonkers, New York.

Funeral services were held Tuesday morning at 9:00 o'clock at St. Mary's Church, with Reverend Charles H. Parquette officiating. As the body was lowered into the grave, Taps was sounded by Armand Lebeau, one of the members of the VFW post. The bearers were Frank X. Vadnais, Antonio Forcier, and Fred St. Onge. Reverend John P. Wodardski officiated at the committal service.

Honored at the Henry Breault Footbridge, part of the Putnam River Trail, Kennedy Drive, Putnam, Connecticut. Photo by the author.

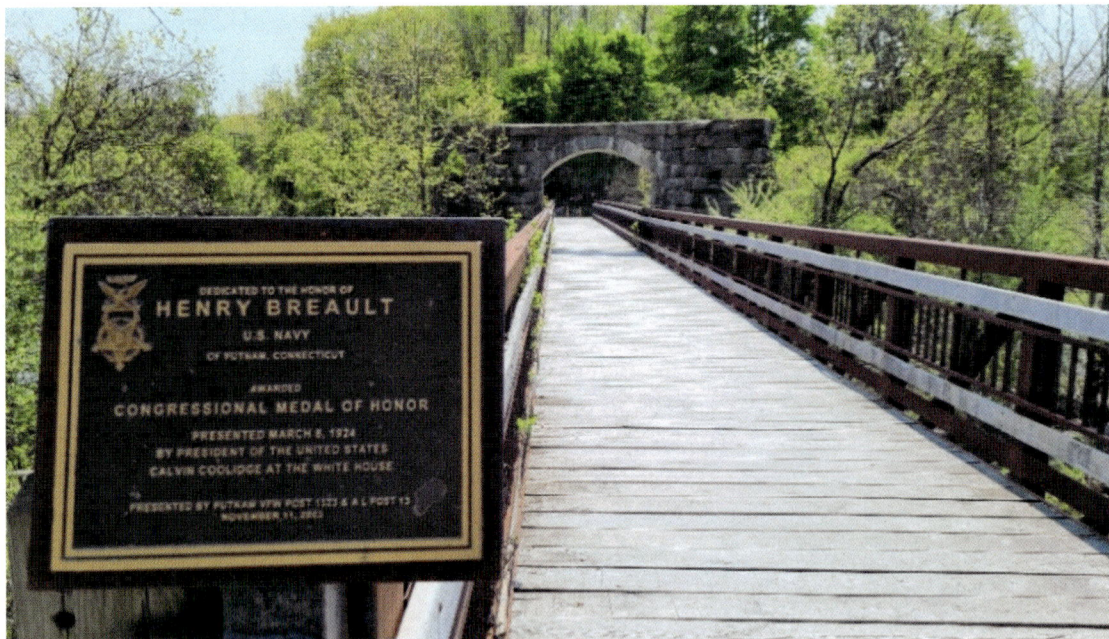

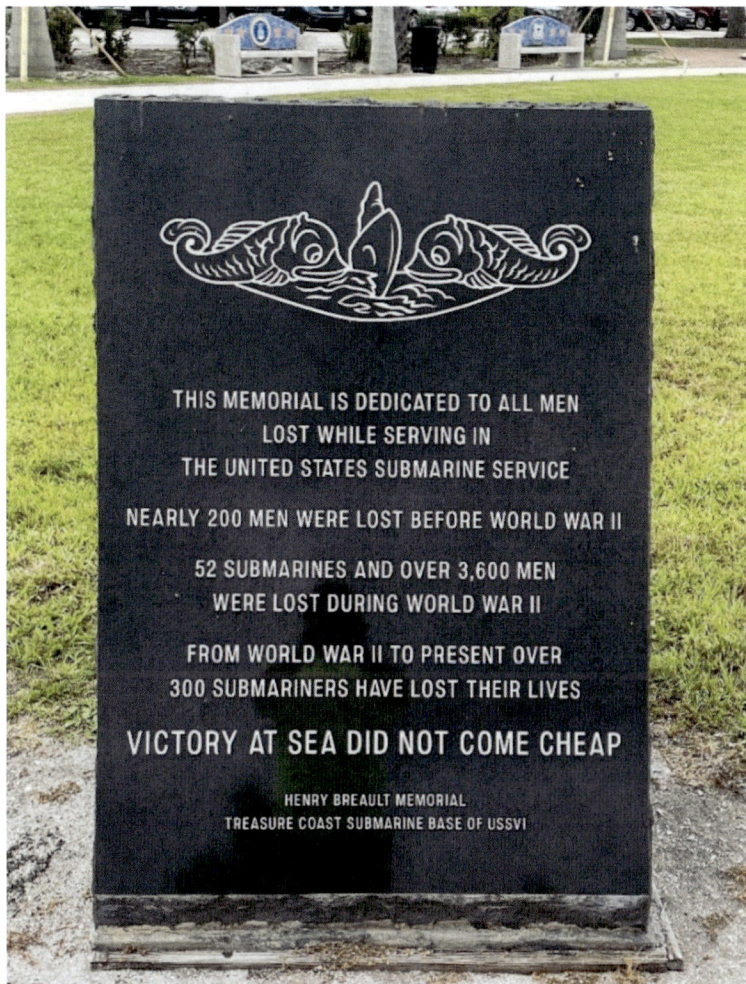

THIS MEMORIAL IS DEDICATED TO ALL MEN
LOST WHILE SERVING IN
THE UNITED STATES SUBMARINE SERVICE

NEARLY 200 MEN WERE LOST BEFORE WORLD WAR II

52 SUBMARINES AND OVER 3,600 MEN
WERE LOST DURING WORLD WAR II

FROM WORLD WAR II TO PRESENT OVER
300 SUBMARINERS HAVE LOST THEIR LIVES

VICTORY AT SEA DID NOT COME CHEAP

HENRY BREAULT MEMORIAL
TREASURE COAST SUBMARINE BASE OF USSVI

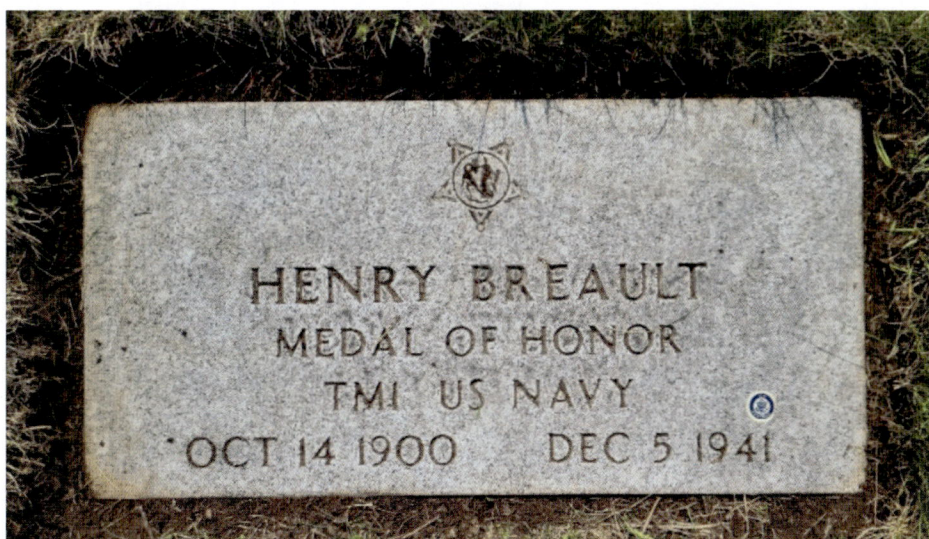

HENRY BREAULT
MEDAL OF HONOR
TM1 US NAVY
OCT 14 1900   DEC 5 1941

61

SERGEANT ELIJAH A. BRIGGS; ARMY

October 26, 1843 (Salisbury, CT) – March 10, 1922 (Beacon, NY); 78 years old

Married Hannah E. Montfort (1851-1931) on June 24, 1874, in Matteawan (Beacon), New York.

One daughter, Marie E. Briggs Hamburger (1891-1973).

Enlisted on July 18, 1862, in Salisbury, Connecticut.

Wounded on June 2, 1864, in Cold Harbor, Virginia.

Mustered out on July 7, 1865.

Born to Gilbert V. (1813-1851) and Jane Atwood Briggs (1810-?). Two sisters, Elizabeth (1840-?) and Martha H. (1847-1847).

MEDAL OF HONOR CITATION

AWARDED FOR ACTIONS DURING: Civil War
BRANCH OF SERVICE: Army
UNIT: Company B, 2nd Connecticut Heavy Artillery
DATE OF ISSUE AND PRESENTATION: May 10, 1865
AGE ON THE DAY OF THE EVENT: 22
CITATION:

The President of the United States of America, in the name of Congress, takes pleasure in presenting the Medal of Honor to Corporal Elijah A. Briggs, United States Army, for extraordinary heroism on 3 April 1865, while serving with Company B, 2nd Connecticut Heavy Artillery, in action at Petersburg, Virginia, for capture of battle flag. Civil War Congressional Medal of Honor Recipient. Served during the Civil War as a Corporal in Company B, 2nd Connecticut Heavy Artillery. He was awarded the CMOH for his bravery at Petersburg, Virginia, on April 3, 1865. His citation reads simply, "Capture of battle flag."

From The Beacon (New York) Daily Herald on Saturday, March 11, 1922

ELIJAH A. BRIGGS CIVIL WAR VETERAN DIED HERE FRIDAY
Well Known G.A.R. Member Succumbed to Illness Of Few Days – 78 Years Old

WILL BE BURIED MONDAY
Was Possessor Of Congressional Medal Of Honor For Bravery – Captured Rebel Flag

Elijah A. Briggs, aged 78 years, one of the few surviving members of Howland Post, Grand Army of the Republic (G.A.R.), passed away at his home, 33 Maple Street, yesterday afternoon shortly after three o'clock following an illness of only a few days.

Mr. Briggs had led an unusually active life and had seldom been ill for any length of time. On Thursday afternoon, he was taken suddenly ill but seemed to recover under treatment administered by Dr. Keating. Yesterday, he was stricken again with the same trouble, and despite all that medical aid could do for him, he answered the final call of death. He was a victim of the harding of the arteries that lead to the heart.

The news of the death of this well-known Civil War veteran and prominent resident of the community was heard in Beacon with sincere sorrow, for Mr. Briggs was widely known in Beacon and well-liked by all with whom he came in contact.

The deceased was born on the 26th day of October 1843 at Lime Rock, Litchfield County, Connecticut, and spent his boyhood days in that county getting his education at the Lime Rock School. When the Civil War broke out, Mr. Briggs had not yet reached his eighteenth year, yet he was filled with the emotion of patriotism that pervaded the country and immediately enlisted to fight for the preservation of the Union.

He enlisted on the 18th day of July 1862 from Litchfield County, Connecticut, to serve three years during the war and was mustered into United States service on the 23rd day of July 1862, at Litchfield Hill, Connecticut, as a private of Captain James Hubbard's Company B, 19th Regiment, Connecticut Volunteers, second artillery, Colonel Leverett W. Wessell, later Colonel Elisha S. Kellogg commanding,

This second artillery was recruited in Litchfield and served as infantry until November 23rd, 1863, when it was changed to an artillery regiment. Gallant and faithful duty was performed by the Connecticut division of which Mr. Briggs was a member and, during the war, lost four hundred and twenty-seven men and officers by death while in service.

The deceased was promoted to Corporal while serving in the gallant army and then to Sergeant and was at all times with his command, except when he was wounded by a gunshot in the forehead at Cold Harbor, Virginia, June 12th, 1864, from the effects of which he was absent for a few weeks, but declined to go to the hospital.

One of Mr. Briggs' most valued possessions was the Congressional Medal of Honor, which was presented him on account of his meritorious service and bravery in capturing a rebel flag at the battle of Sailors Creek on the 6th day of April 1865.

When the war was at an end, Sergeant Briggs took part in the review of the Union's troops at Washington, and on the 7th day of July 1865, he was given his honorable discharge by reason of the end of the war.

Immediately after receiving his discharge, Sergeant Briggs returned to his home at Lime Rock, Connecticut, where he resided for a few years. He then came to the former village of Matteawan (New York), where on the 24th day of June 1874, he was united in marriage to H. Elizabeth Montfort, who survives him, and one daughter, Mrs. William Hamburger. Also, three grandchildren.

He was a member of Howland Post, No. 48, G.A.R., and during his life, held all the offices in the Post. He was also a member of Evergreen Lodge, No. 131, I.O.O.F., and of the First M.E. Church.

Funeral services over the remains will be held at the late home on Maple Street Monday afternoon at two-thirty o'clock and will be conducted by Reverend A.A. Vradenbburgh of the First M.E. Church. Military honors will be given the remains.

Interment will be made in the Fishkill Rural Cemetery.

Undertaker Frederick L. Roosa will direct the funeral arrangements.

CAPTAIN PAUL WILLIAM BUCHA; ARMY

August 1, 1943 (Washington, DC) –
Married Carolyn B. Maynard (1944-) on June 17, 1967.
Four children. Details are unknown.

Born to Paul A. [Colonel, U.S. Army] (1913-1986) and Mary Sikora Bucha (1914-2004). Three sisters, Maryanne P. Bucha Hertzer (1943-), Judith K. Bucha Shelton (1948-), and Sandra L. Bucha Kerscher Rudolph (1954-).

Photos courtesy of the Congressional Medal of Honor Society

MEDAL OF HONOR CITATION

AWARDED FOR ACTIONS DURING: Vietnam War
BRANCH OF SERVICE: Army
UNIT: Company D, 187th Infantry Regiment, 3rd Brigade, 101st Infantry Regiment
GENERAL ORDERS: Department of the Army, General Orders No. 30 (June 5, 1970)
AGE ON THE DAY OF THE EVENT: 24
CITATION:

The President of the United States of America, in the name of Congress, takes pleasure in presenting the Medal of Honor to Captain Paul William Bucha, United States Army, for conspicuous gallantry and intrepidity at the risk of his life above and beyond the call of duty while serving with Company D, 3rd Battalion, 187th Infantry Regiment, 3rd Brigade, 101st Airborne Division, in action against enemy aggressor forces in Binh Duong Province, Republic of Vietnam, from 16 to 19 March 1968. Captain Bucha distinguished himself while serving as Commanding Officer of Company D on a reconnaissance-in-force mission against enemy forces near Phuoc Vinh, and the company was inserted by helicopter into the suspected enemy stronghold to locate and destroy the enemy. During this period, Captain Bucha aggressively and courageously led his men in the destruction of enemy fortifications and base areas and eliminated scattered resistance impeding the advance of the company. On 18 March, while advancing to contact, the lead elements of the company became engaged by the heavy automatic weapon, heavy machinegun, rocket-propelled grenade, Claymore mine, and small-arms fire of an estimated battalion-size force. Captain Bucha, with complete disregard for his safety, moved to the threatened area to direct the defense and ordered reinforcements to the aid of the lead element. Seeing that his men were pinned down by heavy machinegun fire from a concealed bunker located some 40 meters to the front of the positions, Captain Bucha crawled through the hail of fire to single-handedly destroy the bunker with grenades. During this heroic action, Captain Bucha received a painful shrapnel wound. Returning to the perimeter, he observed that his unit could not hold its positions and repel the human wave assaults launched by the determined enemy. Captain Bucha ordered the withdrawal of the unit elements and covered the withdrawal to positions of a company perimeter from which he could direct fire upon the charging enemy. When one friendly element retrieving casualties was ambushed and cut off from the perimeter, Captain Bucha ordered them to feign death, and he directed artillery fire around them. During the night, Captain Bucha moved throughout the position, distributing ammunition, providing encouragement, and ensuring the integrity of the defense. He directed artillery, helicopter gunship, and Air Force gunship fire on the enemy strong points and attacking forces, marking the positions with smoke grenades. Using flashlights in complete view of enemy snipers, he directed the medical evacuation of three air-ambulance loads of seriously wounded personnel and the helicopter supply of his company. At daybreak, Captain Bucha led a rescue party to recover the dead and wounded members of the ambushed element. During the period of intensive combat, Captain Bucha, by his extraordinary heroism, inspirational example, outstanding leadership, and professional competence, led his company in the decimation of a superior enemy force which left 156 dead on the battlefield. His bravery and gallantry at the risk of his life are in the highest traditions of the military service, Captain Bucha has reflected great credit on himself, his unit, and the United States Army.

Presentation Date and Details: May 14, 1970, The White House, presented by President Richard M. Nixon.

Photo contributed by Ryan Pettigrew, AV Archivist, Richard Nixon Presidential Library and Museum.
President Nixon (left), Captain Bucha, his wife Carolyn, and likely his three sisters and parents.

From the Standard Star in New Rochelle, New York, November 9, 1986. The article was written by Virginia Satkowski.

Paul Bucha, West Point graduate, and Medal of Honor recipient, recently spoke in Katonah on behalf of a Westchester Vietnam Veterans' Memorial to be built in Somers.

"Each man who fought knows what he did. For those who didn't, it's important that they understand," he said. Bucha, 43 and a Lewisboro resident, has traveled far beyond Vietnam. But the memory of one night in 1968 is still strong.

With 1,500 North Vietnamese troops surrounding his company of 89 soldiers, Bucha was thinking, "What a hell of a place to die." He and his men were able to fool the enemy into thinking they were a stronger force by building an unorthodox perimeter with the wounded in the center. The men fired grenades randomly, shooting at any noise. When dawn came, the enemy had retreated. For his efforts to protect his men, Bucha received the Medal of Honor.

His brush with danger didn't end in Vietnam, though. After the war, he worked for Electronic Data Systems Corp. in Iran, where in 1978, he narrowly escaped being arrested.

"When the Shah was being pushed out, the left-wing Arab group was anti-high technology and the nouveau-culture the Shah had brought in. This signaled problems for anyone who had done any business with the military, particularly in the high-tech area." Bucha says. Since EDS was computerizing Iranian social security records at the time, it was a prime target.

The story of Bucha's near arrest and EDS Chief Ross Perot's scheme to free two other employees has been told in the book *On Wings of Eagles.* But Bucha, married and the father of four children, says he thinks the Iranians were portrayed inaccurately by U.S. politicians and the press.

He's gone on to form Paul W. Bucha & Co. and is president and CEO of Port Liberte Partners, a Jersey City, N.J.-based development company planning the $750 million Port Liberte condominium and commercial complex for Jersey City.

This Veterans Day finds him far from the international hot spots, but he still thinks about their implications. While Bucha believes the soldiers who fought in Vietnam served their country well, he also believes those who fight must know why they are sent. "Unless you know why, it's not fair to send them," he says.

FIRST LIEUTENANT FREDERICK CLARENCE BUCK; ARMY

1843 * (Poquonock Br, Groton, CT) – July 15, 1905 (Johnson City, TN); 61 years old
Unmarried
Enlisted on August 17, 1862, in Windsor, Connecticut.
Wounded on September 27, 1864, at Fort Harrison, Virginia.
Mustered out on June 16, 1865.

* The exact Date of Birth is unknown.

Born to Daniel (1814-1892) and Mary E. Imlay Buck (1819-1862). Three brothers, Daniel W. (1840-1863), William J. (1842-?), and Charles E. (1845-1880). One sister, Mary E. (1847-1914).

One of five members of the 21st Connecticut to receive the Medal of Honor.

Lt Buck worked as a laborer in Patten, Maine, when he checked into the National Home of Disabled Soldiers in Johnson City, Tennessee.

MEDAL OF HONOR CITATION

AWARDED FOR ACTIONS DURING: Civil War
BRANCH OF SERVICE: Army
UNIT: Company A, 21st Connecticut Infantry
DATE OF ISSUE AND PRESENTATION: April 6, 1865
AGE ON THE DAY OF THE EVENT: 20
CITATION:

The President of the United States of America, in the name of Congress, takes pleasure in presenting the Medal of Honor to Corporal Frederick Clarence Buck, United States Army, for extraordinary heroism on 29 September 1864, while serving with Company A, 21st Connecticut Infantry, in action at Chapin's Farm, Virginia. Although wounded, Corporal Buck refused to leave the field until the fight closed.

Lieutenant Buck spent the last three months of his life in the National Home of Disabled Soldiers in Johnson City, Tennessee. He died at 61 years old due to heart disease, specifically, "cardiac dilation and mitral insufficiency." His grandmother, Susan Buck of Railroad Avenue in Wethersfield, Connecticut, was notified by telegram on July 16, 1905.

The National Home of Disabled Soldiers; photo courtesy of the McClung Historical Collection

The ninth of eleven branches of the National Home for Disabled Volunteer Soldiers (NHDVS), the Mountain Branch was authorized in 1901. The first resident arrived in 1903, a year before the home officially opened. Civil War veterans were the largest population initially. The sprawling complex in Johnson City, Tennessee, covered some 400 acres. Architect Joseph H. Freelander designed the campus, which included administrative and hospital buildings, barracks, staff housing, a mess hall, a chapel, two lakes, and a cemetery. The buildings were constructed in the Beaux Arts style using local timber, brick, and limestone. Freelander's plan remained unchanged until the care of World War I veterans required the construction of new facilities and the repurposing of old buildings. The National Homes were merged with the U.S. Veterans Bureau and Bureau of Pensions to form the Veterans Administration (now the U.S. Department of Veterans Affairs) in 1930.

Buried in Mountain Home National Cemetery, 215 Heroes Drive, Mountain Home, Tennessee; Section F, Row 1, Grave 9. Photo courtesy of Ancestry.com.

BREVET CAPTAIN JOHN KNIGHT BUCKLYN; ARMY

March 15, 1834 (Foster Creek, RI) – May 15, 1906 (Mystic, CT); 72 years old

Married to Mary McKee Young (1841-1907) on January 9, 1864, in Providence, Rhode Island.

Two sons, John Jr. (1865-1925) and Frank A. (1867-1918).

Enlisted on September 30, 1861 at Providence, Rhode Island.

Mustered out February 2, 1865.

Born to Jeremiah P. (1800-1841) and Abigail "Abby" Potter Bucklyn (1798-1880). Four brothers Jeremiah K. (1821-1888), Albert (1823-1888), Henry (1832-1838), Jeremiah (1821-). Four sisters Caroline (1825-1831), Abby A. (1827-1869), Elizabeth "Betsey" F.K. Bucklyn Cooper (1830-1894) and Alma F. (1836-1838).

From Ancestry.com   *Photo courtesy of the Congressional Medal of Honor Society*

MEDAL OF HONOR CITATION

AWARDED FOR ACTIONS DURING: Civil War
BRANCH OF SERVICE: Army
UNIT: Battery E, 1st Rhode Island Light Artillery
DATE OF ISSUE: July 13, 1899 (33 years later)
AGE ON THE DAY OF THE EVENT: 19
CITATION:

The President of the United States of America, in the name of Congress, takes pleasure in presenting the Medal of Honor to First Lieutenant (Field Artillery) John Knight Bucklyn, United States Army, for extraordinary heroism on 3 May 1863, while serving with Battery E, 1st Rhode Island Light Artillery, in action at Chancellorsville, Virginia. Though himself wounded, First Lieutenant Bucklyn gallantly fought his section of the battery under a fierce fire from the enemy until his ammunition was all expended, many of the cannoneers and most of the horses killed or wounded, and the enemy within 25 yards of the guns, when, disabling one piece, he brought off the other in safety.

John Knight Bucklyn was graduated with honors in the class of 1861, at Brown University, Providence, Rhode Island. He served three years in the Civil War, as private, sergeant, Second Lieutenant, First Lieutenant, and Captain of Battery E, 1st Rhode Island Light Artillery. Served one year on the staff of the 6th Corps, and was wounded three times. He was a member of the Loyal Legion Commandery of Philadelphia, Pennsylvania, and a member of the Congressional Medal of Honor Society, and was Past Department Commander of the Connecticut Grand Army of the Republic (G.A.R); he was president of the Mystic Valley E and C Institute for thirty-six years. He was an author and a lecturer. *(The Coggeshalls in America)*

Rhode Island's 1st Regiment Light Artillery's Battery E had three sections, each with two cannons. Bucklyn was in charge of one section.

"Lieutenant Bucklyn, although one of the sections had been engaged less than his, was ordered by Captain Randolph to return up the road in face of the enemy and check the advance. Lieutenant Bucklyn remarked, 'whoever goes up there will not live to return.' Captain Randolph replied, 'I think likely they will not; I must have someone who will stay.' Lieutenant Bucklyn called for volunteers and every man of his section volunteered although believing he was going to certain death."

An entire Mississippi infantry brigade stormed the line where Bucklyn's section of Battery E was positioned. . Bucklyn ordered that the two cannons of his section fire canister shells (shells that were like giant shotgun shells in their action). Half of the men in the section were killed and most of the others wounded from the Confederate direct fire into their position.

Twice Bucklyn had horses shot from under him, as he moved rapidly among the cannons to direct their fire. As he mounted the third horse, the horse was hit with a Confederate artillery shell, and a piece of shrapnel went into Bucklyn's left lung, filling the lung with blood and making him unable to breath effectively. Yet still Bucklyn fought Battery E both bravely and effectively.

As the Confederate infantry brigade closed on his position, and with no Union infantry supporting Battery E, he successfully maintained maximum firepower from his section of the battery. He moved the two cannon to various positions even though most of the horses were dead. The two cannons were fought by him to the last possible moment, as described in the commendation for the Congressional Medal of Honor described at the top of this page. At the last moment possible he had the remaining horses remove one of the cannons to a point of safety behind Union lines, and he remained to disable the other before leaving the field.

Stephen Usler, of Warwick, RI, is writing a biography of John Knight Bucklyn, and has said the following regarding the treatment of Bucklin's wounds at Chancellorsville:

Bucklyn "was taken to a hospital in Georgetown. It was the same hospital described by Louisa May Alcott in her "Hospital Sketches, written while she was a nurse, although she and Bucklyn were not there at the same time. Bucklyn's description of the place and her description corroborate that the conditions were pretty bad.

A soldier of Bucklyn's unit, named Slocum, fed Bucklyn milk with a spoon and a surgeon dressed his wounds. Bucklyn determined that he was not going to stay at the hospital in Georgetown. Slocum put Bucklyn in a boxcar, on a stretcher on top of some coffins of Union soldiers being shipped home. There was a deserter hiding out in the boxcar and he threw Bucklyn off the stretcher and used it to sleep on himself while Bucklyn spent the journey on the floor of the boxcar.

There was nobody helping him. He ended up in a train station in New York all by himself and described having to beat off pickpockets. About six or eight weeks later, he was back at the front with his battery."

Bucklin voluntarily returned to military service with his unit after only about two months for recovery. When Bucklin returned to service, his demonstrated bravery and intelligence earned him the job of Assistant Aide of the Adjutant-General (AAAGen) on the staff of Colonel Thompkins. In that job, Bucklyn had the duty of getting into the thick of battle in the front lines, reorganizing units to fight as battle casualties broke down the effectiveness of a fighting unit or eliminated the unit's commanding officers, reorganizing and recombining remnants of units, and issuing new battle orders on the spot.

During the bloody battle of Shenandoah, in recognition of extreme bravery and effectiveness in battle, he was promoted in the field to the rank of brevet captain on the 19th of October, 1864, "For gallant and meritorious and ofttimes distinguished service before Richmond and in the Shenandoah Valley."

During the latter part of the Civil War, Bucklyn as a Lieutenant (brevet rank of captain) was moved to replace the commander of Battery E, even though on paper the former commander who was moved to a general staff position. Because Bucklyn did not have an actual Congressional commission of a rank needed to command an entire battery, the former Captain remained nominally The Battery E commander on the tables of organization of the artillery.

Rhode Island's Battery E fought continuously in battles from the start to the end of the Civil War. At Gettysburg, Battery E was stationed first at Cemetery Ridge, and later at the Peach Orchard, scenes of perhaps the most intense fighting of the Civil War, his command was exemplary. The appreciation his men had for Bucklyn as their commander on that bloody battleground was illustrated in 1886, when a monument was erected on the Gettysburg battlefield, to mark where Battery E had fought. After the service of dedication, several of the soldiers asked for permission, and were granted permission, to chisel at the bottom of the monument for Battery E's position the additional words: "Lt. J. K. Bucklyn Commanding." *(bucklinsociety.net)*

From The Day (New London, CT) July 28, 1899

Captain J.K. Bucklyn of Mystic received a Medal of Honor several days ago, from the Secretary of War for exceptional gallantry on the memorable battlefield of Chancellorsville in 1863. The Captain was sent on a forlorn hope expedition against the Confederates and in the encounter, every horse or man was killed or wounded.

From The Day (New London, CT) May 16, 1906

DIABETES FATAL TO PROF. BUCKLYN
WELL KNOWN EDUCATOR SUMMONED BY DEATH VILLAGE BRIEFS COLLECTED

Mystic, May 16.

Professor John K. Bucklyn, past Commander of the Connecticut Grand Army of the Republic (G.A.R.), died at his home here Tuesday, aged 72 years. The cause of death was diabetes. For many years he conducted the Mystic Valley institute.

John Knight Bucklyn was a native of Rhode Island, in which state he, was born March 15, 1834. He was educated at the Smithville Seminary and Brown University. Most of his life has been spent at a teacher, preacher, and lecturer. A part of his early manhood was passed in the machinist business. Professor Bucklyn graduated from Brown University in 1861 and was a member of the Phi Beta Kappa Society while in college. Immediately after graduating he enlisted in Battery E, First Rhode Island Light Artillery, and was mustered in September 1, 1861, and won an honorable record In the war. He was commissioned Second Lieutenant on March 1, 1862, and First

Lieutenant in December of the same year. October 19 he was made Captain by brevet for "gallant, meritorious and often distinguished services before Richmond and in the Shanandoah Valley," and received a full commission as Captain in 1865. He participated in 45 battles and was wounded at Fredericksburg. He was also shot while commanding his battery at Gettysburg. In 1864 to 1865 he was on staff duty at the headquarters of the Sixth Corps, Army of Potomac, which was commanded by Connecticut's most distinguished soldier, General Sedgwick.

After returning from the war, he became the principal of the public school in Mystic and remained in that position until 1868. In that year he founded the Mystic Valley institute and has since been principal of the school, which has attained a decided success in its field. The institute was chartered in 1880. During that year Professor Bucklyn traveled in Europe extensively. He had also spent considerable time in visiting the states of the union east of the Rocky Mountains acquiring material for his profession and work. He is a past commander of Williams Post G.A.R., a member of the New London County Historical Society, also of the Rhode Island Historical Society of Soldiers and Sailors, and of the Loyal legion. He was a member of the Baptist church and has been a superintendent of Sunday school work for 20 years. He has held the office of school visitor and was a notary public. In politics he was a Republican. Principal Bucklyn was married by Rev. Dr. Swaine—in the Central Congregational church — in Providence, January 9, 1864. His bride was Miss Mary McKee Young, daughter of Edward R. Young. He has two sons, John K., Jr., and Frank A. Bucklyn, both of whom are graduates of the Mystic Valley Institute and the New York Medical College. Both are practicing [doctors].

__Buried in Lower Mystic Cemetery, 122 New London Road, Groton, Connecticut. Photos by author.__

JOHN K BUCKLYN
MEDAL OF HONOR
1ST LT 1 RI LT BTRY
CIVIL WAR
MAR 15 1834   MAY 15 1906

BRIGADIER GENERAL DANIEL WEBSTER BURKE; ARMY

April 22, 1841 (New Haven, CT) – May 29, 1911 (Portland, OR); 70 years old

Married Sarah J. McBride (1842-1915) on November 17, 1862, in Washington, D.C.

Two daughters, Cornelia Burke Nugent (1856-1934) and Margaret R. Burke (1865-1937).

Enlisted on June 10, 1858.

Retired from the Army on October 21, 1899.

Born to Richard (1816-1880) and Margaret Howard Burke (?-?) [both parents born in County Cork, Ireland, according to General Burke's death certificate]. Two brothers, Richard (1846-1900) and William (1849-?).

Photo courtesy of The Morning Oregonian May 29, 1911

MEDAL OF HONOR CITATION

AWARDED FOR ACTIONS DURING: Civil War

BRANCH OF SERVICE: Army

UNIT: Company B, 2nd U.S. Infantry

DATE OF ISSUE AND PRESENTATION: April 21, 1892 (30 years later)

AGE ON THE DAY OF THE EVENT: 21

CITATION:

The President of the United States of America, in the name of Congress, takes pleasure in presenting the Medal of Honor to First Sergeant Daniel Webster Burke, United States Army, for extraordinary heroism on 20 September 1862, while serving with Company B, 2nd U.S. Infantry, in action at Shepherdstown Ford, Virginia. First Sergeant Burke voluntarily attempted to spike a gun in the face of the enemy.

Civil War Medal of Honor Recipient. He served in the Civil War as a 1st Sergeant in Company B, 2nd United States Regular Infantry. He was awarded the CMOH for his bravery at Shepherdstown Ford, Virginia, on September 20, 1862. During a retreat of a small Union force in the face of a larger Rebel one, a number of artillery pieces had been abandoned and rendered unusable. However, one gun was overlooked. Sergeant Burke volunteered to try to spike it, which he proceeded to attempt to do heedless of the Confederates, who were trying to prevent him from achieving his task. When the fire became too great, he reluctantly returned to the Union lines without being able to disable the gun after repeated attempts. However, he was warmly commended by his superior officers for his coolness and bravery. Later in the War, he was commissioned as a 2nd Lieutenant in the Regular Army and was awarded brevets of Captain, Major, and Lieutenant Colonel for his gallantry during the Battle of Gettysburg, where he was wounded in the fighting in the Wheatfield area. He remained in the Army after the war, retiring with the rank of Brigadier General in 1899. His medal was awarded to him on April 21, 1892.

From Beyer, W. F., & Keydel, O. F. (2000). Deeds of valor: How America's Civil War Heroes won The Congressional Medal of Honor. Smithmark Publishers.

ATTEMPTED TO SPIKE AN ABANDONED GUN

When the Union troops fell back across the Potomac at Shepherdstown Ford, Virginia, on the 20th of September 1862, they had to leave a number of fieldpieces to the advancing Confederates. The enemy, however, gained nothing by their capture, as almost every gun had been spiked. As the Second U.S. Infantry was retiring, an officer of the regiment presently remembered that one large gun had been overlooked and left unspiked.

Who is willing to go and spike that gun?" he inquired.

First Sergeant Daniel W. Burke of Company B, at once offered his services. The fire from the enemy was severe, but nothing daunted, he started out on his perilous task and boldly attempted to unfit this gun for further service. After repeated attempts to fulfill his mission, he saw that the task was impossible of accomplishment and reluctantly returned to his own lines, which he reached in safety. He was thereupon complimented by his superior officers for his display of coolness and courage.

From the Hartford Courant June 2, 1911

General Daniel Webster Burke, U.S. Army, retired, a native of Connecticut, died Tuesday in Portland, Oregon, where he had lived a number of years. He was born on April 22, 1841, and enlisted in the Army June 10, 1858, when only 17 years old. He was a Private, Corporal, and First Sergeant in Companies E and B, Second Infantry, and became a Second Lieutenant when he was 21 and a Captain five years later. He was made a Major of the Twenty-third Infantry on August 13, 1894, Lieutenant Colonel in 1897, and on September 8, 1899, he became Colonel of the Seventeenth Infantry. The following month, he became Brigadier General and shortly afterward retired at the end of more than forty years of service. General Burke was honored for distinguished work in the Army. He was brevetted a Captain on July 2, 1863, and Major on January 22, 1865, for "gallant and meritorious services in the battle of Gettysburg, Pennsylvania." Congress awarded him a medal in 1892 for distinguished gallantry in action at Shepherdstown Ford, West Virginia.

From The Our Sunday Visitor in Lincoln, Nebraska, June 16, 1911

DEATH OF DISTINGUISHED CATHOLIC SOLDIER

General Daniel Webster Burke, retired, who died at Portland, Oregon, on May 30, was 70 years old. He was born in Connecticut on April 22, 1841, and served in the Army as a young man. He rose from the ranks to a Second Lieutenant in the Second Infantry when he was 21 years of age and became a Captain five years later. He was made a Major of the Twenty-third Infantry on August 13, 1894, Lieutenant Colonel in 1897, and on September 8, 1899, achieved the Colonelcy of the Seventeenth Infantry. The following month, he became Brigadier General and shortly afterward retired at the end of more than forty years of service. General Burke was honored for distinguished work in the Army. He was brevetted a Captain on July 2, 1863, and Major on January 22, 1867, for "gallant and meritorious services in the Battle of Gettysburg." Congress awarded him a medal in 1892 for distinguished gallantry in action at Shepherdstown Ford, West Virginia. Of General Burke, the Catholic Sentinel says:

"Although the general had a distinguished career as a soldier of his country, he is more to be esteemed as a soldier of Christ. We are taught by the inspired writer that 'the patient man is better than the valiant, and he that ruleth his spirit, than he that taketh cities.' Self-conquest is, after all, the supreme achievement of every truly commendable life; a man's most formidable enemies are those of his own household, and when these are put to route, the issues of other conflicts are relatively unimportant.

"General Burke was one of those men whom the passing show never distracted from the vivid realization of the meaning and end of his own existence. He was permeated with faith, and in the light of that faith, he aimed steadily at the mark. In all that pertained to the fulfillment of his duties as a Catholic, his faithfulness was well-nigh perfect. Holy Mass and the sacraments were to him fountains of refreshment and delight. He loved his religion and never found its practice irksome. In his private life, he was pre-eminently a man of prayer. He had a special fondness for the rosary and a particular relish for a sermon devoted to the honor of Heaven's Queen. And the piety of his soul manifested itself in the gentleness and amiability of his manner. The fine courtesy that always distinguished him was in him. Christian charity applied at all points of social contact. He was a gentleman, not by artifice or studied affectation, but by reason of the intrinsic goodness of his Christian spirit. The confidence, respect, and affection which he inspired in those who knew him were the reflected beauty of the cultured, righteous soul."

Buried in Arlington National Cemetery, 1 Memorial Drive, Arlington, Virginia; Section 2, Grave 3739. Photo by the author

PRIVATE HETH CANFIELD; ARMY

July 20, 1849 (New Milford, CT) – December 14, 1913 (St. Augustine, FL); 64 years old
Married Jane Louisa Smith (1850-1915) on December 21, 1871.
Three sons, Lawrence H. (1871-1946), Thomas S. (1875-1930), and LeRoy (1879-1923).
Three daughters, Sadie H. Canfield Farris (1880-1913), Annis "Annie" B. (1886-1928), and Louisa E. Canfield Farris (1891-1942). NOTE: When Sadie died in 1913, her husband, Guy W. Farris, then married Sadie's sister Louisa in 1915.
Enlisted on March 15, 1870, in Carlisle Barracks, Pennsylvania.
Discharged on September 11, 1870, in Camp Bingham, Nebraska.

Born to Lawrence (1825-1910) and Sarah A. Marsh Canfield (1826-1907). Two sisters, Urania Canfield Hill (1850-1934) and Mary Louisa Canfield Phillips (1859-1935).

After the service, Heth Canfield became a well-known house builder. He was also President of the St. Augustine [Florida] Improvement Company.

MEDAL OF HONOR CITATION

AWARDED FOR ACTIONS DURING: Indian Campaigns
BRANCH OF SERVICE: Army
UNIT: Company C, 2nd U.S. Cavalry
DATE OF ISSUE AND PRESENTATION: June 22, 1870
AGE ON THE DAY OF THE EVENT: 20
CITATION:

The President of the United States of America, in the name of Congress, takes pleasure in presenting the Medal of Honor to Private Heth Canfield, United States Army, for gallantry in action on __15__ May 1870, while serving with Company C, 2nd U.S. Cavalry, in action at Little Blue, Nebraska.

AUTHOR NOTE: The date of action was corrected to May 17, 1870, by the United States Army's Awards and Decorations Branch in 2012.

On May 17, 1870, Sergeant Patrick Leonard and four men from C Troop were searching the Little Blue River in Nebraska for stray horses when a war party of 50 Indians surrounded the detachment. Racing for cover, Leonard dismounted his men and discovered that Private Thomas Hubbard and two mounts had been wounded. The Indians charged twice, and the troopers repelled them, with one Indian killed and three wounded. Leonard slaughtered the two wounded horses to form a breastwork in time to repulse a third attack in which the cavalrymen killed two more Indians and wounded four others. Within the hour, the Indians retreated. Leonard had to withdraw his patrol on foot because the Indians had killed all the horses during the attack. He then took a settler's family of two women and a child under his charge. While moving to the next settlement, the Indians did not renew their attack. Leonard safely arrived at C Company's bivouac at 2300 hours with his entire patrol and the civilians relatively secure. Private Heth Canfield, along with Sergeant Leonard and fellow Privates Michael Himmelsbeck, Thomas Hubbard, and George Thompson, were all cited for "Gallantry in Action" and awarded Medals of Honor for this action.

Honored on the Cumberland County (Pennsylvania) Medal of Honor Memorial, South Hanover Street, Carlisle, Pennsylvania.

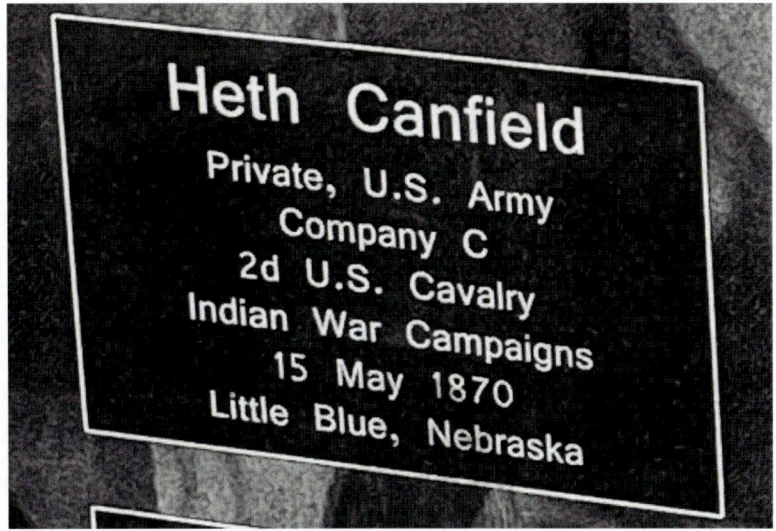

Photo courtesy of HMdb.org and Devry Becker Jones.

Buried in Evergreen Cemetery, 541-599 N. Rodriguez Street, Saint Augustine, Florida; Old Section, Division C, Lot 110. Photos from FindAGrave.com.

HETH CANFIELD
1849 — 1913

HETH CANFIELD
MEDAL OF HONOR
PVT CO C 2 US CAV
INDIAN WARS
1849   1913

ENSIGN TEDFORD HARRIS CANN; NAVY

September 3, 1897 (Bridgeport, CT) – January 26, 1963 (Port Chester, NY); 65 years old
Married Margaret "Marguerite" Maru Powers (1897-1985) on November 13, 1923, in New York City.
Two sons, Tedford J. (1928-2008) and Thomas P. (1933-2017).
Enlisted on April 26, 1917, in New York.
Appointed to Ensign on April 22, 1918.
Discharged on March 3, 1919.
Served aboard the U.S.S. May (SP-164) and U.S.S. Noma (SP-131).

Born to Frank H. (1863-1935) and Alice Goodsell Cann (1872-1938). One brother, Howard G. (1895-1992). Frank was the director of Physical Education at New York University, where both Tedford and his brother Howard attended. Tedford held the AAU 1920 National Championship in 50m, 100m, and 200m freestyle. Howard was an Olympic shot putter who finished 8th in the 1920 games in Antwerp. Howard also was a college basketball and football player. He coached the NYU men's basketball team for 35 years, retiring in 1958 with a record of 429-235, and is in the Basketball Hall of Fame.

Photos courtesy of Ancestry.com and the International Swimming Hall Of Fame

MEDAL OF HONOR CITATION

AWARDED FOR ACTIONS DURING: World War I
BRANCH OF SERVICE: Navy
ASSIGNED TO: U.S.S. May (SP-164)
GENERAL ORDERS: War Department, General Orders No. 366 (1918)
AGE ON THE DAY OF THE EVENT: 20
CITATION:

The President of the United States of America, in the name of Congress, takes pleasure in presenting the Medal of Honor to Seaman Tedford Harris Cann, United States Navy, for courageous conduct while serving on board the U.S.S. May 5 November 1917, at sea between Bermuda and the Azores. Seaman Cann found a leak in a flooded compartment and closed it at the peril of his life, thereby unquestionably saving the ship.

Presentation Date and Details: Unknown date in Brest, France. Presented by Admiral Newton A. McCully.

Ensign Cann's Medal of Honor is in the International Swimming Hall of Fame in Fort Lauderdale, Florida. Photo contributed by Meg Keller-Marvin, Honoree and Olympian Liaison at the International Swimming Hall of Fame.

TEDDY CANN
Honoree Swimmer
WORLD WAR I

Tedford Harris Cann served as an officer in the United States Naval Reserve during World War I and earned the medal for saving his sinking ship. Cann's swimming career began while he was still a teenager. He attended the High School of Commerce in New York City, where he was captain of the basketball and swimming teams and competed in the New York Championships. At age 17, he defeated Hawaiian swimmer Duke Kahanamoku, an event which he later declared was a greater thrill than being awarded the Medal of Honor. While a student at New York University, Cann also excelled in track and field, basketball, and football, where he played halfback as well as becoming a member of the Fraternity of Phi Gamma Delta. He served in the Navy Reserve during World War I, initially as a Seaman. On November 5, 1917, while he was a member of the crew of the patrol vessel U.S.S. May (SP-164), Seaman Cann voluntarily swam into a flooded compartment and repeatedly dived beneath the surface until he had located and closed the leak that endangered the ship. He was awarded the Medal of Honor for this act. In April 1918, Cann was commissioned as an ensign in the Reserves, continuing to serve on the U.S.S. May into July. He spent the rest of World War I as an officer on the U.S.S. Noma (SP-131) and left the service shortly after the conflict's end. Cann resumed his swimming career after the war. Coached by Matt Mann, Cann swam with The New York Athletic Club and later the Detroit Athletic Club. On April 10, 1920, in Detroit, Michigan, he set the world record in the 200-meter freestyle (then called the 220-yard freestyle) with a time of 2:19.8, breaking the previous record of 2:21.6 set by Norman Ross in 1916. His record would stand until 1922 when Johnny Weissmuller swam the distance in 2:15.6. Also in 1920, Cann won the Amateur Athletic Union National Championships in the 50, 100, and 200-meter races, becoming the first person to win all three of those titles in a single year. He had qualified for and was preparing to participate in the 1920 Summer Olympics in Antwerp when he was involved in a serious car accident. Early in the morning of May 11, 1920, Cann and two other Olympic hopefuls were in a taxicab in New York City, returning home from a late night out, when the driver crashed into an elevated railroad pillar. One of Cann's fellow passengers was fatally injured, and Cann's leg was broken in six places. He missed the Olympics due to his injury, which required him to use crutches for more than a year and left him with a permanent limp. Although he was never able to swim as fast as he had before the accident, Cann took up water polo with much success. He participated in the 1924 Summer Olympics in Paris and played with The New York Athletic Club national champion polo team up to the early 1930s. To date, he is the only Olympic water polo player – and among only a few United States Olympians – to hold a Medal of Honor. Cann died at age 65 and was buried in Arlington National Cemetery, Arlington County, Virginia. Four years later, in 1967, he was posthumously inducted into the International Swimming Hall of Fame for his accomplishments as a swimmer.

From the Bridgeport (CT) Times & Evening Farmer August 10, 1916

CRACK SWIMMERS TO CROSS OCEAN TO MEET EXPERTS OF HAWAIIAN ISLANDS

New York, August 9 – The three great swimmers, Herbert Vollmer, Tedford H. Cann of the New York Athletic Club, and Ludy Lander, the Pacific coast champion, are now ready to leave for the long trip to Honolulu to take part in the big water carnival to be held there in September. Considerable interest attaches to the trip because it is practically a certainty that they will again measure strokes with the great Duke Kahanamoku in the coming meet. In fact, despite persistent reports that the Hawaiian wonder swimmer intends to turn professional, it is confidently believed in aquatic circles that he will now retain his amateur standing, at least until he has had a chance to again try conclusion with the New Yorkers. The latter both took his measure conclusively in this country a few weeks ago, and Duke will hardly miss the opportunity to win back his lost laurels, especially as in home waters, the advantage will be entirely on his side. Thus, the prospective clashes are looked forward to with keen anticipation. Vollmer twice lowered the 220-yard indoor world's record last winter, and whether he wins over the Hawaiian or not, there is reason to think he will force the pace to the point of breaking open water standards, at least at the century and furlong. The previous picture shows Vollmer on the left and Cann on the right.

From the New York Times April 27, 1917

CANN BROTHERS ENLIST
Ted and Howard, Prominent Athletes, Join Naval Reserve Corps

Tedford H. Cann, the swimming champion of the New York Athletic Club, and his brother, Howard Cann, New York University's all-around athlete, have enlisted in the Naval Reserve Corps as active members of the mosquito fleet to patrol the waters adjacent to the city. Teddy Cann is the present holder of the national 100-yard swimming championship, and he also holds the metropolitan 100, 220, and 300-yard titles. Howard Cann is an all-around athlete and a football player. He played left halfback on the NYU team for the last two seasons and has been elected Captain of next year's team.

From the Meriden (CT) Record-Journal March 1, 1918

MERIDEN WOMAN'S COUSIN RECEIVES MEDAL OF HONOR
Saved Vessel of the US Naval Reserve From Sinking

Tedford H. Cann, the subject of the following article from the New Yorker, a publication of New York University, is a cousin of Mrs. John G. Nagel of this city:

"Tedford H. Cann is now the proud possessor of the highest military distinction, the Medal of Honor. It was early in November that he saved a ship from sinking.

Soon after war was declared, Ted enlisted and qualified for first-class Quartermaster. He was only 19, yet he longed for the real and truer service "Over there." Consequently, he resigned and enlisted again in the Naval Reserve and was delegated almost immediately to one of the squadrons of submarine chasers.

On November 5, 1917, the ship he was on, the U.S.S. May, flagship of the squadron, sprung a leak. Ted, at the risk of his life, located the leak and stopped it. This action was brought to the attention of Captain McCulley, commander of the squadron. He and Captain Evans of the U.S.S. May wrote to Secretary Daniels and recommended the Medal of Honor as a reward."

From the New York Times May 12, 1920

OLYMPIC ASPIRANTS HURT IN TAXI CRASH
T.H. Cann and Two Other Swimming Champions Among the Five Victims

A. McALEENAN, JR., MAY DIE
Former Diving Title Holder Suffers a Fracture of the Skull

Tedford H. Cann, the first naval reservist to be decorated during the European war, and two other American swimming champions who expected to take part in the Olympic Games in Belgium were seriously injured early yesterday when a taxicab in which they were riding at Jackson and Second Avenues, Long Island City, struck an elevated railroad pillar. One of the champions, Arthur McAleenan, was probably fatally injured, and the driver of the taxi and a man waiting at the corner for the trolley were also badly hurt. Ted Cann is the son of the Physical Education Director of New York University and was a member of the crew of the U.S.S. May during the war. His decoration was won when his ship's bilge was flooded with eight feet of water, and he volunteered to dive and shut off a sea cock, saving the vessel.

The injured men were:

ARTHUR McALEENAN, JR., 28, former Yale student, 13309 Broadway, at one time a national diving champion; fracture of the skull and internal injuries.

STEPHEN RUDDY, 18, 142 East Eighty-Third Street, runner-up for the 200-yard breaststroke swim title; injuries to the head, face, and body, and possible internal injuries.

TEDFORD H. CANN, 22, 2250 Loring Place, the Bronx, present holder of the 50, 100, and 220-yard national titles; fracture of the left leg and internal injuries.

JOHN DAW, 27, 1006 First Avenue, owner and driver of the taxicab; fracture of both legs and internal injuries.

JOHN MARTIN, 25, 849 Second Avenue, Long Island City; lacerations of the face, head, and body, bruises, and contusions.

Cann, McAleenan, and Ruddy had dined with some friends early Monday evening at the New York Athletic Club, and the driver of the taxi said he answered a call to the clubhouse at 1 a.m. He first drove to a place on Lexington Avenue, as directed, and, after remaining there for a short time, proceeded across the Queensboro Bridge to Long Island City. Later, the party started to return to Manhattan, and, according to Daw, he drove down Second Avenue under the elevated train. On Second Avenue, for a distance of several blocks from Jackson Avenue, there is a sharp incline at the foot of which the accident happened. The driver asserted that he was not driving fast and that he did not see the pillar.

AUTHOR NOTE: Arthur McAleenan died on May 15, 1920, three days after the crash.

Buried in Arlington National Cemetery, 1 Memorial Drive, Arlington, Virginia; Section 7, Lot 10118-SS. Photo by the author.

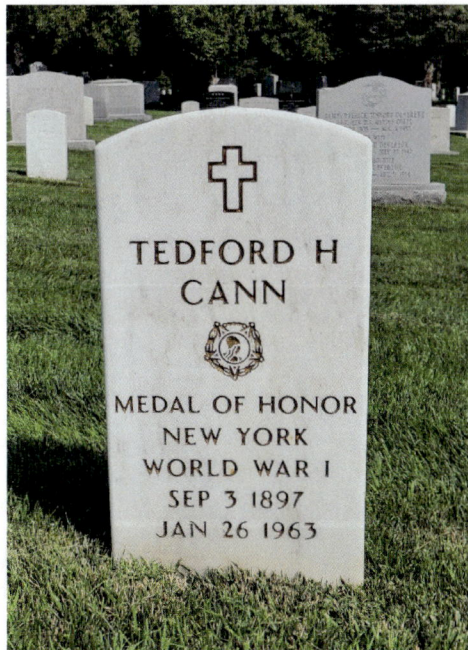

MASTER SERGEANT * JOHN ALLAN "CHAPPY" CHAPMAN; AIR FORCE

* Promoted to Master Sergeant posthumously.

July 14, 1965 (Springfield, MA) – March 4, 2002 (Takur Ghar, Afghanistan); 36 years old
Married Valerie A. Nessel (1968-) on August 22, 1992, in Windber, Pennsylvania.
Two daughters, Madison (1996-) and Brianna (1998-).
Enlisted on September 27, 1985.
Born to Eugene C. [USAF veteran] (1938-2004) and Teresa Marie Chapman Giaccone [remarried in 1994] (1941-).
   One brother, Kevin C. Chapman (1962-). Two sisters, Lori J. Chapman Longfritz (1966-) and Tammy Chapman
   Klein (1967-).

John's sister co-wrote a book, *Alone at Dawn: Medal of Honor Recipient John Chapman and the Untold Story of the World's Deadliest Special Operations Force* by Dan Schilling and Lori Longfritz, available on Amazon.

AUTHOR NOTE: Many thanks to Valerie Nessel Chapman for help with details in MSgt Chapman's biography.

Photo courtesy of the Secretary of the Air Force Public Affairs

Windsor Locks High School Class of '83 yearbook

JOHN ALLAN CHAPMAN

DATELINE: July 14, 1965
LEAD STORY: Var. Soccer 1, 2, 3, 4; Var.
Diving 1, 2, 3, 4; Skiing; parties; Soccer
team clown 4; "6"
HOROSCOPE: To live life to its fullest,
seeing as you only live once
EDITORIAL: "Give of yourself before tak-
ing of someone else."

Anonymous

Windsor Locks High School Soccer Team

THE TEAM — Bottom row, (l-r): F. Jordan, D. Gilbert, J. Chapman, B. Topor, M. Toce, P. Callahan, R. Heim, J. Bologna, M. Masera. Top row: Coach Sullivan, Mgr. D. Christopherson, K. Loughran, C. Losty, D. Piktel, J. Kurmaski, S. Jackson, T. Mandrola, R. Africano, B. O'Boyle, A. Letendre, R. Parry.

Windsor Locks High School Swim Team

THE TEAM — Bottom row (l-r): M. Wabalas, A. Letendre, R. Ferris, D. Curry, A. Green, G. Lawrence, K. Pfaffenbichler, S. Jackson, Coach K. Malone. Top row: B. Kupernick, J. Chapman.

Photo courtesy of the Windsor Locks Hall of Fame

MEDAL OF HONOR CITATION

AWARDED FOR ACTIONS DURING: Global War on Terror
BRANCH OF SERVICE: Air Force
UNIT: 24th Special Tactics Squadron
AGE ON THE DAY OF THE EVENT: 36
CITATION:

The President of the United States of America, in the name of Congress, takes pride in presenting the Medal of Honor (Posthumously) to Technical Sergeant John A. Chapman, United States Air Force, for conspicuous gallantry and intrepidity at the risk of life above and beyond the call of duty. Technical Sergeant Chapman distinguished himself by extraordinary heroism as an Air Force Special Tactics Combat Controller of the 24th Special Tactics Squadron, attached to a Navy Sea, Air, and Land (SEAL) Team conducting reconnaissance operations in Takur Ghar, Afghanistan, on 4 March 2002. During insertion, the team's helicopter was ambushed, causing a teammate to fall into an entrenched group of enemy combatants below. Sergeant Chapman and the team voluntarily reinserted onto the snow-capped mountain into the heart of a known enemy stronghold to rescue one of their own. Without regard for his own safety, Sergeant Chapman immediately engaged, moving in the direction of the closest enemy position despite coming under heavy fire from multiple directions. He fearlessly charged an enemy bunker, up a steep incline in thigh-deep snow and into hostile fire, directly engaging the enemy. Upon reaching the bunker, Sergeant Chapman assaulted and cleared the position, killing all enemy occupants. With complete disregard for his own life, Sergeant Chapman deliberately moved from cover only 12 meters from the enemy, and exposed himself once again to attack a second bunker, from which an emplaced machine gun was firing on his team. During this assault from an exposed position directly in the line of intense fire, Sergeant Chapman was struck and injured by enemy fire. Despite severe, mortal wounds, he continued to fight relentlessly, sustaining a violent engagement with multiple enemy personnel before making the ultimate sacrifice. By his heroic actions and extraordinary valor, sacrificing his life for the lives of his teammates, Technical Sergeant Chapman upheld the highest traditions of military service and reflected great credit upon himself and the United States Air Force.

Presentation Date and Details: August 22, 2018, in the White House, to his widow, by President Donald Trump.

Photos courtesy of the U.S. Air Force; photographer SSgt Rusty Frank.
Bottom photo, left to right, Madison Chapman (daughter), Valerie Nessel (wife), President Trump, Brianna (daughter), and Teresa Chapman Giaccone (MSgt Chapman's mother). Taken on August 22, 2018. That day would have been the Chapman's 26th wedding anniversary.

John Chapman's excellence in diving at Windsor Locks High School earned him winning spots in the Connecticut Interscholastic Athletic Conferences in 1980, 1981, 1982, and 1983 State Championships, winning the Class S event in 1982 and 1983 and placing second in the State Open in 1983. After high school, John attended the University of Connecticut and was on the diving team for one year before changing direction and entering the United States Air Force. John Chapman entered the Air Force in September 1985. After basic training at Lackland Air Force Base, San Antonio., Texas, he was sent to Keesler Air Force Base, Biloxi, Mississippi, in January 1986 for training as an Information Systems Operator. Upon completion of training in March 1986, he was assigned to the 1987th Information Systems Squadron, Lowry Air Force Base, Denver, Colorado, from February 1986 to June 1989. He then cross-trained into the Combat Control career field and served with the 1721st Combat Control Squadron at Pope Air Force Base, North Carolina, from August 1990 to November 1992. His next assignment was as a Special Tactics Team Member with the 320th Special Tactics Squadron at Kadena Air Base, Okinawa, from November 1992 to October 1995. His final assignment was with the 24th Special Tactics Squadron at Pope Air Force Base.

On 10 January 2003, the Secretary of the USAF, James G. Roche, posthumously awarded the Air Force Cross to Technical Sergeant John A. Chapman. He was the first Air Force Combat Controller to be awarded the Air Force Cross [later upgraded].

New technology that allowed a deeper analysis of video of the battle suggested Chapman regained consciousness and resumed fighting Al-Qaeda members who were coming toward him from three directions. Chapman may have crawled into a bunker, shot and killed an enemy charging at him, and then killed another enemy fighter in hand-to-hand combat. *(military.com)*

While the Air Force pushed for Chapman to be recognized, Naval Special Warfare Command allegedly attempted to block Chapman's Medal of Honor as it would result in an admission that Chapman had been left behind. When it became apparent that Chapman's Medal of Honor could not be blocked, it was further alleged that the Navy put the commander of the operation, Britt K. Slabinski, up for the same award, which he received in May 2018. In March 2018, Chapman's family was notified that his Air Force Cross was to be upgraded to the Medal of Honor. *(Newsweek, Task & Purpose, military.com)*

[Valerie] Nessel said that about two or three years ago, when the military was reviewing several cases of valor to see if they merited higher awards, she found out that the technology had advanced to the point that a closer, frame-by-frame analysis of the video of an MQ-1 Predator flying above the battlefield was possible. That video allowed a closer analysis of Chapman's actions at Takur Ghar and was a key piece of evidence in the Air Force's effort to upgrade his Air Force Cross to a Medal of Honor.

"I tell them that he was such a genuine, good-hearted person," Nessel said. "He lived his life — team before self — he lived his life that whole way. The girls and I meant everything to him. When he was home, he was home. He was 110 percent present as a father and as a husband. He was very humble, very kind, very soft-spoken. An amazing man who would be a little embarrassed having this bestowed upon him."

From the Hartford Courant March 8, 2002

BEST FRIEND, AMERICAN HERO

WINDSOR LOCKS – They had grown up together, classmates since kindergarten soccer mates from the time John Chapman's dad rolled out balls for a youth program. And, now, here they were. Freshmen starting for the legendary coach at Windsor Locks [High School] and trying to make sense of him, trying to make sense of it all

John Chapman was the center midfielder.

Mike Toce was the sweeper back.

The year was 1979.

The coach was from a different time. He was 1969.

"We used to joke," Toce said Thursday, "that Sullivan was preparing us for war."

When he retired in 1999, Dan Sullivan was the last three-sport high school coach in Connecticut. He was a soccer coach. He was a basketball coach. He was a baseball coach. He coached for 39 years, winning 1,255 games and, in soccer alone, six state titles.

He was tough, and he never tried to deny it. When Sullivan took the job in 190 at Windsor Locks, he incorporated marching and military drills into his classes. He had been an Army infantry medic, and although the 309th hadn't seen action, Sullivan was sure some of his students would one day. The Vietnam War proved him right.

"By the time we graduated in 1983, there weren't many coaches like him anymore," Toce said. "Playing for Sullivan was brutal at times. He expected a lot of you. On the field, he was tough. Off the field, he was wonderful. You don't see it when you're 16, but the things I learned – the training, discipline, and work ethic – I've incorporated into my life over the years.

"I don't want to make a careless parallel, but I think for John, in a way, it was the start of special forces."

Sullivan watched two jets slam into the World Trade Center on September 11, and he felt white heat shoot through his face and down to his soul. There were dead Connecticut athletes buried in the rubble, among them one of the great lacrosse players in college history and a former Yale football player. The loss of life was incalculable.

"I've never been so hurt and mad in my life," Sullivan said. "War is falling in a battlefield, but innocent kids, mothers, and dads being mowed down? It still upsets me every time I think about it. I was ready to go to Afghanistan myself. These vets, 90 years old, would go right now if they were called.

"I'm a very patriotic man. This is why I'm so proud of John."

This is why Sullivan walked out to the middle of the soccer field at Windsor Locks the other day and found a patch of earth where he knew Chapman once played for him. This is why, at that moment, tears filled the eyes of the tough old coach.

"All of a sudden, it hit me," Sullivan said. "All I could think about were his wife and his two gorgeous little girls. It broke my heart."

"The tough man's voice began to crack. His only remedy is to recover with a barrage of praise.

"He was such a class act," Sullivan said. "He was courageous. He was fearless on the soccer field. And you should have seen him up on that diving board. He'd fly through the air, doing all those tricks. You'd never catch me doing that.

"He was loyal. He was dedicated. He was well-liked by everyone. He'd help me teach skills. John had something special."

"Windsor Locks is the town where aircraft roar to safe Bradley [Airport] landings and little boys grow up to be American heroes. In 1965, Windsor Locks won the Little League World Series in Williamsport. On Monday, half a world away, John Chapman became an American hero in the war on terrorism. A helicopter landing became a controlled crash, and six men fell to the hellfire of al Qaeda and Taliban machine guns and rocket-propelled grenades.

"I was scanning MSNBC on the Internet when I saw John A. Chapman on the list of deceased," Toce said. "I knew he was Air Force Special Operations, but it's not an uncommon name, and I wasn't sure about the A."

Odd about a middle initial, isn't it? You can know a guy since kindergarten and not remember it. His heart pounding, Toce called his wife at home to look it up in his 1983 yearbook.

"His middle name," Toce said, "is Allan."

Tech Sgt John A. Chapman was 36.

"John was a great guy," said David Allen.

Allen wanted to tell everyone that and so much more the other day but was too choked up to speak during a memorial at the high school. David's father, Tom, used to be Chapman's diving coach. A Windsor Locks record Chapman set as a junior, in fact, stands 20 years later.

"My dad has been working to keep what happened off his mind," said David, 16. "He has taken it hard."

Tom Allen thought so much of the young Chapman that he gave his first son the middle name John.

Four years later, he asked Chapman to be David's godfather.

"The day of the memorial at school, we said the Pledge of Allegiance in John's honor," his godson said.

The words never were so important to a town.

Toce and a handful of friends will attend Chapman's funeral in his wife's Pennsylvania hometown on Tuesday. When the tears have been shed and the sorrow spent, surely the time will come to regale those who had not seen him play. The Chapmans are a soccer family. Kevin and Tammy were strong players. Lori was phenomenal, Toce said, better than most of the boys. Kevin had a driver's license and would take John and Toce, three years his junior, all over the state to officiate games. In high school, John led Windsor Locks to the old Central Valley League title. Those were the days when Windsor Locks would battle Glastonbury and all the big state powerhouses.

Gene Chapman, who had preceded his son in the Air Force, played a vital role in building youth soccer in Windsor Locks. Toce calls John's father his source of athletic inspiration. Growing up, he called John something simpler. He called him best friend.

"I was the captain senior year, but John clearly was the best player," Toce said. "He was one of the best high school soccer players I've ever seen."

Sullivan had wondered why he hadn't seen more of Chapman over the years. Toce, in fact, hadn't seen him in 10 years. Isn't that the way it is for so many of us as we move on in life? Or was it because of the secretive nature of special forces, where not even immediate family knows all that is happening?

"All I know is I'm kicking myself in the pants for letting ten years pass," Toce said.

Toce approached the high school about retiring Chapman's Number 6 jersey. He'd like to get one of the fields named after him and start a scholarship. He called Sullivan, and the tough old coach was thrilled about the idea. He knows John Chapman is a hero. He knows John Chapman is his hero.

From the Hartford Courant April 2, 2002

HERO'S FAMILY RESPONDS

Words cannot begin to express the gratitude our family feels for everyone who has helped ease our pain and heartache in this most sorrowful time of our lives since Technical Sergeant John A. Chapman was killed in action in Afghanistan.

We are very fortunate that we live in a place that has such caring people. If the rest of the world were as compassionate, there would be no hatred and wars.

Johnny was truly a gift from God, not because he died saving the lives of his comrades, but because of the person he was. As a child, he was a little rascal who loved life and could make light of any situation. He was also tenderhearted and caring. John carried these characteristics through adulthood. Still, we had no idea he had touched so many lives in such a positive way.

We have been hearing from many people who are sharing stories of how he showed acts of kindness or encouragement through the years, beginning when he was a little boy. We shall treasure these letters.

We have no doubt that God has already found a place for him in heaven, but it will be some time before we can accept the fact that Johnny is no longer with us on Earth. People from Windsor Locks and throughout the state overwhelmed us with their contributions to the beautiful memorial service and celebration of Johnny's life. For this, we are truly grateful to all those who generously gave donations to the memorial trust for our little granddaughters.

The news media were very compassionate and patient with us in our time of sorrow. Everyone went out of their way to be considerate of our feelings.

We would like to ask two things:

> First, like Johnny, never be afraid to show your love for others. Enjoy each day with families and friends to the fullest, and don't be afraid to hug and kiss those who are dear to you.
> Second, please pray for all those who have died, for their families, and for those who continue to fight to preserve our freedom.

TERRY AND NICK GIACCONE; Windsor Locks

NOTE: *Additional family members of John A. Chapman also signed this letter.*

Memorialized at a pavilion near the soccer field at Veteran's Memorial Park in Windsor Locks, Connecticut. Photo courtesy of the Windsor Locks Hall of Fame.

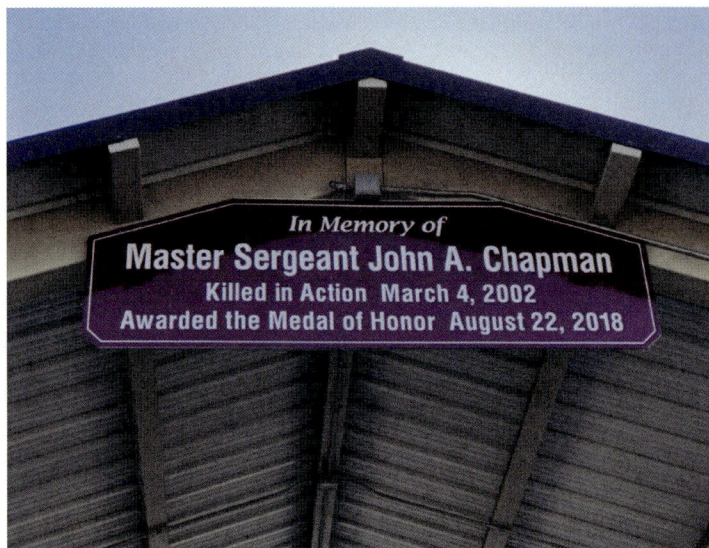

Also memorialized with a plaque at Memorial Hall, 1 South Main Street, Windsor Locks, Connecticut. Photo by the author.

Photo courtesy of msc.navy.mil

MV [Motor Vessel] TSgt John A. Chapman (T-AK-323) was a Buffalo Soldier-class container ship. She was one of the Military Sealift Command's Prepositioning Program. Built in 1978 by Chantier Naval de La Ciotat in La Ciotat, France, she was originally named Merlin. On April 8, 2005, she was renamed for Pope Air Force Base combat controller Technical Sergeant John A. Chapman, a posthumous Medal of Honor recipient.

The TSgt John A. Chapman (T-AK-323) carried Air Force munitions. She featured climate-controlled cocoons on her weather decks, which protect additional cargo from the marine environment. She was owned and operated by Sealift Incorporated under charter to MSC.

She was scrapped on September 4, 2014, at Alang, India.

COLONEL JOSEPHUS SAMUEL CECIL *; ARMY

January 12, 1878 (New River, TN) – August 20, 1940 (Hartford, CT); 62 years old
Married to Emma Caroline Schenck (1883-1942) on September 29, 1904, in Fayette, Kentucky.
One daughter, Emma Caroline S. Cecil Buttram (1919-2003).
Enlisted on July 8, 1898 in the 4th Tennessee Infantry.
Promoted to Colonel on August 9, 1918.
Honorably discharged on March 26, 1920.

Born to Judge Beaty Cecil (1849-1931) and Pauline Elmira "Polly" Buttram Cecil (1858-1938). Five brothers, John R. (1875-1961), Thomas J. (1885-1974), Alexander (1886-1888), Henry (1888-1933), and James J. (1893-1976). One sister, Minnie Cecil Beanblossom Cook (1880-1967).

* Colonel was his rank at retirement. First name is Joseph in some places.

Photo courtesy of FindAGrave.com

MEDAL OF HONOR CITATION

AWARDED FOR ACTIONS DURING: Philippine Insurrection
BRANCH OF SERVICE: Army
UNIT: United States 19th Infantry
GENERAL ORDERS: War Department, General Orders No. 7, February 3, 1913
AGE ON THE DAY OF THE EVENT: 28
CITATION:

The President of the United States of America, in the name of Congress, takes pleasure in presenting the Medal of Honor to First Lieutenant (Infantry) Joseph Samuel Cecil, United States Army, for most distinguished gallantry on 7 March 1906, while serving with 19th Infantry, in action at Mount Bud Dajo, Jolo, Philippine Islands. While at the head of the column about to assault the first cotta under a superior fire at short range, First Lieutenant Cecil personally carried to a sheltered position a wounded man and the body of one who was killed beside him.

<u>Date of Presentation:</u> January 23, 1913 in the White House by President Howard Taft.

From the Tipton (Indiana) Daily Tribune January 24, 1913

FOR GALLANTRY IN ACTION
President Taft Pins Medal on Breast of Tennessee Soldier

Washington, Jan. 24. – President Taft yesterday pinned on the breast of Captain Joseph S. Cecil, Eighteenth Infantry, a native of Tennessee, a congressional medal for "Gallantry in action."

The ceremony took place at the White House and was attended by Secretary of War Stimson and Major General Leonard Wood, Chief of Staff of the Army.

The medal was awarded Captain Cecil for his bravery in the Battle of Bud-Jalo, in the Philippines in 1906, when the officer, then a Lieutenant, led a small detachment of volunteers up to a point within 30 yards of the enemy and drew their fire while the main body of troops executed a flank movement.

From the Hartford Courant August 21, 1940

ARMY HERO TAKES LIFE BY BLUNGE FROM SIXTH FLOOR OF LOCAL HOTEL

A retired colonel of Infantry, United States Army, and holder of a Congressional Medal of Honor, Joseph S. Cecil, 62, plunged to his death shortly after 4 p.m. Tuesday from a window on the sixth floor of the Hotel Bond, to a cement driveway below. Medical Examiner Perry T. Hough, giving a finding of suicide, said death was instantaneous.

Colonel Cecil. of Falmouth, Massachusetts and Washington, DC, appeared at the hotel desk shortly before 4 p.m. and asked for a cool room. according to the assistant manager, Griffith R. Davies. He declined to register, explaining that he would return the following day to take the room. He was perspiring freely and wiped his face frequently with a handkerchief.

A bellhop, Theodore Allegra, took him in the elevator to the sixth 'floor and into one of the hotel rooms on the west side of the building. Allegra opened the window to air out the room. Colonel Gecil, the bellboy later told Detectives Edmund Lowe and Joseph Lynch. raised the screen, leaned out and asked several questions about the names of streets in, the vicinity.

Colonel Cecil suggested that an electric fan would aid in cooling the room. Allegra said he pulled down the screen before leaving the room to get the fan. When he returned the room was empty and the screen raised. He returned to the elevator to learn whether the operator had taken the man down and was informed that the man had been found lying in the concrete drive way on the west side of the hotel.

Hotel authorities immediately called the hotel physician, Dr. F. Arthur Emmett, from his office at 410 Asylum Street, near the hotel. Dr. Emmett found the man dead. Medical Examiner Hough arrived at the scene shortly afterwards. The man's skull and both wrists were fractured, Dr. Hough raid. Hastily 'summoned police officers blocked off the areaway where the body lay and kept a large crowd of spectators on the Asylum Street sidewalk.

Police found only a 1940 membership card of the Army and Navy Legion of Valor, USA. bearing Colonel Cecil's name. a cheap billfold and an eyeglass case stamped with the name of a Somerset, Kentucky. optometrist. in the man's pockets. It was later established, however, that Colonel Cecil had been a patient in various mental hospitals and had recently come here for treatment.

According to the official Army register. Colonel Cecil was retired for disability in line of duty in July 1922, after a career which began in 1888 with his enlistment in the Fourth Tennessee Volunteer Infantry Regiment to serve in the Spanish-American War. During the World War, while a major in the Regular Army, he was elevated to Colonel in the National Army. At the conclusion of the war, he reverted to his former rank and in 1920, was promoted to Lieutenant Colonel. He was given the rank of Colonel upon his retirement.

He leaves his wife. Mrs. Caroline Cecil of Falmouth. Mass, and a brother. Major Thomas J. Cecil, Coast Artillery Corps. retired. of St. Petersburg, Florida.

The body was taken to the funeral home of James P. O'Brien pending funeral arrangements.

Buried in Arlington National Cemetery, 1 Memorial Drive, Arlington Virginia; Section 6, Grave 5718. Photo courtesy of Arlington National Cemetery.

JOSEPH SAMUEL CECIL
JAN. 11, 1878
AUG. 20, 1940

COLONEL OF INFANTRY
UNITED STATES ARMY
CONGRESSIONAL MEDAL
OF HONOR

MAJOR GEORGE WILHELM CORLISS; ARMY

May 8, 1836 (New York City) – May 15, 1903 (New York, NY); 67 years old
Married Catherine A. "Kittie" Bunce (1836-1918) on July 3, 1861, in New Haven,
    Connecticut.
Married Mary H. Munson Corliss (1851-1940).
One son, Reginald Bliss Corliss (1891-1968).
One daughter, Grace W. (1886-1886).
Enlisted on June 21, 1861, in Hartford as a Captain.
He resigned his commission on January 21, 1863.

Born to John B. (1819-1857) and Harriet Pennock Corliss (1817-1853). Four brothers, Samuel W. (1840-1886), John B. (1842-?), Hiram C. (1843-1927), and Henry B. (1849-1856). One sister, Sarah C. (1847-1929).

Photo courtesy of MyHeritage.com

Photo courtesy of Congressional Medal of Honor Society

MEDAL OF HONOR CITATION

AWARDED FOR ACTIONS DURING: Civil War
BRANCH OF SERVICE: Army
UNIT: Company C, 5th Connecticut Infantry
DATE OF ISSUE AND PRESENTATION: September 10, 1897 (35 years later)
AGE ON THE DAY OF THE EVENT: 25
CITATION:

The President of the United States of America, in the name of Congress, takes pleasure in presenting the Medal of Honor to Captain George W. Corliss, United States Army, for extraordinary heroism on 9 August 1862, while serving with Company C, 5th Connecticut Infantry, in action at Cedar Mountain, Virginia. Captain Corliss seized a fallen flag of the regiment, the Color Bearer having been killed, carried it forward in the face of a severe fire, and though himself shot down and permanently disabled, planted the staff in the earth and kept the flag flying.

Photos courtesy of Tasha Caswell of the Connecticut Historical Society. Used with permission.

The wound he sustained was a bullet in the right leg, and it caused him to be captured by the Confederates. After partially recovering in a Confederate hospital, he was sent to the infamous Libby Prison in Richmond, Virginia. When he was finally exchanged, his disability prevented him from further field service, and he resigned on January 21, 1863.

Later, he rejoined the Union war effort in 1864 with a commission of First Lieutenant and Regimental Adjutant of the 3rd Veterans Reserve Corps, eventually brevetted Major, US Volunteers on March 13, 1865. After the war, he served in Vicksburg, Mississippi, in the Bureau of Refugees until 1869, when he resigned. He then became a successful insurance broker.

From the Record-Journal (Meriden, Connecticut) September 15, 1897

MEDAL FOR BRAVERY
AWARDED TO MAJOR CORLISS
OF THE FIFTH CONNECTICUT

Major George W. Corliss of the old Fifth Connecticut has received a medal from Congress for distinguished gallantry in the battle of Cedar Mountain on August 9, 1862. In this hand-to-hand conflict, Major Corliss commanded the color company of the Fifth, which belonged to the Fifth Brigade of the First Division of the Second Army Corps. The regiment occupied the most exposed position possible while advancing in a bayonet charge upon the enemy. Between the positions taken up by the two armies was an open field, which was necessary for the attacking party to cross before the opposing batteries could be assaulted. Advancing with his regiment into the field, Major Corliss charged the enemy down a depression, through which coursed Cedar Run, and then up an elevation into woods and brush, where the Confederates in superior numbers lay concealed in the rear of the obstructions formed of fences. The strong position taken up by the Confederates was fortified with batteries, also concealed from the view of the attacking force.

Major Corliss had stationed himself in front of the line of battle and near the color guard. The bearer of the national flag was killed and fell forward on his face before the line had advanced a few yards. Anxious to employ all the muskets possible, the commander did not detail another bearer but seized the colors himself and bore them forward under a terrific fire of musketry and artillery from the enemy. In battle, the colors are invariably a target for the guns of the foe, and, with a literal shower of bullets whistling around him, Corliss carried the standard at the head of the line until he fell, severely wounded in the right leg.

Despite his injuries, his first thoughts were for the colors. Planting the staff firmly in the ground, he continued to hold up the unfurled flag until he was relieved of it by Sergeant L.A. Palmer. The severity of the engagement is shown in the knowledge that Sergeant Palmer received no fewer than nine wounds within a few seconds after taking possession of the colors.

Major Corliss was captured in the engagement and removed to the Charlottesville Hospital. Afterward, he was confined for several months in Libby prison. After his exchange as a prisoner of war, Major Corliss promptly reported for active duty but was pronounced unfit by the army surgeon and was induced to accept an honorable discharge. After a period of recuperation, however, he returned to the service in April 1864 and was assigned to the brigade of veteran reserves, occupying the fortifications on the Alexandria side of the Potomac, rendering valuable service there until the end of the war. Subsequently, he was appointed to the staff of Major General T. J. Wood at Vicksburg in connection with the Bureau of Refugees, Freedman, and Abandoned Lands. Resigning in 1869, Major Corliss came to New York and established himself in business as an insurance broker. In 1880, he purchased "The Insurance Critic" of Chicago but transferred its publication to New York and has since continued as its proprietor and editor.

The citizens of New Haven, where, at his own expense, he recruited his company, some time ago presented to

Major Corliss an elaborate gold-plated sword and a brace of silver-mounted revolvers as a testimonial of their appreciation of his action at Cedar Mountain.

From The Daily Morning Journal & Courier (New Haven, CT) May 29, 1903

MAJOR G.W. CORLISS
Death of a Former Captain of the Fifth Regiment, C.V. [Connecticut Volunteers]

Major George W. Corliss, edit and proprietor of the "Insurance Critic," well remembered by many old New Haven friends, who died in New York recently, was formerly an officer of the Fifth Connecticut Volunteers. He was a member of the Old Guard, New York, and was buried with Masonic honors after services in the Old Guard Armory. He was a native of the City of New York, where he was born on May 8, 1836. In early life, he was a teacher and accountant, but at the outbreak of the Civil War, he raised Company C of the Fifth Connecticut Volunteers, which he commanded for two years. He was wounded at the Battle of Cedar Mountain and was confined for several months in the Libby prison in Richmond. From 1870 – 1875, Major Corliss was an insurance broker in New York. In the latter years, he became interested in the "Insurance Critic," which he bought and moved from Chicago to New York.

From the Evening Star (Washington, DC) July 10, 1903

DEATH OF MAJOR CORLISS
Union Veteran Who Received Ten Wounds at Cedar Mountain Battle

Word has been received here of the death of Major George W. Corliss at his home in New York a few days ago. Major Corliss formerly resided in Washington and was a brother of Mr. H. C. Corliss of 612 L Street Southwest. During the G. A. R. encampment held here last October, Major Corliss paid his last visit to Washington and took an active part in the sessions of the Grand Army. He was a high-degree Mason and was buried with the honors of that order from the Old Guard Armory in New York.

Major Corliss was sixty-seven years old and a native of New York. He was a Captain In the 5th Connecticut Volunteers, which he recruited at the outbreak of the Civil War. At the Battle of Cedar Mountain, he was wounded ten times. He commanded the color company of the regiment, and after thirteen men had been shot carrying the flag to the top of a high hill, Captain Corliss seized the banner himself and finally planted it on the enemy's breastworks. For this, he was promoted to Major. He was captured and spent several months in Libby prison in Richmond, Virginia, as a prisoner of war.

Buried in Maple Grove Cemetery, 127-15 Kew Gardens Road, Queens, New York; Summit Section, Lot 214, Grave 2. Photos by the author.

LIEUTENANT COMMANDER WILLIAM MERRILL CORRY, JR.; NAVY

October 5, 1889 (Quincy, FL) – October 7, 1920 (Hartford, CT); 31 years old
Unmarried
Graduated from the U.S. Naval Academy in 1910.

Born to William M. Sr. (1860-1927) and Sarah E. Wiggins Corry (1856-1952). Five brothers, Albert D. (1888-1922), James W. (1892-1952), Arthur (1893-1977), Edwin (1898-1898), and Henry E. (1900-1959). One sister, Alice H. (1895-1920).

Lieutenant Commander Corliss was also the recipient of the Navy Cross. The citation reads:

The President of the United States of America takes pleasure in presenting the Navy Cross to Lieutenant Commander William Merrill Corry, Jr., United States Navy, for distinguished and heroic service as an Airplane Pilot, making many daring nights over the enemy's lines, also for untiring and efficient efforts toward the organization of U.S. Naval Aviation, Foreign Service, and the building up of the Northern Bombing project.

Photos courtesy of USNAMemorialHall.org

MEDAL OF HONOR CITATION

AWARDED FOR ACTIONS DURING: Peace Time Awards
BRANCH OF SERVICE: Navy
UNKNOWN PRESENTATION DATE
AGE ON THE DAY OF THE EVENT: 30
CITATION:

The President of the United States of America, in the name of Congress, takes pride in presenting the Medal of Honor (Posthumously) to Lieutenant Commander William Merrill Corry, Jr., United States Navy, for heroic service in attempting to rescue a brother officer from a flame-enveloped airplane near Hartford, Connecticut. On 2 October 1920, an airplane in which Lieutenant Commander Corry was a passenger crashed and burst into flames. He was thrown 30 feet clear of the plane and, though injured, rushed back to the burning machine and endeavored to release the pilot. In so doing, he sustained serious burns, from which he died four days later.

Lieutenant Commander William M. Corry, Jr., USN (1889-1920) William Merrill Corry, Jr. was born on 5 October 1889 in Quincy, Florida. Admitted to the U.S. Naval Academy in June 1906, he graduated in 1910 and spent the next five years serving in the battleship Kansas. In mid-1915, Lieutenant (Junior Grade) Corry began instruction in aviation at Pensacola, Florida, and was designated Naval Aviator # 23 in March 1916. He had a flying position with the armored cruiser Seattle between November 1916 and May 1917, then was an officer in the armored cruiser North Carolina. In August 1917, Lieutenant Corry began World War I service in France, where he commanded Naval Air Stations at La Croisic and Brest during 1918 and early 1919. He was promoted to Lieutenant Commander in July 1918. Corry remained in France for the rest of 1919 and the first half of 1920, involved in removing U.S. Naval Aviation forces from Europe as part of the post-war demobilization. In mid-1920, Lieutenant Commander Corry was assigned as aviation aide to the Commander in Chief Atlantic Fleet, stationed on the Fleet's flagship, U.S.S.

Pennsylvania. While on a flight from Long Island, New York, with another pilot in early October 1920, the plane crashed near Hartford, Connecticut. Though thrown clear of the wreckage, the injured Corry ran back to pull the other officer free of the flaming aircraft. Badly burned during this rescue, William M. Corry died at Hartford on October 7, 1920. He was posthumously awarded the Medal of Honor for his heroism during that accident. Airfields at Pensacola, Florida, and three destroyers have been named in honor of Lieutenant Commander Corry.

From the Hartford Courant October 4, 1920

CROWD AGHAST AT FATAL ENDING OF TRIP TO HARTFORD
Lieutenant A.C. Wagner Dies in Hospital – Commander Corry of Atlantic Air Fleet Is Seriously Burned

FRANTIC ATTEMPT TO SAVE AVIATOR'S LIFE
W.E. Batterson, Col. Horsey and Keane Face Flames – Officers Were Guests of Lieut Col Howard

Lieutenant Arthur C. Wagner, United States Naval Air Service, died about 10 o'clock last night after lingering for nearly eight hours in agony from burns he received when the naval Curtis airplane, which he and Lieutenant Commander William Merrill Corry, commander of the Atlantic Fleet Air Section, were starting on their return journey to Mineola, Long Island, capsized and burned up on the grounds of the Hartford Golf Club yesterday afternoon. Corry received several broken ribs when he was spilled from the machine as it fell, and when he returned to the aid of his comrade, he was terribly burned about the face and hands.

Walter E. Batterson, Colonel Hamilton R. Horsey, former assistant chief of the staff of the Twenty-sixth Division, and Martin Keane, all of this city, were burned while aiding Corry to extricate Wagner from the flaming mass which had been the plane.

The plane had just been started on the return trip to the Mineola Air Station, whence the two aviators had come on Saturday afternoon in a cross-country flight and were receiving all possible attention from a number of club members on the veranda and tennis courts at the time of the accident.

WHAT REMAINS OF THE CURTIS PLANE BENEATH WHICH LIEUTENANT WAGNER WAS PINNED

Photo courtesy of the Hartford Courant October 4, 1920.

Wagner Piloting Plane

Lieutenant Wagner was in the forward or pilot's seat, and Lieutenant Commander Corry was in the rear passenger seat. While there were controls in both seats, Wagner was piloting the plane. People who were gathered around the start disagreed on whether Wagner remarked that the plane was out of order. Some say that he said it was running perfectly.

The start was made in a northerly direction, but when the plane was about fifty feet in the air, it turned completely around and headed southwest. As it passed over the clubhouse, Commander Corry waved to Colonel Horsey and Lieutenant Colonel James S. Howard, secretary of the Travelers Insurance Company, whose guests the two officers had been, and everything appeared to be going well with the machine. Just beyond the club is a large grove of trees, which seemed to the onlookers to be offering interference to the clear flight of the machine. At any rate, just before reaching the grove, the plane swerved sharply to the right and was heading back in a northerly direction when it suddenly made a nose dive from an altitude of about seventy-five feet. Onlookers did not agree on what happened just before the crash, but it was thought that the engine had stopped. This was later found to be the case.

The machine hit the ground at a sharp angle and immediately turned over endwise, the propeller catching in the ground. Commander Corry was catapulted from his seat, but Wagner, who had strapped himself into his seat, was less fortunate. As the machine turned over, it burst into flames, enveloping him in a wash of hissing gasoline from the broken tank.

Corry's Bravery

Commander Corry, picking himself up from the ground, was the first to rush to the aid of his comrade. It was in this way that his coat caught fire with the resulting burns to his hands and face. He was unable to pull Wagner free, and it was not until Walter E. Batterson of the Travelers Insurance Company and Martin Keane, an attaché of the club, added their efforts this was successfully accomplished. Club members rushed from the clubhouse with several gallons of olive and sweet oil and were on hand almost as soon as the stricken man was freed from his seat. While the burning clothing was being removed from Wagner's body, Benjamin Allen, a porter in the club, quickly wrapped his coat around Corry's head and thus cut off any chance of the flames reaching the officer's nose or eyes.

Allen then, with Corry helping, removed the coat and smothered the other smoldering pieces of clothing. Corry's hands and face were burned so badly that not a trace of skin was left untouched. Several ribs were also broken.

Wagner Game

Wagner was rolled over on the ground by willing hands to extinguish the flames, and with the help of the two men who had dragged him from his place beneath the plane, much of his clothing that still remained unburned was stripped from his body to make way for dressings in olive and sweet oil which by this time were available. He was wrapped in swaths of oil-soaked linen and cotton sheeting to allay the agony of his burns. Every scrap of clothing was almost entirely consumed, and his shoes were burned to a crisp. Throughout the process, Wagner, fully conscious, was directing the efforts of the willing helpers despite the fact that his face was burned beyond recognition, with his nose and ears partly burned from his head.

He remained game even up to the time when he was being tenderly lifted to the ambulance, when he thanked those who had helped, telling them that he was sure they had done all they could to aid him.

Corry in Serious Plight

While the work of rescue was going on, William H. Mann, who had been at the tennis court when the crash occurred, appeared on the gulf course with his touring car, which he had driven over knowing that it would furnish quicker transportation than an ambulance. With the help of Lieutenant Colonel Howard, Mr. Mann helped Commander Corry, whose face and hands had been absolutely stripped of skin by the flames, into the car and started for the Hartford Hospital. Wagner was held for the ambulance so that all the aid possible could be given to allay his sufferings and also because it would be impossible to carry him in an open touring car in his condition.

Mr. Mann said after his return from the hospital that he had broken all the speed laws of the state in getting Corry to medical aid and that he was glad to be able to do so. Corry, he said, did not complain of the pain of his burns but did say that they were itching terribly despite the coatings of olive oil on the wounds.

As an indication of the severity of Corry's burns, it was pointed out that his own coat and that of Benjamin A. Allen, which had been wrapped around his head, both burned to ashes.

Wagner Horribly Burned.

The remnants of Wagner's clothing also told a graphic story, with only shreds of the different garments remaining. His shoes were partly freed from his feet, and with the burning of his clothing, every bit of skin on his body was seared off by the heat. The flames partly burned his ears and nose, but miraculously, his eyes were spared, although the lashes and brows, with his hair, were completely burned off. But worst of all, he remained conscious through the entire agony.

Relatives Notified

Lieutenant Wagner was in a condition where it was almost impossible to secure any information from, but the hospital authorities were asked to notify Mrs. Elizabeth Wagner of Wayburn, Saskatchewan, Canada. Whether she is his wife or mother could not be determined by the hospital authorities.

The flier's courage was evident at the hospital. At about 9 o'clock last night, he was able to sip a glass of milk through a tube, and after he finished, he thanked the nurses for the kindness they were showing him.

According to physicians in the hospital, his recovery was highly improbable, but it was said that if there was any chance for any human being to pull through after receiving such burns, that Wagner would surely do it since, from the time of the accident, he had been displaying marvelous willpower and remarkable endurance.

In spite of a heroic fight for life, covering nearly eight hours from the time he received his burns, Wagner died soon after 10 o'clock. The tremendous display of pluck and vitality shown by the man through all of his agony was the marvel of all the physicians and nurses in the hospital.

Corry is Commander

Lieutenant Commander William Merrill Corry Jr., of Quincy, Florida, is the Commanding officer of the aviation section of the Atlantic Fleet, with headquarters at the U.S. Ship Pennsylvania, Admiral Wilson's flagship. He has been a lifelong friend of Colonel Hamilton R. Horsey, whose guests both officers had been from Saturday afternoon to yesterday.

The flight is understood to have been one of the regular cross-country jaunts which are required of all the naval aviators, and it was during their stay in the city that Corry and Wagner were the guests of Colonel Howard and Colonel Horsey. The trip was in direct line of duty, and the stopover factor was included in this, it is understood.

Boy Describes Crash

One of the witnesses of the accident was 14-year-old Harold Johnson of number 73 Tremont Street.

"I was on the golf course when the airplane started at about 3 o'clock." said young Johnson. "The machine did not seem to go just right. I heard some men say the trouble was caused by bad gas. It was not quite up to the level of the tree tops when it tried to come back to the ground. Then it fell straight down, landed on a hillside, and burst into flames. The officer in the back of the machine was thrown out and began walking around with his coat on fire.

Some men rolled him on the ground and threw coats around him, putting the fire out. The other officer was strapped into the machine and was badly burned. Both men were taken to the hospital, and I heard some people say that one of them might die. I also heard the one who was strapped in say he knew what caused the accident but that he would not tell. This was just before they took

him away in an ambulance."

Burns Terrible

Assistant Corporation Counsel Phillip Roberts was among the many witnesses who arrived on the scene shortly after the accident happened. Mr. Roberts, who served with a combat division in France, said last night that he had never during the war seen a more terrible sight than the two aviators yesterday after the fall. He was playing tennis on one of the lower courts when he heard shouts and ran up to see what had happened.

He saw one of the men enveloped in flames rolling down the hill west of the club where the plane crashed, while the other man, also in flames, was being aided by those who had rushed to the spot when they saw the machine sideslip. They were beating out the fire with coats. Both men appeared to be terribly burned.

From the Hartford Courant October 14, 1920

The members of the class of 1910 at the United States Naval Academy have resolved, it is reported, to erect a memorial at Annapolis in memory of their classmate, Lieutenant Commander William Merrill Corry, who died in this city following his injuries when the airplane in which he was riding capsized and was burned at the Hartford Golf Club October 3. Thus, they would honor the memory of a brave gentleman whose death was as heroic as if he had fallen in battle, who unhesitatingly, though vainly, gave his life for his companion and friend.

The public knows of him as a man who, in the immediate call of a great crisis, acted according to the highest traditions of the American Navy. His record of service during the war is likewise public knowledge, a record honorable and distinguished. His private life is not the concern of the rest of us, yet it violates no confidence to say that among the many who came to stand in sorrow at his grave, there was a unanimous tribute to the unusual qualities that made him one of the best-liked men in his class at the Naval Academy and, following that, one of the most popular and respected officers in the Navy.

When the airplane in which he and Lieutenant Arthur C. Wagner were flying fell to the ground, he was hurled free of the machine, which, with Lieutenant Wagner beneath it, immediately burst into flames. In a minute, bruised and shaken, Lieutenant Corry was on his feet. There was not the slightest hesitation. Absolutely unmindful of himself, he rushed into the burning wreckage and tried to rescue Wagner. Later, at the hospital, so horribly burned that there was only the slightest chance for his recovery and enduring terrible agony, his cheerfulness, his hopefulness, and his brave fight for life amazed his doctors and nurses.

It is fitting that there should be erected at Annapolis a memorial to him. There he came, a young man. There, he learned the art of war and the traditions of the service. The boys who yearly enter that institution, who hear of the countless brave deeds of the men whose places they are being trained to fill, can do no better than to hope that, if the crisis presents, in war or in peace, they, like him, will meet it as a man should and, like a hero, die.

From the Pensacola News Journal October 7, 2011, by Hill Goodspeed of the National Naval Aviation Museum

CORRY'S LEGACY SOARS ON

For decades, Pensacola has been known as the Cradle of Naval Aviation, a moniker that reflects its role in the figurative birth of thousands of personnel who have flown and fought for their nation in the cockpits of Naval aircraft. For William Merrill Corry Jr., not only did the launching of his flying career occur in the state of Florida, but so too did life itself. He was the first native Floridian to receive the Wings of Gold.

A product of the rolling farmland of Quincy, Corry entered the Navy as a midshipman at the U.S. Naval Academy in 1906. He proved popular with his Annapolis classmates in the Class of 1910, who called him "one of the best of us and one of the best liked. ... He has a man's head coupled to a boy's heart and live enthusiasm."

Following graduation, Corry went to sea aboard the battleship Kansas (BB 21), yet by the time his ship returned stateside in April 1914, Corry had become disillusioned with the life of a Naval officer, requesting that he be allowed to resign his commission.

The denial of his request came at a time when there was a new line of duty for Naval officers, aviation probably appealing to the "boy's heart and enthusiasm" for which Corry was known. Applying for flight instruction, Corry was accepted and reported to Pensacola Naval Air Station in July 1915, earning his wings as Naval Aviator No. 23 the following year.

After a period of sea duty, he received his first command, reporting overseas to establish a Naval air station at Le Croisic, France. It was the Navy's first operational air station, sending its seaplanes out to hunt for German U-boats operating in the waters off the French coast. He subsequently assumed command of NAS Brest and, by war's end, had been awarded the Navy Cross and French Chevalier, Légion d'Honneur.

Returning to the United States, Corry joined the staff of the Commander, Atlantic Fleet, ready to assume an important place in shaping postwar Naval aviation. Yet, on October 3, 1920, just two days shy of turning 41, he had a more immediate calling, one that revealed the highest character.

While flying as a passenger in a borrowed Army JN-4H "Jenny" landplane, he had just taken off from Hartford, Connecticut, when the engine quit, the plane crashed, throwing Corry 30 feet from the aircraft. Gas began leaking onto the hot engine manifold and ignited, enveloping the forward section of the plane in flames.

Though having broken ribs, Corry immediately dashed into the blaze in an effort to rescue the pilot, Navy Lieutenant Arthur C. Wagner, who managed to free himself from the airplane and stagger away with severe burns. He died later that night. Corry also suffered burns, which resulted in his death on Oct. 7, 1920.

For his actions, Corry received the Medal of Honor posthumously. He was one of six members of the Class of 1910 to lose their lives in aircraft accidents, the names
of two of them — Bronson and Chevalier — joining his as namesakes of Panhandle air stations where subsequent generations of Naval aviators were born.

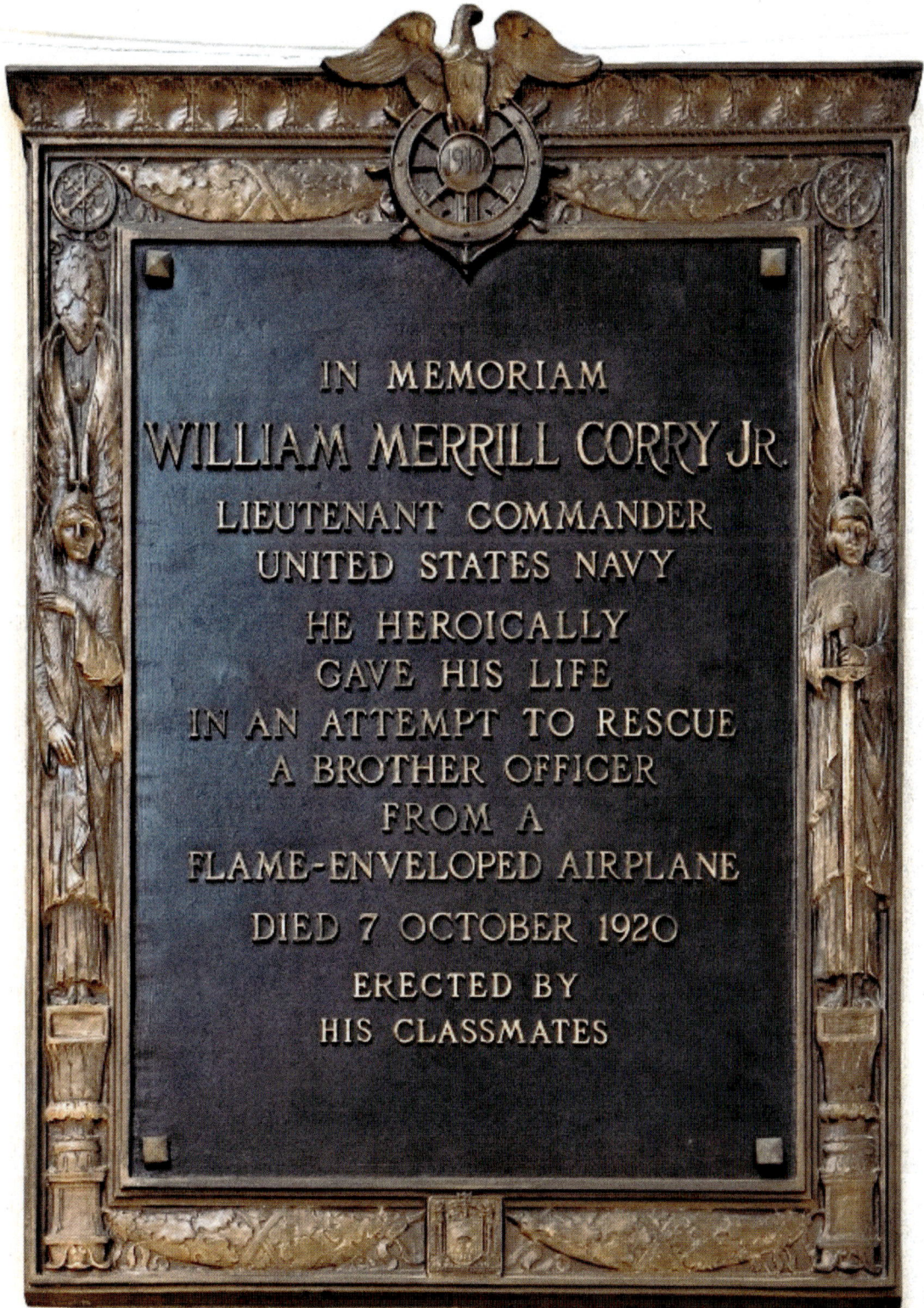

IN MEMORIAM

WILLIAM MERRILL CORRY JR.

LIEUTENANT COMMANDER
UNITED STATES NAVY

HE HEROICALLY
GAVE HIS LIFE
IN AN ATTEMPT TO RESCUE
A BROTHER OFFICER
FROM A
FLAME-ENVELOPED AIRPLANE

DIED 7 OCTOBER 1920

ERECTED BY
HIS CLASSMATES

LIEUTENANT ORSON LEON "SKIPPER" CRANDALL; NAVY

February 2, 1903 (St. Joseph, MO) – May 10, 1960 (St. Petersburg, FL); 57 years old

Married Mary "May" C. Donaldson (1903-1987) in 1929.

Enlisted June 30, 1922, from Connecticut.

Service number 385-23-69.

Retired December 1, 1952.

Born to Marshall J. (1863-1928) and Bertie L. Bennett Crandall (1876-1910). Two brothers, Berne (1897-1933) and Robert (1899-?). One sister, Martha (1899-?). His mother died when he was seven years old, and he was raised by Nehemiah (1841-1917) and Matilda Aldrich (1843-1926).

Orson Crandall was living at 10 Montauk Avenue in New London, Connecticut, at the time of the incident, resulting in him receiving the Medal of Honor.

Photo courtesy of the Congressional Medal of Honor Society

MEDAL OF HONOR CITATION

AWARDED FOR ACTIONS DURING: Peace Time Awards
BRANCH OF SERVICE: Navy
ASSIGNED TO: U.S.S. Falcon (ASR-2)
AGE ON THE DAY OF THE EVENT: 36
CITATION:

The President of the United States of America, in the name of Congress, takes pleasure in presenting the Medal of Honor to Chief Boatswain's Mate Orson Leon Crandall, United States Navy, for extraordinary heroism in the line of his profession as a Master Diver with the Submarine and Rescue Salvage Unit, U.S.S. Falcon, throughout the rescue and salvage operations following the sinking of the U.S.S. Squalus on 23 May 1939. Chief Boatswain's Mate Crandall's leadership and devotion to duty in directing diving operations and in making important and difficult dives under the most hazardous conditions characterize conduct far above and beyond the ordinary call of duty.

Presentation Date and Details: January 19, 1940, Washington, D.C., presented by Secretary of the Navy Charles Edison.

Secretary of the Navy Charles Edison congratulates four divers of the Squalus rescue and salvage operations after presenting them with Medals of Honor. (left to right in dress uniform): Chief Machinist's Mate William Badders; Chief Torpedoman John Mihalowski; Chief Boatswain's Mate Orson L. Crandall; and Chief Metalsmith James Harper McDonald.

The U.S.S. Squalus from history.navy.mil

Orson L. Crandall joined the Navy in 1922 and was trained as a diver from 1932-33. He achieved the designation of a Master Diver in March 1939. He was serving in U.S.S. Falcon (ASR-2) when she supported the rescue and salvage effort on the sunken submarine Squalus (SS-192) in May-September 1939. Chief Boatswain's Mate Crandall was awarded the Medal of Honor for heroism as Master Diver during that operation. During World War II, Crandall became a commissioned officer and served in a variety of salvage and diving-related positions. He transferred to the Fleet Reserve in June 1946 and retired in December 1952.

U.S.S. SQUALUS (SS-192): THE SINKING, RESCUE OF SURVIVORS, AND SUBSEQUENT SALVAGE, 1939

U.S.S. Squalus (SS-192), a diesel-electric submarine built at the Portsmouth Navy Yard, Portsmouth, New Hampshire, and commissioned there on March 1, 1939, suffered a catastrophic valve failure during a test dive off the Isle of Shoals at 0740 on May 23. Partially flooded, the submarine sank to the bottom and came to rest, keel down in 40 fathoms (240 feet) of water. Navy divers and salvage ships responded quickly, and the following day began operations to rescue the surviving 32 crew members and one civilian from the forward sections of the boat. At 1130 on May 24, U.S.S. Falcon (ASR-2) lowered the newly developed McCann rescue chamber – a revised version of a diving bell invented by Commander Charles B. Momsen – and, over the next 13 hours, all 33 survivors were rescued from the stricken submarine. On September 13, after long and difficult salvage operations, Squalus was raised and towed into the Portsmouth Navy Yard. The boat was formally decommissioned on November 15, renamed Sailfish on February 9, 1940, and recommissioned on May 15, 1940.

Photo # NH 97291   Cutaway drawing of McCann Rescue Chamber

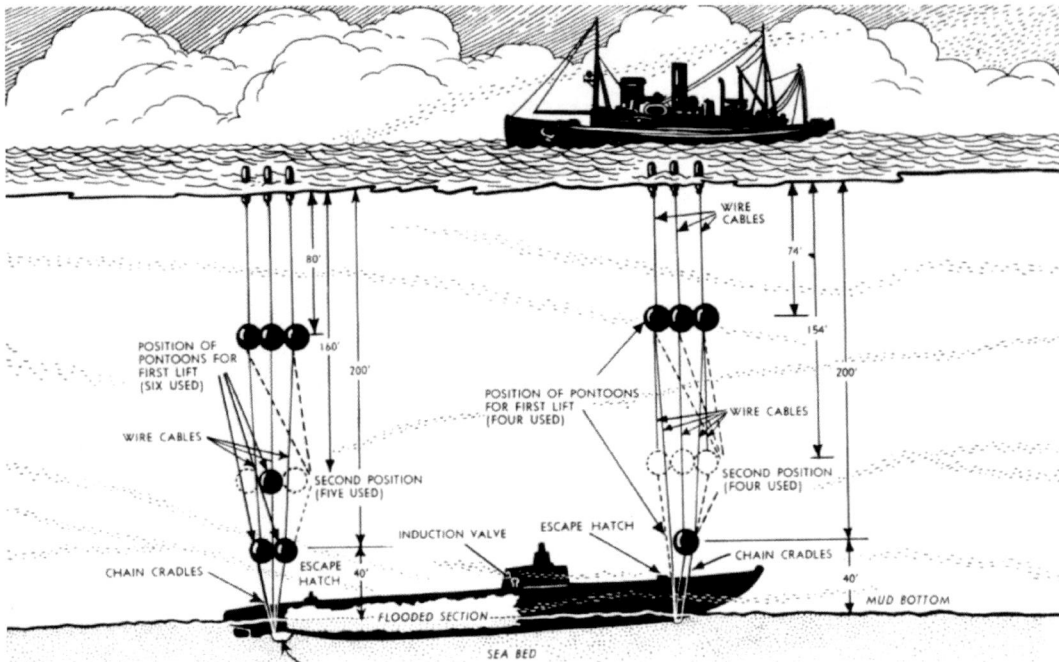

Diagram showing the salvage operation of the sunken USS Squalus (US Navy History & Heritage Command)

From The Evening Sun, Baltimore, Maryland, on May 2, 1952

ROLE IN SQUALUS DISASTER RECALLED BY DIVER

Thirteen years ago yesterday, one of the worst undersea disasters in American peacetime naval history occurred when the ten-ton Sargo class submarine Squalus sank while making a routine dive off the Isles of Shoals near New Hampshire.

Fifty-nine officers and men, one of them a native of Baltimore, were trapped on the bottom beneath 42 fathoms of water. The Squalus and her crew were at the mercy of the weather, tides – and times.

To most, the marine tragedy meant a gripping story in the papers, sympathy for victims and their families, or an opportunity to assail the then-current naval building program.

To Chief Petty Officer Orson L. Crandall, a master diver and navy salvage man, it was a clear-cut call to duty. In the three months that followed the sinking of the Squalus, Chief Crandall made more than sixty dives to the stricken submarine from the decks of the Navy repair ship U.S.S. Falcon.

At Bainbridge Naval Training Center, where today he is an instructor in seamanship, Medal of Honor winner Crandall recalls the sinking clearly.

"We, the U.S.S. Falcon," he explains, "were tied up at New London, Connecticut, for overhaul when we heard the news of the Squalus going down. Within sixteen hours, we were on the spot of the sinking, and by 8 A.M. of the next day, we were ready to dive.

"I remember that the water was rough and that the wind was pretty stiff, but after a while, it calmed down some. The descent was pretty fast – it took only about seven minutes to drop down to the 240-foot level where the submarine lay with her stern in about 12 feet of mud.

"Because of the pressure, we could work for an average of only eighteen minutes at a time. It took three hours to bring us to the surface. It seems like a long time, but it was the only way they could protect us from the bends. The bends, Chief Crandall explained, are when air bubbles form in the bloodstream from too rapid a change in pressure.

From the Tampa Bay Times May 23, 1958

TWO RETIRED NAVY MEN RECALL SQUALUS RESCUE

For the public, it was just an open house. But for two graying Navy career men now living here, a recent visit of the U.S.S. Petrel was old home week. The Petrel was here last weekend for Armed Forces Day.

Aboard a similar vessel 19 years ago, fate threw them together to write a dramatic chapter in Naval history.

On that day, May 24, 1939 – some 24 hours after the submarine Squalus sank off New Hampshire – Torpedoman Third Class Leonard de Medeiros became a living testimonial to the validity of the Navy's then-new submarine rescue procedures. Medeiros and 32 others survived, and 26 died.

Chief Boatswain's Mate Orson L. Crandall, then one of the Navy's top deep sea divers, is partly responsible for Medeiros now being here. For that, Crandall won the nation's top award for valor and courage – the Congressional Medal of Honor.

Crandall retired as a lieutenant several years ago and now lives at 10005 Bay Pines Boulevard. He is a charter boat captain in his time off from personal fishing. Crandall has been invited by President Eisenhower to attend Memorial Day ceremonies on May 30 at Arlington National Cemetery.

Medeiros, now 47, retired last December 1. He now lives at 4707 13th Avenue South. Both he and Crandall are married, but neither has children.

Medeiros, then 28, won no medals for his part in the Squalus saga. But he was chosen at the time to pioneer the "Momsen lung" escape from a sunken submarine.

The Squalus' skipper, Lieutenant Oliver F. Naquin, chose the escape priority list from among his top men. Medeiros was to have had the vital chore of attaching a line from the sub's hull, which his crewmates would have followed hand-over-hand to the surface 240 feet above.

But the rescue crews deemed the use of the McCann "diving bell," an underwater rescue chamber lowered from a surface ship, the better method of rescue.

The diving bell, an inverted pear-shaped object which, with its crew of two, can be lowered by cable and winch to the submarine's escape hatches, was used for the first time in an emergency on the Squalus rescue.

Air pumped into the chamber sustains the men involved, and the chamber still is used by the Navy today.

The pay-off test of the Squalus rescue proved the Navy's theory that trapped submariners should be removed at the earliest possible moment from their sunken ships rather than to try to refloat them with the crew on board.

While no incident as dramatic has been logged in Navy annals since the Squalus' sinking, the Navy still uses the methods and equipment proved by that acid test.

Medeiros recalls his 24 hours trapped beneath the sea primarily as "cold." The other crew members "razzed me for sleeping through most of it," he says with a shrug.

Medeiros and the other survivors were in forward compartments when a faulty valve flooded the Squalus during a test dive. His 26 crewmates, who died, drowned in water-filled aft compartments.

Both Medeiros and Crandall saw combat action in World War II, Crandall as skipper of a salvage and rescue ship and Medeiros as a crewmember on another submarine.

Crandall, whose Medal of Honor citation commends him for "extraordinary heroism," non-committally says the Squalus diving was routine.

The rescue was handled by men inside the diving bell, but divers had to descend first to attach a cable to the sunken sub, which was used extensively to refloat the ship after the rescue.

The late Nat Barrows, a Boston Globe reporter who covered the Squalus rescue and salvage, says in his book "Blow All Ballast" that Crandall's life was saved by chance during the diving operations.

Crandall, a quarterback on a shore-based Navy football team, began calling football signals unconsciously as he lapsed into unconsciousness from an unsuspected buildup of carbon dioxide in his diving helmet.

A teammate, Lieutenant Julian K. Morrison, realized something was wrong and hauled Crandall to the surface.

Lieutenant Morrison died in St. Petersburg on February 11, 1940, a victim of an accidental discharge of a pistol he was cleaning while visiting here aboard the submarine U.S.S. Seahorse.

Orson L. Crandall had a Navy ship named in his honor. The U.S.S. Crandall (YHLC-2) heavy-lift craft was built in Germany in 1942 as the Salvage Barge Ausdauer by Seebeck Werft, in Bremerhaven, Germany. It was leased by the United Nations in 1957 to clear the Suez Canal. It was then purchased by the US Navy in 1967 at Bremerhaven, Germany from Bugsier-, Reederei & Bergungs - AG, Bremerhaven / Hamburg, Germany, named AHLC II and renamed and commissioned U.S.S. Crandall (YHLC-2) in 1967. Assigned to Harbor Clearance Unit One at Naval Station Subic Bay R.P. Decommission date is unknown. Custody was transferred to the Maritime Administration on February 11, 1976, for lay-up in the James River National Reserve Fleet, Lee Hall, VA. Permanent custody was transferred to the Maritime Administration on October 1, 1977. The title was transferred to the Maritime Administration on December 11, 1993. Final Disposition: sold for scrapping on November 28, 2001, to Transforma Marine, Brownsville, Texas.

Photo courtesy of NavSource.org

CAPTAIN HENRY HARRISON CROCKER; ARMY

January 20, 1839 (Colchester, CT) – March 28, 1913 (Washington, NJ); 74 years old

Married Jane "Jennie" Vannatta (1844-1911) on December 6, 1865, in Warren, New Jersey.

Two sons, George O. (1861-1947) and William Q. (1875-1960).

Two daughters, Susan M. Crocker Hampton (1868-1947) and Catherine (1874-?).

Enlisted on March 19, 1863, as a 2nd Lieutenant.

Wounded in action on October 19, 1864, at Cedar Creek, Virginia.

Mustered out on July 20, 1865.

Born to Seth B. (1812-1852) and Laura B. Beckwith Crocker (1816-1866). One brother, John F. (1845-1929). Three sisters, Louisa J. Crocker Coon Doane (1834-1903), Elizabeth R. Crocker Loomis (1837-1880), and Harriet Rosella Crocker Riggs (1849-1875).

Photo courtesy of Ancestry.com

MEDAL OF HONOR CITATION

AWARDED FOR ACTIONS DURING: Civil War
BRANCH OF SERVICE: Army
UNIT: Company F, 2nd Massachusetts Cavalry
DATE OF ISSUE AND PRESENTATION: January 10, 1896 (32 years later)
AGE ON THE DAY OF THE EVENT: 24
CITATION:

The President of the United States of America, in the name of Congress, takes pleasure in presenting the Medal of Honor to Captain Henry H. Crocker, United States Army, for extraordinary heroism on 19 October 1864, while serving with Company F, 2nd Massachusetts Cavalry, in action at Cedar Creek, Virginia. Captain Crocker voluntarily led a charge, which resulted in the capture of 14 prisoners and in which he himself was wounded.

From Beyer, W. F., & Keydel, O. F. (2000). Deeds of valor: How America's Civil War Heroes won The Congressional Medal of Honor. Smithmark Publishers.

TWO RIDERS ON ONE HORSE

When Longstreet and Early planned to annihilate Sheridan's Army in the Shenandoah Valley, the Federal forces were at the little village of Middletown, Virginia, and around the immediate neighborhood between the village and Cedar Creek. The Confederate attack made at early dawn on October 19, 1864, was a complete surprise and came so unexpectedly that many of the Union soldiers had no time to put on their clothes. About ten o'clock in the forenoon, General Sheridan reached the scene of action, and the battle of Cedar Creek, which continued throughout the day, was transformed from defeat, rout, and confusion to order and victory.

The Second Massachusetts Cavalry, Lieutenant-Colonel Caspar Crowninshield commanding, was attached to Lowell's Brigade and was stationed near the village of Middletown. Captain Henry E. Crocker of Company F, a part of the so-called California Battalion attached to this regiment, refers to the battle as follows:

"We were aroused early in the morning by the attack of the enemy. As the enemy came upon us with force, we were compelled to fall back slightly, but as we did so, we inclined toward the pike at our right, thus keeping our line of communication open. It was a bitter contest, the enemy coming at us in several distinct charges, each of which they were repulsed. Colonel Lowell, our brigade commander, who was killed later in the day, rode up and down our line, encouraging the men to stand together and assuring them that General Sheridan would soon be on the field with reinforcements.

"About this time, a body of the enemy was seen to emerge from the woods and advance upon our front. My mind was immediately set on checking those fellows, so I rode up to Colonel Crowninshield and asked permission to charge them. The colonel gave his consent but cautioned me not to advance too far, and 'if possible,' he added, 'come back with a few prisoners.'

"I hurried back to my company and told the boys, very much to their satisfaction, of the work before us. We waited until we knew that the advancing force could give us but one volley before we could reach them, and then I gave the command: 'Forward! Trot! Gallop! Charge!' and away we went with sabers flashing in the sunlight. The expected volley was received, saddles were emptied, and horses went down, but on we went. In less time than it takes to tell it we were among them, their line was broken, and we demanded their surrender. Many ran back into the woods where we could plainly see the enemy in force, but they did not fire upon us for fear of hitting their own men. We brought back fourteen prisoners on the run.

"In the heat of our charge, I had felt a dull, throbbing pain in my left leg and knew that I had been wounded, but that did not prevent me from stopping, on our return, to pick up Lieutenant McIntosh, whose horse had been killed and who was loosening the cinch from his saddle. When he had completed his task, he mounted my horse behind me, and thus, we rode back to our lines just as General Sheridan came dashing along the road on his famous ride from Winchester."

The prisoners captured by Captain Crocker in this charge were, according to the statement of Colonel Crowninshield, the first rebels captured that day and, therefore, of great importance to General Sheridan, who had them questioned closely as to the strength and formation of the opposing army. They also gave valuable and assuring information that General Longstreet had not united forces with General Early, as had been believed by the leaders of the Union forces. This was information of such importance that it naturally changed arrangements of maneuvers, and the expected defeat of the morning was changed into a grand victory by evening.

Excerpt from the Oakland Tribune June 25, 1961

... Massachusetts was paying large bounties for volunteers to fill that state's quota. It was suggested to Governor John A. Andrews that any bounty money be placed in a special fund to be used for paying passage east for a company from California. The Californians offered to provide their own uniforms.

The Massachusetts governor accepted the company to be applied to his state's quota. Recruiting began on October 28, 1862. In a few days, nearly 1,000 men lined up to enroll. Then began the job of sifting out the volunteers to keep the company within the 100 agreed upon. J. Sewell Reed, formerly captain of the First Light Dragoons, was selected to command the company.

Money for the uniforms was raised by popular subscription. The California One Hundred was not clothed in the conventional blue of the Union Army.

Their uniforms were green and adorned with gold. The volunteers must have appeared like something out of a light opera. Besides the green uniforms, the men wore green velvet caps, each adorned by a gold eagle feather. The caps were encircled by a golden band with silver letters "EUREKA" and underneath the silver words "ONE HUNDRED" in a golden laurel wreath.

Cheering thousands saw them leave San Francisco on December 11, 1862, to the ringing tune of Hail Columbia, Happy Land. For gallant, young Captain Reed and many of his men, there was no return.

Enthusiastic welcomes greeted the company in New York and upon arrival at Camp Meigs near Charlestown, Massachusetts. In the camp, the California company was presented with an American flag, hand-sewn by Miss Abbie Lord, a Charlestown dressmaker, who paid for the banner and properly inscribed a silver plate on the staff.

"Many non-commissioned officers and privates of the battalion, all brave and patriotic Californians, were killed in various battles. I regret that the limits of this report will not permit me to mention the names and meritorious services of each. "No better soldiers died for the Union cause during the war."

From the New York Tribune March 28, 1913

Washington, N.J., March 27 – Captain Henry H. Crocker, seventy-four years old, died today at the Easton (Penn.) Hospital from pleuro-pneumonia after an illness of only a week. Besides his wife, who was formerly Miss Jennie Vannatta of Washington, he leaves two sons and a daughter.

Captain Crocker was a veteran of the Civil War. He enlisted in one of the two California regiments and later assigned to the 2nd Massachusetts Cavalry. Two years ago, Congress voted him a medal for distinguished bravery on the field of battle. He was a member of Ute Tribe, 40, I.O. of R.M. (International Order of Red Men), and of Starlight Lodge 112, K. of P. (Knights of Pythias).

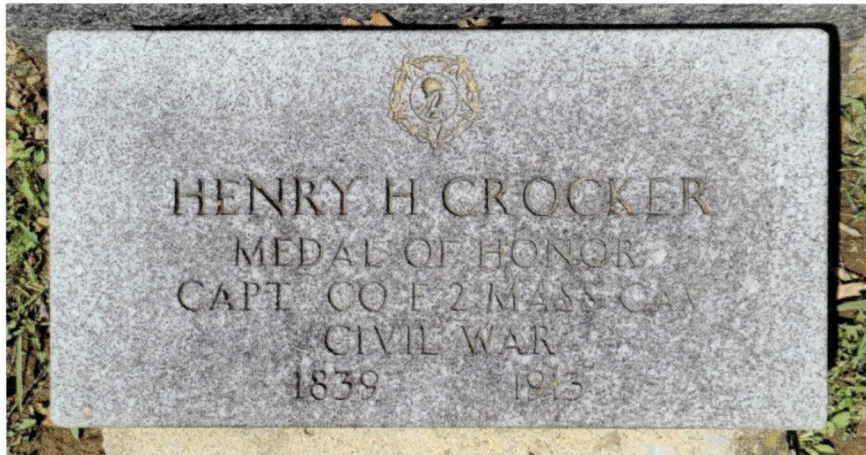

FIRST LIEUTENANT JOHN CALVIN CURTIS; ARMY

April 19, 1845 (Bridgeport, CT) – January 17, 1917 (Bridgeport, CT); 71 years old

Married to Adela/Adeline "Addie" Stuart (1849-1920) on November 8, 1870.

Five sons, Victor S. (1871-1925), Henry S. (1873-1954), John K. (1877-1967), Clapp S. (1884-1889), and Eliot R. (1890-1966).

Four daughters, Adeline "Addie" M. (1876-1881), Vera C. (1879-1962), Gladys H. Curtis Berrien (1881-1953), and Sarah G. Curtis Maugham (1886-1957).

Enlisted on August 17, 1861, in Bridgeport, Connecticut, at just <u>16 years old</u>.

Mustered out on October 29, 1864.

Born to Victory S. (1806-1891) and Susan J. Miles Curtis (1808-1871). Five brothers, Josiah M. (1828-1829), Elliot M. (1831-1894), Cornelius (1837-1918), Frederick (1841-1925), and Victory B. (1848-1929). Three sisters, Susan J. Curtis Beach (1830-1910), Louisa H. Curtis Clark (1834-1899), and Sarah E. Curtis Glover (1839-1903).

Photo courtesy of Ancestry.com

Photo courtesy of the Congressional Medal of Honor Society

MEDAL OF HONOR CITATION

AWARDED FOR ACTIONS DURING: Civil War
BRANCH OF SERVICE: Army
UNIT: 9th Connecticut Infantry
DATE OF ISSUE AND PRESENTATION: December 16, 1896 (34 years later)
AGE ON THE DAY OF THE EVENT: 17
CITATION:

The President of the United States of America, in the name of Congress, takes pleasure in presenting the Medal of Honor to Sergeant Major John Calvin Curtis, United States Army, for extraordinary heroism on 5 August 1862 while serving with 9th Connecticut Infantry, in action at Baton Rouge, Louisiana. Sergeant Major Curtis voluntarily sought the line of battle and, alone and unaided, captured two prisoners, driving them before him to regimental headquarters at the point of the bayonet.

At the outbreak of the Civil War, John Curtis enlisted as a Private in Company I, Ninth Regiment Connecticut Volunteers, and served until he mustered out at the close of the war. He rapidly rose through the various non-commissioned grades to the rank of Sergeant Major and at the time of his discharge, was a First Lieutenant.

From Beyer, W. F., & Keydel, O. F. (2000). Deeds of valor: How America's Civil War Heroes won The Congressional Medal of Honor. Smithmark Publishers.

CAPTURED TWO REBELS

It was at the battle of Baton Rouge, Louisiana, on the 5th of August, 1862, that John C. Curtis, then a Second Lieutenant, performed an act of military daring, which won the plaudits of his comrades, the commendation of officers, and the official recognition of his Government.

Twenty-five hundred Federals faced a foe of twice this strength. For eight hours, the struggle continued with varying success until the Union gunboats Essex, Sumter, and Kineo came to the support of the troops and rendered most valuable assistance.

General Williams, who, in a brilliant charge, led the Yankees to victory, was shot in the chest and killed during this engagement. Under ordinary circumstances, the death of the commander might have caused panic among the troops. The presence of mind of the various officers, however, prevented any such disastrous effect. One of these was Second Lieutenant Curtis. His undaunted courage animated and inspired the men. He was always in the lead, once even approaching the enemy so closely as to be within their own rank. With great coolness and nerve, he captured two rebel soldiers and, at the point of the bayonet, marched them to the regimental headquarters.

From The Bridgeport Times and Evening Farmer January 18, 1917

JOHN C. CURTIS MADE AN ENVIABLE RECORD IN WAR
Prominent Bridgeport Who Died Yesterday Possessed Medal of Honor

SINGLE-HANDED, HE CAPTURED 2 OF HIS FOE
Enlisted at 16 and Performed Valiant Deeds Before He Reached 20

With the death yesterday afternoon of Lieutenant John Calvin Curtis, Civil War hero, former Superintendent of the New England Division of the Adams Express Company, and member of one of the first families to settle in this country, Bridgeport lost one of its most prominent citizens. Mr. Curtis was one of the few soldiers of the Civil War to receive a gold medal from Congress for conspicuous bravery.

Mr. Curtis' health had been gradually failing for the last year. On Sunday, he contracted pneumonia against the ravages of which his enfeebled powers could not long battle, and death followed three days after his serious illness.

Mr. Curtis was born on April 19, 1845, in the house at Main and Arch Streets, built by his father, Victory Curtis, in 1824. His mother was Susan Miles Curtis, who was also of Colonial ancestry.

At the outbreak of the Civil War in 1861, Mr. Curtis, then little past his 16th birthday, enlisted as a private in the Ninth Regiment, Connecticut Volunteers, Infantry.

When only 18 years old, he distinguished himself at Baton Rouge, winning the medal for his brave act. The Military Order, Congress Medal of Honor, Legion of the United States, gives the story of the young man's conspicuous fighting:

"Baton Rouge, situated on the Mississippi River, 75 miles northwest of New Orleans, Louisiana, was captured by Federal forces on May 12, 1862. The city was the scene of a bloody fight on August 5 following, when the Union troops under General Thomas Williams were attacked by the Confederates. After a severe engagement, the enemy was repulsed with heavy loss.

"The Federals lost 200, among them General Williams. The Confederate Brigadier General Charles Clarke also lost his life. The Confederate ironclad gunboat 'Arkansas,' designed to engage the naval force in the river, proved useless and was attacked and destroyed the next day by vessels under the command of David D. Porter.

"At Baton Rouge, Louisiana, August 5, 1862, Lieutenant John Calvin Curtis gained a Congress medal for very conspicuous bravery. He was at the time Lieutenant of Company I in the Ninth Connecticut Infantry and, by his remarkable bravery and coolness in action during the battle, won the plaudits of his comrades. He not only displayed the sterling qualities of a commander, but during a charge on the enemy's lines, during which General Williams was killed, he captured single-handedly two Confederate prisoners. He was a Sergeant Major when he went into the Battle of Baton Rouge. As his equipment only gave a short sword, he put on the equipment of one of the regiment who had fallen.

"When his own regiment was temporarily held in reserve, he requested to go into the engagement and firing line of the Sixth Michigan Regiment on the right. He advised him not to go and urged him to remain with his own regiment, but reluctantly consented, and away the young boy went and was in the midst of the fighting, which was very severe. The Sixth Michigan lost many men and officers. The fighting was in a dense fog, and both lines were very close, thus resulting in many hand-to-hand conflicts. A portion of the regiment was obliged to push back, and young Curtis was compelled to jump a fence and jumped right close to two Confederates, one of whom was a member of a Mississippi Regiment, the other of a Louisiana Regiment. His bayonet was on his gun, and he rushed at them, yelling at the same time to surrender, which they did, as they were so surprised and supposed he was only the forerunner of a larger force. They were taken aback by the sudden rush he made and were his prisoners before they had time to realize their position.

"He rushed them at the point of his bayonet to where the regiment was stationed, and the colonel and regiment set up a great cheer. The colonel first spied the three coming and shouted: 'Great God, see what's coming; see that boy coming in with two Confederate prisoners.' He was commended by the colonel in the official report to the State and War Departments for bravery and received a commission as Second Lieutenant, and later received the Congress medal.

"He was perhaps the youngest commissioned officer in the U.S. Army at the time. The next year, he was promoted to First Lieutenant and was in command of a company most of the time. He received very complimentary appointments while in the service, which seemed to come out of a clear sky. He was appointed and served as Judge Advocate of the military commission held in New Orleans for about a month. Later on, he was appointed and served as Acting Assistant Adjutant General of Brigadier General H.F. Kimberly's brigade at Madisonville, Louisiana, for about six weeks. He left Louisiana and went to Virginia, and was before Petersburg and Deep Bottom and Malvern Hill, and went through the Shenandoah Valley with Sheridan. He was mustered out on the last day of October 1864, having served three years and two months and was then only 19 years and six months of age."

When Mr. Curtis returned to Bridgeport, he entered the employ of the Adams Express Company as a clerk. Henry R. Parrott was at that time First Agent of the company here, and Mr. Curtis eventually worked his way up until he succeeded him. Later, he was made Superintendent of the New England Division of the company, a position which he held for 15 years. During that time, the family resided in Boston, where Mr. Curtis' headquarters were. After his retirement in 1907, they returned to this city and have since made their home at 154 Coleman Street.

Mr. Curtis was very active in the affairs of the city. He was affiliated with the Republican Party and twice served the city as Alderman. He was also prominent fraternally and was a member of St. John's Lodge, Free and Accepted Masons of Stratford, the Elias Howe Jr. Post Number 3, Grand Army of the Republic, the Loyal Legion, a society composed of commissioned officers of the Civil War and officers of the standing army, and the Army and Navy Club. He also belonged to the Sea Side Club. He was much interested in work among the boys of the city and was the founder and first President of the Boys' Club.

John Curtis, who, with his mother Elizabeth and his brother William, came to Connecticut from England in 1639, was the direct ancestor of Mr. Curtis. The family has been prominent in the history of this section of the state ever since they first settled here. Augur Curtis Jr., Grandfather of Mr. Curtis and sixth in line from John Curtis, the original ancestor of the family in this country, was a resident of Stratford. The house, which he built in 1805 when he married Alice Peck, still stands on Booth Street in Stratford. Mr. Curtis was one of the oldest members of the South Congregational Church, of which he was a life-long member. His grandfather was a Deacon in the same church for more than 50 years.

Lieutenant Curtis was married to Miss Adeline Stuart of New Haven. Miss Vera Curtis, his daughter, has distinguished herself in music, having gained a prominent place in the Metropolitan Opera Co. She has the honor of being one of the few American-trained young women ever engaged by that great musical organization. Mr. Curtis is survived by his widow and seven children, all of whom are prominent in the community.

There are three daughters, Mrs. Gladys Curtis Berrien of Bronxville and Misses Vera Cameron Curtis and Sarah Glover Curtis. His four sons are Victor Stuart, Henry Sanford, John K., and Elliot Robertson Curtis.

The funeral will be held at 9:30 tomorrow morning from his late residence. Reverend Henry Dwight Tweedy of Yale, former Pastor of the South Congregational Church of this city, will conduct the services. Delegations will attend from the various organizations of which Mr. Curtis was a member. The services will be carried out simply, and burial will be at the convenience of the family. The bearers will include six of Mr. Curtis' most intimate friends: Judge Morris B. Beardsley, Judge A.B. Beers, Edward W. Harral, William Fairchild, Dr. George L. Porters, and Colonel Richard Fitzgibbon.

The bottom line reads, "A Founder and First President, Boys Club of Bridgeport."

CAPTAIN MICHAEL JOSEPH DALY; ARMY

September 15, 1924 (New York, NY) – July 25, 2008 (Fairfield, CT); 83 years old
Married Margaret N. Wallace Daly (1920-2012) on January 31, 1959, in Fairfield, Connecticut.
One son, Michael (1960-).
One daughter, Deirdre M. Daly Pavlis (1959-).
Enlisted on October 6, 1943.
Service number 31406810.

Born to Paul G. [Colonel, US Army; WWI & WWII veteran; Distinguished Service Cross & Croix de Guerre recipient in WWI and a Legion of Merit in WWII] (1891-1974) and Madeleine Mulqueen Daly (1900-1980). Three brothers, T.F. Gilroy (1931-1996), Daniel (1928-2003), and Dermot (1937-2001). Three sisters, Madeline M. Daly Potter (1922-1955), Bevin Daly Patterson (1926-2011), and Alison Daly Gerard (1932-).
Captain Daly's great-grandfather was Thomas F. Gilroy, an Irish immigrant who was the Mayor of New York City from 1893 to 1894.

Member of the Connecticut Veterans Hall of Fame, Class of 2007.

Georgetown Prep Class of '41

MICHAEL J. DALY
Southport, Connecticut

Sodality, 1-2-3-4; St. John Berchman's Society, 1-2-3-4; Cheerleader, 2-3; Junior Football, 1-2; Varsity Football, 3-4; Baseball, 1-2-3-4; Midget Basketball, 1; Junior Basketball, 2-3; Varsity Basketball, 4; Bellarmine Debating Society, 1-2; Philalethic Debating Society, 3; Rifle, 1.

"With stately triumphs, mirthful comic shows."
—3 Henry VI, v, 7, 43

Photo courtesy of the Fairfield Museum and History Center.
Captain Daly (left), and his father, Colonel Paul G. Daly (right).

Cadet Michel J. Daly in his first and only year at West Point.
Photo courtesy of National Archives Record Group 404.
Thanks to the USMA (West Point) Library Archives and Special Collections.

MEDAL OF HONOR CITATION

AWARDED FOR ACTIONS DURING: World War II
BRANCH OF SERVICE: Army
UNIT: 1st Battalion, 3rd Infantry Division
GENERAL ORDERS: War Department, General Orders No. 77, September 10, 1945
AGE ON THE DAY OF THE EVENT: 21
CITATION:

The President of the United States of America, in the name of Congress, takes pleasure in presenting the Medal of Honor to Captain (Infantry) Michael Joseph Daly (ASN: 0-1692630), United States Army, for conspicuous gallantry and intrepidity in action above and beyond the call of duty while serving with Company A, 1st Battalion, 15th Infantry Regiment, 3rd Infantry Division. Early in the morning of 18 April 1945, Captain Daly led his company through the shell-battered, sniper-infested wreckage of Nuremberg, Germany. When blistering machine gun fire caught his unit in an exposed position, he ordered his men to take cover, dashed forward alone, and, as bullets whined about him, shot the three-man gun crew with his carbine. Continuing the advance at the head of his company, he located an enemy patrol armed with rocket launchers which threatened friendly armor. He again went forward alone, secured a vantage point, and opened fire on the Germans. Immediately he became the target for concentrated machine pistol and rocket fire, which blasted the rubble about him. Calmly, he continued to shoot at the patrol until he had killed all six enemy infantrymen. Continuing boldly far in front of his company, he entered a park, where as his men advanced, a German machine gun opened up on them without warning. With his carbine, he killed the gunner, and then, from a completely exposed position, he directed machine gun fire on the remainder of the crew until all were dead. In a final duel, he wiped out a third machine gun emplacement with rifle fire at a range of ten yards. By fearlessly engaging in four single-handed firefights with a desperate, powerfully armed enemy, Lieutenant Daly, voluntarily taking all major risks himself and protecting his men at every opportunity, killed 15 Germans, silenced three enemy machine guns, and wiped out an entire enemy patrol. His heroism during the lone bitter struggle with fanatical enemy forces was an inspiration to the valiant Americans who took Nuremberg.

Presentation Date and Details: August 23, 1945 at the White House, presented by President Harry S. Truman.

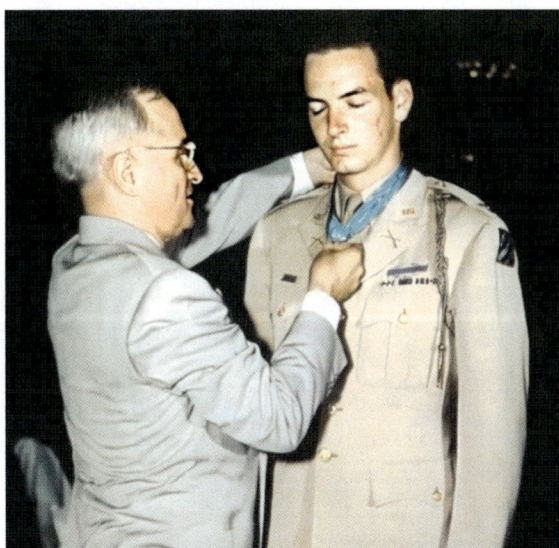

Photo courtesy of the National Archives.

WAR DEPARTMENT
BUREAU OF PUBLIC RELATIONS
PRESS BRANCH
Tol. RE. 6700, BRS. 3425 and 4860 | SIS Release C-261

<u>FUTURE RELEASE</u>

Twice wounded and three times winner of the coveted Silver Star for gallantry in combat, Captain Michael J. Daly of Southport, Connecticut, has been awarded the Medal of Honor, America's highest award for valor, the War Department announced today.

The fighting young Irishman -- he won't be 21 until September 15 -- and son of an Army colonel will have the star-spangled decoration hung around his neck by President Truman in ceremonies at the White House.

The story of Captain Daly's heroics during 48 hectic hours in the danger-infected wreckage of Nuremberg, Germany, reads like a Hollywood script. Actually, the young officer was doing a typical, if bang-up, Infantry job of clearing the doomed city of fanatical Nazi resistance.

At dawn on April 18, Captain Daly (then First Lieutenant) led his Infantry company into the attack on Nuremberg, driving into the city from the north. Ringed with 88-mm guns and flak wagons, the city was also defended by Germans armed with machine guns, pistols, and small arms and dug into the rubble of battered buildings and shell-pitted parks.

Snipers plagued Captain Daly and his men for two days and nights as they engaged with the enemy without pausing for sleep. Always, the young officer advanced ahead of his men, defying blistering fire to destroy German positions single-handedly.

The Doughboys, with Captain Daly 30 yards in advance, first moved toward a railroad station on the outskirts of Nuremberg. By-passing a wrecked railroad bridge, the Captain drew burst after burst of German machine gun fire as he climbed a slight rail embarkment. His company was caught in the open, and Doughboys fell wounded right and left.

Realizing that immediate, aggressive action was necessary to save his men, Captain Daly sprinted through a hail of bullets to a group of shattered buildings to the right of the enemy gun. The fire which followed him plowed a trail of dust at his heels.

He was 50 yards from the enemy gun when he opened fire with his carbine from a standing position and killed one German. Two others turned a machine gun and rifle on him with renewed fury as he sought a new position. But they died as Captain Daly picked them off with his accurate weapon.

Moving, once again, at the head of his Infantrymen, the Connecticut officer spotted a strong German force equipped with bazookas and moving through a block of ruined buildings. He realized the "panzerfaoust" men were a threat to his armor and decided to destroy them.

Captain Daly ran forward to a vantage point in a blasted house. Observing three Germans to his front, he waited until three more came into his gunsights and opened fire. The first Kraut fell dead. The others opened fire on the lone American with their bazookas and machine pistols.

One by one, as bullets struck around him and rockets tore huge holes in the mortar and stone of the house, Captain Daly picked off the Germans. When the brief but the savage fight had ended, every man in the enemy force had been wiped out.

The company commander next moved his Doughboys toward a large city park, the nerve center of enemy activity. Shells crashed all over the area through which he advanced ahead of his men. The streets were raked with knee-high, traversing machine gun fire. Snipers' rifles cracked constantly.

Captain Daly dashed into the park and then called to his men to follow him. But as the men advanced, they met fire from a German machine gun in a well-concealed position. Instantly, Captain Daly started back across the street to find the gun. He spotted it just as the enemy opened up on him from a range of only 50 yards.

The first burst of machine gun fire came so close to the officer that bullets actually passed between his legs.

Firing his carbine, Captain Daly killed the gunner, but another German manned the gun and fired at him.

With deliberate calm, Captain Daly had a machine gun set up in a bomb crater and stood beside it while he directed fire, which knocked out the enemy emplacement and killed the three remaining Germans.

His fourth singlehanded assault took place as he moved back into the park, well ahead of his troops. As he was placing his platoons in line, two Germans suddenly rushed from concealment and shot up a machine gun only 10 yards from where Captain Daly was standing. Instantly, the machine gunner opened fire, and a Doughboy Sergeant fell dead at Daly's feet.

Infuriated, the Captain grabbed an M1 rifle and engaged the enemy at point-blank range. He killed the gunner and silenced the gun, but the assistant gunner, although badly wounded, stumbled to his feet to fire at Captain Daly with a machine pistol. The American officer drilled him with one well-aimed shot, and the Kraut sprawled dead over the body of his comrade.

Thus, in four singlehanded fights in Nuremberg, Captain Daly had killed 15 Germans, destroyed three machine guns, and wiped out an antitank patrol.

The 20-year-old officer also had taken all the major risks himself, for he served his company as first scout during the 48 hours of bitter, hand-to-hand combat.

Of Captain Daly's gallantry, Colonel Hallett D. Edson, commanding officer of the 15th Infantry Regiment, said:

"By his daring, aggressive assaults on the enemy force, Lieutenant Daly destroyed machine guns that threatened to decimate his company. He wiped out a strong antitank group, thus providing his armor with a comparatively safe corridor of attack. Driving forward relentlessly despite all odds, he infected his men with some measure of heroism and demoralized the enemy by the uniform deadliness of his fire.

"The actions of this company commander were beyond the requirement of duty, and had he neglected to do what he did, I should not have censured him. His heroism towered above the courage of those around him; it will stand out and long be remembered in the annals of this regiment."

First Sergeant Roy A. Kurtz, of R.F.D. 2, Mohnton, Pennsylvania, said of his company commander:

Captain Daly smashed a path into the heart of Nuremberg by performing the combat duties normally done by a full company."

This sentiment was echoed by Staff Sergeant Ivan Kotron of R.F.D. 2, Surgoinsville, Tennessee. He declared:

"If it hadn't been for what Captain Daly did at Nuremberg, I don't know how many of us would have pulled through. There was no fear in him as he rushed strong enemy positions all by himself to save us from being cut to pieces. He showed he is a great soldier and a great combat leader."

Major Burton S. Barr, of 2621 Northeast 21st Avenue, Portland, Oregon, another eyewitness, added that the captain's heroism during the battle for Nuremberg "will never be forgotten by the officers and enlisted men who fought there."

The intrepid young officer was seriously wounded in the head the day after he completed his series of raids on German positions in Nuremberg. He had been less seriously injured in an earlier action.

Captain Daly wears the Silver Star with the two Oak Leaf Clusters for earlier gallantry in action against the Germans -- each time risking his life to go ahead of his men when the fighting was roughest.

He is the son of Colonel and Mrs. Paul G. Daly, Hull Farms Road, Southport, and had attended the United States Military Academy at West Point for a year before he was sent to Fort McClellan, Alabama, for basic Infantry training. He joined the 18th Infantry Regiment of the 1st Infantry Division in January 1943 as an enlisted man with the rank of Private First Class. He was commissioned a Second Lieutenant last December 18 in the European theater and saw five months of combat duty before he was wounded the second time. He is now back in the United States, having recovered from his wounds.

From The Hartford Courant July 27, 2008

MEDAL OF HONOR RECIPIENT DIES

FAIRFIELD – A Fairfield man who was awarded the Medal of Honor for heroism as a 20-year-old lieutenant in World War II has died at the age of 83.

A funeral home confirmed Saturday that Michael J. Daly died at his home on Friday.

Daly was awarded the Medal of Honor by Present Truman for valor in combat. The award was for actions Daly took on April 18, 1945, in Nuremberg, Germany.

According to the Medal of Honor Society website, Daly engaged in 4 single-handed firefights to protect his men, killing 15 Germans, silencing three enemy machine guns, and wiping out an entire enemy patrol.

Daly was later promoted to Captain.

"I'm no hero," Daly often said, according to the Connecticut Post. "The heroes are those who gave their lives."

During World War II, which he entered as an 18-year-old private after leaving West Point, Daly was also awarded three Silver Stars, two Purple Hearts, and a Bronze Star with "V" for acts of bravery.

Daly was modest about his military accomplishments and circumspect about his particular role.

"Anybody would have done what I did," he later told a friend. "Luck is important in life, but in combat, it is crucial. The bravest things are often done with God as the only witness."

After the war, Daly returned to Fairfield and began a business career as a manufacturer's representative and entrepreneur. He devoted a substantial part of his life to St. Vincent's Medical Center in Bridgeport.

He was one of the hospital's first lay trustees and served on its board for more than 30 years. He was known as the "conscience of the hospital" for his commitment to the poor and palliative care for the terminally ill.

He was also instrumental in developing financial support for the hospital.

Ronald J. Bianchi, St. Vincent's corporate senior vice president, said, "Michael Daly was the finest person I've ever known. He was responsive on a daily basis to people in need."

Bianchi also announced that the new St. Vincent's emergency wing will be named after Daly.

Funeral services are set for Tuesday.

AUTHOR NOTE: The St. Vincent's Michael J. Daly Center for Emergency and Trauma Care, 2800 Main Street, Bridgeport, CT, is a full-service Level II Trauma Center.

From WWII History Magazine, June 2014. Used with permission from the magazine and the author, Dr. Stephen J. Ochs.

THE PATH OF HEROISM

On the morning of April 18, 1945, amid street fighting in rubble-strewn Nuremberg, Germany, 20-year-old U.S. Army Captain Michael J. Daly, who had not slept in 24 hours and was running on pure adrenalin, had one overriding goal in mind: to protect his men.

Pinned down by enemy fire, Daly ordered them to stay put and then went forward alone, "a long-tall boy (6-3)," according to a Mississippi machine gunner in Daly's company, "running stooped-over with his carbine." Daly engaged in four single-handed firefights, killing 15 Germans, silencing three enemy machine guns, and wiping out an entire enemy patrol.

For his conspicuous "gallantry and intrepidity" that day, Michael Daly was later awarded the Medal of Honor by President Harry Truman—one of 467 bestowed for action during World War II, 60 percent of them posthumously. Indeed, a member of the armed forces cannot receive the Medal of Honor for simply acting under orders, no matter how bravely he or she executes them. Michael Daly was a member of that select group.

Daly's heroism was not a one-time occurrence. Rather, it represented the culmination of 11 months of selflessly courageous acts from June 6, 1944, when he landed at Omaha Beach, to April 19, 1945, when he suffered a near fatal wound in Nuremberg. Daly served in the European Theater of Operations (ETO) first as an enlisted man in the 18th Infantry Regiment of the 1st Division and then as an officer in the 15th Infantry Regiment of the 3rd Division. During that time, he was awarded two Purple Hearts, the Bronze Star with V attachment for valor, three Silver Stars for valor, and the Medal of Honor. He also advanced in rank from Private to Captain and from assistant squad leader to company commander. He embodied a quality absolutely essential to the ultimate triumph of Allied arms: the initiative to close with and aggressively engage the enemy. He did all of this before the age of 21 and on the heels of hell-raising teenage hijinks that led to his dismissal from Portsmouth Priory School and then the United States Military Academy at West Point.

Daly's path to redemption for his West Point fiasco and other teenage failings would pass through the crucible of an often overlooked but nevertheless brutal campaign on the Alsatian plain in eastern France. Its purpose was to close a German salient west of the Rhine River centered on the Alsatian city of Colmar, France, and known as the Colmar Pocket. The Battle of the Colmar Pocket would last from January 20, 1945, to February 9, 1945. Daly's development as an officer in the 15th Infantry Regiment during the Colmar campaign previewed his extraordinary actions later in Nuremberg and provided a prism through which to view the closing months of the war in an often forgotten part of the European Theater.

A Troublesome Teenager

Tall and handsome, Michael Daly came from a privileged, lace curtain, Irish Catholic Connecticut family. His father, Paul G. Daly (known by family and neighbors as "the Major"), cultivated the air of a country squire as he practiced law in New York City and raised steeplechase horses on his Connecticut farm. Paul Daly was also a highly decorated officer in World War I, having received the World War I equivalent of the Silver Star, the Distinguished Service Cross, and a nomination for the Medal of Honor, among other commendations. The elder Daly sought to inculcate in his son values of courage, patriotism, selflessness, and leadership. He regaled young Michael with stories drawn from military history and from legends and myths.

Mike also learned from his father how to manage fear. Like his father, Mike developed a love for riding horses and eventually competed in the steeplechase. Paul and Mike took long horseback rides together, and horsemanship became an arena for moral instruction and character development.

But hell raising rather than heroism seemed more the order of the day as Mike entered his teenage years, becoming headstrong, rebellious, and self-centered. His father enrolled him in the Jesuit Georgetown Preparatory School, the nation's oldest boys' Catholic high school located in the Maryland countryside near Washington, D.C. There, he proved himself a solid student, a likable, popular man on campus (elected president of the senior class), and often a thorn in the side of the Jesuit Prefect of Discipline, the Reverend Bernard F. Kirby. Mike was not mean-spirited, insolent, or ill-mannered. Most of his disciplinary infractions involved the school dress code, lateness, and hijinks in class.

Off to West Point

Daly graduated in the Prep class of 1941 at the age of 16 and faced an important crossroads. His father wanted him to attend the United States Military Academy at West Point. Mike did not wish to do so, but he never indicated that to his father because he did not want to disappoint him. Since Mike had been advanced from third to fifth grade during his grade school days, he was still too young to attend West Point immediately after high school graduation.

Therefore, Paul Daly, who had subsequently reentered the Army as a lieutenant colonel after Pearl Harbor, arranged for a postgrad year for his son at Portsmouth Priory, a Benedictine boarding school located outside Portsmouth, Rhode Island. There, Daly grew taller and more muscular, played football, did little studying, and capped a desultory semester with an unexcused night excursion to a bar in Portsmouth that resulted in his immediate expulsion.

Nevertheless, because of his father's political and social connections, Mike was still able to secure a Senatorial appointment to West Point. He also passed the entrance exam for the Academy, one that he had expected to fail. On July 15, 1942, he reported to West Point. He had no problem with the physical rigors of training at the Academy, but he hated the regimentation and hazing that were an integral part of life for plebes. He struggled with math and mechanical drawing in the classroom and bridled at what he perceived to be the arbitrary power wielded by upperclassmen, most of whom he came to loathe. Instead of maintaining a low profile, he took every opportunity to tweak them.

Ultimately, Daly did fail math for the second semester and faced dismissal unless he could pass a reentrance test at the end of the summer. At the urging of his father, Mike enrolled in remedial classes during the summer at the home of a tutor who lived in the Bronx.

"To Hell With This! I'm Going to War."

George S. Patton IV, a classmate of Mike's and the son of America's most flamboyant general, was taking the tutorial also. According to Patton, on a steamy afternoon with the mercury approaching 100 degrees, Daly stood up, threw his books in the corner, and declared, "To hell with this! I'm going to war."

Eager for combat and yearning for redemption in the eyes of his father for his failure at West Point, Mike enlisted in the infantry. For him, basic combat training at Fort McClellan, Alabama, proved liberating. Freed from what he regarded as the arbitrary and pointless hazing of West Point and already in excellent physical condition—he had grown another inch and now stood at 6-3 and weighed about 190 pounds—Daly excelled. He could see the rationale behind the training regimen at Fort McClellan, even including the tirades by sergeants because they were preparing their men for the rigors of war.

Landing on the Continent

In the spring of 1944, Mike was designated an infantry replacement and sent to Fort Shanks, New Jersey, to await passage to Britain. On arriving in Britain, Mike found himself assigned shortly before D-Day to his father's old regiment, the 18th Infantry, 1st Division. Paul Daly had pulled some strings to get his son into his old unit and into action as soon as possible. Landing in the second wave at Omaha Beach on June 6, 1944, Private Daly pulled a wounded man through the surf and then struggled along with his compatriots across the beach and eventually up the heights.

Within two weeks of landing in Normandy, Daly's actions exposing himself to enemy fire as a forward observer resulted in his being awarded a Silver Star for valor. He subsequently fought his way from Normandy to Belgium, earning the commendation of his commanding officers for his bravery, combat skill, aggressiveness, and initiative in volunteering for the most dangerous assignments, such as taking the point during patrols and serving as a forward observer or as a sniper.

In July 1944, following the Allied breakout from Normandy that shattered Hitler's armies in the West and sent them reeling across France, Daly and some other decorated American servicemen were tapped to appear on an armed services radio broadcast originating with Ernie Pyle in Paris. As they entered the city, Daly and his compatriots experienced firsthand the jubilation of liberated Parisiennes. A deliriously joyful crowd of young women lifted the Americans from their jeep and passed them over their heads—an exhilarating experience for the 19-year-old Daly. To many, including General Dwight Eisenhower, Supreme Commander Allied Expeditionary Force, it appeared that the war might be won by Christmas.

Taking a Commission With the 7th Army

The heady Allied optimism of the summer, however, dissipated as autumn approached and the resistance of

German troops stiffened closer to their homeland. Daly experienced this firsthand near Battice, Belgium, on September 6, 1944, when he was wounded in the leg by shrapnel during a mortar barrage. Sent for treatment to a British hospital, Daly was then invited by General Alexander McCarrell "Sandy" Patch, the commander of the 7th Army and a close friend of his father, to finish his convalescence at Patch's headquarters located in Épinal in the Lorraine region of eastern France.

Meanwhile, throughout the fall of 1944, gloom deepened among Allied forces as they experienced a bloody stalemate all along the Western Front capped by the German counterattack in the Ardennes early on the mist-shrouded morning of December 16. Daly was at Patch's headquarters when the momentous Battle of the Bulge commenced to the north. Patch attempted to return Daly by plane to the 1st Division, but terrible weather thwarted three separate attempts.

Patch, who had recently lost his son in combat, took this as a sign that Daly should be transferred to the Seventh Army. After reviewing glowing reports and recommendations from Daly's commanding officers, Patch offered Mike a commission as a second lieutenant and a job as his personal aide. Daly accepted the commission but insisted on returning to combat. Patch acquiesced, and on December 28, Mike joined Able Company, 1st Battalion, 15th Regiment, 3rd Division. The regiment was just ending a desperately fought and bloody, five-day battle for control of Sigolsheim, a town on the western Alsatian plain just east of the last line of the Vosges Mountains.

Holding Ground "At All Cost"

Daly had become a member of one of the most battle-tested divisions in the United States Army. The 3rd had fought in North Africa, Sicily, and at Anzio Beach in Italy, and then had landed in southern France as part of Operation Anvil-Dragoon in June 1944. It had subsequently battled up the Rhône River Valley and through the Vosges Mountains with the rest of the Seventh Army. The commander of the 3rd Division was Major General John W. "Iron Mike" O'Daniel. Stocky, gruff, gravel-voiced, and outspoken, O'Daniel carried a bayonet scar on his cheek from combat during World War I. O'Daniel's troops admired him as a man of great personal courage who understood them and who himself had suffered the loss of a son during the war.

On the day Daly joined Able Company, the Germans were resisting fiercely, their artillery and mortar fire reducing Sigolsheim to rubble, but by the next day, the 15th Regiment had taken the town. The 15th Regiment's determined victory had opened the gates to the plain of Alsace to the east. The Ardennes offensive, however, forced General Jacob Devers's 6th Army Group in the south to halt all offensive operations and extend its front northward. With an attack possible at any time, the 15th Regiment took up defensive positions with orders to hold the recently won ground "at all costs."

On New Year's Eve, the German high command launched Operation Nordwind, the southern counterpart to the Ardennes campaign. A major armor and infantry offensive against Patch's overextended Seventh Army, Nordwind was designed to link up with German forces engaged in the Ardennes. The Germans also forced a crossing of the Rhine River just north of Strasbourg that threatened to recapture that city. A stubborn but flexible defense, however, wore the German forces thin, and by January 25, Nordwind had ended in defeat. Fortunately for Daly, the 15th Regiment sector had remained quiet. The division sat perched in Alsace, ready to close a German salient known as the Colmar Pocket.

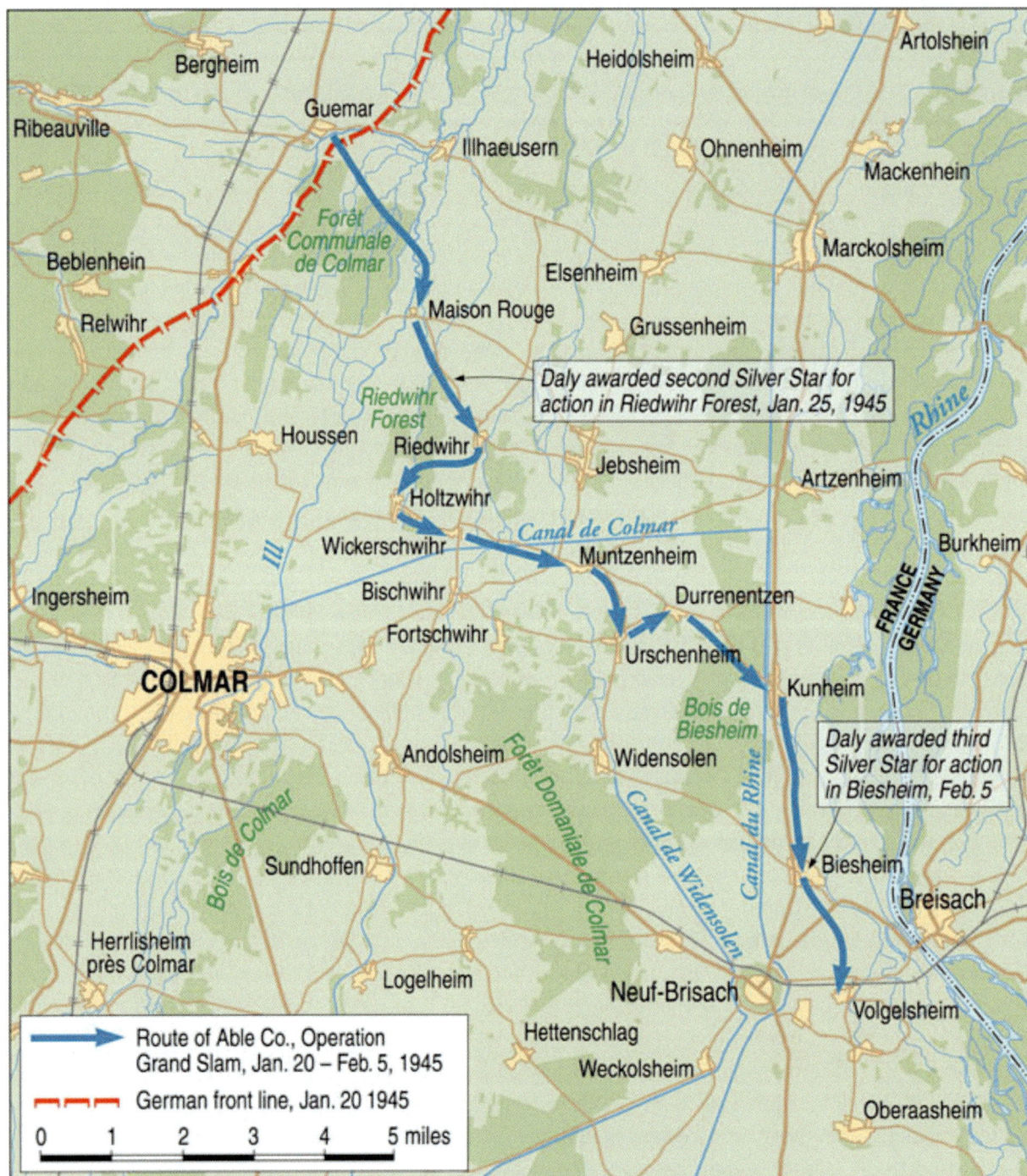

*The arduous route that Captain Michael J. Daly and Able Company followed
during the reduction of the Colmar Pocket in France resulted in lengthy
periods of contact with the Germans and episodes of heavy fighting.*

Daly found the men of his new platoon receptive and friendly, but many expressed astonishment at their new lieutenant's youth and boyish appearance. "The first time I saw him, he was a tall kid," remembered Sergeant Troy Cox. "He had wavy hair when he took off his helmet. I couldn't believe he could be an officer and a leader."

While some of the men of the regiment were seasoned veterans, Daly had also demonstrated his own mettle as a warrior during his four months of combat from June to early September 1944. The members of his platoon knew he had served as an enlisted man, had seen combat, had received the Silver Star and the Purple Heart, and had attained an officer's commission, all of which increased his credibility with them.

In January 1945, following the defeat of Hitler's counterattacks, General Eisenhower ordered General Devers and his VI Corps in Alsace to launch a major offensive (Operation Cheerful) to eliminate the Colmar Pocket. This German salient west of the Rhine River, which took its name from the city of Colmar, measured 45 miles at its base on the Rhine and extended 25 miles into the Vosges Mountains. The perimeter around the pocket, which measured 130 miles, enclosed 850 square miles. Creating a 50-mile gap in the Rhine front of the First French Army, the German presence in the pocket threatened the rear of both the Third and the Seventh Armies and, thereby, the entire Allied position in Alsace. It also drained Allied troops from what Eisenhower considered the more important front farther north, where he hoped for a deep breakthrough into Germany.

The American and French forces sought to strike the pocket simultaneously from the north and south, push along the Rhine plain, and then pinch off the salient, thereby cutting off, trapping, and eliminating an array of German units that had concentrated west of the Rhine. Committed to holding the Colmar Pocket, the Germans brought in the elite 2nd Mountain Infantry Division from Norway and ordered their forces to hold the salient.

At the beginning of the Colmar offensive, Daly and the men of the 3rd Division found themselves attached to II Corps of the First Army under French General Jean de Lattre de Tassigny. In addition to German arms, Daly and his men faced a formidable foe in the weather. De Lattre graphically described the situation faced by both the Allied and German forces during the Colmar campaign as "frightful" and almost impossible to imagine.

Closing the Colmar Pocket also required offensive operations in terrain ideally suited to defense. Small villages, towns, and extensive wood patches dotted the flat Alsatian plain that spread eastward from the base of the Vosges Mountains to the Rhine. In addition, numerous canals, irrigation ditches, and unfordable streams crisscrossed the area. German troops armed with Panzerfaust shoulder-fired antitank weapons posed a deadly threat to American armor.

The offensive called for coordinated attacks on both shoulders of the pocket by American and French forces. The main objective, however, was not the city of Colmar but rather the town of Neuf-Brisach and the nearby bridge over the Rhine. Neuf-Brisach and the bridge lay seven miles east of Colmar. The Brisach Bridge had proven invulnerable to earlier Allied air attack, and now Devers and de Lattre hoped to secure it and to trap as many Germans within the pocket as possible. The four regiments of O'Daniel's 3rd Division (7th, 15th, 30th, and attached 254th) would thrust at Neuf-Brisach from the northwest shoulder of the pocket. In an operation called Grand Slam, the 3rd Division would cross the Fecht River at Guémar, then the River Ill at Maison-Rouge, and finally the Colmar and Rhine-Rhone Canals to cut off the city of Colmar, thus assuring its fall. After that, troops would then move southward between the Rhone and Rhine Canals to capture the town of Neuf-Brisach and the Brisach Bridge over the Rhine.

General Siegfried Rasp's Nineteenth Army

Opposing them were the men of the German Nineteenth Army under the command of General Siegfried Rasp. Rasp hoped to tie down Allied forces west of the Rhine to afford the German Army time to redeploy units to the Eastern Front and to reorganize those units remaining east of the Rhine. The Nineteenth Army had been battered by the U.S. Seventh Army and Free French forces during the Vosges Mountains campaign. Its divisions were understrength, underequipped, and undertrained. They possessed only about 65 operational tanks and assault guns.

Still, Rasp had some advantages that would allow him to slow the Allies. He possessed some 22,500 highly motivated troops, whereas the Allies thought he had only 15,000. His army, moreover, possessed plentiful supplies of mines, food, and small-arms ammunition, the advantage of short, interior lines of communication, a secure rear area, and the ability to transform the numerous small Alsatian towns into formidable defensive strongpoints. And then, of course, there were the great equalizers: weather and terrain. The Colmar Pocket would be no Allied cakewalk. Of that, Daly and the men of Able Company needed no convincing.

The Maison-Rouge

On January 20, the I Corps of the French First Army began the operation, attacking northward from Mulhouse in a driving snowstorm with strong armor and infantry forces. This action drew armor of the German Nineteenth Army and the arriving 2nd Mountain Division to the southern part of the pocket. Two days later, on the night of January 22, the anniversary of the Anzio landings in Italy, O'Daniel committed his 3rd Division in Operation Grand Slam. In the early morning hours, the 7th and 30th Infantry Regiments, with the 15th Regiment in reserve, staged a surprise crossing of the Fecht River at Guémar before the Germans could react and then positioned themselves for an attack to the south. By noon, the 7th and 30th had captured Ostheim, cleared the Colmar forest, and arrived at the River Ill, which the infantry crossed using rubber boats.

Troops of the 30th then proceeded down the east bank of the River Ill and, after a brief skirmish with a small detachment of German troops, captured a 100-foot-long timber bridge and, about a mile away, a crossroads. The location was known as Maison-Rouge because of a nearby farm complex painted red. The Germans believed they had to deny the Allies access to the bridgehead across the Ill because, according to a later Army study, it opened "like the neck of a funnel into the whole area of German resistance around the Colmar Canal," and once captured "might well become [as it in fact did] the distributing point for American forces pushing to the Rhine."

Disaster For the 30th Regiment

At Maison-Rouge, however, the Americans encountered near disaster. The bridge over the Ill collapsed under the weight of a Sherman tank attached to the regiment. Until the engineers extracted the tank and repaired the bridge, the troops on the east side of the river had no armor support—a dangerous situation, especially in light of the Germans' seemingly uncanny ability to extract a terrible price for Allied mistakes.

The Germans showed themselves masters of active defense, ceding ground slowly, stubbornly, and bitterly as they conducted a fighting retreat that battered the Americans with tanks, artillery, and mortars. The German Army built its defensive doctrine around persistent local counterattacks. The units staging these counterstrikes, which varied in strength from company to battalion size, often used tanks and tank destroyers closely integrated with infantry. With lengthening nights and sometimes limited air observation and photography during the day, the enemy could mass forces in an assembly area close to U.S. lines and still avoid detection. Then, taking advantage of the morning fog or haze, they could engage U.S. forces quickly. Enemy artillery fire also increased appreciably, one of the most significant changes since the Normandy operations. The same weather conditions that limited aerial observation and photography made it more difficult for American artillery to locate and thus neutralize enemy guns.

The 30th Regiment, however, could not delay its offensive while the engineers worked frantically on the bridge over the Ill. It had to coordinate its attack with simultaneous drives by the French on its left and the 7th Regiment on its right. Using a footbridge laid across the Ill north of the helpless tank, the 1st and 3rd Battalions of the 30th moved south and east across 1,000 yards of snow-white flatland, entering a section of woods on the outskirts of the villages of Reidwihr and Holtzwihr. Unfortunately, fierce resistance elsewhere had held up both the French and the 7th Regiment, leaving the 1st and 3rd Battalions with dangerously exposed flanks and facing a powerful enemy. At 4:30 p.m., the hammer blow fell. The Germans counterattacked ferociously with infantry and armor and routed the 1st and 3rd Battalions, which had no supporting armor of their own.

On receiving news of the disaster that had befallen the 30th, O'Daniel sent the 15th Regiment hurrying to the site of the footbridge over the Ill. He instructed the regiment to assume the mission of the 30th and to counterattack at once, even though he knew that his infantry, absent armor, would be chewed up. He believed, however, that he had no choice. He had to try to keep the enemy at bay while the engineers repaired the bridge and could not let the Germans seize the initiative and concentrate their power.

At 3 a.m. on January 24, Companies I and K of the 15th Regiment's 3rd Battalion moved across the Ill to press the attack and suffered the same results as the 30th on the previous day. At about noon on January 24, Daly's 1st Battalion entered the fray with his Able Company in reserve. Still lacking armor, they moved into the woods north of Riedwihr and were crushed, albeit with far fewer casualties than the 3rd Battalion had suffered. The 1st Battalion had maintained an orderly retreat because it had been able to call in supporting artillery fire. By late afternoon, the 1st Battalion had regrouped and was preparing to counterattack, this time thanks to the repaired bridge, accompanied by tanks and tank destroyers and by a ferocious artillery barrage that sent shells into roads, junctions, and trail crossings in the Riedwihr woods.

Towering above several of the sergeants he found alongside in the Colmar Pocket, the 6'3" Michael Daly grins during a brief respite from bitter combat during the waning days of the Third Reich.

In his first combat role as an officer, Daly led Able Company as part of the 1st Battalion thrust southward from the road junction at Maison-Rouge in an attack on the woods. As Daly later recalled, the forest was dense, and though most trees were bare of leaves in the winter, there were evergreens. Maintaining formation in the woods proved difficult. To do so, a man had to keep the soldier next to him in sight. Because the Americans were pressing the offensive, they were more vulnerable to ambush. When those attacks occurred, GIs would fire into bushes and at trees, but often they were unable to see the Germans who were clad in their winter-white parkas and pants— "spook suits"—that blended into the snowy terrain. Sometimes, fighting involved individual duels between American and German soldiers separated by a few yards, each sniping at the other from behind trees. Sometimes, hand-to-hand combat ensued. Tree bursts from German artillery proved especially lethal, sending flaming branches and red-hot shrapnel to the forest floor.

As it happened, both Able and Charlie Companies ran into fierce opposition from enemy infantry and tanks at the edge of the forest, became disorganized, and suffered heavy casualties as the Germans employed a large number of tanks. Daly found himself in a desperate situation and momentarily confused about whether to fight or to flee. He hated to "let people down by retreating" but realized that he had to extricate his men from the woods so that they all could live to fight another day. He gave the order to pull out and made sure that his men, running downhill as fast as they could in knee-deep snow, got out. Then he followed them. Paul Daly would have approved.

Daly described the withdrawal as "urgent," not "panic-stricken." Although the Germans did not pursue the Americans out of the woods, they did keep firing at them, hitting several more of Daly's troops. When Daly and company reached the Ill River, they had to swim or ford the stream. Icicles dripped from the soaked uniforms of the shivering men. Daly felt relief at having extricated his platoon from an untenable situation and at having gotten them to safety, but he felt embarrassment at having been shot during the retreat. His first major engagement as an officer had ended in near calamity. Armored battles raged throughout the night as Daly's platoon and the whole company, much reduced in size by casualties, regrouped.

German Armored Counterattack

All companies in the battalion had suffered numerous casualties and found themselves seriously weakened. When Able and Charlie Companies were combined, for example, they still numbered only a handful of men. In that precarious condition, the 1st Battalion dug in at the edge of the woods. Reorganizing the scattered companies took almost all day.

At mid-morning on January 25, German infantry, accompanied by armor, counterattacked Able Company, which lacked both armor and antitank weapons. The Germans breached the line, driving some men back and isolating others while opening a gap through which their infantry tried to move. Daly's platoon sergeant, Kenneth W. Johns, however, remained in his foxhole and defended his position with his carbine against heavy small arms and automatic weapons fire from infantrymen seeking to exploit the opening. Six hours of grueling battle ensued, at the end of which the remaining men of Able Company forced the Germans to withdraw, even though one of their tanks continued to roam about in the woods, shooting up whatever it found.

Capturing Riedwihr

By 3:00 p.m. on January 25, the 15th Regiment prepared to attack again. The 3rd Battalion would take Riedwihr while the 1st and 2nd Battalions eliminated resistance in the northeast and northwest woods, respectively. The drained 1st Battalion had only 60 riflemen, with Able and Charlie Companies still merged. In the dark of night, Daly led 24 of his men 300 yards against a strongpoint at the edge of the woods that consisted of dug-in troops around a machine gun.

The Germans often located strongpoints in an opening in the woods or near a wide path where supporting troops dug in. Sometimes, they were backed by mortars or one or two tanks. Advancing to within 30 yards of the German machine gun and "with bullets striking inches away from him," Daly killed the gunner, enabling his men to capture the weapon. He then led his platoon 300 yards over "heavily shelled and bullet-swept terrain" to clear the objective in three-quarters of an hour.

Twenty Germans died in the attack, and "many more were captured or wounded through his [Daly's] inspiring and aggressive leadership." Daly "went after the other guy, and it was every man for himself." The next day, he and his men helped repulse yet another German counterattack of infantry and armor. Meanwhile, the 3rd Battalion took Riedwihr.

"Inspiring Attack"

Looking tired and dirty, Captain Michael J. Daly returns from a patrol near Schweinfurt, Germany, in March 1945. According to Sergeant J. Leon Lebowitz, the company clerk who snapped this photo, Daly was 'the best officer and bravest man I ever knew.'

After the capture of Riedwihr, Daly and another man from Able Company trudged their way to Major General O'Daniel's headquarters for a regimental awards ceremony. On a snowy field, O'Daniel pinned an oakleaf cluster representing a second Silver Star on Daly's jacket. He made some encouraging comments and then asked the Lieutenant if he was "ready to go back in there and get this thing over with."

Mike's mumbled "I think so" was less gung-ho than O'Daniel had hoped for, and he made his dissatisfaction apparent. But this rolled off Daly's back. The laconic second lieutenant had nothing to prove; his actions said it all. Numbed by cold, fatigue, and combat, Daly and his companion turned around and made their way back through the snow to company quarters. The headline in the Bridgeport newspaper back home read, "Lieutenant M.J. Daly of Fairfield Cited for 'Inspiring' Attack."

In two days of fighting against continuous counterattacks and stubborn resistance, the 15th Regiment had saved the Ill River bridgehead, broken through the German defense, pushed south over difficult terrain, and established a line from which the offensive could be carried across the Colmar Canal to the immediate front. But the regiment paid dearly in casualties among officers, NCOs, and enlisted men. Some companies numbered only 15 men. Many 3rd Division veterans of the Anzio beachhead pronounced the fighting in the Colmar Pocket, especially around Maison-Rouge, as "just about as severe as anything they had yet gone through."

The Bloodiest Month in Northwest Europe

Indeed, in the Colmar Pocket, a dark mood prevailed. Daly recognized that in addition to brutal combat and high casualties—January would prove the bloodiest month for casualties in northwest Europe—the cruel winter weather of the Colmar Pocket endangered not only his men's health but also their morale by increasing the physical and psychological difficulties of military operations. Daly looked back on the Colmar Pocket campaign as his most difficult combat, the dug-in veteran German units, the death and wounding of his men, snow and cold, the frostbite and trench foot. "We had to fight the weather as well as the Germans," he later recalled.

"Some genius decided that we would wear white sheet covers for camouflage," Daly remembered, "but the damn things flopped around, got wet, and then froze at night," making movement difficult and sleep impossible. Daly and many others quickly discarded the sheets.

As Daly's men fought their way into the streets of the Bavarian city of Nuremberg, these troops of the U.S. 15th Infantry Regiment moved forward warily on April 18, 1945. Nuremberg was considered the cradle of Nazism.

There seemed no escape from the cold. Trigger mechanisms on rifles froze, as did oil on the weapons. When troops slept on the floors of abandoned schoolhouses or warehouses, they curled in the fetal position, hands clasped together and pressed between the knees. Essential clothing included long johns and gloves (or trigger-finger mittens), along with knit woolen caps and scarves, windbreaker trousers to be worn over the standard olive drab, and M1944 Shoepac boots. With leather uppers, rubber lowers, and moisture-absorbing insoles, these boots provided far better protection against water, especially in static positions, than the standard combat boot. But the early versions, which had no heels and gave no support to the arch of the foot, proved terrible for walking. The "paddle-foot shuffle" seen in the ranks of American infantrymen that winter signified not just bulky clothing, inadequate arch support, and numbed or frozen feet but also psychological demoralization.

By March 1945, more men were missing from the lines because of trench foot than for any other reason. The 46,000 cold weather injuries constituted 9.25 percent of all casualties in the European Theater, the equivalent of more than three divisions. Daly later recalled "the constant challenge" that feet presented. He and his fellow platoon leaders and their NCOs minimized the incidence of trench foot in Able Company by insisting that the men change their socks regularly and by personally seeing to it that they did.

Operation Kraut

Fearing an American breakthrough, the Germans mustered what reserves remained east and southeast of Jebsheim. The Americans, however, shifted southward to the Colmar Canal, a 50-foot-wide, six-foot-deep waterway with 12-foot embankments and slow-moving water that had not frozen. The canal passed just north of the city of Colmar, connecting it with the Rhine River to the northeast. Well-dug emplacements protected the canal, and the fortified towns of Muntzenheim and Bischwihr lay nearby. These proved no match, however, for Allied air power and artillery. Allied planes bombed for two days, and on the cold, clear night of January 29, eight battalions of artillery pummeled the target area.

As a result, in an operation dubbed "Kraut," Allied forces quickly crossed the Colmar Canal and made short work of the dazed, disorganized force on the opposite shore. Daly's Able Company, held in reserve along with the rest of the 1st Battalion during the initial crossing, later led the 1st Battalion across the footbridges to join in the broadening offensive to clear the remainder of the Colmar Pocket and isolate the city of Colmar. The Americans would accomplish the latter task by occupying the area east and south of the city to the Rhine River. In the face of the combined American-French offensive, with the Americans driving to the center of the pocket and the French increasing pressure at both the northern and the southern ends, the Colmar Pocket began to disintegrate. As the German 2nd Mountain Division was ground down and then shattered, the 15th Regiment and the rest of the 3rd Division "encountered only scattered, piecemeal units and no cohesive battle order or defensive organization." Those piecemeal units, however, remained deadly.

"An Interminable Series of Local Collisions"

In the first hour of February 1, the third phase of operations opened with an offensive to the Rhine designed to cut the pocket in two. This meant crossing yet another strategic water barrier, the Rhine-Rhone Canal, which ran in a north-south direction. Able Company's objective was to take the bridge leading into Kunheim. During the first phase of the attack through the Durrenentzen woods west of Kunheim, all company officers senior to Daly became casualties. He took command of Able Company and pressed ahead toward the town.

The Germans were well armed with tanks, artillery, mortars, and rockets and committed themselves to defending the approaches to the bridge. They had created strong points at its foot by sending reinforcements to man thick-walled houses just west of the span. A 24-hour battle ensued. After several hours, word arrived that the French had taken Artzenheim and its bridge a mile and a half north, making seizure of the bridge at Kunheim unnecessary. The 15th Regiment's objective changed from crossing the canal to clearing Germans from the area up to the canal and from the bridge itself.

An American machine gunner sprints for cover while carrying his Browning .30-caliber machine gun as an ammunition carrier follows, his rifle slung across his back. This photo was taken in the French arrondissement of Sarreguemines at the height of the fighting in the Colmar Pocket during early February 1945.

An American machine gunner sprints for cover while carrying his Browning .30-caliber machine gun as an ammunition carrier follows, his rifle slung across his back. This photo was taken in the French arrondissement of Sarreguemines at the height of the fighting in the Colmar Pocket during early February 1945.

As Daly and Able Company attempted to traverse a clearing near the bridge at Kunheim, they encountered a withering hail of machine-gun and small-arms fire as well as heavy mortar concentrations. Daly extricated his men from their untenable position, reorganized them, and then led them on a new route through woods infested by determined German opposition. Staying in the lead, Daly encouraged his men and impelled them forward in the face of a hail of fire until he found it impossible to move farther. He then directed his men to dig in and hold their ground. He personally supervised and checked the placement of their positions, enabling them to withstand intense fire from the fearsome German 88mm guns that night.

Daly's company also suffered numerous casualties as a result of machine-gun fire directed from tanks at a range of 150 yards and barrages of 150mm rockets, known to GIs as "Screaming Meemies," fired from Nebelwerfers, combination mortar, and rocket launchers. The firing abated in the early morning hours, and at dawn, Daly discovered that the Germans had withdrawn under cover of darkness, leaving behind many casualties.

Coming off the line, Daly moved his company into a former German barracks in the woods. There, he thoroughly reorganized the men after their engagement, painstakingly checking their equipment and seeing to it that they were able to rest and bathe. The next day, he turned over a fresh, victorious, and tightly organized fighting unit to the returning company commander. Meanwhile, the 7th Infantry had taken Kunheim after the battered German forces withdrew from the town.

Daly, however, had no sense of elation or victory. When one town fell, there was always another, and then another, and another after that. Max Hastings captured the nature of battle in northwest Europe when he described it not as a clash of mighty armies after the fashion of Waterloo or Gettysburg but rather as "an interminable series of local collisions involving a few hundred men and a score or two of armored vehicles, amid some village or hillside or patch of woodland between Switzerland and the North Sea."

The Death of Joseph Daly

On the morning of February 3, Daly and his men returned to action, moving southward the three or four miles between Kunheim and Biesheim along a slushy, muddy road flanked by fields and interspersed with enemy pillboxes.

The 1st Battalion was charged with eliminating enemy forces in the rear of the 7th Infantry, some of whose units were engaged in the town of Biesheim, where fighting grew more intense. The Germans knew that if Biesheim fell, Neuf-Brisach, the communications center, could not hold out. Its capitulation, in turn, would sever key communications and supply lines, sealing the fate of the Colmar Pocket and providing the Allies a possible springboard into Germany. The combat that ensued, including street fighting, bombing, and strafing by Allied planes and artillery barrages from both sides, reduced much of Biesheim to rubble.

Daly's company pushed to approximately 200 yards north of the town when fire from three or four machine guns, manned by what was characterized as "fanatical infantry," hit the flanks and the front, pinning down the forward elements. There ensued one of the most harrowing nights of the war for Daly. It also highlighted an ugly reality and leadership challenge faced by company officers such as Daly in the war's final months, the fate of 18-year-old "greenhorns" pressed into service as combat replacements because of manpower shortages. One such youngster bore his Lieutenant's last name.

Private Joseph Daly joined the platoon in the midst of the battle for the Colmar Pocket and was clearly frightened, insecure, and inexperienced. Daly tried to reassure him and told him to stay close to his sergeant and do exactly what the sergeant directed. While the company was pinned down north of Bisheim, Joseph Daly suffered a grievous wound to his back. There was no way to evacuate him, and Daly helplessly watched him die a slow, agonizing death as a medic valiantly but vainly tried to ease his suffering and provide some comfort. That scene seared its way into Daly's consciousness. He never forgot Joseph Daly, whose memory helped inspire Daly's efforts years later on behalf of the indigent and dying in Fairfield, Connecticut. The terrible experience also reinforced Daly's determination to do everything he could to bring his men home safely.

Battling Through the Mud

At daylight, Able and Charlie Companies called in armor, and three tanks helped wipe out the enemy positions. The small units of the experienced 3rd Division earned well-deserved praise for their skillful use of infantry-tank teams. In the words of one historian, they "almost unconsciously perfected their … teamwork to a fine art, enabling them to overcome the physical fatigue that most of the soldiers… felt."

On February 5, the final mission began, moving southward to secure the vital bridges across the Rhine at Neuf-Brisach and thus cut the enemy's last remaining avenue of escape from the crumbling pocket. Daly and his company, their uniforms covered with so much mud that only the shape of their helmets distinguished them from the Germans, slogged down a slushy road southeast of the village as part of the

1st Battalion's drive to the south.

After trudging across 800 yards of flat, mucky, open field while enduring fire from 88s and heavy mortars that inflicted numerous casualties, Daly's platoon spotted a German strongpoint about 200 yards ahead. At a crossroads southeast of the town stood a fortified two-story stone house protected by barbed wire and surrounded by a low stone wall interspersed at intervals with stone columns. At least 25 German soldiers were entrenched in the structure.

Three enemy machine guns opened up and caught Daly and his men in a crossfire. By that time, only nine of Daly's 22-man platoon remained unwounded. Reacting quickly, Daly directed his men to withdraw down a ditch. Meanwhile, he stood up squarely in the middle of the road, firing his pistol to draw the concentrated fire of the enemy upon himself while his men retreated. For 30 minutes, he moved about in plain view of enemy machine gunners and infantrymen armed with the MP40 machine pistol. They fired a hail of bullets at him. As he danced around, they ricocheted at his feet. At the same time, he noticed a 15-man German patrol approaching on his flank, and he started firing his pistol at them. Killing two, he alerted his men to fight off the rest. Finally, he broke contact and raced toward his platoon, most of whom were crawling on their hands and knees toward the edge of town and the cover of two machine guns set up there.

Daly, meanwhile, worked his way among the more seriously wounded, who were lagging behind the others, helping and encouraging them. Not until he knew that every wounded man had made it back safely did Daly himself enter the company area. He then gave a concise and calm report on the enemy situation to his company commander. For his action in the road that day, Daly received a second oak leaf cluster on his Silver Star. He felt particularly proud of the Silver Star, later calling it the "infantryman's or workhorse medal," indicating valor in a specific instance, not just meritorious service.

Because Daly's company had not dislodged the Germans from the strongpoint, they once again received orders to seize it. The depleted 60-man company attacked across 500 yards of open field. Troy Cox recalled, "We couldn't run at all in the mud and would fall because it was so soft." When he fell, he also dropped his machine gun into the mire. The quarter-size openings in the barrel meant to cool the weapon became packed with mud, rendering the gun useless, but Cox still carried it as he continued to slip-slide across the field.

The deadly crossfire from the German machine guns and numerous submachine guns mowed down 41 of the men. Only 19 reached the position. When an American tank moved up and blasted a hole in the wall, both the 2nd and 3rd Platoons charged forward in an attempt to storm the opening. But a German gunner on the other side, in combination with the continuing deadly crossfire, repelled two attempts. Finally, rifleman Deland Payne worked his way to within 50 yards of the breach, stood up amid a hail of fire, and blazed at the gunner with his M1 rifle until he killed him.

"Shoot the Bastards!"

After an enemy grenade wounded the commander of Able Company, Daly leaped to the front amid the confusion and led the last assault. Grappling with the nearest German, he shot him dead with his pistol and then ran from man to man, directing them toward German positions. Finally, he led his men inside the stone wall surrounding the house and into the house itself. Firing his weapon, he yelled for his men to "Shoot the bastards!" inciting them to their utmost in the bitter close-range fighting. The result: nine enemy dead, six wounded, and nine prisoners.

A German counterattack ensued shortly thereafter. As fire from enemy self-propelled artillery began wrecking the house, Daly directed his men to dig in and hold the position. The Germans maintained fire on the house, the crossroads, and the roads to the rear in an attempt to deny the Americans use of them. Then, as Able Company fanned out to secure other houses in the area, German tank and artillery fire took them down one after another while continuing to zero in on the crossroads. The company clerk, Sergeant J. Leon Lebowitz, recorded approximately 25 missing or killed in action that day.

While Daly and his company hung on at the crossroads, other companies of the 1st Battalion, along with those of the 2nd and 3rd Battalions, captured Fort Mortier, which commanded the northern approaches to the Rhine River bridge sites. The Americans swept southward to the bridges themselves, only to find that the Germans had demolished them.

More Than 4,500 Casualties

By nightfall on February 5, the shelling had ceased, and the 15th Regiment had secured all its objectives. The next night, the 30th Regiment scaled the walls of the old fortress town of Neuf-Brisach. The Americans now firmly controlled the designated area east of Colmar, including the approaches to the damaged railroad and highway bridges across the Rhine. A staff officer of the 136th Mountain Regiment of the German 2nd Mountain Division stated that by the first few days of February, the German supply system had broken down completely, lack of gasoline being the major consequence.

A captured officer said that large numbers of casualties were the result of accurate and intense U.S. artillery fire. Still, the 15th Regiment suffered 744 battle casualties and more than 1,000 additional casualties from disease, exhaustion, frostbite, and trench foot. The 3rd Division as a whole suffered more than 4,500 casualties. Unable to retreat across the bridges, only 3,000 to 4,000 combat infantry of the now virtually destroyed German Nineteenth Army managed to escape to the east bank of the Rhine. The remnants of the German Army were mopped up, and resistance in the division sector came to an end after the 17-day campaign.

Heroism in "America's Unknown Battle"

Daly had distinguished himself as a platoon leader during the Colmar campaign, adding two oakleaf clusters to his Silver Star, and his commanding officers sang his praises. Writing on February 7, less than two months after Daly had joined the company, Major Kenneth B. Potter, commander of the 1st Battalion, characterized the young lieutenant's service as "exemplary, evidencing a very high degree of leadership, aggressiveness, and organizational ability under the most difficult of conditions."

In recommending Daly for promotion from second to first lieutenant shortly after the actions at Kunheim and Biesheim, Potter not only praised Daly's initiative in twice assuming command of the company during a battle but also identified essential elements of the young officer's leadership: "a very high degree of aggressiveness, cool courage and calculated daring, high organizational ability under the most difficult of circumstances, and the utmost devotion to his men both in the height of combat and in the lull ensuing."

As Daly observed later, "You have to take the chance to get things moving."

Sergeant Lebowitz snapped a photo of an exhausted Daly returning from a night patrol. He later mounted it into a scrapbook and wrote a caption describing Daly as "the best officer and bravest man I ever knew."

In the "frozen crust" of the Colmar Pocket, during what one historian termed "America's unknown battle," Daly and his fellow citizen-soldiers had prevailed over a battered yet skilled enemy. Famed war correspondent Ernie Pyle attributed the victory to the foot soldiers who had demonstrated "real heroism—the uncomplaining acceptance of unendurable conditions." Amid those "unendurable conditions," Daly had mastered the role of platoon leader. Now, he and his men had a chance to rest and to train for the next phase, the battle for Germany that would also include Daly's rendezvous with the Medal of Honor.

The quote on the stone in the first photo reads, "When the smoke clears from the last battlefield, we will stand face to face with our own humanity, our need to respect and help one another."

LANDSMAN LORENZO DEMING *; NAVY

* Last name is Deming by birth, Denning by service record

September 6, 1843 (Granby, CT) – February 8, 1865 (Salisbury, NC); 21 years old
Married Sarah J. Hubbard (1838-1906) on January 19, 1864, in New Britain, Connecticut.
One daughter, Inez E.A. Deming Langley (1864-1941).
Enlisted on September 8, 1864, two days after his 21st birthday. He died in prison five months later.

Born to Gideon (1803-1877) and Louisa Bidwell Deming (1805-1896). Three brothers, Lucius (1825-1850), James (1827-1890), and Julius (1841-1918). Three sisters, Martha Deming Drake (1829-1904), Mary S. Deming Stebbins (1839-1906), and Sarah A. (1846-1859).

MEDAL OF HONOR CITATION

AWARDED FOR ACTIONS DURING: Civil War
BRANCH OF SERVICE: Navy
ASSIGNED TO: U.S.S. Chicopee, U.S. Picket Boat #1
GENERAL ORDERS: War Department, General Orders No. 45 (December 31, 1864)
AGE ON THE DAY OF THE EVENT: 21
CITATION:

The President of the United States of America, in the name of Congress, takes pride in presenting the Medal of Honor (Posthumously) to Landsman Lorenzo Denning, United States Navy, for extraordinary heroism in action while serving on board the U.S. Picket Boat No. 1 in action near Plymouth, North Carolina, 27 October 1864, against the Confederate ram Albemarle which had resisted repeated attacks by our steamers and had kept a large force of vessels employed in watching her. The picket boat, equipped with a spar torpedo, succeeded in passing the enemy pickets within 20 yards without being discovered and then made for the Albemarle under a full head of steam. Immediately taken under fire by the ram, the small boat plunged on, jumped the log boom which encircled the target, and exploded its torpedo under the port bow of the ram. The picket boat was destroyed by enemy fire, and almost the entire crew was taken prisoner or lost.

From the Hartford Courant May 24, 1991

CIVIL WAR RECIPIENT OF MEDAL OF HONOR

NEW BRITAIN — A daring Civil War naval attack and bitter accusations of a wife's infidelity resulted Thursday in a ceremony honoring Lorenzo Deming for winning the
Medal of Honor.

At Fairview Cemetery, local veterans gathered with flags at the Deming family plot around a new marble stone commemorating Deming's long-forgotten heroism.

Thomas F. Durning Jr. of North Haven, who researched Deming's accomplishments and tracked him to New Britain through letters attacking the character of Deming's wife, stood in a Civil War uniform and told the crowd what Deming did to earn the country's highest military award.

In September 1864, just two days after his 21st birthday, Deming enlisted in the Navy in New Britain. He volunteered almost immediately for a hazardous mission to attack the Confederate ironclad ship Albemarle,

Durning said.

Deming steamed down the Atlantic Coast from New York in one of three tiny open boats commanded by Lieutenant W.B. Cushing. Under cover of darkness, the little boat Deming was on rammed the Albemarle at full speed with a bomb attached to the end of a pole on its bow. The explosion sank the Albemarle.

Deming was captured and taken to a Confederate prison camp in Salisbury, North Carolina.

The troops lived in holes in the ground. They were starving," Durning said. Deming died on February 5, 1865, one of 11,700 Union troops to die in the camp. His body was dumped into a mass grave.

Back in New Britain, Deming apparently was given no special honors, Durning said, and he is not sure why. Deming's name was not even included on a Civil War memorial
possibly because, although his parents lived in the city, his last address was New Haven.

In 1985, Durning, secretary-treasurer of the Connecticut Sons of Union Veterans of the Civil War, began researching Civil War recipients of the Medal of Honor from Connecticut. He acted at the request of a national group trying to find recipients' gravesites so the Veterans Administration could put markers on them.

Deming's name was misspelled in federal records, and he was listed as coming from New York. But Durning learned Deming had been born in East Granby.

After a few lucky breaks, Durning obtained in federal archives copies of letters that Deming's relatives in the city had written, asking the government to reduce the pension to Deming's widow, Sarah. The letters said Sarah had had a child by another man but claimed it was Deming's to get more money.

Durning had the marker installed this spring in the Deming family plot, between the graves of Deming's mother and sister. "It looks like they just left that space open for him," he said.

From Beyer, W. F., & Keydel, O. F. (2000). Deeds of Valor: How America's Civil War Heroes Won The Congressional Medal of Honor. Smithmark Publishers.

THE BLOWING UP OF THE ALBEMARLE

While Admiral Porter was fitting out the fleet which he was to command in the intended attack on Fort Fisher in the fall of 1864, the Navy Department was greatly troubled on account of the Confederate ram Albemarle, repairing at Plymouth, N. C. The reputation the Albemarle had gained in the North by her sinking the Southfield, disabling the Miami, and her engagement with the "double ender" squadron of Captain Melanchthon Smith in Albemarle Sound in the spring of this same year was the cause of this alarm.

Admiral Porter, having been apprised of the views of the department in this matter, suggested a plan to blow up the Albemarle with steam launches and by means of torpedoes. The plan was approved, and details arranged forthwith for the building of three steam launches by Naval Engineers Wood and Lay.

Lieutenant Porter selected the young and indefatigable lieutenant, William D. Cushing, for the command of this hazardous expedition. Cushing accepted rejoicingly and started with the three launches about the middle of October from the New York Navy Yard for Hampton Roads. Here he arrived on the 24th with one badly battered launch, he and his crew utterly exhausted from the week's trip. Of the other two launches, one had foundered shortly after leaving New York, the second had run ashore on account of a terrible storm in Chesapeake Bay and surrendered to the Confederates. Cushing alone, storm or no storm, pushed ahead and reached his destination. Admiral Porter ordered Cushing and his men to rest while the battered launch was put in ship-shape again.

Just at that time, the admiral was ordered to prefer charges against Cushing for the supposed violation of some neutral rights while in command of a vessel in those waters. Cushing felt greatly distressed about this, but the admiral, after a brief investigation, reported the young officer free from blame, and at the designated time, Cushing, in his launch, started on his forlorn-hope trip, jubilant at having so fortunately, slipped off from a possible court-martial. Passing through the Dismal Swamp Canal, Cushing, on the 27th of October, reached the Roanoke

River in Albemarle Sound and reported to Captain Macomb on the flagship Shamrock.

This same night, he completed his arrangements and started up the Roanoke to find his prey. It was said that at the wreck of the Southfield, about seven miles up the river, there was a guard of armed schooners. So, Cushing took with him against them, in case they should discover him, an armed boat from the Shamrock. His own launch carried fourteen volunteers, officers, and enlisted men from Captain Macomb's squadron, mainly from Picket Boat No. 1. The Albemarle was made fast to a wharf about a mile above where the Southfield lay. The attackers knew that her crew and all the pickets along the banks of the Roanoke kept a sharp lookout against any surprises, for an unsuccessful torpedo attack had been made against the ram on the 25th of May by a party of daring men from the Wyalusing.

The weapon Cushing intended to use was a boom torpedo. When the daring party shoved off from the Shamrock, all of its members, as well as those in the squadron, were convinced that the Albemarle would be destroyed or they would never return. Such was the reputation of young Cushing's unbending and daring nature.

The launch with the Shamrock's boat in tow proceeded up the river unmolested, although the infantry pickets had a good many fires burning on the banks, which were hardly 200 yards apart. The Southfield was reached and passed without disturbing or rousing anybody.

Soon, a dark object loomed up before the anxious men, who kept the keenest lookout. It was the Albemarle. Cushing cast loose the armed boat, with instructions to take care of armed hostile boats which might come to interfere with him, and then made for the ram. When within twenty yards of her, he saw that she was protected against a torpedo attack by a boom of logs extending about ten yards from her sides. At this moment, a sentry from aboard hailed them.

Cushing, standing ready at the torpedo boom, which was raised, started his launch at full speed against the obstruction. The sentry gave the alarm. In a moment, the deck of the ram swarmed with men. Two field guns discharged a hail of grapes at the launch. Sharpshooters also opened a hot fire. But while the launch was pushing the logs under and Cushing was lowering the torpedo boom, he had his 12-pound howitzer in the bow of his boat fire canister into the human mass on board, which drove them for a moment under shelter. In the next second, there was a tremendous roar, and a huge column of water rose high in the air, lifting the Albemarle several feet. Then, the ram settled in a sinking condition from a fatal wound in her side. The little launch was swamped by the falling water and drifted down the river with some of her crew still on board while others, among them Cushing, were struggling in the water, trying to get beyond the light of the fires and the reach of the rifles of the infantrymen.

The following men composed Cushing's crew: From picket boat No. 1 – William Howarth, master's mate; William Stotesbury, assistant engineer; Bernard Harley, Edward Houghton, William Smith, seamen; R. H. King, Lorenzo Demming, Henry Wilkes, landsmen; Samuel Higgins, fireman; R Hamilton, coalheaver. From Otsego – T.S. Gay, master's mate; C. S. Steever, assistant engineer; F. Swan, assistant paymaster. From Commodore Hull - John Woodman, master's mate.

Cushing, Woodman, and Higgins left the launch or were hurled out of her. The rest of the crew, with the exception of Houghton, some of them wounded, were picked up by the Confederates and taken prisoners. Cushing himself had been wounded in the wrist. He drifted in the icy cold water until his strength nearly gave out. He came across Master's Mate Woodman, who was crying for help. Cushing's strength, although he tried to save the man, failed, and Woodman was drowned. Fireman Higgins, too, lost his life in the river. The bodies were afterward found washed on shore and buried by the Confederates.

Finally managing to reach the bank, Cushing hid in a dense swamp half a mile below Plymouth. Here, his hiding place being near a path leading alongside the river bank, he heard two passing rebel officers talking about the sinking of the Albemarle, whose smokestack only remained visible above the water. The exhausted man remained in the swamp until the next evening, when, having obtained some reliable information from a faithful old negro, he continued his toilsome wandering down the river, coming finally to a small creek, where he found an empty boat.

He took it, and, pulling, exhausted as he was, all the following day until late into the night, he came towards 11 o'clock within hailing distance of a Federal gunboat. It proved to be the Valley City. He called for help and collapsed unconscious in the boat. It took some time for the suspicious crew of the Valley City to overcome their distrust and sent a boat down to the drifting object. Somebody recognized Cushing, and he was saved. Soon afterward, he was able to make his way back to his admiral's flagship at Hampton Roads and report the details of his daring achievement. Cushing and Houghton were the only two members of the expedition who escaped imprisonment or death.

Cushing was promoted to Lieutenant Commander for this most heroic act. From his men, the following, all of Picket Boat No. 1, were awarded the Medal of Honor: Bernard Harley, William Smith, Edward J. Houghton, seamen; Lorenzo Demming, Henry Wilkes, R. H. King, landsmen; R. Hamilton, coalheaver. These formed the original crew which had brought the boat from New York.

Landsman Demming was captured at the destruction of the rebel iron-clad ship Albermarle on November 27, 1864, and was taken to Salisbury National Cemetery, where he died.

Artist's rendering of Salisbury Prison

BIRD'S EYE VIEW OF CONFEDERATE PRISON PEN
AT SALISBURY, N.C. — TAKEN IN 1864

Courtesy of the Library of Congress Geography and Map Division Washington, D.C.

Lorenzo Deming was buried along with 11,700 unknowns in long trenches in Salisbury National Cemetery, 501 Statesville Boulevard, Salisbury, North Carolina.

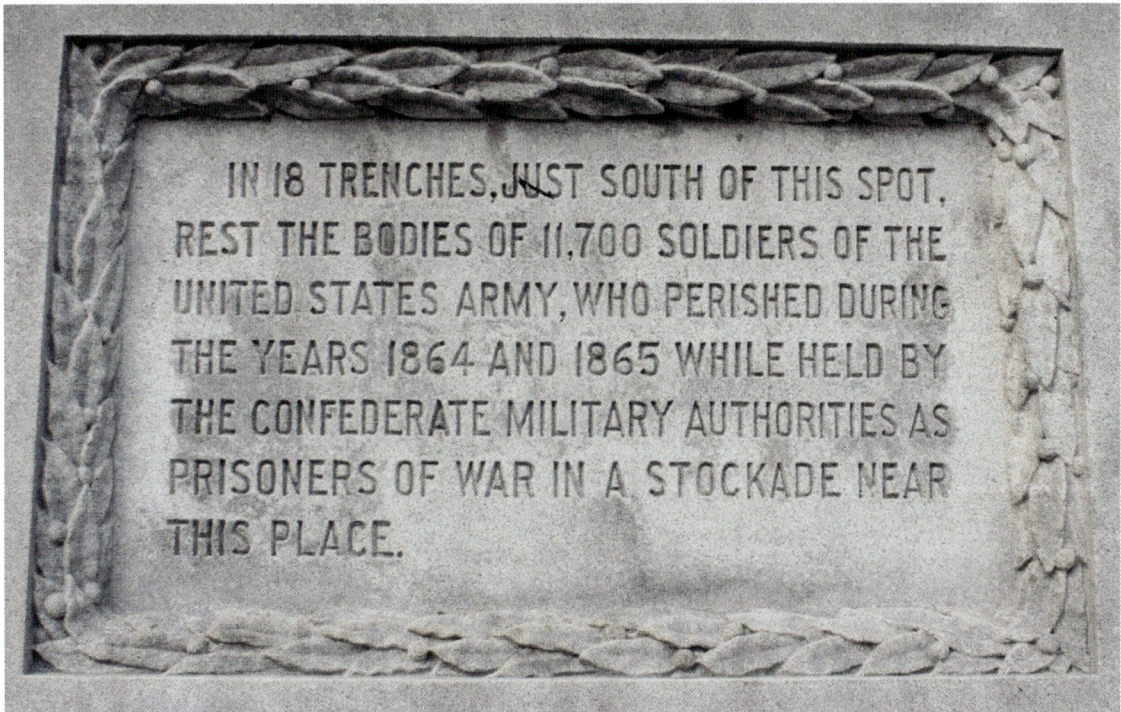

IN 18 TRENCHES, JUST SOUTH OF THIS SPOT, REST THE BODIES OF 11,700 SOLDIERS OF THE UNITED STATES ARMY, WHO PERISHED DURING THE YEARS 1864 AND 1865 WHILE HELD BY THE CONFEDERATE MILITARY AUTHORITIES AS PRISONERS OF WAR IN A STOCKADE NEAR THIS PLACE.

"In Memory Of" marker in the family plot in Fairview Cemetery, 120 Smalley Street, New Britain, Connecticut; Section 3. First two photos by author.

LORENZO DEMING
BORN SEPT. 6, 1843.
JOINED U.S. NAVY.
SEPT. 8, 1864,
CAPTURED AT PLYMOUTH N.C.
AT THE DESTRUCTION OF
THE REBEL
IRON CLAD ALBERMARLE.
NOV. 27 1864,
AND DIED IN REBEL PRISON
AT SALISBURY N.C.,
FEB. 5, 1865.
"He died at his Post."

DEMING

IN MEMORY OF
LORENZO DEMING
MEDAL OF HONOR
LDS US NAVY
PICKET BOAT 1
1843
1865

Photo courtesy of the author.

Photo courtesy of FindAGrave.com

158

Photo courtesy of the author

PRIVATE/WAGONER WILLIS H. DOWNS; ARMY

September 10, 1865 (Mount Carmel, CT) - September 16, 1929 (Jamestown, ND); 59 years old
Married to Nellie B. Eaton (1879-1949).
Two daughters, Helen T.E. Downs Carter (1910-1987) and Samantha H. (1921-?).
Enlisted in 1898.
Discharged on September 25, 1899.

Born to Mark W. (1831-1922) and Sarah J. Alatey Downs (1829-1912). Two brothers, Walter E. (1861-1918) and John H. (1866-1912). One sister, Sarah J. (1856-1912).

MEDAL OF HONOR CITATION

AWARDED FOR ACTIONS DURING: The Philippine Insurrection
BRANCH OF SERVICE: Army
UNIT: Company H, 1st North Dakota Volunteer Infantry
DATE OF ISSUE AND PRESENTATION: February 16, 1906 (7 years later)
AGE ON THE DAY OF THE EVENT: 34
CITATION:

The President of the United States of America, in the name of Congress, takes pleasure in presenting the Medal of Honor to Private Willis H. Downs, United States Army, for most distinguished gallantry on 13 May 1899, while serving with Company H, 1st North Dakota Volunteer Infantry, in action at San Miguel de Mayumo, Luzon, Philippine Islands. With 11 other scouts, without waiting for the supporting battalion to aid them or to get into a position to do so, Private Downs charged over a distance of about 150 yards and completely routed about 300 of the enemy who were in line and in a position that could only be carried by a frontal attack.

From the Bismarck (ND) Tribune February 22, 1906

BRAVERY REWARDED BY CONGRESS

Jamestown – W.H. Downs received this morning from the War Department in Washington the Congressional Gold Medal and Medal of Honor ribbon, awarded by act of Congress, March 3, 1903, to each of 12 scouts for most distinguished gallantry in action at San Miguel de Mayumo, Luzon, Philippine Islands, May 13th, 1899, which resulted in the complete rout of three hundred of the enemy. On this occasion, Private Downs and eleven other scouts, without waiting for the supporting battalion to aid them or to get into a position to do so, charged over a distance of about 150 yards and completely routed about 300 of the enemy, who were in line and in a position that could only be carried by a frontal attack.

It is a handsome medal and is engraved on the back, "presented by the Congress to Willis H. Downs," and giving the date and place of the occurrence for which it is given. Mr. Downs is naturally very proud of it.

From The Jamestown Sun October 3, 1986

CONGRESSIONAL MEDAL OF HONOR RECIPIENTS GRAVE UNMARKED

Nearly 400 Congressional Medal of Honor recipients, including a Jamestown veteran, have unknown or improperly marked graves, according to a state AmVets official.

The stone over the grave of Medal of Honor recipient Private Willis H. Downs, Jamestown, typifies improperly marked graves, according to David Erbstoesser, 2nd Vice Commander of the North Dakota AmVets.

"Research has shown that the 400 Medal of Honor recipients are buried in unknown graves in this country," Erbstoessder, who has been studying the history of military medals for six years, said.

Erbstoesser called LeRoy Wegenast, President of the Jamestown Vietnam Veterans of America Chapter 145, and asked him to visit Highland Homes Cemetery in Jamestown Saturday to find Downs' grave.

Wegenast and two members of the chapter board, Daryl Neumiller and Chuck Lyche, both of Jamestown, found the grave on the north side of the cemetery.

They also discovered that, besides a tarnished military emblem, the only distinction to the military-style gravestone is the letters "M.H."

"We didn't know what "M.H." stood for at first," Wegenast said. "It didn't hold any significance for us. I expected the inscription to read 'Medal of Honor for valor recipient,' which would be more befitting a war hero.

"Sometimes we forget the tremendous number of veterans who served to protect our freedom and, in some instances, gave the supreme sacrifice of their lives to allow us to live in a free society," he said.

Upon hearing of the condition of the stone, Erbstoesser said he would contact officials of the Congressional Medal of Honor Historical Society about appropriate action. Such action might include working with Jamestown veterans organization in replacing the stone with one that reads "Medal of Honor."

Erbsoteeser said he has not been able to locate any surviving relatives of Downs.

Downs was born in Mount Carmel, Connecticut, in 1843," he said. At the age of 19, he moved to Jamestown. In 1899, he joined Company H of the First North Dakota Volunteer Infantry.

While stationed near San Miguel de Mayaomo in the Philippine Islands, Downs and 11 other soldiers, without waiting or troop or battery support, rushed 150 yards into enemy lines and routed 300 with a frontal attack.

For "conspicuous gallantry and intrepidity at the risk of his life," Downs was presented the Medal of Honor.

He died September 15, 1929, at the age of 63, while seeking medical treatment in Grand Forks. He had been a conductor with the Northern Pacific Railroad.

Buried in Highland Home Cemetery, 3309 Highway 281 SE, Jamestown, North Dakota; Old Section, Plot D-L-19.
Photo from FindAGrave.com.

APPRENTICE FRANK DUMOULIN; NAVY

1850 or 1851 * (Philadelphia, PA) – unknown date of death
Enlisted on January 21, 1867, in Philadelphia, Pennsylvania, at 16 years old.

* The exact Date of Birth is unknown.

Born to Augustus M. (1815-?) and Adeline du Moulin (1820-1859). One sister, Augusta (1845-?). Two brothers, Charles (1844-1901) and Harry (1851-1878).

AUTHOR NOTE: The incident resulting in the award of the Medal of Honor to Frank DuMoulin happened in Connecticut, in New London Harbor, thus the inclusion in this book. There isn't much information on Frank Du Moulin or his family. There are some accounts of a Frank Du Moulin in Philadelphia who had frequent run-ins with police between 1869 and 1886. The circumstances of his death are unknown. It's possible he may have changed his name as his name isn't found anywhere past October 1886, when he was sentenced to four months in jail for stealing a box of cigars. His brother Harry died in Eastern State Penitentiary in Pennsylvania.

MEDAL OF HONOR CITATION

AWARDED FOR ACTIONS DURING: Peace Time Awards
BRANCH OF SERVICE: Navy
ASSIGNED TO: U.S.S. Sabine
GENERAL ORDERS: War Department, General Orders No. 84, October 3, 1867
AGE ON THE DAY OF THE EVENT: 16 or 17
CITATION:

The President of the United States of America, in the name of Congress, takes pleasure in presenting the Medal of Honor to Apprentice Frank DuMoulin, United States Navy, for gallant and heroic conduct on the 5th of September 1867. Apprentice Du Moulin jumped overboard and saved from drowning Apprentice D'Orsay, who had fallen from the mizzen topmast rigging of the U.S.S. Sabine in New London Harbor, Connecticut, and was rendered helpless by striking the mizzen rigging and boat davit in the fall.

U.S.S. Sabine. Public domain photo.

At the Pennsylvania State Capitol, Commonwealth Avenue, and State Street Harrisburg, Pennsylvania, is the state's Medal of Honor Memorial. The memorial lists the names of each Medal of Honor recipient, including those from the Civil War. Photo by Sam Kiebach. Used with permission.

BREVET COLONEL ANDREW HENRY EMBLER; ARMY

June 29, 1834 (Montgomery, NY) – July 28 1918 (New Haven, CT); 84years old
Married to Maria Eleanora Dickerson (1839-1927).
Four sons, Ralph (1868-1943), Howard W. (1869-1943), Simon (1872-1918), and Marshall J. (1875-1940).
Seven daughters, Mildred A. Embler Loomis (1866-1921), Harriet Embler Sanford (1871-?), Esther E. (1874-1963), Alice V. (1878-1961), Grace Embler Voight (1880-1912), Tennie Embler Merwin (1881-1950). and Jennie (1882-?).
Enlisted on April 19, 1861.
Discharged on March 21, 1865.

Born to Adam Embler (1788-1865) and Hannah Weller Embler (1795-1843).Eight sisters, Mary Ann Embler Puff (1808-1881), Letita Embler Moore (1813-1882), Catherine M. (1814-1852), Mary (1815-1835), Harriet W. (1818-1854), Martha T. (1823-1845), Sarah (1824-1851), and Catherine (1843-?). One brother, Adam H. (1820-1879).

 After the Civil War he returned to his home in Montgomery, Orange County, New York, but eventually moved to Connecticut. He was an officer and one of the founders of the Southern New England Telephone Company and was Adjutant General of Connecticut under Connecticut Governor Morgan C. Bulkeley. As a result, he was always referred to as "The General" or "General Embler." He was also a Major in the First Company Governor's Foot Guard of Connecticut. Around June of 1918, he attended a memorial service for the members of the Old New Haven Blues, who had fallen in France, and contracted pneumonia, which later contributed to his weakening health, and he passed away in July of that year.

Photo courtesy of Ancestry.com

Photo courtesy of FindAGrave.com

MEDAL OF HONOR CITATION

AWARDED FOR ACTIONS DURING: Civil War
BRANCH OF SERVICE: Army
UNIT: Company D, 59th New York Infantry
DATE OF ISSUE AND PRESENTATION: October 19, 1893 (29 years later)
AGE ON THE DAY OF THE EVENT: 30
CITATION:

The President of the United States of America, in the name of Congress, takes pleasure in presenting the Medal of Honor to Captain (Infantry) Andrew Henry Embler, United States Army, for extraordinary heroism on 27 October 1864, while serving with Company D, 59th New York Infantry, in action at Boydton Plank Road, Virginia. Captain Embler charged at the head of two regiments, which drove the enemy's main body, gained the crest of the hill near the Burgess House and forced a barricade on the Boydton road.

From The Meriden Daily Republic October 23, 1893

GENERAL EMBLER HONORED
A MEDAL FROM THE GOVERNMENT FOR GALLANTRY

General A.H. Embler, ex-adjutant general of the state, has received from the Secretary of War, a medal for distinguished gallantry at Boydton Plank Road, Virginia, on October 27, 1864. The medal is made from the metal of old cannon captured from the Confederates during the war, and is one of the most valuable testimonials given by this government to its brave old soldiers. The lower or star part of the medallion upon one side is embellished with raised figures enclosed with a circle, depicting the symbol of Liberty putting down rebellion, while upon the opposite side is engraved the following inscription:

The Congress to Brevet Colonel Andrew H. Embler, United States Volunteers, for distinguished gallantry in action at Boydton Plank Road, Virginia, October 27, 1864.

General Embler upon receiving the medal remembered that in 1863 Congress passed the law noted in the letter accompanying the medal, but as he had not expected to receive such a high testimonial, it had passed completely from his mind until its receipt. How it is that the War Department has been so long carrying out the act, General Embler himself is unable to explain.

From the Hartford Courant June 12, 1913

EMBLER TELLS VETS OF GETTYSBURG
GIVES GRAPHIC ACCOUNT OF PICKETT'S CHARGE
General A.H. Embler Tellis his Recollections of the battle
Exchanges Reminiscences with Reverend J.H. Twichell

General A, H. Embler of New Haven, formerly a resident of this city and the second commander of Robert O. Tyler Post, G.A.R., addressed his comrades in Grand Army Hall, Brown, Thomson & Co. building, last evening on the battle of Gettysburg, with especial reference to the third day's fight in which he was a participant, being at that time assistant adjutant in the Second Division, Second Corps, Hancock's. The meeting was open and the hall was well filled.

A large map, showing the field on the third day, had been prepared and this General Embler explained with a brief introduction covering the results of the three days' fight, in which 50,000 men were killed, wounded or j missing. He spoke of the causes which made Gettysburg the scene of the greatest fight in the Civil War, saying that it was first brought about | by the trivial fact that the Confederates under Heth wanted shoes and went to Gettysburg in the hope of finding them and secondly because once an engagement had begun there 'it was found a suitable place at which to mass troops, as ten roads led into the town. seven. of which were held through the fight by Lee's forces and three, the Emmetsburg Road, in Taneytown Road and the Baltimore Turnpike, were in possession of the Union forces.

Reynolds, in common with the Union forces which first reached, Gettysburg and passed beyond it for a matter of two miles early on July 1, the first day, saw the importance of the ground and it was due largely to the report which he sent back to Meade that the great conflict was forced there. During the first day's fighting, in which General Reynolds was killed, the Eleventh Corps was badly hammered and fell back so that the Confederates occupied the city from that time until their retreat. The first day ended with the Confederates in possession of the field and with the Eleventh Corps in possession of a ridge south of the town, known as Cemetery Ridge, and of Culp's Hill.

As Meade's men arrived, they prolonged the line to the southward, taking in two rocky hills at the end of the Cemetery Ridge, known as Round Top and Little Round Top, which saw some of the fiercest of the fighting on the second day. Before going on to the second day General Embler spoke of certain features of the first day's fight, alluding to John Burns, the old farmer who put on his Sunday suit, took an old smooth-bore musket and fought with the Wisconsin Iron Brigade, being wounded three times in the course of the day. It was explained that his ire was aroused because some of Ewells' Confederates had milked his cows. He added, to illustrate the fierceness of the first day's contest, that Company C, Twentieth North Carolina, went into the battle with three officers and eighty-four men and came out of it with one private and no, officers.

Coming to the second day General Embler said that the morning was spent in correcting position by both armies, but that General Sickles, not satisfied with his position, went forward to the Emmetsburg Road and left both his flanks up in the air, an act which cost many lives. Longstreet attacked him at 4 o'clock In the afternoon, though the fight around the Round Top had begun much earlier and these were safe at 4. Longstreet finally broke through and Sickles lost a lor in this contest. During this fight the First Minnesota Regiment charged three Mississippi regiments under Barksdale and lost 215 men out of 260.

The gap in the Union lines was finally closed and both sides were fairly exhausted. At sunset Johnson's Confederates took Culp's Hill, the Union forces having been drawn away from it, but Johnson was driven out the next morning.

Coming to the last day, July 3, General Embler said that the morning was perfectly quiet except for four hours of fighting incident to the retaking of Culp's Hill, and then a Sunday calm lasted until about 1 o'clock in the afternoon, by which time Lee had determined to send Pickett with his fifteen regiments of Virginians against the Union center. At 1 o'clock the greatest artillery duel of the war began, over 100 cannon on each side being worked. After two hours of this it ceased und Pickett's charge began, the men having a march of a little over a mile before they reached the crest of Cemetery Hill and the Union infantry. He said that neither tongue nor pen could do justice to the magnificent valor of that charge in the face of a direct two oblique and an enfilading fire from the Union guns. The point of contact was Webb's Philadelphia brigade, which Armistead finally reached with his brigade of Virginians. The fight then, he said, became a melee in which the commands of the officers could not be heard and in which they were not needed. It lasted hut a short time and then the men separated, the Confederates either raising their hands in token of surrender or falling back down the hill, leaving their dead and wounded and thirty-three battle flags on the field.

On July 4, General Embler said parties were going over the field picking up the muskets and sticking the bayonets in the ground. the guns standing up like trees in a nursery. The fight was over.

After the address the request was made that veterans who had been in the fight might arise. and nine, including Rev. Joseph H. Twichell. stood up. Rev. Mr. Twichell. once General Embler's pastor. was greatly interested in the address and the map and pointed out on the latter the site of the Trostle house, which he recalled. He spoke later briefly. as did Chaplain W. F. Hilton and William A. Willard the latter a member of the Citizens' 'Corps of Robert O. Tyler Post.

From the Hartford Courant July 29, 1918

GEN. A.H. EMBLER DIES IN NEW HAVEN
Many Years Treasurer of Southern New England Telephone Co.
VETERAN OF THE CIVIL WAR
Once Resident of Hartford and Major of First Company, Governor's Foot Guard

(Special to The Courant.)

General Andrew Henry Embler of New Haven, adjutant general under Governor Morgan G. Bulkeley, once Major of the First Company Governor's Foot Guard, and former treasurer of the Southern New England Telephone Company, died in New Haven yesterday. He was 84 years old. General Embler's death came after a severe attack of pneumonia contracted about six weeks ago as the result of a vis.t to a cemetery to attend a memorial service for the members of the old New Haven Blues, now incorporated with the 102nd Infantry, who have fallen in France. General Embler apparent ly recovered from pneumonia, but was not in vigorous health after his illness.

General Embler was born in New York City June 29, 1834, and was educated in the public schools of that city. At the outbreak of the Civil War in 1861 he enlisted as a Private in the second corps of New York infantry and during the war was wounded three times at Bull Run, Gettysburg and Appomattox. He received a medal for bravery in action, and was present at the Appomattox Courthouse at Lee's surrender. He was breveted Lieutenant Colonel by Secretary of War Stanton in 1865.

After the war he came to Hartford. In 1871 he was a member of the firm of H. P. Blair & Embler, whose place of business was at No. 178 Asylum street. The firm became Embler & Bosworth, with N. A. Bosworth as the other member, in 1872 and later, in 1875, A. H. Embler & Co. Its store was then at No. 442 Asylum street, while General Embler lived on Niles Street. He had previously lived in Windsor.

He was major of the First Company, Governor's Foot Guard, about forty years ago and later was connected with the Second Company in New Haven.

On his retirement from the Southern New England Telephone Company in 1913, General Embler was the only remaining members of the original executive officers of the company. When he first became connected with the Connecticut Telephone Company, which later became the Southern New England Telephone Company, the entire executive force was located in one room in the Palladium building on Orange street, New Haven, the only other members of the force besides the officers being a bookkeeper and two young women clerks. The Southern New England Telephone Company had ninety-six stockholders in 1882. General Embler has seen two general superintendents and one general manager of the company in authority. He was a pioneer in the telephone business, being made treasurer of the Connecticut Telephone Company in 1882 and taking the same office with the Southern New England, a place he held more than thirty years.

General Embler was long an enthusiastic member of the New Haven Blues, Company D. He served in the National Guard as Private, Captain and Major, and had a record of forty-two years as a citizen-soldier. In 1890 he was appointed Adjutant General after the resignation of Adjutant General Lucius B. Barbour.

Besides his wife General Embler leaves nine children, Mrs. Mildred Loomis, Ralph H. Embler, Howard W. Embler, Mrs. Harris M. Sanford, Simms Embler, Esther E. Embler, Marshall J. Embler, Olive V. Embler and Mrs. A. D. Merwin. A daughter, Mrs. Grave Voight, died a number of years ago.

Buried in Evergreen Cemetery, 769 Ella T Grasso Boulevard New Haven, Connecticut; Larch Avenue, Plot 13, Grave 3. Photos by author.

PRIVATE CHARLES DENNISON ENNIS; ARMY

August 8, 1843 (Stonington, CT) – December 29, 1930 (Potter Hill, RI); 87 years old

Married Mary E. Tucker (1839-1893) on November 29, 1865, in Providence, Rhode Island.

Four sons, Charles W. (1866-1938), Alvin L. (1868-), William N. (1873-1941), and Frank E. (1877-1966).

Two daughters, Mary E. (1870-?) and Alzada G. (1875-1917).

Enlisted on August 1, 1862, in Charleston, Rhode Island.

Mustered out on June 24, 1865.

Born to Joseph (1802-1845) and Susannah Burdick Ennis (1804-1901). Six brothers, William (1826-1907), Varnum S. (1829-1904), Joseph F. (1831-1895), Thomas N. (1836-1891), Edwin O. (1838-1847), and George H. (1840-1931). Two sisters, Susan F. Ennis Burdick (1831-1914) and Phoebe A. Ennis Potter (1834-1906).

MEDAL OF HONOR CITATION

AWARDED FOR ACTIONS DURING: Civil War
BRANCH OF SERVICE: Army
UNIT: 1st Rhode Island Light Artillery
DATE OF ISSUE AND PRESENTATION: June 28, 1892 (27 years later)
AGE ON THE DAY OF THE EVENT: 22
CITATION:

The President of the United States of America, in the name of Congress, takes pleasure in presenting the Medal of Honor to Private Charles D. Ennis, United States Army, for extraordinary heroism on 2 April 1865, while serving with Company G, 1st Rhode Island Light Artillery, in action at Petersburg, Virginia. Private Ennis was one of a detachment of 20 picked artillerymen who voluntarily accompanied an infantry assaulting party and who turned upon the enemy the guns captured in the assault.

From Beyer, W. F., & Keydel, O. F. (2000). Deeds of Valor: How America's Civil War Heroes Won The Congressional Medal of Honor. Smithmark Publishers.

MADE GOOD USE OF THE ENEMY'S WEAPONS

At about ten o'clock on the night of April 1, 1865, Captain G. W. Adams of Battery G, First Rhode Island Light Artillery, was detailed to select a detachment of twenty men from his battery to advance with the Sixth Army Corps in its intended assault on the enemy's works in front of Petersburg, Virginia, and with this detachment take command of all the captured guns and turn them on the enemy.

Late that night, Captain Adams called his battery together and asked for volunteers for this hazardous duty, at the same time pointing out to them what it meant to go into the enemy's works with only ramrods, sponge staffs, lanyards, friction primers, and gun spikes; that, should they be unable to work the captured guns, they would have no means of defending themselves, except with these implements.

Twenty men nevertheless promptly volunteered, and at the outset of the assault, when the captain asked whether any of the twenty wished to remain with the battery, only three fell out, thus leaving seventeen to perform the duty laid out for them.

At daybreak of the 2nd, the assaulting column moved upon the fortifications of the enemy amid a shower of shot and shell with such resistless force that the works were carried and the enemy driven back. Here followed the little volunteer detachment of

seventeen, scaling the works and at once taking possession of twelve large guns, but when they began to work them, it was necessary to fire along the line of works in order to drive the enemy out of the embrasures at the end of the pits, and consequently only one gun, a twenty-four pounder Napoleon, could be used. It was in an exposed position, and the brave cannoneers received heavy fire from the rebels in the embrasures of the forts they still retained. But the gun was kept hot by the rapid fire with which the little band poured one hundred or more shots into the enemy, causing them to become demoralized and retire. Some of the detachment were wounded, while others were under cover, but the seven who served this gun so nobly, standing up unflinchingly before the terrific fire of the enemy - Sergeant John

H. Havron, Sergeant Archibald Molbone, Corporal James A. Barber, Corporal Samuel E. Lewis, Privates Charles D. Ennis, John Corcoran, and George W. Potter -were rewarded for their bravery and daring with the Medal of Honor soon after this eventful day.

SERGEANT CHRISTOPHER J. FLYNN; ARMY

December 15, 1829 (County Westmeath, Ireland) – October 15, 1889 (Sprague, CT); 60 years old
Married Catherine Spratt (1836-1912) on November 24, 1852, in Blackstone, Massachusetts.
Four sons, Joseph T. (1863-1943), John (1859-1939), James (1861-?), and Thomas E. (1874-1964).
Five daughters, Anna J. Flynn Craig (1863-1939), Catherine V. Flynn Welch (1865-1942), Sarah C. (1868-?), Teresa
    (1872-?), and Marie E. Flynn Finnup (1873-1952).
Enlisted on August 12, 1862, in Connecticut.
Wounded on May 10, 1964, at Laurel Hill, Virginia.
Mustered out on May 31, 1865, at Alexandria, Virginia.

According to his death certificate, he was born to Michael Flynn and Ann Cosgrave. Their exact details are unknown.

MEDAL OF HONOR CITATION

AWARDED FOR ACTIONS DURING: Civil War
BRANCH OF SERVICE: Army
UNIT: Company K, 14th Connecticut Infantry
DATE OF ISSUE: December 1, 1864
AGE ON THE DAY OF THE EVENT: 34
CITATION:

The President of the United States of America, in the name of Congress, takes pleasure in presenting the Medal of Honor to Corporal Christopher Flynn, United States Army, for extraordinary heroism on 3 July 1863, while serving with Company K, 14th Connecticut Infantry, in action at Gettysburg, Pennsylvania, for capture of flag of 52nd North Carolina Infantry (Confederate States of America).

Presentation Date and Details: December 6, 1864, by Major General George G. Meade, at a review of the 2nd Army Corps Headquarters, Peebles' House, near Petersburg, Virginia.

From the Fourteenth Regiment, Connecticut Volunteer Infantry, Regimental History

... The men, now careless of shelter, stood erect and, with loud shouts, continued to fire into the retreating army as long as they were within range. Many of the retreating column lay down behind stones and hillocks, and even the dead bodies of their comrades, to be protected from the Union shots. Presently. As by one common impulse, bits of white cloth and handkerchiefs were waved as signals of surrender. In response to these signals, our men leaped over the wall and advanced toward the retreating foe. When they reached the point where the enemy's advance had halted, rebels wounded, and unwounded in large numbers rose up and surrendered themselves. One of the first to leap over the wall was Corporal Christopher Flynn of Company K, who, advancing far down toward the retreating line, picked up a battle flag which they had dropped in their flight. Corporal E.W. Bacon of Company F also seized the flag of the Sixteenth North Carolina. Several others were subsequently picked up, making five in all, which were credited to the regiment. The claim has also been made that six flags were captured, although Major Ellis speaks of only five in this official report. Some have claimed that the sixth flag was a beautiful silk flag, which was not given to the proper officers. Major Hincks, Corporal Flynn of Company K, and Corporal Bacon of Company F afterwards received the United States Medal of Honor for deeds of special bravery.

COMMISSARY SERGEANT* THOMAS HALL FORSYTH JR.; ARMY

* During the Civil War, Commissary Sergeants were one of three Non-Commissioned Staff Sergeants, along with the Quartermaster Sergeant and Sergeant Major. The Commissary Sergeant was responsible for helping the Assistant Commissary of Subsistence, typically a Captain or Lieutenant, with overseeing the distribution of rations to the soldiers. Future President, and at the time, 19-year-old William McKinley, served as the Commissary Sergeant of the 23rd Ohio Volunteer Infantry.

December 17, 1842 (Hartford, CT) – March 22, 1908 (San Diego, CA); 65 years old
Married Mary E. Strickland (1850-1937) in 1870 in Fort Leavenworth, Kansas.
Eight daughters, Amanda S. (1870-1937), Clara W. Forsyth Fisher (1871-1951), Mary E. Forsyth Barrett (1874-1940), Isabella Forsyth Platt (1881-1938), Margaret J. (1883-1949), Pauline (1886-1886), Mabel A. Forsyth Hartigan [twin of Thomas H. III] (1887-1928), and Patience Forsyth Rowan May (1890-1953).
Three sons, Henry H. (1879-1929) and George A. "Harvey" (1885-1972), and Thomas H. III [twin of Mable] (1887-1957).
Enlisted on July 20, 1861.

Born to Thomas H. Sr. (1808-1865) and Isabella Macaulay Forsyth (1819-1865). One sister, Jean "Jennie" Forsyth Rolshouse (1843-1908). In 1900, he retired from the Army and became a rancher in Silver City, New Mexico.

Sgt. Thomas Hall Forsyth and family. Back row (left to right): niece Beulah Rolhouse Wylie, Clara Wharton Forsyth, Mary Elizabeth Forsyth, Henry Hall Forsyth. Center row: Sgt. Thomas Forsyth, Margaret Forsyth, Mary Elizabeth Strickland Forsyth (wife) holding Thomas Hall Forsyth. On the floor: George "Harvey" A. Forsyth, Mabel Agnes Forsyth (Thomas Hall's twin sister), and Isabella Forsyth. Not pictured is Patience, born in 1890 after this photograph was taken. Photograph from the Fort Davis Archives, AB-8.

MEDAL OF HONOR CITATION

AWARDED FOR ACTIONS DURING: Indian Campaigns
BRANCH OF SERVICE: Army
UNIT: Company M, 4th U.S. Cavalry
DATE OF ISSUE AND PRESENTATION: July 14, 1891 (15 years later)
AGE ON THE DAY OF THE EVENT: 33
CITATION:

The President of the United States of America, in the name of Congress, takes pleasure in presenting the Medal of Honor to First Sergeant Thomas Hall Forsyth, United States Army, for extraordinary heroism on 25 November 1876, while serving with Company M, 4th U.S. Cavalry, in action at Powder River, Wyoming. Though dangerously wounded, First Sergeant Forsyth maintained his ground with a small party against a largely superior force after his commanding officer had been shot down during a sudden attack and rescued that officer and a comrade from the enemy.

From "Morning Star Dawn: The Powder River Expedition and the Northern Cheyenne's (1876)

As it became apparent that some of the warriors, trying to save the ponies from capture, had been pressed into the gulch near the base of the Red Butte and were trying to move up that rugged zigzag defile to escape,9 Mackenzie sent Lieutenant Henry W. Lawton to direct two companies (H of the Third Cavalry and M of the Fourth, operating as the rear units of Gordon's battalion but far in advance of Mauck's second battalion reserves) to thwart the movement and intercept the Indians. Immediately, the units raced ahead, rounded the Red Butte on its north side, and approached the largely unseen ravine in column of fours. Company M led the way with Memphis-born First Lieutenant John A. McKinney, an 1871 West Point graduate, out in front, and Company H of the Third under Captain Henry W. Wessels following close behind. As the troops, pistols raised, closed on the gulch, they suddenly drew point-blank gunfire from fifteen or twenty warriors hidden therein, a volley that ripped into the thirty-year-old McKinney, knocking him from his saddle with four gunshot wounds, three of them mortal. McKinney's horse was shot under him, and as the lieutenant fell, he screamed to his men, "Fall back! Fall back!" Two men, First

176

Sergeant Thomas H. Forsyth and Private Thomas Ryan dismounted and rushed to the officer's side, their weapons blazing at the Indians. Two others, Sergeant Frank Murray and Corporal William J. Linn, also hurried forward. Within moments, a bullet grazed Forsyth's head and another struck Linn in the right hip joint, yet both were able to continue to discharge their weapons into the ravine while protecting the fallen lieutenant. The abruptness of the assault, together with the succeeding volley, caused Company M to reel to the right, back from the ravine, and many of the panicked cavalrymen started to retreat up a rise twenty or so yards to the rear. Adding to the confusion, the wounded horse of McKinney's trumpeter, George Hicks, slumped atop its rider, pinning the man's leg and trapping him, but using the animal as a breastwork, he was able to twist around and open fire on the warriors in the gorge. At the roar of gunfire and the sudden halting and repulse of McKinney's first ranks, the men of Wessels's Company H, riding directly behind, skewed their mounts sharply to the right to avoid a collision with McKinney's horses and pulled up along the ravine on their flank, tumbling from their saddles at Wessels's barked command to "Dismount and Fight on Foot!" and mixing in with the remaining horsemen of Company M. Although McKinney's second in command, Second Lieutenant Harrison G. Otis, soon moved up and managed to help restore order, it had been Wessels's prompt action near the ravine that had saved the teetering command from a possible rout.

Meanwhile, Forsyth and Linn, both wounded, remained at the scene close to the ravine, and with Sergeant Murray and Private Ryan, they surrounded and protected the stricken McKinney until he could be moved to the rear. Their action in staying at the ravine also most certainly saved Trumpeter Hicks from being killed. Forsyth's head injury shortly rendered him unconscious. Things now happened rapidly, confusedly. The led horses were rushed to a point east of the Red Butte out of the line of fire, and the remaining soldiers of the two companies—seemingly moving in undisciplined bunches—advanced on the ravine and opened a fusillade that killed some of the tribesmen. "Just as we swung out of the saddle," remembered Sergeant McClellan, "those in the gully poured in another volley, which passed over our head." By the time of McKinney's fall, Mackenzie had individual honors for the soldiers who attacked Morning Star's people were not presently forthcoming. No soldiers were immediately nominated for the Medal of Honor. The closest such distinction came on November 30, 1876, when Lieutenant Harrison G. Otis, Company M, Fourth Cavalry, presented to Mackenzie a recommendation to recognize three of the individuals who had shielded Lieutenant McKinney as he lay unconscious at the edge of the ravine following his wounding. "I have the honor to call the attention of the Regimental Commander to the gallant conduct of 1st Sergeant Thomas H. Forsyth, Sergeant Frank Murray, and Corporal William J. Linn, Co. M, 4th Cavalry, as displayed in their successful efforts to defend the person of 1st Lieutenant John A. McKinney, 4th Cavalry, mortally wounded, from being outraged by the Indians during the fight of November 25, 1876. While thus engaged, 1st Sergeant Forsyth and Corporal Linn were wounded, yet all three maintained their positions, protecting the body of Lieutenant McKinney until its recovery, and I take great pleasure in recommending them to the Regimental Commander for honorable mention." Despite this endorsement, none of the men won recognition for their valor for some time, and Private Thomas Ryan, Company M, Fourth Cavalry, who had played an important role during the moments following McKinney's fall, did not even receive mention in Otis's citation. But in 1880, Ryan received a Certificate of Merit for "extraordinary gallantry," entitling him to two dollars extra pay each month for "maintaining his stand with but two of his comrades, one of them disabled, thus rallying the troop in time to rescue the body of his commanding officer." By that time, however, Murray and Linn, mentioned in Otis's initial communication, had left the service and received nothing. In 1891, following a petition by former adjutant Joseph H. Dorst and others, Forsyth was granted a Medal of Honor – the only such recognition accorded any participant in the engagement. Finally, six officers received brevet commissions in 1894 for their performances at the Red Fork. Besides the deceased McKinney, they were Second Lieutenant Hayden DeLany, Ninth Infantry; Second Lieutenant Homer W. Wheeler and Captain Wirt Davis, Fourth Cavalry; and Captains John M. Hamilton and Walter S. Schuyler, Fifth Cavalry.

Sergeant Thomas Hall Forsyth, one of Fort Davis's most interesting characters, was a member of both the Good Templars' and Oddfellows' lodges. A Civil War veteran, Hall's heroic action in protecting the body of his commanding officer in 1876 was later rewarded with the Medal of Honor. The sergeant married in 1871 and had eleven children, one of whom wed a Third Cavalryman at Fort Davis. From a wealthy family, he enjoyed dancing, music, and chess and subscribed to several Eastern newspapers. Forsyth became commissary sergeant at the post on the Limpia in 1885. Holding down one of the army's most honored noncommissioned slots, Forsyth was allotted an individual adobe house befitting his position.

The following are letters obtained from the Arizona Historical Society, Forsyth papers, MS 1090, Box 1, Folder 15. Used with permission.

Fort Davis, Texas.
March 9th, 1891.

To Capt. J. H. Dorst,
4th Cavalry.

Sir:

I see by Act of Congress that the law awarding certificates of merit to privates for acts of a meritorious character has been amended so that all classes of enlisted men can obtain this recognition, and since reading this amended law, I have been debating in my mind the propriety of asking for it and have at last concluded to do so for this reason.

I am now in a position in which it is almost impossible to render any distinguished or meritorious service that would meet the requirements. I, of course, can render faithful service, which I hope to do, but that will not answer, so I have to call on my service in the old Regiment, which is a matter of record. I believe that General MacKenzie, were he alive, would endeavor to procure me the recognition he failed to get at Garland in 1880. I presume you will call it to mind as you were Adjutant at the time.

I would like to leave my children something besides my name when I answer the last roll call, and anything that could bear testimony to bravery and gallantry on the part of their father in action would be the best and noblest remembrance that a soldier's children could have,

To this end, I respectfully ask that you take the matter in hand, in conjunction with the old officers of the 4th who remember me and try to obtain for me what I deserve.

The Regimental records will give you full information to guide you in this matter, or if you so desire, I will send you copies from the extracts given me by you when I was made Company Sergeant. I do not particularly care for the money consideration accompanying the certificate of merit would far rather be recognized in some other way, and men have been decorated for less cause, but if I cannot obtain the decoration, will gladly accept the other,

Trusting that you will take this into favorable consideration, I am, sir.

Very Respectfully
Your obedient servant
T.H. Forsyth
Company Sergeant U.S.A.

Captain J. H. Dorst,
4th U.S. Cavalry,
Presidio of San Francisco, Cal,

Sir:

Yours of 28th March at hand, and in reply, I enclose your copies of endorsements, etc., bearing on the matter in question.

Your recollection of the affair is fairly correct, except that instead of having five or six, I was only able to get two. Sergeant Murray and Captain Limm are to stay with me. The number of Indians I do not know. Some of the men say thirty, others say about twenty-five. I was too busy working my carbine to count them, but think your estimate of fifteen is about right. There was that many, at least, but it would have been the same if there had been fifty.

The facts are thus.

On entering the broken ground from the mouth of the canyon, I removed my overcoat and fur gloves and strapped them to my saddle. Lieutenant McKinney, watching me, asked what I was doing that for, and I told him I thought it would be warm enough without them when we got into the fight. He followed suit and told me to stick to him no matter what happened. I told him I would, and I believe I kept my word.

When the Indians opened on us, we were in a column of fours with drawn pistols. The head of the column received the first volley. Lieutenant McKinney and Trumpeter Hicks went down. The Lieutenant ordered us, "fall back," "fall back." The Company, except Private Ryan and myself, who had dismounted, instantly turned by the right flank and retreated up the little hill about twenty yards in rear of us. I had ordered the Company to halt, dismount, and deploy to the front as skirmishers. Sergeant Murray and Corporal Limm remained with me. Private Ryan and myself had opened with our carbines, and so far, all the credit is due to him as had he not acted as he did, the Indians would, in all probability, either killed me or driven me back. The Company, under Lieutenant Otis, had by this time recovered from the momentary panic and advanced with "F" Co, under the command of Captain Davis. Corporal Linn and I were both wounded, but we could still handle our arms and covered Lieutenant McKinney's body until it was it was recovered and carried back. I fainted from the loss of blood about then end, remember nothing further until I found myself with other wounded men back out of the line of fire.

The above facts are, so far as my memory serves me correctly, giving Col Lawton, I think, observed the whole or part of the affair related and can verify my statement.

Now, as to my making application for this, I do not think that I should do so for this reason that a soldier cannot himself say what is distinguished gallantry on the battlefield. Consequently, it would come with poor grace from me to apply for a certificate for such services when my commanding officers have not thought fit to do so: the application should come from some officer who was then and is cognizant of the facts, and you and Colonel Lawton are the only officers I know of whom I could ask to do this, have not written to Colonel Lawton and would much rather you would make the recommendation to the Colonel commanding the Regiment, and have it referred to Col. Lawton for such remarks as he may deem fit. Then, have him return it to Regimental Headquarters and, from there, forwarded to the proper authority.

I know I am putting you to considerable trouble, but if you deem my services at the time worthy of recognition, you will not, I believe, regard the time and trouble given to obtain for me what I should always be proud of.

I am sir,
Very Respectfully
Your obedient servant
T. H, Forsyth
Commissary Sgt, U.S.A.

Troop "K" 4th Cavalry
Presidio of S. F. Calif
May 10, 1892

The Adjutant General, U.S.A.
Washington, D.C.
Post Headquarters

Sir: I have the honor to forward herewith two letters from Commissary Sergeant T.H. Forsyth U.S.A., late Sergeant Major of the 4th Cavalry, and certain papers in connection with them. The letters explain themselves, and the statements in the one dated April 6th concerning certain incidents in an affair with hostile Indians near the Sioux Pass of the Big Horn Mountains, Wyoming, on November 25, 1876, I am sure, are correct. I know of but three officers now in the service who were with the regiment in that fight. They are Lieutenant Colonel Lawton, Inspector General's Department, Major Wirt Davis of the 5th Cavalry, and myself. Colonel Lawton was then 1st Lieutenant and Regimental Quartermaster, Major Davis was a captain, and I was a 2nd Lieutenant and adjutant, though my appointment as adjutant was afterward revoked by orders from Washington because there was a supernumerary 1st Lieutenant in the regiment. The troops engaged were six troops, 4th Cavalry, two 3rd Cavalry, and two 5th Cavalry, with Colonel Mackenzie, 4th Cavalry, commanding the whole.

The Indians were the whole of the northern Cheyennes, then numbering about 1,500 people and a few Sioux. The village lay in a deep canyon in the heart of the mountains and was attacked at daylight. Sergeant Forsyth was the late Sergeant of Troop M, 4th Cavalry, Lieutenant John McKinney commanding. The troop was the sixth in the column, and all were delayed so long in reaching the village by having to cross a very boggy stream and then pick their way through a wild growth of high and almost impenetrable brush that the head of the column was engaged for some time before the rear troops could come into action. They had to advance about half a mile after getting clear of the brush. The village lay on the left side of the canyon on the stream. The canyon was probably 600 yards wide with precipitous walls on either side, that on the right being at least 800 feet high. The ground between that side and the village sloped toward the stream was uneven and cut up by ravines heading at the right side of the canyon and running towards the stream. These ravines were washed-out gullies, about twenty feet deep with almost vertical sides, and were not noticeable until they were nearly reached.

When the troops at the head of the column rushed through the village, the Indians fled in all directions, and many ran up into the ravines for shelter and followed them up to get under the cover of the rocks and trees on the side of the canyon.

I am aware of only the following facts concerning the matter in question. After the fighting commenced, Colonel MacKenzie sent me back with some instructions for the troops in the rear coming up. While going back, I was passed by Troop M moving to the front at a fast gallop in a column of fours with Lieutenant McKinney at the head. While I was returning, I saw Troop "M" several hundred yards in front of me, falling back on some disorder. It came possibly 80 or 100 yards and then rallied. When I came up with it, I saw about a dozen wounded men lying about that belonged to different troops, and Lieut, McKinney was dying, having received six wounds. I learned afterward that Lieutenant Me Kinney had come upon one of the ravines, which in the gray of the morning was not seen until it was reached, and he had then encountered one of the bands of Indians that were running up the ravine for shelter. The ravine was too deep and wide, and the sides too nearly vertical for the columns to cross it mounted, and he turned to the right, evidently to go around its head. The column was within eight or ten feet of the ravine, and just as the column turned, the Indians fired. At the lowest estimate, this band numbered fifteen men, but some said the number was greater. As the Indians fired, Lieutenant McKinney called out "all back" and fell from his horse, The horse of Trumpeter Hicks Troop "M" was killed and fell on him so that he could not get away. Hicks was not hurt, and the horse served as a breastwork till the Indians were driven away. Second Lieutenant Otis, the other officer with the troop, had his cap torn by a bullet and started back with nearly all the troop as ordered, not noticing that Lieutenant McKinney was hurt but Sergeant Forsyth and a few men that remained with him by his orders, stopped when the troop fell back, opening fire on the Indians and alone kept them from getting Lieutenant McKinney's body and killing Trumpeter Hicks. Sergeant then Corporal Linn was shot in the hip joint while dismounting to help Sergeant Forsyth, and before relief came, the latter was himself shot in the head. For a long while, it was uncertain that he would live, and I know that he suffered from the wound up to the time he was made Commissary Sergeant in 1880. The speedy succor of these men was due to Lieutenant now Lieutenant Colonel Lawton, who noticed the disorder in the troops, at once assumed command of it, rallied it, and took it back to the place it had fled from.

Of the men mentioned by Sergeant Forsyth, I think that Sergeant Murray is now out of the service. Sergeant Linn was discharged in '78 or '79 for disability, and Private Ryan was lately a member of Battery B, 5th Artillery, at this post. He was discharged for disability about a month ago and died in Oakland while on his way to the Hot Springs of Arkansas. There was no officer who was cognizant of everything Sergeant Forsyth did. The above statements were common talk at the time and are a summary of the statements made to Colonel MacKenzie by Lieutenant Lawton, Lieutenant Otis, and a number of enlisted men when he was investigating the circumstances of Lieutenant McKinney's death.

Private Ryan received a certificate of merit for his conduct that day, but as those certificates could only be given to privates, soldier Sergeant Forsyth was not recommended for one. I know that Colonel Mackenzie wished him to have one and preferred to recommend for that instead of for a Medal of Honor because the certificate carried extra pay with it, and the Sergeant, being a married man, needed the money.

I know Sergeant Forsyth well, having had him as Sergeant Major for three years while I was regimental adjutant, and I know that he is honest, brave, modest, sensitive, and conscientious in every respect. I have as high a degree of respect for him as I have for any man, and it is only because he knows I understand him that a man so quiet and unassuming would write me so freely. I do not believe that under the law, he can get a certificate of merit now for gallant conduct fifteen years ago. But there are precedents for granting Medals of Honor long after they were won. It is reported by the newspapers that only a short time ago, General Martin T. McMahon received one for his gallantry in the Civil War. I believe that Gen Mackenzie, who was most of the praise, would recommend this soldier for one now. Without stopping to count the Indians opposed to him when his commander was shot down, and his other officer and all but one man was retreating and while under hot fire from a greater superior force at a distance of not more than 10 yards, he had the resolution and moral and physical courage to stand his ground and keep other men with him and by his action, protected his body from desecration and saved the life of a comrade. In doing so, he received a wound that, for a long time, threatened his life and caused him suffering for years. I think he is fully entitled to a medal and request that these papers be submitted to Lieutenant Colonel W. Lawton, Inspector General U.S.A., for his report and opinion.

Very Respectfully-
Your Obedient Servant
W.H. Dorest, Captain 4th Cavalry, Troop K

From Motor Travel Magazine for July 1930, pp. 15-18; these items are in blocked-off inserts in an article titled "A Day with the 'Fighting Cheyennes'."

"Gallant Conduct Promptly Acknowledged"

Company M, 4th Cavalry, Camp on
Crazy Woman's Creek, Wyoming Territory
November 30, 1876.

Colonel R.S. Mackenzie
Commanding 4th Cavalry.

Sir:

I have the honor to call the attention of the Regimental Commander to the gallant conduct of 1st Sergeant Thomas H. Forsyth, Sergeant Frank Murray, and Corp. William J. Linn, Co. M, 4th Cavalry, as displayed in their successful efforts to defend the person of 1st Lieutenant John A. McKinney, 4th Cavalry, mortally wounded, from being outraged by the Indians during the fight of November 25, 1876.
While thus engaged, 1st Sergeant Forsyth and Corp. Linn were wounded, yet all three maintained their positions, protecting the body of Lieutenant McKinney until its recovery, and I take great pleasure in recommending them to the Regimental Commander for honorable mention.
Very respectfully, your most obedient servant,

(Signed) H.G. Otis, 2nd Lt.,
4th U.S. Cavalry, Commanding Co, M,

An excellent type of heroic non-commissioned officers of the Old Army, Sergeant Forsyth carried with him into the Powder River Expedition of 1876 scars from wounds received in the Civil Wars and also had the experience of service under Colonel Mackenzie in the Southwest during the early 1870s. When Lieutenant McKinney's company was ordered into the charge, Forsyth was in the forefront of the attack, and after McKinney had been killed, he, with two comrades, beat back the savage warriors and rescued the body of his former commander, for which a Congressional Medal of Honor was well bestowed.

Born at Hartford, Conn., December 17, 1842; first enlistment at Harrisburg, Pennsylvania, July 20, 1861; eighth enlistment, October 14, 1897; placed on the retired list after long and faithful service, December 20, 1898; died at San Diego, California, March 22, 1908. A wound in the back, made by a bullet which struck his spine sideways during the Civil War, and one in his temple received in the Dull Knife fight, undoubtedly hastened his death. Sergeant Forsyth had other but less severe wounds. It would be difficult to find a better record than his. Mrs. Forsyth, the widow who married the sergeant in 1871, still resides in San Diego.

"A Medal of Honor for the Dull Knife Fight"

Particularly in view of the number of officers, several of high rank, participating in that engagement, it is interesting to note that the only Medal of Honor ever bestowed by the Government for conspicuous gallantry in action was to a non-commissioned officer, Thomas H. Forsyth. This was granted to him on July 14, 1891, with the following citation:

FORSYTH, Thomas Hall, Commissary Sergeant: for distinguished gallantry in action against hostile *Sioux Indians near the Sioux Pass* (see note below) of the Big Horn Mountains, Wyoming Territory, November 25, 1876, where he was dangerously wounded, maintaining his ground with a small party against a largely superior force of Indians during a sudden attack, after his commanding officer had been shot down, and rescuing that officer # (see note below) and a comrade from the enemy; while serving as 1st Sergeant, Troop M., 4th Cavalry.

* an incidental error--should have stated Northern Cheyenne Indians; reference to the "Sioux Pass" corresponds with Colonel Mackenzie's report of November 26, 1876, as to the march on the hostile village having been "in a southwesterly direction toward the Sioux Pass of the Big Horn Mountains." Now correctly defined as along the Red Fork of Powder River at the eastern edge of those mountains near Barnum, Johnson Co., Wyoming.

\# Lieutenant John A. McKinney, commanding Troop M in that engagement and the only commissioned officer killed in it.

Wirt Davis, then Captain, Company F, 4th Cavalry, received a Brevet Commission (February 27, 1890) as Lieutenant Colonel for gallant service in action in Texas (1872) and in the Dull Knife fight; and Walter S. Schuyler, then 1st Lieutenant, 5th Cavalry, a Brevet Commission (February 27, 1890) as Captain for gallantry in action in the Dull Knife fight -- Sergeant Forsyth's Medal of Honor and these two brevet commissions being the only official honors from that engagement.

Buried in Mount Hope Cemetery, 3751 Market Street, San Diego, California; Masonic Section P, Lot 5, Grave 6B. Photos from FindAGrave.com.

SERGEANT WILLIAM "BILLY" GRANT FOURNIER; ARMY

June 21, 1913 (Norwich, CT) – January 10, 1943; 29 years old
Unmarried
Enlisted on September 12, 1940, in Bangor, Maine.
Service number 11014123.
He also served in the Navy in the early 1930s under the name William Grant Gadrow.
Born to Alfred C. Sr. (1877-?) and Olive S. Gadrow Fournier (1874-1914). One brother, Alfred C. Jr. (1910-1939). Two half-brothers from his mother's first marriage, Charles Michaud (1897-1948) and Ernest Michaud (1905-1987). One half-sister, Olive Michaud Drake (1900-1983).

While still a baby, William was adopted by Henry (1873-1954) and Amelia A. Pashley Gadrow (1886-1937). He was raised with Theodore J. (1899-1979), Lawrence H. (1910-1944), Harold D. (1918-1962), Mary M. Gadrow Barker (1898-1954), and Lillian V. Gadrow Harford (1925-1990).

Namesake of VFW Post 916, 155 High Street, Wakefield, Rhode Island.

Photos courtesy of FindAGrave.com. Navy on the left, Army on the right.

MEDAL OF HONOR CITATION

AWARDED FOR ACTIONS DURING: World War II
BRANCH OF SERVICE: Army
UNIT: Company M, 35th Infantry Regiment, 25th Infantry Division
GENERAL ORDERS: War Department, General Orders No. 28 (June 5, 1943)
AGE ON THE DAY OF THE EVENT: 29
CITATION:

The President of the United States of America, in the name of Congress, takes pride in presenting the Medal of Honor (Posthumously) to Sergeant William Grant Fournier, United States Army, for gallantry and intrepidity above and beyond the call of duty on 10 January 1943, while serving with Company M, 35th Infantry Regiment, 25th Infantry Division, in action at Mount Austen, Guadalcanal, Solomon Islands. As leader of a machinegun section charged with the protection of other battalion units, his group was attacked by a superior number of Japanese, his gunner killed, his assistant gunner wounded, and an adjoining guncrew put out of action. Ordered to withdraw from this hazardous position, Sergeant Fournier refused to retire but rushed forward to the idle gun and, with the aid of another soldier who joined him, held up the machine gun by the tripod to increase its field action. They opened fire and inflicted heavy casualties upon the enemy. While so engaged, both these gallant soldiers were killed, but their sturdy defensive was a decisive factor in the following success of the attacking battalion.

Presentation Date and Details: October 28, 1943, at Rhode Island State College, presented by Major General Sherman Miles, Commanding General of the First Service Command, to Sergeant Fournier's foster father, Henry Gadrow of Wakefield, Rhode Island.

The inset photo is of Sergeant Fournier when he served in the Navy.
Left to right, Governor J. Howard McGrath, Major General Sherman Miles,
Henry Gadrow, Fournier's foster father, and two unknown Army officers.
Photo courtesy of the Providence Journal, October 29, 1943.

William Grant Fournier was born on June 21, 1913, to parents Olive Gadrow and Alfred Cyril Fournier in Norwich, Connecticut. Not much is known about his early life, as his mother passed away when he was roughly one year old on Christmas Day due to breast cancer.

According to his great-nephew, Fournier's father was not present in his life. Sometime after his mother's death, Fournier moved to live with his aunt, Amelia Pashley Gadrow, and uncle, Henry Gadrow. He grew up with his cousins around the town of South Kingstown. He attended grammar school until the eighth grade and eventually worked in a store installing radios. When he was 18, he moved to Maine to work as a hired hand and driver.

In 1931, Fournier enlisted in the U.S. Navy from Winterport, Maine. In 1937, his aunt and adopted mother passed away, and in 1939, his brother Alfred Cyril Fournier, Jr. died in an ice fishing accident. Just a year following the events, Fournier enlisted in the U.S. Army.

His great-nephew described him as a restless soul, someone who was trying to enjoy life and not take it too seriously during his travels in the Navy. Fournier served in the Navy for less than a decade, but he seemingly fell in love with the Pacific region. He eventually returned to Maine after leaving the Navy but did not stay there long.

In September 1940, Fournier re-enlisted, this time in the U.S. Army, with hopes to return to the Pacific. Sergeant Fournier was assigned to the 25th Infantry Division, 35th Infantry Regiment "The Cacti," Company M, and was stationed at the Schofield Barracks, Oahu, Hawaii. Following the Japanese attack on December 7, 1941, the American island-hopping campaign was put in motion. The 25th Infantry Division was deployed to Guadalcanal to relieve the first Marine Division. The 35th Infantry Regiment would soon find themselves located on a ridge referred to as "Sea Horse" and were tasked with attacking a Japanese defensive line and setting up a line of their own.

This American line fell under Japanese attack on January 8, 1943, and on January 10, in an attempt to stop the Japanese from flanking the regiment, Sergeant Fournier and the rest of his patrol opened machine gun fire onto the attacking Japanese. The Japanese were on the verge of overrunning the patrol, and a retreat was called for due to almost everybody in the patrol being wounded by the attackers.

Sergeant Fournier and Technician Fifth Grade Lewis R. Hall, some of the only non-wounded men, did not withdraw and instead worked together to lift a machine gun, aim the muzzle, and operate the trigger. Their efforts killed 46 Japanese soldiers and broke the attack.

Technician Fifth Grade Lewis R. Hall was killed helping Sergeant Fournier hold the line, and Sergeant Fournier died three days later due to the wounds he received protecting his vulnerable brothers in arms. Sergeant Fournier was posthumously awarded the Medal of Honor, Purple Heart, Combat Infantryman Badge, Asiatic-Pacific Service Medal, and the World War II Victory Medal. *(nhdsilentheroes.org)*

Sergeant Fournier's Medal of Honor was presented posthumously at an award ceremony at the University of Rhode Island in 1943, and his family donated it to the Veterans of Foreign Wars Post 916 in Wakefield, which has as its namesake William G. Fournier.

From The Bangor Daily News May 27, 1943

Winterport Man Recommended For Posthumous Award

WINTERPORT, May 26 – Stephen D. Perkins of this town has received a letter from the commander of the regiment in which Sergeant William G. Fournier was serving in the South Pacific when he was killed in action, expressing the sympathy of the officers and men of his regiment, and stating that his commanding officer had recommended that Sergeant Fournier be awarded a citation for extraordinary heroism in combat.

Sergeant Fournier, a native of Rhode Island, was employed by Mr. Perkins here several years ago. He had no close relatives. He was sent to Hawaii soon after his enlistment in September 1940 and was at Pearl Harbor at the time of the Japanese attack on December 7, 1941. He was killed in action on January 13, 1943.

The letter follows:

> *"My Dear Mr. Perkins:*
> *"By this time, you have, no doubt, received official notification that your friend, William G. Fournier, was killed in action on January 13, 1943. I am writing this letter to offer you the sincere sympathy of myself and the officers and men of your friend's regiment and to do what little I can to soften your grief.*
> *"Your friend was killed in brave performance of duty against the enemy. I assure you that you can be proud in the knowledge that his actions were willing, loyal, and courageous in making the noblest sacrifice a man can give – his life for his country. For his act of unselfish bravery, I have recommended that he be*

awarded a citation for extraordinary heroism in combat.

"Only in a small way can this letter ease your sorrow. You can be certain, however, that your grief is shared by those of us who lived and worked and fought with your friend as fellow soldiers. This pledge we make to you – we shall do our best to make certain that his sacrifice was not in vain.

Sincerely yours:
Robert B. McClure
Colonel, 35th Infantry, Commanding

From The Providence Journal October 29, 1943, with thanks to Cassidy Santos in the Robert L. Carothers Library & Learning Commons at the University of Rhode Island.

MEDAL OF HONOR AWARDED TO SERGEANT WILLIAM FOURNIER POSTHUMOUSLY AT KINGSTON.

Sergeant William G. Fournier, Wakefield leader of a machine gun section who was killed at Guadalcanal while inflicting such heavy casualties on superior forces of Japanese that the attack of his battalion later succeeded, was awarded posthumously the Congressional Medal of Honor at Rhode Island State College yesterday.

The 31-year-old soldier, whose manning of a machine gun after his regular gunner was killed and the assistant wounded, was termed "gallantry and intrepidity above and beyond the call of duty," brought the first award of the Congressional Medal of Honor to any Rhode Islander in this war.

Fourth to New Englander

It was the fourth such award to any New Englander in this war, and the ceremony, originally planned for Washington, was the first of its kind in New England in this war.

Major General Sherman Miles, the commanding general of the First Service Command for President Roosevelt and the War Department, pinned the medal on the coat of Sergeant Fournier's foster father, Henry Gadrow, of Wakefield.

Other members of the family, Governor J. Howard McGrath, college officials, and ranking military officers were present against the impressive background furnished as 1000 troops of the Narragansett Bay Harbor Defenses and the Army Specialized Training Program unit at Kingston stood at attention on the wind-swept athletic field. All classes at the college were suspended, and more than 500 students and former neighbors of the gallant soldier were in the stands.

Major Winthrop Reads Citation

As the citation, which told the story of Fournier's heroic last minutes, in which he disregarded all orders to retire, was read by Major Fred Winthrop, an aide to General Miles, the foster father stood proudly erect, looking straight ahead, except when his glance strayed to the wind-whipped flag.

The citation said Sergeant Fournier died last January 10 at Mount Austen, Guadalcanal, Solomon Islands, where "as a leader of a machine gun section, charged with the protection of other battalion units. His group was attacked by a superior number of Japanese. His gunner was killed, his assistant gunner was wounded, and an adjoining gun crew was put out of action. Ordered to withdraw from this hazardous position, Sergeant Fournier refused to retire but rushed forward to the idle gun and, with the aid of another soldier who joined him, held up the machine gun by the tripod to increase its field action.

Both Soldiers Killed

"They opened fire and inflicted heavy casualties upon the enemy. While so engaged, both these gallant soldiers were killed, but their sturdy defensive was a decisive factor in the following success of the attacking battalion." The citation was signed by Secretary of War Henry L. Stimson.

Battalions from Fort Greene, commanded by Lieutenant Colonel Francis Spry and headed by the 243rd Coast Artillery Band, marched onto the field shortly after 2 o'clock and after the official party was seated. Colonel Spry presented the troops to General Miles. Six hundred soldiers in the ASTP unit at State College were massed in battalion formation behind the reviewing party.

After the presentation of troops by the commanding officer, General Miles, Brigadier General Thomas E. Trolland, commanding officer of the Fifth District, comprising the State of Rhode Island; Governor McGrath; Major George W. Gage, commandant at State College; Dr. Harold W. Browning, vice president of the college, representing Dr. Carl R. Woodward, president. who is in Chicago attending a national conference of the American Association of Land Grant Colleges, and other Army officers trooped the line.

Presentation of Award

This formality was followed by the presentation of the award to Mr. Gadrow. After the reading of the citation, arms were presented, and the band played the National Anthem. Then General Miles stepped out of the line to pin the medal upon Mr. Gadrow.

Members of the family who were the honored guests, besides Mr. Gadrow, were his wife, Mrs. Hulda I. Gadrow; a daughter, Mrs. Lillian N. Harford; a half-sister of Sergeant Fournier, Mrs. Clarice Drake; two half-brothers, Ernest Michaud, and Charles Michaud; a sister of Mr. Gadrow, Mrs. Agnes Holloway, and a brother, Levi Gadrow.

Others In the reviewing stand were Adjutant General Peter L. Cannon of the State of Rhode Island; Lieutenant Colonel Morton Smith, chief of the ASTP division of the First Service Command; Major Robert C Beckett. of the college ASTP; Captain Carl F. Haussler of the staff of General Trolland; Captain Margaret V. Knox, of the WAC, attached to General Trolland's staff; Staff Sergeants Frederick W. Guinness and John P. McConnon, and Rev. Leo P. McKenna, assistant pastor of St. Francis Church, Wakefield.

Initially buried in the Guadalcanal Cemetery. Repatriated and buried on January 28, 1949, in the National Memorial Cemetery of the Pacific (Punchbowl) 2177 Puowaina Drive, Honolulu, Hawaii; Section C, Grave 462. Photo courtesy of FindAGrave.com.

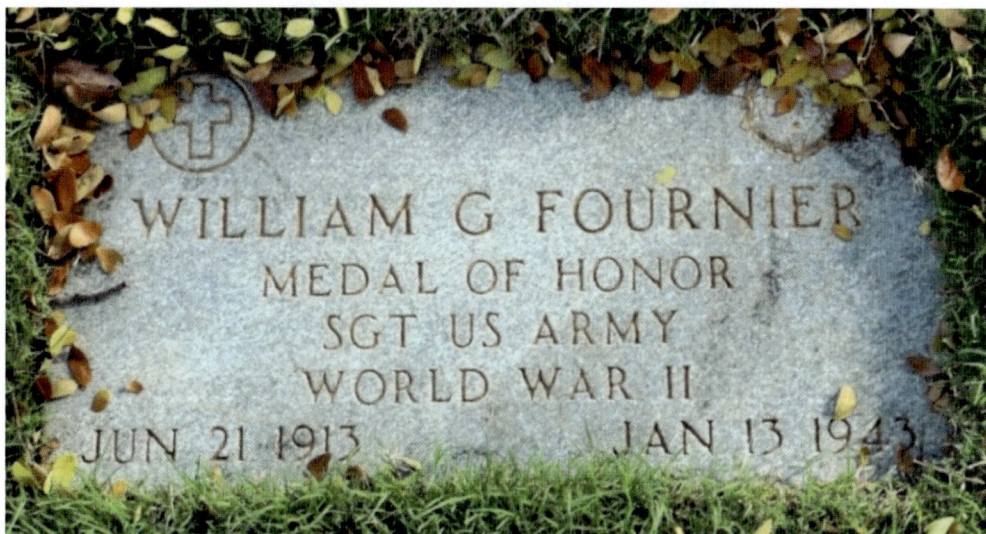

189

PRIVATE NICHOLAS FOX; ARMY

November 6, 1844 (Oldcastle, County Meath, Ireland) – October 2, 1929 (Port Chester, NY); 84 years old

Married to Catherine S. Simcox (1857-1923).

Five sons, Thomas G. (1872-?), Arthur L. (1880-1891), Gerald G. (1880-1943), Alfred E. (1888-1942), and Lester C. (1898-1986).

Eight daughters, Minnie (1874-1930), Florence E. (1876-?), Agnes G. Fox Gagan (1880-?), Frances C. (1881-?), Olivia (1886-?), Isabelle Fox Nugent (1887-?), Viola G. (1891-?), and Vera (1893-?).

Mustered into Company H, 28th Connecticut Infantry, on November 15, 1862, in New Haven, Connecticut.

Mustered out of the 28th Connecticut Infantry on August 28, 1863, in New Haven, Connecticut.

Enlisted in Company F, 22nd New York Cavalry, on April 5, 1865.

Mustered out on August 1, 1865, at Winchester, Virginia.

Born to Patrick (1798-1887) and Catherine Gibney Fox (1818-1891). Six brothers, John (1844-1930), Luke (1846-1921), Conrad (1852-1922), Patrick (1856-1892), Thomas (1859-1931), and James C. (1861-1931). Three sisters, Anne Fox Finn (1848-1929), Julia Fox Higgins (1851-1911), Margaret Fox Dorsey (1854-1922),

Photo courtesy of Ancestry.com

MEDAL OF HONOR CITATION

AWARDED FOR ACTIONS DURING: Civil War
BRANCH OF SERVICE: Army
UNIT: Company H, 28th Connecticut Infantry
DATE OF ISSUE AND PRESENTATION: April 1, 1898 (35 years later)
AGE ON THE DAY OF THE EVENT: 18
CITATION:

The President of the United States of America, in the name of Congress, takes pleasure in presenting the Medal of Honor to Private Nicholas Fox, United States Army, for extraordinary heroism on 14 June 1863, while serving with Company H, 28th Connecticut Infantry, in action at Port Hudson, Louisiana. Private Fox made two trips across an open space, in the face of the enemy's concentrated fire, and secured water for the sick and wounded.

From The Port Chester Journal April 7, 1898

NICHOLAS FOX HONORED
He Was a Brave Soldier Under Rebel Fire

In these times of agitation and war, removed from the piping times of peace, it is most pleasurable to recall the heroic act of a Port Chester resident and the tardy acknowledgment of the government of the United States. Nearly 35 years ago, Nicholas Fox, our fellow citizen of North Main Street, Past Commander of Charles Lawrence Post No. 378 Grand Army of the Republic, and for many years, one of the Superintendents of the Russell, Burdsall & Ward factory at Pemberwick, almost gave up his life that he might alleviate the sufferings of comrades and preserve their lives.

The story of Mr. Fox's valor forms a chapter of much interest. Like the brave boys who responded to their country's call, Mr. Fox, in the early sixties, joined Company H, 28th Regiment, Connecticut Infantry. It was the lot of his company in 1863 to be a part of the army that was selected to force the surrender of Port Hudson, Louisiana, or capture it by assault. The mere statement of facts can hardly convey what the undertaking was. Port Hudson, like Vicksburg, was a Sebastopol. It was a fortified town on a high bluff overlooking the Mississippi River, and the army of invasion was forced to fight their way up a steep declivity with the furious fire of the enemy falling like a hurricane of lead and iron in their faces. On June 14, 1863, was made one of the gallant attacks on Port Hudson, and the Union Army was repulsed with severe consequences. Many of the boys of the 28th Connecticut Infantry fell in that charge, and some of them badly wounded and laid between the rebel fortifications and the redoubts where the besieging Federal soldiers were. The day was one of those sultry, burning days only found in the South, and the suffering of the Federal wounded under rebel guns was frightful. The cries of the unfortunates were heart-rending. Several parties were formed and made an effort to relieve their comrades, but almost as fast as they crossed the Union fortification, they were shot and killed by rebel sharpshooters. This necessarily made a few of the boys anxious to try to relieve their unfortunate comrades. Yet after the deadly bullets had worked such havoc, Private Nicholas Fox volunteered to go to the rescue of the wounded. Securing all the canteens he could find, he filled them with water, and weight down almost beyond his capacity, he made a dash for the field where lay the wounded, and though he twice repeated the daring errand, he escaped unhurt, In his work, Mr. Fox was also able to save the life of Colonel Payne, whom he found in the dangerous ground seriously wounded and was able later to lead a rescuing party to the officer's relief.

From an Act of Congress passed in 1863, Mr. Fox was entitled to a medal for bravery because his act of heroism had been publicly announced in the order of the General of his Brigade. A sense of delicacy prevented Mr. Fox from obtaining the medal that was his due, though finally importuned by friends and relatives, he made an application, according to the Act of Congress before alluded to, for a medal of merit. The application was first intended to be placed in the hands of ex-Congressman Fairchild, but after consuming considerable time, the application was given to Congressman Ward. The matter dragging, Mr. Fox thought it more proper that the application should be placed in the hand of Congressman Hill of Connecticut, from whose District Mr. Fox had enlisted. The Connecticut Congressman was not long in securing Mr. Fox what the Government had promised all those who had distinguished themselves in the service.

On March 23, 1898, Mr. Fox received the following communication:

SUBJECT: -- Medal of Honor.
WAR DEPARTMENT
WASHINGTON
File No. – R. & P. 608,474 March 22, 1898
Mr. Nicholas Fox, Port Chester, N.Y.
Sir: --

You are hereby notified that by direction of the President and under the provisions of the Act of Congress approved March 3, 1863, providing for the presentation of Medals of Honor to such officers, non-commissioned officers, and privates a have most distinguished themselves in action, A CONGRESSIONAL MEDAL OF HONOR has this day been presented to you for MOST DISTINGUISHED GALLANTRY in action, the following being a statement of the particular service, viz:

"At Port Hudson, Louisiana, June 15, 1863, this soldier, then a private in Company H, 28th Connecticut Volunteers, participated in the assault on the enemy's works, but the troops were repulsed, leaving between the lines many wounded who were helpless and exposed to the enemy's fire and the heat of the sun. After several men had been killed in attempting to relieve the sufferings of the wounded, Fox volunteered to carry water to them and, loading himself with canteens, made two trips in plain view and under the hot fire of the enemy, his act being praised at the time by his brigade commander."

The medal will be forwarded to you by registered mail as soon as it shall have been engraved.
Respectfully,
R.A. ALGER
Secretary of War."

Saturday afternoon, the medal, a handsome bronze affair made by Tiffany, reached Mr. Fox. It is a five-pointed star about two inches from one extreme point to another and is dependent from a bar and attached to a ribbon of the national colors, but consisting of a narrow white stripe in the center, with a broad blue stripe each side of the white, and red stripes of equal width with the blue on the outside. The ribbon, depending from the bar, is about one inch wide. The bar is a shield. In the center of the two ornate corners, with laurel branches on each side of the shield. An eagle with outstretched wings, having in its talons two unmounted guns and a pyramid of balls, surmounts the star, which has two figures on its face, on an ideal picture of the Goddess of Mercy, with a shield in her arm extended over the half prostrate body of a man. Following in the inscription on the reverse of the medal:

THE CONGRESS TO
PRIVATE NICHOLAS FOX
Co. H., 28th Conn. Inf.
For GALLANTRY at
Port Hudson, La.
June 14, 1863.

It is fortunate that Mr. Fox is long-lived, or he might have never had the satisfaction of looking upon the medal and the autograph.

From The Daily Item (Port Chester, NY) October 4, 1929

AN EARNED TRIBUTE

If, by any chance, Port Chester, through its civic officials and patriotic organizations, failed to pay notable tribute to the late Nicholas Fox when his remains are carried to their last resting place tomorrow, then Port Chester will have cause for shame. Few men in all the history of this community have so deserved the respect and admiration of their fellows.

Nicholas Fox was a poor man – had been poor all his days. Nor was he a powerful man in the sense that he had been able, by affluence or position, to exact the fawning regard of his neighbors. In a word, there was nothing about him to exact tribute – but there was much about him which did and does deserve tribute. The extent of the symbolic respect which we pay him, dead, will be the measure of our community's character.

A mere boy, not long since he arrived in this country from his native Old World country, he responded to the call of Lincoln for defenders of the Union. The spirit of American patriotism burned in his mind and heart. His surpassing bravery in devotion to his adopted flag won for him the highest honor which personal valor can win for an American – the Congressional Medal of Honor, conferred by an act of the national legislature and illuminated by the personal praise of the President of the United States. Only a handful of men in all the wars in all the history of the United States achieved such distinction. In spirit and example, therefore, Nicholas Fox was a truly great American.

But there is even more about the record of Nicholas Fox's life to commend him to our esteem – in civilian life, he typified the homely virtues which have made this one of the most powerful nationals of all time. He married early and established a home and a family to which he gave unaltering loyalty until the moment of his death. He was intelligent and industrious in his daily toil and supremely loyal to his employers – for seventy-two years, almost three-quarters of a century. He was a dependable, valuable factor in a great industry, contributing to his usefulness in the scheme of American life. Citizens such as him determine and sustain the character of a nation.

True, Nicholas Fox has passed beyond the cognizance of worldly honors – there is now nothing Port Chester can do for him. The tribute we offer him now can have naught of value to him – but will have great value to us and to those who will come after him and us. Whether or not the native and naturalized Americans in Port Chester express their appreciation of the fundamental virtues Nicholas Fox possessed will decide for countless young people and for many older people new to the life and customs of this country whether or not they shall deem it worthwhile to emulate him.

Nicholas Fox deserves our tribute because he has earned it – he commands it because we, as patriots, are bound in the circumstances of our American citizenship to demonstrate our faith in and fealty to the essentials of patriotism for which he stood. When we cease to appreciate heroes, we shall have lost the characteristics which make heroes.

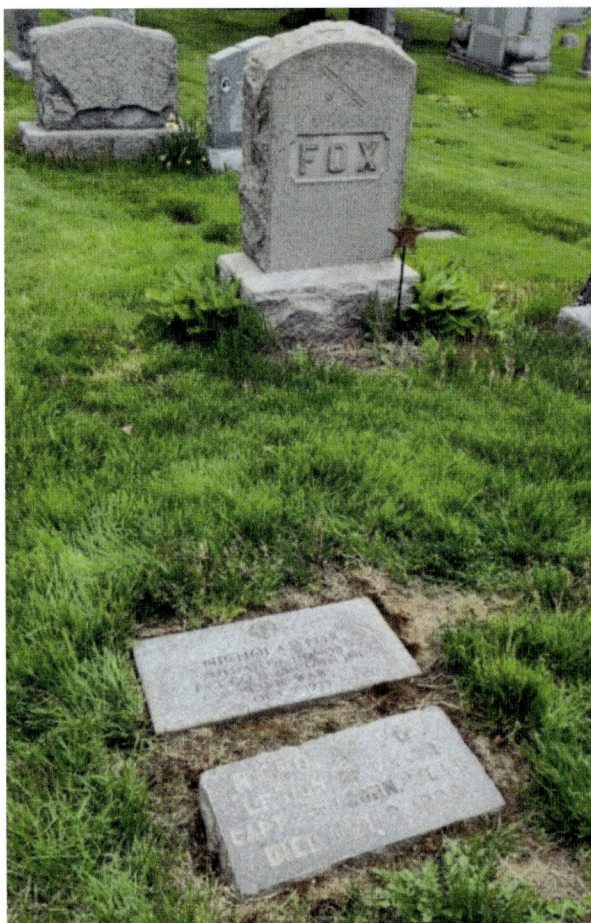

NICHOLAS FOX
MEDAL OF HONOR
PVT CO H 28 CONN INF
CIVIL WAR
OCT 2 1929

CORPORAL* FRANK ROCCO FRATELLENICO; ARMY

* Posthumously promoted to Corporal

July 14, 1951 (Sharon, CT) – August 19, 1970; 19 years old
Unmarried
Enlisted on September 23, 1969, in Albany, New York.
Service number: 069440577.
Tour Start Date May 5, 1970.
MOS: 11B10, Infantryman.
On The Wall at Panel 08W, Line 124.
Home of Record: Chatham, New York.

Born to Joseph [WWII Navy veteran] (1928-1995) and Marie Xicart Fratellenico (1928-2001). One sister, Donna M. (1952-1989).
Also received the Purple Heart Medal and is on the Roll of Honor at the National Purple Heart Museum in Vail's Gate, New York. In addition, he received the Bronze Star, Army Commendation, Good Conduct, National Defense Service, and Vietnam Service Medals.

Photo (left) courtesy of the Congressional Medal of Honor Society. Photo (right) courtesy of Facebook.

1968 Chatham (NY) High School photo. Corporal Fratellenico is on the far right of 2nd row. His sister Diane is seated in the middle of the first row.

MEDAL OF HONOR CITATION

AWARDED FOR ACTIONS DURING: Vietnam War
BRANCH OF SERVICE: Army
UNIT: Company B, 2nd Battalion, 502nd Infantry Regiment, 1st Brigade, 101st Airborne Division
GENERAL ORDERS: Department of the Army, General Orders No. 37 (September 6, 1974)
AGE ON THE DAY OF THE EVENT: 20
CITATION:

The President of the United States of America, in the name of Congress, takes pride in presenting the Medal of Honor (Posthumously) to Corporal Frank Rocco Fratellenico, United States Army, for conspicuous gallantry and intrepidity at the risk of his life above and beyond the call of duty while serving as a rifleman with Company B, 2nd Battalion, 502nd Infantry Regiment, 1st Brigade, 101st Airborne Division, in action against enemy aggressor forces at Fire Base Barnett, Quang Tri Province, Republic of Vietnam, on 19 August 1970. Corporal Fratellenico's squad was pinned down by intensive fire from two well-fortified enemy bunkers. At great personal risk, Corporal Fratellenico maneuvered forward and, using hand grenades, neutralized the first bunker, which was occupied by a number of enemy soldiers. While attacking the second bunker, enemy fire struck Corporal Fratellenico, causing him to fall to the ground and drop a grenade which he was preparing to throw. Alert to the imminent danger to his comrades, Corporal Fratellenico retrieved the grenade and fell upon it an instant before it exploded. His heroic actions prevented death or serious injury to four of his comrades nearby and inspired his unit, which subsequently overran the enemy position. Corporal Fratellenico's conspicuous gallantry, extraordinary heroism, and intrepidity at the cost of his life, above and beyond the call of duty, are in keeping with the highest traditions of the military service and reflect great credit on him, his unit, and the United States Army.

Presentation Date and Details: August 8, 1974, at the Blair House, presented by Vice President Gerald R. Ford to his family. **AUTHOR NOTE:** This was the same day Richard Nixon resigned as President.

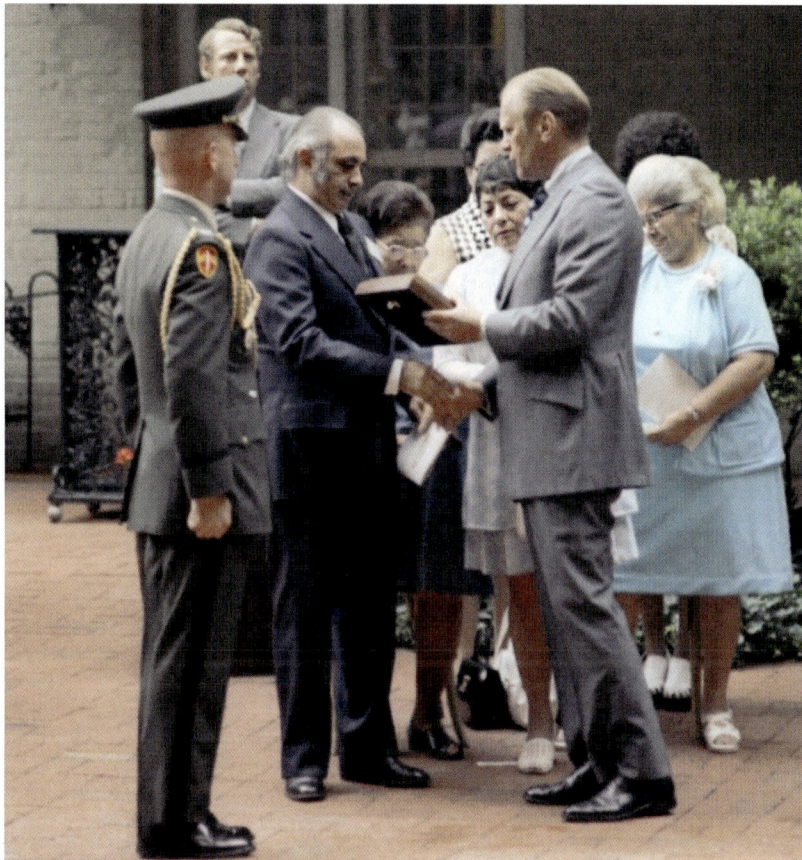

Photo contributed by Elizabeth Druga, Archivist, Gerald R. Ford Presidential Library and Museum.
From left to right, an unknown Army officer and an unknown person behind him.
Corporal Fratellenico's father, Joseph, his mother, Marie, an unknown woman, President Ford,
and an unknown woman in the blue dress.

From the Register-Star (Hudson, NY) August 14, 1974

CHATHAM - One month and five days after his 19th birthday, Frank R. Fratellenico of Chatham died in a remote jungle of Vietnam, sacrificing his life so four comrades would live, an action that four years later brought him the Medal of Honor.

Established by a Joint Resolution of Congress on July 12, 1862, the nation's highest award has been bestowed upon only one other Columbia County serviceman, Civil War Calvary Capt. John W. Blunt.

One of the latest awards was presented posthumously to the young soldier's parents by then Vice President Gerald Ford in ceremonies at the Blair House in Washington, D.C.

In August 1970, Joseph and Jenny Fratellenico of Route 203 were notified by military authorities that their only son had received fatal wounds during combat.

Military officials again visited the wood-framed farmhouse to inform them "Frankie" had been nominated for the medal. However, it was not until minutes before the ceremony that the Fratellenicos learned the nature of their son's heroic deed. "... for conspicuous gallantry and intrepidity in action at the risk of his life above and beyond the call duty in the Republic of Vietnam."

The citation says: "Corporal Frank R. Fratellenico distinguished himself on August 19, 1970, while serving as a rifleman with Company B, 2nd Battalion, 502nd Infantry, 1st Brigade, 101st Airborne Division."

"During an assault that day against a North Vietnamese Army company near Fire Base Barnett, Quang Tri Province, Corporal Fratellenico's squad was pinned down by intensive fire from two well-fortified enemy bunkers."

"At great personal risk, Corporal Fratellenico maneuvered forward and, using hand grenades, neutralized the first bunker, which was occupied by a number of enemy soldiers."

"While attacking the second bunker, enemy fire struck Corporal Fratellenico, causing him to fall to the ground and drop a grenade which he was preparing to throw. Alert to imminent danger to his comrades, Corporal Frank Fratellenico retrieved the grenade and fell upon it an instant before it exploded."

"His heroic actions prevented death or serious injury to four of his comrades nearby and inspired his unit, which subsequently overran the enemy position."

"Corporal Fratellenico's conspicuous gallantry, extraordinary heroism, and intrepidity at the cost of his life, above and beyond the call of duty, are in keeping with the highest traditions of the military service and reflect great credit to him, his unit, and the United States Army."

Two months prior to his death, the young Chatham GI had displayed similar courage by subjecting himself to hostile fire while enabling his squad to capture one enemy sniper and silence another.

For that action, Corporal Fratellenico was presented with the Bronze Star.

The teenage soldier was born in Sharon, Connecticut, on July 14, 1951, and at the age of eight, moved with his parents and three sisters to Chatham.

A slim, muscular youth, Corporal Fratellenico enjoyed hunting, having received his first rifle at the age of nine.

The youth quit Chatham Central School while in the 11th grade and enlisted in the Army in 1969.

Following basic training at Fort Dix, New Jersey, Frank underwent advanced training at Fort Gordon, Georgia.

Following the footsteps of his father and uncles, he then volunteered for airborne training, undertaking the rigorous paratrooper course at Fort Benning, Georgia.

He was assigned in May 1970 to Vietnam, where his 11-month military career ended a short time later.

The Fratellenico family is a close-knit group with a special relationship between father and son.

Joseph Fratellenico was reared in a tough East Harlem neighborhood and was fighting in the Army at the age of 15.

He is proud that he taught his son "how to use his hands...like my father taught me... Frankie was a fighting son of a gun, and he feared no one."

"He wanted to be the man his father was," Mrs. Fratellenico said, "he wanted to be strong and as tough as his father."

There was another side to the young soldier, a young man fighting for his life in the jungles of a faraway country who took the time to write "beautiful, lovely poems" to his mother.

Corporal Fratellenico also wrote personal letters to his father, the last one after the youth's 19th birthday.

The soldier's father keeps the letter in his nightstand and frequently rereads it.

The Medal of Honor filled the parents with pride, cloaked with sorrow, "as many old memories were brought back...it wasn't easy."

Fratellenico was unable to place into words the emotions he felt when learning of the award. "No words can express it...how can I tell you how beautiful the air is - I can't see it.

The award presentation was an emotional occasion for the parents and daughter Diane, but it was a memorable one.

What impressed the family most was "Jerry," Vice President Ford, who, 26 hours after the presentation, would become the 38th President of the United States.

The family arrived in Washington Wednesday as a guest of the government, housed near the White House.

They met President Ford "casually" before the presentation. After the awards, however, the Vice President took his time and mingled with the guests.

101st Airborne, 2nd Brigade gymnasium is named in his honor. Photo contributed by Bernetta Prather, Fort Campbell, Kentucky.

From vvmf.org, posted on June 25, 1999, by James A. (Tony) Woods, Sergeant Major, US Army (retired)

Rest in Peace, Brave Soldier: I was Rocky's Squad Leader the day he died. He and I were clearing a bunker complex, going from one to the other, taking turns. There are very few days or weeks that go by that I don't think of him and that day. One of many we try to forget. But not the people. August 19, 1970, at about 11:30 a.m.

From vvmf.org, posted on May 29, 2006, by Dick Hudson

Unlikely Hero: I have learned a lot about life and heroes from Frank's death. I served with him in training at Fort Gordon, Georgia. We didn't treat him very good because he was cocky, and thought he was tough. Truth is, he ended up being tough.

I wish we had treated him better. I was as close as anyone to being a friend to him in AIT. But he was hard to get to know.

I have learned not to judge others. We never know who is gonna come through in the clutch. I only hope I will be as courageous as him if my turn ever happens.

I miss him and think of him a lot.

From vvmf.org, posted on August 31, 2014, by George R. Kern.

Tragic Loss of a Friend: Frank and I were from the same small town in upstate NY. We attended the same high school, and I knew him well. I had done my tour a year before him and was a couple of weeks from ETS when Frank was killed. His family was devastated, especially his dad, who had been hard on him. I used to pass by his gravesite a lot and always wondered how he would have turned out had he survived. I still think of him from time to time.

Memorial marker to Corporal Fratellenico in front of St. Peter's Presbyterian Church, 5219 County Road 7, Chatham, New York. Photo by the author.

In May 1985, he was reinterred to his father's private land in Spencertown, New York. From the Berkshire Eagle on May 25, 1985:

10—The Berkshire Eagle, Saturday, May 25, 1985

Alan Solomon

CONGRESSIONAL MEDAL OF HONOR recipient Frank R. Fratellenico, who died in Vietnam Aug. 19, 1970, was buried in new grave yesterday in Spencertown, N.Y., with ceremony conducted by local posts of Veterans of Vietnam War and American Legion. Fratellenico was only Columbia County recipient of the Medal of Honor since the Civil War. The soldier covered exploding grenade with his own body to save his buddies. To right of firing squad is his father, Joseph Fratellenico, and stepmother, Daehanne. New grave is on father's private land and required permission from governor. Memorial is planned.

In 1997, likely because of the death of his father in 1995, Corporal Fratellenico's remains were exhumed and cremated, and his ashes were taken to Thailand.

CAPTAIN WILLIAM S. GARVIN; NAVY

1835 (Canada) * – unknown

* One of 30 Canadians who received the Medal of Honor.

Enlisted in the Army on February 24, 1864, in Bridgeport, Connecticut.
Assigned to the Connecticut, 8th Infantry, Company H.
Transferred to the Navy on May 4, 1864, in Plymouth, Connecticut.
Discharged from the Navy on January 29, 1866, in Fair Oaks, Virginia.

As "Captain of the Forecastle" on the U.S.S. Agawam, William Garvin was in charge of the anchors as well as the head sails.

MEDAL OF HONOR CITATION

AWARDED FOR ACTIONS DURING: Civil War
BRANCH OF SERVICE: Navy
ASSIGNED TO: U.S.S. Agawam
GENERAL ORDERS: War Department, General Orders No. 45 (December 31, 1864)
AGE ON THE DAY OF THE EVENT: 28 of 29
CITATION:

The President of the United States of America, in the name of Congress, takes pleasure in presenting the Medal of Honor to Captain of the Forecastle William Garvin, United States Navy, for extraordinary heroism in action while serving on board the U.S.S. Agawam, as one of a volunteer crew of a powder boat which was exploded near Fort Fisher, North Carolina, 23 December 1864. The powder boat, towed in by the Wilderness to prevent detection by the enemy, cast off and slowly steamed to within 300 yards of the beach. After fuses and fires had been lit and a second anchor with short scope let go to assure the boat's tailing inshore, the crew again boarded the Wilderness and proceeded a distance of 12 miles from shore. Less than two hours later, the explosion took place, and the following day, fires were observed still burning at the fort.

AUTHOR NOTE: One of five recipients of the Medal of Honor from Connecticut who were aboard the U.S.S. Agawam. The others were Robert Montgomery, John Neil, James Roberts, and James Sullivan.

U.S.S. Agawam (1864-1867). In the James River, Virginia, July 1864. Photographed by Brady & Company, Washington, D.C. Collection of Surgeon Herman P. Babcock, USN. Donated by his son, George R. Babcock, in 1939. U.S. Naval History and Heritage Command Photograph.

No other information is known about William Garvin's life.

SERGEANT WESLEY GIBBS; ARMY

July 24, 1842 (Sharon, CT) – May 29, 1917 (Winsted, CT); 74 years old

Married Mary Flannagan (1847-1910).

Two sons, Wilber A. (1876-1878) and William H. (1885-?).

Four daughters, Bertha E. Gibbs Alling (1871-?), Blanche Gibbs Boorom (1884-1955), Alice Gibbs Brothwell (1881-1962), and Anna Gibbs Eaton (1888-1978).

Enlisted on August 8, 1862, and assigned to the 19th Connecticut Infantry, Company B, which was redesignated the 2nd Heavy Artillery

Reduced to the rank of Private on June 16, 1865, for an unknown cause

Mustered out on July 7, 1865.

Born to Lemuel III (1790-1872) and Beulah Boland Gibbs (1799-1866). Nine brothers, George W. (1818-1900), Homer A. (1822-1885), Myron B. [died in the Civil War and is interred in Andersonville, Georgia] (1825-1864), Francis J. (1828-1861), Goodrich S. (1830-1883), John B. (1832-1873), Eber S. (1833-1907), Henry H. (1836-1838), and Henly L. (1839-1842). One sister, Lydia M. Gibbs Pendleton (1820-1892).

Photo courtesy of Wikimedia Commons. Public domain.

MEDAL OF HONOR CITATION

AWARDED FOR ACTIONS DURING: Civil War

BRANCH OF SERVICE: Army

UNIT: Company B, 2nd Connecticut Heavy Artillery

DATE OF ISSUE AND PRESENTATION: May 10, 1865

AGE ON THE DAY OF THE EVENT: 22

CITATION:

The President of the United States of America, in the name of Congress, takes pleasure in presenting the Medal of Honor to Sergeant Wesley Gibbs, United States Army, for extraordinary heroism on 2 April 1865, while serving with Company B, 2nd Connecticut Heavy Artillery, in action at Petersburg, Virginia, for capture of flag.

Excerpts From One Medal of Honor Too Many at the Breakthrough; Edward Alexander

Sergeant Wesley Gibbs, 2nd Connecticut Heavy Artillery, who was a deserved recipient of the Medal of Honor, though not for the battle stated on his citation.

In August 1862, Gibbs enlisted into Company B of the 19th Connecticut Infantry. This unit was sent to the Washington defenses and redesignated the 2nd Heavy Artillery. They remained in the nation's capital until the middle of May 1864, when the heavy losses of the Overland Campaign necessitated the transition back to infantry and transfer into the field.

For their brave actions, on April 2, 1865, thirty-six members of the corps received the Medal of Honor. Sergeant Wesley Gibbs is counted among this. His citation stated that he received it for the capture of a flag on April 2, 1865. Thirteen others in Horatio Wright's VI Corps received the medal for capturing a Confederate flag that day. All of those cases can be properly verified, but a clerical error incorrectly placed Gibbs among that number.

But Wright had forwarded on April 16th a list of flags captured by the VI Corps in the engagements on the 2nd and 6th. This was the first time it was stated: "Battle-flag (regiment unknown), captured by Sergeant Wesley Gibbs, Company B, Second Connecticut Heavy Artillery, in the enemy's works near Petersburg, April 2, 1865."

Wright's adjutant must have bungled the dates, which affected Gibbs' Medal citation and ought to bring the Medal of Honor recipients for the Breakthrough down to a *measly* thirty-five. The "smoking gun" in this admittedly boring investigation into a clerical error is a September 23, 1906 article in the *Springfield Republican* – "Medal of Honor Legion Holds Annual Meeting This Week–Story of Modest Man and Lost Medal."

The correspondent interviewed the veteran Gibbs and reported, "during the memorable attack on Gen. Lee at Sailor's Creek, VA., April 6, 1865, Gibbs rushed from the Connecticut ranks in front of the 121st New York and captured a rebel flag, carrying half the staff away with him under fire."

The Museum of the Confederacy now preserves the flag captured by Gibbs on April 6, 1865

As the title of the article implies, Gibbs didn't care much for the medal he was issued on May 10, 1865. He had been summoned along with the other recipients in the corps to Washington and received a thirty-day furlough from Secretary of War Edwin M. Stanton. After his return to the regiment, Adjutant Theodore F. Vaill called the men out and presented Gibbs with his medal. "I didn't want it, but the adjutant insisted on my accepting it and pinned it on me," Gibbs recalled.

A friend, Henry Ayres, had received a furlough and would be passing by the Gibbs' house in Salisbury, Connecticut, on his way home. Wesley asked if Henry could take the medal and give it to his mother. Gibbs was then demoted to private, for reasons unknown, just before his own mustering out of the army.

When he returned home, his mother said she had seen neither Ayres nor the medal. Ayres confessed that he had indeed lost the medal but was unsure where. Gibbs let the matter pass until the turn of the twentieth century when he advertised the loss in the *National Tribune*. In 1905, he received a response from Pennsylvania veteran John M. Berry, who had found the medal in a knapsack at a Washington train station on his way home from the war. "Though lost to me more than 40 years, I never bothered my head about the medal," Gibbs admitted.

From The Hartford Courant May 24, 1905

SOLDIER GETS TRACK OF LONG LOST MEDAL
Winsted Veteran Locates His Property in Pennsylvania

(Special to The Courant.)
Winsted, May 23.

Wesley Gibbs of this place, who was a Sergeant in Company B, Second Connecticut Heavy Artillery, has succeeded, after a forty years' search, in getting track of a medal which was presented to him for an act of bravery during the Civil War.

Mr. Gibbs, at the battle of Cedar Creek, shortly before the close of the war, captured a Confederate flag for which Congress awarded him a medal. The medal was pinned to his coat by Adjutant Vaill, who now resides in Litchfield. An item in the "National Tribune" was the first intimation Mr. Gibbs had of the whereabouts of the medal, which he had given to a comrade to care for. The item Mr. Gibbs read was:

"Comrade Jonn M. Berry, Eighteenth Regiment, P. R. C., of Eighty Four, Pennsylvania, has a medal belonging to Sergeant Wesley Gibbs, Company B, Second Connecticut Heavy Artillery, which he would return to this soldier or his friends."

Mr. Gibbs wrote to Comrade Berry and hopes to secure the medal in a few days.

<hr>

From The Hartford Courant June 3, 1905

Wesley Gibbs of Main Street received a medal yesterday, which had been lost to him for over forty years. The medal was given to Mr. Gibbs, then a sergeant in Company B, Second Connecticut Heavy Artillery, for an act of bravery, that of capturing a Confederate flag during the battle of Cedar Creek. Congress awarded him a medal for this act, and he afterward placed it in the hands of a comrade to bring home to his mother. The medal never reached Winsted, and Mr. Gibbs had no intimation of its whereabouts until a few days ago when he noted an item in the "National Tribune" that John M. Berry of Eighty-Four, Pennsylvania, had a medal belonging to Sergeant Wesley Gibbs. Mr. Gibbs wrote to Mr. Berry and received the medal yesterday. He says that it is a great satisfaction to recover the medal, for he prizes it highly.

<hr>

Buried in Forest View Cemetery, 171 Rowley Street, Winsted, Connecticut; GAR Section. Photos by the author.

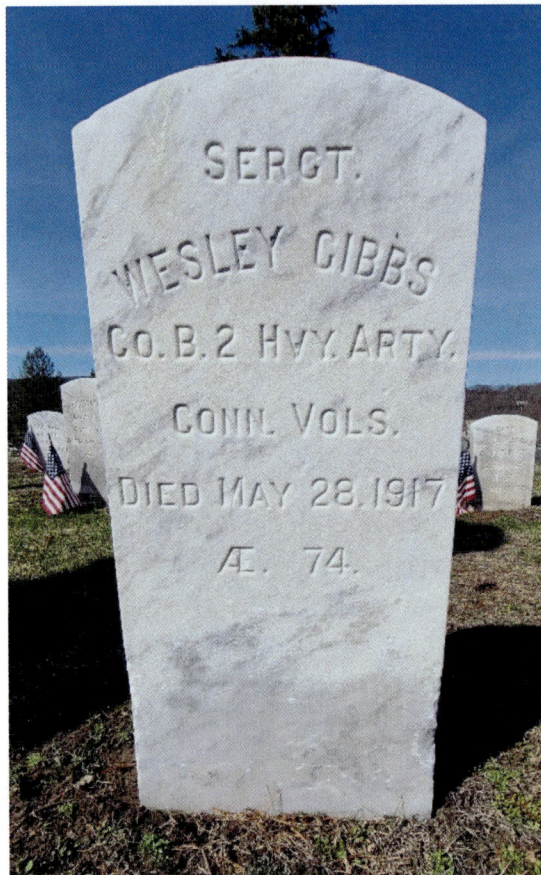

FIRST LIEUTENANT DONALD JOSEPH GOTT; ARMY AIR FORCE

June 3, 1923 (Arnett, OK) – November 9, 1944 (Hattonville, France); 21 years old
Unmarried
Enlisted on September 21, 1942, in Hartford, Connecticut.
Serial number O-763966

Born to Joseph E. (1880-1959) and Mary L. Hanlon Gott (1887-1978). Two brothers, Clarence (1912-1913) and Otto J. (1918-1983). Two sisters, Hazel C. Gott Peil (1910-1991) and Lucile M. Gott Compton (1914-1986).

When Donald Gott registered for the draft on June 30, 1942, he worked at U.S. Aluminum Company at 2190 Post Road in Bridgeport, Connecticut. On his draft card, he listed his mailing address as 905 Howard Avenue in Bridgeport.

Also, the recipient of the Air Medal with three oak leaf clusters, the Purple Heart Medal, the European-African-Middle Eastern Campaign Medal with two Bronze Service Stars for participation in the Northern France and Rhineland Campaigns, and the World War II Victory Medal.

MEDAL OF HONOR CITATION

AWARDED FOR ACTIONS DURING: World War II
BRANCH OF SERVICE: Army Air Forces
ASSIGNED TO: 729th Bombardment Squadron 452nd Bombardment Group, 8th Air Force
GENERAL ORDERS: War Department, General Orders No. 38 (May 16, 1945)
AGE ON THE DAY OF THE EVENT: 20
CITATION:

The President of the United States of America, in the name of Congress, takes pride in presenting the Medal of Honor (Posthumously) to First Lieutenant (Air Corps) Donald Joseph Gott (ASN: 0-763996), United States Army Air Forces, for conspicuous gallantry and intrepidity in action above and beyond the call of duty while serving with the 729th Bombardment Squadron, 452nd Bombardment Group (H), Eighth Air Force in action over Saarbrucken, Germany, on 9 November 1944. On a bombing run upon the marshaling yards at Saarbrucken, a B-17 aircraft piloted by First Lieutenant Gott was seriously damaged by anti-aircraft fire. Three of the aircraft's engines were damaged beyond control and on fire; dangerous flames from the No. 4 engine were leaping back as far as the tail assembly. Flares in the cockpit were ignited, and a fire raged therein, which was further increased by free-flowing fluid from damaged hydraulic lines. The interphone system was rendered useless. In addition to these serious mechanical difficulties, the engineer was wounded in the leg, and the radio operator's arm was severed below the elbow. Suffering from intense pain, despite the application of a tourniquet, the radio operator fell unconscious. Faced with the imminent explosion of his aircraft and death to his entire crew, mere seconds before bombs away on the target, First Lieutenant Gott and his copilot conferred. Something had to be done immediately to save the life of the wounded radio operator. The lack of a static line and the thought that his unconscious body striking the ground in unknown territory would not bring immediate medical attention forced a quick decision. First Lieutenant Gott and his copilot decided to fly the flaming aircraft to friendly territory and then attempt to crash land. Bombs were released on the target, and the crippled aircraft proceeded alone to Allied-controlled territory. When that had been reached, First Lieutenant Gott had the copilot personally inform all crewmembers to bail out. The copilot chose to remain with 1st Lieutenant Gott in order to assist in landing the bomber. With only one normally functioning engine and with the danger of explosion much greater, the aircraft banked into an open field, and when it was at an altitude of 100 feet, it exploded, crashed, exploded again, and then disintegrated. All three crewmembers were instantly killed. First Lieutenant Gott's loyalty to his crew, his determination to accomplish the task set forth to him, and his deed of knowingly performing what may have been his last service to his country was an example of valor at its highest.

Presentation Date and Details: June 18, 1945, to his mother, Mrs. Joseph Gott, by Major General Robert B. Williams, at Fargo High School, Fargo, Oklahoma

---

From The Daily Oklahoman June 8, 1945. Contributed by Carolyn Krumanocker, Library Technician, Oklahoma Historical Society, Oklahoma City, Oklahoma.

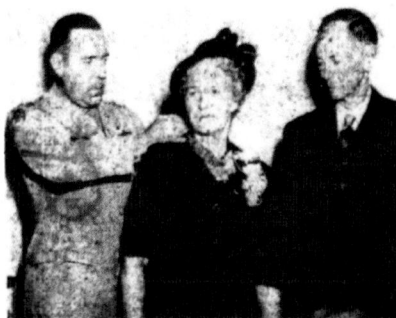

FARGO, June 17. – The nation's highest award, the Congressional Medal of Honor, was awarded Sunday posthumously in Fargo to Lieutenant Donald J. Gott, Ellis County bomber pilot who died trying to save the lives of injured crewmen during a raid on Saarbrucken, Germany, last November 9.

The medal was presented to Mrs. Joseph Gott, mother of the 21-year-old Lieutenant, here by Major General Robert B. Williams, Commanding General of the Second Air Force, in a simple but impressive ceremony in the Fargo High School auditorium where four years ago, her son had stood as valedictorian of his graduating class.

Friends and neighbors crowded the school auditorium to witness the presentation, the first ceremony of its kind ever held in Oklahoma.

"One who has never flown down the enemy flak alley or met enemy fighters cannot conceive of sustained courage, day after day, of our fliers such as Lieutenant Gott," General Williams said. "He truly lived up to the tradition of the air forces – mission complete."

And, as he prepared to lace the beribboned medal about the neck of Mrs. Gott, the Second Air Force Commander, himself, a veteran of the European air war, remarked, "I consider it a great honor to have been selected by General H.H. Arnold, Army Air Forces Commander, to represent the President of the United States in paying this tribute to Lieutenant Gott."

As the audience which overflowed the auditorium stood reverently, Captain John E. Jordan, Catholic Chaplain from Will Rogers Field, prayed, and a Will Rogers field bugler sounded Taps, many eyes were moist in memory of the farm youth who chose to fly his crippled B-17 bomber back from enemy territory in an attempt to make a crash landing that possibly would have saved the life of a badly wounded radio operator.

"We are here today to pay tribute to a gallant flier," Chaplain Jordan said. "Lieutenant Gott rose above the call of duty so conspicuously that our nation has bestowed upon him its highest honor."

The Ellis County youth, flying his 28th mission over German territory, was piloting a bomber over the Saarbrucken marshaling yards when enemy fire disabled three of the four motors, a citation by President Truman said.

The craft was damaged beyond control and was on fire. The engineer was wounded in the leg, and the radio operator's arm was severed below the elbow.

Knowing that the wounded radioman could not be parachuted to safety, Lieutenant Gott and the co-pilot decided to fly the flaming aircraft to friendly territory and attempt to crash land. Other crew members bailed out. Then, with their goal in sight, the plane exploded, crashed, and burned. The pilot, co-pilot, and radio operator were killed.

With the mother on the auditorium stage was the flier's father, Joseph Gott, Ellis County farmer of the Harmon community, his brother, O.J. Gott, Los Angeles aircraft plant mechanic, and two sisters, Mrs. Lucille Compton of Arnett, and Miss Hazel Gott of Los Angeles.

It was a proud day for Fargo, a farming community that has felt the war deeply, and at the same time, it was a sad one. Donald, popular as a student and a leader in his classes, was a favorite here.

After the presentation, other grey-haired mothers came to press Mrs. Gott's hand briefly.

"I pray every night that no more of our sons will have to go," one said.

After the ceremony, the parents and other relatives drove to the Woodward Army Airfield, where they inspected the B-17 bomber, which brought General Williams here from Colorado Springs. The visit to the field was at the request of Mrs. Gott, who was eager for others to see the big bomber, similar to the one Donald piloted.

The plane, an overseas veteran with patched flak holes along the fuselage, was piloted by General Williams on a trip here.

Taking off from the Woodward Field, the general wagged his wings at the crowd.

"Donald always said he would do that if he flew over our place," Mrs. Gott said. "But I told him not to."

The Gotts and their children will go to Oklahoma City next Tuesday for a second ceremony at Tinker Field. There, they will receive the Air Medal and oak-leaf clusters awarded posthumously to their son.

They will be guests at a luncheon at noon Tuesday at Will Rogers Field, with Colonel John E. Bodle, commanding officers, as their host.

Colonel and Lieutenant William M. Silbert, public relations officer at Will Rogers Field, arranged the ceremony here Sunday.

Crew Members of the Lady Jeanette, #42-97904

1st Lt Donald J. Gott, Pilot, Oklahoma, Medal of Honor, Air Medal, Purple Heart; **KIA**
2nd Lt William E. Metzger Jr., Copilot, Ohio, Air Medal, Purple Heart, Medal of Honor; **KIA**
2nd Lt Joseph F. Harms, Bombardier, New York, Air Medal, Purple Heart
2nd Lt John A. Harland, Navigator, Illinois, Air Medal, Purple Heart
TSgt Russell W. Gustafson, Flight Engineer, New York, Air Medal, Purple Heart
TSgt Robert A. Dunlap, Radio Operator, California, Air Medal with 2 Oak Leaf Clusters, Purple Heart; **KIA**
SSgt James O. Fross, Belly Gunner, Texas, Air Medal, Purple Heart
SSgt William R. Robbins, Gunner, Massachusetts, Air Medal
SSgt Herman B. Krimminger, Tail Gunner, North Carolina, Air Medal, Purple Heart; **KIA**

From "Air Support for Operation Madison" in Airman Magazine, 1961, Vol 5. Used with permission.

Two young men who were destined to fly side by side to immortality were among the new class of cadets reporting to preflight school at Santa Ana, California, on March 23, 1943.

From opposite sides of the nation, the two had traversed completely different paths to their initial meeting, and from this point forward, they would do likewise until once more united on an explosive ride to a common death.

The dual story of Donald Joseph Gott and William Edward Metzger, Jr., properly begins in the fall of 1942. On September 21, Don Gott, a native of Oklahoma, was sworn into the Enlisted Reserve Corps in the grade of Private and alerted to await his call for cadet training.

Exactly two weeks later, Bill Metzger was inducted from his native state of Ohio. Shortly after being assigned to the 83rd Ordnance Battalion at Camp Young, California, he, too, applied for cadet training.

Both men were called to begin their pursuit of wings and commission the following March. However, they were not destined to finish even this first phase of training together. By June, Cadet Gott had completed his first training phase and moved on to primary school at Glendale, Arizona. Illness, meanwhile, forced Cadet Metzger to remain behind, and it was not until July that he proceeded to primary at Twentynine Palms, California.

On January 7, 1944, Donald J. Gott was awarded pilot wings and was commissioned a second lieutenant upon graduation from advanced two-engine school at Stockton, California.

In the meantime, William E. Metzger, Jr., also continued with his training and finally graduated from the advanced school at Douglas Field, Arizona, on March 11, 1944. He, too, received pilot wings but was awarded the grade of flight officer rather than a commission.

Two weeks later, Lieutenant Gott completed another course and graduated with honors from B-17 transition school at Hobbs Field, New Mexico. Their diverging paths were now destined to take them even further apart when, late in July, Lieutenant Don Gott departed for England. While he underwent combat crew replacement training, Flight Officer Bill Metzger was being shuttled between several assignments within the Zone of the Interior (ZI).

On August 17, 1944, however, their paths, now widely separated, once more began to bend toward a meeting. On that date, Lieutenant Gott was assigned to the 729th Bombardment Squadron, 452nd Bomb Group.

Within days, he began his combat career, piling up mission after mission. Early in October, he passed the 20-mission mark, was promoted to First Lieutenant, and rightly laid claim to the title of veteran combat pilot. Having reached such a respected plateau in mid-October, he was selected to transition to a new arrival to his crew. The new copilot was Lieutenant William Metzger (he had been promoted in August.)

During the next two weeks, Metzger learned the ins and outs of combat at the side of his former preflight buddy and began to fit neatly into an already tightly knit group.

While this drama of limited scope was unfolding, one of much wider consequence was taking place on the battlefields of Continental Europe.

Allied ground forces had pushed deeper and deeper into Festung Europa (Fortress Europe) since D-Day and were now poised for the final drive into Germany proper. Early the second week in September, American forces penetrated the German wall at Aachen. By mid-October, Allied forces presented a solid front of advancing troops which threatened, at any moment, to erupt into a tidal wave which would inundate Hitler's Germany.

Allied commanders began to concentrate on support for these troops in the all-important breaching of the Rhine River. Among the coordinated efforts against this immediate goal was *Operation Madison*.

Launched from the Aachen area on November 8, 1944, the plan called for General George Patton's tank forces to exert pressure on both southern and northern flanks of the Metz salient. South of Metz, the XIIth Corps was to begin its drive northeastward toward the Rhine to establish a bridgehead in the Darmstadt area and, concurrently, north of Metz, the XXth Corps was to strike toward the Saar basin and the Mainz-Frankfurt area.

Major aerial support was to be flown to protect this two-pronged attack. In addition to P-38s, 51s, and 47s and the B-25s of the 9th Air Force, the B-17s and 24s of the 8th were also assigned a major role in this mission. Their primary aim was to attack east of the point of the drive "to neutralize enemy troops, destroy their defensive fortresses, and wipe out bridges, supply dumps, and similar installations."

On the morning of November 9, the second day of the drive, 1,295 B-17s and 24s attacked targets in the battle zone. Among them was the B-17 Flying Fortress piloted by Lieutenants Gott and Metzger.

Their immediate objective was Thionville, but since visual bombing proved to be impossible in this area, 308 of the Forts were diverted to secondary targets in the marshaling yards at Saarbrucken.

Identical citations, contained in General Order 38, published on May 16, 1945, contain a graphic description of the action which involved the Gott-Metzger B17.

On a bombing run upon the marshaling yards at Saarbrucken, a B-17 aircraft piloted by Lieutenant Gott was seriously damaged by anti-aircraft fire. Three of the aircraft's engines were damaged beyond control and on fire; dangerous flames from the No. 4 engine were leaping back as far as the tail assembly. Flares in the cockpit were ignited, and a fire raged therein, which was further increased by free-flowing fluid from damaged hydraulic lines. The interphone system was rendered useless. In addition to these serious mechanical difficulties, the engineer was wounded in the leg, and the radio operator's arm was severed below the elbow. Suffering from intense pain, despite the application of a tourniquet, the radio operator fell unconscious. Faced with the imminent explosion of his aircraft and death to his entire crew, mere seconds before bombs away on target, Lieutenant Gott and his copilot (Lieutenant Metzger) conferred. Something had to be done immediately to save the life of the wounded radio operator. The lack of a static line and the thought that his unconscious body striking the ground in unknown territory would not bring immediate medical attention forced a quick decision. Lieutenant Gott and his co-pilot decided to fly the flaming aircraft to friendly territory and then attempt to crash land. Bombs were released on the target, and the crippled aircraft proceeded alone to Allied-controlled territory. When that had been reached, Lieutenant Gott had the copilot personally inform all crew members to bail out. The copilot chose to remain with Lieutenant Gott in order to assist in landing the bomber. With only one normally functioning engine and with the danger of explosion much greater, the aircraft banked into an open field, and when it was at an altitude of 100 feet, it exploded, crashed, exploded again, and then disintegrated. All three crew members were instantly killed. Lieutenant Gott's loyalty to his crew, his determination to accomplish the task set forth to him, and his deed of knowingly performing what may have been his last service to his country was an example of valor at its highest.

This dual award, the most recent in Air Force annals, marked the fourth multiple presentation of the Medal of

Honor to Air Force personnel in WW II and the fifth in USAF history. It brought the roll of Medal of Honor recipients to a total of 38, all but five of which had been awarded since the infamous attack on Pearl Harbor.

Memorialized by "1st Lt Donald J. Gott Memorial Highway", Ellis County, Oklahoma. Specifically on U.S. Highway 60 / Oklahoma State Highway 51, between Arnett and Harmon in Ellis County, in northwestern Oklahoma.

From the Ellis County (OK) Capital August 27, 1948

RE-BURIAL OF LT. GOTT MONDAY MORNING AT 11

Remains of the late 1st Lieutenant Donald J. Gott, son of Mr. and Mrs. Joseph E. Gott, Arnett, Oklahoma, who was killed on November 9, 1944, in Metz, France, and was the first Oklahoman to receive the Congressional Medal of Honor posthumously, will arrive in Woodward, Friday, August 27th, 1948 at 6:55 p.m. by Santa Fe.

Donald was born at the family home eight miles east of Arnett, Oklahoma, on June 3, 1923. He attended grade school at Kennebeck School near his home but attended high school at Fargo, where he graduated as valedictorian of his class in 1941 and received a medal for being an all-around boy student.

In March 1943, while working in a defense plant in Bridgeport, Connecticut, he volunteered for active duty with the U.S. Air Corps and, within six months, was called for training. He took his Army primary Flight Training course at Thunderbird Field No. 1 at Glendale, Arizona; his Pilot School Basic in the West Coast training center, Gardner Field, California; advanced Pilot School training at Stockton Field, California, where he received his wings and commission. He received his four-engine pilot training course at Hobbs, New Mexico. In July 1944, he flew overseas and joined the 8th Air Force and was awarded the Air Medal and three Oak Leaf clusters. In October, he was promoted to 1st Lieutenant and made squadron leader and expected to complete his missions in time to be home for Christmas. On November 9, 1944, when he was on his 28th mission and was returning from a bombing run at the marshaling yards in Saarbrucken, Germany, his B-17 was seriously damaged from antiaircraft fire and exploded and crashed as he attempted a landing, killing him instantly.

Besides his parents, Mr. and Mrs. Joseph E. Gott, Arnett, Oklahoma, he is survived by two sisters, Mrs. Hazel Peil, Fair Oaks, California; Mrs. Lucille Compton, Arnett, Oklahoma; and one brother, O.J. Gott, Los Angeles, California; and five nephews and two nieces.

Requiem Mass will be Monday, August 30th, 1948, at 9:30 a.m. in the St. Peter's Catholic Church in Woodward by Father Joseph McGurk. Burial will be in the family plot in Fairmont Cemetery, Harmon, Oklahoma, at 11:00 a.m. Monday, with Oca J. Collar Post No. 313 of the American Legion at Arnett in charge of military rites at the grave. The body will lie in state in the Stetcher Mortuary in Woodward from train time until Sunday morning, when he will be taken to his home for the day.

IST. LT. DONALD J. GOTT
AWARDED THE MEDAL OF HONOR
BORN JUNE 3, 1923
DIED NOV. 9, 1944

SERGEANT ROBERT A. GRAY; ARMY

September 21, 1834 (Philadelphia, PA) – November 22, 1906 (Groton, CT); 72 years old
Married Evaline Tuttle (1839-1864) on September 13, 1860.
Remarried Mary J. Wilcox (1845-1915) in 1871.
No children.
Enlisted on August 8, 1862, in Groton, Connecticut.
Discharged on June 23, 1865.

Born to Joseph Gray (1810-1850) and Emeline H. Morgan Gray (1815-1898). One brother, Charles (1836-1878). Four sisters, Emeline "Emma" Gray Shepherd (1839-1890), Caroline "Carrie" M. Gray Gould (1842-1889), Lucy A. Gray Seeley (1844-1863), and Alice (1849-1916).

One of five members of the 21st Connecticut to receive the Medal of Honor.

Photo courtesy of FindAGrave.com

MEDAL OF HONOR CITATION

AWARDED FOR ACTIONS DURING: Civil War
BRANCH OF SERVICE: Army
UNIT: Company C, 21st Connecticut Infantry
DATE OF ISSUE AND PRESENTATION: July 13, 1897 (33 years later)
AGE ON THE DAY OF THE EVENT: 29
CITATION:

The President of the United States of America, in the name of Congress, takes pleasure in presenting the Medal of Honor to Sergeant Robert A. Gray, United States Army, for extraordinary heroism on 16 May 1864, while serving with Company C, 21st Connecticut Infantry, in action at Drewry's Bluff, Virginia. While retreating with his regiment, which had been repulsed, Sergeant Gray voluntarily returned, in the face of the enemy's fire, to a former position and rescued a wounded officer of his company who was unable to walk.

After the war, Sgt Gray returned to Groton, where he spent the rest of his life. He resided on Ramsdell Street in Groton Bank and became a partner in the Groton-based granite and marble quarry business, Merritt, Gray & Company. He took an active interest in community civic life, serving as a representative to the General Assembly in 1880-1881 and vice president of the Groton Heights Centennial Committee in 1881. He was an active worker and participant in the perpetuation of the historic Fort Griswold. He is buried in Colonel Ledyard Cemetery, where, ironically, he had worked for over ten years cutting grass, removing and burying stumps, and building walls.

From Beyer, W. F., & Keydel, O. F. (2000). Deeds of valor: How America's Civil War Heroes won The Congressional Medal of Honor. Smithmark Publishers.

RESCUED HIS LIEUTENANT

During the hotly contested battle of Bluff, when the Union troops were compelled to fall back, a small squad of Federal soldiers - fifteen in all - were left on the field. They were members of Company C of the Twenty-first Connecticut Infantry, under the command of Lieutenant Dutton, who, having no orders to fall back, had no choice but to brave the situation. Rapidly, however, their position became more and more untenable; the enemy was fast closing in on the little band; already, several of them had fallen under the increasing murderous fire from the Confederates. Lieutenant Dutton finally was forced to order a retreat but had no sooner uttered the words than, struck by a bullet, he sank to the ground. Sergeant Robert A. Gray was five rods away from him when he noticed the Lieutenant's absence and, looking back, saw that the officer was disabled and sure to fall into the hands of the enemy, who were no more than twenty rods away from him. With a few leaps, he was by his side and found him shot through the leg. He helped him up and managed to retreat with him. The brave sergeant assisted the wounded lieutenant to a place of comparative safety and then hurried back to his regiment.

From The Day (New London, CT) September 21, 1904

THREE SCORE AND TEN ON TUESDAY

LONG AND USEFUL LIFE OF ROBERT A. GRAY – ERRATIC HIGHWAYMAN

Groton, September 21 – Robert A. Gray, one of Groton's oldest and most respected residents, celebrated in a quiet way his seventieth birthday at his home in the borough Tuesday. He was born in Philadelphia. His mother was Emeline Morgan, wife of Joseph Gray. At the age of 11 months, Mr. Gray's parents moved to New London, where they resided until 1845 when they moved across the river and took up residence in Groton Bank. When a young man, Gray went to work in the quarry of B.N. Greene in Groton. It was there that he learned his trade as a stone cutter. Later, he went to California, where he was assistant superintendent of the Colton marble yards at Colonton, California. He also practiced his trade in the state of Maine for several years. In 1860, he married Eveline Tuttle of Willimantic. In the year of 1862, Gray enlisted in Company C, Twenty-first Regiment, Connecticut Volunteers. From 1862 until the close of the war in 1865, he saw hard service. He was one of few men to receive a Medal of Honor for bravery in action. He was a recipient of a medal voted by Congress for the gallant rescue of S.A. Dutton of Durant, Iowa, in the conflict at Drury's Bluff, Virginia. Comrade Dutton is still living, and correspondence is still carried on between the two men.

AUTHOR NOTE: Lieutenant Samuel A. Dutton died on December 26, 1928, at 85 years old, a father of 5 sons and 3 daughters.

His first wife died in 1864. In 1870, he established the granite works now owned and operated by John Salter and Son. He was connected with the granite works in Groton for many years. In 1871, he was married again. His second wife was Mary I. Wilcox of Groton.

During the years of his retirement, he had faithfully served his town and state by holding various offices. He served as a representative from the town in the 1880-81 session. He was always a consistent member of the Groton Heights Baptist Church and, for many years, was a deacon in the church. Mr. Gray's name has been placed on the senatorial committee by his Republican friends for 24 consecutive years, and during this time, he has not failed to act at each occasion. He has always prided himself in being, as he terms it, "a straight out and out Republican." He has also served for ten years as a member of the congressional committee. For 25 years, he served as chairman of the Groton Monument Association. This was done in addition to and in connection with five successive terms as president of the association. In 1881, he superintended the work of placing the cap on the shaft. The last work that he performed upon the shaft was to take 30 of the large granite blocks from the monument and replace them with new ones.

Mr. Gray is a familiar figure upon the streets of the borough. No man in the vicinity is better informed concerning the living members of the companies in the Connecticut Volunteer regiments.

Gray Soldier's Monument, 316 Monument Street, Groton, Connecticut.

A monument next to the Fort Griswold battlefield honors Groton's Civil War veterans.

The Gray Soldiers' Monument was a posthumous gift by Robert A. Gray, a Groton native and Civil War veteran who received a Medal of Honor for courage during fighting at Drewry's Bluff, Virginia.

The monument, which features an infantryman standing atop a granite base, bears a dedication on its front (south) face reading, "Erected by Robert A. Gray and dedicated to the memory of his brave comrades who offered their lives for their country in the war of 1861-1865."

The south face also bears the Connecticut and United States shields near its base and also honors the battle of Fredericksburg, Virginia. The east face honors the battle of Port Hudson, Louisiana. Gettysburg is listed on the north face, and Drewry's Bluff is honored on the west face.

The monument was dedicated July 4, 1916, thanks to a posthumous donation. Robert A. Gray, a Groton stonecutter, had served with the 21st Regiment, Connecticut Volunteer Infantry. Gray was awarded the Medal of Honor for rescuing an injured officer during fighting at Drewry's Bluff.

The Soldiers' Monument, near the corner of Park Avenue and Smith Street, stands almost in the shadow of the Groton Battle Monument and Museum in Fort Griswold State Park.

The monument was supplied by the Smith Granite Works in nearby Westerly, R.I., and may have been among the last Civil War monuments purchased from the firm.

Gray's Soldier's Monument, 316 Monument Street, Groton, Connecticut. Photos by the author. The monument commemorates soldiers who died in the Civil War. It was erected by Robert A. Gray, a partner in the Groton firm of Merritt, Gray & Company, granite and marble works, and a representative in the State Legislature. The battles listed on the monument are those in which he fought. Gray gave the monument to the Groton Monument Association by testamentary gift.

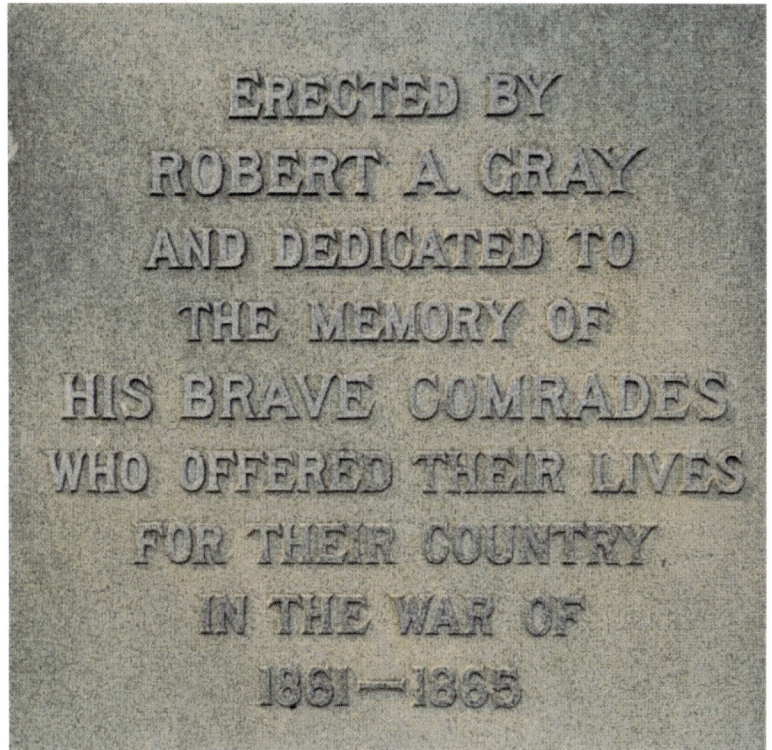

Buried in Colonel Ledyard Cemetery, 240 Mitchell Street, Groton, Connecticut. Photos by the author.

ORDINARY SEAMAN LUKE M. GRISWOLD; NAVY

1837 * (Bloomfield, CT) – March 18, 1892 (Springfield, MA); 54 or 55 years old
Married Margaret E. Colton (1835-1913) in Springfield, MA, on July 20, 1864.
One daughter, Hattie M. (1873-1873).
Enlisted on August 12, 1862, in Boston, Massachusetts
Discharged on September 3, 1863, in Springfield, Massachusetts.

* The exact Date of Birth is unknown.

Born to Zophar (1800-1877) and Joanna R. (1800-?). Two sisters, Eunice J. Griswold Hayes (1826-1857) and Maria J. (1835-1835).

In a sad footnote of a hero's life, Seaman Griswold died, apparently penniless, in 1892. His wife, Margaret, later died in the Springfield poor house.

MEDAL OF HONOR CITATION

AWARDED FOR ACTIONS DURING: Civil War
BRANCH OF SERVICE: Navy
ASSIGNED TO: U.S.S. Rhode Island
GENERAL ORDERS: War Department, General Orders No. 59 (June 22, 1865)
CITATION:

The President of the United States of America, in the name of Congress, takes pleasure in presenting the Medal of Honor to Ordinary Seaman Luke M. Griswold, United States Navy, for extraordinary heroism in action while serving on board the U.S.S. Rhode Island, which was engaged in saving the lives of the officers and crew of the U.S.S. Monitor, 30 December 1862 near Cape Hatteras, North Carolina. Participating in the hazardous rescue of the officers and crew of the sinking Monitor, Ordinary Seaman Griswold, after rescuing several of the men, became separated in a heavy gale with other members of the cutter that had set out from the Rhode Island and spent many hours in the small boat at the mercy of the weather and high seas until finally picked up by a schooner 50 miles east of Cape Hatteras.

From the Wilmington Journal January 15, 1863

Official Report of Commander Trenchard of the Rhode Island
U.S. Steamer Rhode Island, Hampton Roads, January 3, 1863.

Sir: I have the honor to report, in conformity with your orders of the 24th, that the Rhode Island proceeded to sea with the iron-clad steamer Monitor in tow, and half-past two p.m., of the 29th, the being light from the southward and Westward with a smooth sea. The weather continued favorable during the night, and the Monitor towed easily, with speed ranging between five and six miles per hour. At one p.m. of the 30th, made Cape Hatteras lighthouse, bearing WSW fourteen miles distant. The weather during the day continued the same. At sunset, when seventeen miles Southeast of Cape Hatteras, made the steamer State of Georgia with the Passaic in tow to the Northward and Eastward of us, the wind being light at the time from Southward and Westward with indications of good weather. Between eight and nine p.m., the wind freshened, hauling more to the Southward, and attended with rainy and squally weather.

At nine p.m., the Monitor made signals to stop. We stopped the engines, starting them again soon after. During the interval, the Monitor appeared to be lying in the trough of the sea, laboring heavily, the sea making a complete breach over her. The steamer was then brought head to wind and sea under easy steam, and the Monitor rode much easier and made better weather. About two hours afterwards (eleven p.m.), when about twenty miles South Southwest of Cape Hatteras, Commander Bankhead made signals for assistance, and upon hailing, we learned the Monitor was in a sinking condition. We lowered our launch and first cutter without delay and commenced getting her crew on board.

While so engaged, the Monitor ranged upon our port quarter, staving in the launch, and to prevent a serious collision, by which the Rhode Island would have been badly injured, it was necessary to force the steamer ahead a little. While under our quarter, ropes were thrown on board the Monitor, but so reluctant did the crew appear to leave their vessel that they did not take advantage of this opportunity to save themselves.

The vessels now being separated, and a third boat was then lowered to assist the others in getting the crew on board. Acting Master's Mate Brown, the officer in charge of the first cutter, deserves special credit for the skillful manner in which he managed his boat, having made two trips to the Monitor and rescuing a number of her men. Encouraged by the success attending them, Mr. Brown started on another trip and soon after was hailed and directed to lie on his oars or drop astern and be towed up as the Rhode Island would steam for the Monitor as soon as the men could be got on board from the boats alongside and the boats hoisted up. Mr. Brown, perhaps not understanding the order, proceeding on in the direction of the Monitor, whose red light from her turret was still visible, but by the time the steamer was ready to turn her wheels, the light had unfortunately disappeared.

1:30 p.m., on the 30th – The steam proceeded slowly in the direction which the Monitor bore when last seen and endeavored to keep her position as near as possible through the night, burning Coston's night signals at intervals.

After daylight, not seeing anything of the missing boat, I decided to cruise between the position she had separated from us and Cape Hatteras and the extremity of its shoals, with the hope of falling in with her. This plan was carried out, and the day (31st), without success. It is possible, however, that the boat may have been picked up by one of the numerous vessels that were seen off the coast on that day. The boat was buoyant, had a good crew, and no doubt well-managed, and I entertain hope that her daring crew have been saved by some passing vessel.

Acting Ensign Taylor, the officer who had charge of the launch, which had rendered good service, speaks the high praise of the gallant conduct of acting Master's Mate Stevens, who, when the launch was manning, went quietly into the boat, took one of the oars, and while alongside the Monitor, in striving to save others, was himself washed from the boat, was rescued by the first cutter. Mr. Taylor also speaks in the highest terms of David T. Compton, cockswain of the launch, who, when the boat was stove and rendered unfit for service, oarlocks broken, declared he would not leave the boat, but would go to the Monitor even if he had to scull the boat.

I enclose herewith a list of the men in the missing boat belonging to the Rhode Island.

I am, very respectfully, your obedient servant.

Stephen D. Trenchard,

Commander.

Acting Rear Admiral S.P. Lee, commanding North Atlantic Blockading Squadron Hampton Roads.

Accession #: NHHC 1957-2-S
Circa: 1862
Size: 2 x 2.5
Medium: Bronze
Location: Headquarters Artifact Collection, Naval History, and Heritage Command
Obverse: Five-pointed bronze star tipped with trefoils containing a crown of laurel and oak. In the center is Minerva, the Roman goddess of wisdom and warfare, standing with left hand resting on fasces and right hand holding a shield blazoned with the escutcheon of the United States. She repulses discord, represented by a male figure holding snakes. It is made of solid red brass, oxidized, and buffed.

Reverse: engraved "Personal Valor / Luke M. Griswold / O. Seaman / U.S.S. Rhode Island / Loss of the Monitor / Dec. 31 1862."

NAMES OF THE MISSING FROM THE USS RHODE ISLAND.

The following is a list of the men missing in the first cutter from the United States steamer Rhode Island:

Acting Master's Mate J. Rodney Brown in charge,
Charles H. Smith, Coxswain
Maurice Wagg, Coxswain
Hugh Logan, Captain After Guard
Lewis A. Horton, Seaman
John Jones, Landsman
Luke M. Griswold, Ordinary Seaman
George Moore, Seaman.

Buried in Oak Grove Cemetery, 424 Bay Street, Springfield, Massachusetts; Section A, Grave 297. The Medal of Honor marker was installed in May 2013. It was paid for with private funds. The VA rejected his application as a Next Of Kin could not be found. Photo by the author.

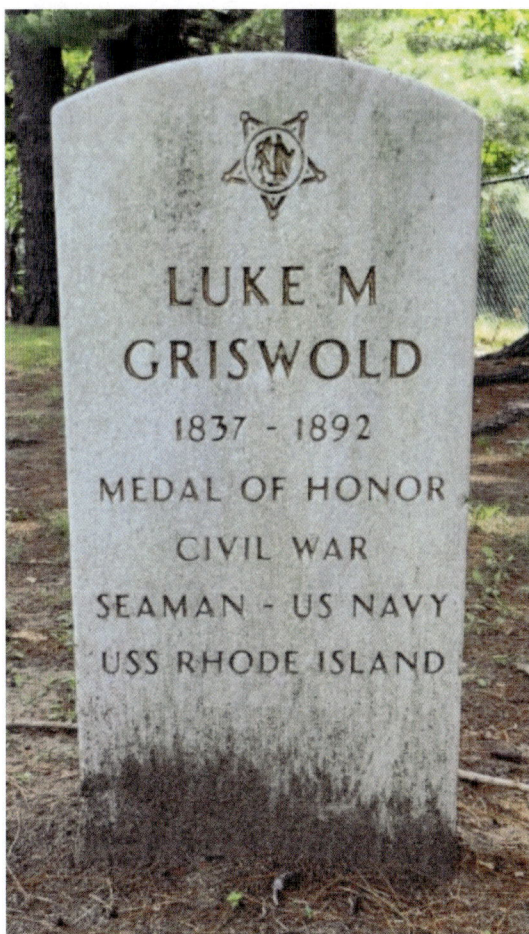

CAPTAIN FORECASTLE THOMAS HARDING; NAVY

1837 * (Middletown, CT) – December 15, 1911 (Cheyenne, WY); 74 years old
Married to Margaret "Maggie" Berry (1850-1924).
Three sons, John (1875-1961), Thomas (1880-1894), and Steven (1882-1957).
Two daughters, Alice Harding Skinner (1877-1966) and Maggie M. (1882-1910).

* The exact Date of Birth is unknown.

Parent and sibling information is unknown.

MEDAL OF HONOR CITATION

AWARDED FOR ACTIONS DURING: Civil War
BRANCH OF SERVICE: Navy
ASSIGNED TO: U.S.S. Dacotah
GENERAL ORDERS: War Department, General Orders No. 45 (December 31, 1864)
CITATION:

The President of the United States of America, in the name of Congress, takes pleasure in presenting the Medal of Honor to Captain of the Forecastle Thomas Harding, United States Navy, for extraordinary heroism in action, serving as Captain of the Forecastle on board the U.S.S. Dacotah on the occasion of the destruction of the blockade runner Pevensey, near Beaufort, North Carolina, 9 June 1864. Learning that one of the officers in the boat, which was in danger of being, and subsequently was, swamped, could not swim, Captain of the Forecastle Harding remarked to him: "If we are swamped, sir, I shall carry you to the beach, or I will never go there myself.'" He did not succeed in carrying out his promise but made desperate efforts to do so, while others thought only of themselves. Such conduct is worthy of appreciation and admiration--a sailor risking his own life to save that of an officer.

Photos of Thomas Harding's Medal of Honor contributed by Kristie DaFoe, Associate Registrar for Acquisitions, Curator Branch, Naval History and Heritage Command.

The inscription reads, "Personal Valor; Thomas Harding; Captain of Forecastle; U.S.S. Dacotah; Wreck of the Pevensey; June 9, 1864

From the Laramie Boomerang July 22, 2017

In today's society, most 16-year-olds are buying their first car, working their first job, or adjusting to high school, but in 1864, 16-year-old Thomas Harding Sr. was awarded the Medal of Honor.

Born in Connecticut, Harding was buried in Laramie in 1911.

However, for more than a century, his simple gravestone in Greenhill Cemetery sat bereft of any indication the valorous commendation he earned in service to his country.

"Mr. Harding was a Union Navy Sailor in the American Civil War, who received the U.S. military's highest decoration — the Medal of Honor — for attempting to save an officer from drowning," American Legion Post No. 14 member E.J. McDonald said. "It's never too late to honor courage."

After the boiler on a nearby ship exploded on June 9, 1864, off the North Carolina coast, McDonald said Harding and other crew members of the U.S.S. Dacotah used a small boat to try to retrieve some of the destroyed ship's cargo and personnel.

"The small boat started to take on water and sink," he said. "Captain of the Forecastle Harding tried to help acting Master's Mate Jarvis G. Farrar, who could not swim but was unsuccessful, and Farrar drowned."

In the attempt, McDonald said Harding remarked, "If we are swamped, sir, I shall carry you to the beach, or I will never go there myself."

Although Harding failed to keep his promise, McDonald said his official award citation states he made desperate attempts to save the officer "while others thought only of themselves."

Harding was awarded the Medal of Honor six months later.

An obituary in the Laramie Republican states Harding was a lamplighter for the Union Pacific Railroad in Cheyenne when he died in 1911.

McDonald said the American Legion Post No. 14 was notified of Harding's story in late 2016 by the Medal of Honor Historical Society of the United States.

The society is a nonprofit organization dedicated to researching, preserving, and documenting the individuals who have been awarded the Medal of Honor.

"At the time, I was a member of the (American Legion Post No. 14 Board of Trustees), and I kind of just took over the event," McDonald said. "It took some time to research the group that informed us and dig up what we could about Harding."

Once McDonald validated the society's information and found Harding's grave, he said he went to the other veterans groups in town for help putting together the ceremony.

"I think most of the ceremonies outside of the day-to-day stuff is a collaborative effort among the veteran community," he said. "Things like this are really important."

After visiting Montgomery-Stryker Funeral Home to order the Medal of Honor marker now accompanying Harding's grave, McDonald said he was struck by John Montgomery's generosity.

"When I asked him how much the bill was, he said, 'Don't even worry about it. It's just the right thing to do,'" McDonald said.

With the grave marked, he said the site will be honored with a flag and a token each Memorial Day.

"Veterans here are proud," said Karl Lankford, a Vietnam War veteran and Albany County resident. "Being a part of this is an honor for all the veterans in the community."

Buried in Greenhill Cemetery, 455 N 15th Street, Laramie, Wyoming; Row K, Lot 84, Space 1. Photo from FindAGrave.com.

FIRST LIEUTENANT LEE ROSS HARTELL; ARMY

August 23, 1923 (Philadelphia, PA) – August 27, 1951; 28 years old
Married Margaret "Peggy" A. Burns (1921-2020) on May 17, 1947, in Danbury, Connecticut.
One son, Lee J. (1950-2013).
Two daughters, Sharon L. Hartell Siegel (1948-) and Sandra J. Hartell Barry (1949-).
His original enlistment was in 1940 at 17 years old.
Service number: O-944579
Born to Andrew R. Sr. (1898-1990) and Dorothy Jackson Hartell (1899-1999). Three brothers, Andrew S. Jr. (1922-1999), Leonard (1931-2001), and Charles E. (1932-2022).

Lee Hartell was born August 23, 1923, in Pennsylvania and grew up in Danbury, Connecticut. He attended local schools, went to church with his family, and was active in the Boy Scouts between the ages of 10 and 17. Hartell was not a physically imposing figure. He seized playing football following a broken clavicle. Even as an adult, he stood only 5'8" and weighed only 135 pounds. Yet, young Lee was a steady youth with great endurance, prefiguring his military career. At age 15, he broke his neck in a swing accident but ignored the pain for several days until he was overcome by paralysis. A six-week hospitalization resulted in a discharge with a brace he was expected to wear for the rest of his life. Hartell worked himself to a full recovery, and the brace was removed in three months. At 17, he joined the Connecticut National Guard, although he was too young to enlist. He was a good student at Danbury High School, but the arrival of World War II caused him to earn his diploma in the Army. The Hartell family had a long tradition of military service. Lee's father, Andrew Hartell Sr., served in the Navy in World War I and would again in World War II. His grandfather saw service in the Spanish-American War, and his great-grandfather was a veteran of the Civil War. Three of Lee's brothers also served in the armed forces. Hartell's father recalled following Lee's death, "We've always been a militia family."

Lee Hartell enlisted in the Connecticut National Guard on June 20, 1940, in the 192nd Field Artillery Battalion. He transferred to active duty on September 22, 1942, and was wounded in action in the South Pacific on June 19, 1943. He then transferred to Battery C of the 31st Battalion, 8th Field Artillery training regiment at Fort Sill, Oklahoma, and was discharged from active duty on July 1, 1945. He was discharged from the Connecticut National Guard the following day.

On August 8, 1946, he rejoined the Connecticut National Guard as a Second Lieutenant and served as an artillery officer with the 963rd Field Artillery Battalion. He was then discharged from the National Guard on January 12, 1948, to enter active duty service. He was deployed to Korea as part of Battery A, 15th Artillery Battalion of the 2nd Infantry Division.

In addition to the Medal of Honor, Lt Hartell is the recipient of the Distinguished Service Cross, the Air Medal with 6 Oak Leaf Clusters, the Good Conduct Medal, the Purple Heart with 2 Oak Leaf Clusters, the Korean Service Medal, the United Nations Service Medal, the National Defense Service Medal, the Korean War Service Medal, and the World War II Victory Medal.

MEDAL OF HONOR CITATION

AWARDED FOR ACTIONS DURING: Korean War
BRANCH OF SERVICE: Army
UNIT: Battery A, 15th Field Artillery Battalion, 2nd Infantry Division
GENERAL ORDERS: Department of the Army, General Orders No. 16 (February 1, 1952)
AGE ON THE DAY OF THE EVENT: 28
CITATION:

The President of the United States of America, in the name of Congress, takes pride in presenting the Medal of Honor (Posthumously) to First Lieutenant (Field Artillery) Lee Ross Hartell (ASN: 0-944579), United States Army, for conspicuous gallantry and intrepidity at the risk of his life above and beyond the call of duty while serving with Battery A, 15th Field Artillery Battalion, 2nd Infantry Division, in action against enemy aggressor forces at Kobangsan-ni, Korea, on 27 August 1951. During the darkness of early morning, the enemy launched a ruthless attack against friendly positions on a rugged mountainous ridge. First Lieutenant Hartell, attached to Company B, 9th Infantry Regiment, as forward observer, quickly moved his radio to an exposed vantage on the ridge line to adjust defensive fires. Realizing the tactical advantage of illuminating the area of approach, he called for flares and then directed crippling fire into the onrushing assailants. At this juncture, a large force of hostile troops swarmed up the slope in banzai charge and came within ten yards of First Lieutenant Hartell's position. First Lieutenant Hartell sustained a severe hand wound in the ensuing encounter but grasped the microphone with his other hand and maintained his magnificent stand until the front and left flank of the company were protected by a close-in wall of withering fire, causing the fanatical foe to disperse and fall back momentarily. After the numerically superior enemy overran an outpost and was closing on his position, First Lieutenant Hartell, in a final radio call, urged the friendly elements to fire both batteries continuously. Although mortally wounded, First Lieutenant Hartell's intrepid actions contributed significantly to stemming the onslaught and enabled his company to maintain the strategic strongpoint. His consummate valor and unwavering devotion to duty reflect lasting glory on himself and uphold the noble traditions of military service.

Presentation Date and Details: January 16, 1952, at the Pentagon, by the Secretary of Defense Robert A. Lovett to his widow.

Mrs. Margaret E. Hartell, of Danbury, Connecticut, receives the Congressional Medal of Honor, which was awarded posthumously to her husband, 1st Lt Lee R. Hartell, who was killed in Korea. Defense Secretary Robert Lovett (left) made the presentation at the Pentagon. Photo from the author's personal files.

From The News (Paterson, NJ) September 19, 1951

KILLED DIRECTING BANZAI DEFENSE

EAST CENTRAL FRONT, Korea, Sept. 19 (UP) – A bullet crashed into 1st Lt Lee R Hartell's chest as he stood, microphone in hand, unflinching at the North Korean banzai charge.

He had just said: "Keep firing both batteries. I think they have got us."

The bullet but a period to the sentence and his life. But his crisp order from a forward artillery post saved the lives of others.

Allied guns responded with a fire curtain. It checked the enemy advance while an isolated infantry company with Hartell obtained fresh ammunition.

The young lieutenant from Danbury, Connecticut, moved forward to the exposed position overlooking "Bloody Ridge" on the dark, rainy morning of August 27. The saddle-shaped slope north of Yanggu was already drenched with the blood of thousands.

Whistle-blowing North Koreans broke through the Allied defense. Hartell carefully made adjustments and called for fire from 105-millimeter howitzers to the rear.

He ignored hand grenades bursting a few yards from his open position. He refused to leave his radio or to use a rifle in his own defense.

A bullet shattered his right hand. He jammed it under his left armpit to stem the flow of blood and called again for artillery fire. Throughout, he continued to make adjustments for accurate fire.

Hartell lived up to the reputation he established as an artillery plane spotter. He was known to "kick the back seat out of his plane" whenever he spotted a good target.

The man, called "The Sparrow" among his friends because of his quick, bright movements, was assigned as a forward observer with a rifle company hard pressed for replacements.

He leaves a wife, two daughters, and a son he never saw behind in Danbury.

From the Hartford Courant January 17, 1952

AWARD GIVEN TO WIDOW OF DANBURY MAN

LOVETT PRESENTS HONOR MEDAL TO MRS. HARTELL IN PENTAGON CEREMONY

WASHINGTON, January 16 (AP) – Two New Englanders, First Lieutenant Lee R. Hartell, 28, of Danbury, Connecticut, and Corporal Clair Goodblood, 21, of Burnham, Maine, today were awarded posthumously, the Medal of Honor.

The blue-starred ribbons and medals were presented in a Pentagon ceremony by Secretary of Defense Robert Lovett to Mrs. Margaret E. Hartell, widow of Lieutenant Hartell, and Mrs. Emily S. Goodblood, mother of the corporal. Lovett also presented Medals of Honor to relatives of eight others who died in Korean fighting.

Hartell was killed near Kobansan-Ni, Korea, on the night of August 27 when Reds attacked his unit. He crawled to a forward position, called for flares to illuminate the attacking force, and directed artillery fire against them. Although badly wounded, he continued to call back, firing directions while the enemy was only 30 feet from him.

Mrs. Hartell wore a black suit and hat and a corsage of gardenias presented by the Defense Department. She listened with a set expression as the citation for her husband was read by Brigadier General John A. Klein, deputy adjutant General.

In the Pentagon auditorium audience were her three children, Sharon Lee, 3; Sandra Jean, 2; John Lee, 1; and Hartell's parents, Mr. and Mrs. Andrew R. Hartell, all of Danbury.

Sharon Lee and Sandra Jean wore tiny red, white, and blue corsages on their dark blue suits. The three youngsters, sitting with their grandparents, seemed puzzled by the bright lights and the cameras.

Senators McMahon and Benton and Representative Morano of Connecticut were present at the ceremony and personally expressed their sympathy and pride in Hartell's heroism to the family. Morano also spoke for Governor John Davis Lodge of Connecticut.

From the Danbury News Times May 30, 2021

DANBURY — Sandra Barry doesn't remember her dad.

She was only 2 when First Lieutenant Lee Hartell was killed in the Korean War on Aug. 27, 1951, on a rugged terrain now known as "Bloody Ridge."

But remembrances of him are throughout Danbury, the United States, and Korea. Hartell is the only Danbury resident since the Civil War to be posthumously awarded with the prestigious Congressional Medal of Honor.

"We just remember seeing pictures, and that really didn't mean anything to us," said Barry, whose brother was just under one and sister was three when their father died. "Because he was over in Korea for a year before that, almost a year."

The Medal of Honor is the country's highest award for military valor in action, with more than 3,500 recipients nationwide and 82 recipients from Connecticut, according to federal and state figures.

"You end up becoming...kind of a hero to other veterans," said Daniel Hayes, director of veterans affairs in Danbury. "That's way above and beyond the call of duty."

Nathan Hickok, from the Army, and James Sullivan, from the Navy, are the only other Danbury residents to earn this medal, both because of their service in the Civil War. Sgt. Major Allan Jay Kellogg, Jr., of Bethel, and Capt. Paul Bucha, of Ridgefield, received the medal for their service during the Vietnam War.

Hartell, who was born in Pennsylvania but grew up in Danbury, joined the Connecticut National Guard at 17 in 1940 and was called to Camp Blanding, Fla. At 18, he reportedly became the youngest corporal in the 43rd Division and was deployed to New Zealand in October 1942 to fight in the Pacific Theater operations during World War II,

232

according to the state military department.

After World War II, he married Margaret Burns "Peggy" Hartell in May 1947. They had three children, Sharon, Sandra, and Lee.

He was deployed to Korea in 1950 and led a forward observation team to support Company B, earning the nickname "Colonel Hilltop" because he shot at the enemy while calmly standing at the top of a hill, the state said.

Communist forces attacked predawn on Aug. 27 near Kobanson-ni, and Company B was surrounded on all sides. From his position, Hartell could see where the enemy was and called for flares, shooting at the attackers as they approached within 10 yards of him.

"First Lieutenant Hartell sustained a severe hand wound in the ensuing encounter but grasped the microphone with his other hand and maintained his magnificent stand until the front and left flank of the company were protected by a close-in wall of withering fire, causing the fanatical foe to disperse and fall back momentarily," the citation for his medal reads.

The enemy regrouped and overran an outpost.

That's when Hartell was shot through the chest.

"Keep firing both batteries. I think they've got us," he said in a final radio call, according to the state.

Hartell's actions "contributed significantly to stemming the onslaught and enabled his company to maintain the strategic strongpoint," the medal citation reads.

When Hartell's remains returned to Danbury, schools and businesses closed, and flags were flown at half-mast, the Danbury War Memorial describes on its website.

The Connecticut National Guard carried his flag-draped casket through the city streets, followed by a parade of soldiers, veterans' organizations, and civic groups, the state said. Hartell was buried in St. Peter's Cemetery.

But the city didn't do much else to remember her dad when she was a kid, Barry said.

"It was just something that happened," said Barry, adding she didn't look forward to going to the Memorial Day parade yearly as a kid. It's something she misses this year, with the parade canceled for the second year in a row due to COVID-19.

But the city later named the connector between White and Crosby Streets as Lee Hartell Drive and put a monument for him there.

"I would have rather they didn't do that at all," Barry said.

Kids would sit, stand, and jump off the monument, she said. In 1997, the monument was moved to its current place between the Vietnam and Korean War memorials outside the Danbury War Memorial.
"That's where it belonged," Barry said.

A photograph of Hartell is displayed in the lobby of the War Memorial building. The Disabled Americans Veterans Lee Hartell, Chapter 25 in Danbury, is named after him, and a plaque inside the building, as well as a sign outside, bears his name.

The Hartell chapter was formed in 1954 and sought to recognize his service.

"If it wasn't for him, a lot of guys would have died," said Chuck Gartland, commander of the organization who graduated from Danbury High School and served in the Marine Corps during the Vietnam War.

There's a Camp Hartell in Windsor Locks, as well as in Munsan-ni, Korea. The Hartell House serves as a general officer's mess hall for U.S., South Korean, and United Nations military personnel. A road at Fort Sill, Oklahoma, was renamed Hartell Boulevard.

Although Hartell died in August, his body was not returned to the family until January, Barry said. It came in a sealed coffin, she said. Her mother couldn't believe he was gone because many other soldiers who had been missing were returning alive.

"My mother didn't talk about my father at all," Barry said. "It was kind of a sad situation because, for many years, she just didn't accept the fact he was gone."

Barry recalled her grandparents on both sides of the family helping to watch her and her siblings.

"It was rough growing up," Barry said. "She put a lot of good faith on."

Her mom — who died at 99 last December — served three terms as city treasurer with then-Mayor John Define, according to her obituary. She worked at the John McLean store on Main Street around Christmastime for many years and every year at the Great Danbury State Fair, her daughter said.

"She loved working at the fair," Barry said

After Gartland returned home from Vietnam, he lived near the Hartells — although, at the time, he didn't know them or their connection to the first lieutenant. He said he often saw a woman, who he thinks was either Hartell's mother or wife, walking her dog with a "look of loneliness" on her face, so he always said hello.

Bernie Rotunda was drafted into the Korean War in 1951 and served for a year and four months. He never met Hartell but became friends with his wife, who laid a wreath for her husband each time the veterans read his name during ceremonies.

"She was very friendly and very helpful to the Korean War veterans," said Rotunda, who is the first vice commander for the Catholic War Veterans Post 1042 in Danbury.

Barry doesn't know what made her dad join the service. Her grandfather and uncles were in the Navy, with her grandfather, Andrew Hartell, Sr., serving in World War I and II.

"Kind of back in those days, it was something you did," Barry said. "He just had a real drive."

Barry's two sons sought to go into the military. One of her sons went into the Air Force but was injured during his training and could not continue. Her other son became a Navy SEAL.

She doesn't know if he was inspired by her father, but her son grew up hearing her grandfather's stories from the Navy.

She recalled her son once arguing with a kid, who refused to believe the photo hanging in the War Memorial building where they had camp was of the boy's grandfather. Barry settled the fight by confirming the photo was of her dad.

"He [my son] was quite proud of it," Barry said.

Lee Hartell Drive in Danbury, Connecticut

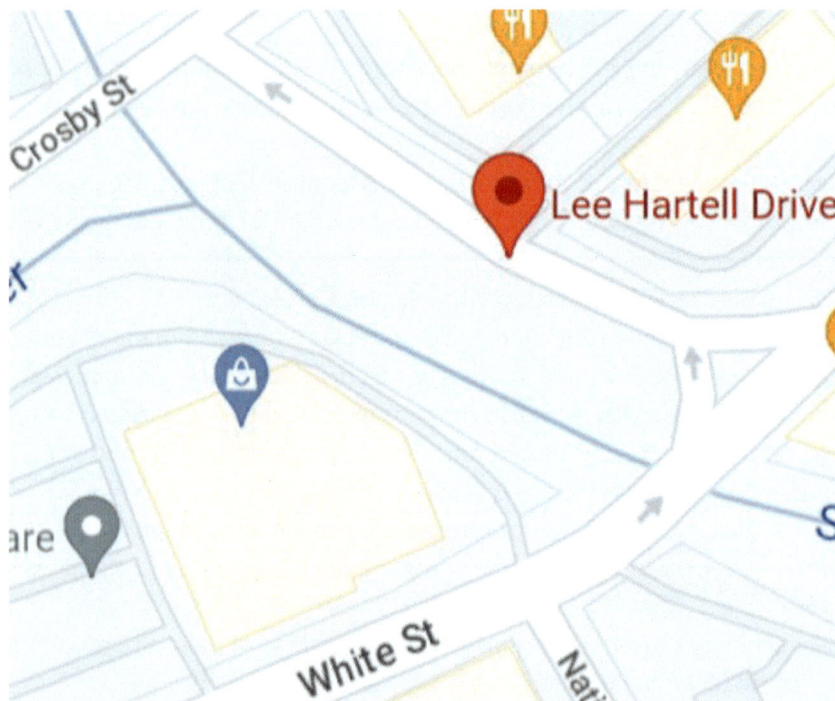

Memorial at the Danbury War Memorial, 1 Memorial Drive, Danbury, Connecticut. Photo by the author.

Buried in St. Peter's Cemetery, 71 Lake Avenue Extension, Danbury, Connecticut; Section 20, Grave 197. Photos by the author.

MACHINIST'S MATE SECOND CLASS GEORGE FRANCIS HENRECHON; NAVY

November 22, 1885 (Hartford, CT) – August 16, 1929 (New Orleans, LA); 43 years old
Married to Hattie Kesler (1877-?) on December 2, 1916, in Detroit, Michigan
No children.

Born to John B. (1852-1937) and Elizabeth J. "Eliza" Breen Henrechon (1861-1940). Three brothers, John F. (1888-1947), Joseph L. [WWI and WWII veteran] (1891-1978), and Arthur E. [WWI veteran] (1893-1944). Four sisters, Elizabeth C. "Lizzie" Henrechon Murphy (1883-1938), MaryAnn A. "May" Henrechon Dowd (1890-1970), Esther E. Henrechon Kennedy (1895-1963), Ruth M. "Emma" Henrechon Christie (1897-1976), Philomen E. (1899-1915), Madeline D. Henrechon Hotchkiss (1901-1952), and Florence L. (1906-1928).

Photo courtesy of the Congressional Medal of Honor Society

Photo courtesy of Ancestry.com

U.S.S. Pampagna (PG-39) courtesy of NavSource.org. Public domain photo.

MEDAL OF HONOR CITATION

AWARDED FOR ACTIONS DURING: Philippine Insurrection (1911)
BRANCH OF SERVICE: Navy
ASSIGNED TO: U.S.S. Pampanga
GENERAL ORDERS: War Department, General Orders No. 138 (December 13, 1911)
AGE ON DATE OF EVENT: 25
CITATION:

The President of the United States of America, in the name of Congress, takes pleasure in presenting the Medal of Honor to Machinist's Mate Second Class George Francis Henrechon, United States Navy, for extraordinary heroism in action while attached to the U.S.S. Pampanga. Machinist's Mate Second Class Henrechon was one of a shore party moving in to capture Mundang, Philippine Islands, on 24 September 1911. Ordered to take station within 100 yards of a group of nipa huts close to the trail, Henrechon advanced and stood guard as the leader and his scout party first searched the surrounding deep grasses, then moved into the open area before the huts. Instantly, enemy Moros opened point-blank fire on the exposed men, and approximately twenty Moros rushed the small group from inside the huts and from other concealed positions. Henrechon, responding to the calls for help, was one of the first on the scene. When his rifle jammed after the first shot, he closed in with rifle, using it as a club to break the stock over the head of the nearest Moro and then, drawing his pistol, started in pursuit of the fleeing outlaws. Machinist's Mate Second Class Henrechon's aggressive charging of the enemy under heavy fire and in the face of great odds contributed materially to the success of the engagement.

From The Indianapolis News January 20, 1912

MEDALS OF HONOR AWARDED TO MEN WHO FOUGHT OUTLAWS TO FINISH

General Order Received From Navy Department Tells of Acts of Heroism on the Island of Basilan – Ensign, Dying, Said "Get on the Job, McGuire."

In a general order received from the Navy Department by the naval recruiting station in this city, an announcement is made of the awarding of a Medal of Honor and a gratuity of $100 each to Jacob Volz, a Carpenter's Mate Third Class; Fred Henry McGuire, Hospital Apprentice; Bolden Reush Harrison, Seaman; George Francis Henrechon, Machinist's Mate Second Class, and John Hugh Catherwood, Ordinary Seaman, "for their extraordinary heroism while operating against outlaws on the island of Basilan, Philippine Islands, September 24, 1911." The order does not give the names of the cities of which these men were residents before enlistment.

The order sets forth an extract from the report of the commanding officer of the U.S.S. Pampanga, which, though brief, is full of action. It says that Ensign Hovey left his camp at Tablas at about 3:30 a.m., September 24, 1911, to act in conjunction with Lieutenant A. Cody, P.S. [Philippine Service], in the capture of Mundang. He had with him a Yacan guide, Private Nisperes of the Thirty-fourth Company, P.S., as an interpreter, and the five men of his own detachment to whom the medals and the money have been awarded.

Continuing, the report says: "At about 6 a.m. on the morning of September 24, 1911, the guide discovered several shacks or nipa houses ahead near the trail. This was the rancheria of Lapurap. Ensign Hovey went forward with the guide and the scout soldier to reconnoiter, leaving Volz, Catherwood, Harrison, Henrechon, and McGuire in the trail about three hundred yards in the rear. Ensign Hovey then sent the guide back to bring up ten more men. Harrison and Volz answered this call. In about five minutes, Ensign Hovey came back and ordered McGuire, Henrechon, and Catherwood to take station within one hundred yards of the houses and allow no one to get past them. Ensign Hovey then went up to the houses accompanied by the guide, the scout solder, and Catherwood. Before they reached the houses, this party went off the trail into the cogon grass for about fifteen steps as if in search of something. They then retraced their steps and halted in front of the houses. Ensign Hovey had no sooner halted than the Moros opened fire. As soon as the first shot was fired, the Moros charged from the cogon grass, from inside the house, and from behind trees. Ensign Hovey emptied his .45 caliber revolver at the attacking Moros. The number of Moros attacking was estimated at from fifteen to twenty.

"Ensign Hovey called for help, and Henrechon, McGuire, Volz, and Harrison advanced to the rescue. Henrechon and McGuire arrived on the scene first and found Ensign Hovey, Catherwood, and the scout soldier on the ground but still fighting. The guide was killed at the first volley. McGuire emptied his trifle and then sprang in with clubbed rifle."

"Henrechon's rifle jammed after the first shot, and he also clubbed his rifle, breaking the stock over the head of the nearest Moro, and then drawing his pistol, he started in pursuit of one of the fleeing Moros. Harrison and Volz had, meanwhile, arrived on the scene, firing with shotgun and rifle as they charged. Harrison, with a double-barreled shotgun, blew off the heads of three of the attacking Moros, and Volz accounted for several more. Our men rallied around the bodies of Ensign Hovey, Catherwood, and the scout soldier, and the Moros fled through the high cogon grass. On the arrival of Volz and Harrison on the field, McGuire, the hospital apprentice, having fired his last shot, went to Ensign Hovey's assistance to give him first aid, the last words of Ensign Hovey were, "Get on the job, McGuire.""

"The hospital apprentice, seeing that Ensign Hovey was dead, went to the assistance of Catherwood and the scout solder. The hospital apprentice had finished rendering first aid to Catherwood when the company of scouts arrived. The sanitary private with the company assisted in caring for the wounded. There were no wounded among the attacking Moros, all on the field being dead.

"The heroism and coolness shown by our men cannot be too highly commended and should receive recognition from the department. J.H. Catherwood, Ordinary Seaman, though severely wounded, did all he could to beat off the Moros attacking Ensign Hovey. F.H. McGuire, Hospital Apprentice, though wounded himself, gave immediate aid to the wounded and undoubtedly saved the lives of the scout soldier and Catherwood. The coolness and bravery shown by Henrechon, Volz, and Harrison in charging against the odds cannot be praised in too strong terms.

I recommend that Catherwood, McGuire, Volz, Harrison, and Henrechon be given a Medal of Honor. The scout soldier, Private Nisperes, had his right arm shot off above the elbow and was knocked down. He dug the stump of his arm in the ground and kept firing his rifle. A flag, three guns, and numerous spears and knives were captured from the enemy."

Buried in Mount St. Benedict Cemetery, 1 Cottage Grove Road, Bloomfield, Connecticut; Section F, Grave 430. Photos by the author.

JOHN B. HENRECHON
1852 — 1937
ELIZA J BREEN
HIS WIFE
1861 — 1940
1899 PHILOMEN L 1915
1906 FLORENCE L 1928
1888 JOHN L 1942
1891 JOSEPH L 1978

SERGEANT NATHAN E. HICKOK; ARMY

1839 or 1840 * (Danbury, CT) – unknown date in 1864 #
Marital status is unknown.
Enlisted on October 1, 1861.
Reenlisted on December 24, 1863.

His father is Nathan H. Hickok (1805-?), and his mother is unknown. One brother, Edward E. (1845-?). One sister, Eliza Hickok Wood (1836-1869).

* The exact dates of birth and death are unknown.
# Nathan Hickok's last known battle was the Second Battle of Fair Oaks in Virginia, October 27-28, 1864. Union records list him as "Captured October 29, 1864, Fair Oaks, Virginia." There are no Confederate records of him being a prisoner of war.

MEDAL OF HONOR CITATION

AWARDED FOR ACTIONS DURING: Civil War
BRANCH OF SERVICE: Army
UNIT: Company A, 8th Connecticut Infantry
DATE OF ISSUE AND PRESENTATION: April 6, 1865
AGE ON THE DAY OF THE EVENT: 25 or 26 years old
CITATION:

The President of the United States of America, in the name of Congress, takes pleasure in presenting the Medal of Honor to Corporal Nathan E. Hickok, United States Army, for extraordinary heroism on 29 September 1864, while serving with Company A, 8th Connecticut Infantry, in action at Chapin's Farm, Virginia, for capture of flag.

In 1861, Hickok, 22, volunteered to serve in the Union Army. He was assigned as a sharpshooter to Company A in the 8th Connecticut Infantry. In June of 1864, Hickok was transferred to a new unit composed entirely of sharpshooters, who fought with new Sharp rifles that allowed them to fire repeatedly far more often than soldiers with muzzle-loading muskets.

The name is inscribed on a monument and plaque honoring local men in unknown graves – Wooster Cemetery, 20 Ellsworth Avenue, Danbury, Connecticut; Section G. Photos by the author.

Also honored with a monument in Veterans Walkway of Honor, 1 Memorial Drive, Danbury, Connecticut. Photo by the author.

PRIVATE FRANK HILL; MARINE CORPS

August 13, 1864 (Hartford, CT) – unknown date of death
Unmarried
Enlisted on May 29, 1893, in New Haven, Connecticut

After his enlistment with the Marine Corps ended, he joined the Army and served with Company B, 5th Infantry, and Company E, 15th Infantry. Discharged September 1, 1903, for disability at Ordinance Barracks, Benicia, California. No other information is known.

MEDAL OF HONOR CITATION

AWARDED FOR ACTIONS DURING: Spanish-American War
BRANCH OF SERVICE: Marine Corps
ASSIGNED TO: U.S.S. Nashville (PG-7)
GENERAL ORDERS: War Department, General Orders No. 521 (July 7, 1899)
PRESENTED ON: August 15, 1899
AGE ON THE DAY OF THE EVENT: 33
CITATION:

The President of the United States of America, in the name of Congress, takes pleasure in presenting the Medal of Honor to Private Frank Hill, United States Marine Corps, for extraordinary heroism in action on board the U.S.S. Nashville during the operation of cutting the cable leading from Cienfuegos, Cuba, 11 May 1898. Facing the heavy fire of the enemy, Private Hill displayed extraordinary bravery and coolness throughout this action.

The U.S.S. Nashville (PG-7). Public domain photo.

From The Hartford Courant February 25, 1915

Hill Or Hills Wanted.

Information is wanted by the commandant of the United States Marine Corps as to the present whereabouts of Frank Hill or Hills, who enlisted in the Marine Corps in 1898 and was awarded a medal of honor for cutting cables at Cienfuegos in that year. He said his father's name was I. Hill and gave his address at Hartford.

Frank Hill's burial location is unknown. He is one of 314 Medal of Honor recipients whose final resting place is a mystery.

MAJOR WILLIAM BLISS HINCKS; ARMY

September 8, 1841 (Bucksport, ME) – November 7, 1903 (Bridgeport, CT); 62 years old
Married Mary L. Hart (1843-1890)
Three sons, Edward B. (1869-1890), William T. (1870-1931), and Robert (1875-1935).
Enlisted on July 22, 1862, in Connecticut.
Mustered out on May 31, 1865, in Alexandria, Virginia.

Born to John W. (1817-1875) and Sarah A. Blodgett Hincks (1820-1864). Brothers Edward Y. (1844-1927), Enoch P. (1846-1915), John H. (1849-1804). One sister, Jane I. (1856-1929).

From the 14th Regimental History Book

MEDAL OF HONOR CITATION

AWARDED FOR ACTIONS DURING: Civil War
BRANCH OF SERVICE: Army
UNIT: 14th Connecticut Infantry
DATE OF ISSUE: December 1, 1864
AGE ON THE DAY OF THE EVENT: 21
CITATION:

The President of the United States of America, in the name of Congress, takes pleasure in presenting the Medal of Honor to Sergeant Major William B. Hincks, United States Army, for extraordinary heroism on 3 July 1863, while serving with the 14th Connecticut Infantry, in action at Gettysburg, Pennsylvania. During the high-water mark of Pickett's charge on 3 July 1863, the colors of the 14th Tennessee Infantry C.S.A. were planted 50 yards in front of the center of Sergeant Major Hincks' regiment. There were no Confederates standing near it, but several were lying down around it. Upon a call for volunteers by Major Ellis, commanding, to capture this flag, this soldier and two others leaped the wall. One companion was instantly shot. Sergeant Major Hincks outran his remaining companion, running straight and swift for the colors amid a storm of shot. Swinging his saber over the prostrate Confederates and uttering a terrific yell, he seized the flag and hastily returned to his lines. The 14th Tennessee carried 12 battle honors on its flag. The devotion to duty shown by Sergeant Major Hincks gave encouragement to many of his comrades at a crucial moment of the battle.

Presentation Date and Details: December 6, 1864, by Major General George G. Meade, at a review of the 2nd Army Corps Headquarters, Peebles' House, near Petersburg, Virginia.

After moving to Bridgeport with his family, William established a career for himself as a writer, and on July 22, 1862, he enlisted in the 14th Connecticut Infantry as the unit's adjutant (aka secretary).

After the war, he became a wealthy bank executive and prominent citizen in his hometown of Bridgeport, Connecticut, and through his assistance to circus showman and fellow Bridgeport native P.T. Barnum, was able to found the Barnum Museum (which still exists today) and the Bridgeport Hospital. He also established a book business in partnership with Hobart Brinsmade under the name of Brinsmade & Hincks, purchasing his partner's interests in 1871. He was interested in American history and contributed to many of the nation's leading magazines (Harpers, Hearth & Home) and, in 1876, wrote *"Bridgeport and Vicinity in the Revolution and the War of 1812"*.

In later life, Hincks became one of Bridgeport's most respected citizens, serving on the boards of a large number of Bridgeport businesses in his capacity as treasurer of the City Savings Bank of Bridgeport. He served as co-executor of P.T. Barnum's estate, which amounted to more than $5 million at the time.

Buried in Mountain Grove Cemetery, 2675 North Avenue, Bridgeport, Connecticut; Section 1, Mausoleum 17. Photos by the author.

246

QUARTERMASTER SERGEANT WILLIAM BEANEY HOOPER; ARMY

August 14, 1840 (Willimantic, CT) – January 16, 1870 (Caldera, Chile); 29 years old
Married to Margaret L. Long (1817-1880) on October 14, 1863.
Enlisted on February 24, 1864, in Jersey City, New Jersey
Mustered out on July 2, 1865

Born to John C.M. (1815-1894) and Mary A. Reed Hooper (1817-1880). One brother, George S. (1837-1892). One sister Helen E. Hooper Root (1843-1915).

MEDAL OF HONOR CITATION

AWARDED FOR ACTIONS DURING: Civil War
BRANCH OF SERVICE: Army
UNIT: Company L, 1st New Jersey Cavalry
DATE OF ISSUE AND PRESENTATION: July 3, 1865
AGE ON THE DAY OF THE EVENT: 24
CITATION:

The President of the United States of America, in the name of Congress, takes pleasure in presenting the Medal of Honor to Corporal William B. Hooper, United States Army, for extraordinary heroism on 31 March 1865, while serving with Company L, 1st New Jersey Cavalry, in action at Chamberlain's Creek, Virginia. With the assistance of a comrade, Corporal Hooper headed off the advance of the enemy, shooting two of his Color Bearers; also posted himself between the enemy and the lead horses of his own command, thus saving the herd from capture.

Others in the 1st Regiment, New Jersey Cavalry to receive the Medal of Honor

Sergeant James T. Clancy, C Company - Vaughan Road, 1 October 1864
Private Lewis Locke, A Company - Paine's Crossroads, 5 April 1865
Sergeant William Porter, H Company - Sayler's Creek, 6 April 1865
Sergeant John C. Sagelhurst, B Company - Hatcher's Run, 6 February 1865
Sergeant David Southard, C Company - Sayler's Creek, 6 April 1865
1st Sergeant George W. Stewart, E Company - Paine's Crossroads, 5 April 1865
Private Christian Streile, I Company - Paine's Crossroads, 5 April 1865
Sergeant Charles Titus, H Company - Sayler's Creek, 6 April 1865
Sergeant Aaron B. Tompkins, G Company - Sayler's Creek, 5 April 1865
Sergeant Charles E. Wilson, A Company - Sayler's Creek, 6 April 1865
Sergeant John Wilson, L Company - Chamberlain's Creek, 31 March 1865

From an unknown newspaper dated Monday, October 10, 1988

NEW HEADSTONE HONORS MYSTERY MAN AND HERO

WINDHAM — A Congressional Medal of Honor headstone was put in place Friday in the Old Willimantic Cemetery for Wilham B. Hooper — 118 years after he died.

The special stone is the first and only one of its kind in Windham.

The Medal of Honor star is etched in glistening gold leaf into the white Georgia marble stone. The simple stone indicates Hooper lived from 1841-1870 and was a
quartermaster sergeant in the 1st New Jersey Cavalry during the Civil War.

The new stone was placed in front of a large family headstone just left of the entrance to the cemetery at the intersection of Routes 32 and 66.

The inscription on the larger headstone states only that Hooper died in Caldera, Chile, on January 16, 1870, at the age of 29. Other names on the stone also are from the Hooper family, including John C. Hooper and Mary A. Hooper (possibly William's parents), John Root and Helen Hooper Root, and a George Hooper, who all died after William.

The two stones and a citation in the office of Hugh MacKinnon, Windham veterans' advisor, are the only accounts that could be found of William Hooper's ground. The citation states Hooper was awarded the Medal of Honor as a corporal for action in a battle at Chamberlain's Creek, Virginia, during the Civil War, MacKinnon said.

The rest of Hooper's history, including why he was given the highest decoration bestowed on Army personnel, remains a mystery. MacKinnon, who only learned of the special stone on Friday, said the Medal of Honor is only given to individuals who go beyond the call of duty. 'He had to do something outstanding to achieve this medal," MacKinnon said.

The medal is a special honor for U.S. Army or Marine personnel, he said, adding that the first Medal of Honor recipients were 15 Union Army men sent on a mission into the South by President Lincoln.

The story of how the stone came to Willimantic also was rather mysterious, according to two local men who got involved in the stone's placement.

Leonard Delehanty, town cemetery maintenance crew chief, said about two years ago, someone inquired about the location of Hooper's gravestone. He helped the person find the grave and then forgot about it.

Last spring, another man, who also did not give his name, asked Delehanty about the
grave and indicated that Hooper was to receive a Medal of Honor monument. The same man also visited George Rice, owner of Tri-County Memorials of Windham, asking him if he would install the headstone. The man said he would handle all the paperwork involved, so Rice also put the visit out of his mind until last week when the 20-pound marble stone, fully inscribed, arrived by truck at his offices on Windham Road.

All that came with the stone was an invoice and the bill for placing the stone, which he is to send to the Department of Veterans Affairs in Rocky Hill.

"I thought it was rather unique 118 years later to finally get a monument," said Rice
Friday as he and his son, Erik, marked the spot where the new stone would be placed.

Rice and Delehanty said they were glad the stone would be in such a prominent place in the Cemetery since it is one of a kind.

Mae Libera from the veteran's affairs office said Friday the headstone was indeed legitimate and was one of several being placed around the country for the first time to
mark the graves of Medal of Honor recipients.

Libera also revealed that the name of the mystery man who had inquired about Hooper's grave. He is Thomas F. Durning of New Haven, a member of the Sons of Union Veterans of the Civil War, who has been searching out the graves of Medal of Honor recipients all along the East Coast, Libera said. He has done the extensive research on his own, she added.

Libera had no information on Hooper, and Durning could not be reached for comment.

To add to the mystery of William Hooper, Delehanty said Hooper's remains are not buried in the Willimantic Cemetery, "He's not here. We have no record of his death."'

No one could answer the question of why Hooper died in South America. But Delehanty said Hooper was probably buried in Chile as bodies were not normally transported at that time.

Unknown burial location. He is one of 314 Medal of Honor recipients whose final resting place is a mystery. An 'In Memory Of' government-issued headstone is in the Hooper plot, Old Willimantic Cemetery, 1385 Main Street, Willimantic, Connecticut. Attempts to get information from the U.S. Embassy in Santiago, Chile, turned up no additional information. One of 314 Medal of Honor recipients whose final resting place is a mystery.

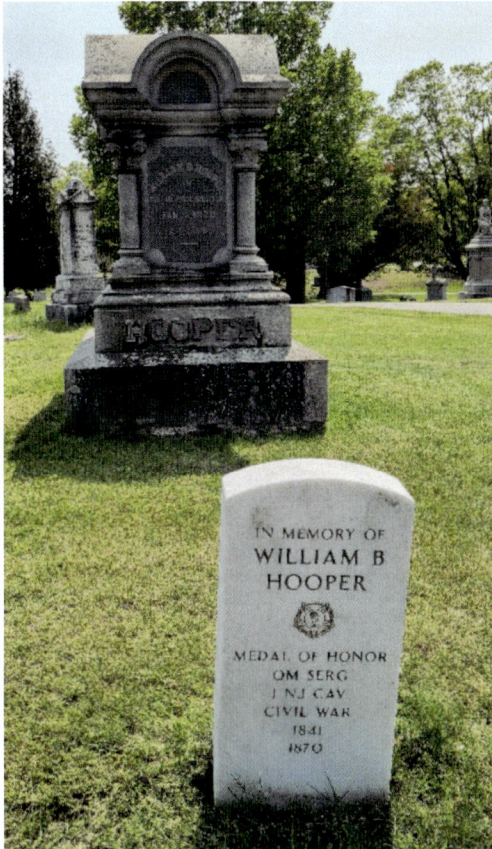

COLONEL SAMUEL BELTON HORNE; ARMY

March 3, 1843 (Tullamore, County Offaly, Ireland *) – September 18, 1928 (Winchester, CT); 85 years old
Married Etta D. Bartlett Horne (1852-1930) in 1872.
One son, Frank B. (1873-1874).
One daughter, Belle B. Horne Lawton (1872-1954)
Enlisted on April 22, 1861, in Winsted, Connecticut
Mustered out on November 17, 1864.

* There are inconsistencies regarding where Colonel Horne was born. On his 1899 passport application, he listed "Farbane, Kings County, Ireland." His death certificate lists "Tullamore, Ireland."

Born to Anthony (1808-1873) and Ann Horne (1808-1892). One sister, Matilda Horne Abel (1839-1897). Three brothers, William A. (1840-1918), John J. [Civil War veteran] (1845-1915), and Robert E. (1849-1914).

After his enlistment in 1861, he quickly rose through the enlisted ranks to First Sergeant. He subsequently was commissioned a Second Lieutenant in August 1863. He was wounded in September 1862 at Antietam, June 1864 at Cold Harbor, Virginia, and again at Chapin's Farm, Virginia, in September 1864. He was discharged due to those wounds in November 1864.

MEDAL OF HONOR CITATION

AWARDED FOR ACTIONS DURING: Civil War
BRANCH OF SERVICE: Army
UNIT: Company H, 11th Connecticut Infantry
DATE OF ISSUE AND PRESENTATION: November 19, 1897 (33 years later)
AGE ON THE DAY OF THE EVENT: 21
CITATION:

The President of the United States of America, in the name of Congress, takes pleasure in presenting the Medal of Honor to Captain (Infantry) Samuel Belton Horne, United States Army, for extraordinary heroism on 29 September 1864, while serving with Company H, 11th Connecticut Infantry, in action at Fort Harrison, Virginia. While acting as an Aide and carrying an important message, Captain Horne was severely wounded and his horse killed, but he delivered the order and rejoined his general.

From Beyer, W. F., & Keydel, O. F. (2000). Deeds of valor: How America's Civil War Heroes won The Congressional Medal of Honor. Smithmark Publishers.

A MESSAGE DELIVERED UNDER DIFFICULTY

With two dangerous wounds in his body, Lieutenant Samuel B. Horne of Company H, Eleventh Connecticut Infantry, was carried off the field at Cold Harbor, Virginia, on June 3, 1864, and sent to a hospital. Though his recovery proceeded slowly, he could not bear to be confined to his bed and three months later returned to his regiment, though still an invalid. Ten days later, at Chapin's Farm, Virginia, on September 29, 1864, he won his medal by a display of courage almost superhuman. It happened thus: Upon his return to the regiment, he was attached to the staff of General Ord as aide-de-camp and, during the attack on Fort Harrison, was sent to deliver a verbal message to the colonel of one of the advancing regiments.

"Though my injuries still pained me very much, I obeyed the order cheerfully," Lieutenant Horne goes on to tell. "I spurred my horse forward and soon came within range of the enemy's guns. While going at full gallop, my horse was killed by grapeshot and fell upon me with crushing weight, cracking some of my ribs, injuring me internally, and pinioning me to the ground. Here, I lay perfectly helpless and suffering intense pain until Colonel Wells rode up and relieved me from my precarious position. Still, the message had to be delivered, and although lacerated, in great pain, and partly denuded, I proceeded on foot to carry out my mission. I could only advance slowly and with difficulty and had to pass under the very guns of the fort before I reached the colonel of the advancing regiment. I reported to General Ord and was with him when he was wounded on the parapet and with him was taken to the rear."

Samuel Horne, writing under the letterhead of 'Peck & Horne, Counselors at Law and Solicitors in Chancery of Grand Rapids, Michigan' on April 5th, 1870, commenced a claim for compensation in respect of his Civil War service as he had not been correctly recorded as Captain nor paid in recognition of his promotion to the rank of Captain. His rank was officially corrected under Special Order No. 282, Headquarters of the Army, on December 9, 1885. The financial reimbursement for such rank was rectified in the 54th Congress by Bill H.R.7696 in the House of Representatives on March 27, 1896, and S.2720 in the Senate on April 2, 1896.

Horne received a letter from the Secretary of War dated November 4, 1897, which stated, "You are hereby notified that by direction of the President and under provisions of the Act of Congress approved March 3, 1863, providing for the presentation of Medals of Honor to such officers, non-commissioned officers and privates as have most distinguished themselves in action, a Congressional Medal of Honor has this day been presented to you for Most Distinguished Gallantry in Action, the following being a statement of the particular service, viz: At Fort Harrison, Virginia, September 29th, 1864, this officer, then serving as First Lieutenant 11th Connecticut Volunteers, and acting as aide-de-camp to General Ord, while carrying an important message on the field was wounded and his horse killed; but notwithstanding his severe wounds and sufferings, he continued on his way, delivered the order, and then joined his General but had to be taken to the rear on account of injuries received. The medal will be forwarded by registered mail as soon as it shall have been engraved."

In fact, it was sent on November 19 and received by Horne on November 23, 1897.

On January 31, 1908, the War Department advised Horne that he was to be issued with another Medal of Honor of the new design to be engraved,

The Congress To
Captain Samuel B. Horne
Co. H, 11th Conn. Inf. Vols
Fort Harrison, Va.
Sept. 29, 1864.

The new medal was sent to him on February 21, 1908, and received on March 2, 1908.

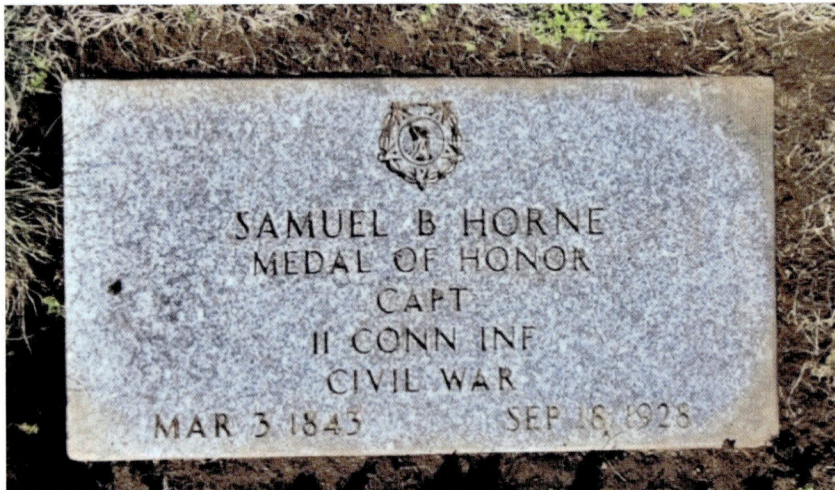

BREVET MAJOR WILLIAM STONE HUBBELL; ARMY

April 19, 1837 (Wolcottville, CT) – August 28, 1930 (Plymouth, MA); 93 years old
Married to Caroline Southmayd (1840-1922)
Two sons, William S. II (1874-1901), and DeWitt (1876-1952).
Two daughters, Mary C. (1867-1947) and Susan (1869-1958).
Enlisted on August 30, 1862, in North Stonington, Connecticut
Commissioned in November 1862
Wounded on May 16, 1864, at Drewry's Bluff, Virginia
Mustered out November 24, 1862

Born to Reverend Stephen (1802-1884) and Martha E. Stone Hubbell (1814-1856). One sister, Mary E. (1833-1854). One brother, Edward S. (1839-1839).

One of five members of the 21st Connecticut to receive the Medal of Honor.

Photo courtesy of FindAGrave.com

MEDAL OF HONOR CITATION

AWARDED FOR ACTIONS DURING: Civil War
BRANCH OF SERVICE: Army
UNIT: Company A, 21st Connecticut Infantry
DATE OF ISSUE AND PRESENTATION: June 13, 1894 (30 years later)
AGE ON THE DAY OF THE EVENT: 27
CITATION:

The President of the United States of America, in the name of Congress, takes pleasure in presenting the Medal of Honor to Captain (Infantry) William Stone Hubbell, United States Army, for extraordinary heroism on 30 September 1864, while serving with Company A, 21st Connecticut Infantry, in action at Fort Harrison, Virginia. Captain Hubbell led out a small flanking party and by a clash and at great risk, captured a large number of prisoners.

William Stone Hubbell, son of Rev. Stephen (Yale, 1826) and Martha (Stone) Hubbell, was born in Wolcottville, Litchfield County, Connecticut, April 19, 1837. He was prepared for College by E. L. Hart, Farmington, Connecticut, and entered the Class on July 24, 1854.

From October 1858, he was engaged in surveying in Will and Kankakee Counties, Illinois, until June 1859, and then returned to the East. During the Autumn of 1859 and Winter of 1859 and '60, he studied Engineering at Yale. During part of the Spring and Summer of 1860, he taught at a private school at Stonington, Connecticut. In September 1860, he entered the Junior Class in the Andover Theological Seminary and remained until August 1862. August 30, 1862, he enlisted as a private in the 25th Connecticut Infantry, was promoted to be 2nd Lieutenant in the 21st Connecticut Infantry November 24, 1862, 1st Lieutenant February 5, 1864, and Captain September 23, 1864. He was twice wounded; May 16, 1864, at Drury's Bluff, by a shell in the right thigh, and September 30, 1864, at Chapin's Farm (Fort Harrison) by a musket ball entering the back and left side, skipping over and behind the spine, and reentering and passing out through the right shoulder. He was for the last year detailed as A. A. G. of his brigade, at one time the third in the First Division, 18th Corps, and at another, in the Third Division, 24th Corps. He was discharged July 1, 1865, with his regiment, and in the following September, commenced his third and last year at Andover and wrote, "My morals are on the rise."

He is a descendant, in the seventh generation, of Richard Hubbell of Fairfield, Connecticut, who was born in 1627-8.

On February 1, 1898, he became Secretary of The New York Sabbath Committee at 31 Bible House.

"The object of this Society, which was formed in 1857, is to protect and promote Sunday Rest and Observance, and to awaken public sentiment so as to secure the prudent enforcement of existing laws and new legislation when necessary and to guard against unfavorable legislation: to prevent unnecessary work and illegal public amusements on Sunday: and in general, to save the Rest Day from destruction by greed, pleasure, and irreligion.

"With this strenuous task, I have been busy for the past ten years, making a multitude of addresses in New York State and elsewhere, conducting fifty public hearings before the legislature and the mayor, campaigning for the Sunday closing of Expositions at Buffalo, Omaha, St. Louis, Jamestown, and Seattle, taking part in various Sunday Rest Congresses in this country and in Europe, consorting with commissioners and other police authorities in New York, and acting as the complainant in many courts, serving as President of the Federation of the eleven Sunday Rest Societies in the United States and Canada for four years, and issuing many reports and other documents meanwhile.

"It has been a difficult and delicate business, from which I would gladly withdraw if allowed to do so. During this period, I have visited Europe seven times with most of my family."

He edited and prepared The Story of the Twenty-First Regiment, Connecticut Volunteer Infantry, Stewart Printing Company, Middletown, Connecticut, 1900.

He is serving his eighth term as Chaplain of the New York Commandery of the Loyal Legion: is Chaplain of the Medal of Honor Legion, of George Washington Post, No. 103, G.A.R., and of the Military Society Department of the Gulf. He is a member of the Army and Navy Club and is Vice-President of the Quill Club.

From the Democrat and Chronicle (Rochester, New York) June 27, 1884

UTICA, June 26, -- Twenty-three graduates of the class of forty-nine members that left Clinton in a body last winter took part in the commencement exercises at Hamilton College today. The Kellogg Commencement Prize was awarded to Reuben L. McGuicken of Utica. The following honorary degrees were conferred: Ph.D. – Professor Francis Brown of the Union Theological Seminary in New York; Doctorate of Divinity – Reverend William Stone Hubbell of Buffalo, Reverend Amory Howe Bradford of Montclair, New Jersey, and Reverend William Henry Palmer of Penn Yan, New York; LLD (Doctor of Law) – Judge Glenni William Scofield of the United States Court of Claims in Washington and William F. Cogswell of Rochester.

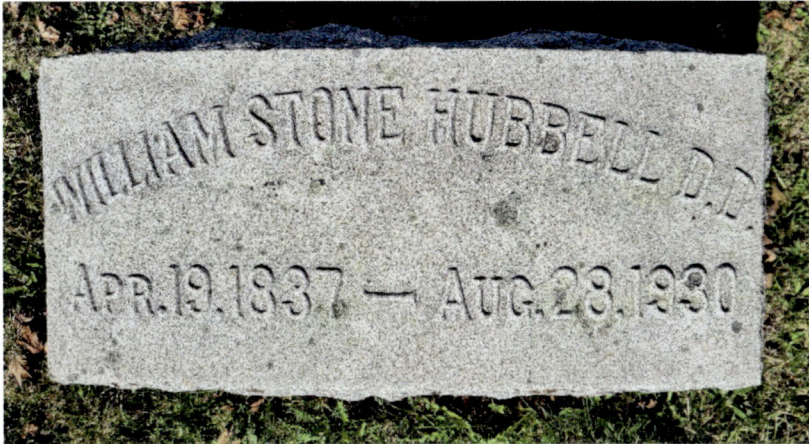

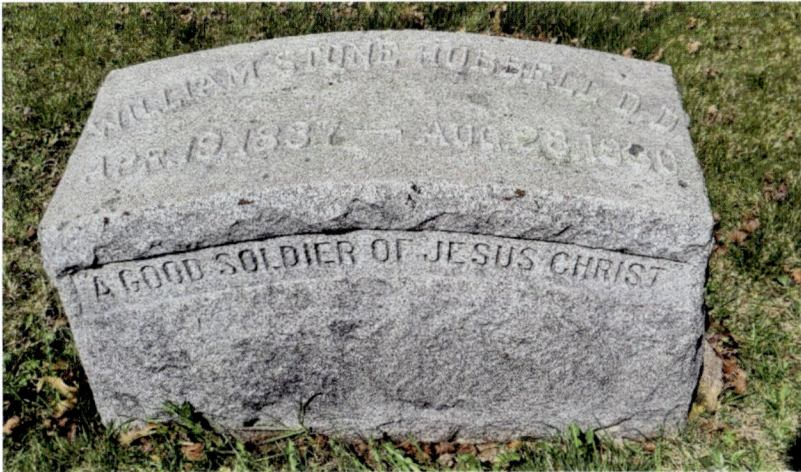

SERGEANT MAJOR FREDERICK RANDOLPH JACKSON; ARMY

February 18, 1844 (North Haven, CT) – February 14, 1925 (Smithville, NY); 80 years old

Married Emma L. Gibbs (1846-1872) on February 2, 1865, in Washington, DC.

Three daughters, Maude I. Jackson Crumb (1866-1953), Emma G. Jacson Burch (1868-1958), and Harriet W. (1871-1872).

Enlisted on August 29, 1861, in New Haven, Connecticut.

Imprisoned on June 16, 1862, at James Island, South Carolina.

Mustered out on October 19, 1862, due to a wound to the elbow by a canister shot.

Born to Benjamin H. (1813-1888) and Harriet Bradley Jackson (1816-1903). One brother, William "Willie" E. (1854-1906).

Photo courtesy of Ancestry.com   *Photo courtesy of the Congressional Medal of Honor Society*

MEDAL OF HONOR CITATION

AWARDED FOR ACTIONS DURING: Civil War
BRANCH OF SERVICE: Army
UNIT: Company F, 7th Connecticut Infantry
DATE OF ISSUE AND PRESENTATION: 1863
AGE ON THE DAY OF THE EVENT: 18
CITATION:

The President of the United States of America, in the name of Congress, takes pleasure in presenting the Medal of Honor to First Sergeant Frederick Randolph Jackson, United States Army, for extraordinary heroism on 16 June 1862, while serving with Company F, 7th Connecticut Infantry, in action at James Island, South Carolina. Having his left arm shot away in a charge on the enemy, First Sergeant Jackson continued on duty, taking part in a second and a third charge until he fell exhausted from the loss of blood.

From Beyer, W. F., & Keydel, O. F. (2000). Deeds of valor: How America's Civil War Heroes won The Congressional Medal of Honor. Smithmark Publishers.

When the Seventh Connecticut Infantry was storming Fort Lamar, James Island, South Carolina, at daybreak June 16, 1862, Sergeant Jackson was in command of Company F. He was struck above the elbow with a canister shot from an eight-inch columbiad, and his left arm was shattered. With his right hand, Jackson seized his splintered arm, pressed it tightly to prevent, as much as possible, the flow of blood, and dashed forward with his men. The regiment retired, rallied again, and went forward on the second charge, only to be again repulsed. Once more, the

regiment rallied, and in this charge, Sergeant Jackson fell, fainting from the loss of blood.   He lay on the field from five o'clock in the morning until half-past ten at night, only a hundred feet from the fort, neither Federals nor Confederates daring to succor their wounded, so fierce was the firing. During more than seventeen hours, he remained unable to move, all the while exposed to the fire from the Union forces but too near the fort to be in range of the enemy's missiles.

FREDERICK R. JACKSON,
1st Serg't., Co. F.,
7th Conn. Inf.
Highest rank attained; Major, U. S. V.
Born at New Haven, Conn.

Referring to this part of his experience, he writes:

"Of the fourteen comrades who came under the Confederate surgeon's knife as prisoners, only myself and one other lived to reach home. I was put under the influence of chloroform, and when I became conscious again, discovered two surgeon's knives and another instrument lying across my breast. Among those in the room were General Gist, commanding the Confederates, and the colonel in charge of the fort. On regaining consciousness, someone asked me:

"How many troops have your forces got?"

"Go over and count them," I replied.

"We will go over, and we shall get them all," said he.

"The surgeon was Doctor Bellinger, the son of one of the most famous surgeons in the South at that time. He said to me:

"The Southern Confederacy is not abundantly supplied with chloroform and will not throw any away on you."

"Before beginning to amputate my arm, they divided some of my clothing among themselves. The first thing taken was a pair of new boots which had been sent from home by my father. My uniform was also disposed of, and they gave me a shabby suit of clothes in case I should ever need any more. Then the surgeon proceeded to cut off my arm, and, true to his word, he did not waste any of the Southern Confederacy's chloroform on me."

"I was made acquainted with six of the Southern prisons and was graduated from Libby [prison] October 14, 1862."

From "New York's North Country and the Civil War: Soldiers, Civilians and Legacies" Shampine, D. (2012)

As he was being discharged from the Army, he met the president, who had been informed by other soldiers of Mr. Jackson's heroics and his injury. In a letter written by Mr. Jackson nearly three decades later, he quoted the president. "I want to give this brave boy a Medal of Honor, and I wish you would personally see that he has one," Mr. Lincoln said to Secretary of War Edwin M. Stanton. Then, dismissing the soldier, Mr. Lincoln promised him a commission."

Buried in Smithville Cemetery, north side of County Route 71 (Penney Road), just past the intersection of Sand Road, Smithville, New York. Photos from FindAGrave.com.

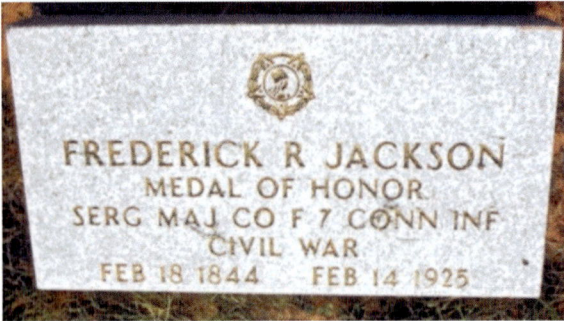

258

PRIVATE FIRST CLASS WILLIAM JAMES "JIMMY" JOHNSTON SR.; ARMY

August 15, 1918 (Trenton, NJ) – May 29, 1990 (Newington, CT); 71 years old
Married Dorothy G. Clark Johnston (1921-2005) on August 8, 1942, in Colchester, Connecticut
One son, William J., Jr. (1943-).
Three daughters, Dorothy "Dottie" E. Johnston O'Meara (1946-), Diane J. Johnston Carragher (1950-2014), and
    Donna L. (1954-).
Enlisted on March 13, 1943.
Serial number 31009365.
Basic training at Fort McClellan, Alabama. Infantry training at Camp Rooker, Alabama.
Discharged on September 9, 1944, after a seven-month hospital stay.

Born to John G. (1881-1961) and Mary A. Watson Johnston (1888-1922). John was born in Scotland, and Mary in
England. Mary died when PFC Johnston was three years old. Three brothers, Robert G. (1910-1996), John J. (1914-
1960), and Charles O. (1920-1998). One sister, Elizbeth G. Johnston Cohen (1912-1994).

Following his discharge from the Army, PFC Johnston had a long career with the Veterans Administration. He was
also the VFW Department of Connecticut Commander in 1952-1953, representing Post 6990 in Amston.

Member of the Connecticut Veterans Hall of Fame, Class of 2006.
In a meeting between the author and daughter Dottie O'Meara, she said, "We were buddies." She went on to say
her father was a quiet man. The shrapnel that injured her father entered his chest and exited his side. Half of one
lung was removed because of this event.

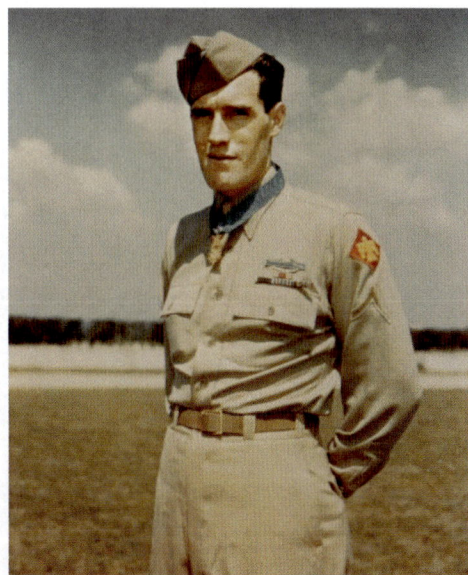

Photos courtesy of the Congressional Medal of Honor Society

MEDAL OF HONOR CITATION

AWARDED FOR ACTIONS DURING: World War II
BRANCH OF SERVICE: Army
UNIT: Company G, 180th Infantry Regiment, 45th Infantry Division

GENERAL ORDERS: War Department, General Orders No. 73, September 6, 1944
AGE ON THE DAY OF THE EVENT: 26
CITATION:

The President of the United States of America, in the name of Congress, takes pleasure in presenting the Medal of Honor to Private First Class William James Johnston, Sr., United States Army, for conspicuous gallantry and intrepidity at risk of life above and beyond the call of duty on February 17 - 19, 1944, while serving with Company G, 180th Infantry Regiment, 45th Infantry Division. On 17 February 1944, near Padiglione, Italy, Private First Class Johnston observed and fired upon an attacking force of approximately 80 Germans, causing at least 25 casualties and forcing withdrawal of the remainder. All that day, he manned his gun without relief, subject to mortar, artillery, and sniper fire. Two Germans individually worked so close to his position that his machine gun was ineffective, whereupon he killed one with his pistol the second with a rifle taken from another soldier. When a rifleman protecting his gun position was killed by a sniper, he immediately moved the body and relocated the machine gun in that spot in order to obtain a better field of fire. He volunteered to cover the platoon's withdrawal and was the last man to leave that night. In his new position, he maintained an all-night vigil, the next day causing seven German casualties. On the afternoon of the 18th, the organization on the left flank, having been forced to withdraw, he again covered the withdrawal of his own organization. Shortly thereafter, he was seriously wounded over the heart, and a passing soldier saw him trying to crawl up the embankment. The soldier aided him to resume his position behind the machine gun, which was soon heard in action for about ten minutes. Though reported killed, Private First Class Johnston was seen returning to the American lines on the morning of 19 February, slowly and painfully working his way back from his overrun position through enemy lines. He gave valuable information of new enemy dispositions. His heroic determination to destroy the enemy and his disregard of his own safety aided immeasurably in halting a strong enemy attack, caused an enormous amount of enemy casualties, and so inspired his fellow soldiers that they fought for and held a vitally important position against greatly superior forces.

Presentation Date and Details: August 30, 1944, in Washington, D.C., presented by President Franklin D. Roosevelt and Undersecretary of War Robert P. Patterson, Jr.

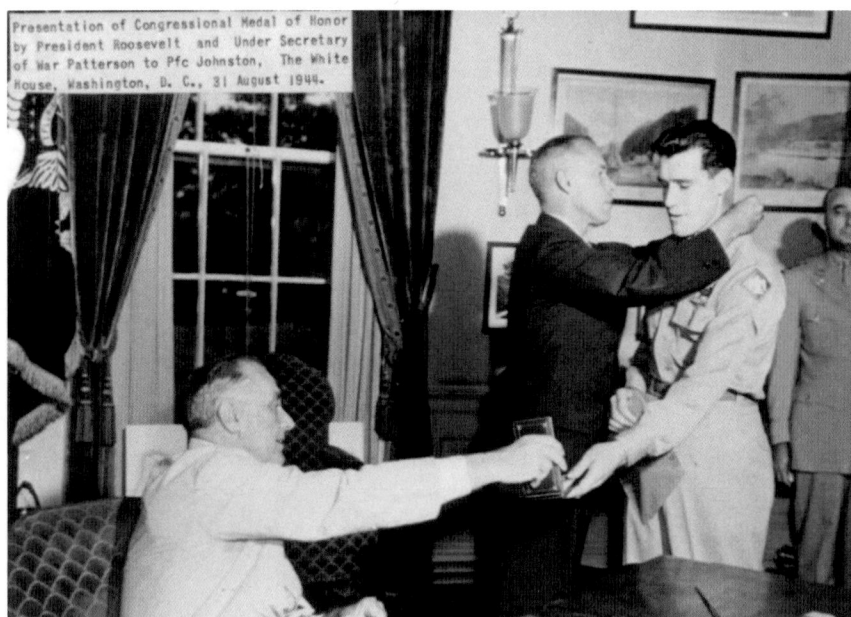

Photo courtesy of the Congressional Medal of Honor Society

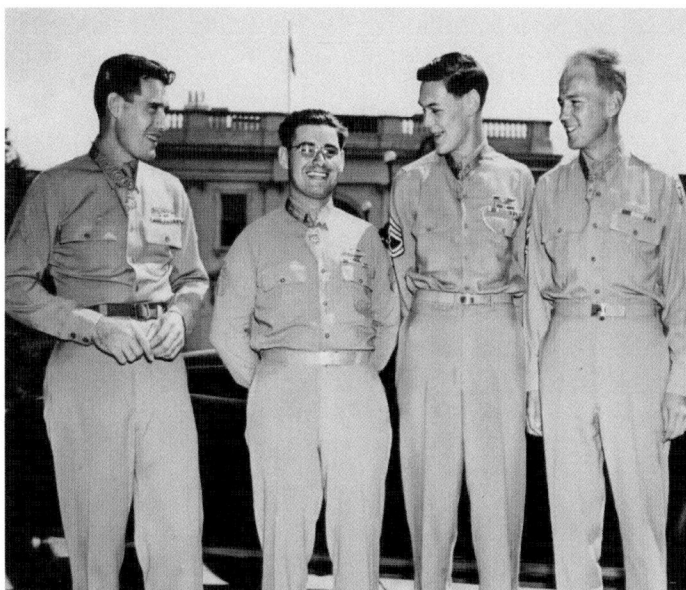

Photo courtesy of LittleRock.gov; photo credit to ACME. On the White House lawn are four Medal of Honor recipients: (left to right) PFC William J. Johnston, Colchester, Connecticut; SSgt Jesse R. Drowley, Luzerne, Michigan (1919-1996); TSgt Forrest L. Vosler, Livonia, N.Y. (1923-1992); and 1st Lt Arnold L Bjorklund (1918-1979), Seattle, Washington.

From the 180th Infantry Division History. All three Medal of Honor recipients listed survived the war.

Roll of Honor

CONGRESSIONAL MEDAL OF HONOR

1st LT. JACK C. MONTGOMERY   PFC. WILLIAM J. JOHNSTON
2nd LT. ERNEST CHILDERS

DISTINGUISHED SERVICE-CROSS

LT. COL. CHESTER G. CRUIKSHANK	CAPT. BENJAMIN BLACKMER
CAPT. MILTON JARROLD	CAPT. CLIFTON MC CLAIN, JR
CAPT. RODERIC G. MORERE	1st LT. CYRIL MURPHY
1st LT. JOHN B. MYERS	2nd LT. CHARLES A. BRANDT
2nd LT. JOHN H. HAYS	2nd LT. PAUL L. PETERSON
2nd LT. JACK L. TREADWELL	T/SGT. ROBERT O. ALEXANDER
T/SGT. BILLY MCMILLIAN	T/SGT. WALTER E. ROBINSON
S/SGT. JOHN C. GAZZETTI	S/SGT. TROY E HOTTINGER
S/SGT. SALVADOR J. LARA	S/SGT. CHARLES W. SHIELDS
SGT. CHARLIE L. CASEY	SGT. EDWIN L. HURD
SGT. MILTON I. RUSSELL	SGT. MARTIN N. SCHRECK
CPL. CHARLES E. MACEK	TEC/5 SHERRILL LACKEY
PFC. BARRY CRANFILL	PFC. LLOYD C. GREER
PFC. JOHN KOZEJ	PFC. ALPHONSE LAUDATO, JR.
PFC. DOMINGO MARTINEZ	PFC. HENRY C. SALLEY
PVT. ALLEN LANGILLE	

LEGION OF MERIT

LT. COL. DANIEL K. AHERN	LT. COL. EVERETT DUVALL
MAJOR WILLIAM T. BROGAN	MAJOR KIRK A. MEADERS
CAPT. ROBERT C. CATES	CAPT. EARL M. COOPER
CAPT. THOMAS B. FINAN	CAPT. JAMES O. SMITH
1st LT. HOWARD M. RICHIE	T/SGT. CARL R. FORCE
T/SGT. WILLIAM SCHWEIKHARD	T/SGT. ARNOLD W. SMITH
S/SGT. FRANKLIN ADAMS	T/SGT. HENRY WEINBERGER
S/SGT. WILLARD BERGMAN	S/SGT. UEAL F. ALLEN
SGT. CHARLES F. LEEPER	SGT. MELVIN C. BROWN

The Medal of Honor and certificate are from a display case in the William J. Johnston Middle School lobby. Photos by the author.

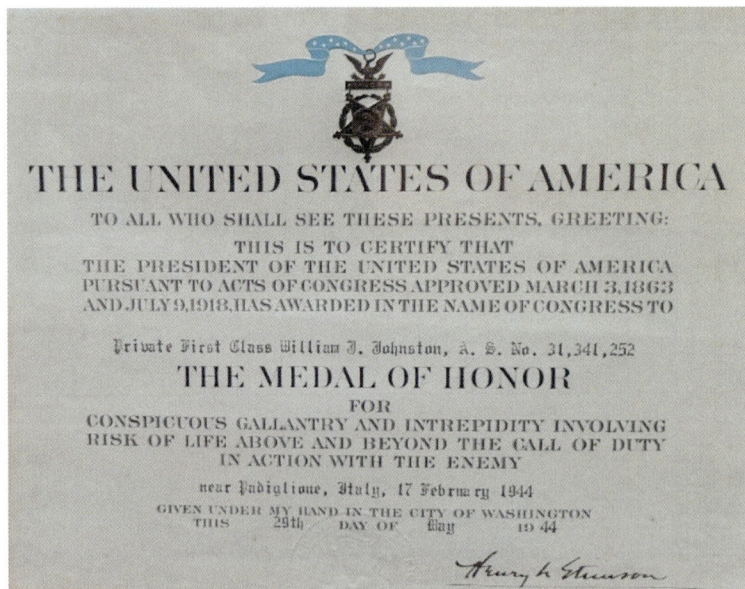

He was also awarded the Bronze Star Medal for action during the Naples-Foggia Campaign. Certificate and medal are from a display in the William J. Johnston Middle School lobby. Photos by the author.

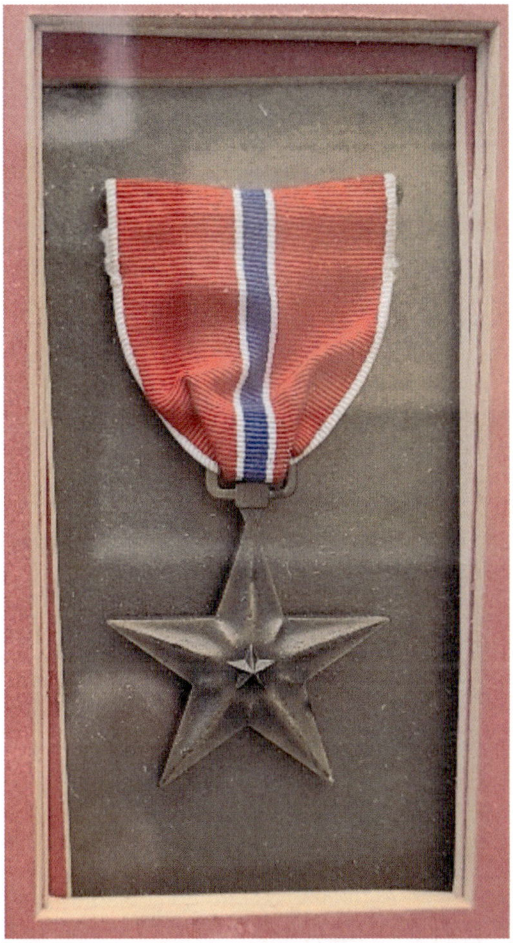

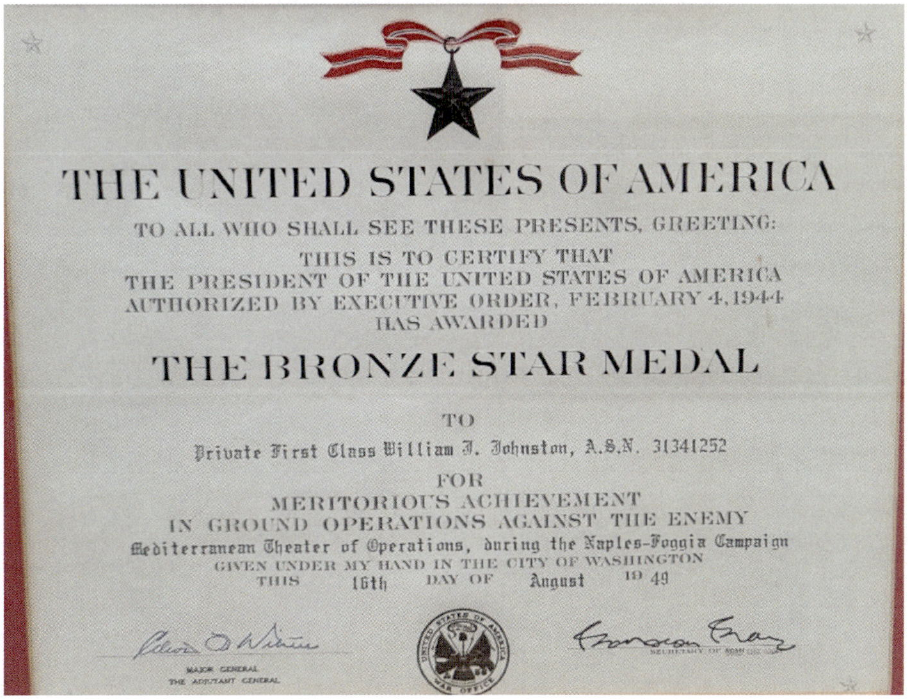

THE UNITED STATES OF AMERICA

TO ALL WHO SHALL SEE THESE PRESENTS, GREETING:

THIS IS TO CERTIFY THAT
THE PRESIDENT OF THE UNITED STATES OF AMERICA
AUTHORIZED BY EXECUTIVE ORDER, FEBRUARY 4, 1944
HAS AWARDED

THE BRONZE STAR MEDAL

TO

Private First Class William J. Johnston, A.S.N. 31341252

FOR
MERITORIOUS ACHIEVEMENT
IN GROUND OPERATIONS AGAINST THE ENEMY
Mediterranean Theater of Operations, during the Naples-Foggia Campaign
GIVEN UNDER MY HAND IN THE CITY OF WASHINGTON
THIS 16th DAY OF August 1949

UNITED STATES OF AMERICA
WAR OFFICE

MAJOR GENERAL
THE ADJUTANT GENERAL

SECRETARY OF [illegible]

Purple Heart Medal from display in William J. Johnston Middle School lobby. Photo by the author.

This is the Purple Heart
received by Mr. Johnston
because he was
wounded in battle

TRANSLATION OF THE CERTIFICATE

MINISTRY OF WAR

Umberto of Savoy Prince of Piedmont Lieutenant General of the Kingdom with His Decree dated 15 September 1945.

Having regard to the Royal Decree 4 November 1932, no 1423 subsequent modifications, on the proposal of the Minister Secretary of State for Affairs. Of the war;

He conferred the Motu Troprio.
Military Cross
to PFC Johnston, William J.

IN THE ITALIAN COUNTRYSIDE HE WAS DISTINGUISHED FOR VALOR AND HIGH SPIRIT OF SACRIFICE

    The Minister Secretary of State for War Affairs hereby releases this document to certify the conferred honorary badge.

Rome, October 5, 1944

Namesake of William J. Johnston Middle School at 360 Norwich Avenue, Colchester, Connecticut.

Front of William J. Johnston Middle School. Photo by the author.

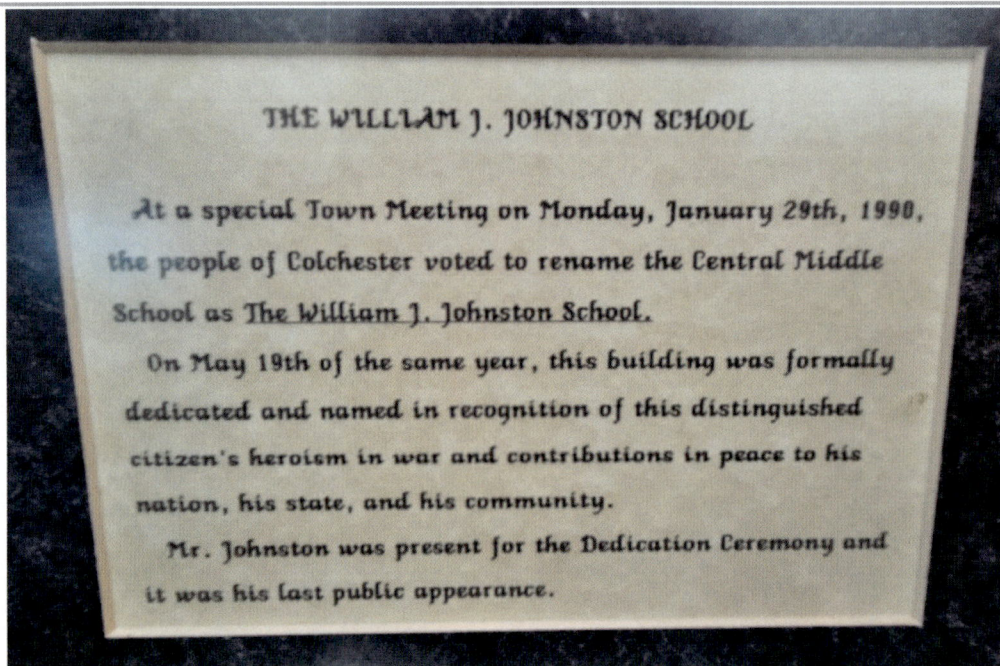

THE WILLIAM J. JOHNSTON SCHOOL

At a special Town Meeting on Monday, January 29th, 1990, the people of Colchester voted to rename the Central Middle School as The William J. Johnston School.

On May 19th of the same year, this building was formally dedicated and named in recognition of this distinguished citizen's heroism in war and contributions in peace to his nation, his state, and his community.

Mr. Johnston was present for the Dedication Ceremony and it was his last public appearance.

Plaque in the lobby of William J. Johnston Middle School. Photo by the author.

On May 19, 1990, Central Middle School was renamed the William J. Johnston Middle School in honor of Colchester's World War II Congressional Medal of Honor recipient, William J. Johnston. Mr. Johnston, a native of Colchester, received the nation's highest award for his conspicuous gallantry and intrepidity at risk of life, above and beyond the call of duty, in action against the enemy.

President Franklin D. Roosevelt presented the Medal of Honor to Private First Class Johnston on May 29, 1944. Following his discharge from the Army, Mr. Johnston built a career with the Veteran's Administration as a service officer. He was also a former Selectman of the Town of Colchester and an active member of the American Legion and the Veterans of Foreign Wars.

Mr. Johnston's message for the students of Colchester was to "respect each other" and to respect the right to disagree without being disagreeable, to be decent, and to be willing to accept other people's opinions.

Mr. Johnston passed away on May 29, 1990, forty-six years after he received his most prestigious honor.

From the River East News Bulletin October 12, 2007. Author: Jim Salemi. Used with permission.

COLCHESTER HIGHWAY NAMED IN JOHNSTON'S HONOR

The section of Lebanon Avenue between Broadway and the Lebanon town line was dedicated as the William J. Johnston Memorial Highway last Friday (October 5, 2007) on the town green, near where the green sign stands.

Family and friends of World War II veteran and Congressional Medal of Honor recipient William J. Johnston Sr. gathered on the green for the formal ceremony, flanked on one side by the Antique Veterans Color Guard.

Johnston died 17 years ago, but if he had been in attendance, he might have simply shaken his head over all the fuss, just as he did on the very same green 60 years ago when the town threw a celebration in his honor after returning from Europe, a hero.

"Sixty years ago, after he returned and healed, there was a big celebration for him on the town green. The whole town was there. The whole town was so proud of him." said American Legion commander and VFW member Ray Ryan, a veteran of the Korean War era.

"People were heaping on the praise and appreciation," Ryan continued, "and all he could do was sit there and wonder what all the hoopla was about. To him, he was just doing his job."

Ryan, who served as master of ceremony last Friday with VFW Commander Joe Burba, also read Johnston's Medal of Honor citation by President Roosevelt:

"On 17 February 1944, near Padigilone, Italy, he observed and fired upon an attacking force of approximately 80 Germans. causing at least 25 casualties and forcing withdrawal of the remainder." Ryan read. "All that day, he manned his gun without relief, subject to mortar, artillery, and sniper fire. ... When a rifleman protecting his gun position was killed by a sniper, he immediately moved the body and relocated the machinegun in that spot in order to obtain a better field of fire. ... Shortly thereafter, he was seriously wounded over the heart, and a passing soldier saw him trying to crawl up the embankment. The soldier aided him to resume his position behind the machine gun, which was soon heard in action for about 10 minutes..."

Other details in the citation include accounts of when Johnston killed soldiers who had worked their way so close to him that his fixed machine gun was ineffective. He killed one with his pistol and another with a rifle taken from another soldier.

State Rep. Linda Orange presented Johnston's family with a replica of the sign naming the road for Johnston.

William Johnston Jr. and his wife Judy, as well as Johnston Sr.'s daughter Dottie O'Meara and her husband Thomas, were among the family members in attendance.

Orange acknowledged the veteran's groups, former First Selectman Jenny Contois and State Senator Eileen Daily, for making the memorial possible.

"This is a great honor bestowed upon your father," Orange said to Johnston Jr. and O'Meara.

State Rep. Linda Orange speaks at last week's William J. Johnston Memorial Highway dedication. Also shown are Johnston's son, William J. Johnston Jr., and daughter Dottie O'Meara.

While Johnston is recognized for earning the Medal of Honor recipient, he also received other awards, including the Purple Heart, the Combat Infantry Badge, the Italian Medal of Honor, and the Bronze Star during his relatively brief service.

Johnston was born in 1918 in Trenton, New Jersey, came to Connecticut with his family in 1919, and settled in Amston.

In 1922, his mother died, and Johnston was taken in by the Harrison Foote family in Colchester. Johnston went to the Unionville School for his elementary education and attended Bacon Academy from 1933-37, where he was active in sports, playing on the basketball and baseball teams.

After high school, Johnston went to work for Bacon Brothers in Middletown as an apprentice plumber. He later worked as a truck driver and then went to work for United Aircraft in East Hartford in 1939.

Johnston married Dorothy Clark from North Westchester on August 8. 1942. He entered the service on March 23, 1943, and was discharged on September 9, 1944. After working again as a truck driver for a year, Johnston went to work for the Veterans' Administration in Hartford in 1945, remaining with them until he retired. He had four children: William Jr., Dorothy, Diane, and Donna.

Johnston was also involved in the Colchester community. He served as a selectman, coached basketball at Bacon Academy, and was a member of the VFW, American Legion, the Legion of Valor, and the Colchester Fish and Game Club. He died on May 29, 1990.

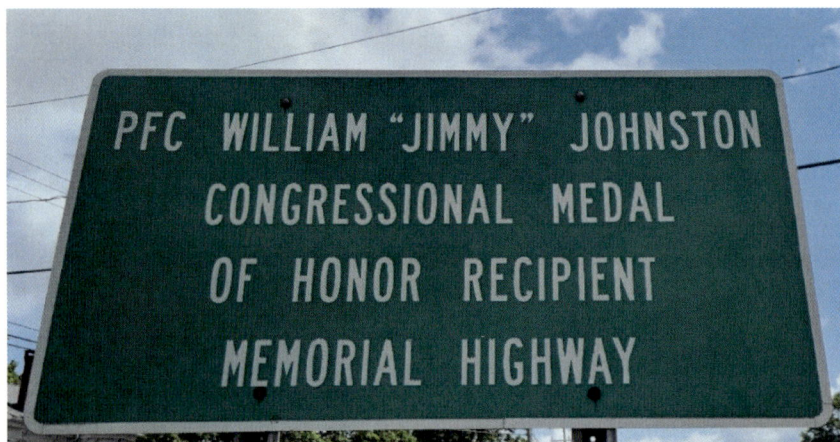

Photo by the author

From The Regional Standard June 2, 1990

COLCHESTER MOURNS DEATH OF WILLIAM J. JOHNSTON
War Hero's Memory Lives In School Recently Dedicated In His Honor

So we're glad
Not that our friend is gone
But that the world he loved and lived upon
Was our world, too.
That we had closely known and loved him
And that our love we'd shown.
Tears over his departure?
Nay, a smile that we had walked with him a little while.

- Poem, unknown author, and title, quoted by Dr. Franklin Gross

COLCHESTER - War hero and Colchester native William J. Johnston Sr. died Tuesday (May 29), 10 days after the middle school was dedicated and renamed in his
honor.

Johnston, 71, had suffered from a lung condition for a number of years, and according to his wife, Dorothy, his condition had been getting worse. He was admitted to the U.S. Veterans Medical Center in Newington on Sunday.

"I'm so glad he lived to see the dedication," she said, noting that it was becoming impossible for his lungs to expel carbon dioxide as the muscles had lost their elasticity. By Tuesday, his heart and kidneys had failed.

"Just before he died, he was the most peaceful man you would want to see," she said. "The whole family was with him at the end, and it was really beautiful." Dorothy Johnston said she has all good memories and believes the "Lord has been good to us."

The Board of Selectmen has declared May 30 to June 6 a period of mourning in Johnston's memory and "further proclaim that this shall be a period of reflection on his life."

Calling Johnston a good friend, First Selectman F. Duncan Green said, "If I ever could say I loved a man, I loved Bill and admired him."

Johnston was awarded the Congressional Medal of Honor in September 1944 by President Franklin D. Roosevelt for an act of bravery under fire against the Germans near Padiglione, Italy, during the Anzio invasion in February 1944. For two days, he manned a machine gun without relief and held off the enemy despite being seriously wounded. Eventually, after being reported killed, Private First Class Johnston worked his way back to the American lines.

"They talk about what I did with a machine gun," Johnston once said. "The truth of the matter is I never qualified in basic training to use a machine gun, and my sergeant was always on me about that."

When talk about naming a school for him started, he thought his friends were joking. Overwhelmed at the prospect, he said it reminded him of the time he walked into the Oval Office to meet President Roosevelt. "My knees were shaking," he had recalled. "Now that was scary."

But his town honored him for more than winning a medal. Over the years, he dedicated his life to his country, state, and town. "He was such a kind man," Margaret Fuchs said. "He helped so many veterans, and after talking to him, they all came away feeling so much better."

Fuchs said she believes that people should give flowers to one another when they are alive, not after they have died. As one of the residents who spearheaded the move to rename the school, she thanked God that "Jimmy lived long enough to be there.

"I knew him since he was about two years old," Fuchs added, "All the old-timers called him Jimmy - I guess he preferred it." Fuchs' comment about Johnston living long enough to attend the ceremony was echoed by many others as word of his death spread.

"How wonderful that he was there," Louis Amara said. "I brought my children (to the dedication) and would like them to remember what he represented."

Dr. Franklin Gross, who came to know Johnston fairly well in recent years, said he immediately thought of Jacqueline Kennedy's words after President John F. Kennedy was shot. "For one brief shining moment, there was Camelot," he said. Happily, Bill Johnston had his Camelot while he was alive."

During his lifetime, Johnston preferred to talk about his years in Colchester, nor his war experiences. "I love this town, and I very much like the new people who are moving in," he said not long ago. "They have many new ideas we ought to listen to."

Johnston was born August 15, 1918, in Trenton, New Jersey, the son of the late John and Mary (Watson) Johnston. Married for almost 48 years to his childhood sweetheart Dorothy Clark, whom he wed on August 8, 1942, in Colchester, Johnston also said that in looking back on his life, he would not change a thing "if I had my life to live over."

Johnston was retired from the State of Connecticut Treasury Department, Veterans Bonus Division. He served as a commissioner of the Rocky Hill Veteran's Home and Hospital and was retired from the Veterans Administration in Hartford.

Active in the Veterans of Foreign Wars, the American Legion, the Legion of Valor, and the Disabled American Veterans, Johnston was also a member of the Purple Heart and Medal of Honor Society. He had served on both the

Board of Selectmen and the Borough Board of Burgesses and was an active member of the Colchester Fish and Game Club and the St. Andrews Holy Name Society.

In addition to his wife, Johnston is survived by four children - a son, William J. Johnston Jr. of Newtown and three daughters. Dorothy O'Meara of Colchester, Diane Carragher of Colchester, and Donna Johnston of New York – and six grandchildren. He was predeceased by a brother, John Johnston.

Funeral services were held June 1 at St. Andrews Roman Catholic Church in Colchester; he was buried in the Connecticut State Veteran's Cemetery on Silver Street in Middletown. Donations may be made in his memory to the St. Andrew's Improvement Fund, Norwich Avenue, Colchester 06415.

From an unknown newspaper. Clipping is held in the Congressional Medal of Honor Society archives. Used with permission.

A HERO IN OUR MIDST

Dear Sir:

I want to thank the community of Colchester for the dedication of the William J. Johnston School. The ceremony was most impressive, memorable, thoughtfully planned, and presented. I wish to you all for the honor you have bestowed on me.

Sincerely,
William J. Johnston

That 5-word letter to the editor from Bill Johnston is a true reflection of the man himself. It's a brief, simple, yet eloquent message written straight from the heart.

Mr. Johnston died in a veteran's hospital on May 29, a little more than one week after the town renamed the middle school after him. That letter includes his last words to his fellow townspeople, who must take comfort in knowing how much the honor meant to him. He will most certainly be missed by everyone who knew him, but perhaps those people who never met Mr. Johnston or know little about his town could stand to know more.

Mr. Johnston's courage in serving as a private in the U.S. Army during World War II has become locally famous. He was wounded just above the heart while covering his platoon's withdrawal during a battle in Italy. He was reported killed, but the true story was that he fended off the enemy by firing at an attacking troop of some 80 German soldiers, killing at least 25 of them.

This Colchester native returned here to a hero's welcome in September 1944, his Congressional Medal of Honor in tow. He had been credited for his courage by his fellow soldiers, superior officers, and President Franklin D. Roosevelt, yet he changed little. He remained modest, and his service to the Armed Forces continued until his death. He was a Veterans Administration employee and a lifetime member of the VFW, where he served as commander for many years.

The word 'hero' is so grossly overused today that you can't help but be leery upon hearing the term. Heroes are not paid a fortune for their work. They do not seek fame or personal gain. But think of some of the people deemed heroes: athletes, movie stars, rock musicians, and politicians. Unfortunately, this overuse has somewhat diluted a wonderful title.

That was not the case when you were around Mr. Johnston. He was an impressive man, yet without pretense, as he did not try to be anything more than he was – a rock-solid citizen of America. What made him the perfect hero was the fact that you did not have to know about him to respect him.

Flags will be flown at half-staff this week in his honor, and that is quite appropriate. After all, red, white, and blue were his favorite colors.

William James Johnston Sr., 71, a recipient of the Congressional Medal of Honor, of 64 Clark Lane, Colchester, died Tuesday (May 29) at the U.S. Veteran's Medical Center, Newington. He was born August 15, 1918, in Trenton, New Jersey, the son of the late John and Mary (Watson) Johnston. He was married on August 8, 1942, at St. Andrew's Catholic Church, Colchester, to Dorothy Clark. He was a U.S. Army veteran of World War II. He was retired from the Connecticut State Treasury Department for the Veteran's Bonus Division. He was a commissioner of the Rocky Hill Veteran's Home and Hospital. He was retired from the Veteran's Administration, Hartford. He was a member of the VFW, the American Legion, the Legion of Valor, and the DAV, and was also a member of the Purple Heart and Medal of Honor Society. Besides receiving the Congressional Medal of Honor, he received a Purple Heart Medal. He served on the Board of Selectman and the Board of Burgesses for the Town of Colchester. He was an active member of the Colchester Fish and Game Club and the St. Andrew's Holy Name Society. Besides his wife, he is survived by a son, William J. Johnston Jr. of Newtown; three daughters, Mrs. Thomas (Dorothy) O'Meara of Colchester, Diane J. Carragher of Colchester, and Donna L. Johnston of New York; two brothers, Robert and Charles Johnston, both of Colchester; a sister, Mrs. Ruban (Elizabeth) Cohen of Colchester; six grandchildren; numerous nieces and nephews. He was predeceased by a brother, John Johnston. A mass of Christian burial will be celebrated Friday, 10 a.m., at St. Andrew's R.C. Church. Interment will follow in the Connecticut State Veteran's Cemetery, Middletown. Calling hours are today, 2-4 and 7-9 p.m., at the Belmont Funeral Home, 144 S. Main Street, Colchester. Donations may be made in his memory to the St. Andrew's Improvement Fund, Norwich Avenue, Colchester, 06415.

Honored with a small monument at the main flagpole at the Connecticut State Veterans Cemetery, 317 Bow Lane, Middletown, Connecticut. Photo by the author. He is the only Medal of Honor recipient buried there.

From The Regional Standard (Colchester, CT) June 2, 2002

Whereas the entire Town of Colchester is saddened at the death of William J. Johnston, we, the Selectmen of the Town, wish to offer our condolences and the sympathy of the entire town to the family and friends of this great American Hero.

It was our honor to have known and worked with Bill. He was always a willing servant of his fellow man. His life was dedicated to service to his Country, his State, and his Community. His record of service will never be forgotten by his fellow townspeople.

Just ten days ago, it was our privilege to take part in the ceremonies indicating our new middle school, and that dedication was a fitting man who had given so much to his fellow man. Now, the William J. Johnston School lives on as a permanent memorial to that life of service.

Now, therefore, we, the Board of Selectmen of the Town of Colchester, do hereby proclaim that the seven days between May 30, 1990, and June 6, 1990, shall be a period of mourning in the Town of Colchester and that all flags in Colchester shall be flown at half-mast in remembrance of William J. Johnston. We further proclaim that this shall be a period of reflection on his life of service, and we suggest that all citizens of the Town of Colchester should strive to emulate that service for the betterment of our Town, our State, and our Country.

Signed and sealed this twenty-ninth day of May, nineteen hundred and ninety, at Colchester, Connecticut.

> First Selectman F. Duncan Green Jr.
> Selectman Adam Piekarz
> Selectwoman Patricia Barton
> Colchester

Buried in Connecticut State Veterans Cemetery, 317 Bow Lane, Middletown, Connecticut; Section 72, Row F, Grave 17. Photo by the author.

LANDSMAN JOHN JONES; NAVY

August 25, 1841 (Bridgeport, CT) – August 14, 1907 (Portsmouth, NH); 65 years old
Married Catherine Power (1842-1904).
Four sons, William H. (1873-1941), Edward (1877-1889), Thomas (1879-1898), and James (1880-1899).
Four daughters, Mary (1872-1884), Elizabeth (1876-?), Teresa G. (1883-1955), and Margaret B. (1891-1952).
Enlisted in the Navy on May 13, 1861, in Acton, Massachusetts.

Born to James (1805-?) and Abigail "Abba" Granville Jones (1815-?). Two sisters, Abigail (1842-?) and Mary (1846-1918). One brother, Michael (1844-?).

Photo courtesy of the Congressional Medal of Honor Society

MEDAL OF HONOR CITATION

AWARDED FOR ACTIONS DURING: Civil War
BRANCH OF SERVICE: Navy
ASSIGNED TO: U.S.S. Rhode Island
GENERAL ORDERS: War Department, General Orders No. 59 (June 22, 1865)
AGE ON THE DAY OF THE EVENT: 21
CITATION:

The President of the United States of America, in the name of Congress, takes pleasure in presenting the Medal of Honor to Landsman John Jones, United States Navy, for extraordinary heroism in action while serving on board the U.S.S. Rhode Island, which was engaged in saving the lives of the officers and crew of the U.S.S. Monitor near Cape Hatteras, North Carolina, 30 December 1862. Participating in the hazardous rescue of the officers and crew of the sinking Monitor, Landsman Jones, after rescuing several of the men, became separated in a heavy gale with other members of the cutter that had set out from the Rhode Island and spent many hours in the small boat at the mercy of the weather and high seas until finally picked up by a schooner 50 miles east of Cape Hatteras.

From the Portsmouth Herald August 14, 1907. Contributed by Katie Czajkowski, Special Collections, Portsmouth Public Library. Used with permission.

MEDAL OF HONOR MAN

Death of John Jones, Solider of the Republic

John Jones, one of the best-known and most respected citizens of this city, passed away early this morning at his home on Stark Street, aged sixty-five years, four months, and nine days.

Mr. Jones was a native of Bridgeport, Connecticut, but had resided in this city nearly all his life. As a veteran of the Civil War, he was known as a Medal of Honor man, and his bravery during the dark days from '61 to '65 has often been related by shipmates and officials.

He enlisted on December 24, 1861, at Portsmouth as a landsman and served on the U.S.S. Tioga, the South Carolina, the Niagara, and the Rhode Island. He was one of the first volunteers of the crew of the Rhode Island, which, on the night of December 30, 1862, saved the lives of the officers and crew of the old Monitor.

His gallantry and zealous desire to save lives on that night, stand without question, and this act of John Jones and his comrades is recorded in the annals of the Navy as one of the bravest deeds of the Civil War. He was promoted for his work by the Navy Department.

When he finished his term of enlistment in 1864, he came back to Portsmouth and, for twenty-five years or more, had charge of a department at the Eldredge Brewing Company's plant. The firm and his fellow workmen highly respected him. No man was more honest, no man was more generous, and no man was more loyal to his friends than John Jones. His word was as good as gold, and an enemy was a stranger to him.

He is survived by one son, William, and three daughters, Elizabeth, Margaret, and Theresa. His funeral will be held from the Church of the Immaculate Conception on Saturday morning.

From the Portsmouth Herald, October 16, 1907. Also contributed by Katie Czajkowski, Special Collections, Portsmouth Public Library

The funeral for John Jones was held from the Church of the Immaculate Conception this morning at nine o'clock and was attended by a large number of lifelong friends and acquaintances, who came to pay the last tribute of respect to a man universally admired during life.

Reverend Father Edward J. Walsh offered requiem mass in memory of the soul of Mr. Jones, and the music was tendered by the children's choir.

The floral tokens were numerous and beautiful, attesting to the keen sorrow of many friends and relatives.

The pallbearers were from the Kearsarge Naval Veterans, Storer Post, Grand Army, and the Eldredge Brewing Company. Interment was in St. Mary's Cemetery under the direction of undertaker W.P. Miskell.

The inscription reads:

This memorial was erected during the 150th anniversary year of the Immaculate Conception Parish in memory of Civil War Veterans known to be buried in unmarked graves in this cemetery.

Patrick Adams   6th NH Inf
William Danielson   2nd MA HA & 17th MA Inf
James Hahr   2nd NH Inf & 10th NH Inf
Patrick Quinn   10th NH Inf & 2nd US Cav

John Harris USMC	James Mates USN
William Barnes USN	Patrick O'Connor USN
Martin Garrity USN	John O'Donnell USN
Michael Jones USN	Michael Stack USN

AND
John Jones   USN – Congressional Medal of Honor Holder

SERGEANT MAJOR ALLAN JAY KELLOGG JR.; MARINE CORPS

October 1, 1943 (Bethel, CT) – present

Married Carol D. Haviland (1942-2002) on October 4, 1969, in Bethel, Connecticut.

Two sons, Allan J. III (1967-) and Aaron [U.S. Army Ranger] (?-).

Three daughters, Tanya (1972-), Meagan Kellogg Soderholm (1979-), and Maile (1986-).

Two stepdaughters Rhonda Haviland (1962-) and Kristin (1964-)

Born to Allan J. Sr. (1907-1969) and Sarah E. Blaney Kellogg (1915-1966). Three sisters, Marie M. Kellogg Williams Schneeburger (1938-), Edna G. Kellogg Fox Frank (1941-2020), and Mary Ann Kellogg Williams (1946-). One brother, Richard C. [U.S. Army] (1947-).

Also the recipient of the Bronze Star Medal with V device for valor, the Purple Heart Medal with two devices, the Combat Action Ribbon, the Presidential Unit Citation, the Navy Meritorious Unit Commendation with two devices, the Marine Corps Good Conduct Medal with 9 devices, the National Defense Medal with one device, the Armed Forces Expeditionary Medal, Vietnam Service Medal with four devices, Korean Defense Service Medal, Vietnamese Military Merit Medal, Vietnam Gallantry Cross with silver star, Vietnam Gallantry Cross Unit Medal, Vietnam Civil Actions Unit citation, and the Republic of Vietnam Campaign Medal.

Photos courtesy of the Congressional Medal of Honor Society

MEDAL OF HONOR CITATION

AWARDED FOR ACTIONS DURING: Vietnam War
BRANCH OF SERVICE: Marine Corps
UNIT: 1st Marine Division (Rein.) (FMF), 2nd Battalion, 5th Marines, Company G
AGE ON THE DAY OF THE EVENT: 26
CITATION:

The President of the United States of America, in the name of Congress, takes pleasure in presenting the Medal of Honor to Gunnery Sergeant Allan Jay Kellogg, Jr. (MCSN: 1927666), United States Marine Corps, for conspicuous gallantry and intrepidity at the risk of his life above and beyond the call of duty while serving as a platoon sergeant with Company G, Second Battalion, Fifth Marines, FIRST Marine Division (Reinforced), Fleet Marine Force, in connection with combat operations against the enemy on the night of 11 March 1970 in Quang Nam Province, Republic of Vietnam. Under the leadership of Gunnery Sergeant Kellogg, a small unit from Company G was evacuating a fallen comrade when the unit came under a heavy volume of small arms and automatic weapons fire from a numerically superior enemy force occupying well-concealed emplacements in the surrounding jungle. During the ensuing fierce engagement, an enemy soldier managed to maneuver through the dense foliage to a position near the Marines and hurled a hand grenade into their midst, which glanced off the chest of Gunnery Sergeant Kellogg. Quick to act, he forced the grenade into the mud in which he was standing, threw himself over the lethal weapon, and absorbed the full effects of its detonation with his body, thereby preventing serious injury or possible death to several of his fellow Marines. Although suffering multiple injuries to his chest and his right shoulder and arm, Gunnery Sergeant Kellogg resolutely continued to direct the efforts of his men until all were able to maneuver to the relative safety of the company perimeter. By his heroic and decisive action in risking his life to save the lives of his comrades, Gunnery Sergeant Kellogg reflected the highest credit upon himself and upheld the finest traditions of the Marine Corps and the United States Naval Service.

Presentation Date and Details: October 15, 1973 the White House, presented by President Richard M. Nixon

Photo contributed by Ryan Pettigrew, AV Archivist, Richard Nixon Presidential Library and Museum. In front from the left, President Nixon, Sergeant Kellogg, his wife Carol, daughter Tanya in Carol's arms, sister Krissie, and sister Rhonda. In the back, Sgt Kellogg's sister Edna, wearing glasses, Sgt Kellogg's mother-in-law Florence Jacobsen, and father-in-law Vincent Maroldi. The two men in the back are unconnected to the family.

TOMB OF THE UNKNOWNS AT ARLINGTON NATIONAL CEMETERY

The Tomb of the Unknowns at Arlington National Cemetery in Arlington, Virginia, is also known as the Tomb of the Unknown Soldier and has never been officially named. The Tomb of the Unknowns stands atop a hill overlooking Washington, D.C.

On March 4, 1921, Congress approved the burial of an unidentified American soldier from World War I in the plaza of the new Memorial Amphitheater.

The white marble sarcophagus has a flat-faced form and is relieved at the corners and along the sides by neo-classic pilasters, or columns, set into the surface. Sculpted into the east panel, which faces Washington, D.C., are three Greek figures representing Peace, Victory, and Valor. Inscribed on the back of the Tomb are the words: HERE RESTS IN HONORED GLORY AN AMERICAN SOLDIER KNOWN BUT TO GOD

The Tomb sarcophagus was placed above the grave of the Unknown Soldier of World War I. West of World War I Unknown are the crypts of unknowns from World War II, Korea, and Vietnam. Those three graves are marked with white marble slabs flush with the plaza.

THE UNKNOWN OF WORLD WAR I

On Memorial Day, 1921, four unknowns were exhumed from four World War I American cemeteries in France. U.S. Army Sergeant Edward F. Younger, who was wounded in combat, highly decorated for valor, and received the Distinguished Service Medal in "The Great War, the war to end all wars," selected the Unknown Soldier of World War I from four identical caskets at the city hall in Chalons-sur-Mame, France, October 24, 1921.

Sergeant Younger selected the unknown by placing a spray of white roses on one of the caskets. He chose the third casket from the left. The chosen unknown soldier was transported to the United States aboard the U.S.S. Olympia. Those remaining were interred in the Meuse Argonne Cemetery in France.

The Unknown Soldier lay in state in the Capitol Rotunda from his arrival in the United States until Armistice Day, 1921. On November 11, 1921, President Warren G. Harding officiated at the interment ceremonies at the Memorial Amphitheater at Arlington National Cemetery.

THE UNKNOWNS OF WORLD WAR II AND KOREA

On August 3, 1956, President Dwight D. Eisenhower signed a bill to select and pay tribute to the unknowns of World War II and Korea. The selection ceremonies and the interment of these unknowns took place in 1958. The World War II Unknown was selected from remains exhumed from cemeteries in Europe, Africa, Hawaii, and the Philippines.

Two unknowns from World War II, one from the European Theater and one from the Pacific Theater, were placed in identical caskets and taken aboard the U.S.S. Canberra, a guided-missile cruiser resting off the Virginia capes. Navy Hospitalman 1st Class William R. Charette, then the Navy's only active-duty Medal of Honor recipient, selected the Unknown Soldier of World War II. The remaining casket received a solemn burial at sea. Four unknown Americans who died in the Korean War were disinterred from the National Cemetery of the Pacific in Hawaii. Army Master Sgt. Ned Lyle made the final selection. Both caskets arrived in Washington on May 28, 1958, where they lay in the Capitol Rotunda until May 30.

That morning, they were carried on caissons to Arlington National Cemetery. President Eisenhower awarded each the Medal of Honor, and the Unknowns were interred in the plaza beside their comrades from World War I.

THE UNKNOWN OF VIETNAM

The Memorial Bridge, leading from Washington, D.C., to Virginia, is lined with a joint-service cordon as the remains of the Vietnam War Unknown are taken by a motor escort to Arlington National Cemetery for interment in the Tomb of the Unknowns.

The Unknown service member from the Vietnam War was designated by Medal of Honor recipient U.S. Marine Corps Sergeant Major Allan Jay Kellogg, Jr. during a ceremony at Pearl Harbor, Hawaii, May 17, 1984.

Transported aboard the U.S.S. Brewton to Alameda Naval Base, California, the remains were then sent to Travis Air Force Base, California, on May 24. The Vietnam Unknown arrived at Andrews Air Force Base the next day.

From the Honolulu Star-Advertiser October 5, 2012

Kristen Wong | Hawaii Marine

Retired Sgt. Maj. Allan J. Kellogg Jr. holds his hand over his heart during the Kaneohe Klipper Memorial Ceremony on Marine Corps Base Hawaii, Dec. 7, 2010.

At age 15, Allan J. Kellogg Jr. wanted to do two things — "get tattoos and be a MO-reen." Today, the Medal of Honor recipient has done both.

Kellogg, a current Kailua resident and a native of Bethel, Connecticut, joined more than 50 Medal of Honor recipients in Honolulu for the 2012 Medal of Honor Convention events this week.

Kellogg said he was very impressed by the Kaneohe Bay Air Show, which he and other recipients attended on Saturday, and also attended a ceremony at the National Memorial of the Pacific on Wednesday, dedicated to all fallen Medal of Honor recipients.

Born on October 1, 1943, Kellogg attended Bethel High School for only two years before enlisting in the Marine Corps in 1960. He has been stationed in various places, including Marine Corps Base Camp Lejeune, N.C., as part of the 3rd Battalion, 8th Marine Regiment, and Marine Corps Base Camp Pendleton, Calif., as part of the 1st Battalion, 4th Marine Regiment.

As a Staff Sergeant, Kellogg was deployed to the Republic of Vietnam. On March 11, 1970, while leading a platoon of nine in Quang Nam Province, Kellogg and his fellow Marines encountered a booby trap. The trap wounded three of his men and killed one.

A helicopter evacuated the three wounded, but the platoon was told another would arrive for the deceased due to limited space.

"It started getting dark out, and the area I was in was no place to be after sundown," Kellogg said.

The platoon later found itself in an ambush of 45 to 50 enemy forces attacking with multiple weapons, from machine guns to rocket-propelled grenades.

"They were closing in on us," Kellogg said. "They snuck up on me and reached over the dike and dropped a grenade right in my lap."

Kellogg remembers shouting "GRENADE!" and attempting to smother it by forcing it down into the mud. When it detonated, he lost consciousness.

When he came to, Kellogg remembers breathing in the mud of the paddy he had fallen in, moaning quietly for help, thinking he was going to die. But in the end, Kellogg made it out of Vietnam and was awarded a Medal of Honor for his actions.

Retired Lieutenant Colonel Jon Gangloff of Friendswood, Texas, called Kellogg an "exceptional individual."

Gangloff was Kellogg's company commander in the 4th Battalion, 9th Marine Regiment, in Okinawa, Japan. He said Kellogg always made himself available to support junior Marines.

"He never used excuses," Gangloff said. "He was always a first-class individual. He's still helping Marines today ... I think he deserves a lot of credit for that."

In 1990, Kellogg retired after serving as 1st Marine Expeditionary Brigade Sergeant Major when the brigade was headquartered in Hawaii.

That same year, Kellogg became a permanent resident of Hawaii. Of his 30 years of service, he said he was most proud of having earned his rank as a senior enlisted leader.

In 1995, he started working as a benefits counselor at the local Department of Veterans Affairs.

He said he chose to work for the VA to continue what he did in the Corps, which was helping veterans and people in need.

Now 69 years old and a widower with seven children, Kellogg is an incarcerated veteran's re-entry specialist and also does homeless veteran outreach. He supports homeless veterans with food, clothes, identification cards, and more.

Kellogg said the average veteran he supports is around 61 years old, and some turned to drug and alcohol abuse. He said the most rewarding aspect of his job is when a veteran released from jail manages to quit drugs and alcohol and transition successfully into society, though it doesn't always happen.

"I can only do so much for a homeless veteran and an incarcerated veteran," Kellogg said. "At some time, the veteran has to take a step forward and help himself."

For retired Sergeant Major Robert W. Holub, Kellogg has been a support system both in and out of the service. Holub, a Sergeant Major of U.S. Marine Corps Forces, Pacific until 2001, said he frequently sought Kellogg's advice.

"When I first made Sergeant Major, I wanted an infantry battalion in the worst way," said Holub, 56. "He said, 'No matter what job you get, do your best. Take care of your Marines.'"

While supporting Marines, Kellogg was also always straightforward with his peers. Holub called Kellogg an example of "the utmost in professionalism."

"If you weren't cutting the mustard or if you weren't living up to the standards of the staff noncommissioned officer, he'd come down on you," Holub said. "By God, you always knew where you stood with him."

Kellogg also interviewed Holub at the VA when he retired from the military.

Today, as Kellogg continues his work at the VA and attends various ceremonies such as Medal of Honor Convention events.

"He didn't quit taking care of Marines when he retired," Holub said. "He still takes care of them every day."

But it's not every day a service member is able to meet a Medal of Honor recipient. For those currently serving in the military or who hope to be in the military someday, Kellogg shared these words with the Hawaii Marine.

"Keep your act together and be prepared for whatever might happen. You never know what might be around the corner."

FIRST LIEUTENANT AARON STEVEN LANFARE; ARMY

September 9, 1824 (Branford, CT) – August 19, 1875 (at sea Sulawesi Tengah, Indonesia); 51 years old

Married Eliza J. Purse (1826-1903) on March 4, 1851.

Three daughters, Agnes S. Lanfare Woodward (1855-1894), Mary E. (1857-1926), and Adella M. Lanfare Thompson (1858-1889).

One son, Jesse F. (1862-1870).

Enlisted on November 16, 1861, in Branford, Connecticut.

Mustered out August 2, 1865.

Born to Oliver Jr. (1782-1873) and Lois Willard Lanfare [also seen as Lanphere, Lamphier, Lanphier, and Landphier] (1792-1825). Four sisters, Martha (1810-1870), Mary Ann (1812-1870), Betsy Lamphier Peck (1816-1822), and Louisa Lanfare Dodd (1818-). Three brothers, William S. (1814-1816), William S. (1820-1890), and Henry (1822-).

Photos from FindAGrave.com.

MEDAL OF HONOR CITATION

AWARDED FOR ACTIONS DURING: Civil War

BRANCH OF SERVICE: Army

UNIT: 1st Connecticut Cavalry, Company B

DATE OF ISSUE AND PRESENTATION: May 3, 1865

AGE ON THE DAY OF THE EVENT: 20

CITATION:

The President of the United States of America, in the name of Congress, takes pleasure in presenting the Medal of Honor to First Lieutenant (Cavalry) Aaron Steven Lanfare, United States Army, for extraordinary heroism on 6 April 1865, while serving with Company B, 1st Connecticut Cavalry, in action at Deatonsville (Sailor's Creek), Virginia, for capture of flag of 11th Florida Infantry (Confederate States of America).

Aaron Lanfare was a sea captain for the Trowbridge family in New Haven. He was a master of a vessel that supplied goods from New Haven to the Caribbean, West Indies, Barbados, Bermuda, and so on. He was a Civil War volunteer, and after the war, he returned to the Trowbridge fleet as Master of Vessels and was lost at sea in 1875 on a voyage to the West Indies. A headstone was placed by his descendants in 1985 in Branford Center Cemetery.

Photo of the telescope courtesy of Jane P. Bouley. Description courtesy of the Branford Historical Society

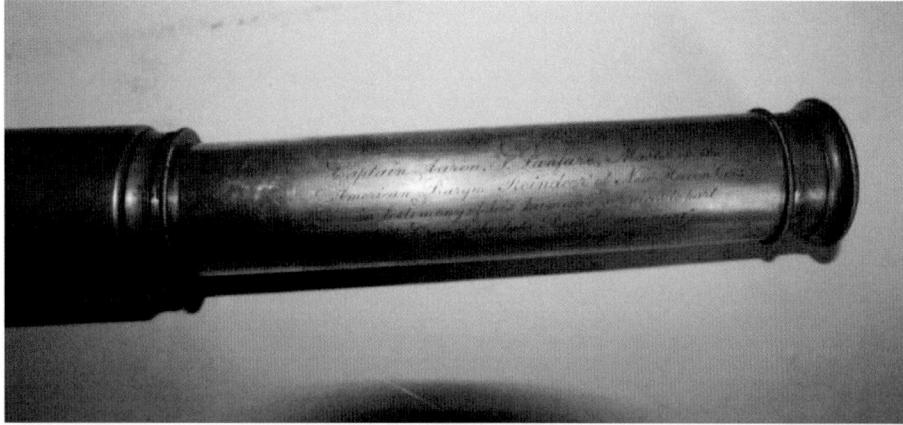

The Lanfare/Lanphier telescope was donated first to the Blackstone Library by three sisters, all granddaughters of Aaron Lanfare. When the library started breaking up its museum, the sisters requested that the telescope be returned to them, and they, in turn, donated it to the Branford Historical Society. The telescope has been proudly displayed ever since at the Harrison House.

The telescope was presented to Aaron Lanfare by Queen Victoria, and the engraving reads as follows:

*Presented by the British Government
to Captain Aaron S. Lanfare,
master of American Barque "Reindeer"
of New Haven, Conn:
In testimony of his humane services
to part of the crew of the late
Brig "Dominica" of Exeter on the
2nd April 1860.*

From The Branford Review October 17, 1990

LANFARE RECEIVED MEDAL OF HONOR

Aaron Steven Lanfare was born in 1824 in Branford, one of 15 children born to Oliver Lanfare (1782-1873) of Short Beach. Aaron's grandfather, Oliver Lanfare (1749-1812), served in the Revolutionary War as master of the ship "Chloe Ann," which patrolled the coastal waters throughout the conflict. Like his ancestors, Aaron took to the sea and, before the Civil War, was master of the barque "Reindeer" out of New Haven. In 1860, he was given a telescope by Queen Isabella of England for his service to the British brig "Dominica." The telescope was later donated to the James Blackstone Memorial Library by the Lanfare family.

At the outbreak of the Civil War, Aaron Lanfare, at the age of 37, enlisted in Company B, First Connecticut Cavalry. The cavalry division saw action in Virginia at Cedar Creek, Winchester, Sailor's Creek, and Appomattox. During the battle of Sailor's Creek, Aaron Lanfare captured the flag of the 11th Florida Infantry on April 6, 1864. On the day he was mustered out, May 3, 1865, First Lieutenant Aaron S. Lanfare was awarded the Congressional Medal of Honor.

After the Civil War, the Lanfare family lived in New Haven, and Aaron was a spice merchant and captain of vessels that traded goods to the West Indies. On one such voyage in August of 1875, he was lost at sea.

Branford has paid tribute to Aaron Lanfare on several occasions. A plaque in his memory was placed at the flagpole at the old Post Office on Montowese Street in 1961. The plaque was rededicated at the new Post Office on Park Street in 1984, with several of Aaron Lanfare's great-granddaughters in attendance. A memorial stone was placed in Center Cemetery in 1984 next to Aaron's grandfather, Oliver Lanfare (Lamphier). Aaron Steven Lanfare remains Branford's only native son to receive the Congressional Medal of Honor.

A plaque was placed at Branford's old Post Office in 1961, then moved to the new and current Post Office in 1984. About 20 years ago, the plaque at the Post Office was being vandalized and skateboarded on, and the town had a new one made, which is now to the right front of Town Hall, 1019 Town Hall Drive, Branford, Connecticut.

In memory marker in Branford Center Cemetery, 161 Montowese Street, Branford, Connecticut; front right corner of the cemetery along Montowese Street. Photo by the author.

In Memory marker in Fair Haven Union Cemetery, 149 Grand Avenue, New Haven, Connecticut; Avenue D, East Side. Photo by the author.

285

WARRANT OFFICER JUNIOR GRADE JOHN "JACK" CRIDLAND LATHAM; ARMY

March 3, 1888 (Windermere, South Lakeland District, Cumbria, England) – November 2, 1975; 87 years old
Married to Alice Witman Nash (1895-1965).
One son, John N. Latham (1924-2001). One daughter, Constance E. Latham Coonan, (1921-1993).
Enlisted on May 4, 1917.
Serial number 1212528.
Discharged on April 2, 1919.

Born to Thomas (1862-1902) and Elizabeth Latham (1865-1906). Four sisters, Katherine (1891-?), Lucy (1893-?), Frances (1894-?), and Mary (1896-?). One brother, Reginald (1899-1918).

Also received the Purple Heart Medal and the French Croix de Guerre with bronze palm.

One of twenty English-born Medal of Honor recipients.

Photo courtesy of FindAGrave.com.

MEDAL OF HONOR CITATION

AWARDED FOR ACTIONS DURING: World War I
BRANCH OF SERVICE: Army
UNIT: Machine Gun Company, 107th Infantry Regiment, 27th Infantry Division
GENERAL ORDERS: War Department, General Orders No. 20 (January 30, 1919)
AGE ON THE DAY OF EVENT: 30
CITATION:

The President of the United States of America, in the name of Congress, takes pleasure in presenting the Medal of Honor to Sergeant John Cridland Latham (ASN: 1212528), United States Army, for extraordinary heroism on 29 September 1918, while serving with Machine Gun Company, 107th Infantry, 27th Division, in action at Le Catelet, France. Becoming separated from their platoon by a smoke barrage, Sergeant Latham, Sergeant Alan L. Eggers, and Corporal Thomas E. O'Shea took cover in a shell hole well within the enemy's lines. Upon hearing a call for help from an American tank that had become disabled 30 yards from them, the three soldiers left their shelter and started toward the tank under heavy fire from German machineguns and trench mortars. In crossing the fire-swept area, Corporal O'Shea was mortally wounded, but his companions, undeterred, proceeded to the tank, rescued a wounded officer, and assisted two wounded soldiers to cover in the sap of a nearby trench. Sergeants Latham and Eggers then returned to the tank in the face of the violent fire, dismounted a Hotchkiss gun, and took it back to where the wounded men were keeping off the enemy all day by effective use of the gun and later bringing it with the wounded men back to our lines under cover of darkness.

Presentation Date and Details: February 4, 1919, Chaumont, France, presented by General John J. Pershing

---

From the South Bergenite (NJ) on August 6, 2009

Editor's note: This article is the beginning of a series of articles by Rutherford borough historian Rod Leith, who will
share historical figures and moments with the South Bergenite monthly.

> *"Jack, I'm proud to belong to such a splendid outfit and prouder still to belong to such a fine company as the MG (Machine Gun) is."*

Those are the words of Sgt John C. Latham, who, for bravery demonstrated on a French battlefield on September 29, 1918, won the highest military honors bestowed by America, France, and Great Britain in World War 1. As a member of the Machine Gun Company, 107th Infantry, 27th Division, Sgt. Latham, with two comrades, both from Summit [New Jersey] heard a call for help from a disabled America tank. Under heavy fire behind the enemy's line near le Catelet, France, Latham, and his two colleagues rescued the tank's officer and two soldiers and brought the three wounded men to safety. Then, with one comrade, Latham returned to the tank, dismounted its Hotchkiss gun, carried it back to where the wounded men were, and held off the enemy all day by effective use of the Hotchkiss. Later, under cover of darkness, they brought the wounded and the gun back to American lines. One of Latham's comrades, Thomas E. O'Shea, was mortally wounded and received the Congressional Medal of Honor posthumously. The third of the brave trio, Sgt Alan Louis Eggers, also received America's highest military honor. After Sgt Eggers came home to Summit, they named a street in honor of his conduct in World War I.

But John Cridland Latham, born in Windemere, England, on March 3, 1888, is still pretty much an unsung hero in the community of Rutherford, which he called home for much of a decade. After he came here in 1909, Latham was employed by Lambertus C. Bobbink, who recognized the Englishman's promising shills as a landscape gardener and hired him to work for Bobbink & Atkins, the venerable horticultural service in East Rutherford. In 1917, Latham enlisted in the U.S. Army. For his "conspicuous gallantry and intrepidity above and beyond the call of duty in action with the enemy..." Latham not only was awarded America's highest honor, but he also received the French Croix de Guerre and the Médialle Militaire. From Great Britain, Latham won the Distinguished Service Medal.

While recovering in a French hospital from wounds received on September 29, 1918, Latham wrote to John "Jack" Jennings, his old friend and former boss at Bobbink & Atkins, and colorfully described the events of that crucial day:

"Jack, that stunt we pulled off on the 29th was a hell-hole, and no mistake about it. We tackled the toughest part of the Hindenburg line, and smashed it, too, and in such a way that Fritz (the Germans) saw the beginning of the end when that drive commenced. It was a wonderful sight to see the barrage working and eating its way into the Hun lines and a more glorious one when we received the order to go over the top."

During his time in Rutherford, John Latham lived in a boarding house at 171 Montross Ave., run by Emily Ahsler. Ironically, at the time Latham went off to war, silent film director Douglas Fairbanks chose Rutherford for a production called "In Again, Out Again," which was a spoof on the American anti-war movement. Fairbanks, who played a character named Teddy Rutherford in the 1917 film, could be seen climbing to a second-story window of 171 Montross Avenue, trying to break in tow in the charms of his sweeties (Helen Greene). Emily Ahsler owned the house through this period and later managed another boarding house at 63 Highland Cross, where Latham was listed as a resident in 1920. Latham later moved to Connecticut, where he married and raised a family in Darien. He died in Stamford, Connecticut, on November 5, 1975.

From The Stamford Advocate, September 23, 2018, by James A. Sparrow

'JACK' LATHAM HONORED — Bedford Park is now John C. Latham Park, renamed Saturday to honor John Latham for his 40 years as a merchant on Bedford St. and his service to his country in World War I as a Congressional Medal of Honor winner. From left to right, T. Frank Cowlin, chairman of the Park Commission; Mr. Latham; and Edward R. Mallozzi president of the Bedford St. Association. (Advocate Photo by Roberts)

Latham Park has gotten a lot of ink this past summer because of various sculptures, events, and, of course, "Marilyn Monroe." It is a beautiful inner city park, and I am very happy it is being used. I go by it every day, and people are always there and seem to be enjoying themselves.

And now, here comes the "but."

288

Several times, I have walked around the park asking different people what or who the park is named after. What or who is Latham? "It might be the name of this section of town" or "It might be the name of a former mayor" are common guesses.

Most of what I got was simply, "I have no idea." At the southern point of the park is a stone about a foot and a half high and about 3 feet wide with a bronze plaque that reads John Latham Park, CMH, (which stands for Congressional Medal of Honor; however, the right term is just Medal of Honor) along with the date Sept. 29, 1918, which is the date of the action for which he was awarded the Medal of Honor. That was 100 years ago this week. Thanks to our parks department, the park is well-groomed. However, the beautiful flowers in front of the stone and plaque have now covered up the information.

Latham is John Cridland Latham. He ran the Latham Florist Shop on Bedford Street for 30 years after World War I. He was born on March 3, 1888, In Windermere, England. He immigrated to the United States and joined the U.S. Army to serve in World War I.

On September 29, 1918, he was serving as a sergeant in the machine gun company of the 107th Infantry Regiment of the 27th Infantry Division. His Medal of Honor citation for that day reads: "Becoming separated from their platoon by a smoke barrage, Sergeant Latham, Sergeant Alan L. Eggers, and Corporal Thomas E. O'Shea took cover in a shell hole well within the enemy's lines. Upon hearing a call for help from an American tank that had become disabled 30 yards from the, the three soldiers left their shelter and started toward the tank under heavy fire from German machine guns and trench mortars. In crossing the fire-swept area, Corporal O'Shea was mortally wounded, but his companions, undeterred, proceeded to the tank, rescued a wounded officer, and assisted two wounded soldiers to cover in the sap of a nearby trench. Sergeants Latham and Eggers then returned to the tank in the face of the violent fire, dismounted a Hotchkiss gun, and took it back to where the wounded men were keeping off the enemy all day by effective use of the gun and later bringing it with the wounded men back to our lines under cover of darkness."

His awards are the Medal of Honor, Purple Heart, and the World War I Victory Medal, with three Bronze Service stars to denote credit for the Somme Offensive, Ypres-Lys, and Defensive Sector battle clasps.

And that's just what he received from the United States.

He also was awarded the Distinguished Conduct Medal from Great Britain, The Médaille Militaire and Croix de guerre with bronze palm from the French Republic, the Croce al Merito di Guerra from Italy, the Medal for Military Bravery from the Kingdom of Montenegro and the Medalha da Cruz de Guerra from the Portuguese Republic.

What a man! A true combat hero who went on to operate a florist shop in Stamford. I think there is a big message in that. So, the next time you are on Bedford Street, maybe going to the Avon Theatre or window shopping, just check out that little corner of Latham Park and give a nod.

From the Hartford Courant November 4, 1975

STAMFORD (AP) – John C. Latham of Darien, a Congressional Medal of Honor winner for leading a daring rescue mission in France during World War I, died Sunday in a convalescent home. He was 87.

A sergeant commanding a platoon of machine gunners in the 107th Regiment of the 27th Infantry Division in 1918, in France, Latham and several of his men found themselves cut off by the enemy near La Catelet.

He and two others left cover to rescue three Americans in a tank, then held their position using a machine gun taken from the tank.

Despite a side wound, he and the platoon captured several German machine gun nests. Under cover of darkness, he led 2 men, some of them wounded, back to allied lines.

A native of England, he came to this country in 1909 to work on a Greenwich estate. He operated a Stamford flower shop for 30 years.

A park in Stamford bears his name.

He leaves a son, John N. Latham of Darien, a daughter, Mrs. Constance Coonan of Suffield (Connecticut), a sister in England, and four grandchildren. The funeral will be held Wednesday in the Noroton section of Darien.

Honored on a plaque in Fort Stamford Park, 900 Westover Road, Stamford, Connecticut

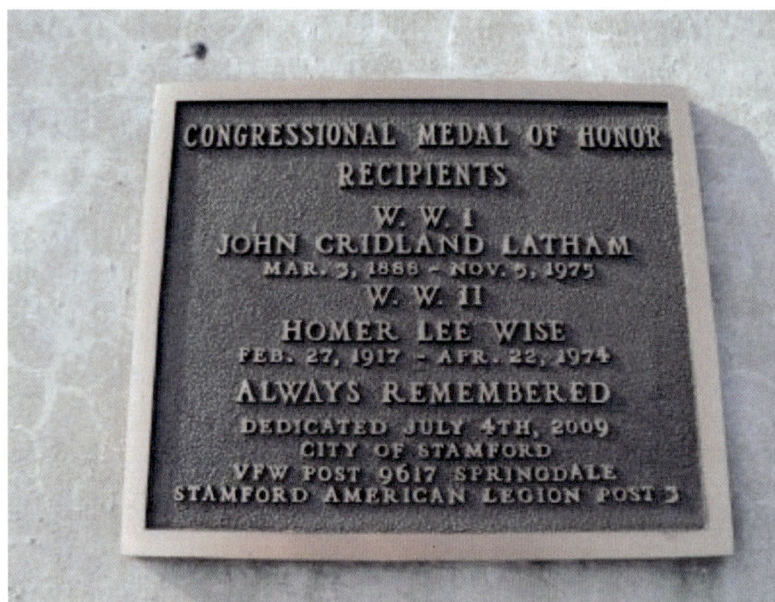

Buried in Arlington National Cemetery, 1 Memorial Drive, Arlington, Virginia; Section 35, Grave 1127. Photo from FindAGrave.com.

SERGEANT JOHN LEE LEVITOW; AIR FORCE

November 1, 1945 (Hartford, CT) – November 8, 2000 (Rocky Hill, CT); 55 years old
Married to Barbara A. Corbeil (1949-) on July 19, 1969, in Glastonbury, Connecticut.
One son, John L. Jr. (1973-).   New Hampshire   wife, Lucy
One daughter, Corrie L. Levitow Wilson Santelises (1975-).
Enlisted on June 6, 1966.
Discharged on April 3, 1970.

Born to Leonard T. (1912-1983) and Marion V. Winialski (1911-2001). One sister, Mary L. Levitow Constantine (1946-2004).

He was also the recipient of the Air Medal with 8 Oak Leaf Clusters, the Purple Heart Medal, and the Vietnam Cross of Gallantry with Bronze Star.

Member of the Connecticut Veterans Hall of Fame, Class of 2008.

Glastonbury High School Class of '65 yearbook

JOHN LEE LEVITOW
"Leetoe" . . . who's the cute redhead? . . . typical college dresser . . . drag that Rambler much? . . . his constant jokes match his personality.

Photo (Left) A1C John Lee Levitow, United States Air Force. (United States Air Force 120517-F-DW547-010). Photo (Right) is a public domain photo.

Spooky 71, a Douglas AC-47D gunship, U.S. Air Force serial number 43-49770, at Bien Hoa Air Base, RVN, 24 February 1969. (U.S. Air Force 120517-F-DW547-011)

MEDAL OF HONOR CITATION

AWARDED FOR ACTIONS DURING: Vietnam War
BRANCH OF SERVICE: Air Force
UNIT: 3rd Special Operations Squadron
GENERAL ORDERS: Department of the Air Force, Special Order GB-476 (June 23, 1970)
AGE ON THE DAY OF THE EVENT: 23
CITATION:

The President of the United States of America, in the name of Congress, takes pleasure in presenting the Medal of Honor to Sergeant [then Airman First Class] John Lee Levitow, United States Air Force, for conspicuous gallantry and intrepidity in action at the risk of his life above and beyond the call of duty serving with the 3rd Special Operations Squadron, 14th Special Operations Wing, in the air over Long Binh Army Post, Republic of Vietnam, on 24 February 1969. Sergeant Levitow, U.S. Air Force, distinguished himself by exceptional heroism while assigned as a loadmaster aboard an AC-47 aircraft flying a night mission in support of Long Binh Army post. Sergeant Levitow's aircraft was struck by a hostile mortar round. The resulting explosion ripped a hole two feet in diameter through the wing, and fragments made over 3,500 holes in the fuselage. All occupants of the cargo compartment were wounded and helplessly slammed against the floor and fuselage. The explosion tore an activated flare from the grasp of a crewmember who had been launching flares to provide illumination for Army ground troops engaged in combat. Sergeant Levitow, though stunned by the concussion of the blast and suffering from over 40 fragment wounds in the back and legs, staggered to his feet and turned to assist the man nearest to him, who had been knocked down and was bleeding heavily. As he was moving his wounded comrade forward and away from the opened cargo compartment door, he saw the smoking flare ahead of him in the aisle. Realizing the danger involved and completely disregarding his own wounds, Sergeant Levitow started toward the burning flare. The aircraft was partially out of control, and the flare was rolling wildly from side to side. Sergeant Levitow struggled forward despite the loss of blood from his many wounds and the partial loss of feeling in his right leg. Unable to grasp the rolling flare with his hands, he threw himself bodily upon the burning flare. Hugging the deadly device to his body, he dragged himself back to the rear of the aircraft and hurled the flare through the open cargo door. At that instant, the flare separated and ignited in the air, but clear of the aircraft. Sergeant Levitow, by his selfless and heroic actions, saved the aircraft and its entire crew from certain death and destruction. Sergeant Levitow's gallantry, his profound concern for his fellowmen, at the risk of his life above and beyond the call of duty, are in keeping with the highest traditions of the U.S. Air Force and reflect great credit upon himself and the Armed Forces of his country.

Presentation Date and Details: May 14, 1970 the White House, presented by President Richard M. Nixon

President Richard M. Nixon awards the Medal of Honor to Sergeant John Lee Levitow at The White House on May 14, 1970. Left to right, President Nixon, John Levitow, father Leonard, wife Barbara, sister Mary, and mother Marion.

John Levitow's Medal of Honor from the archives at the Congressional Medal of Honor Society.

John Levitow decided to join the Navy after high school because the Army and the Marines required a lot of walking, and to him, that seemed like too much work. But when he showed up at the Navy recruiting office and had to wait because the recruiters were busy, he went next door and joined the Air Force.

Levitow was sent to Vietnam as a loadmaster for C-130s. On the night of February 24, 1969, he was asked to fill in for the regular loadmaster on an AC-47 called Spooky 71. An adaptation of the famous DC-3 airliner, the specially outfitted gunship carried three 7.62-mm mini guns that could accurately spray up to six thousand rounds a minute. It could also, in a few seconds, light up the darkness for GIs below—each of its MK-24 flares burned at three thousand degrees and provided two million candlepower intensity.

After cruising for more than four hours, Spooky 71 received orders to go to the Bien Hoa area, where North Vietnamese troops had come out of their jungle sanctuaries under the cover of darkness to launch attacks on U.S. troops. Banking in tight circles about one thousand feet above the ground, the plane dropped several of its twenty-seven-pound flares out of the open cargo door, then raked the enemy with bursts from its mini-guns that sounded like loud zippers.

Suddenly, Spooky 71 was rocked by a violent explosion. The plane had flown directly into the path of an enemy mortar round, and shrapnel had ripped holes in its wings and body. As the aircraft lurched wildly, the pilot struggled to keep control. The five crewmen in the hold were all wounded. Airman First Class Levitow had been struck by more than forty shell fragments on his right side just as he was arming a flare. The crew member who had been about to throw the flare out of the plane was on his back, and the flare was bouncing wildly through the hold.

With the plane gyrating in a 30-degree turn, Levitow, despite the numbness overtaking his body, got to one of the gunners who was about to fall out of the open cargo door and dragged him back from the bay by his uniform.

Then he went after the flare; he knew it would detonate within about twenty seconds, burn through the metal floor of the cargo hold, explode the ammunition, and destroy the plane.

The plane pitched and bucked, throwing Levitow from side to side. Twice, the smoking flare rolled just beyond his grasp. Then he fell on top of the two-foot canister and trapped it. Hugging it to his body, he crawled toward the cargo door and heaved the canister out. It exploded a split second later. The pilot of Spooky 71 later reconstructed what had happened in the hold by the pattern of the blood Levitow had left on the floor.

John Levitow recovered from his wounds after a brief hospital stay. He flew twenty more missions in Vietnam before being discharged in 1969. On May 14, 1970, he was awarded the Medal of Honor by President Richard Nixon. He was the first enlisted man in the Air Force to receive this honor. The Air Force later named its outstanding graduate award, given by each enlisted professional military education class, the John L. Levitow Award.

John Lee Levitow worked for federal and state veterans' agencies for more than two decades after leaving the Air Force. He was the legislative liaison and director of planning for the Connecticut Department of Veterans Affairs at the time of his death.

From The Hartford Courant January 29, 1969

U.S. Air Force Sergeant John L. Levitow, son of Mr. and Mrs. Lee T. Levitow, 38 Kimberly Lane, South Glastonbury, has been decorated with the Vietnamese Cross of Gallantry with Bronze Star at Bien Hoa Air Base in South Vietnam.

Levitow was recognized for his heroic defense of the Phuoc Tan outpost during an enemy assault last September 1968. Overcoming the handicaps of darkness, adverse weather, and intense anti-aircraft fire, Levitow and his crew dropped flares to light the area and flew close turns in order to fire and repel the assault.

Levitow, a member of the 3rd Special Operations Squadron, flies the modified C-47 Skytrain. He is a 1965 graduate of Glastonbury High School.   **AUTHOR NOTE:** The incident in the previous article happened the month before the incident, resulting in his receiving the Medal of Honor.

Honored at the Connecticut State Veterans Cemetery in Middletown, Connecticut, at the main flagpole in the cemetery. Photo by the author.

Honored at Green Park, Green Cemetery Road, Glastonbury, Connecticut.

Honored with a marker on Oneal Avenue, Hurlburt Field Memorial Air Park, Hurlburt Field, Florida.

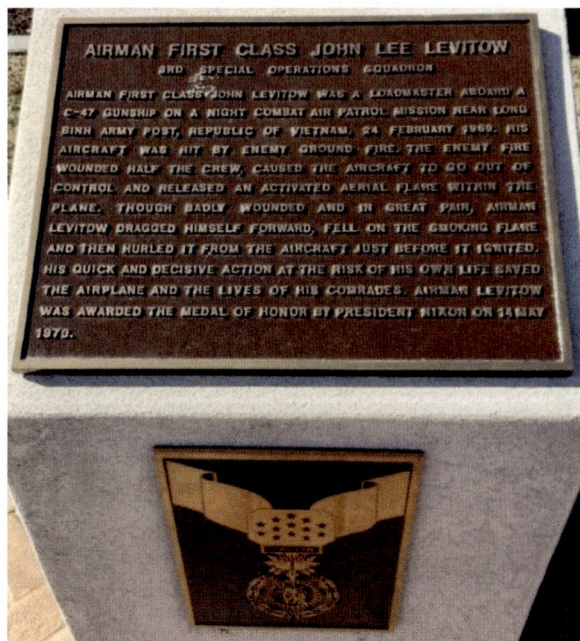

Photo courtesy of HMdb.org and Mark Hilton.

SERGEANT GEORGE DALTON LIBBY; ARMY

December 4, 1919 (Bridgton, ME) – July 20, 1950; 30 years old
Unmarried
Enlisted on November 13, 1945, in New Haven, Connecticut
MOS 3729 - Combat Construction Specialist

Born to Benjamin F. (1873-1947) and Blanche M. Seavey Libby (1890-1942). Two sisters, Gladys M. Libby Hillertz (1916-1979) and Madelyn E. Libby Birt (1921-2006). Half-sister Grace E. Merrifield (1890-1973).

The first Medal of Honor recipient during the Korean War.

Photo courtesy of FindAGrave.com

MEDAL OF HONOR CITATION

AWARDED FOR ACTIONS DURING: Korean War
BRANCH OF SERVICE: Army
UNIT: Company C, 3rd Engineer Combat Battalion, 24th Infantry Division
GENERAL ORDERS: Department of the Army, General Orders No. 62 (August 2, 1951)
AGE ON THE DAY OF THE EVENT: 30
CITATION:

The President of the United States of America, in the name of Congress, takes pride in presenting the Medal of Honor (Posthumously) to Sergeant George Dalton Libby (ASN: 31153010), United States Army, for conspicuous gallantry and intrepidity above and beyond the call of duty while serving with Company C, 3rd Combat Engineer Battalion, 24th Infantry Division, in action against enemy aggressor forces at Taejon, Korea, on 20 July 1950. While breaking through an enemy encirclement, the vehicle in which he was riding approached an enemy roadblock and encountered devastating fire, which disabled the truck, killing or wounding all the passengers except Sergeant Libby. Taking cover in a ditch, Sergeant Libby engaged the enemy and, despite the heavy fire, crossed the road twice to administer aid to his wounded comrades. He then hailed a passing M-5 artillery tractor and helped the wounded aboard. The enemy directed intense small-arms fire at the driver, and Sergeant Libby, realizing that no one else could operate the vehicle, placed himself between the driver and the enemy, thereby shielding him while he returned the fire. During this action, he received several wounds in the arms and body. Continuing through the town, the tractor made frequent stops, and Sergeant Libby helped more wounded aboard. Refusing first aid, he continued to shield the driver and return the fire of the enemy when another roadblock was encountered. Sergeant Libby received additional wounds but held his position until he lost consciousness. Sergeant Libby's sustained, heroic actions enabled his comrades to reach friendly lines. His dauntless courage and gallant self-sacrifice reflect the highest credit upon himself and uphold the esteemed traditions of the U.S. Army.

Presentation Date and Details: June 21, 1951, at the Pentagon, presented by General Omar N. Bradley to Sergeant Libby's sister, Mrs. Gladys Hillertz.

General of the Army Omar N. Bradley, presents the Medal of Honor to Gladys Hillertz, sister of George Libby. Courtesy of the National Archives, photo no. 111-SC-367440_001.

Photo of Taejon, South Korea, after the battle

From the Evening Express June 21, 1951

SISTER OF CASCO SOLDIER-HERO ACCEPTS HIS MEDAL OF HONOR

Sgt George Libby One of 11 To Get Highest Award

Washington, June 21 (AP) – General Omar Bradley said today that in Korea, "the free nations gained at least one precious year to prepare for whatever may come."

He told the kinfolk of 11 gallant men of the Army – one of them Sergeant George D. Libby of Casco, Maine – to whom he gave the Medal of Honor, the Nation's paramount military decoration, that these men made an "eminent contribution" to attaining that period of grace.

Ten of the men – infantrymen, engineers, a medic, men, and officers – are dead, and one is missing in action. Of 23 Medals of Honor awarded to Army soldiers who fought in Korea, only three have been alive and present to receive them.

The valor of these 11, above and beyond the call of duty, was demonstrated on what Bradley said was "that grim battleground" of Korea. He said their deeds had placed their names on the roll of courageous, patriotic Americans whose exploits will never be forgotten."

For their deaths and for their daring, the five-star general of the Army offered "the deep sympathy and profound gratitude of our Nation."

The Chairman of the Joint Chiefs of Staff recalled that "three days less than a year ago," the North Korean Communists crossed the 38th Parallel to wage war on the Republic of Korea. This was "part of the continuing Community plan to test the fortitude of the United Nations and the sincerity underlying their pledge taken at San Francisco five years before," Bradley said.

He continued: World War III was a distinct possibility when the 38th Parallel was violated that morning in June 1950. Any sign of weakness on the part of the United States and her Allies – any shrinking from the challenge – most certainly would have indicated that the free world was ripe for conquest.

"But the challenge was accepted. The armies of North Korea and later of Red China – puppet armies sided in every way possible short of actual employment of Soviet Union forces – were resisted immediately, firmly, and courageously.

"Doubtlessly, this earnest stand deterred the Communists from engaging in an all-out war caused them to pause – momentarily perhaps, but pause nevertheless – in their plan for world domination.

"The free nations gained at least one precious year to prepare for whatever may come. During that year, they achieved complete cooperation and unity of understanding. During that year, they began to build the forces and equipment needed to bring their strength to the level needed for their collective security.

"That precious period of grace was earned by the strong, determined position which the United Nations took in Korea and by the achievement of their forces on that grim battleground.

"The gallant men whom we honor today each made an eminent contribution to those attainments, and I deem it a great privilege that I am permitted to participate in this ceremony and present their decorations as the representative of our President and commander-in-chief."

With the awards today, the list of Army Medal of Honor winners in the Korean War has grown to 23 – of whom only three are alive and not missing. All those awarded today were to men either dead or missing.

The Army awards have gone to both soldiers and officers of four branches of service – 18 to infantrymen, two to engineers, two to members of armored outfits, and one to a hero of the Army Medical Service.

TARO LEAFERS PROUDLY OUTLIVE COMMIES' PROPHECY

Ill-Equipped, Under-Strength Division Now Potent Fighting Force

WITH U.S. 24TH DIV (UP) – Seoul City Sue boasted on more than one occasion that the North Korean Communists would destroy the U.S. 24th Division.

But the war is one year old today, and the "Taro Leaf" Division is still around. In fact, almost 12 months of combat have transformed it from an ill-equipped, under-strength, occupation-softened garrison outfit into a seasoned, veteran fighting force considered the most potent of the United Nations divisions in Korea.

The Communists have good reason to wish for the annihilation of the 24th combat-wise troopers. Since the first two and one-half companies of the division were committed at Osan, South Korea, last July 5th, it has cut down the flower of the North Korean and Chinese Communist forces.

It has killed 38,253, wounded 61,120, and captured 28,006 Reds – a total of 127,329. And those figures do not include the months of July and November for which records have been lost.

A conservative estimate of the overall toll made by Lieutenant Colonel Thomas J. Marsden, Rye Beach, New Hampshire, division officers, is "at least 150,000." Compared to the approximately 10,000 casualties – killed, wounded, and missing – suffered by the 24th, the ratio is 15 to one.

The most colorful pages in the history of the Korean War have been written by the 24th. The tiny original force, which stood eight and one-half hours against three Communist divisions at Osan, marked the first instance of the United Nations meeting force with force in combatting unwarranted aggression.

The bloody struggle at Taejon added many legends to American military history. The most colorful and often-quoted is the saga of Major General William Dean, who stayed behind with his rear guard and was last seen attacking an enemy tank with only a hand grenade.

And there was Sergeant George Dalton Libby, an engineer, who fought as an infantryman. He loaded wounded men on a tractor and shielded the only man who could drive it as the lumbering vehicle crashed through an enemy roadblock. Although wounded several times, Libby refused any aid and continued to shield the driver and return enemy fire until he fell dead from loss of blood.

Both he and General Dean were awarded the Congressional Medal of Honor.

Under a new commander, Major General John J. Church, the 24th held on the Naktong River and annihilated the Fourth North Korean Division in the bitter fighting. The 34th regiment was all but wiped out and was replaced by the Fifth Regimental Combat Team from Hawaii. The 21st Regiment earned the nickname "Fire Brigade" because of its quick shifts to plug dangerous gaps in the shaky perimeter.

The 24th broke out of the perimeter on September 18 and didn't stop until it was within 14 miles of Sinuiju on the Yalu River in November. It was forced to pull back when the Chinese entered and made it a new war.

It fought rear guard actions for the evacuation of Pyongyang in early December and Seoul in January.

The "Taro Leafers," under the command of Major General B.M. Bryan, were prominent in the renewed northward drive ordered by General Matthew B. Ridgway last winter. The doughfeet fought cross-country through knee-deep snow and sub-zero temperatures to slaughter fanatical Chinese fighting to the death for each hill.

It swept the Reds from south of the Han River and was within sight of Kumhwa when the Chinese launched their abortive spring counteroffensive. It fell back only when exposed flanks made its flanks untenable and contained the thrust north of the Han.

The division has earned two Presidential Unit Citations for its part in the Korean conflict, and each of the original men who landed with it last summer has been awarded the Bronze Star Medal.

General Bryan, in a special war anniversary statement, saluted the division as "The greatest infantry outfit ever to walk on its own two feet."

On May 30, 2001, Nature Coast Korean War Veterans Association Chapter 174 made a special presentation during the Veterans of Foreign Wars Memorial Day services at Florida Hills Memorial Gardens in Spring Hill. The chapter's president, John McMillan, presented a certificate of special congressional recognition to the family of Sergeant George Dalton Libby, a Korean War Medal of Honor recipient.

Nature Coast Chapter #174 of Florida

John McMillan (left), poses with Mr. and Mrs. Birt. Mrs. Birt, sister of Sgt. Dalton Libby, MOH, was presented a special Congresional Recognition.

Legacy naming

1) Libby Army Reserve Center in New Haven, Connecticut
2) Sierra Vista Municipal Airport – Libby Army Airfield Fort Huachuca, Arizona
3) George Dalton Libby Complex, Fort Leonard Wood – houses engineers in training
4) Monument at the Waterbury, Connecticut War Memorial, 1892 Thomaston Avenue

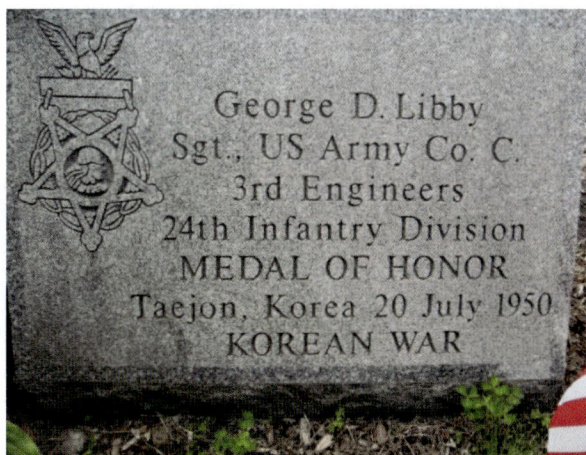

George D. Libby
Sgt., US Army Co. C.
3rd Engineers
24th Infantry Division
MEDAL OF HONOR
Taejon, Korea 20 July 1950
KOREAN WAR

Photo courtesy of HMdb.org

5) Libby Bridge in Korea: The Libby Bridge spans the Imjin River north of the Spoonbill region. The bridge is the work of the 84th Engineer Battalion and is one of the largest troop construction projects on record in Korea. It was built during the Korean War and used as a military road that also served as a travel path for farming residents in the north of the Civilian Control Line. It was shut down for safety reasons in 2016. Taking National Route 37, you can see the overall view of the Libby Bridge on the way to the upper stream of the Imjingang River. The City of Paju is currently working to have the Libby Bridge registered as a Modern Cultural Heritage and to develop the Bridge as a tourist site.

Libby Bridge in Korea courtesy of KoreaDMZVets.com

Buried in Arlington National Cemetery, 1 Memorial Drive, Arlington, Virginia; Section 34, Grave 1317. Photo by the author.

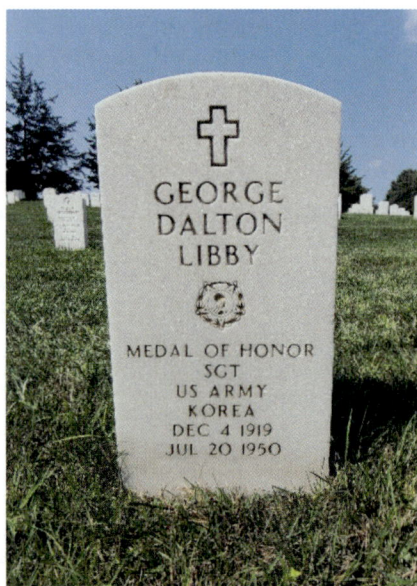

304

CAPTAIN OF THE TOP * ALEXANDER MACK; NAVY

May 17, 1834 (Rotterdam, Netherlands) – September 25, 1907 (New London, CT); 73 years old
Married to Margaret O'Neil (1840-1914).
One son, John F. Mack.

* Captain of the Top rank was one of two petty officers, placed in charge of the foremast or mainmast.

MEDAL OF HONOR CITATION

AWARDED FOR ACTIONS DURING: Civil War
BRANCH OF SERVICE: Navy
SHIP: U.S.S. Brooklyn
GENERAL ORDERS: War Department, General Orders No. 45 (December 31, 1864)
AGE ON THE DAY OF THE EVENT: 30
CITATION:

The President of the United States of America, in the name of Congress, takes pleasure in presenting the Medal of Honor to Captain of the Top Alexander Mack, United States Navy, for extraordinary heroism in action while serving on board the U.S.S. Brooklyn during successful attacks against Fort Morgan, rebel gunboats and the ram Tennessee in Mobile Bay, Alabama, on 5 August 1864. Although wounded and sent below for treatment, Captain of the Top Mack immediately returned to his post and took charge of his gun and, as heavy enemy return fire continued to fall, performed his duties with skill and courage until he was again wounded and totally disabled.

From The Day (New London, CT) September 25, 1907

DEATH CAME TO OLD NAVAL HERO
BOATSWAIN MACK PASSES AWAY AFTER LONG ILLNESS – HIS GREAT CAREER

Alexander Mack, Chief Boatswain in the United States navy, retired, died Tuesday afternoon about 5 o'clock at his home, Montauk avenue. He leaves a widow and one son, John Mack. Boatswain Mack has been ill for several months and of late the services of a nurse has been constantly required. Dr. H. H. Heyer has been attending physician and the aged veteran's son, John, has been an unfailing source of help to his father the latter's sufferings.

Boatswain Mack was born at sea, off Holyhead, in the Irish channel, on May 17, 1836. Born on the water it was but natural that he should follow the sea for a livelihood. It was not surprising, therefore, that he began when he was 10 years of age and that during his boyhood days, he made a trip around Cape Horn. During 1854 he was in the English Navy and was one of the crew of H. M.S. Algiers. During this period, he served in the Crimean War.

It was during the Civil war, in 1863, that the intrepid sailor and fighter entered the United States Navy, joining the ship Brooklyn. He was given the rating of captain of the maintop. During the Battle of Mobile Bay Boatswain Mack was one of the crew with Admiral Farragut and distinguished himself by conspicuous gallantry. During the fighting he lost his left arm and was injured in 31 different places about his body. He had to be dragged from his post in order that his life might be saved. For service with Farragut, he was awarded a medal of honor by Congress.

Boatswain Mack was retired from the United States Navy on December 12, 1864, on account of disability. Again in 1872 Boatswain Mack joined the Navy and received his commission as Chief Boatswain. He served on various ships and at the New London Naval station for over six years. It was while stationed here that he decided to make his home in New London. Upen his final retirement in 1899, he took up his residence in Montauk Avenue. For several years Boatswain Mack has been the only commandant at the station up the river. But in recent months he had retired from any active participation of the management of the yard.

Aside from his service to this country. Boatswain Mack was a good citizen and was generally respected by his neighbors and fellow citizens.

From The Day (New London, CT) September 27, 1907

BORNE TO THE GRAVE
Boatswain Mack's Body Taken to Fall River For Interment

With the casket enwrapped with the American flag, the body of Boatswain Alexander Mack was taken to Fall River, Massachusetts today for burial. There was no service at the house, but a mass will be celebrated in the latter city. The bearers were Jacob R. Fisher, Thomas W. Casey, Philip Spelman and F.M. Barrows, the latter pay director's clerk. The Navy Department was represented by the presence of Chief Boatswain Duffy, who recently arrived here to take charge of the New London Naval Station. The body was taken to the Union Station in time to be placed aboard the 9:40 train. The funeral arrangements were in charge of Caulkins & Prentis.

Buried in St. Patrick's Cemetery, 2233 Robeson Street, Fall River, Massachusetts; Section 11, Lot 172.

CHIEF BOATSWAIN'S MATE JOHN SPEARS MACKENZIE; NAVY

July 7, 1886 (Bridgeport, CT) – December 26, 1933 (Holyoke, MA); 47 years old
Married to Jean Harris (1922-1977).
One son, James (1921-1985).
One daughter, Jessie D. MacKenzie Fuller [Navy veteran] (1922-2007).
Enlisted on December 20, 1902.
Discharged on July 6, 1907.
Reenlisted in May 1917.

Born to James (1851-1944) and Mary McCall MacKenzie (1853-1925) [both born in Scotland]. Three sisters, Christina S. MacKenzie Smith Lamberton (1879-1974), Mary MacKenzie Burckard (1881-1962), and Margaret (1893-1907). Two brothers, James (1878-1975) and George (1883-1919).

Photo (left) courtesy of Transcript-Telegram (Holyoke, MA). Photo (right) courtesy of the Congressional Medal of Honor Society.

MEDAL OF HONOR CITATION

AWARDED FOR ACTIONS DURING: World War I
BRANCH OF SERVICE: Navy
ASSIGNED TO: U.S.S. Remlik
GENERAL ORDERS: War Department, General Orders No. 391 (1918)
CITATION:

The President of the United States of America, in the name of Congress, takes pleasure in presenting the Medal of Honor to Chief Boatswain's Mate John MacKenzie, United States Navy, for extraordinary heroism while serving on board the U.S.S. Remlik, on the morning of 17 December 1917, when the Remlik encountered a heavy gale. During this gale, there was a heavy sea running. The depth charge box on the taffrail aft, containing a Sperry depth charge, was washed overboard, the depth charge itself falling inboard and remaining on deck. Chief Boatswain's Mate MacKenzie, on his own initiative, went aft and sat down on the depth charge, as it was impracticable to carry it to safety until the ship was headed up into the sea. In acting as he did, Chief Boatswain's Mate MacKenzie exposed his life and prevented a serious accident to the ship and probable loss of the ship and the entire crew.

From The Springfield Republican; unknown date

HOLYOKE MAN GIVEN ITALIAN WAR CROSS
John MacKenzie Already Holder of United States Congressional Medal of Honor

Holyoke, January 27 — John Mackenzie of 112 Nonotuck Street, Formerly of South Hadley Falls, has received from the Italian government the Italian War Cross. He already held the Congressional Medal of Honor for saving the crew of the U.S. converted yacht Remlik when a depth bomb got loose and began to roll about the deck. Mackenzie seized the bomb and held it until it could be secured. Depth bombs are not considered healthful play-things, and his deed was noticed by the government.

Letter from John MacKenzie describing the incident for which he was awarded the Medal of Honor. From a typescript in the collection of John MacKenzie, held by the Naval Historical Center.

10 Bolton St.
South Hadley Falls, Massachusetts
September 28, 1922

Mr. H. Reuterdahl
Lieutenant Commander U. S. N. R.F. Retired,
800 Boulevard E.
Weehawken, N.J.

It has taken me some little time to make up my mind as to whether or not to write giving you the information which you requested in your letter of September 8th, and have decided that what I think of the affair personally must take second place when the traditions of the Navy are considered. To begin with, I wish to state that I did not consider that my act warranted the award of the Medal of Honor, but as my Commanding Officer, Isaac C. Johnson, thought differently, I decided to abide by his decision.

You are no doubt familiar with weather conditions in the Bay of Biscay during the month of December, and I would like to give you some idea of the conditions existing when my little affair took place. We left Queiberon Bay at 4 P.M. on December 15, 1917, with a northbound convoy for Brest and Channel Ports. The convoy consisted of 45 ships and the patrol. A northeaster was kicking things up in good style when we cleared Belle Isle, and by 7 P.M., the entire convoy had vanished from sight. We had in the Remlik a sturdy little craft, and she managed to worry along through the night and all of the following day. By the night of the 16th, we had about worn ourselves out, and the battering the Remlik was receiving did not help matters any.

At about 7:30 A.M. December 17, 1917, the lookout aloft forward sighted a periscope on our starboard beam at about 500 yards distance. I was standing on the bridge talking with Captain Johnson when General Quarters sounded. As I had charge of the Machine Guns and there was no chance to use them owing to the seas running, I remained on the Bridge. The seas were breaking over us from stern {stem?} to stern, and naturally, the decks were awash all of the time. The Gun Crews were knee-deep in water and, with the rolling and pitching of the Remlik, were prevented from landing the U Boat. The general opinion at that time was that she, like ourselves, had become lost in the storm and was not looking for a fight, but for objects from which to take bearings. However, she had no more than vanished than a tremendous sea broke over our stern. I stood on the Bridge looking aft, and as the old salt would have said, that sea shivered our timbers and carried away the depth charge cradle carried aft on the taffrail. After the freeing ports had disposed of some of the water, I could see friend Depth Bomb cavorting around on the Gun Platform between the Port rail and the Steering Engine. Knowing that it would hardly do to let our little pet bump many times, I ran down from the bridge and aft. After several attempts and as many duckings, I finally got a toe hold on the Gun Platform and my arms around the bomb. I then made the discovery that the safety pin had come out of the bomb and had visions of the buoy section getting away from me. Could feel the cold chills chasing up and down my spine. Fortunately, I got the pin back into place at the first attempt. After several more attempts, I swung the Bomb with such a position that I could both sit on it and, at the same time, hold on to the Gun Platform. The ship was then headed up into the sea, and Patrick Danahee, Fireman First Class, helped me to lash the bomb to the Gun Platform.

I am enclosing herewith a copy of Captain Johnson's original letter to the Department.

Since receiving your letter, I have received from the Italian Government the Italian War Cross.

Very truly yours, JM*CS

From "Holyoke In the Great War" by Charles Zack (1919)

Chasing a U-boat while fighting a 100-mile gale and having a depth bomb break loose from its fastening and go rolling about the decks, in imminent danger of exploding and blowing up the ship, was one of the experiences of the crew of the U.S.S. converted yacht Remlik.

And then, as the full realization of their peril was sweeping over the officers, into the picture springs a figure that wrestles with the deadly missile, filled with TNT, and holds it until it can be safely secured.

Thus, did Chief Boatswain's Mate John Mackenzie of South Hadley Falls rescue his ship and its 80 officers and men from certain destruction, later to receive the commendation of his commander and a citation with the Medal of Honor from the Secretary of the Navy.

"There wasn't much to it; it was simply a case of go get it," Mate Mackenzie said when cornered in his cubbyhole office at Battery Wharf, Boston. He was much more communicative concerning the heroic achievements of the officers.

"Their acts of bravery will never be written," he said. "Why, take our captain, for example, now Lieutenant-Commander Isaac C. Johnson. When we sailed out of New York, it was freely predicted we would never reach the other side. Our commander never had his clothes off during our whole trip across and never went to his quarters to sleep. I have seen him standing with one arm thrown around a stanchion, snatching a nap, having given orders that if he was wanted to touch his arm. And all through the Navy, there are hundreds of such incidents that history will never record."

To understand the great danger of a depth bomb, it is necessary to explain its mechanism. In this instance, it was of the old Sperry type, resembling an ash can in form, but now practically obsolete. It is in two sections, the top for about a quarter of the length of the cylinder being the buoy. The lower section is filled with about 100 pounds of TNT and is the mine. The sections are held together by a wire running from the mine up through the center of the buoy to its top, where it is fastened by a cotter pin. The wire can be fixed to pay out to any depth desired. In this case, it was set for fifty feet. When the bomb is dropped overboard, the safety pin is pulled out; the buoy and mine separate, the mine, of course, dropping until the limit of the wire is reached when the pull detonates the charge. This particular bomb was resting in a U-shaped cradle at the stern.

Chief Mackenzie's own story of the incident is this:

"We were convoying in the Bay of Biscay and had been a day and a half in a gale. We had just sighted a submarine, and everybody was ordered on deck. I happened to be walking aft when I saw a big wave break over the stern and smash the cradle. The depth bomb was let loose and started rolling around the decks. I threw myself on it, grabbed it in my arms, braced my feet against the gun platform, and was able to hold it fast."

309

This laconic tale of the heroic deed takes no account of the dangers he was facing other than from the bomb itself, the chances of being swept into the sea by each receding breaker, his safety depending wholly upon the length of time he could retain his foot grip upon the timbers of the gun platform, since, as the official report states it, there was no way to get assistance to him "until the ship could be headed into the sea and the after part made more secure for passage."

But in the Navy records of the World War will be found this official report from Lieutenant Commander Johnson of the Remlik:

"The depth charge box on the taffrail, containing a Sperry depth charge, was washed overboard on December 17, 1917, the depth charge itself falling inboard and remaining on deck. It was impossible for anyone to carry it to safety, and it was even dangerous for anyone to go to that part of the ship due to the seas washing over the stern. Mackenzie, on his own initiative, went aft and sat down on the depth charge until the ship was headed into the sea.

"After the depth charge was carried to a place of safety, it was found that the safety pin had become detached, and had it remained on deck and been washed around with the sea, the buoy section of the depth charge would, no doubt, have become detached and the depth charge detonated had not Mackenzie acted immediately as he did.

"Mackenzie exposed his life and prevented a serious accident to the ship and probable loss of the ship and entire crew.

"The action of Mackenzie in this case is most highly recommended for the serious consideration of the department."

Chief Boatswain's Mate Mackenzie's "extraordinary heroism in the line of his profession" was made the subject of general orders in the navy. Following this came the citation from the Secretary of the Navy.

"You have upheld the best traditions of the naval service, and the department heartily commends you. The department will also award you a Medal of Honor," wrote Secretary Daniels.

Mate Mackenzie also received the $100 gratuity that accompanies awards for "extraordinary heroism." Later, he received a check for the same amount from Willis S. Kilmer, owner of the yacht Remlik. The inscription on the medal reads: "Awarded to John Mackenzie. U. S. N. F., for extraordinary heroism, U.S.S. Remlik, December 17, 1917. Saved ship from destruction by securing depth bomb."

Chief Mackenzie may be classed with the veterans of the Navy. He served as a naval apprentice from 1902 to 1907, during which his cruises carried him over 66,000 miles of sea. After leaving the Navy, he engaged in the automobile accessory business at Springfield. He re-entered the naval service on May 12, 1917, and served overseas in convoy work and submarine chasing.

From the Transcript-Telegram (Holyoke, Massachusetts) December 26, 1933

JOHN MACKENZIE DIES OF HEART ATTACK; WAS MEDAL OF HONOR MAN

Won Highest Distinction In World War While Serving In Navy

John MacKenzie, 47, of 62 Norwood Terrace, World War naval hero who won the Congressional Medal of Honor for saving a ship from destruction by holding on to a depth bomb, died in his home this afternoon of a heart attack suffered in his High Street restaurant at 1:45 p.m.

A veteran of the Navy, MacKenzie served as a naval apprentice from 1902 to 1907. He left the service to go into the auto accessory business in Springfield and reenlisted in 1917 as America entered the World War.

In the 66,000 miles he traveled all over the world in naval ships, he was distinguished by qualities of courage and seamanship that finally saved 80 lives in the storm-tossed Bay of Biscay on December 17, 1917.

MacKenzie was a Boatswain's Mate on the U.S.S. Remlik, a converted yacht on duty off the French coast. As the small craft was buffeted by the seas, a depth bomb containing 100 pounds of TNT broke from its cradle on the afterdeck and careened around the deck, adding its terror to the stormy plight of the ship. Only a small pin needed to be pulled out to explode the bomb.

MacKenzie threw himself on it and held it until it could be again secured.

Mr. MacKenzie was born July 7, 1886, in Bridgeport, Connecticut, and moved to South Hadley Falls when he was a boy. He received his education there. He was married 13 years ago, last July 7, to Jean L. Harris. The couple had two children, James and Jessie, both at home. He had been the proprietor of MacKenzie's Home Lunch on High Street for the past eight years.

He was a member of the Mount Tom Lodge of Masons, the Shriners, the American Legion, Elks, Veterans of Foreign Wars, holder of the Legion of Valor, and a Congressional Medal of Honor given by the U.S. Navy.

He was a member of Grace Church and, for many years, sang in the choir there. Besides his father, James MacKenzie, he leaves two sisters, Mrs. Christina S. Lamberton of this city and Mrs. Lorin Burkhardt of San Jose, California. The funeral will be held on Friday, the time to be announced later.

The official record of MacKenzie's deed follows:

"The depth charge box on the taffrail containing a Sperry depth charge was washed overboard on December 17, 1917, the depth charge itself falling inboard and remaining on deck. It was impossible for anyone to carry it to safety, and it was even dangerous for anyone to go to that part of the ship due to the seas washing over the stern. MacKenzie, on his own initiative, went aft and sat down on the depth charge until the ship was headed into the sea.

"After the depth charge was carried to a place of safety, it was found that the safety pin had become detached, and had it remained on deck and been washed around with the sea, the buoy section of the depth charge would, no doubt, have become detached and the depth charge detonated had not MacKenzie acted immediately as he did.

"MacKenzie exposed his life and prevented a serious accident to the ship and probable loss of the ship and the entire crew.

"The action of MacKenzie in this case is most highly recommended for the serious consideration of the department. Chief Boatswain's Mate MacKenzie's "extraordinary heroism in the line of his profession" was made the subject of general orders in the Navy. Following this came the citation from the Secretary of the Navy.

"You have upheld the best traditions of the naval service, and the department heartily commends you. This department will also award you a Medal of Honor," wrote Secretary Daniels.

Boatswain's Mate MacKenzie also received the $100 gratuity that accompanies awards for "extraordinary heroism." Later, he received a check for the same amount from Willis S. Kilmer, owner of the yacht Remlik. The inscription on the medal reads:

"Awarded to John MacKenzie, U.S.N.F. [United States Naval Force], for extraordinary heroism, U.S.S. Remlik, December 17, 1917. Saved ship from destruction by securing depth bomb.

Photo # NH 98030   USS Remlik during World War I

Photo courtesy of the U.S. Navy (U.S. Navy photo NH 98030).

Honored with the naming of MacKenzie Stadium next to Holyoke High School's North Campus at 500 Beech Street, Holyoke, Massachusetts.

Previously known as "The Range" and later known as "Beech Street Grounds," Mackenzie Stadium, built as a Works Progress Administration project, was dedicated on Labor Day, September 4, 1939, in memory of the late John S. MacKenzie. MacKenzie was awarded the Congressional Medal of Honor for extraordinary heroism on the U.S.S. Remlik, December 17, 1917. It was Holyoke's first enclosed stadium and hosts numerous sports teams/events. The Valley Blue Sox, a collegiate summer baseball team and member of the New England Collegiate Baseball League plays its home games at Mackenzie Stadium. The Memorial is located on the east side near the Beech Street gate.

Medal of Honor monument in Veterans Memorial Park, 163 Maple Street, Holyoke, Massachusetts.

Photo courtesy of WayMarking.com

PRIVATE FIRST CLASS JOHN DAVID MAGRATH; ARMY

July 4, 1924 (Norwalk, CT) – April 14, 1945; 20 years old
Unmarried
Last local address: 17 Wallace Avenue, East Norwalk
Enlisted on April 4, 1943
Service number: 31326858

Born to Gerry C. (1876-1959) and Anna M. Radzimanowski Magrath (1885-1940). Three brothers, Frederick C. (1916-2005), Gerry A. (1918-1996), and William B. (1922-2012).

Photo (left) courtesy of the Congressional Medal of Honor Society. Photo (right) courtesy of the Magrath family.

MEDAL OF HONOR CITATION

AWARDED FOR ACTIONS DURING: World War II
BRANCH OF SERVICE: Army
UNIT: Company G, 85th Infantry Regiment, 10th Mountain Division
GENERAL ORDERS: War Department, General Orders No. 71, July 17, 1946
AGE ON THE DAY OF THE EVENT: 20
CITATION:

The President of the United States of America, in the name of Congress, takes pride in presenting the Medal of Honor (Posthumously) to Private First Class John D. Magrath, United States Army, for conspicuous gallantry and intrepidity above and beyond the call of duty on 14 April 1945, while serving with Company G, 85th Infantry Regiment, 10th Mountain Division when his company was pinned down by heavy artillery, mortar, and small arms fire, near Castel d'Aiano, Italy. Volunteering to act as a scout, armed with only a rifle, Private First Class Magrath charged headlong into withering fire, killing two Germans and wounding three in order to capture a machinegun. Carrying this enemy weapon across an open field through heavy fire, he neutralized two more machinegun nests; he then circled behind four other Germans, killing them with a burst as they were firing on his company. Spotting another dangerous enemy position to this right, he knelt with the machinegun in his arms and exchanged fire with the Germans until he had killed two and wounded three. The enemy now poured increased mortar and artillery fire on the company's newly won position. Private First Class Magrath fearlessly volunteered again to brave the shelling in order to collect a report of casualties. Heroically carrying out this task, he made the supreme sacrifice -- a climax to the valor and courage that are in keeping with the highest traditions of military service.

<u>Presentation Date and Details</u>: September 7, 1946, Mathews Park, Norwalk, Connecticut, presented by Major General James G. VanFleet to Gerry Magrath, PFC Magrath's father.

Photo from an unknown newspaper courtesy of the Magrath family.
Left to right, Major General Van Fleet, Casper Lowenstein, who helped organize
the event for the City of Norwalk, Mrs. Marion Magrath, stepmother,
and Gerry Magrath, father.

The son of Gerry C. and Anna Magrath, John David Magrath was born in East Norwalk, Connecticut, on July 4, 1924. He took up scouting in 1937 and earned twenty-one merit badges. As a Boy Scout, he served as patrol leader, troop scribe, and assistant scoutmaster for East Norwalk's Troop 16. He became an Eagle Scout on February 8, 1943. Magrath was an active member of Christ Episcopal Church, which sponsored the scout troop. He also sang in the church choir.

Magrath entered the U.S. Army during his junior year in high school, along with three friends. The four young men were all members of the Norwalk Ski Club who volunteered in order to join the ski troops. Magrath was sworn in on March 4, 1943, at Hartford, Connecticut. Two of his brothers, Gerry and William, were already serving in the U.S. Army.

Magrath joined the 10th Mountain Division at Camp Hale, Colorado, and continued his training at Camp Swift, Texas. Initially, Magrath was assigned to the 86th Infantry Regiment, where he served in Companies A, F, and M.

Later, he transferred to the 85th Infantry Regiment, Company G. Senator Bob Dole was a 2nd Lieutenant in the 10th Mountain Division and was wounded in action in April 1945 at Castel d'Aiano, the same battle as PFC Magrath.

Magrath served as a radio operator during combat operations in Italy. On April 14, 1945, Company G was ordered to attack German positions on Hill 909 near the town of Castel d'Aiano. The attack bogged down under intense German artillery fire, which caused numerous casualties. Magrath volunteered to accompany his company commander on a reconnaissance. When they encountered German small-arms fire, Magrath charged the German positions with only his rifle. He is credited with single-handedly silencing several enemy machine gun emplacements with a captured German machine gun. Later that day, Magrath volunteered to make contact with each platoon in the company to compile a casualty report. While moving under heavy artillery fire, he was killed in action.

For his gallantry, Magrath was posthumously awarded the Medal of Honor. He was the only member of the 10th Mountain Division and the only citizen of East Norwalk, Connecticut, to be so honored during World War II. A monument in his honor was dedicated at Fort Riley, Kansas, on August 17, 1955, and an elementary school at Norwalk, which opened on March 15, 1956, was also named in his honor. Later, the school was purchased by the state of Connecticut for the site of the East Campus of Norwalk Community College. The college maintains a memorial display in Magrath's honor.

In June 1995, Fort Drum, New York, home of the 10th Mountain Division, renamed its Soldiers Sports Complex the John D. Magrath Gymnasium. A plaque and portrait at Magrath Gym honor his memory.

Until September 2009, PFC Magrath was the only member of the 10th Mountain Division to be awarded the Medal of Honor. The others were Captain William D. Swenson, honored in 2013 for his actions during a six-hour battle on Sept. 8, 2009, in the Ganjgal valley of eastern Afghanistan, Sergeant First Class Jared C. Monti, posthumously honored in September 2009 for his actions in Afghanistan in June 2006, and Staff Sergeant Travis W. Atkins for his actions on June 1, 2007, in support of Operation Iraqi Freedom.

From pietredellamemoria.it regarding a memorial in Italy to John Magrath

Nation: Italy
Region: Emilia Romagna
Province: Bologna (BO)
Common: Castel d'Aiano
Fraction: Riodomello
Address: Via Riodomello
Postal code: 40034
Place of placement: Wooded area near the Riodomello block
Placement date: May 30, 2009
Materials (Generic): Bronze, stone
Materials (Detail): Bronze slab on a sandstone boulder.
Conservation status: Great
Entity in charge of conservation: Municipality of Castel d'Aiano
News and historical contextualization (translated from Italian):
On April 14, 1945, a 19-year-old young man serving in the 85th G. Infantry Company of the 10th Mountain Division distinguished himself for an act of great courage, sustained at the risk of life and beyond his duty. His company was immobilized because of the heavy fire of the enemy artillery. He volunteered for an exploratory action and armed with a single rifle, he managed to overpower 2 German soldiers by taking possession of their machine gun. With this, he responded to enemy fire, neutralizing three more posts. Back inside his company, on which the rain of blows was intensifying, he volunteered again to come out and collect the list of victims. After heroically completing

this painful task, he also left his life on the field, in an extreme gesture of value and courage, in observance of the highest tradition of military service. For these reasons, the President of the United States has awarded the chosen soldier John D. Magrath the posthumous Ad Honorem Medal, and for the same reasons now, in the exact place where this valiant young man gave his life, this recognition is dedicated to him.

Registration: The President of the United States of America, authorized by the Act of Congress, on March 3, 1963, bestowed the Posthumous Ad Honorem Medal on behalf of Congress to the SOLDIER JOHN D. MAGRATH OF THE UNITED STATES ARMY
For his great courage and fearlessness of action at the risk of his life beyond his duty: the chosen soldier John D. Magrath of the United States Army, distinguished himself in action on April 14, 1945, while he was serving in the 85th Company G. Infantry of the 10th Mountain Division.

The chosen Magrath soldier showed great courage and fearlessness above and beyond his duty when his company was immobilized by heavy artillery fire, mortar, and small arms near Castel D'Aiano, Italy. He volunteered and, as an explorer, armed only with a rifle, loaded headlong into the chilling fire, killing two Germans and injuring three, to take possession of a machine gun. Transporting this enemy weapon through an open field in the middle of the enemy fire, neutralizing two other machine gun positions, and then encircling four other Germans who were shooting at the Company, killing them with a burst.

Detecting another enemy position on his right, he knelt with the machine gun and fired on the Germans, killing two and injuring three. The enemy increased the mortar and artillery attack on the Company and its newly acquired position. The chosen soldier, Magrath, intrepidly volunteered again to bravely face the cannonade and to be able to collect the list of victims. He carried out this task in a heroic way, and it was the last supreme sacrifice, the culminating point of value and courage that are in observance of the highest tradition of military service.

Symbols: Symbol of the Municipality of Castel d'Aiano and the X Mountain Division

Personal comments: We wanted to connect the 2 stems of Monte della Spe and Riodomello in a single "memory" to remember the dramatic days between March and April 1945 when our town of Castel D'Aiano was at the center of one of the most important fronts of the Second World War. We also wanted to remember the sacrifice of the American soldiers who, on that fateful April 14, 1945, moved from Monte della Spe to conquer, after bitter battles, the heights of Riodomello and the Serre D'Aiano, breaking through the last German defensive line and thus freeing, in a few days, the whole of Northern Italy. Near the two steles, the trenches used by the soldiers and recently renovated are still visible.

From the Star Democrat, Easton, Maryland (stardem.com), June 28, 2009

ITALIAN TOWNSPEOPLE REMEMBER MAGRATH WITH A MONUMENT

Giancarlo Bendini, right, poses with a friend next to a monument in Castel d'Aiano, Italy, honoring PFC John Magrath

The townspeople of Castel d'Aiano, Italy, haven't forgotten what the American soldiers of the 10th Mountain Division did for them. And now, they definitely will not forget about the heroics of PFC John Magrath.

John's brother, Bill Magrath of St. Michaels (Maryland), recently received a letter and photographs of the dedication of a monument in Castel d'Aiano in early June. The monument honors the memory of John's service in their country.

The 10th Mountain Division was the U.S. Army's first mountain infantry division. Its 12,000 men included ski teachers, Russo-Finnish war veterans, fur trappers, rock climbers, and Jewish refugees. Recruits learned to ski with packs and rifles, walking up every hill and then skiing down. The training succeeded as patrols on skis led to the 10th's breakthrough of the German Army's Gothic Line in the Apennine Mountains of Italy.

On April 14, 1945, the 85th and 87th Regiments, leading the 10th Mountain Division, attacked toward Po Valley, Italy, spearheading the Fifth Army drive. The fighting was fierce, with 553 mountain infantrymen killed, wounded, or missing by the end of the day. One of the soldiers killed was 20-year-old John D. Magrath.

Magrath was the only soldier from the 10th Mountain Division to receive a Medal of Honor, the highest award for valor by an individual serving in the U.S. armed forces. The new monument includes the wording, in both English and Italian, written on John's original Medal of Honor citation, which was signed by Harry Truman:

"Private Magrath, radio operator, Company G, 85th Infantry, on 14 April 1945 displayed conspicuous gallantry and intrepidity above and beyond the call of duty when his company was pinned down by heavy artillery, mortar, and small arms fire near Castel d'Aiano, Italy. Volunteering to act as a scout, armed with only a rifle, he charged headlong into the withering fire, killing two Germans and wounding three in order to capture a machine gun. Carrying this enemy weapon across an open field through heavy fire, he neutralized two more machine gun nests; he then circled behind four other Germans, killing them with a burst as they were firing on his company. Spotting another dangerous enemy position to this right, he knelt with the machine gun in his arms and exchanged fire with the Germans until he had killed two and wounded three. The enemy now poured increased mortar and artillery fire on the company's newly-won position. Private Magrath fearlessly volunteered again to brave the shelling in order

318

to collect a report of casualties. Heroically carrying out this task, he made the supreme sacrifice a climax to the valor and courage that are in keeping with the highest traditions of the military service."

Giovanni Sulla arranged to have the monument erected near the spot where John was killed.

In a letter to Bill, Giancarlo Bendini wrote: " was a little bit exciting ceremony (sic); and for me is one good and important event, precious historical and memory for the next generations."

COMUNE DI CASTEL d'AIANO

MEDAL OF HONOR

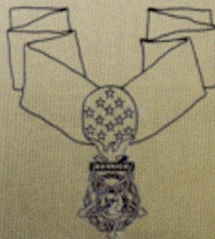

PFC John D. Magrath
Co. G, 85th Infantry, 10th Mountain Division
KIA 14 April 1945 at Castel d'Aiano

The President of the United States of America, authorized by Act of Congress, March 3, 1863, has awarded in the name of The Congress the Medal of Honor posthumously to

PRIVATE FIRST CLASS JOHN D. MAGRATH
UNITED STATES ARMY

for conspicuous gallantry and intrepidity in action at the risk of his life above and beyond the call of duty.

Private First Class John D. Magrath, United States Army, distinguished himself in action on 14 April 1945 while serving with Company G, 85th Infantry, 10th Mountain Division.

Private Magrath displayed conspicuous gallantry and intrepidity above and beyond the call of duty when his company was pinned down by heavy artillery, mortar, and small-arms fire, near Castel d'Aiano, Italy. Volunteering to act as a scout, armed with only a rifle, he charged headlong into withering fire, killing two Germans and wounding three in order to capture a machine gun. Carrying this enemy weapon across an open field through heavy fire, he neutralized two more machine-gun nests. He then circled behind four other Germans, killing them with a burst as they were firing on his company. Spotting another dangerous enemy position to his right, he knocked out the machine gun in his area and exchanged fire with the Germans until he had killed two and wounded three. The enemy now poured increased mortar and artillery fire on the company's newly won position. Private First Class Magrath fearlessly volunteered again to brave the shelling in order to collect a report of casualties. Heroically carrying out this task, he made the supreme sacrifice - a climax to the valor and courage that are in keeping with highest traditions of the military service.

Il Presidente degli Stati Uniti d'America, autorizzato dall'Act of Congress del 3 Marzo 1863, ha conferito a nome del Congresso la Medaglia ad Honorem postumo al

SOLDATO SCELTO JOHN D. MAGRATH
DELL'ESERCITO DEGLI STATI UNITI

per il grande coraggio ed intrepidità di azione a rischio della propria vita al di là del proprio dovere.

Il Soldato Scelto John D. Magrath, dell'Esercito degli Stati Uniti, si è distinto in azione il 14 Aprile 1945, mentre era in servizio presso la 85ª Compagnia G. di Fanteria della 10ª Divisione di Montagna.

Il Soldato Scelto Magrath ha dimostrato grande coraggio ed intrepidità al di sopra e al di là del proprio dovere quando la sua Compagnia fu immobilizzata da fuoco di artiglieria pesante, mortaio ed armi leggere nei pressi di Castel d'Aiano, Italia. Si offrì volontario a come esploratore, armato solo di fucile, caricò a capofitto nel raggelante fuoco, uccidendo due Tedeschi e ferendone tre, per impossessarsi di una mitragliatrice. Trasportando quest'arma nemica, attraverso in campo aperto in mezzo al fuoco nemico, neutralizzando altre due postazioni di mitragliatrice per poi accerchiare altri quattro Tedeschi che stavano sparando sulla Compagnia, uccidendoli con una raffica. Rilevando un'altra postazione nemica sulla sua destra, si ingranchiò con la mitragliatrice e sparò sui Tedeschi uccidendone due e ferendone tre. Il nemico incrementò l'attacco con mortaio ed artiglieria sulla Compagnia e la sua nuova posizione appena acquisita. Il Soldato Scelto Magrath, intrepidamente, si offrì nuovamente volontario per affrontare coraggiosamente il cannoneggiamento e poter raccogliere l'elenco delle vittime. Partì a termine questo compito in modo eroico, e fu l'ultimo supremo sacrificio, punto culminante di valore e coraggio che sono nell'essenza della più alta tradizione del servizio militare.

Castel d'Aiano 30 Maggio 2009

Honored on the "Soldiers of the Summit" marker on the Blue River Bike Trail, West Adams Avenue, Breckenridge, Colorado. Map three on the plaque says, "This time, there is no surprise, and the division has its bloodiest day in spite of an extensive preparatory bombardment by our artillery and aircraft. 2nd Lieutenant Robert Dole (85-I) is seriously wounded on Hill 913. Pfc. John Magrath (85-G) knocks out four German machine guns on Hill 909 and then volunteers for another mission in which he is killed by mortar fire. For these heroic acts, Magrath will receive the posthumous award of the 10th Division's only Medal of Honor."

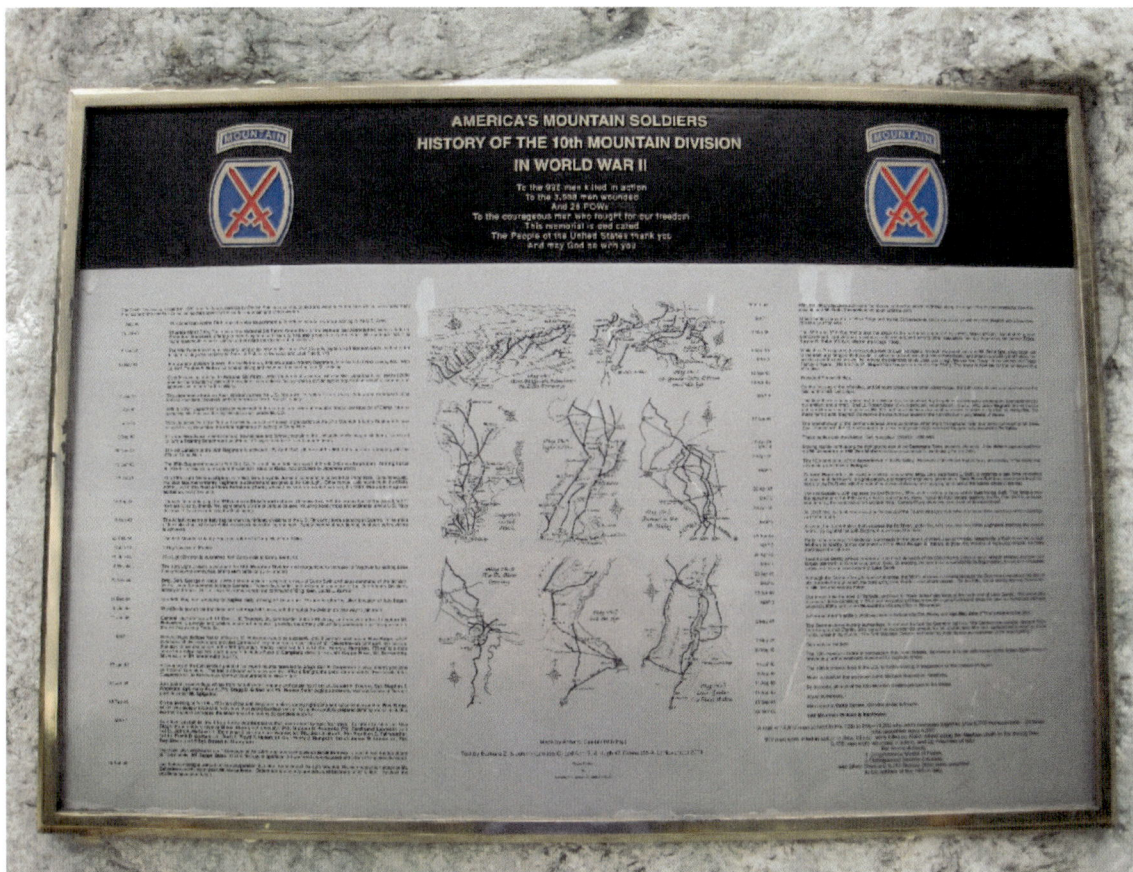

Photo courtesy of HMdb.org and Kevin W. (no last name given)

PFC Magrath is buried at Riverside Cemetery, 81 Riverside Avenue, Norwalk, Connecticut; Section 20, Plot 185. Photos by the author.

Plaque in honor of John Magrath at the Shea – Magrath Memorial and Wall of Remembrance, 55 Calf Pasture Beach Road, Norwalk, Connecticut.

QUARTERMASTER HENRY J. MANNING; NAVY

September 17, 1859 (New Haven, CT) – unknown *

One of 314 Medal of Honor recipients whose final resting place is a mystery.

Enlisted on March 8, 1876, in Baltimore, Maryland, at 16 years old.
Discharged on September 18, 1880, in New Haven, Connecticut.
Also served aboard the U.S.S. Juniata.

Parent and sibling information is unknown.

MEDAL OF HONOR CITATION

AWARDED FOR ACTIONS DURING: Peace Time Awards
BRANCH OF SERVICE: Navy
ASSIGNED TO: U.S. Training Ship New Hampshire
GENERAL ORDERS: War Department, General Orders No. 326 (October 18, 1884)
CITATION:

The President of the United States of America, in the name of Congress, takes pleasure in presenting the Medal of Honor to Quartermaster Henry J. Manning, United States Navy, for gallant and heroic conduct while serving on board the U.S. Training Ship New Hampshire, off Newport, Rhode Island, 4 January 1882. Jumping overboard, Quartermaster Manning endeavored to rescue Jabez Smith, Second Class Musician, from drowning.

The U.S.S. Juniata in 1862

When Henry Manning enlisted, his initial rank was "2nd class boy," and his original service expiration date was September 17, 1880 - his 21st birthday.

Prior to the Second World War, the Navy offered minority enlistments in which a young man could be enlisted until his 21st birthday, when he would reach the legal age of majority and could decide for himself if he wished to continue his career in the Navy.

His physical description was that he was five foot two and one half inches tall, grey eyes, dark brown hair, and dark complexion.

By January 4, 1882, he was serving as a quartermaster on the training ship U.S.S. New Hampshire. On that day, while New Hampshire was off Coaster's Harbor Island in Newport, Rhode Island, he and another sailor, Ship's Printer John McCarton, jumped overboard in an attempt to save Second Class Musician Jabez Smith from drowning. For this action, both Manning and McCarton were awarded the Medal of Honor two and a half years later, on October 18, 1884.

Nothing is known of Henry Manning's life after he received the Medal of Honor.

PRIVATE CHARLES H. MARSH; ARMY

1840 * (Milford, CT) – January 25, 1867 (New Milford, CT); 27 years old

Married to Sarah E. Kramer (1844-1935).

One son, Oliver C. (1864-1888).

One daughter, Carrie V. Marsh Kellogg (1867-1926).

Enlisted on April 20, 1861, in New Milford, Connecticut.

Discharged on August 2, 1865.

* The exact Date of Birth is unknown.

Born to Oliver C. (1811-1883) and Caroline Davis Marsh (1815-1880). One brother, Philip G. (1837-1922).

Member of St. Peter's Masonic Lodge #21 in New Milford. Wounded and imprisoned on August 7, 1862, at Gordonsville, Virginia.

Photos courtesy of the New Milford Historical Society

MEDAL OF HONOR CITATION

AWARDED FOR ACTIONS DURING: Civil War
BRANCH OF SERVICE: Army
UNIT: Company H, 1st Connecticut Cavalry
DATE OF ISSUE AND PRESENTATION: January 23, 1865
AGE ON THE DAY OF THE EVENT: 24
CITATION:

The President of the United States of America, in the name of Congress, takes pleasure in presenting the Medal of Honor to Private Charles H. Marsh, United States Army, for extraordinary heroism on 31 July 1864, while serving with Company D, 1st Connecticut Cavalry, in action at Back Creek Valley, West Virginia, for capture of flag and its bearer.

From the Hartford Courant November 17, 1864

CAPTURE OF A BLACK FLAG
Summary of Late Captures In the Shenandoah Valley

WASHINGTON, Nov. 16 – General Tyler has forwarded to the Adjutant General's office the black flag captured from [Confederate General Jubal] Early's command last August near North Mountain. He says the flag was in charge of two rebels and set up against a tree. One of the rebels went in search of water. C.H. Marsh, a detective who had been watching the flag from nightfall, determined to get it if possible and sprung upon the man left alone, secured him, took the flag from the pole, and brought it and the prisoner safely within our lines.

From The Danbury News-Times June 11, 1989. The clipping was found in the Congressional Medal of Honor Society archives. Used with permission.

NEW MILFORD -- The year was 1862, and Union spy Charles Marsh was in a Virginia prison awaiting execution. Beside him lay another war prisoner, a man on his deathbed.

In the dark of night and with the help of the prison doctor, Marsh changed places with the dying man. The following day, "Marsh" was found dead in bed.

Friends who thought Marsh had been hanged at Aldie, Virginia, were shocked when he turned up in Baltimore a few months later, paroled under his assumed name.

Less than a year later, Marsh, a Union Corporal who often passed himself off as a Confederate soldier, was again captured. But the New Milford man was released to continue a story-book career that earned him a footnote in Civil War history.

For his reliable intelligence reports and the daring capture of a prized Confederate flag, Marsh was one of few soldiers to earn the Congressional Medal of Honor during the Civil War.

"When I read what he did, it was unbelievable," said Thomas Durning of North Haven, who is researching Medal of Honor recipients. Although thousands received the medal after the war, Durning said Marsh was one of about 150 who received the highest military honor during the war.

"Last year, During placed a monument containing the Medal of Honor insignia over Marsh's grave in a Quaker cemetery near the intersection of Route 7 and Sullivan Road.

By the time Marsh died, the Quaker cemetery had become less a religious burying ground than a neighborhood cemetery, according to Joseph Lillis, the town historian. Lillis said Marsh lived on nearby Lanesville Road.

Durning said Marsh's reports on Confederate troop movements made their way to top commanders in Washington. Marsh's inclusion of names of the commanders of the Confederate units was a bonus for Union generals because it gave them a better idea of what to expect from their opponents, Durning said.

The highlight of Marsh's career came when he spotted a Confederate flag in Back Creek Valley, Virginia, in 1864. Marsh waited nearby until one of the guarding the flag left for a drink of water. He then overpowered the remaining guard and brought both the guard and the flag back through Confederate lines.

A company flag was an important signal because it was a rallying point for troops.

On another foray, Marsh returned with several deserting rebels.

Marsh eluded the enemy for several years but contracted tuberculosis during the war and died at the age of 27 in 1867. He left a widow, Sara, and three children, Oliver, Carrie, and Sara.

Sara remained in New Milford until she died in 1935.

Durning found the references to Marsh's exploits in the Official Records of the War of the Rebellion.

In 1977, the town dedicated a bridge at Lover's Leap in Marsh's memory after local historian Norman Flayderman searched through records to find a local hero.

Marsh's grandson's widow, Dorothy Kellogg, spoke at the Marsh Bridge dedication in 1977. Kellogg said Sara had felt that the town had forgotten her husband's exploits and had hoped for recognition for him.

Durning did his research as part of his crusade to identify and honor the state's Medal of Honor winners. He began the task when he was asked to find the grave sites of Civil War Medal of Honor winners but expanded it when he found that medal winners from all wars were interred in poorly marked graves.

Durning, in fact, found the grave of Ridgefield Brigadier General Wilbur Wilder only by chance. After searching the graveyard several times, Durning happened to notice Wilder's broken marker under a bush.

From The Connecticut Post May 30, 2010

CIVIL WAR MEDAL OF HONOR WINNER HAD TIES TO MILFORD

MILFORD -- A second U.S. Medal of Honor winner once called Milford home, but apparently not for long.

Charles H. Marsh, born here in 1840, won the highest U.S. military honor for "capturing a Confederate flag and its bearer" on July 31, 1864, at Back Creek Valley, Virginia.

But Marsh, who after the Civil War moved to Pawling, N.Y., and is buried in New Milford, had been at several key battles with the famed 1st Connecticut Calvary, Company D, including the pivotal confrontation at Spotsylvania.

The only other Milford resident known to have received the Medal of Honor, Gen. William Baird, also served in the Civil War but won his decoration for bravery a decade later fighting on the Great Plains against the Nez Perce Indians and their leader, Chief Joseph.

Former Mayor Joel Baldwin, who serves on the Milford Hall of Fame Committee, provided the research on Marsh to the committee last week. The Hall of Fame annually inducts a Milford native or resident from each of the five centuries of the community's existence.

Marsh, whose time as a city resident as well as his life were both brief, could be considered for future induction, organizers said.

He won the medal, the highest military honor that the country bestows, in a raid against Confederate Gen. Jubal Early's troops in a contested section of western Virginia. During the war, that part of the state, including Harper's Ferry, joined the Union as West Virginia.

However brave Marsh may have been that day, his letters pleading to be exchanged after he was taken prisoner are also part of his war record. A Dec. 1, 1862, letter to James Seddon, the secretary of war for the Confederacy, argues that when he was captured that October near Haymarket, he was within an area controlled by federal troops.

"Am I not then a prisoner of war? And if so, why should I not be exchanged? I am here without friends or money," Marsh wrote from prison. "True, I am, but a poor private, and that must be the reason I am overlooked. But I am confined with all classes of criminals, and I respectfully solicit an inquiry into my case."

Seddon asked the superintendent of Castle Thunder prison to investigate and was told that Marsh was being held as a spy. Another letter, taken from Marsh, "was deemed of itself sufficient to establish a grave suspicion and to warrant his detention," replied George Alexander, the provost marshal of the prison.

Nonetheless, Marsh was part of a group of Union soldiers exchanged for Confederate POWs later that year. In light of his heroism on the battlefield two years later, the Southerners may have regretted the decision to let him go.

Marsh was living in New Milford when he enlisted in the Connecticut Cavalry, which also fought at Cold Harbor and Port Republic. The unit escorted Gen. Ulysses S. Grant to receive Lee's surrender at Appomattox, according to the website www.civil-war-history.com/, and suffered a 56 percent casualty rate.

Marsh died in Pawling on January 25, 1867, at age 27, from "disease contracted in the war," according to his entry in the Official Records and Correspondence of the War of Rebellion.

329

City Historian Richard Platt said that the town of New Milford, in the northwestern section of the state, was founded by people from Milford and that there was considerable movement between the two communities in the 19th century.

Honored on the New Milford Civil War Memorial, New Milford Town Green, 25 Main Street, New Milford, Connecticut.

CAPTAIN OF THE AFTERGUARD* ROBERT WILLIAM MONTGOMERY; NAVY

* Petty officers are divided into two classes: petty officers of the line and petty officers. The petty officers of the line, in order of rank, are as follows: Boatswain's Mates, Gunner's Mates, Signal Quartermaster, Coxswain to Commander in Chief, Captains of Forecastle, Quartermasters, Quarter Gunners, Coxswains, Captains of Main-top, Captains of Fore-top, Captains of Mizzen-top, Captains of Afterguard.

1838 # (Liverpool, England) – January 22, 1899 (Liverpool, England); 61 years old
Unmarried
Enlisted on August 29, 1863, as William Montgomery into the 8th Connecticut Volunteer Infantry and then
    transferred to the Navy on May 4, 1864. He was discharged from the Navy on January 25, 1866, as Robert
    William Montgomery.

The exact Date of Birth is unknown.

Entered the service from Norwich, Connecticut.

MEDAL OF HONOR CITATION

AWARDED FOR ACTIONS DURING: Civil War
BRANCH OF SERVICE: Navy
ASSIGNED: U.S.S. Agawam
GENERAL ORDERS: War Department, General Orders No. 45 (December 31, 1864)
AGE ON THE DAY OF THE EVENT: 25 or 26
CITATION:

The President of the United States of America, in the name of Congress, takes pleasure in presenting the Medal of Honor to Captain of the Afterguard Robert William Montgomery, United States Navy, for extraordinary heroism in action while serving on board the U.S.S. Agawam, as one of a volunteer crew of a powder boat which was exploded near Fort Fisher, North Carolina, 23 December 1864. The powder boat, towed in by the Wilderness to prevent detection by the enemy, cast off and slowly steamed to within 300 yards of the beach. After fuses and fires had been lit and a second anchor with short scope let go to assure the boat's tailing inshore, the crew again boarded the Wilderness and proceeded a distance of 12 miles from shore. Less than two hours later, the explosion took place, and the following day, fires were observed still burning at the fort.

Presentation Date and Details: May 12, 1865, off of New Bern, North Carolina, on board the U.S.S. Agawam

AUTHOR NOTE: One of five recipients of the Medal of Honor from Connecticut who were aboard the U.S.S. Agawam. The others were William Garvin, John Neil, James Roberts, and James Sullivan.

U.S.S. Agawam (1864-1867). In the James River, Virginia, July 1864. Photographed by Brady & Company, Washington, D.C. Collection of Surgeon Herman P. Babcock, USN. Donated by his son, George R. Babcock, in 1939. U.S. Naval History and Heritage Command Photograph.

Buried in Ford Cemetery, also known as the Liverpool Catholic Cemetery, Ford; Borough of Sefton, Merseyside, England; Public Lot, Section B, Grave 2414 (unmarked). Photo from FindAGrave.com.

SERGEANT JAMES T. MURPHY; ARMY

July ?, 1840 * (Canada) – January 11, 1904 (New Haven, CT); 65 years old
Unmarried
Enlisted on December 27, 1861, in New Haven, Connecticut
Wounded at Petersburg, Virginia, on March 29, 1865
Discharged May 11, 1865

* The exact Date of Birth is unknown.

Listed in the 1900 census as living in the Springside Home, a widower, and born in July 1840 in Canada.

MEDAL OF HONOR CITATION

AWARDED FOR ACTIONS DURING: Civil War
BRANCH OF SERVICE: Army
UNIT: Company L, 1st Connecticut Heavy Artillery
DATE OF ISSUE AND PRESENTATION: October 29, 1886 (21 years later)
AGE ON THE DAY OF THE EVENT: 24
CITATION:

The President of the United States of America, in the name of Congress, takes pleasure in presenting the Medal of Honor to Private James T. Murphy, United States Army, for extraordinary heroism on 25 March 1865, while serving with Company L, 1st Connecticut Artillery, in action at Petersburg, Virginia. A piece of artillery having been silenced by the enemy, Private Murphy voluntarily assisted in working the piece, conducting himself throughout the engagement in a gallant and fearless manner.

From "History of the First Connecticut Artillery; 1862-1865

I have received a letter from Capt. J. M. Deane, 29th Massachusetts Veteran Volunteers, wrote to call attention to the gallant conduct of Private James T. Murphy of Co. L, who volunteered to serve a light gun in Fort Haskell when its officer and all but two of the detachment were killed or wounded, and the gun was silenced. Private Murphy served at the piece with gallantry during the rest of the fight. The loss of the company was 2 enlisted men killed, 5 wounded, and 13 missing.

From the Morning Journal-Courier (New Haven, CT) January 15, 1904

James T. Murphy, the only Civil War soldier to be individually awarded a medal by Congress, died at the New Haven poorhouse at Springside Wednesday and has been saved from a pauper's grave by Owen Colwell, of 439 Congress Avenue, who belonged to the same regiment with Murphy.

Murphy was frequently referred to as the bravest man in the war. He was a New Havener and joined Company I, Second Regiment, for its three months campaign. Later, he joined Company L, Heavy Artillery. Murphy was made a captain for his bravery at Fort Steadman. General Grant said that his bravery at Fort Steadman shortened the war by at least six months.

Mr. Colwell learned of Captain Murphy's death and immediately made efforts to save his comrade from Potter's Field. The funeral will be at Flynn's undertaking establishment on Grand Avenue this afternoon.

From the Morning Journal-Courier (New Haven, CT) January 16, 1904

A military funeral with all honors befitting his rank was accorded the late Captain James Murphy, who was once said to have been the bravest man in the Civil War, was given him yesterday. The services were held at the Flynn undertaking establishment on Grand Avenue and were conducted by the Reverend Father Russell of St. Patrick's Church. There was a large attendance of men connected with the military of this city who have been instrumental in raising sufficient funds to prevent the deceased from occupying the obscurity of a pauper's grave. This would have been his fate as Murphy died penniless at Springside Home several days ago. At the funeral, a record of his noble and brave exploits was read, and they were interesting in the extreme.

The pallbearers were Robert Hollinger, James E. McGann, Al Hurley, D.J. O'Leary, Owen Colwell, and Lieutenant Duffy. The burial was in the soldiers' lot in St. Bernard Cemetery.

Buried in St. Bernard's Cemetery, 604 Ella Grasso Boulevard, New Haven, Connecticut; Civil War Section. Photos by the author.

JAMES T. MURPHY
MEDAL OF HONOR
SERG CO L 1 CONN HV ARTY
CIVIL WAR
JAN 11 1904

QUARTER GUNNER* JOHN NEIL; NAVY

* Quarter gunners were supervised by the gunner's mates. Most ships carried one quarter gunner for every four guns. Their duties were similar to those of the gunner's mates, but they were also considered prime seamen and often found themselves keeping watch and supervising tricky sail handling maneuvers.

1837 # (Newfoundland, Canada) – unknown Date of Death #
Enlisted on September 5, 1863, in Norwich, Connecticut. Transferred to the Navy on May 4, 1864, in Hampton Roads, Virginia. Discharged on January 26, 1866.

The exact Dates of Birth and Death are unknown.

Parent and sibling information are unknown.

MEDAL OF HONOR CITATION

AWARDED FOR ACTIONS DURING: Civil War
BRANCH OF SERVICE: Navy
ASSIGNED TO: U.S.S. Agawam
GENERAL ORDERS: War Department, General Orders No. 45 (December 31, 1864)
AGE ON THE DAY OF THE EVENT: 24
CITATION:

The President of the United States of America, in the name of Congress, takes pleasure in presenting the Medal of Honor to Quarter Gunner John Neil, United States Navy, for extraordinary heroism in action while serving on board the U.S.S. Agawam, as one of a volunteer crew of a powder boat which was exploded near Fort Fisher, North Carolina, 23 December 1864. The powder boat, towed in by the Wilderness to prevent detection by the enemy, cast off and slowly steamed to within 300 yards of the beach. After fuses and fires had been lit and a second anchor with short scope let go to assure the boat's tailing inshore, the crew again boarded the Wilderness and proceeded a distance of 12 miles from shore. Less than two hours later, the explosion took place, and the following day fires were observed still burning at the fort.

Presentation Date and Details: May 12, 1865, off New Bern, NC, on board the U.S.S. Agawam

AUTHOR NOTE: One of five recipients of the Medal of Honor from Connecticut who were aboard the U.S.S. Agawam. The others were William Garvin, Robert Montgomery, James Roberts, and James Sullivan.

U.S.S. Agawam (1864-1867). In the James River, Virginia, July 1864. Photographed by Brady & Company, Washington, D.C. Collection of Surgeon Herman P. Babcock, USN. Donated by his son, George R. Babcock, in 1939.

John Neil was born in Newfoundland. It is believed by some, and disputed by others (including the Congressional Medal of Honor Society), that his grave and final resting place is at the Mare Island Cemetery in Vallejo, California. The next article shows some inconsistencies (*italics and underlined*) in that it says Neil was born in Ireland; however, the article does say he received a Congressional Medal of Honor. There was only one John Neil who received the medal.

From the San Francisco Examiner October 18, 1893

SUICIDE OF JOHN NEIL ON THE INDEPENDENCE

VALLEJO, October 17 – John Neil, a seaman of the United States Navy serving on board the receiving ship Independence at Mare Island, committed suicide this morning between 11:15 a.m. and 12 noon in the bag room on board the receiving ship. The cause which led Neil to take his life is said to be despondency. Some days ago, Neil was granted a leave of absence, going to Vallejo, where he indulged rather freely, causing him to overstay his leave. Yesterday, Captain Cotton sent some of Neil's shipmates on shore to bring him off to the ship. This morning, Neil was summoned to the mast before Captain Cotton, who reduced Neil in classification and restricted him to the ship for a period of forty days.

Nothing unusual was observed in his appearance, and he was allowed the freedom of the ship.

Evidently, he went below and, taking a pistol, placed the muzzle to his right temple, pulled the trigger, and ended his life. When found, the deceased was seated in an easy chair in the bag room while by his side lay the revolver.

Neil was a native of *Ireland* and sixty years of age. He entered the service in 1861, serving with meritorious distinction with Admiral Farragut at Mobile Bay and numerous other naval engagements, for which he *received a Medal of Honor from Congress*. He was a member of the Grand Army of the Republic and an officer of the local garrison of the Army and Navy Union. Officers at the Navy yard speak in the highest terms of his bravery and mourn his death. He will be buried with full naval honors at the Naval Cemetery.

One of 314 Medal of Honor recipients whose final resting place is a mystery.

COLONEL ROBERT BURTON NETT; ARMY

June 13, 1922 (New Haven, CT) – October 19, 2008 (Columbus, GA); 86 years old
Married to Frances Kabler [Army Nurse Corps veteran] (1918-2012).
One son, Robert B. Jr. [Army veteran] (1954-2012).
Connecticut National Guard from June 13, 1940 – September 29, 1940.
Commissioned a 2nd Lieutenant on December 26, 1942.
Retired on July 31, 1973.

Born to Matthew M. (1882-1935) and Emma L. Miller Nett (1883-1951). One brother, Joseph F. (1909-?), and one sister, Doris M. Nett Manion (1916-2003).

He also received the Legion of Merit, Purple Heart Medal, Bronze Star Medal w/V for valor, and two Oak Leaf Clusters.

Member of the Connecticut Veterans Hall of Fame, Class of 2007.

Photos courtesy of the Congressional Medal of Honor Society

MEDAL OF HONOR CITATION

AWARDED FOR ACTIONS DURING: World War II
BRANCH OF SERVICE: Army
UNIT: Company E, 2nd Battalion, 305th Infantry Regiment, 77th Infantry Division
GENERAL ORDERS: War Department, General Orders No. 16 (February 8, 1946)
AGE ON THE DAY OF THE EVENT: 22
CITATION:

The President of the United States of America, in the name of Congress, takes pleasure in presenting the Medal of Honor to Captain (Infantry) Robert Burton Nett (ASN: 0-1305818), United States Army, for conspicuous gallantry and intrepidity in action above and beyond the call of duty while Commanding Company E, 2nd Battalion, 305th Infantry Regiment, 77th Infantry Division, in action at Cognon, Leyte, Philippine Islands, on 14 December 1944. Captain Nett commanded Company E in an attack against a reinforced enemy battalion which had held up the American advance for two days from its entrenched positions around a three-story concrete building. With another infantry company and armored vehicles, Company E advanced against heavy machine gun and other automatic weapons fire, with Lieutenant Nett spearheading the assault against the strongpoint. During the fierce hand-to-hand encounter which ensued, he killed seven deeply entrenched Japanese with his rifle and bayonet and, although seriously wounded, gallantly continued to lead his men forward, refusing to relinquish his command. Again, he was severely wounded but, still unwilling to retire, pressed ahead with his troops to assure the capture of the objective. Wounded once more in the final assault, he calmly made all arrangements for the resumption of the advance, turned over his command to another officer, and then walked unaided to the rear for medical treatment. By his remarkable courage in continuing forward through sheer determination despite successive wounds, Lieutenant Nett provided an inspiring example for his men and was instrumental in the capture of a vital strong point.

Presentation Date & Details: February 8, 1946, in New Haven, Connecticut, presented by Lieutenant General Oscar W. Griswold

---

Honorary naming

Camp Nett, Connecticut National Guard training center in Niantic, Connecticut.

Colonel Robert B. Nett building, The Fort Benning OCS classroom.

Colonel Robert B. Nett Leadership Award is awarded to the Distinguished Leadership Graduate (DLG), the second highest honor bestowed upon a Candidate at OCS.

Colonel Robert B. Nett Medal of Honor Highway, a 5-mile stretch of US 280/SR 520 (Martha Berry Highway) through Fort Benning.

Colonel Robert Nett Leadership Hall, the leadership hall for the Connecticut National Guard at Camp Nett in Niantic.

Nett Warrior, a dismounted battle command system (Ground Soldier®), was named for Colonel Nett in 2010.

ACTS AND RESOLUTIONS OF THE GENERAL ASSEMBLY OF THE STATE OF GEORGIA 1992

1992 Vol. 1 -- Page: 2203

ROBERT B. NETT MEDAL OF HONOR HIGHWAY— DESIGNATED.

No. 71 (Senate Resolution No. 485).

A RESOLUTION

Designating the Robert B. Nett Medal of Honor Highway; and for other purposes.

WHEREAS, 48 years ago, in one of World War II's many fierce firefights, Colonel (Retired) Robert B. Nett of Columbus, Georgia, (then Lieutenant) distinguished himself as a cut above most men when courage and bravery are measured and earned for himself this country's highest award of valor -- the Medal of Honor; and

WHEREAS, on December 14, 1944, as commander of Company E, he is credited with killing seven Japanese soldiers with the bayonet of his M-1 rifle and with leading his company through a major enemy defensive line on Leyte Island in the Philippines; and

WHEREAS, he suffered three bullet wounds that day: one that grazed his jugular vein, which was patched with a butterfly bandage by a medic; another bullet caught him in the right side of the chest, carrying away part of a lung; and the third bullet "blew out a rib" in his back and put him out of operation; and

WHEREAS, the citation accompanying his Medal of Honor states that "by his remarkable courage in continuing forward through sheer determination despite successive wounds, Lieutenant Nett provided an inspiring example for his men and was instrumental in the capture of a vital strongpoint" and

WHEREAS, Colonel Nett is one of only 208 [in 1992] living winners of the military's most cherished medal; and

WHEREAS, for his outstanding bravery and unflinching determination in the face of desperately dangerous conditions, Colonel Nett merits the recognition of the State of Georgia, and it is only fitting that his name be perpetuated in an appropriate fashion.

NOW, THEREFORE, BE IT RESOLVED BY THE GENERAL ASSEMBLY OF GEORGIA that the portion of U. S. Highway 27 beginning at the point where it crosses I-185 east to the Muscogee County line is designated as the Robert B. Nett Medal of Honor Highway.

BE IT FURTHER RESOLVED that the Department of Transportation is authorized and directed to place and maintain appropriate markers so designating said highway.

BE IT FURTHER RESOLVED that the Secretary of the Senate is authorized and directed to transmit an appropriate copy of this resolution to the commissioner of transportation and to Colonel (Ret.) Robert B. Nett.

Approval Date: April 17, 1992.

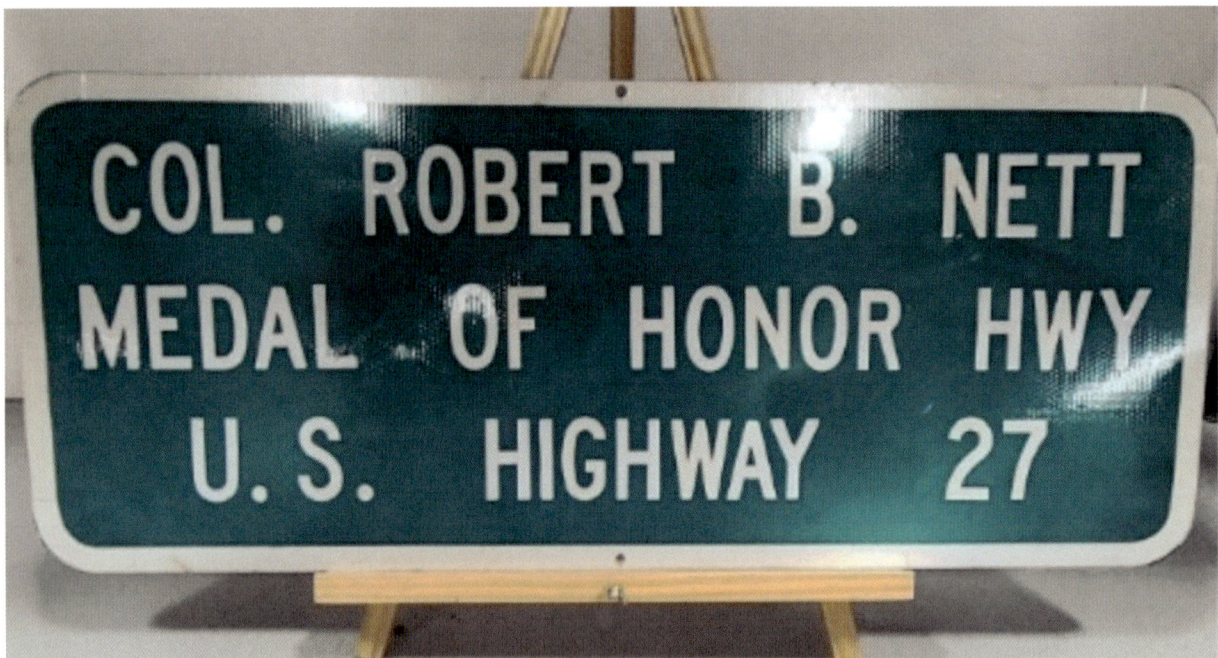

Sign on display in the West Haven (CT) Veterans Center. Photo by the author

Retired Col. Robert B. Nett, the last of five Medal of Honor recipients who resided in Columbus, died Sunday. He was 86.

Nett enlisted in the Connecticut National Guard in 1940 and graduated from Officer Candidate School in 1942. His distinguished career included service in World War II, the Korean War, and Vietnam.

Nett earned the nation's highest military award for valor on Dec. 14, 1944, for heroic actions during hand-to-hand fighting with Japanese soldiers at their heavily fortified stronghold on the west coast of Leyte near Cognon in the Philippines. The Commander of E Company, 305th Infantry Regiment, 77th Infantry Division, Nett spearheaded the assault, killing seven Japanese soldiers with his rifle and bayonet. Though he was seriously wounded three times during the attack, he was later able to rejoin his company and participate in the Okinawa campaign.

"He was the greatest patriot that ever lived in Columbus, Ga.," said Nett's long-time friend Jim Rhodes.

Retired U.S. Army Col. Ralph Puckett, considered one of the founders of the modern Rangers, said the inclusion of Nett's name on the Ranger Memorial located near Infantry Hall at Fort Benning and his membership in the Army Ranger Hall of Fame elevated the prestige of the battalion.

"We've lost a real American hero," he said.

Inspiring generations

Following his retirement from the Army in August of 1973 after 33 years of service, Nett taught for 17 years in the local school system. He held a bachelor
of science degree and teaching certificates in social science and industrial arts. He was named Teacher of the Year in 1985. Two years later, he retired from teaching.

Nett was a frequent lecturer at the Officer Candidate School and a speaker at the 75th Ranger Regiment on Fort Benning. He was also a member of the Officer Candidate School Hall of Fame.

"Our relationship was one of great respect and admiration for what he had done on active duty and what he continued to do with the OCS battalion," Puckett said.

Lieutenant Colonel John Shattuck, commander of OCS, called Nett a "hallowed hero" who, up until last spring, took the time to mentor the school's officer candidates.

"He talked about his experiences and what it meant to be a leader of soldiers in combat," Shattuck said. "When you have an opportunity to spend time with a Medal of Honor recipient, it's an honor for anybody."

Puckett said he saw Nett last week in the hospital.

"I thought how sad it was that such a great soldier, such a great warrior, was lying in that bed, and I knew that we would lose him shortly," Puckett said. "He was such a great individual, someone who is irreplaceable."

Rhodes spoke with Nett two weeks ago, just before the colonel was hospitalized at Martin Army Community Hospital. He asked his friend to be an honorary guest at an upcoming Pearl Harbor remembrance ceremony he's helping to organize.

"Colonel Robert Burton Nett will long be remembered for his heroism, his willingness to step forward when America needed him, and his distinguished military
service," his family stated in a release. "Equally important, however, are his contributions to the community. His mentoring and guidance to the countless students he served in the public school system and his tireless assistance and advice to veterans who came to him for help have earned him the friendship of more people than even he could recall. To virtually his last day, he found himself greeted by those whose lives he had touched and who still had the greatest respect for this great American."

Former Columbus mayor and retired U.S. Col. Bob Poydasheff called Nett a mentor, a father figure, and a friend. "We just liked each other," Poydasheff said. His relationship with Nett dates back more than 50 years, when Poydasheff was a second lieutenant. "As an infantry officer, he helped me moderate my arrogance," Poydasheff said with a laugh.

The Columbus attorney said Nett was active in various veterans organizations and in his church. He loved to teach and endeavored to impart on his students the qualities that Puckett, Poydasheff, and Rhodes said Nett personified: Integrity, decency, and love of country.

"I know Colonel Nett, and he didn't care what your color was or what your religion was. If you were a soldier, he'd support you and bring you to the highest heights," Poydasheff said.

The repercussions of Nett's service and generosity were also felt in his home state of Connecticut. Gov. M. Jodi Rell issued the following statement Monday: "Colonel Nett served bravely and honorably throughout his distinguished career. His contributions to his fellow soldiers and community are the hallmarks of dedication. Connecticut is justifiably proud of this native son. He was inducted into the state Veterans Hall of Fame last year, and the leadership hall at Camp Rell bears his name. Our deepest sympathies go out to the Nett family along with our gratitude for his lifetime of valor and service."

In addition to the many military awards and decorations he earned throughout his career, Nett was selected to receive the Spirit of Hope Award in 2005. It is presented several times annually by the USO to men and women of the United States Armed Forces, entertainers, organizations, and corporations that epitomize the values of the USO in its efforts to support and enhance the quality of life for military servicemen and women and their families and whose patriotism and service reflects that of Bob Hope. Past winners include U.S. Sens, Strom Thurmond and Daniel K. Inouye, longtime CBS News anchor Walter Cronkite, and the Dallas Cowboy Cheerleaders, who have entertained the troops for 20 years.

Nett was preceded in death by his parents, Matthew Martin Nett and Emma Miller Nett; his brother, Joseph Frederick Nett; and his sister Doris Nett Manion. He is survived by Frances K. Nett, his wife of 66 years; his son Dr. Robert B. Nett, Jr., and wife Patti Ann Nett, and his grandchildren Erica and Nicholas Nett of San Antonio, Texas; and by his daughter Frances Anne Randall, of Roswell, N.M., and husband Doyle, and his granddaughter Yvonne Michelle Randall of Las Vegas, Nev.

A rosary service will be held at Striffler-Hamby Mortuary on Macon Road at 6 p.m. on Wednesday. Visitation will be held at Striffler-Hamby Mortuary from 7-9 p.m., Wednesday. His funeral Mass will be held at the Catholic Chapel on Ingersoll Street, Fort Benning, at 10 a.m. Thursday.

CAPTAIN EDWIN MICHAEL NEVILLE; ARMY

January 27, 1843 (Waterbury, CT) – October 4, 1886 (Waterbury, CT); 43 years old
Unmarried
Enlisted on January 13, 1864, in Waterbury, Connecticut
Discharged August 2, 1865
Born to Michael (1805-1866) and Ann Delaney Neville (1807-1877). Brothers, Timothy (1837-1898), Matthew F. (1846-1909), and John J. (1850-1936). One sister, Margaret Neville Dougherty (1841-1910).

Photo from FindAGrave.com

MEDAL OF HONOR CITATION

AWARDED FOR ACTIONS DURING: Civil War
BRANCH OF SERVICE: Army
UNIT: Company C, 1st Connecticut Cavalry
DATE OF ISSUE AND PRESENTATION: May 3, 1865
AGE ON THE DAY OF THE EVENT: 22
CITATION:

The President of the United States of America, in the name of Congress, takes pleasure in presenting the Medal of Honor to Captain (Cavalry) Edwin Michael Neville, United States Army, for extraordinary heroism on 6 April 1865, while serving with Company C, 1st Connecticut Cavalry, in action at Deatonsville (Sailor's Creek), Virginia, for the capture of flag.

The photo is courtesy of the Mattatuck Historical Society. Gift of Timothy Sample, in memory of his uncle, Edwin Lawrence Clark, 2019. The Mattatuck Historical Society is forever grateful to the following individuals and organizations who contributed to the donation and conservation of his medal and creation of a period-correct replacement ribbon -- Timothy and Jan Sample, Frank Monterio, Drew International, Kathryn Tarlenton and Charlotte Hamlin of ConText Inc., and Susan Holbrook of Holbrook & Hawes.

From The Town and City of Waterbury

Edwin Michael Neville, second son of Michael and Ann (Delaney) Neville, was born in Waterbury on January 27, 1843. After a course at the High school, he entered St. John's College, Fordham, New York, in September 1859 and continued his studies there until 1862. At the age of eighteen, he went to visit his brother, Timothy F. Neville, at Providence, and while there, enlisted in the Third Regiment of Rhode Island Infantry under Col. Welcome B. Sayles. After a few months service, he was discharged for disability, as it was thought he could not live. On his recovery, he joined the First Connecticut Cavalry as Second Lieutenant and was soon after promoted to captaincy. To have been a soldier in this regiment was in itself equivalent to a brilliant record, as it was engaged with the enemy, in some way, over ninety times, and suffered loss at the enemy's hands, in killed, wounded, or missing, on over eighty different occasions. The place of the regiment was with Sheridan, in the division commanded by Wilson and afterward by Custer. It fought cavalry, infantry, and artillery in the field and behind breastworks, and its capture of prisoners, guns, and flags was very considerable. It was detailed to escort Gen. Grant when he went to receive Lee's surrender. When mustered out, it was allowed to return to its state-mounted, a privilege granted to no other regiment in the service. Captain Neville was on Custer's staff and fought under Sheridan, who said that he was one of the bravest soldiers under him.

The spirit of the man is revealed in such testimonials as the following, tenderly cherished by his kindred:

Headquarters First Connecticut Cavalry
Ashland, Virginia, March 15, 1865.
Captain E. M. Neville, Commanding Squadron.

Captain: The gallant manner and noble bearing of yourself and men on today's reconnaissance, under the trying circumstances and position in which you were placed, call from your commanding officer his thanks and hearty approbation. Please obtain for us a nominal list of the men who were actually under the infantry fire.
I am, Captain, very respectfully, etc.,
E. W. Whitaker.
Lieutenant Colonel commanding First Connecticut Cavalry.

Another occasion on which he exhibited marked bravery was at the battle of Sailor's Creek on April 6, 1865, in which he captured one of the enemy's flags. The recognition his services at that time received is recorded in the following communication:

War Department, Adjutant-General's Office.
Washington, May 3, 1865.

Sir: Herewith I enclose the Medal of Honor which has been awarded you by the Secretary of War, under the Resolution of Congress, approved July 12, 1862, "to provide for the presentation of Medals of Honor to the enlisted men of the army and volunteer forces who have distinguished or may distinguish themselves in battle during the present rebellion." Please acknowledge its receipt.

Very respectfully, your obedient servant,
U. A. Nichols,
Assistant Adjutant-General.
Captain Edwin M. Neville,
Co. H, First Connecticut Cavalry.

Captain Neville's name is frequently mentioned in the history of the regiment to which he belonged. After the war, he was adjutant-general on General Kellogg's staff in 1867 and 1868 and adjutant of the Sixty-ninth New York regiment, National Guard, under Colonel Kavanagh, in 1871 and 1872. He also received a testimonial as "Companion of the first class" from the military order of the Loyal Legion of the United States for having been especially distinguished "for faithful service in maintaining the honor, integrity, and supremacy of the government of the United States," dated November 7, 1870, signed by Gen. Cadwalader, commander-in-chief.

In 1869, he went to Paris as an agent for the Remington Firearms Company to sell arms to the French government. He negotiated a large contract and was ready to leave the city when he found it in a state of siege and was one of a few who escaped in a balloon. On returning home, he studied law in the office of his brother, T. F. Neville, and was admitted to the New York bar in June 1872. He was successful in his practice and continued it until his last illness. He died in Waterbury on October 4, 1886, and was buried here with military honors.

From the Hartford Courant October 6, 1886

Captain Edwin M. Neville, formerly of Waterbury, died at that place on Monday, aged 44. At the age of 19, he enlisted in the Third Rhode Island Cavalry and afterward was recruited as a company for the First Connecticut Cavalry. He served through the war and, near its close, was appointed to General Custer's staff. After the war, he was sent for some time in Hartford as one of the staff of the Post. He then studied law. The American says: "He was admitted to the bar at the general term in New York City in 1872. He applied himself closely to the practice of his profession in New York after being admitted and had been engaged in many important cases. He was one of the American officers who left Paris in a balloon during the Franco-Prussian War, he having gone there in the interest of an American company dealing firearms. His war record was a good one. Congress voted him a medal for his brave capture of a rebel flag during a skirmish, and his bravery was heartily commended by his comrades. Captain Neville was a member of the Loyal Legion of New York, had been Adjutant of the Sixty-Ninth Regiment, New York militia, and was a member of General Kellogg's staff in the old Connecticut brigade. He was also an active member of the Grand Army of the Republic."

From the Morning Journal-Courier (New Haven, Connecticut) October 8, 1886

FUNERAL OF CAPTAIN NEVILLE.

The funeral of Captain Edwin M. Neville of New York City took place from the residence of his sister, Mrs. T. D. Doherty, at 70 N. Main Street Waterbury, to the Catholic church of the Immaculate Conception, at 9:30 a.m. yesterday. The remains were enclosed in a very neat broadcloth-covered casket with silver handles and trimmings. The house was crowded with sympathizing neighbors and friends, including many out-of-town people, and not a few who had enjoyed the friendship of the deceased since boyhood. There was a profusion of flowers, including a very beautiful wreath from Dr. A. McDonald, medical superintendent of the insane at Ward's Island (N. Y.). The G. A. R. was represented at the funeral by an escort under Commander Oscar W. Cornish, and the Loyal Legion of New York by Captain D. B. Hamilton and Major F. A. Spencer. The pallbearers were Captain D. B. Hamilton, John O'Neill, Jr., Thomas Donahue, Major Keefe of New Haven, and Majors Bannon and Spencer of Waterbury. The interment was in the family lot at St. Joseph's Cemetery.

The family are in receipt of numerous telegrams of condolence touching upon the death of Captain Neville, which to many of his associates in New York City was a complete surprise. They bear the signatures of ex-Judge George M. Curtis, Colonel Hatch, Dr. A. W. McDonald, Major J. J. Hagerty of the New York Assembly, Thomas J. Montgomery of the Bash Electric Light company, Major McGrath of the Twenty-second regiment and Frederick Uhlman of the stock board, all of New York, and the Rev. J. J. McCabe and the Rev. J. J. Creedon, pastors at

Providence and Moosup, Rhode Island.

   The deceased was about twenty years ago connected with the Hartford Post and an officer on the staff of General Kellogg when the latter was commander of the brigade, of which the Second regiment formed a part. He was well known, and his friendship was treasured by many friends in this city. His genial, kindly disposition and warm heart gave him a host of friends.

Honored with a monument in Veterans Memorial Park, 1892 Thomaston Avenue, Waterbury, Connecticut. Photo by the author.

Buried in Old St. Joseph's Cemetery, 480 Hamilton Avenue, Waterbury, Connecticut; Section D, top of the hill. Photos by the author.

EDWIN M NEVILLE
MEDAL OF HONOR
CAPT CO C 1 CONN CAV
CIVIL WAR
JAN 27 1843   OCT 4 1886

FIRST LIEUTENANT ELLIOTT MALLOY NORTON; ARMY

June 15, 1834 (Connecticut *) – January 5, 1899 (North Shade, MI); 64 years old

Married to Lucinda "Lucy" L. Bennett (1844-1917) on March 12, 1868 in Alamo, Michigan

Five sons, Elliott M. (1872-1960), Claude B. (1874-1933), Seward J. (1879-1959), Ralph S. (1887-1965), and Maxwell "Maxie" (1891-1907).

Two daughters, Effie M. (1871-1879) and Abby B. Norton Jamison (1869-1955).

Enlisted on November 21, 1862, in Grand Rapids, Michigan.

Discharged on March 10, 1866.

Sergeant, April 1, 1863; Sergeant Major, August 6, 1864; Second Lieutenant; First Lieutenant, January 4, 1865. Transferred to First Cavalry November 7, 1865. Mustered out March 10, 1866, in Salt Lake City, Utah.

* The exact city of birth is unknown.

Born to Asa A. (1805-1885) and Barbara Hurlburt Norton (1909-1900). Five brothers, August (1835-1885), Edwin H. (1839-1921), Albert O. (1847-1865), Frank E. (1848-1915), and Frederick B. (1853-1914). Three sisters, Carolyn M. Norton Beebe (1838-1910), Mary Norton Huntley (1843-1887), and Nellie E. Norton Belcher (1846-1933).

Photo courtesy of Ancestry.com

MEDAL OF HONOR CITATION

AWARDED FOR ACTIONS DURING: Civil War
BRANCH OF SERVICE: Army
UNIT: Company H, 6th Michigan Cavalry
DATE OF ISSUE AND PRESENTATION: May 3, 1865
AGE ON THE DAY OF THE EVENT: 30
CITATION:

The President of the United States of America, in the name of Congress, takes pleasure in presenting the Medal of Honor to Second Lieutenant Elliott Malloy Norton, United States Army, for extraordinary heroism on 6 April 1865, while serving with Company H, 6th Michigan Cavalry, in action at Deatonsville (Sailor's Creek), Virginia. Second Lieutenant Norton rushed ahead of his column and captured the flag of the 44th Tennessee Infantry (Confederate States of America).

Buried in Liberty Street Cemetery, 7730 W-G Avenue, Alamo, Michigan. Photo from FindAGrave.com

CORPORAL WILLIAM O'NEILL; ARMY

1848 (Tariffville [Simsbury], CT) – unknown *
Enlisted on March 21, 1870, in New York City
Discharged on March 21, 1875.

* Exact Dates of Birth and Death are unknown.

No family information could be found.

MEDAL OF HONOR CITATION

AWARDED FOR ACTIONS DURING: Indian Campaigns
BRANCH OF SERVICE: Army
UNIT: Company I, 4th U.S. Cavalry, Company
DATE OF ISSUE AND PRESENTATION: November 19, 1872
AGE ON THE DAY OF THE EVENT: 23 or 24 years old
CITATION:

The President of the United States of America, in the name of Congress, takes pleasure in presenting the Medal of Honor to Corporal William O'Neill, United States Army, for bravery in action on 29 September 1872, while serving with Company I, 4th U.S. Cavalry, in action at Red River, Texas.

At some point in his life, William O'Neill moved to New York City, where he enlisted in the U.S. Army. In September 1872, O'Neill was among the cavalry troopers who followed Colonel Ranald Slidell Mackenzie in an expedition over the Staked Plains of Texas. After a one-day march to reach the North Fork of the Red River, his regiment encountered a large encampment of 280 Comanche warriors on September 29. Although the cavalrymen attempted to take the enemy by surprise, the Indians' ponies stampeded at the soldiers approached, alerting the camp. Engaged in fierce combat with the Comanche, O'Neill and his company led the advance and were able to secure the camp with the loss of only one trooper killed and three others wounded. The Mow-wi tribe of Comanche, who lost 23 braves in the battle, were humbled by this victory and surrendered at Fort Sill, ending 17 years of continuous warfare.

One of 314 Medal of Honor recipients whose final resting place is a mystery. "In Memory Of" marker in Fort Concho National Historic Landmark, 630 South Oakes Street, San Angelo, Texas. Photos from HMdb.org and Cosmos Mariner. In May 1992, burial sites for five soldiers were unknown, and special permission was given to place these headstones at a fort where all five served. Photos from FindAGrave.com.

THE HIGHEST UNITED STATES MILITARY
DECORATION, THE MEDAL OF HONOR, IS AWARDED
IN THE NAME OF CONGRESS FOR ACHIEVEMENTS
ABOVE AND BEYOND THE CALL OF DUTY.
ALTHOUGH NOT REPRESENTING THE ACTUAL
BURIALS, THESE "IN MEMORY OF" HEADSTONES
PAY HOMAGE TO FIVE MEDAL OF HONOR
RECIPIENTS WHO SERVED AT FORT CONCHO. AT
THE TIME OF THE DEDICATION IN MAY 1992,
THEIR BURIAL SITES WERE UNKNOWN AND
SPECIAL PERMISSION WAS GIVEN TO PLACE THESE
HEADSTONES AT A FORT WHERE ALL FIVE
SERVED. EACH SOLDIER SERVED HERE PRIOR TO
OR AFTER THE ACTION FOR WHICH THEY
EARNED THIS DISTINCTION.

PRIVATE WILLIAM O'NEILL
CITATION : BRAVERY IN ACTION
PLACE AND DATE : AT RED RIVER, TEX., 29 SEPT. 1872
DATE OF ISSUE : 19 NOV. 1872

PRIVATE GREGORY MAHONEY
CITATION : GALLANTRY IN ATTACK ON A LARGE PARTY
OF CHEYENNES
PLACE AND DATE : NEAR RED RIVER, TEX., 26 - 28 SEPT. 1874
DATE OF ISSUE : 13 OCT. 1875

SERGEANT EDWARD BRANAGAN
CITATION : GALLANTRY IN ACTION
PLACE AND DATE : AT RED RIVER, TEX., 29 SEPT. 1872
DATE OF ISSUE : 19 NOV. 1872

CORPORAL WILLIAM McCABE
CITATION : GALLANTRY IN ATTACK ON A LARGE PARTY
OF CHEYENNES
PLACE AND DATE : NEAR RED RIVER, TEX., 26 - 28 SEPT. 1874
DATE OF ISSUE : 13 OCT. 1875

PRIVATE JOHN O'SULLIVAN
CITATION : GALLANTRY IN A LONG CHASE AFTER INDIANS
PLACE AND DATE : AT STAKED PLAINS, TEX. 8 DEC. 1874
DATE OF ISSUE : 13 OCT. 1875

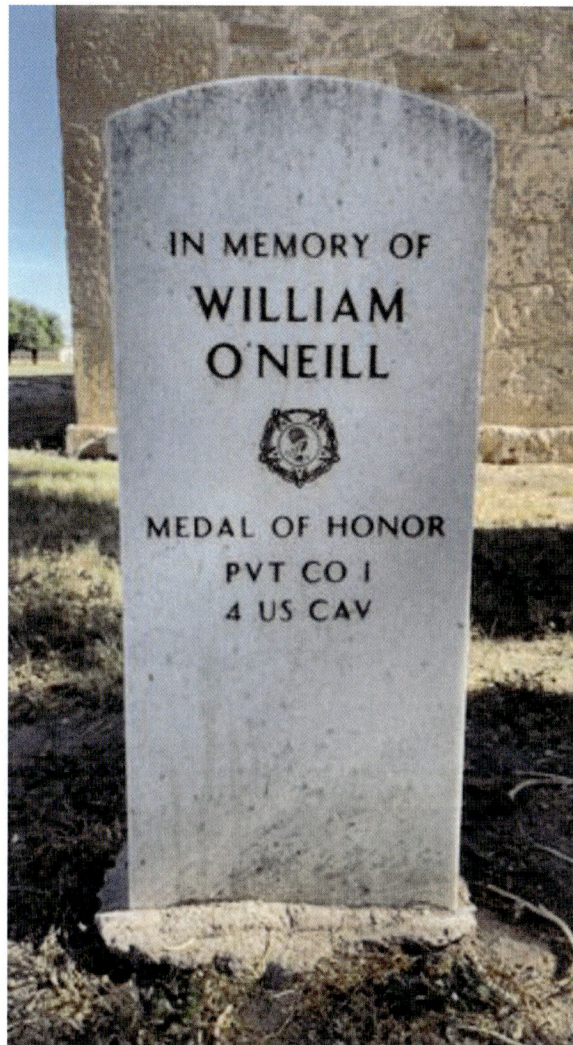

IN MEMORY OF
WILLIAM
O'NEILL

MEDAL OF HONOR
PVT CO I
4 US CAV

CORPORAL JOHN GIDEON PALMER; ARMY

October 14, 1845 (Montville, CT) – November 17, 1901 (New Haven, CT);
Married Elvira A. Grover (1846-1929)
One son, Charles N. (1869-?).
Three daughters, Eunice G. (1873-), Emma G. (1874-), and Ola S. (1890-).
Enlisted on August 6, 1862, in Montville, Connecticut, at just 16 years old.
Discharged on September 24, 1864.

Born to William H. (1821-1901) and Clarissa A. Stanton Palmer (1820-1880). Two brothers, William H. (1843-1916) and Charles S. (1852-1862). Two sisters, Clarissa M. (1847-1882) and Marian E. Palmer Markham (1849-1928).

One of five members of the 21st Connecticut to receive the Medal of Honor.

A descendant of Private Matthew Turner (1733-1824), who served in Captain George Markham's Connecticut Troops in 1781. A member of the Sons of the American Revolution.

MEDAL OF HONOR CITATION

AWARDED FOR ACTIONS DURING: Civil War
BRANCH OF SERVICE: Army
UNIT: Company F, 21st Connecticut Infantry
DATE OF ISSUE AND PRESENTATION: October 30, 1896 (34 years later)
AGE ON THE DAY OF THE EVENT: 17
CITATION:

The President of the United States of America, in the name of Congress, takes pleasure in presenting the Medal of Honor to Corporal John Gideon Palmer, United States Army, for extraordinary heroism on 13 December 1862, while serving with Company F, 21st Connecticut Infantry, in action at Fredericksburg, Virginia. Corporal Palmer was the first of six men who volunteered to assist the gunner of a battery upon which the enemy was concentrating its fire and fought with the battery until the close of the engagement. His commanding officer felt he would never see this man alive again.

From Beyer, W. F., & Keydel, O. F. (2000). Deeds of valor: How America's Civil War Heroes won The Congressional Medal of Honor. Smithmark Publishers.

An example of dashing bravery and courage, which General Daniel E. Sickles designates "a heroic act," was furnished by Corporal John G. Palmer and Private Wallace A. Beckwith of Company F, Twenty-first Connecticut Infantry. The story is interestingly told by Corporal Palmer:

"At the time of Burnside's great battle of Fredericksburg, I was a boy seventeen years of age and a member of Company F, Twenty-first Connecticut Infantry. We were held in reserve in the streets of the city until the last afternoon of the desperate fight. At 4:30 P.M., we received a hurry order to go to the support of the Second Division. Away we went, glad to take an active part, as we had been under fire more or less for two or three days. As soon as we cleared the streets of the city, we were exposed to a perfect shower of bullets and exploding shells from a general attack which was now taking place all along the front. Amidst this terrible fire we formed and moved rapidly towards the line of battle, our company marching for two or three blocks through the backyards of houses and dwellings. We had a most lively time
pulling up and scaling numerous fences to keep up with that part of the line which was meeting with less obstructions. We advanced to the scene of operations until the right of the regiment reached the railroad at the depot, the line extending to the left through some brick kilns. A light battery of four pieces, situated on a low ridge in front of the left of the regiment, was shelling the enemy, whose fronts were near, as fast as they could fire their guns.

"We were ordered to lie down, which we did in short order, and settled ourselves into the soft clay of the brickyard, which offered some degree of shelter from the iron and lead which were flying so furiously around and dangerously near our heads.

"After a time, the fire slackened. Our assault had met with a bloody repulse. Maneuvers were immediately ordered with a view of making one more grand final charge and ending the battle.

"As the attack ceased and the firing had become desultory, I raised up on my elbows; the colors of the regiment brushed my face. Pushing the flag aside, I glanced up and down the line. Our regiment appeared like two rows of dead men, everyone except the colonel, with his head face down in the mud as low as possible.

"Presently, the captain of a battery came running towards our regiment and hurriedly saluting the colonel, said: 'For God's sake, colonel, give me six men, quick, tho know something about firing a gun. I haven't men enough left to work my battery in the coming charge.'

"Our colonel faced the colors and repeated the call. Though I was the youngest member of the company, I had heard and seen enough for several days, and especially during the previous hour, to know the seriousness of the situation, to realize the probable consequences of the act, and to compare the exposure on the knoll with the safety of the shelter of the brick kilns.

"It took but a few moments for me to determine what to do. By the time the colonel had pronounced the word 'men,' I stepped from the ranks, closely followed by Comrade Beckwith and four others. We had but a few moments to look over the field and receive instructions from the sergeant when the captain, reading the signals from the church belfry, gave the order to stand by the guns, ready for action.

"The troops that were selected to make the final attack moved forward to the charge.

357

"Suddenly, the enemy opened with every gun and musket that could be brought to bear. As we occupied the only rise of ground on our side and were the only battery in action on our left, we found that several of the enemy's batteries were paying us particular attention and that we had to take their concentrated fire. The battle grew more fierce.

"Twilight came on; twilight passed to darkness. It was a grand and awe-inspiring spectacle - one mighty and thundering roar.

"Around us rained a perfect shower of bullets, which completely riddled a board fence in front of the knoll. They struck the guns and splintered the spokes of the wheels.

Shells exploded constantly over and around us and knocked down several of my comrades. Many officers and men were killed, and a great number, including several in my own regiment, were wounded in our immediate rear. We kept our little battery

barking. Our commander said that our shells were bursting squarely in the ranks of the enemy, but our army could not accomplish the impossible. The heights were too strong with earthworks, cannons, and men, and the assault ended the battle for the night.

"We lived through the entire attack uninjured. Sunday morning, the captain of the battery thanked us heartily for our services and told us to return to our regiment. Our colonel said, as he received us: 'I am proud of my men.'"

Fredericksburg. - In December 1862, General Burnside, superseding McClellan as commander-in-chief of the Union Army, directed an attack against Fredericksburg, Virginia, on the southern bank of the Rappahannock. The town is situated on the steep slopes of one of the three wooded terraces in the narrow valley. The battle took place on the second terrace, while on the third, the enemy under Lee had gathered a force of 90,000 men.

Burnside, stationed at Falmouth, was occupied from December 11 to 13 in building bridges and throwing across the river the two divisions of Franklin and Sumner. On the 13th, assaults were made by these divisions, which were repulsed with great loss. Hooker, ordered across, had the same experience. The Union troops were gathered at Fredericksburg and withdrawn across the river.

Burnside's losses amounted to 13,000 men, while the Confederate loss was not more than a third of that number.

From the Hartford Courant November 19, 1901

John G. Palmer, superintendent of the Arawana Mills in Middletown, died Sunday morning at the home of his son-in-law, Harvey Howard, in New Haven, where he had been for a few days for treatment. He had suffered for some time from cirrhosis of the liver. He was a prominent businessman, a member of the board of trade, and, for several years, a member of the board of education. He had also served on the common council. He was born at Montville, October 4, 1845, and enlisted as a corporal in Company F, Twenty-first Connecticut Volunteers on August 6, 1862, and was discharged on November 30, 1865, at Charleston, South Carolina, by expiration of term of service, having been transferred to the Second Company Provisional Cavalry, Veteran Reserve Corps, September 24, 1864, at Washington, D.C. Mr. Palmer was in the Battles of Fredericksburg, Virginia, the sieges of Suffolk and Bermuda Hundred, and was disabled January 24, 1864, at Brandon Farms, Virginia by a left inguinal hernia, and was in several hospitals before he was discharged. Corporal Palmer was one of the few men who was especially honored by Congress by receiving the Medal of Honor for distinguished bravery in battle aside from regular duty. This was won by bravery at the Battle of Fredericksburg. Phillips's Massachusetts Battery was at an important point, and all its men were killed or wounded. Volunteers were called for, and Mr. Palmer served on that battery during the battle and helped to save the day. The following are the principal points in his military record: He served in three branches of the Army: Twenty-first Connecticut Volunteers, Phillips's Massachusetts Battery, and Second Company, Provincial Cavalry, Veteran Reserve Corps. He served with this company as President Lincoln's bodyguard in the latter part of the war. He was detached by special orders, No. 8 War Department, on January 5, 1865, to

358

accompany Major General D.E. Sickles on a diplomatic mission — to Bogota, United States of Colombia. He also served in a confidential position with General Sickles in Boston until September 1865. Afterward, he was at Charleston, South Carolina, until he was discharged. Mr. Palmer was a member of Mansfield Post, Grand Army of the Republic, of Middletown, and in 1893, was an aide on the staff of the National Commander. Last year, he was President of the Twenty-first Regimental Association. He was also a member of St. John's Lodge, No, 2, A.F. and AM [Free and Accepted Masons], and Mattabesset Council, Royal Arcanum, of Middletown. Mr. Palmer is survived by a father, W. H. Palmer of Middletown; a brother, ex-Senator W. H. Palmer of Norwich, an uncle, I.E. Palmer of Middletown, with whom he had been associated since the close of the War, a wife, two daughters, Mrs. Harvey Howard of New Haven, and Miss Ola of Middletown, and a son, Charles. The funeral will be held this afternoon at his home on Lincoln Street, Middletown, with Reverend E.C. Acheson officiating, and the interment will be in Indian Hill Cemetery.

Buried in Indian Hill Cemetery, 209 Vine Street, Middletown, Connecticut; GAR plot. Photos by the author.

JOHN G. PALMER
MEDAL OF HONOR
CORP CO E 21 CONN INF
CIVIL WAR
1845   1901

SECOND CLASS BOY* OSCAR EDWARD PECK; NAVY

* The rank of Second Class Boy is for boys aged 15 to 17 rated as such on entry to a training ship. Such entry was conditional on a boy's adequate physical height, weight, medical fitness, and evidence of being of 'good character.'

March 1, 1847 (Bridgeport, CT) – October 23, 1906 (Noroton Heights, CT); 59 years old
Married to Eva Husted (1869-1957).
One son, Russell O. (1903-1905).
Enlisted on January 24, 1862, in New York City at 15 years old.

Born to William (1809-1885) and Caroline Sherwood Peck (1816-1896). Three sisters, Julia (1839-), Harriet E. (1844-), and Mary Caroline (1851-). Two brothers, Elias S. (1842-1921) and Albert M. (1853-).

He is the youngest to be awarded the Medal of Honor from Connecticut.

MEDAL OF HONOR CITATION

AWARDED FOR ACTIONS DURING: Civil War
BRANCH OF SERVICE: Navy
ASSIGNED TO: U.S.S. Varuna
GENERAL ORDERS: War Department, General Orders No. 11 (April 3, 1863)
AGE ON THE DAY OF THE EVENT: 15
CITATION:

The President of the United States of America, in the name of Congress, takes pleasure in presenting the Medal of Honor to Second Class Boy Oscar E. Peck, United States Navy, for extraordinary heroism in action while serving as Second Class Boy on board the U.S.S. Varuna during an attack on Forts Jackson and St. Philip, Louisiana, 24 April 1862. Acting as powder boy of the after rifle, Second Class Boy Peck served gallantly while the Varuna was repeatedly attacked and rammed and finally sunk. This was an extremely close-range action, and although badly damaged, the Varuna delivered shells abaft the Morgan's armor.

Photo # NH 57822   USS Varuna.   Artwork by R.G. Skerrett

The U.S.S. Varuna. Courtesy of the Navy Art Collection.

Some months since, the writer of this suggested, through the columns of a contemporary, that some of the appointments at West Point and the Naval Academy should be made from the soldiers and sailors who were distinguishing themselves in this war. The bill for the organization of the Naval Academy was so changed as to allow the President to choose three. He has done so. Here is the record of one. F.A. ROE, Executive officer of the United States ship Pensacola at New Orleans, reports thus to Capt. MORRIS, date April 30:

"I must make special mention of THOMAS FLOOD, (boy) who acted as my aid on the bridge. He was swept from my side along with the signal quartermaster, MURRY, who had his leg shot away by a shell which burst near them. FLOOD, finding himself unhurt on the deck below the bridge, assisted the signal quartermaster to get below. After getting him into the hands of the Surgeon, FLOOD promptly returned to my side and assisted me very materially by taking the duties of signal quartermaster upon himself. This duty he performed with the coolness, exactitude, and fidelity of a veteran seaman. I cannot speak too warmly of FLOOD and would be glad to see him appointed a midshipman in the Navy. His intelligence and gentle character arc of a high order."

Here is the record of another boy who did not get appointed. It is the report of Captain BOGGS, of the Varuna, in the same fight:

"I would particularly commend to the notice of the Department OSCAR PECK, second-class boy and powder boy of the after rifle, whose coolness and intrepidity attracted the attention of all hands. A fit reward for such services would be an appointment at the Naval School."

We hope that a similar rule will be adopted in West Point and that the places not filled from the rebel districts may be filled by the loyal young soldiers now fighting In the Union ranks, volunteer or regular, with no preference but that of merit.

The question has often been asked – how is it that the Navy makes so much more progress than the Army? The answer is simple enough. No person is commissioned for the lowest grade of command unless he has some knowledge, through practice, as a sailor. That, of course, has taught him some discipline and the necessity of coolness in danger. But the army appointments are made even of the higher grades of stumping lawyers, without any military knowledge, and under Mr. CAMERON, the grossest favoritism and nepotism prevailed, so much so that Mr. STANTON was obliged to issue an order running into the other extreme, which I may comment on another time. G.W.B.

Spring Grove Cemetery monument at the main flagpole in honor of Oscar Peck. Photos by the author.

The inscription reads: Civil War; In Memory Of; Oscar E. Peck; Dedicated – 2012; Congressional Medal of Honor Recipient; Powder Boy – U.S. Navy – U.S. Varuna; "For conspicuous gallantry and intrepidity at risk of life above and beyond the call of duty in action against the enemy."

Buried in Spring Grove / Veterans Cemetery, 41 Hecker Avenue, Darien, Connecticut; Veterans Section. Photo by the author.

Civil War
In Memory Of:
OSCAR E. PECK
Dedicated ~ 2012

Congressional Medal of Honor Recipient
Powder Boy ~ U.S. Navy ~ U.S.S. Varuna
"For conspicuous gallantry and intrepidity
at risk of life above and beyond the call
of duty in action against the enemy."

PRIVATE GEORGE WARREN POTTER; ARMY

December 11, 1843 (Coventry, RI) – November 30, 1918 (Sterling, CT); 74 years old
Married Susan A. Yeaw (1852-1927) on December 21, 1866, in Coventry, Rhode Island.
Lucy Ann Burdick Smith (1854-1926) on September 21, 1884, in Scituate, Rhode Island.
One son with Susan, William F. (1868-1944).
Enlisted on February 26, 1862.
Reenlisted on March 5, 1864.
Mustered out June 24, 1865.
Wounded at Petersburg, Virginia on April 2, 1865.

Born to George A. (1792-1865) and Susan A. Weaver Potter (1807-1879). No siblings.

Photo courtesy of Ancestry.com.

MEDAL OF HONOR CITATION

AWARDED FOR ACTIONS DURING: Civil War
UNIT: Battery G, 1st Rhode Island Light Artillery
DATE OF ISSUE: March 4, 1886
AGE ON THE DAY OF THE EVENT: 21
CITATION:

The President of the United States of America, in the name of Congress, takes pleasure in presenting the Medal of Honor to Private George W. Potter, United States Army, for extraordinary heroism on 2 April 1865, while serving with Company G, 1st Rhode Island Light Artillery, in action at Petersburg, Virginia. Private Potter was one of a detachment of 20 picked artillerymen who voluntarily accompanied an infantry assaulting party and who turned upon the enemy the guns captured in the assault.

Buried in Swan Point Cemetery, 585 Blackstone Boulevard, Providence, Rhode Island; Group 374, Lot 52. Photos by the author.

GEORGE W. POTTER
MEDAL OF HONOR
PVT CO G.1 RI LT ARTY
CIVIL WAR
DEC 11 1843   NOV 30 1918

PRIVATE HERBERT IRVING PRESTON; U.S. MARINE CORPS

August 6, 1878 (Berkeley, NJ) – December 8, 1928 (Norwalk, CT); 50 years old
Married to Edith L. Pennoyer Preston (1885-1958) on April 29, 1906 in Westport, Connecticut
Two sons, Harry F. (1909-1994) and Irving W. (1912-1965).
Lived at 40 First Street, East Norwalk, when he registered for the WWI draft in 1918
Enlisted on June 29, 1899.
Assigned to League Island, Pennsylvania.

Born to Joseph H. (1838-1918) and Ester "Ettie" A. Hitchcock Preston (1844-1890) of Vermont. Brothers Henry M. (1862-1914), Adam (1864-1930), Hiram (1865-1893), Wilbur F.H. (1867-1943), and Franklin C. (1873-1937). Sister Ester C. Preston Davis (1869-1930).

Worked as a ship carpenter for Lake Torpedo Company on Seaview Avenue, Bridgeport, CT.

There is evidence Herbert Preston deserted while assigned to the USS Oregon on November 7, 1901, in Bremerton, Washington.

MEDAL OF HONOR CITATION

AWARDED FOR ACTIONS DURING: China Relief
BRANCH OF SERVICE: Marine Corps
ASSIGNED TO: U.S.S. Oregon
GENERAL ORDERS: War Department, General Orders No. 55 (July 19, 1901)
AGE ON THE DAYS OF THE EVENT: 21
CITATION:

The President of the United States of America, in the name of Congress, takes pleasure in presenting the Medal of Honor to Private Herbert Irving Preston, United States Marine Corps, for extraordinary heroism in action in the presence of the enemy during the action at Peking, China, 21 July to 17 August 1900. Throughout this period, Private Preston distinguished himself by meritorious conduct.

During the Boxer Rebellion in China (November 2, 1899 – September 7, 1901), 59 American servicemen received the Medal of Honor for their actions. Four of these were for Army personnel, twenty-two went to Navy sailors, and the remaining thirty-three went to Marines. Private Preston was assigned to the U.S.S. Oregon at the time of the actions, resulting in him receiving the Medal Of Honor.

From The Norwalk Hour, December 10, 1928

ALTON W. "BINK" REYNOLDS DIES A HERO IN HARBOR
AS HERBERT I. PRESTON ALSO LOSES LIFE IN STORM

The body of Alton W. "Bink" Reynolds, 35, of Gregory Boulevard, one of Norwalk's most popular residents, had been recovered today from the waters of the Norwalk harbor, where he bravely met death Saturday evening battling his way ashore in an effort to get help for his companions, Herbert I. Preston, 50, of 47 Second Street, who also lost his life, and Reynolds' own son, Alton W. Reynolds Jr., 14 years of age, who was saved hours later from the waters off Peach Island. The body of Preston, whose numbing form was washed by a wave off of an overturned ten-foot rowboat to which he and the boy were clinging, was sought by grapplers this afternoon. The boy, saved in a miraculous manner, rallied in a surprising way at the Norwalk Hospital and was to be taken home today to the grieving mother, the former Miss Hazel Blascer, who herself has been confined to the home for several weeks by illness. She collapsed upon being informed of the tragedy but rallied, and it is felt that the knowledge of the son's escape saved her from death upon receiving word of her husband's loss.

From The Norwalk Hour December 11, 1928

The body of Herbert Preston was recovered shortly after 4 o'clock yesterday afternoon on the low tide. It was within a few hundred feet of the overturned skiff which figured in the double tragedy and which had been left anchored where it was at a market. The body was found by a searching party consisting of Alfred J. Boerum, Wallace Radfan, Captain Frederick F. Lovejoy, and Crawford Jessup. Shortly after the quartet arrived at the scene of the double fatality, Boerum, who is the proprietor of the Boerum garage, saw the body with one hand at the surface. The body was lifted into the boat and taken to the public dock at the Washington Street drawbridge, where it was removed to the funeral parlors of LeGrand Raymond.

Marker for Wife Edith Preston and "In Memory Of" footstone for Herbert I. Preston, Riverside Cemetery, 81 Riverside Ave, Norwalk, Connecticut; Section 12, Grave 700. Photos by the author. Herbert Preston isn't buried here. He is buried in an unmarked grave in Norwalk Union Cemetery, 90 Ward Street, Norwalk, Connecticut.

IN MEMORY OF
HERBERT I PRESTON
MEDAL OF HONOR
PVT USMC
CHINA EXPEDITION
1878   1928

CHIEF RADIOMAN, THOMAS JAMES REEVES; NAVY

December 9, 1895 (Thomaston, CT) – December 7, 1941; 45 years old
Unmarried
Brother listed at 31 Godwin Court, Thomaston (house is no longer there)
Enlisted on July 20, 1917
Discharged on August 21, 1921, and on October 12, 1921, he reenlisted in the Navy, making it his career.

Born to William Reeves (1850-1938) and Mary O'Riley Reeves (1858-1939) [both born in Ireland]. Sister, Rosetta Reeves (1882-1905). Four brothers, Joseph (1885-1972), Leo (1889-1967), William (1892-1949), and Frederick (1898-1970).

MEDAL OF HONOR CITATION

AWARDED FOR ACTIONS DURING: World War II
BRANCH OF SERVICE: Navy
ASSIGNED TO: U.S.S. California (BB-44)
AGE ON THE DAY OF THE EVENT: 45
CITATION:

The President of the United States of America, in the name of Congress, takes pride in presenting the Medal of Honor (Posthumously) to Radio Electrician Thomas James Reeves, United States Navy, for distinguished conduct in the line of his profession, extraordinary courage and disregard of his own safety during the attack on the Fleet in Pearl Harbor, Territory of Hawaii, by Japanese forces on 7 December 1941. After the mechanized ammunition hoists were put out of action in the U.S.S. CALIFORNIA (BB-44), Radio Electrician Reeves, on his own initiative, in a burning passageway, assisted in the maintenance of an ammunition supply by hand to the anti-aircraft guns until he was overcome by smoke and fire, which resulted in his death.

Presentation Date and Details: In March 1942, the Medal of Honor was mailed to his brother's home in Thomaston, Connecticut, by Secretary of the Navy William F. Knox.

U.S.S. California after the attack on December 7, 1941. Official US Navy photograph 80-G-32740, courtesy of Naval History and Heritage Command.

Photo of CRM Reeves' Medal of Honor on permanent display in Thomaston Town Hall, 158 Main Street, Thomaston, Connecticut. Photo by the author.

THOMAS JAMES REEVES, the son of Mr. and Mrs. William Reeves of Thomaston, Connecticut. He attended local schools and, before entering the service, was the chief operator for Western Union at Waterbury, CT. Thomas enlisted in the U.S. Navy on July 10, 1917. He saw service in WWI in the Transportation Service. In the following years, he had service on the U.S.S. American, Whipple, Seattle, Texas, Chicago, Maryland, New Mexico, and California. He also served in Staff Headquarters of the 3rd Naval District and with the Naval Mission to Brazil. He also taught radio in Rio de Janeiro. Thomas intended to retire in 1939 with more than 22 years of service completed. He had accepted an appointment as a ground engineer with the Civil Service. The day before his retirement was to take effect, President Roosevelt declared a Limited Emergency, and all persons were prohibited from leaving the Navy. Thomas then re-enlisted at San Pedro for another four years. At the time of Pearl Harbor, he was on the Admiral's staff on board the U.S.S. California.

A remembrance letter written by Thomas Mason. Transposed from the original letter on display in the Town Hall in Thomaston, Connecticut.

A remembrance of Chief Radioman Thomas J. Reeves, Medal of Honor

One day in the summer of 1941, Chief Reeves called me over to the supervisor's desk in the radio room of the battleship California. We were moored to Berth F-3 at the head of the battle line in Pearl Harbor.
"Mason, I'm giving you a promotion," he said. "I'm sending you to the main top for your battle station."
"That's great, Chief!" I enthused. "What do I do there?"
"When our planes are up, you copy their spotting reports," he said. "By hand. They're used for correcting main-battery fire."
"What do I do when the planes aren't up?"
"Enjoy the scenery." He smiled. "You're going to like it up there, Mason. Lots of fresh air."
The chief -- who ran the 90-man radio gang of both the ship and the admiral's flag complement with an awesome competence -- had given me more than a promotion. He had, it is quite likely, given me my life. Otherwise, I would have been in main radio, located on the platform deck below the third deck, port side, on December 7 when the Japanese attacked Pearl Harbor. After it flooded and was abandoned following the deadly impact of two torpedoes, I would have been with my best friend, Melvin G. Johnson, near the ship's service store when a bomb hit there, killing him and about fifty other shipmates. Or -- had I been a better man than I probably was -- with Chief Reeves in a burning passageway on the third deck.
When main radio was abandoned, Chief Reeves was the last man out. After helping some men to relative safety, he returned to the burning, rapidly flooding the third deck. Realizing the desperate need for ammunition at the anti-aircraft batteries, he plunged into the smoke and flames with every able-bodied man he could muster. It was there on the starboard side of the third deck, less than fifty feet from the entrance to the radio room he had supervised so long and so ably that he was overcome by smoke and fire, collapsed, and died. He won the nation's highest award for valor, the Medal of Honor. Of this medal, Harry Truman said: "I would rather have it than be President."
The last time I saw the chief was on the late evening of December 5, 1941, in front of Wo Fat's restaurant on Hotel Street in Honolulu.
"He was one of those men of above-medium height and large frame who become corpulent but never look fat," I later wrote. "He had a round, smooth face under a full head of thick, iron-gray hair that gave him a leonine look despite the military haircut. His piercing, hawk-like eyes could have been those of a surgeon -- or a riverboat gambler.
"Even then, he was a near-legendary figure. A pioneer during the primitive days of the arc transmitter, he was a man who scorned the easy shore billet that could have been his for one of the toughest jobs in the enlisted Navy: chief in charge of the radio gang, Commander Battle Force. He ran the C-D Division with a

discipline that was firm without being oppressive... Reputedly, he had turned down a commission of at least two stripes, which was certainly understandable, for no junior officer in a battleship had anything like his real authority and prestige. The chief alone decoded when and where you stood watch, what your battle station was when you went on liberty, and when you were ready for a faster radio circuit or an advance in rating. Within his division, he was more feared and respected than the captain himself."

On this Friday evening of December 5, Johnson and I were nearly broke. Spotting the chief, I ran across the street and explained my problem.

"Well, Mason," he said without hesitation, "let me make you a small loan." He pulled a bill from one of his pockets and handed it to me. "That enough?" he asked.

I was holding a twenty dollar bill -- a third of a month's pay for a third-class petty officer. I must have stammered in explaining that I didn't need so much, that a five would be plenty.

"That's all right, Mason," he said with a wave of the hand and a flash from the large diamond ring he wore on his little finger. "Keep it."

A Japanese task force prevented me from repaying that loan, but I never forgot the obligation. My assignment to the main top by Chief Radioman Thomas J. Reeves of Thomaston, Connecticut, enabled me to survive the attack on Pearl Harbor and later to attend college on the G.I. Bill. Decades later, it made possible the repayment of my debt in coin of a different kind. When I was asked by the Naval Institute Press to write Battleship Sailor, I was, at last, able to pay tribute to my gallant chief radioman of the California and to include his name in the book's dedication.

"The battleship Navy was gone as an overwhelming physical force," I wrote in my memoir, "but I knew that some of its intangible legacies would remain. What would live for others to emulate and for history to admire were the qualities of men like Reeves. To such men, defeat was unendurable, failure was not acceptable."

I am proud to have known and served with Chief Radioman Thomas J. Reeves, Medal of Honor.

- Theodore C. Mason

AUTHOR NOTE: Theodore Charles Mason survived the war and died in 2004 at 82 years old.

From The Hartford Courant July 12, 1942

Thomaston, July 11. – (AP) – Thomas Reeves is to have a United States Navy escort vessel named in his memory, according to a letter received today by his brother, Fred D. Reeves, from the Secretary of the Navy, Frank Knox. Mr. Reeves, whose memory was honored at special ceremonies here on May 30 and who was posthumously awarded the Navy Medal of Honor, died December 7 in the Japanese attack on Pearl Harbor. He was a Chief Radioman in the Navy.

U.S.S. Reeves (DE-156/APD-52) was a Buckley-class destroyer escort of the United States Navy, named in honor of Chief Petty Officer Thomas J. Reeves (1895–1941).

The first Reeves was laid down by the Norfolk Navy Yard, Portsmouth, Virginia, on February 7, 1943; launched on April 23, 1943; sponsored by Miss Mary Anne Reeves, niece of Chief Radioman Reeves; and commissioned on June 9, 1943, Lieutenant Commander Mathias S. Clark in command.

Memorialized on his parent's headstone. The stone is located in St. Thomas Cemetery, 55 Altair Avenue, Thomaston, Connecticut; Section B, Plot 283. Photo by the author.

Chief Reeves was buried on January 28, 1949, in the National Military Cemetery of the Pacific, 2177 Puowaina Dr, Honolulu, Hawaii; Section A, Grave 884. Photo from FindAGrave.com.

SEAMAN JAMES ROBERTS; NAVY

February 14, 1837 (England) – October 19, 1908 (Bath, NY); 71 years old
Unmarried
Enlisted on September 5, 1863, in Hartford, Connecticut, into Company K, 8th Connecticut Infantry. Enlisted in the U.S. Navy on May 3, 1864.
Discharged on April 15, 1865.
He lived in Bristol, Connecticut, when he enlisted in 1863.

Family information is unknown.

MEDAL OF HONOR CITATION

AWARDED FOR ACTIONS DURING: Civil War
BRANCH OF SERVICE: Navy
ASSIGNED TO: U.S.S. Agawam
GENERAL ORDERS: War Department, General Orders No. 45 (December 31, 1864)
AGE ON THE DAY OF THE EVENT: 27
CITATION:

The President of the United States of America, in the name of Congress, takes pleasure in presenting the Medal of Honor to Seaman James Roberts, United States Navy, for extraordinary heroism in action while serving on board the U.S.S. Agawam, as one of a volunteer crew of a powder boat which was exploded near Fort Fisher, North Carolina, 23 December 1864. The powder boat, towed in by the Wilderness to prevent detection by the enemy, cast off and slowly steamed to within 300 yards of the beach. After fuses and fires had been lit and a second anchor with short scope let go to assure the boat's tailing inshore, the crew again boarded the Wilderness and proceeded a distance of 12 miles from shore. Less than two hours later, the explosion took place, and the following day fires were observed still burning at the fort.

AUTHOR NOTE: One of five recipients of the Medal of Honor from Connecticut who were aboard the U.S.S. Agawam. The others were William Garvin, Robert Montgomery, John Neil, and James Sullivan.

U.S.S. Agawam (1864-1867). In the James River, Virginia, July 1864. Photographed by Brady & Company, Washington, D.C. Collection of Surgeon Herman P. Babcock, USN. Donated by his son, George R. Babcock, in 1939. U.S. Naval History and Heritage Command Photograph.

From the Democrat and Chronicle (Rochester, NY) October 20, 1908

THREE BATH HOME VETERANS ARE DEAD BY VIOLENT MEANS

Bath, Oct 19 – James Roberts, a member of the state Soldiers' and Sailors' Home, was found at an early hour this morning lying in the Conhocton River near the home. The presence of the body in the water, near the D.L.&W. railroad bridge, coupled with the fact that Roberts's skull is fractured and his body bears cuts and wounds, gives rise to the theory that he was struck by a D.L.&W. train as he was walking on the railroad bridge, and his body thrown off the bridge into the river.

Roberts was about 60 years old. He served during the war with a Massachusetts regiment of volunteers and also in the Navy. For many years, he was a resident of Buffalo before his entrance to the home in 1903. Coroner John E. Hasson was summoned, and at his direction, the body was removed to the home morgue. The coroner will conduct an inquest.

Buried in Bath National Cemetery, San Juan Avenue, Bath, New York; Section I, Row 26, Grave 2. Photo from FindAGrave.com.

AUTHOR'S NOTE: The New York State Soldiers and Sailors Home was established in 1878 to care for "him who shall have borne the battle," in Lincoln's words. It served as a retirement home, nursing home, or poorhouse for New York State veterans of the Civil War. Residents from other states lived in the home, presumably men who had served in or with New York units. Spanish War veterans were later admitted, and then a broad range of New York State veterans. As the Civil War population declined, the facility was federalized in the 1920s, even before there was a Veterans Administration.

Due to its proximity to the home, there are five Medal of Honor recipients buried in Bath National Cemetery:

Private George Grueb, 158th New York Infantry
Section A, Row 2, Grave 3

Sgt John Kiggins, 149th New York Infantry
Section H, Row 32, Grave 9

Private George Ladd, 22nd New York Cavalry
Section C, Row 6, Grave 6

Sgt Charles E. Morse, 62nd New York Infantry
Section J, Row 4, Grave 24

And Seaman James Roberts --

LIEUTENANT COMMANDER GEORGE HARRY ROSE; NAVY

February 28, 1880 (Stamford, CT) – December 7, 1932 (Teaneck, NJ); 52 years old
Married to Augusta Bogen (1887-1921).
Married to Eva M. Wintermute (1902-1975).
Two daughters, Florence R. Rose Burton (1906-1969) and Anna (1908-?).
One son, George H. (1911-1996).

Parent's and sibling's information were not found.

MEDAL OF HONOR CITATION

AWARDED FOR ACTIONS DURING: China Relief
BRANCH OF SERVICE: Navy
ASSIGNED TO: U.S.S. Newark
GENERAL ORDERS: War Department, General Orders No. 55 (July 19, 1901)
AGE ON THE DAYS OF THE EVENT: 20
CITATION:

The President of the United States of America, in the name of Congress, takes pleasure in presenting the Medal of Honor to Seaman George Harry Rose, United States Navy, for extraordinary heroism in action in the presence of the enemy during the battles at Peking, China, 13, 20, 21 and 22 June 1900. Throughout this period, Seaman Rose distinguished himself by meritorious conduct. While stationed as a crewmember of the U.S.S. Newark, he was part of its landing force that went ashore off Taku, China. On 31 May 1900, he was in a party of six under John McCloy (MH), which took ammunition from the Newark to Tientsin. On 10 June 1900, he was one of a party that carried dispatches from LaFa to Yongstsum at night. On the 13th, he was one of a few who fought off a large force of the enemy, saving the Main baggage train from destruction. On the 20th and 21st, he was engaged in heavy fighting against the Imperial Army, being always in the first rank. On the 22nd, he showed gallantry in the capture of the Siku Arsenal. He volunteered to go to the nearby village, which was occupied by the enemy, to secure medical supplies urgently required. The party brought back the supplies carried by newly taken prisoners.

U.S.S. Newark (C-1). Photo courtesy of U.S. National Archives and Records Administration (NARA).

From The Courier-News (Plainfield, NJ) December 8, 1932

CAPT G.H. ROSE, MUNSON SKIPPER, COMMITS SUICIDE

TEANECK (AP) – A hero's burial in Arlington Cemetery has been requested for Captain George H. Rose, skipper of the Munson liner Western World and retired naval officer who was decorated for bravery in the Boxer Rebellion.

His body was found yesterday in the bedroom of his home by his wife, Eva. A bullet had pierced his heart. Police said he committed suicide. Mrs. Rose said he had been long ill, and six weeks ago, a serious kidney ailment developed.

Born in Stamford, Connecticut, 52 years ago, Captain Rose enlisted in the Navy in 1898 and served three years. He was decorated with the Congressional Medal of Honor for bravery in carrying messages through Chinese lines in four battles in the Boxer Rebellion.

In 1901, he entered the merchant service and, in 1917, re-enlisted in the Navy, rising to the rank of Lieutenant in the World War and Lieutenant Commander in the reserve after the Armistice.

As pilot of the Pan-American on an emergency run from New York to Nassau made necessary by crippling the regular steamship on the run, Captain Rose rescued eighty-three passengers on January 20, 1929, from the Dollar Line vessel President Garfield, which had grounded in a fog on a reef off the Bahama Islands.

Captain Rose picked up the SOS at 7:30 a.m. when 200 miles away and steamed 90 miles of his course to transfer the passengers, mail, and baggage from the President Garfield to his ship before 5 p.m. the same day.

He entered the Munson service as a Captain in 1919. The Western World was to have sailed for South American ports on Saturday.

The widow and three children, George Jr., Anna, and Florence, survive.

Buried in Arlington National Cemetery, 1 Memorial Drive, Arlington, Virginia; Section 7, Grave 9978-ES. Photo by the author.

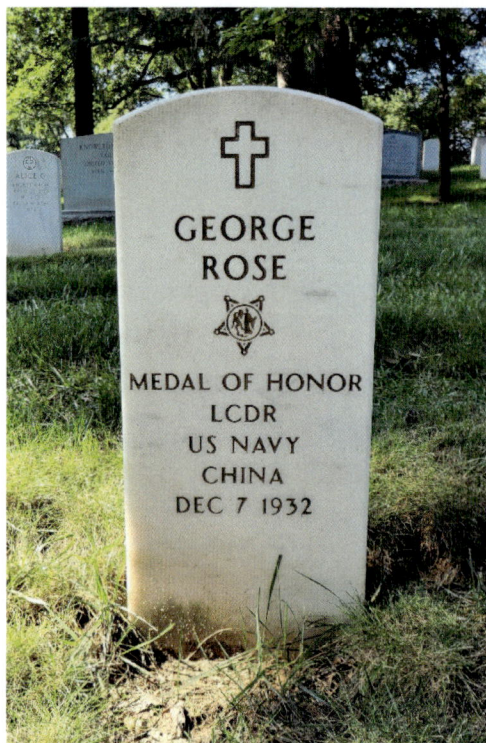

ORDINARY SEAMAN RICHARD RYAN; NAVY

1853 * (Waterbury, CT) – December 16, 1933 (Staten Island, NY); 80 years old
Unmarried
Enlisted on August 17, 1875

* The exact Date of Birth is unknown.

Born to Richard (1820-?) and Annie Ryan (1823-?) [both born in Ireland]. Two sisters, Margaret Ryan White (1849-1927) and Mary (1850-?). Two brothers, John (1852-?) and Edward (1857-?).

MEDAL OF HONOR CITATION

AWARDED FOR ACTIONS DURING: Peace Time Awards
BRANCH OF SERVICE: Navy
ASSIGNED TO: U.S.S. Hartford
GENERAL ORDERS: War Department, General Orders No. 207 (March 23, 1876).
AGE ON THE DAY OF THE EVENT: 22 or 23
CITATION:

The President of the United States of America, in the name of Congress, takes pleasure in presenting the Medal of Honor to Ordinary Seaman Richard Ryan, United States Navy, for distinguished and heroic conduct while serving on board the U.S.S. Hartford. Ordinary Seaman Ryan displayed gallant conduct in jumping overboard at Norfolk, Virginia, and rescuing from drowning one of the crew of that vessel 4 March 1876.

U.S.S. Hartford. Photo from Conways All the Worlds Fighting Ships 1860-1905.

From The Waterbury Democrat December 18, 1933

Richard Ryan, a native of this city and well-known to older residents, died Saturday at the Sailors' Home, Snug Harbor, Staten Island, New York. He was born here and spent his early life in this city. He was a brother of the late Mrs. John White of Walnut Street.

The body is being removed to the Bergen Funeral Home, 290 East Main Street, where friends may call tomorrow night. The funeral will be held Wednesday morning at 8:30, with services at the Sacred Heart Church at 9 o'clock. Burial will be in old St. Joseph's Cemetery.

Mr. Ryan leaves a number of nieces and nephews in Ansonia and New Haven, as well as several relatives in this city.

Buried in St. Joseph's Cemetery, 480 Hamilton Avenue, Waterbury, Connecticut; Section L, Lot 19. Photos by the author.

SERGEANT PATRICK SCANLAN *, ARMY

1838 (Ireland) – September 5, 1903 (Farmington, CT); 64 or 65 years old
Married to Ellen Scanlan (?-1917).
Enlisted on December 9, 1863 in Massachusetts.
Mustered out on November 14, 1865 in Richmond, Virginia

Born to Conor (1800-1850), and Mary Killoran Scanlon (1800-?)

* Last name also spelled Scanlon in some places.

MEDAL OF HONOR CITATION

AWARDED FOR ACTIONS DURING: Civil War
BRANCH OF SERVICE: Army
UNIT: Company A, 4th Massachusetts Cavalry
DATE OF ISSUE: January 21, 1897 (33 years later)
AGE ON THE DAY OF THE EVENT: 25 or 26 years old
CITATION:

The President of the United States of America, in the name of Congress, takes pleasure in presenting the Medal of Honor to Private Patrick Scanlan, United States Army, for extraordinary heroism on 24 May 1864, while serving with Company A, 4th Massachusetts Cavalry, in action at Ashepoo River, South Carolina. Private Scanlan volunteered as a member of a boat crew which went to the rescue of a large number of Union soldiers on board the stranded steamer Boston, and with great gallantry assisted in conveying them to shore, being exposed during the entire time to a heavy fire from a Confederate battery.

From the Fall River Globe January 20, 1897

AFTER MANY YEARS
Medals Bestowed on Union Soldiers for Gallantry During the War

WASHINGTON, D.C., Jan. 20. – Nearly 38 years ago. on May 24, 1864, steamer Boston. with a large number of Union soldiers on board was stranded ed in the Ashepoo river, and a volunteer boat's crew went to their rescue through a storm of rebel missiles. Dr. George W. Brush. now of Brooklyn New York, then captain of the fourth United States Infantry, voluntarily commanded the boat's crew, and with great gallantry succeeded in conveying them to the shore, being exposed during the entire time to a heavy fire from a rebel battery.

Captain Brush at this late day had been awarded a medal of honor, and medals have also been awarded to the following soldiers, who voluntarily participated in the rescue, as members of the boat's crew: Patrick Scanian, late Sergeant Company A, Fourth Massachusetts Volunteers; John Duffy, late Private Company B, Fourth Massachusetts Cavalry Volunteers; William Downey. late Private Company B, Fourth Massachusetts Cavalry Volunteers (probably now of New Bedford), and David Gifford, late Private Company B, Fourth Massachusetts Cavalry Volunteers.

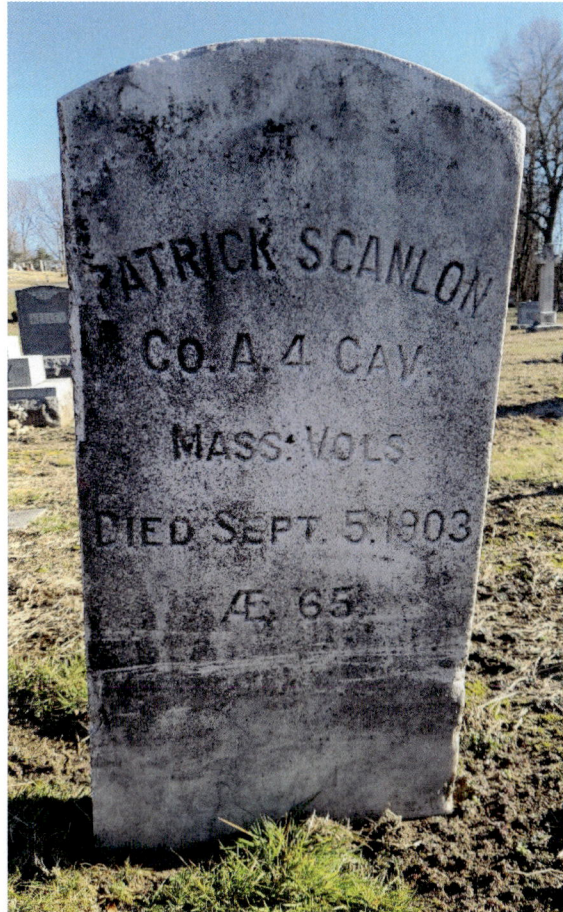

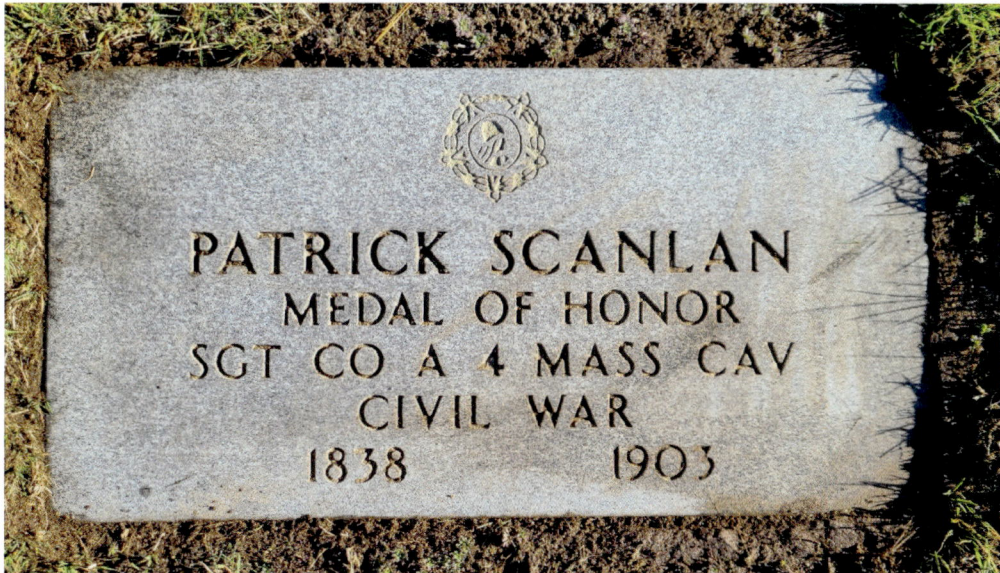

REAR ADMIRAL HERBERT EMERY SCHONLAND; NAVY

September 7, 1900 (Portland, ME) – November 13, 1984 (New London, CT); 84 years old

Married to Alice "Claire" Mills (1908-1997) on November 29, 1932, in New London, Connecticut.

One daughter, Dianne Morgan Schonland Sims (1938-).

One son, Rodney C. (1947-).

Entered the Navy on June 9, 1920.

Retired on December 31, 1946.

Graduated from the U.S. Naval Academy in 1925.

Born to Richard R. (1861-1952) and Helene L. Geisler Schonland [born in Germany] (1862-1947). Two brothers, Carl (1886-1912) and Richard P. (1897-1968). Two sisters, Helene Schonland Mabry (1889-1974), and Mildred L. Schonland Keefe (1892-1974).

The only member of the U.S. Naval Academy, Class of 1925, to be awarded the Medal of Honor.

Photo (left) courtesy of the Congressional Medal of Honor Society. Photo (right) U.S. Naval History and Heritage Command Photograph Photo #: NH 106452-A

MEDAL OF HONOR CITATION

AWARDED FOR ACTIONS DURING: World War II
BRANCH OF SERVICE: Navy
ASSIGNED TO: U.S.S. San Francisco (CA-38)
AGE ON THE DAYS OF THE EVENT: 41
CITATION:

The President of the United States of America, in the name of Congress, takes pleasure in presenting the Medal of Honor to Commander Herbert Emery Schonland, United States Navy, for extreme heroism and courage above and beyond the call of duty as Damage Control Officer of the U.S.S. San Francisco (CA-38) in action against greatly superior enemy forces in the battle off Savo Island, 12 – 13 November 1942. In the same violent night engagement in which all of his superior officers were killed or wounded, Lieutenant Commander Schonland was fighting valiantly to free the San Francisco of large quantities of water flooding the second deck compartments through numerous shell holes caused by enemy fire. Upon being informed that he was commanding officer, he ascertained that the conning of the ship was being efficiently handled, then directed the officer who had taken over that task to continue while he himself resumed the vitally important work of maintaining the stability of the ship. In water waist deep, he carried on his efforts in darkness illuminated only by hand lanterns until water in flooded compartments had been drained or pumped off and watertight integrity had again been restored to the San Francisco. His great personal valor and gallant devotion to duty at great peril to his own life were instrumental in bringing his ship back to port under her own power, saved to fight again in the service of her country.

Presentation Date and Details: January 5, 1943, at the White House (Oval Office), presented by President Franklin D. Roosevelt

Photo taken by the Associated Press. The author purchased the photo.
Commander Herbert E. Schonland has the Medal of Honor placed about his neck by his wife,
Alice Schonland. Looking on is the Schonland's daughter, Dianne, 4 years old at the time.

389

The U.S.S. San Francisco (CA-38). U.S. Navy Bureau of Ships photo 19-N-73588.

From the Kennebec (Maine) Journal March 17, 1920

Herbert Emery Schonland, Portland High School, 1919, will enter Annapolis Naval Academy in June, having passed examinations after fitting the past six months at Severn in Maryland. He made the school letter there also, as well as at Portland High, where he played football. He is a son of Mr. and Mrs. Richard R. Schonland, 54 Cumberland Avenue West. His sister married Lieutenant J.H. Keefe of Portland, a naval officer. Schonland received his appointment from Senator Bert M. Fernald.

From the Los Angeles Times November 19, 1984

HEROIC ADMIRAL HERBERT SCHONLAND DIES

NEW LONDON, Conn. – Retired Rear Admiral Herbert E. Schonland died Tuesday, 42 years to the day after a sea battle in which he opted to stay at his station rather than assume command of his sinking ship.

The Medal of Honor winner was 84. He was among the first to win the nation's highest award after the start of World War II.

Schonland died at Lawrence and Memorial Hospitals here and was to be buried Friday with full military honors in Arlington National Cemetery.

He was the damage control officer on the cruiser San Francisco during a three-day naval battle off Savo Island in the South Pacific.

Brave and Humble

He was cited for bravery and humility when he passed up an opportunity to become commander of his stricken vessel on November 13, 1942, when all others above him in rank either were killed or wounded.

He chose Bruce McCandless [USNA, Class of '32], the ship's communications officer, to command the ship and continued his successful efforts to remove seawater from the vessel. McCandless was also given the Medal of Honor, as were Rear Admirals Daniel J. Callaghan and Norman Scott, who were killed in the battle.

The major naval engagement near Guadalcanal resulted in the Japanese losing 2 battleships, 3 destroyers, and 11 transports. The United States lost two cruisers and seven destroyers. But the sinking of the Japanese transports meant that their garrisons on Guadalcanal could no longer be effectively resupplied., The battle ultimately was credited with speeding the Japanese surrender of that Solomon Island bastion in February 1943.

Schonland was a member of the U.S. Naval Academy's Class of 1925 and helped start the Navy's first damage control schools in Philadelphia and San Francisco.

Retired in 1947

He retired with the rank of Rear Admiral on January 1, 1947, with a medical disability because of an eye injury received in combat.

After retirement, he taught for several years at the University of Santa Clara and was the principal of the Drew School in San Francisco before moving in 1958 to New London.

A hall at the naval base in Newport, Rhode Island, home of the Surface Warfare Officers Damage Control School, is named for him. Only four other times in Navy history has the service named a facility for a living person.

From The Westerly (RI) Sun, April 4, 2020. Written by Steven Slosberg. Used with permission.

POSTSCRIPTS: THE MEDAL OF HONOR WINNER WHO ONCE ROAMED THE HALLS AT STONINGTON HIGH SCHOOL

In the decades following World War II, it was not unusual to find retired military officers teaching in public school classrooms here.

At Norwich Free Academy, from which I graduated in 1965, the math department counted among its teachers retired Navy Capt. Frank Lynch of Stonington and retired Navy Cmdr. Arthur Jerbert of Ledyard.

Likely more unusual was to have a retired Navy flag officer — a rear admiral — teaching physics to high-schoolers, and it had to have been hands down unique to be taught by a retired Navy rear admiral who had been awarded the United States military's highest decoration — the Medal of Honor.

But there was Herbert E. Schonland in the classroom at Stonington High School, teaching physics and science in the early 1960s.

Few of his students knew about his medal or how he earned it, and from what I've heard, he never talked about it. The nation tries to remember — March 25 was National Medal of Honor Day.

One of the students at Stonington High when Schonland was there but who didn't have him as a teacher was William Previty, who, like Schonland, went to the United States Naval Academy, Class of 1965, and from 1982 through 1985 was commanding officer of the nuclear fast-attack submarine San Francisco (SSN-711).

Previty, who retired as a captain and settled in Boise, Idaho, did some research into the history of Navy vessels named San Francisco after he assumed command of the sub and read about the World War II heavy cruiser San Francisco and its involvement in the Battle of Guadalcanal in November 1942.

Four Medals of Honor, rare in itself, were awarded — two posthumously — to officers aboard the San Francisco, and among those decorated was a name that Previty remembered: Herbert Schonland.

"We were very fortunate to have such a distinguished person as a teacher at Stonington," Previty said in a telephone conversation the other day. "I didn't have him as a teacher, but I remember him as very friendly, never having a military air about him."

What Schonland, as damage control officer aboard the San Francisco, did have about him during the battle was his wits.

According to the Naval narrative accompanying the award of the Medal of Honor, "While battling a greatly superior Japanese force that included two battleships, San Francisco was badly damaged by enemy gunfire. Rear

Admiral (Daniel J.) Callaghan and the ship's Captain, Cassin Young, were among those killed, leaving Commander Schonland as the senior surviving officer.

"Though command thereby devolved on him, he was already engaged in vital damage control efforts. Recognizing that Lieutenant Commander Bruce McCandless was skillfully conning the cruiser, Schonland remained at his post below, where his efforts were critical to saving the ship."

Waist-deep in water and in the pitch dark, Schonland quickly assessed that the ship's second-deck pumps were inadequate to pump out water pouring in from the shells fired by the Japanese. So he directed the seawater to be sent down to the lower decks where the higher-capacity bilge pumps would be able to handle the task. He first alerted the crew below that a wall of water was about to descend, then opened the hatches to the lower decks.

As another account of the battle put it: "Not only did his plan work, but sending the water to the bottom decks actually helped lower the center of gravity, giving the ship greater stability during the effort to save it."

Medals of Honor were awarded by President Franklin D. Roosevelt to the two deceased officers, Callaghan and Young, and to McCandless and Schonland.

Ironically, the San Francisco had been docked at Pearl Harbor on December 7, 1941, but was unscathed during the Japanese attack.

Schonland was promoted to captain in August 1944 and retired from the Navy in 1947, being promoted to rear admiral in recognition of his distinguished combat record.

He and his wife, Claire Mills Schonland, decided to return to New London, where they had met and married in 1932. Claire Schonland's father was an Army officer stationed on Fishers Island, and Schonland was stationed at the submarine base here.

Diane Schonland Sims, the couple's daughter who lives today in New London, said before moving back to New London, her parents had been in San Francisco where her father was a damage control instructor at the Naval Training School there and taught at the University of Santa Clara and at a private school in the city.

Back in Connecticut, he earned teacher certification at the University of Connecticut, eventually joining the faculty at Stonington High for several years.

He died of a heart attack in 1984 at age 84. Both he and his wife, who died in 2000, are buried at Arlington.

Bruce Greene, of North Stonington, a member of the Class of 1964 at Stonington High, took Schonland's physics class.

"I knew him and liked him as any 17-year-old would," said Greene. "We knew he had won the Medal of Honor, but he never boasted about it. He never mentioned his past."

Schonland's daughter suspects her father may never have gotten over the horror he saw that night at Guadalcanal.

"It didn't make him a hard person," she told me. "He was the most gentlemanly person. He never complained. He went through what no person should have seen or been through."

CHESS CLUB

The purpose of the Chess Club is to teach members that ancient parlor game and to arouse interest and promote proficiency in it.

President — Richard Songdahl
Vice-President — Earl Smith

Mr. Schonland

Stonington High School, Pawcatuck, Connecticut, 1961 yearbook. Physics and Science teacher and faculty advisor to the Chess Club

AUTHOR NOTE: Dianne Sims, Herbert Schonland's daughter, shared with me that the sailors who served with him were dedicated and devoted to him, and he to them. They would call him later in life for advice or a recommendation for a job. She said he was "remarkable" and "a gentleman." High praise.

Buried in Arlington National Cemetery, 1 Memorial Drive, Arlington, Virginia; Section 7A, Grave 168. Photo by the author.

QUARTERMASTER SERGEANT DAVID H. SCOFIELD; ARMY

December 10, 1840 (Mamaroneck, NY) – September 30, 1905 (Bath, NY);
Married Nellie W. Noyes (1842-1922) on May 5, 1867, in Stamford, Connecticut.
Two sons, Linus W. (1869-1947) and Clayson N. (1873-1879).
One daughter, Elizabeth M. Scofield Lewis (1881-?).
Enlisted on October 22, 1861, in Stamford, Connecticut
Discharged on July 19, 1865, in Winchester, Virginia

Born to David (1817-1841) and Sarah B. Slater Scofield (1819-1907). One sister, Mary D. (1837-1922). One sister, Mary D. Scofield Bailey Downs (1837-1922). Sarah remarried John E. Crabb of Stamford. One half-sister, Ella J. (1855-1864). Six half-brothers, David H. Crabb (1841-), George W. Crabb (1847-1925), Elbert Crabb (1850-1854), Jerome E. (1852-1854), Elbert J. (1858-1911), and John (1860-1918).

MEDAL OF HONOR CITATION

AWARDED FOR ACTIONS DURING: Civil War
BRANCH OF SERVICE: Army
UNIT: Company K, 5th New York Cavalry
DATE OF ISSUE AND PRESENTATION: October 26, 1864
AGE ON THE DAY OF THE EVENT: 23
CITATION:

The President of the United States of America, in the name of Congress, takes pleasure in presenting the Medal of Honor to Quartermaster Sergeant David H. Scofield, United States Army, for extraordinary heroism on 19 October 1864, while serving with Company K, 5th New York Cavalry, in action at Cedar Creek, Virginia, for capture of flag of 13th Virginia Infantry (Confederate States of America).

Buried in Slawson Cemetery, 107 Hanson Road, Darien, Connecticut. Photos by the author.

BREVET MAJOR GENERAL* ALEXANDER SHALER; ARMY

* Brevet rank in the Union Army, whether in the Regular Army or the United States Volunteers, during and at the conclusion of the American Civil War, may be regarded as an honorary title which conferred none of the authority, precedence, nor pay of real or full rank. The vast majority of the Union Army brevet ranks were awarded posthumously on or as of March 13, 1865, as the war was coming to a close.

March 19, 1827 (Haddam, CT) – December 28, 1911 (New York, NY); 84 years old

Married Mary McMurray (1829-1920) on March 31, 1847, in New York City

One son, Ira A. (1862-1902).

Five daughters, Camilla J. Shaler Jussen (1848-1933), Emma (1850-), Martha W. Shaler Penney (1857-1932), Matilda
     (1860-), and Mary V. Shaler Shailer (1852-1925).

Enlisted on April 17, 1861, as a Major in New York City.

Born to Captain Ira Shaler (1788-1866) and Jerusha Arnold Shaler (1788-1874). Nine sisters, Louise L. Shaler Brockway (1809-1896), Pamelia (1811-1861), Ariette M. (1814-1868), Jerusha (1816-1842), Martha E. (1819-1851), Tamzin (1821-1844), Henrietta (1825-1847), Mary (1828-?), and Ariadna W. (1829-1855).

*Photos courtesy of the Library of Congress; left photo LC-DIG-ppmsca-85709
and right, photo LC-DIG-ppmsca-74527.*

Photo courtesy of CivilWarTalk.com.

MEDAL OF HONOR CITATION

AWARDED FOR ACTIONS DURING: Civil War
BRANCH OF SERVICE: Army
UNIT: 65th New York Infantry
DATE OF ISSUE AND PRESENTATION: November 25, 1893 (30 years later)
AGE ON THE DAY OF THE EVENT: 36
CITATION:

The President of the United States of America, in the name of Congress, takes pleasure in presenting the Medal of Honor to Colonel Alexander Shaler, United States Army, for extraordinary heroism on 3 May 1863, while serving with the 65th New York Infantry, in action at Marye's Heights, Fredericksburg, Virginia. At a most critical moment, the head of the charging column being about to be crushed by the severe fire of the enemy's artillery and infantry, Colonel Shaler pushed forward with a supporting column, pierced the enemy's works, and turned their flank.

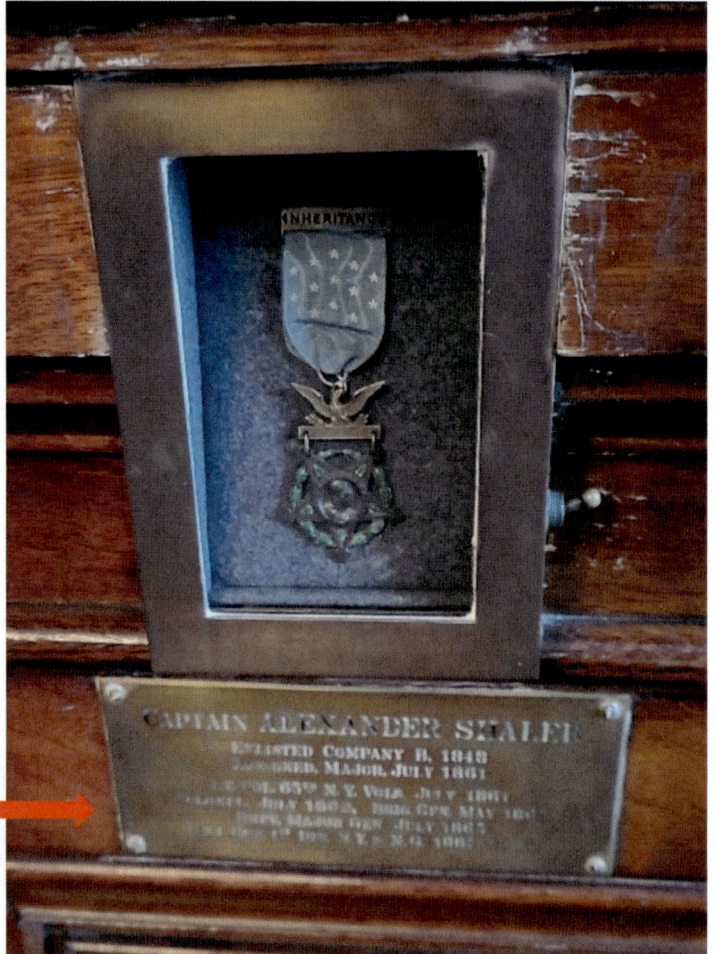

Note the medal mounted into the wall under the portrait. Photos by the author.

CAPTAIN ALEXANDER SHALER

ENLISTED COMPANY B, 1848
RESIGNED, MAJOR, JULY 1861

LT. COL. 65TH N. Y. VOLS. JULY 1861
COLONEL, JULY 1862, BRIG. GEN. MAY 1863
BREV. MAJOR GEN. JULY 1865
MAJ. GEN. 1ST DIV. N.Y.S.N.G. 1867 - 1886

SHALER, Alexander, soldier, b. in Haddam, Connecticut, 19 March 1827. He was educated in private schools, entered the New York militia as a Private in 1845, and became a Major of the 7th New York Regiment on December 13, 1860. He was appointed Lieutenant Colonel of the 65th New York Volunteers in June 1861, became Colonel, on 17 July 1862, and commanded the military prison at Johnson's Island, Ohio, during the winter of 1863-64. He served with the Army of the Potomac, participating in all its battles, until 6 May 1864, when he was taken prisoner at the Battle of the Wilderness and was held in Charleston, South Carolina, during the summer of that year. After his exchange, he commanded a division in the 7th Corps and the post of Duval's Bluffs, Ark., serving in the southwest until he was mustered out on 24 August 1865. He was commissioned Brigadier General of Volunteers on 26 May 1863 and brevetted Major General of Volunteers on 27 July 1865. From 1867 to 1870, he was President of the Board of Commissioners of the Metropolitan Fire Department and Commissioner of the Fire Department of New York City from 1870-1878. He was a consulting engineer to the Chicago Board of Police and fire in 1874, being charged with the reorganization and instruction of the fire department in that city. From 1867 until 1886, he was Major General of the 1st Division of the National Guard of New York and was an organizer and president of the National Rifle Association of the United States. While a member of the board for the purchase of sites for armories, he was accused of bribery; but, although he was tried twice, the jury disagreed. Gen. Shaler published a "Manual of Arms for Light Infantry using the Rifle Musket." (New York, 1861).

From Beyer, W. F., & Keydel, O. F. (2000). Deeds of valor: How America's Civil War Heroes won The Congressional Medal of Honor. Smithmark Publishers.

Alexander Shaler was colonel of the Sixty-fifth New York Volunteer Infantry, and in the spring of 1863, commanded the First Brigade Third Division, Sixth Corps, Army of the Potomac. While General Hooker was engaging the enemy at Chancellorsville, the Sixth Corps was on the Rappahannock River below Fredericksburg. On the night of May 2nd, under orders from Hooker to move out on the plank road leading from Fredericksburg to Chancellorsville and attack Lee's rear, the Sixth Corps entered Fredericksburg but was unable to advance farther in the darkness and fog on account of the formidable, defensive works of the enemy on Marye's Heights back of Fredericksburg, through which the plank road passed.

COLONEL SHALER AT CHANCELLORSVILLE.

At nine o'clock on the morning of May 3rd, the Corps was formed for an assault. On the right were two columns, ordered to charge over the two roads leading up to Marye's Heights. All the troops to the left of these columns were in deployed lines. The enemy's batteries completely enfiladed the two roadways which led from the city over an open plain about a quarter of a mile wide up the height. The column on the extreme right was composed of the Sixty-first Pennsylvania Volunteers, Colonel George C. Spear, and the Thirty-first New York, Colonel Baker, supported by the Eighty-second Pennsylvania, Colonel Isaac Bassett, and the Sixty-seventh New York, Colonel Nelson Cross, all formed in the order named. Colonel Shaler was ordered to accompany the two last-named regiments which belonged to his brigade.

Upon a given signal, the troops advanced. As soon as the head of the right column debouched from the city, it received fire from the enemy's infantry in the rifle pits at the base of the hill and from the batteries, one of which was placed in the middle of the road, delivering a terrific hail of grape and canister. This momentarily checked the column's advance, but Colonel Spear, with great gallantry, rallied and carried it to a small bridge about halfway across the open ground. Here, Colonel Spear fell at the head of his column, mortally wounded, and his two regiments were practically dissolved. The demoralization which ensued greatly imperiled the success of the movement at that point, as the surging column was threatened with destruction from the severe fire of the infantry and artillery. The Eighty-second Pennsylvania, next in the column, seemed unable to make any headway. Seeing this, Colonel Shaler caught up the standard of the regiment, rushed forward, calling upon the two regiments of his brigade to follow him, forced the passage, advanced up the hill, and captured two guns, one officer, and a few men of the Washington Battery of artillery, of New Orleans, posted in a redoubt on the right of the road. The other regiments of this brigade, soon after, greeted him within the enemy's works with cheers and congratulations. His men had not expected to see him alive.

Colonel Shaler's bravery was reported to President Lincoln the night of the same day by Doctor Hosmer, the Herald correspondent with the Sixth Army Corps, who witnessed the assault and started for Washington immediately thereafter to report the success of the Sixth Corps in capturing all the enemy's works around Fredericksburg. Colonel Shaler was promptly made a Brigadier General of Volunteers and subsequently received the Congressional Medal of Honor for this act of bravery.

From The Brooklyn Daily Eagle December 29, 1911

The Civil War made many reputations and wrecked some. Perhaps in the history of that war and of the years following it, there is no finer example of opportunities uprightly improved than in the life of Alexander Shaler, who has just died at the age of 84 years.

A young businessman who had come from Haddam, Connecticut, and enlisted in the Washington Greys in 1847, he transferred to the Seventh Regiment a little later and became a Captain in that regiment in January 1850, accepted it in November 1860. When Sumter was fired on, he was the first militia officer from any state to offer his services to President Lincoln. He went to the front. He devised the regiment rifle tactics, which were later, in 1874, embodied in Upton's Tactics. In July 1861, he was commissioned as Lieutenant Colonel of the Sixty-fifth New York Volunteers. He fought bravely at Williamsburg, Fair Oaks, and Malvern Hill. Soon after Fredericksburg., where he had commanded a brigade, he was made a Brigadier General. He was taken prisoner at the Battle of the Wilderness in May 1864 and was confined in Charleston until August of that year, when he was exchanged. He was mustered out in July 1865 as Major General of Volunteers. He continued as an officer in the National Guard. He was President of the National Rifle Association for several years and did much to encourage marksmanship. His only part in political life before the war had been as a supervisor of New York County in 1866. After the war, he was made President of the Metropolitan Fire Department, and to him, it is largely due to the credit of making the New York department the best in the world. Later, for three years, he gave his rare abilities as an organizer to the Health Department as President. His old age was quiet and peaceful.

The incidents of such a career are worth recalling. They are an inspiration to American youth and manhood that cannot be too highly appreciated.

From the Brooklyn Daily Eagle January 2, 1912

Editor The Brooklyn Daily Eagle:

I read with much pleasure the editorial on Alexander Shaler in your issue of Friday, December 29, 1911. It was a just tribute to a true man, an upright citizen, a brave soldier, and a loyal comrade. It was particularly gratifying to the members of the New York Association of Union Ex-Prisoners of War, of which General Shaler had been a member for many years. He was a past commander of the association and, at the time of his death, Chairman of its executive committee.

We knew him, not as the ordinary world knows each other, but as a comrade in all which the name implies, one tested under conditions impossible to describe, and in which he was found to be unflinchingly faithful. There was no dross or shoddy in or about Alexander Shaler. He was eminently an American, both as a citizen and a soldier, one of the types of which the nation should be proud and the youth of our land taught to emulate.

On behalf of his surviving comrades of the prison pens of the Confederacy, I thank you most cordially for the editorial. The enclosed letter, of which General Shaler was one of the signers, may be of interest to your readers.

JOSEPH L. KILLGORE,
Commander of the New York Association
of Union ex-Prisoners of War.

Headquarters Borough Hall, Brooklyn,
Brooklyn, January 1, 1912.

This was the letter referred to. It was addressed to Adjutant General Thomas at Washington and was sent North through the Confederate lines with the sanction of Major General J.G. Foster, Commanding the Department of the South:

Charleston, S.C.
July 1, 1864

We desire respectfully to represent, through you, to our authorities our firm belief that a prompt exchange of the prisoners of war in the hands of the Southern Confederacy, if exchanges are to be made, is called for by every consideration of humanity. There are many thousands confined at Southern points of the Confederacy, in a climate to which they are unaccustomed, deprived of much of the food, clothing, and shelter they have habitually received, and it is not surprising, from these and other causes that need not be enumerated here, much suffering, sickness and death should ensue. In this matter, the statements of our own officers are confirmed by those of Southern journals. And while we cheerfully submit to any policy that may be decided by our government, we would urge that the great wills that must result from said delay that is not desired should be obviated by the designation of some point in this vicinity at which exchanges might be made; a course we are induced to believe, that would be accepted to by the Confederate authorities.

H.W. WESSELS, Brig. Gen. U.S. Vols.
H.P. Scammon, Brig. Gen. U.S. Vols
Alexander Shaler, Brig. Gen. U.S. Vols
T. Seymour, Brig. Gen. U.S. Vols
C.A. Heckman, Brig. Gen. U.S. Vols.

Shaler Boulevard in Ridgefield, New Jersey, is named in his honor. It runs 1.2 miles from State Route 9 to East Harriet Avenue.

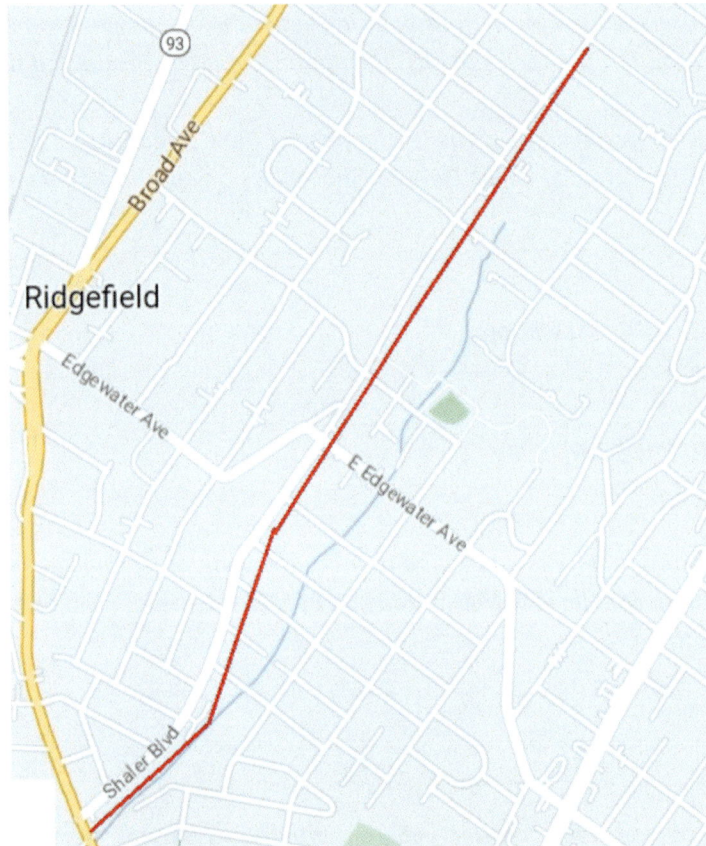

Honored on a plaque at Stop 7 of the Wilderness Battlefield Historic Site, 35347 Constitution Highway, Orange, Virginia. Photo courtesy of HMdb.org and Craig Swain.

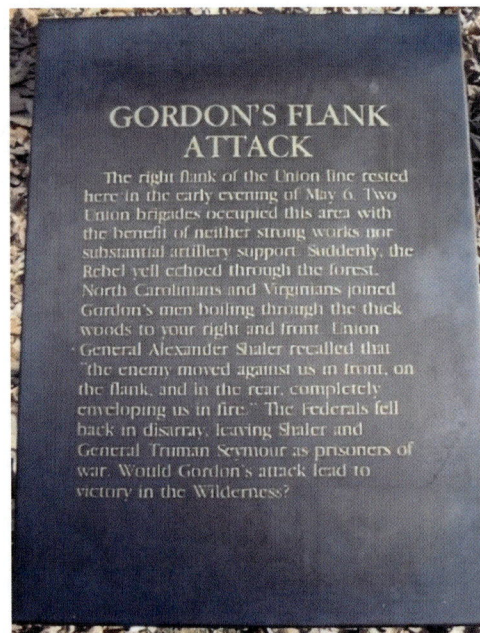

GORDON'S FLANK ATTACK

The right flank of the Union line rested here in the early evening of May 6. Two Union brigades occupied this area with the benefit of neither strong works nor substantial artillery support. Suddenly, the Rebel yell echoed through the forest. North Carolinians and Virginians joined Gordon's men boiling through the thick woods to your right and front. Union General Alexander Shaler recalled that "the enemy moved against us in front, on the flank, and in the rear, completely enveloping us in fire." The Federals fell back in disarray, leaving Shaler and General Truman Seymour as prisoners of war. Would Gordon's attack lead to victory in the Wilderness?

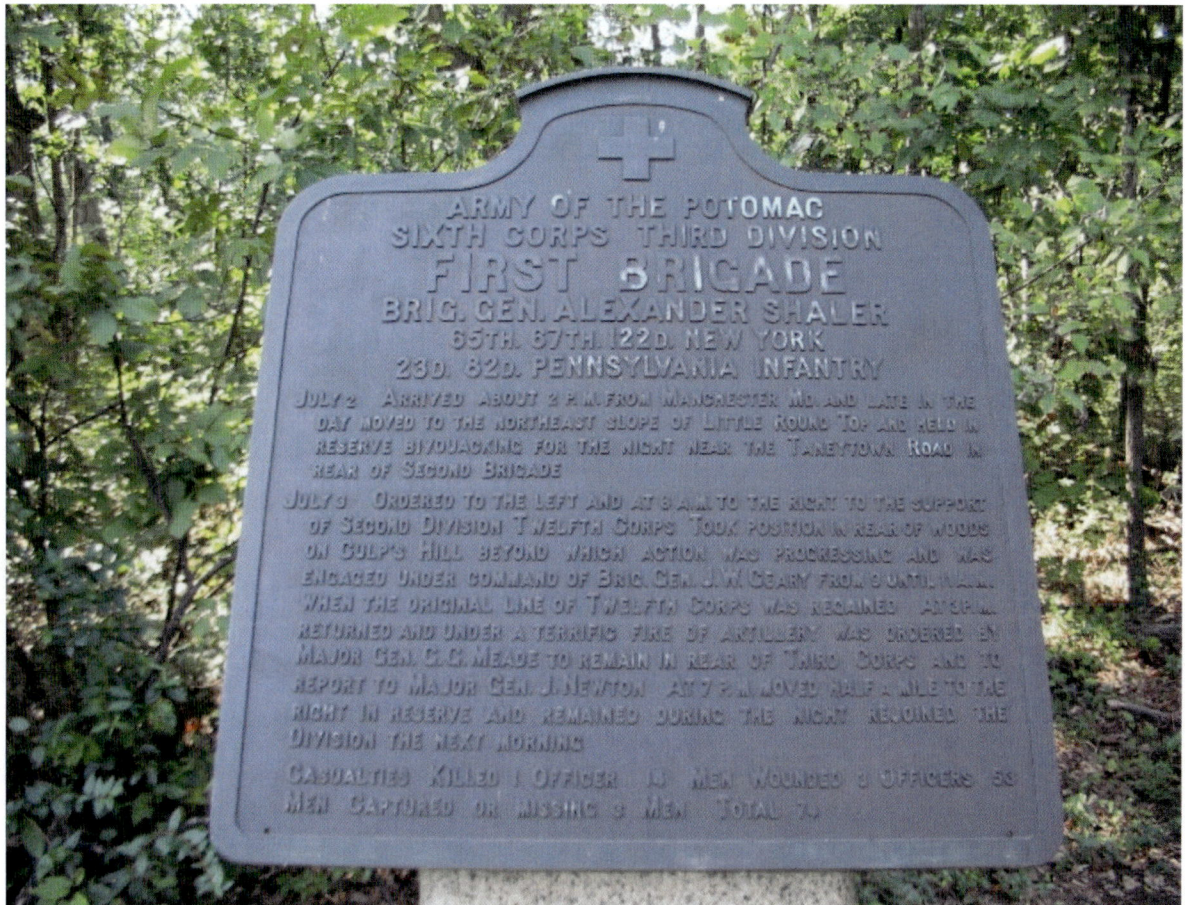

The plaque reads:

Brig. Gen. Alexander Shaler
65th 67th 122nd New York
23rd 82nd Pennsylvania Infantry

July 2 Arrived about 2 p.m. from Manchester Md and late in the day moved to the northeast slope of Little Round Top and held in reserve bivouacking for the night near the Taneytown Road in rear of Second Brigade.

July 3: Ordered to the left and at 8 a.m. to the right to the support of Second Division Twelfth Corps. Took position in rear of woods on Culp's Hill, beyond which action was progressing, and was engaged under command of Brig. Gen. J.W. Geary from 9 until 11 a.m. when the original line of Twelfth Corps was regained. At 3 p.m., returned and, under a terrific fire of artillery, was ordered by Major Gen. G.G. Meade to remain in rear of Third Corps and to report to Major Gen. J. Newton. At 7 p.m., moved half a mile to the right in reserve and remained during the night, rejoined the Division the next morning.

Casualties. Killed - 1 officer, 14 men. Wounded - 3 officers, 53 men. Captured or missing - 3 men. Total 74.

Honored on the New York State Auxiliary Monument, Hancock Avenue, Round Top, Pennsylvania – part of Cemetery Ridge in Gettysburg National Military Park. Photo courtesy of HMdb.org and Craig Swain.

Buried in English Neighborhood Reformed Church Cemetery, 1040 Edgewater Avenue, Ridgefield, New Jersey. Photos by the author.

ALEXANDER SHALER
MEDAL OF HONOR
BVT MAJ GEN 65 NY INFANTRY
CIVIL WAR
MAR 19 1827   DEC 28 1911

ALEXANDER SHALER
BORN MARCH 19 1827 DIED DECEMBER 28 1911
BRIGADIER GENERAL AND BREVET MAJ. GENERAL
U. S. ARMY   CIVIL WAR
MAJOR GENERAL NATIONAL GUARD S. N. Y.
PRESIDENT FIRE DEPARTMENT AND
HEALTH DEPARTMENT CITY OF NEW YORK
MASTER OF GRANGE OF FREEFIELD
CONFLICT AT CHANCELLORSVILLE

MARY
WIFE OF ALEXANDER SHALER
DIED ...

SHALER

PRIVATE FIRST CLASS DANIEL JOHN SHEA; VIETNAM WAR

January 29, 1947 (Norwalk, CT) – May 14, 1969; 22 years old
Unmarried
Last local address: 5 St. John Street, East Norwalk
Entered the service on April 24, 1968, in New Haven, Connecticut.
Service number: 52725281
MOS: 91A10, Corpsman
Tour Start Date: March 27, 1969
Unit: Americal Division, 196th Infantry Brigade, 21st Infantry, 3rd Battalion, Headquarters and Headquarters
    Company

Born to Raymond Paul (1914-1950) and Olive Stow Shea Salancy (1918-2003). Olive remarried Alex Salancy on August 30, 1963. One brother, Dennis (1949-), and one sister, Paula Ray Shea June (1951-).

Casualty Location: Quang Tin Province, South Vietnam. Daniel is on the Vietnam Veterans Memorial Wall at Panel 24W, Line 12.

Photo courtesy of the Congressional Medal of Honor Society

MEDAL OF HONOR CITATION

AWARDED FOR ACTIONS DURING: Vietnam War
BRANCH OF SERVICE: Army
UNIT: HQ & HQ Company, 3rd Battalion, 21st Infantry Regiment, Americal Division
GENERAL ORDERS: Department of the Army, General Orders No. 13 (March 9, 1971)
AGE ON THE DAY OF THE EVENT: 22
CITATION:

The President of the United States of America, in the name of Congress, takes pride in presenting the Medal of Honor (Posthumously) to Private First Class Daniel John Shea (ASN: 52725281), United States Army, for conspicuous gallantry and intrepidity at the risk of his life above and beyond the call of duty while serving as a Medical Aidman with Headquarters & Headquarters Company, 3rd Battalion, 21st Infantry Regiment, 196th Infantry Brigade, Americal Division, in action against enemy aggressor forces during a combat patrol mission in Quang Tri Province, Republic of Vietnam, on 14 May 1969. As the lead platoon of the company was crossing a rice paddy, a large enemy force in ambush positions opened fire with mortars, grenades, and automatic weapons. Under heavy crossfire from three sides, the platoon withdrew to a small island in the paddy to establish a defensive perimeter. Private First Class Shea, seeing that a number of his comrades had fallen in the initial hail of fire, dashed from the defensive position to assist the wounded. With complete disregard for his safety and braving the intense hostile fire sweeping the open rice paddy, Private First Class Shea made four trips to tend to wounded soldiers and to carry them to the safety of the platoon position. Seeing a fifth wounded comrade directly in front of one of the enemy strong points, Private First Class Shea ran to his assistance. As he reached the wounded man, Private First Class Shea was grievously wounded. Disregarding his welfare, Private First Class Shea tended to his wounded comrade and began to move him back to the safety of the defensive perimeter. As he neared the platoon position, Private First Class Shea was mortally wounded by a burst of enemy fire. By his heroic actions, Private First Class Shea saved the lives of several of his fellow soldiers. Private First Class Shea's gallantry in action at the cost of his life were in keeping with the highest traditions of the military service and reflect great credit upon himself, his unit, and the United States Army.

Presentation Date and Details: February 16, 1971 at the White House, presented by President Richard M. Nixon, presented to his family.

Photo contributed by Ryan Pettigrew, AV Archivist, Richard Nixon Presidential Library and Museum. Left to right, President Nixon, Daniel Shea (brother), Olive Selancy (mother), Alex Selancy (stepfather), and Paula Shea (sister).

Plaque at the Shea – Magrath Memorial and Wall of Remembrance at Calf Pasture Beach, 55 Calf Pasture Beach Road, Norwalk, Connecticut.

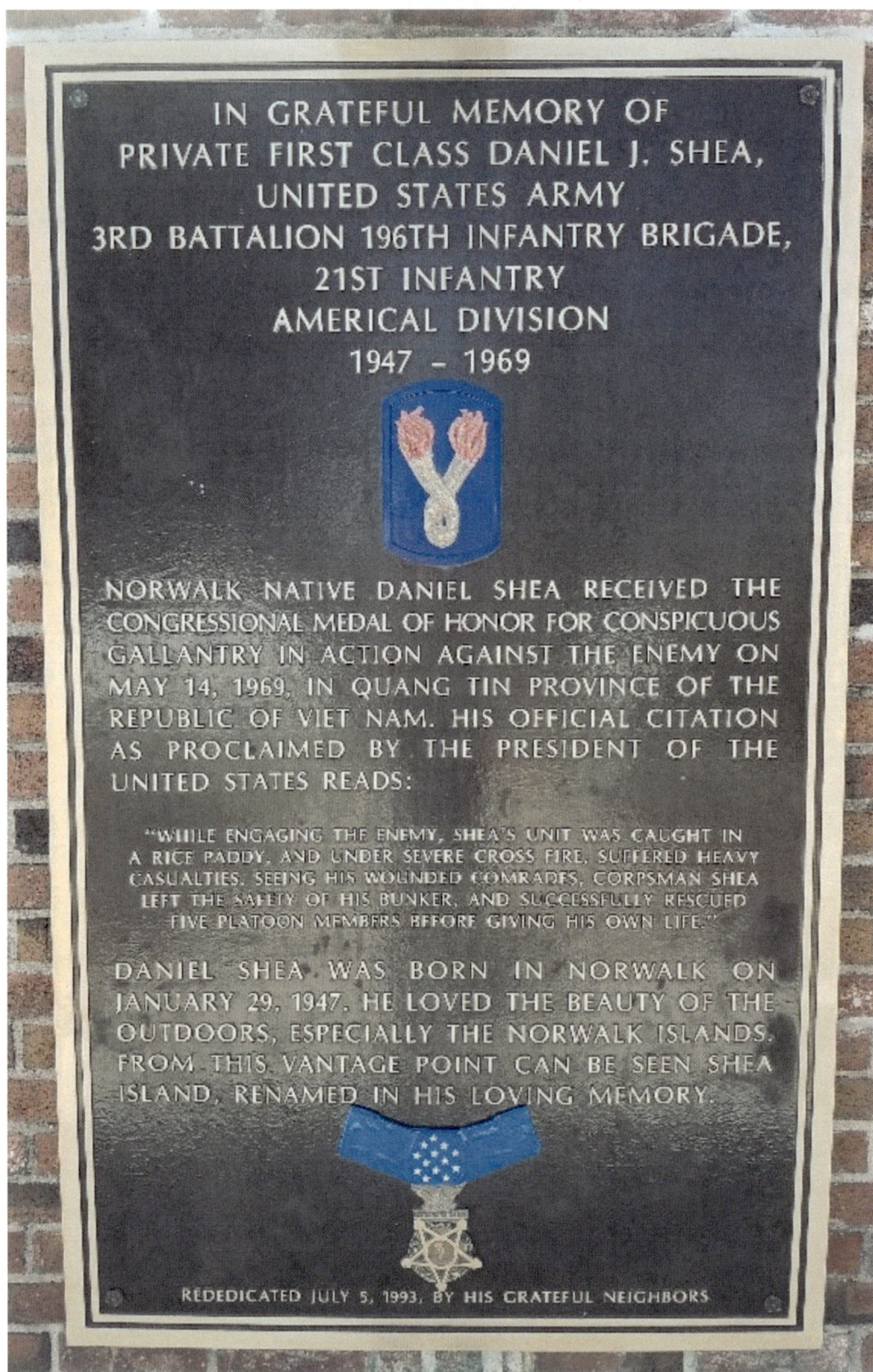

IN GRATEFUL MEMORY OF
PRIVATE FIRST CLASS DANIEL J. SHEA,
UNITED STATES ARMY
3RD BATTALION 196TH INFANTRY BRIGADE,
21ST INFANTRY
AMERICAL DIVISION
1947 – 1969

NORWALK NATIVE DANIEL SHEA RECEIVED THE
CONGRESSIONAL MEDAL OF HONOR FOR CONSPICUOUS
GALLANTRY IN ACTION AGAINST THE ENEMY ON
MAY 14, 1969, IN QUANG TIN PROVINCE OF THE
REPUBLIC OF VIET NAM. HIS OFFICIAL CITATION
AS PROCLAIMED BY THE PRESIDENT OF THE
UNITED STATES READS:

"WHILE ENGAGING THE ENEMY, SHEA'S UNIT WAS CAUGHT IN
A RICE PADDY, AND UNDER SEVERE CROSS FIRE, SUFFERED HEAVY
CASUALTIES. SEEING HIS WOUNDED COMRADES, CORPSMAN SHEA
LEFT THE SAFETY OF HIS BUNKER, AND SUCCESSFULLY RESCUED
FIVE PLATOON MEMBERS BEFORE GIVING HIS OWN LIFE."

DANIEL SHEA WAS BORN IN NORWALK ON
JANUARY 29, 1947. HE LOVED THE BEAUTY OF THE
OUTDOORS, ESPECIALLY THE NORWALK ISLANDS.
FROM THIS VANTAGE POINT CAN BE SEEN SHEA
ISLAND, RENAMED IN HIS LOVING MEMORY.

REDEDICATED JULY 5, 1993, BY HIS GRATEFUL NEIGHBORS

Photo used with permission from Rich Bonenfant Photography.

From The Norwalk Hour May 19, 1969

DANIEL J. SHEA, U.S. ARMY MEDIC, KILLED IN VIETNAM

"The mountains around Chu Lai are so beautiful you wouldn't believe a war is being fought here." Private First Class Daniel J. Shea, 22, of 5 St. John Street, wrote that sentence to his mother recently upon arriving at the U.S. base in Chu Lai. He died in those mountains Wednesday night while on a search and destroy sweep with Company C, 196th Regiment of the Americal Division. Mrs. Olive Stow Shea Salancy received word of the death Saturday morning when an Army sergeant visited her East Norwalk home. Confirmation came later in the day when an Army colonel reiterated the fact. Still later, on Sunday, a telegram from the Department of the Army gave added corroboration. It said that PFC Shea had been "killed while at a night defensive position." It thanked Mrs. Shea in the name of the President and the Secretary of the Army. Mrs. Salancy was courageous this morning when talking about the event and about her oldest son. "I have a lot of feelings, but I keep them inside. I hope President Nixon can solve the Vietnam problem, but I hope the solution doesn't give the country to the Communists. We've spent too much there. It wouldn't be right." PFC Shea had been in the Far East only six weeks and in the Army just two weeks more than a year. He was a medic, a job he learned at Fort Sam Houston in Texas after previous training at Fort Bragg in North Carolina. He had also been stationed at Fort Leonard Wood in Missouri. His mother described him as a quiet young man who had enjoyed most to be around boats on the East Norwalk waterfront. He didn't like war and didn't look forward to Vietnam, but he said little about these feelings, and when the time came to shoulder the burden, he did so without fuss. A younger brother, Marine Lance Corporal Dennis Shea, had enlisted two years before and had already served a tour in Vietnam. He expects to be discharged soon. Daniel's late father, Raymond Paul Shea, had served illustriously in World War II, especially during the Normandy invasion, where he had received the Bronze Star Medal and several Unit Citations. Mr. Shea suffered multiple wounds in battle, and they may have contributed to his early death in 1950. Also surviving are a sister, Paula Ray Shea; an uncle, Everett Stow of Rowayton; and his paternal grandmother, Mrs. Helen Shea of Port Chester, New York. Arrangements are incomplete and will be announced by the Collins Funeral Home.

Just three days before the nation pauses to pay tribute to its dead from all wars, Norwalk paid final honors to Private First Class Daniel J. Shea, its 13th son to fall in combat in Vietnam. Between the time his family was informed of his death and the services were held Tuesday, still, another Norwalk GI, Specialist 4th Class Willie Davis, was added to the casualty list. Full military honors were given to the young medic, who died during enemy action while on a search and destroy mission with the 196th Regiment of the Americal Division. He had been in the Army just over a year and had arrived in the combat zone about six weeks before his death. Representatives of veteran organizations, city officials, and a large contingent of uniformed policemen and firemen were on hand for the funeral. The flag-draped casket was borne between the ranks of uniformed men by an Army detachment from Fort Hamilton, New York. The sun shone brightly on the knot of mourners assembled on the flat plain of St. John's Cemetery, where the interment took place. Earlier, a requiem mass had been celebrated in St. Thomas the Apostle Church, the home parish of the young GI whose mother, Mrs. Olive Stow Shea Salancy, lives at 5 St. John Street. Reverend John Smiley, assistant pastor, was the celebrant, and Right Reverend John F. Cavanaugh, pastor, was seated in the sanctuary. At the cemetery, committal prayers were read by Father Smiley.

From The Norwalk Hour February 17, 1971

SMILES, TEARS AS MOTHER RECEIVES SON'S MEDALS

"I want to thank you for your dedication and love of country." These words of thanks and praise were given to Mrs. Olive S. Salancy of this city Tuesday by President Richard M. Nixon as he presented her the Congressional Medal of Honor awarded posthumously to her son, PFC Daniel J. Shea, for extraordinary gallantry in Vietnam. Mrs. Salancy was flanked by her son, Dennis, and daughter, Mrs. Walter June, as she stood before the President in the East Room of the White House. She was smiling through tears as the President took her hand firmly and offered the framed decoration and plaque representing the nation's highest military honor. She took the frame tenderly and looked at it admiringly as the President shook hands with Dennis and Mrs. June before moving to another bereaved family receiving identical honors. There were some 400 people in the East Room when the President walked in, accompanied by Defense Secretary Melvin Laird, Army Secretary Stanly Resor, Navy Secretary John Chaffee, and Air Force Secretary Dr. Robert Seaman. The President remained in the room for almost an hour, making the 12 awards and shaking hands with every member of every family. The press was excluded from the ceremony, and this account was furnished by Representative Stewart McKinney of Fairfield, who was present. He reported it was a somber event. Little advance notice had been afforded of the citation by which PFC Shea had merited the Medal of Honor. White House aides explained this by noting that President Nixon believes it is the right of the family to know the citation in person before it is released to the press. It was with some difficulty that The Hour learned of the citation Tuesday just before the press run, again through the efforts of Mr. McKinney. Mrs. Salancy and her children were the guests of the federal government while in Washington for three days. They were housed at the Mayflower Hotel. They were not registered by name, and it was impossible to reach them for comment. They are scheduled to return here tonight. Accompanying them throughout their trip from Kennedy International Airport were two Army officers and one enlisted man. PFC Shea is the second Norwalker ever awarded the Medal of Honor and the second Connecticut man to be awarded it in the Vietnam War. Marine Captain Harvey Barnum of Cheshire is also a recipient. He also received it posthumously. Decorations were unpopular during the nation's early years because many people considered them symbols of European monarchies. The establishment of the Medal of Honor by Congress in 1861 evoked much debate. More than 1,900 servicemen received it during the Civil War and Indian Wars. The Medal of Honor remained the only U.S. decoration until World War I, when Congress created others and restricted its award to persons who performed only the most extraordinary acts of heroism. The medal is predated

411

only by the Badge of Military Merit, which General George Washington created in 1782 to honor soldiers for extraordinary bravery during the Revolutionary War. Only three people received it. This decoration became the Purple Heart in 1932 by Presidential decree in celebration of Washington's birthday. It had not been awarded in the intervening years.

From The Bridgeport Telegram April 15, 1971

DANIEL SHEA DAY RITES, JUNE 13 ON RAM ISLAND

Extensive plans to honor local posthumous Congressional Medal of Honor recipient PFC Daniel Shea were announced at Tuesday night's Common Council meeting by Councilman Thomas C. O'Connor and William A. Collins. Mr. O'Connor said that President Richard M. Nixon has been invited to attend the ceremonies on June 13 (Daniel Shea Day), at which Ram Island will be renamed Shea Island, and a stone and bronze "working memorial" on Beach Road in Calf Pasture Park will be unveiled. Ram Island was chosen for renaming because young Shea had grown up as a local boating and water sports enthusiast and spent much of his time on the island. The memorial, which is being designed by Norwalk architect James Conte, was described as a three-walled court holding two bronze tablets commemorating Shea and 14 other Norwalk servicemen killed in Vietnam. Located adjacent to the Coast Guard station, the memorial will face out to Ram Island and might also include a flag pole and an "eternal flame." Tuesday night, James Romano of the Norwalk Building Trades Council said his organization will provide free labor, and Mr. O'Connor said local merchants will provide free building materials. Mr. O'Connor said some $2,000 to pay for the two plaques will be sought from public donations. For that day, Mr. O'Connor said he has asked Mr. Nixon for a naval vessel to fire a salute, a fly-over of jets, and an Army band. The day will also feature a boat parade and fireworks, he said. PFC Shea was killed in May of 1969 while serving in Vietnam. His mother, Mrs. Olive Salancy of 5 St. John Street, was presented the Medal of Honor by the President at a White House ceremony this January.

Buried in St. John's Cemetery, 223 Richards Avenue, Norwalk, Connecticut; Section A, Lot 113, Grave 2. Photos by the author.

SERGEANT CHARLES SHEPPARD *; ARMY

November 27, 1854 (Connecticut) – November 17, 1921 (Los Angeles, CA); 67 years old
His death certificate said he was "widowed." No evidence of a marriage could be found.
Enlisted in St. Louis, Missouri

* Last name spelled Shepherd, Sheppard, and Shepard in various places. His death certificate listed his father as John Shepard of Canada. His mother's information was blank.

MEDAL OF HONOR CITATION

AWARDED FOR ACTIONS DURING: Indian Campaigns
BRANCH OF SERVICE: Army
UNIT: Company A, 5th U.S. Infantry
DATE OF ISSUE AND PRESENTATION: April 27, 1877
AGE ON THE DATES OF THE EVENT: 27
CITATION:

The President of the United States of America, in the name of Congress, takes pleasure in presenting the Medal of Honor to Private Charles Sheppard, United States Army, for gallantry in engagements at Cedar Creek, Montana, and other campaigns during the period 21 October 1876 to 8 January 1877, while serving with Company A, 5th U.S. Infantry.

From the Los Angeles Herald November 21, 1921

HOLD FUNERAL FOR INDIAN FIGHTER

Funeral services for Charles Shepherd, 63, of 502 Molino Street, were held at the Odd Fellows Cemetery. Shepherd, a noted Indian fighter who possessed a congressional medal for valor in the Battles of Cedar Creek and Wolf Mountain, died at the county hospital after a long illness. Shepherd was accredited with having slain the Indian chieftain Crazy Horse at the Battle of Wolf Mountain on January 8, 1877. In memoirs left with a friend, Burt Anderson of 409 Molino Street, the plainsman told of viewing the massacre of General Custer's detachment of troopers.

SECOND LIEUTENANT WILLIAM EDGAR SIMONDS; ARMY

November 24, 1842 (Collinsville, CT) – March 14, 1903 (Hartford, CT); 60 years old

Married Sarah J. Mills (1844-1909) on October 17, 1867, in Collinsville, Connecticut.

Two sons, William E. (died in infancy) and Caspar (1876-1909).

One daughter, Katherine "Kitty" (1878-1882).

Enlisted on August 18, 1862, in Canton, Connecticut.

Wounded on June 14, 1863, in Port Hudson, Louisiana.

Discharged on August 26, 1863.

Born to John (1812-1845) and Tryphena Converse Simonds Creighton (1811-1884). One sister, Adelaide Simonds Jones (1838-1911). One brother, John C. (1840-1845). One half-sister, Ellen E. Creighton (1848-1852).

Photo (left) courtesy of the Evening Post Annual, 1885, Biographical sketches with portraits. Photo (right) courtesy of Ancestry.com.

MEDAL OF HONOR CITATION

AWARDED FOR ACTIONS DURING: Civil War

BRANCH OF SERVICE: Army

UNIT: Company A, 25th Connecticut Infantry

DATE OF ISSUE AND PRESENTATION: February 25, 1899 (36 years later)

AGE ON THE DAY OF THE EVENT: 20

CITATION:

The President of the United States of America, in the name of Congress, takes pleasure in presenting the Medal of Honor to Sergeant Major William Edgar Simonds, United States Army, for extraordinary heroism on 14 April 1863 while serving with the 25th Connecticut Infantry, in action at Irish Bend, Louisiana. Sergeant Major Simonds displayed great gallantry, under heavy fire from the enemy, in calling in the skirmishers and assisting in forming the line of battle.

Before military service, William attended public school and Collinsville High School and graduated from Connecticut State Normal School in New Britain in 1860. He enlisted in August 1862 and was promoted to Second Lieutenant of Company I of his regiment on April 24, 1863. After his military service, he attended Yale University and graduated from Yale Law School in 1865. He was admitted to the bar and commenced the practice of law in Hartford, Connecticut. In 1883 and 1885, and served as Speaker in 1885. In 1889, he was elected as a Republican to the 51st U.S. Congress, served until 1891, and was a United States Commissioner of Patents (1891-93). Author of Simonds' Manual of Patent Law, Simonds on the Law of Design Patents, and the Digest of Patent Decisions.

From The Hartford Courant March 16, 1903

The Honorable William Edgar Simonds, formerly a congressman from this district, well known in Grand Army and political circles, a member of the Hartford County bar, and prominent in patent law and agricultural interests, died at his rooms in the Linden, No. 427 Main Street, shortly after 9 o'clock Saturday morning. Mr. Simonds had been critically ill for several weeks and had been in ill health for several months. His death was caused by a complication of diseases. Ever since leaving the volunteer Army in 1863, Mr. Simonds had suffered from stomach trouble, which he attributed to dyspepsia and which was probably a symptom of one of the diseases which ultimately caused his death. His home was in Canton, but he had occupied rooms at the Linden in the winter for several years.

Brief funeral services will be held at the Linden at 11:30 o'clock this morning, and the body will be taken to Collinsville on the train leaving the Central New England railway station at 12:35 p.m. Funeral services will be held at the Congregational Church in Collinsville at 1:30, the Episcopal service being used. The interment will be in Canton Center. The honorary bearers will be: Captain Edwin E. Marvin of the Fifth Regiment, C. V., Judge John H. White, Judge William S. Case, Meigs H. Whaples, treasurer of the Collins Company; Francis B. Allen, vice-president of the Hartford Steam Boiler Inspection and Insurance Company; John H. Thatcher, assistant adjutant 'general of the Department of Connecticut, Grand Army of the Republic, with Mr. Allen, representing also Robert O. Tyler Post, No. 50; N. G. Williams of Bellows Falls, Vermont, and George W. Flint of Arlington Heights, Massachusetts.

The active bearers will be Edward H. Sears, president of the Collins Company; Harry E. Harrie, Dr. J. Warren Harper, L. P. Waldo Marvin, Emerson A. Hough, and M. Stanley Neal. The services will be conducted by Rev. James P. Faucon, assistant rector of Christ Church, assisted by Rev. C. E. Cooledge of Collinsville.

Mr. Simonds was born in Collinsville on November 24, 1842, and was descended through his father from the families of Simonds and (Daniel) Webster and through his mother from the families of Weaver and Converse, the latter tracing an unbroken line from Roger de Ceigneries, who went to England from Normandy with William the Conqueror. Mr. Simonds's father died when he was 4 years old, leaving his wife with three children, of whom Mr. Simonds was the youngest. Mrs. Simonds was without resources other than the work of her hands but managed to educate her children. William was educated in the public schools of his native village and, when 16 years old, entered the employ of the Collings Company and thus was able to save enough money to take a course of study at the Normal School in New Britain, lasting a year. He then taught school until the summer of 1862, when he enlisted in Company A, Twenty-fifth Regiment, Connecticut Volunteers. He was soon appointed Sergeant Major of the regiment and was mustered into the United States service in that grade. He served with the regiment in the Department of the Gulf and, for distinguished gallantry at the battle of Irish Bend, Louisiana, on April 14, 1863, was promoted to Second Lieutenant of Company J. At a reunion of the regiment held in this city twenty-five years later, the late Colonel George P. Bissell, who was in command of the regiment at the battle of Irish Bend, highly complimented Lieutenant Simonds, with others, for the part they took in the battle, especially referring to the formation of a regimental line by Major Thomas McManus, Adjutant Ward, and Sergeant Major Simonds when the regiment was under a sharp fire. Mr. Simonds was promoted on the field for his coolness and bravery on that occasion.

Lieutenant Simonds was mustered out with his regiment on August 26, 1863, and decided to study for the law. He entered Yale Law School and graduated therefrom in 1865 with the degree of bachelor of law. He practiced law by himself for about two years and then became interested in patent law, which branch he followed all during his subsequent career at the bar. Mr. Simonds was the author of several works on patent law, which have been accepted by the legal profession as standards. They include the following works: "Design Patents," "Digest of Patent Office Decisions," "Summary of Patent Law," and "Digest of Patent Cases," the latter of which embraced all patent cases decided by the federal and state courts since the foundation of the republic. In 1884, Mr. Simonds was appointed a lecturer on patent law at Yale Law School, which position he filled for many years. He also held a similar position at the Columbian University in Washington, D. C.: His recognized position as a leading patent lawyer brought him a large practice which included causes before the United States Supreme Court and the circuit courts of the United States in several districts in the Eastern states.

Mr. Simonds was always a Republican in politics and was elected a representative from the town of Canton in the General Assembly of 1883. He was one of the leaders of the party at that session owing to his natural ability and his position as House chairman of the important committee on railroads. He was influential in the passage o of the "short haul" bill and in other measures of considerable importance. His action on the "short haul" bill was much appreciated by the manufacturers of the State. Mr. Simonds wasn't re-elected to the House in 1885 and elected speaker, a position which he filled with good judgment and to his credit. He was an earnest advocate of the bill which established the Storrs Agricultural College, now the Connecticut College, and aided materially in the passage of the bill at that session. He was made a trustee of the college, a position which he continued to fill until recently by successive re-election by the General Assembly.

Mr. Simonds was considered an authority on the subject of agriculture and had delivered many public addresses on that important subject. He gave close attention to the subject of political economy and published several interesting articles on that subject. "Discontent Among the Laboring Classes," which was published in the state labor report for 1888, and an article on "Wool and Woolens," written about that time, are two of the most important articles written by Mr. Simonds in that line.

Mr. Simonds's legislative experience brought him into prominence politically, and in 1888, he was nominated for Congress by the First District Republican convention and was elected, defeating the sitting Democratic member. He served as a member of the Fifty-first Congress from March 4, 1889. to March 4, 1891. His service in Congress was signalized by his successful efforts on behalf of international copyright law. It was the first international copyright law in the country, although the subject had been agitated in Congress and before the country ever since the days of Henry Clay, who began the agitation of the subject seventy-five years or more ago. Mr. Simonds was unanimously renominated for Congress in 1890 but was carried down in the Democratic landslide of that year.

In 1891, President Harrison appointed Mr. Simonds United States Commissioner of Patents, which position he held for two years. The administration of the office during that period was distinguished by the introduction of reforms in methods of administration and by many valuable reports to Congress. He rendered many judicial decisions, some of them on important causes which had held the attention of the patent office for many years.

Mr. Simonds was an orator of no mean repute. He delivered an oration on the late ex-Governor Marshall Jewell in 1883, a celebrated speech on the Gettysburg appropriation in 1885, the Memorial Day address in this city on May 30, 1887, a historical address on the centennial of the First Company Governor's Foot Guard in 1889, and the Memorial Day address at Arlington Military Cemetery in 1993. He had delivered a great number of Memorial Day addresses in many cities and towns in the state. Mr. Simonds was quite popular among Grand Army men and with associations of old soldiers. He was one of the charter members of Nathaniel Lyon Post, No. 2, Grand Army of the Republic (GAR) of this city and retained his membership in that body until transferred to Robert O. Tyler Post, No. 50, about three years ago. He was a member of the Loyal Legion of the United States and several social and benevolent organizations. He was elected department commander of the Grand Army in 1898 and served his term of one year with credit to the organization. During the early days of the Connecticut Western Railroad, Mr. Simonds was an agent for the town of Canton regarding its loan to the road, succeeding his father-in-law, Honorary A. O. Mills, in that capacity.

Mr. Simonds's membership in fraternal organizations included the Sons of the American Revolution, Village Lodge, A. F., and A. M., of Collinsville, Pythagoras Chapter, R. A. M., Washington Commandery, No. 1. Knights Templars and Sphinx Temple, Nobles of the Mystic Shrine.

Mr. Simonds was married on October 17, 1877, to Miss Sarah J. Mills, the daughter of Honorary Addison O. Mills of Canton, by whom he had three children, one of whom, Casper J. Simonds, with Mrs. Simonds, survives him. He also leaves a brother, Albert Simonds of Stafford Springs, and a sister, Mrs. Leroy Jones of Collinsville.

From Canton Today Magazine + Today Publishing article, Simonds' Civil War heroics merited Medal of Honor; David K. Leff; April 2019. Used with permission.

CANTON HISTORY – APRIL 1863 — Rising stiff and chilled on the morning of April 14, 1863, 20-year-old Canton native William Edgar Simonds awakened to a gray morning in Louisiana, where he was camped with several units of Union troops during the Civil War.

After a hasty breakfast, the men set out on a winding road following Bayou Teche. Eventually, they entered an immense sugar cane field in a place called Irish Bend. It was crowded with desiccated, breast-high stalks from the previous year.

On orders of the commanding officer, Col. George P. Bissell, they marched down the field, right wing deployed ahead as skirmishers. Suddenly, there was gunfire from the dense wood of magnolia, cottonwood, briars, vines, and palmettos growing nearby. Lead raked the dry, brown canes with a sound like hail on a window.

With the skirmishers helplessly pinned down ahead, the colonel shouted for the men to hit the dirt, load, and rise up and fire at an enemy who was all but invisible among the trees.

Simonds thought of the ambushed skirmishers cringing on the ground up front under threat of certain death. They'd been through a lot together since leaving Connecticut. Without warning or even knowing why, Simonds got up.

Bullets whizzing overhead, he kept low and painstakingly worked his way up from the rear through a hazardous no man's land of muddy furrows and brittle cane stalks to where his compatriots were trapped under a withering enfilade.

The air was thick with acrid smoke when Simonds found his Civil War heroics merited the Medal of Honor, the trapped men. Breathing heavily, blood pounding in his ears, his face and uniform were spattered with muck. Startled by his appearance, the troops stared as if at a ghost.

Finally finding his wind, Simonds mustered an authoritative voice that commanded obedience and ordered the skirmishers to move. Urging them to keep low, he hurried the isolated patrol through the canes and safely back to the regiment under unrelenting enemy fire.

Although outnumbered and outgunned as exploding artillery shells rained down, Simonds and the other troops were eventually saved by reinforcements just as the end was drawing near. With fresh men on the field, the Union turned the tide of battle. For his gallantry in uniting the unit under fire, Bissell promoted Simonds from Sergeant-Major to Lieutenant. Following a congressional investigation 36 years later, Simonds was awarded the Medal of Honor, the highest military award for bravery bestowed by the United States.

The Congressional Medal of Honor Society believes Williams Simonds' Medal of Honor is in the Canton Historical Museum in Canton, Connecticut. On a visit to the museum, it was discovered the medal wasn't there. The photos that follow are part of a display in honor of William Simonds in the Canton Museum. They were taken by the author on a visit to Canton to document Lt Simonds' final resting place.

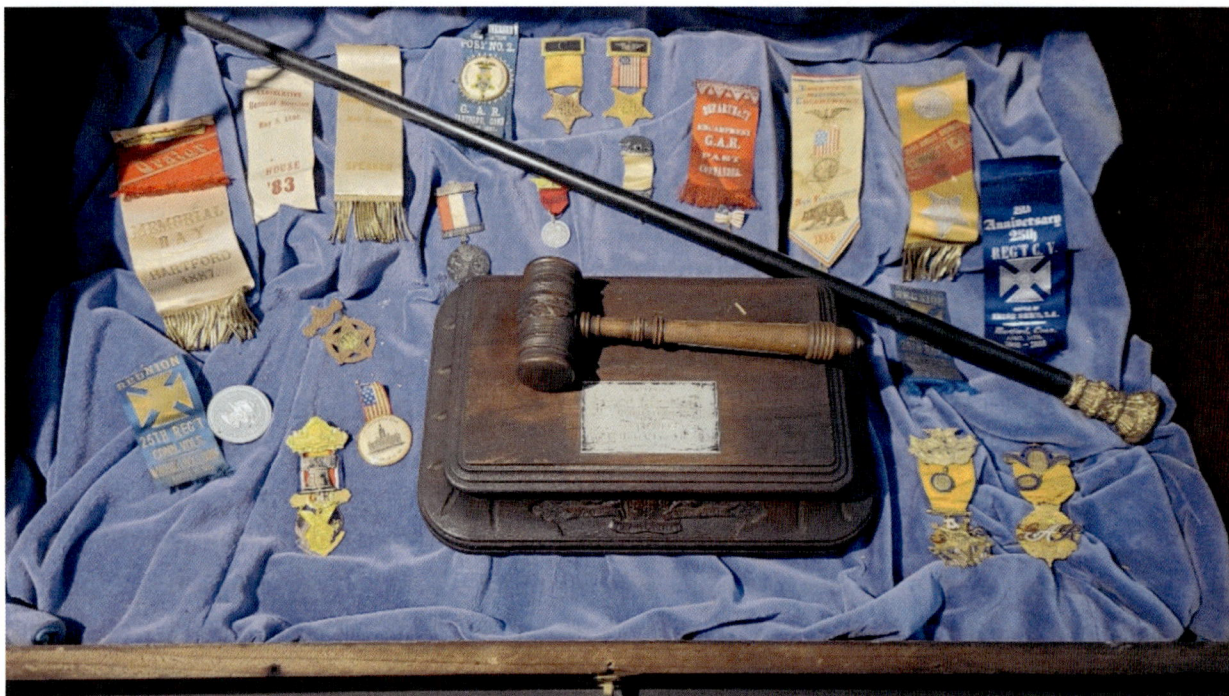

PRESENTED
BY THE
House of Representatives
OF
CONNECTICUT
To The
Speaker,
Hon. William Edgar Simonds
Session of 1885.

SECOND LIEUTENANT SHERROD "ROD" EMERSON SKINNER, JR.; MARINE CORPS

October 29, 1929 (Hartford, CT) – October 26, 1952 (South Korea); 22 years old
Unmarried
Service Number: 054537
MOS: 802, Field Artillery Officer

Born to Sherrod E. Sr. (1896-1977) and Abigail E. Leete Skinner (1897-1992). Two sisters, Martha L. Skinner Cargill (1922-2012) and Shirley Y. Skinner Sherrill Young (1924-2001). One brother, David C. [also a USMC veteran and twin of Sherrod] (1929-2012).

In 1991, Skinner Hall at Quantico, Virginia, was dedicated in his honor.

Milton Academy, Milton, Massachusetts, Class of 1947

SHERROD EMERSON SKINNER, JR.
625 Wildwood Drive, East Lansing, Michigan
"Rod", "Little Fella"

Age: 17   College Choice: Harvard

Upton House, 1943-47   Festival Chorus, 1946
Blue Club   Dramatic Society, 1946-47
Student Council, 1946-47   Football Squad, 1945
Orange and Blue Sports Editor,   Soccer Team, 1946
    1946-47   Wrestling Squad, 1943-44
Glee Club, 1944-47   Wrestling Team, 1944-47
Choir, 1945-47   Baseball Team, 1946-47
Warren Hall Glee Club, 1944

Milton Academy wrestling team; seated, 3rd from right.

Milton Academy soccer team, middle row, 4th from left or right

Milton Academy Dramatic Club, top row, far left.

Harvard University Class of 1951; one of 18 Harvard graduates to receive the Medal of Honor, including President Theodore Roosevelt and his son Theodore Roosevelt Jr.

SHERROD E. SKINNER, JR.
Born October 29, 1929 in Hartford, Connecticut. Prepared at Milton Academy. Entered Harvard as a Freshman in September 1947. Home address: 625 Wildwood Drive, East Lansing, Michigan. Baseball. Golf. Wrestling. Harvard Publications. Glee Club. Member of Marine Corps Reserve. Field of Concentration: History and Literature.

Photo courtesy of the Congressional Medal of Honor Society.

MEDAL OF HONOR CITATION

AWARDED FOR ACTIONS DURING: Korean War
BRANCH OF SERVICE: Marine Corps
UNIT: Battery F, 11th Marines, 1st Marine Division (Reinforced)
AGE ON THE DAY OF THE EVENT: 22
CITATION:

The President of the United States of America, in the name of Congress, takes pride in presenting the Medal of Honor (Posthumously) to Second Lieutenant Sherrod Emerson Skinner, Jr. (MCSN: 0-54537), United States Marine Corps Reserve, for conspicuous gallantry and intrepidity at the risk of his life above and beyond the call of duty as an artillery forward observer of Battery F, Second Battalion, Eleventh Marines, FIRST Marine Division (Reinforced), in action against enemy aggressor forces in Korea on the night of 26 October 1952. When his observation post in an extremely critical and vital sector of the main line of resistance was subjected to a sudden and fanatical attack by hostile forces, supported by a devastating barrage of artillery and mortar fire which completely severed communication lines connecting the outpost with friendly firing batteries, Second Lieutenant Skinner, in a determined effort to hold his position, immediately organized and directed the surviving personnel in defense of the outpost, continuing to call down fire on the enemy by means of radio alone until his equipment became damaged beyond repair. Undaunted by the intense hostile barrage and the rapidly closing attackers, he twice left the protection of his bunker in order to direct accurate machinegun fire and to replenish the depleted supply of ammunition and grenades. Although painfully wounded on each occasion, he steadfastly refused medical aid until the rest of the men received treatment. As the ground attack reached its climax, he gallantly directed the final defense until the meager supply of ammunition was exhausted and the position overrun. During the three hours that the outpost was occupied by the enemy, several grenades were thrown into the bunker, which served as protection for Second Lieutenant Skinner and his remaining comrades. Realizing that there was no chance for other than passive resistance, he directed his men to feign death even though the hostile troops entered the bunker and searched their persons. Later, when an enemy grenade was thrown between him and two other survivors, he immediately threw himself on the deadly missile in an effort to protect the others, absorbing the full force of the explosion and sacrificing his life for his comrades. By his indomitable fighting spirit, superb leadership, and great personal valor in the face of tremendous odds, Second Lieutenant Skinner served to inspire his fellow Marines in their heroic stand against the enemy and upheld the highest traditions of the U.S. Naval Service. He gallantly gave his life for his country.

Presentation Date and Details: September 9, 1953, at Marine Corps Barracks, Washington, D.C., presented by Vice President Richard M. Nixon to his parents.

Photo contributed by Ryan Pettigrew, AV Archivist, Richard Nixon Presidential Library and Museum.
VP Nixon (left), father, Sherrod Sr. (middle), and mother, Abigail (right).

Personal remembrance on KoreanWar.org by Emmett Edgar (Ed) Potts on October 11, 2012

I was with Lieutenant Skinner on the night of the Battle Of The Hook. We were in the FO Bunker when the Chinese hit us.

I was a radioman for the 4.2 Mortar Forward Observer by the name of Jim Sloan. I looked out the aperture and saw that the Chinese were about 50 yards from us.

Lieutenant Skinner told me to radio the guns and to fire "Box Me In Fire." He also told his radioman, Frank Roy, to do the same. All hell broke loose, and I was screaming into my radio, "Fire on Our Position," "Fire On Our Position."

Our bunker was being destroyed, and we had to get out. When the incoming and our own guns let up, we dug our way out of the bunker. Outside, we started receiving small arms fire, and the lieutenant was hit but was still on his feet.

We worked our way back to a trench that went down to the Lt's CP bunker. He told us to stay put as he proceeded down to the CP bunker. Our rifles had been buried in the FO bunker, and all Sloan and I had was .45 sidearms and two grenades.

Sloan and I became separated. I proceeded to another bunker, which later I found out was a supply bunker. While taking cover behind the bunker, I was hit in the right knee and left ankle when a round of incoming hit beside me.

Later, I made it down to an Aid Bunker. I was taken back to a Field hospital and was later transferred to the hospital ship at Inchon. I later found out that the Lieutenant and another man were killed when the Lieutenant threw his body on a grenade. I think Roy made it out that night later and survived the war.

Honored with a monument and flagpole at the intersection of Corbin Avenue and Monroe Street, New Britain, Connecticut. Photos by the author.

IN MEMORY OF
SECOND LT. SHERROD EMERSON SKINNER, JR.
UNITED STATES MARINE CORPS RESERVE
OCTOBER 29, 1929 · · · OCTOBER 26, 1952

KILLED IN ACTION IN KOREA AND AWARDED THE CONGRESSIONAL
MEDAL OF HONOR BY THE PRESIDENT OF THE UNITED STATES
FOR CONSPICUOUS GALLANTRY AND INTREPIDITY AT THE RISK
OF HIS LIFE ABOVE AND BEYOND THE CALL OF DUTY.

"BY HIS INDOMITABLE FIGHTING SPIRIT, SUPERB LEADERSHIP AND GREAT
PERSONAL VALOR IN THE FACE OF TREMENDOUS ODDS, SECOND LIEUTENANT
SKINNER SERVED TO INSPIRE HIS FELLOW MARINES IN THEIR HEROIC STAND
AGAINST THE ENEMY AND UPHELD THE HIGHEST TRADITIONS OF THE UNITED
STATES NAVAL SERVICE. HE GALLANTLY GAVE HIS LIFE FOR HIS COUNTRY."

ERECTED BY THE CITIZENS OF NEW BRITAIN,
CONNECTICUT, IN GRATEFUL REMEMBRANCE
OF ALL THOSE WHO GAVE THEIR LIVES IN KOREA.

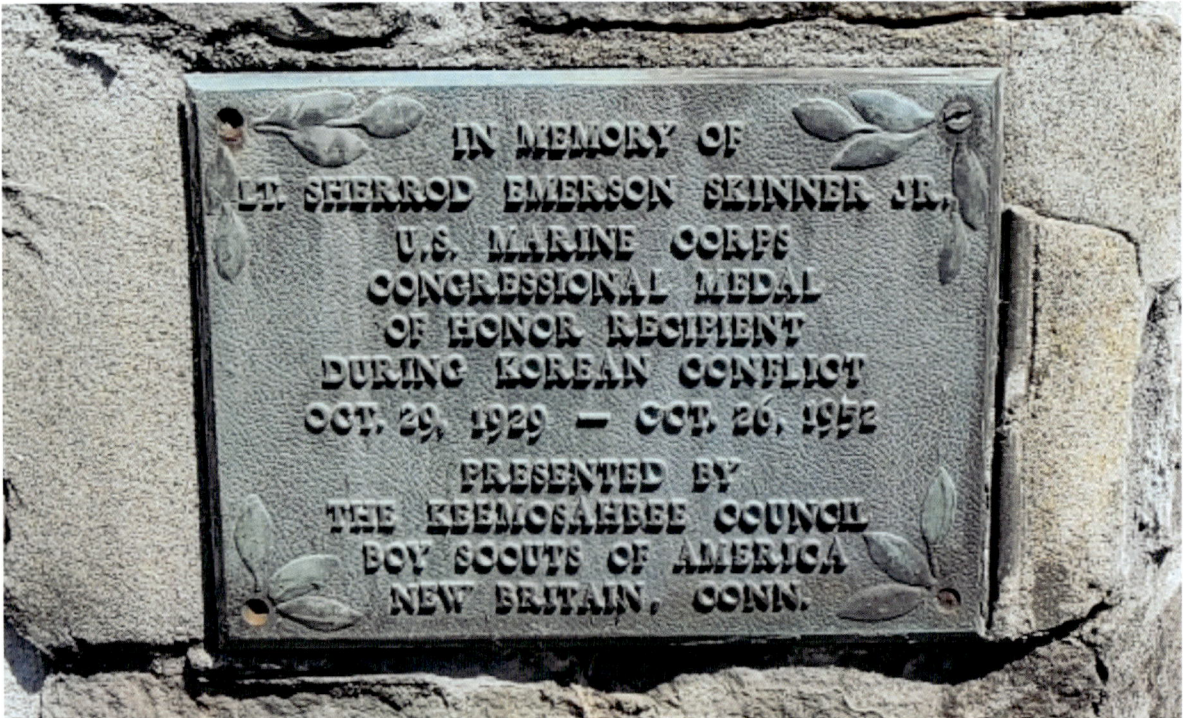

IN MEMORY OF
LT. SHERROD EMERSON SKINNER JR.
U.S. MARINE CORPS
CONGRESSIONAL MEDAL
OF HONOR RECIPIENT
DURING KOREAN CONFLICT
OCT. 29, 1929 — OCT. 26, 1952
PRESENTED BY
THE KEEMOSAHBEE COUNCIL
BOY SCOUTS OF AMERICA
NEW BRITAIN, CONN.

428

PRIVATE FIRST CLASS WILLIAM ADOLPH SODERMAN; ARMY

March 20, 1912 (West Haven, CT) – October 20, 1980 (West Haven, CT); 68 years old
Married to Virginia R. Leake (1917-2003) on June 10, 1939, in West Haven, Connecticut
One son, Peter W. (1945-2022).
One daughter, Susan Soderman Sandrock (1948-1998).
Enlisted on August 23, 1943, in New Haven, Connecticut
Army Serial Number: 31405086

Born to Gustave L. [born in Sweden] (1884-1961) and Anna L. Peterson Soderman [born in Finland] (1893-1972).
One sister, Anna "Florence" Soderman Carlson Johnson (1918-2003).

In e-mails with Jude Soderman Chewning, granddaughter of PFC Soderman, she shared that he built his own home at 35 Sorenson Road in West Haven. "Pop Pop had help from his father-in-law during construction, putting up a few beams in the basement, but, according to my dad, Pop pop built everything else by himself. He also made a lot of their furniture. He made arched doorways leading into the living and dining rooms as well as all the cabinets, a screened porch, etc."

Photos courtesy of the Congressional Medal of Honor Society.

MEDAL OF HONOR CITATION

AWARDED FOR ACTIONS DURING: World War II
BRANCH OF SERVICE: Army
UNIT: Company K, 9th Infantry Regiment, 2nd Infantry Division
GENERAL ORDERS: War Department, General Orders No. 97 (November 1, 1945)
AGE ON THE DAY OF THE EVENT: 32
CITATION:

The President of the United States of America, in the name of Congress, takes pleasure in presenting the Medal of Honor to Private First Class William Adolph Soderman, United States Army, for conspicuous gallantry and intrepidity in action above and beyond the call of duty while serving with Company K, 9th Infantry Regiment, 2nd Infantry Division. Armed with a bazooka, Private First Class Soderman defended a key road junction near Rocherath, Belgium, on 17 December 1944, during the German Ardennes counteroffensive. After a heavy artillery barrage had wounded and forced the withdrawal of his assistant, he heard enemy tanks approaching the position where he calmly waited in the gathering darkness of early evening until the five Mark V tanks which made up the hostile force were within point blank range. He then stood up, completely disregarding the firepower that could be brought to bear upon him, and launched a rocket into the lead tank, setting it afire and forcing its crew to abandon it as the other tanks pressed on before Private First Class Soderman could reload. The daring bazooka man remained at his post all night under severe artillery, mortar, and machinegun fire, awaiting the next onslaught, which was made shortly after dawn by five more tanks. Running along a ditch to meet them, he reached an advantageous point and there leaped to the road in full view of the tank gunners, deliberately aimed his weapon, and disabled the lead tank. The other vehicles, thwarted by a deep ditch in their attempt to go around the crippled machine, withdrew. While returning to his post, Private First Class Soderman, braving heavy fire to attack an enemy infantry platoon from close range, killed at least three Germans and wounded several others with a round from his bazooka. By this time, enemy pressure had made Company K's position untenable. Orders were issued for withdrawal to an assembly area, where Private First Class Soderman was located, when he once more heard enemy tanks approaching. Knowing that elements of the company had not completed their disengaging maneuver and were consequently extremely vulnerable to an armored attack, he hurried from his comparatively safe position to meet the tanks. Once more, he disabled the lead tank with a single rocket, his last, but before he could reach cover, machinegun bullets from the tank ripped into his right shoulder. Unarmed and seriously wounded, he dragged himself along a ditch to the American lines and was evacuated. Through his unfaltering courage against overwhelming odds, Private First Class Soderman contributed in great measure to the defense of Rocherath, exhibiting to a superlative degree the intrepidity and heroism with which American soldiers met and smashed the savage power of the last great German offensive.

Presentation Date and Details: October 12, 1945, at the White House, presented by President Harry S. Truman

William Soderman's Medal of Honor. On display in the West Haven Veterans Museum, 30 Hood Terrace, West Haven, Connecticut. Photo by the author.

Press Release

WAR DEPARTMENT
Bureau of Public Relations
PRESS BRANCH
Tel. RE 7600, Brs. 3425 and 4860

SIS Release C-531

<u>FUTURE RELEASE</u>

An infantry bazooka gunner, Private First Class William A. Soderman of West Haven, Connecticut, has been awarded the Medal of Honor, the War Department announced today, in recognition of outstanding heroism when he stood alone against enemy tanks, knocking out three of them, last December 17 and 18 during the furious German Ardennes counteroffensive.

The 33-year-old Private's heroic action contributed greatly to the defense of Rocherath, Belgium, while his comrades of the 2nd Infantry "Indian Head" Division were fighting a defensive battle against the rejuvenated German army.

Private Soderman's assistant gunner had been wounded during the heavy artillery barrage while the two Company K, 9th Infantry Regiment, soldiers were defending a key road junction leading to the town of Rocherath.

Private Meredith E. Oliver, Route 3, Box 51, Indianapolis, Indiana, was one of two men who observed Private Soderman's gallant stand against Nazi tanks on three separate occasions.

"Rather than abandon his position, even though his assistant was wounded," Private Oliver related, "Private Soderman decided to remain at his post alone to prevent enemy tanks from penetrating the position and endangering the town.

"Soon, five Mark V 'Panther' tanks came into sight, and with utter disregard for his personal safety, Private Soderman stood up when the lead tank was opposite him and fired his bazooka into the bogie wheels, disabling the tank. My companion and I killed the German tank crew as they climbed out of the vehicle.

The daring bazookaman remained at his post all night under severe artillery, mortar, and machinegun fire, awaiting the next onslaught, which came shortly after dawn. The early morning action was described by Private James Shuttleworth, Route 3, Box 149, Grafton, West Virginia, and the other riflemen who witnessed the man versus machine battle.

"The next morning, five more Panther tanks rumbled into view through the fog," Private Shuttleworth revealed. When the lead tank came abreast of Private Soderman, he jumped out on the road and fired point blank, shattering the tracks. I saw the four remaining tanks, unable to get by the wrecked vehicle because of a deep ditch, turn around and head back in the direction from which they came."

"While returning to his post, Private Soderman, braving heavy fire to attack an enemy infantry platoon from close range, killed at least three Germans and wounded several others with a round from his trusty bazooka.

Once more, during that second day, Private Soderman heard enemy tanks approaching. Knowing that elements of his company had not yet completed their withdrawal and were highly vulnerable to an armored attack, the Connecticut Yankee sallied forth once again from his comparatively safe position to meet the tanks. Once more, he disabled the lead tank with a single rocket, his last.

But before he could reach cover, machinegun bullets from the tank ripped into his right shoulder. Unarmed and seriously wounded, Private Soderman dragged himself along a ditch to the American lines.

Privates Oliver and Shuttleworth turned in this report to their commanding officer:

"At no time during our two days with him did Private Soderman show fear but was always grim and determined in his efforts to halt the enemy tanks. All throughout the battle, Private Soderman displayed heroism that far exceeded the deeds of an ordinary soldier. If it were not for his cool and courageous acts, we are certain that our position and probably that of the entire unit would have been overrun."

"The heroic soldier was born March 20, 1912, in West Haven. His wife, Virginia, resides at 548 First Avenue, and his parents, Mr. and Mrs. Gustave Soderman, at 203 First Avenue in West Haven. He entered the Army on September 13, 1943, at Fort Devens, Massachusetts.

Unknown newspaper clipping found in the archives at the Congressional Medal of Honor Society. Used with permission.

MANY MOURN SODERMAN

WEST HAVEN – The telephone rang early Tuesday morning. It was a call Peter Nugent would rather not have received.

Nugent, retired veterans affairs coordinator, is known by thousands of area veterans, having helped many of them obtain military benefits some may never have received without that aid.

One of those soldiers, Private First Class William A. Soderman, who went on to become West Haven's only Congressional Medal of Honor recipient, earning the country's highest military award during the Battle of the Bulge in Belgium in 1944.

A tall, rugged individual and stalwart tackle on the 1931 football team at West Haven High School, Soderman single-handedly defended a key road junction, killed three German soldiers, wounded several others, disabled a lead attack tank, and forced others to take cover and retreat as he fired a bazooka with deadly precision.

Soderman died Monday night in the Veterans Administration Hospital, where he worked for many years. News of his death spread quickly throughout the city, and those who knew him were deeply saddened.

Mayor Robert Johnson ordered the flags in front of City Hall and on the Green flown at half-staff.

"I'm deeply saddened by Bill's death," said Nugent.

A retired member of the Veterans' Administration staff, Nugent recalled his first meeting with Soderman when he appeared before the draft board and was inducted.

Perhaps Nugent remembered best the parade and the thousands of people who turned out on November 4, 1945, to pay tribute to the returning Medal of Honor winner. Nugent served as chairman for the event, "Bill Soderman Day," which was proclaimed by then-First Selectman Elmer Scranton.

The bunting flew on city buildings, and flags flapped in the chilly winds as a steady rain fell, but the clouds did not disrupt the ceremonies and day for a returning hero.

The townspeople, through Nugent, gave Soderman and his wife a substantial monetary gift to get the young couple started on a new life.

President Harry Turman presented the medal at a White House ceremony on October 12, 1945.

Nugent worked with Soderman for 15 years and was responsible for getting him into the Veterans Administration and later assigned to the hospital here.

"He was quiet, unassuming, and shunned publicity," Nugent said Tuesday, his voice choking, "I've lost a real friend."

Johnson said the city is saddened by the loss of our "most famous veteran and leading citizen – Bill Soderman."

Soderman shared a spot on the reviewing stand last Memorial Day with the mayor, and according to Johnson, Soderman said "too much fuss was being made over him," and he was embarrassed.

Those who knew Soderman at the hospital were shocked and saddened by his passing.

Paul Eule, assistant chief of staff there, called Soderman a "loyal veteran and one who was dedicated and did a tremendous job.

"I remember," Eule said, "when Bill was called from Washington, and he didn't want to go to receive his award. It took a lot of effort to make him go."

Everyone who knew Soderman said the same.... – humble, quiet, unassuming, and dedicated.

Soderman made many friends with the community and in his role as an adviser to men in the military, a job for which he was tutored by his closest friend, Nugent.

Funeral services will be private for Mr. Soderman, 68, of 35 Sorenson Road. He was the husband of Virginia Leake Soderman.

A Masonic service by the Annawon Lodge No. 115 AF& AM will be conducted this evening at 7:30 at West Haven Funeral Home at the Green. Burial will be in the family plot in Oak Grove Cemetery, West Haven. Memorial donations may be made to the Masonic Home and Hospital, Wallingford, Connecticut 06492, or to the First Congregational Church of West Haven on the Green Book of Remembrance.

Mr. Soderman was born in West Haven on March 20, 1912, the son of the late Gustave A. and Anna Pettersson Soderman.

Besides his wife, he leaves a son, Peter Soderman of Wallingford; a daughter, Susan L. Soderman of Baltimore, Maryland; a sister, Florence Carlson of New Britain; and two grandchildren.

IN MEMORIAM:
WILLIAM A, SODERMAN, U.S. ARMY-WWII

On Tuesday, October 20, 1980, William Soderman of West Haven, CT, died. The following article, reprinted from the New Haven Register of December 19, 1976, was the last comprehensive interview Soderman granted.

Thirty-two years ago, last Friday, Army Private William A. Soderman sat in a foxhole in a snowy field clutching a bazooka, waiting in silence for the German tanks.

He had no way of knowing that in the next 12 hours, he would earn the Medal of Honor, the Purple Heart, the Bronze Star, the Belgian Croix de Guerre, and the Belgian Order of Leopold.

He waited calmly, thinking about death - his own - and the four remaining bazooka rockets he had.

The silence was broken at sunset with the sound of approaching German tanks. As the first passed only feet away, he jumped from his foxhole and launched a rocket at the lead tank, setting it afire.

Soderman dove back into the foxhole, reloaded, and waited as the remaining tanks withdrew. Hours passed, and shortly before sunrise, the Germans launched their second attack. As five more tanks approached, Soderman ran along a ditch, leaped onto the road, and fired at the first tank, disabling it and again forcing the other tanks to retreat.

Now under infantry fire himself, Soderman ran back to his position. With his third bazooka rocket, he killed at least three German soldiers and wounded others. By now, his company, K of the 9th Infantry, 2nd Infantry Division, had been ordered to retreat, but in the distance, Soderman heard yet more tanks coming.

Knowing his troops were vulnerable, he ran from his safe position and, with his last rocket, blew up the lead tank. Before he reached cover, Nazi machine gun bullets ripped into his right shoulder. Now unarmed and wounded, he dragged himself along the ditch to safety.

Ten months later, on October 12, 1945, civilian William Soderman stood before President Truman to receive the Medal of Honor. His citation praised the veteran for exhibiting "to a superlative degree the intrepidity and heroism with which American soldiers met and smashed the savage power of the last great German invasion."

Now, at age 64, Bill Soderman, retired and happy, remembers back to that long day and night in the field in Belgium as "just another day in my life." He no longer discusses the battle itself. The account of his role in the Battle of the Bulge is reported from a copy of his Medal of Honor citation. An intensely modest man, Soderman says he is proud of his Medal of Honor - "I stood up to what was demanded of me" – but he doesn't let it go to his head.

He marches in Memorial Day parades when invited and occasionally attends veteran's events, but mostly he prefers to stay out of public life. One of the most pleasant Memorial Day parades he recalls was at Lake George, NY, when he stood in the crowd with his family as other soldiers of bygone wars marched through the streets.

He avoids many of the trappings that go along with the Medal. He doesn't give speeches. He rarely makes public appearances. Next month, he will not go to Washington to sit in the Medal of Honor winners' reviewing stand at President-elect Carter's inauguration.

He has made it to Washington only twice since he received his medal from Truman; once for Eisenhower's second inauguration and the other for a party the President gave in May 1963. "These things don't impress me much," he said in his West Haven home this week. "To be a public figure, that's foreign to me. You have to be a glad-hander, and I'm not."

Soderman, a thin man who looks years younger than 64, sees the medal as giving him an opportunity to lead a different kind of life from the one he had before he was drafted in 1943 when he was a butcher. From 1945 until his retirement four years ago, he worked at the VA Hospital, assisting patients in processing claims and helping them secure benefits. Before he earned the medal, he never thought he would hold a desk job.

Since his retirement, Soderman stays close to home with his wife, Virginia, venturing away from West Haven only to visit his children, who now live in Baltimore and Boston. "As I get older, my family comes first," he says.

He credits his earning the medal to some advice given to him years ago by his father, Gustave, who is now dead. Soderman recalls, "My father used to tell me two things: 'Never let it go to your head, and when other people get excited, keep your head.'"

Soderman was born in West Haven on March 20, 1912. He was survived by his wife, son Peter, daughter Susan L., a sister, and two grandchildren. He was buried in the family plot in Oak Grove Cemetery.

Honored with a marker and flagpole on the Veterans Walk of Honor, Bradley Point Park, 469 Captain Thomas Boulevard, West Haven, Connecticut. Dedicated on Sunday, July 1, 1984

William A. Soderman
Congressional Medal of Honor

On December 17, 1944, Pfc. William A. Soderman, of West Haven, Company K, 9th Infantry, 2nd Infantry Division armed with a bazooka, defended a key road junction near Rocherath, Belgium.

As the German artillery barrage pinned down troops around him, Soderman faced five Mark V tanks. "He stood up completely disregarding the fire that could be brought to bear on him..." His rocket dismantled the lead tank.

Near dawn, five more tanks appeared. Running along a ditch, he jumped to the road in full view of the gunners, disabled the lead tank with a rocket and forced the others to withdraw. He then fired another rocket that silenced the machine guns of a nearby German infantry platoon.

Then, after Company K was ordered to fall back under mounting enemy pressure, more tanks moved down the road. Fully exposed, Soderman once again disabled the lead tank with his last rocket. Before he could reach cover, machinegun bullets from the tank ripped into his right shoulder. Unarmed and seriously wounded, he dragged himself along a ditch to the American lines.

For his display of "intrepidity and heroism" Pfc. Soderman received the Congressional Medal of Honor from President Truman during a ceremony at the White House on October 12, 1945.

The three previous photos by the author.

USNS Soderman Naming Ceremony, October 25, 1997, San Diego, California.

With the solemnity befitting the remembrance of a war hero, the USNS William A. Soderman was christened in the shipyard of the National Steel and Shipbuilding Company (NASSCO), San Diego, two weeks ago.

The new ship is the eighth and final "Strategic Sealift" ship to be built by the Navy. The "roll-on, roll-off" ships, as they are called, will be used to transport men and machines when and where necessary.

Sporting a length of 950 feet with a beam of 105 feet, the ships are the largest ever launched down a sliding ways in the United States, according to NASSCO, and the largest to traverse the Panama Canal.

This is technically the second USNS Soderman. The first was a converted liner that was commissioned in October 1997. "That one is going to the Marines," said Virginia "Ginny" Soderman, widow of the city's only Medal of Honor winner.

"This new ship is so big. I felt like a cricket when standing next to it," said Soderman.

Along with Soderman was the couple's niece, Kristina Carlson Fletcher. The nighttime christening had the traditional champagne bottle smashed into the bow. It was then the two women got a perspective on how big the ship was. "We were on a platform 60 feet high," Soderman said. "We had to hit a 'strike box' to get the ship to slide down to the water. It was just so big."

The ceremony was capped off by a fireworks display and celebration, but it was more muted than in 1997. "This had a much more solemn tone to it," said Soderman, "it wasn't like the last one."

She said the ship is now undergoing construction of its fittings and equipment. The christening also served a very practical purpose. "Now that it's in the water, they'll be able to see if there are any leaks or problems, but it's got the name on it," she said excitedly.

Strategic sealift ships are large, medium-speed, roll-on, roll-off vessels (LMSRs). The USNS William A. Soderman boasts more than 390,000 square feet of cargo space. It will be part of the Navy's Military Sealift Command and carry U.S. Army tanks, armored vehicles, tractor-trailers, and other combat equipment and supplies.

The story of Soderman's heroics is legendary. On December 17-18, 1944, near Rocherath, Belgium, he defended a key junction armed only with a bazooka. Soderman remained at his post under severe artillery fire and disabled three German tanks. Despite a shoulder wound, he was able to crawl back to American lines with the help of two companions.

He was awarded the Congressional Medal of Honor on October 12, 1945. Soderman was part of the famed 2nd Infantry Division, stationed at Fort Sam Houston, Texas. It was nicknamed the Indianhead Division.

It was transferred to Ireland in October 1943 and was part of the June 6, 1944, D-Day operation at Normandy's Omaha Beach. Soderman's division was then positioned in Belgium and throughout the famous Battle of the Bulge.

USNS Soderman. Picture courtesy of the Department of Defense

Buried in Oak Grove Cemetery, 881 Campbell Avenue, West Haven, Connecticut; Oakdale Section, Lot A56-1.
Photos by the author.

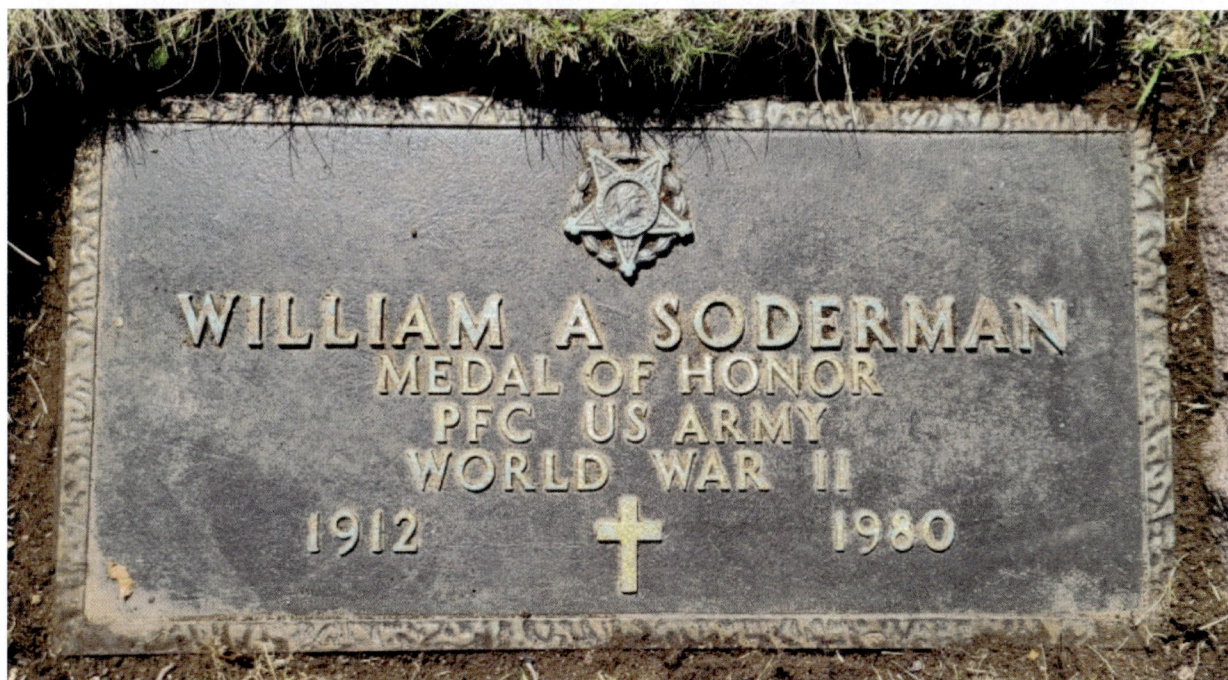

ORDINARY SEAMAN JAMES SULLIVAN*; NAVY

* His name at birth was Peter Van Hoesen. He entered the Navy under the alias of James Sullivan at Danbury, Connecticut. He previously served in the 18th New York Infantry, Company B, and the 7th Connecticut Volunteer Infantry, Company H, as a Private.

January 24, 1831 (Albany County, NY) – May 10, 1918 (South Bethlehem, NY); 90 years old
Married Nancy Acker (1840-1875) in 1858.
Married Charlotte I. Mansfield (1848-1908) in 1875.
Three daughters, Hannah M. Van Hoesen Snyder (1860-1941), Helen J. Van Hoesen Hurst (1867-1942), and Anna
    Van Hoesen (1872-1875).
Three sons, Henry (1863-?), Garret (1865-?), and Peter (1873-?).

Born to John (1795-1860) and Elizabeth Wiedman Van Hoesen (1803-1865). Two brothers, William (1822-1914) and Henry (1836-1913). Two sisters, Elizabeth J. (1837-?) and Catherine (1846-).

Lived in Danbury, Connecticut, and entered the service in October 1863 in Bridgeport, Connecticut; thus, his inclusion in this book.

   After his service in the war, Van Hoesen stopped using the alias James Sullivan and tried to file for his veteran pension. He was denied his pension due to his desertion while he was in the Albany Barracks. He died on May 10, 1918, without ever getting his pension and without recognition for receiving the Medal of Honor, and was buried in Coeymans Hollow Cemetery in Albany, New York. His service in the Civil War was mentioned at his funeral, but nothing about his Medal of Honor. On August 27, 2016, ninety-eight years after he died, he was finally recognized as a Medal of Honor recipient by a new tombstone bearing the Medal of Honor marker.

MEDAL OF HONOR CITATION

AWARDED FOR ACTIONS DURING: Civil War
BRANCH OF SERVICE: Navy
ASSIGNED TO: U.S.S. Agawam
GENERAL ORDERS: War Department, General Orders No. 45 (December 31, 1864)
CITATION:

The President of the United States of America, in the name of Congress, takes pleasure in presenting the Medal of Honor to Ordinary Seaman James Sullivan, United States Navy, for extraordinary heroism in action while serving on board the U.S.S. Agawam as one of a volunteer crew of a powder boat which was exploded near Fort Fisher, North Carolina, 23 December 1864. The powder boat, towed in by the Wilderness to prevent detection by the enemy, cast off and slowly steamed to within 300 yards of the beach. After fuses and fires had been lit and a second anchor with short scope let go to assure the boat's tailing inshore, the crew again boarded the Wilderness and proceeded a distance of 12 miles from shore. Less than two hours later, the explosion took place, and the following day fires were observed still burning at the fort.

Presentation Date and Details: May 12, 1865, off New Bern, North Carolina, on board the U.S.S. Agawam. The others were William Garvin, Robert Montgomery, John Neil, and James Roberts.

U.S.S. Agawam (1864-1867). In the James River, Virginia, July 1864. Photographed by Brady & Company, Washington, D.C. Collection of Surgeon Herman P. Babcock, USN. Donated by his son, George R. Babcock, in 1939. U.S. Naval History and Heritage Command Photograph.

From The Hitching Post, The Newsletter of the Ravena Coeymans Historical Society; Volume 9, Number 2, Summer 2011; Harry A. Sturges

Mr. Donald Morfe, a member of the Medal of Honor Historical Society, contacted me asking for my assistance in locating the burial site of a veteran of the Civil War and possible MOH recipient named Peter Van Hoesen. It was believed that Peter may have been buried in the Coeymans Hollow cemetery, but the society had no actual proof that this was true. Morfe's organization, a not-for-profit volunteer group, devotes its time locating the burial sites of recipients of the Medal of Honor and thereafter, if it had not previously been done, making sure that an appropriate marker is placed on the graves honoring such heroes. It reads,

> *"The Department of Veterans Affairs, upon proper application and with ample proof of identity, after themselves doing due diligence to ascertain the information as accurate, will furnish at no cost to the cemetery a marker to be placed on the grave commemorating the serviceman's designation as a MOH recipient."*

A map of the Coeymans Hollow Cemetery, prepared by the American Legion Post #114 of Ravena, identifies the gravesites of veterans from various wars. Peter Van Hoesen's site was clearly marked, as well as the graves of 23 other Civil War veterans. The Record of Enlistments prepared by Town Clerk John Whitbeck in 1865 lists 137 Civil War veterans from the Town of Coeymans, including 12 who were in the U.S. Navy, 11 who died from disease (mostly in Louisiana), five who died from combat wounds, two deserters, and one who had hired a replacement.

Van Hoesen's gravestone contains the following information: "Peter Van Hoesen, Co. H, Regiment 7, Connecticut Volunteers, Died May 10, 1918, aged 86 years." His wife is buried just to the right of Peter. Her stone reads: "Charlotte Mansfield, wife of Peter Van Hoesen, 1849-1908." The information on his and his wife's gravestone seemed to verify that we had found the correct Peter Van Hoesen, as his military record almost perfectly matched the information on his stone. I say almost because the military has his death as May 9, 1918, instead of May 10.

I took several pictures of the gravestones and e-mailed them to Mr. Morfe. He felt positive enough about the identity that he sent me a copy of the VA's application for a MOH marker. The application was completed with the help of Town Clerk Diane Millious and her staff and with additional assistance from Richard Houghtaling, a town employee working in the Parks Department.

One piece of information missing from Peter Van Hoesen's stone is the fact that, besides serving in the Grand Army of the Republic, he had also served in the U.S. Navy as an Ordinary Seaman. It was during his naval service that he earned the MOH.

Van Hoesen served aboard the U.S.S. Agawan, which was a wooden, double-ended side-wheel gunboat with a complement of 145 officers and men under the command of Commander Alexander Rhind. She was commissioned on March 9, 1864, and left port on May 6, two days after the Army of the Potomac crossed the Rapidan River to begin General Grant's offensive against Richmond. This action was designed to place unrelenting pressure on General Robert E. Lee's Army of Northern Virginia until it was bottled up in the siege of Richmond and possibly forced to surrender. The Agawan performed most of her Civil War service in support of that mission.

Early in July, Lieutenant George Dewey (later Admiral Dewey, the hero of Manila Bay) temporarily relieved the command of the Agawan. It was Lieutenant Dewey's first command. Commander Rhind left the Agawan for a short time to take command of the Louisiana, a steamer selected to perform an unusual and seemingly important task. Rhind took with him a carefully selected small group of volunteers, including Peter, to man this vessel. The Louisiana was towed to Wilmington, North Carolina, for use as a giant bomb against the fortification at Fort Fisher. I can't imagine walking atop that steamer's deck lighting fires and fuses, knowing that any malfunction, one short fuse or one slip, would blow me to kingdom come. The purpose of this dangerous mission was to cause a concussion and/or fire severe enough to detonate the fort's powder magazine, causing mass damage to the fort and heavy casualties to the enemy. Although fires were reported burning at the fort for several days after the blast, the mission failed in its attempt to cause the more desired results. (The above information was taken from various sources located on the web).

For Peter Van Hoesen's act of bravery on that day, December 22, 1864, he was awarded the MOH. On May 12, 1865, the medal presentation ceremony took place aboard the Agawan off New Bern, North Carolina.

There are many websites dedicated to the MOH, including one that lists the names of all MOH recipients. You will not find Peter's name on that list. There is also a site naming all the seamen who served aboard the U.S.S Agawan. You will not find Peter's name on that list, either. His military record lists his name as James Sullivan, aka Peter Van Hoesen, with a notation "deserted." There were a million reasons why men from both sides deserted, and there were thousands and thousands listed as deserters who, in fact, never did so. But that is another story. It appears that after James Sullivan completed his military enlistments, he adopted the named Peter Van Hoesen and lived with that name until his death.

I have no personal information of Peter Van Hoesen or his wife, Charlotte. I do not know exactly where his home was when he died, what he did for a living, if he had children, or know why he and his wife were buried in the Coeymans Hollow Cemetery.

I do know that he was an infantry soldier in the Grand Army of the Republic, an ordinary seaman in the U.S. Navy, and a recipient of the Medal of Honor, the highest award for valor in action against an enemy our country bestows. For that, I honor him.

From PorcupineSoup.com, an online digital newspaper, September 30, 2021; Tracing Your Roots in Greene County: Civil War hero Peter Van Hoesen; written by Sylvia Hasenkopf, historian, North River Research.

It was December 23, 1864, a dark, murky night off the coast of North Carolina, when a volunteer crew from the U.S.S. Agawam boarded the U.S.S. Louisiana. They set the fuses and kindled a fire in the aft of the boat, escaping in small boats afterward. The hopes were that the explosion of this "powder boat" would destroy Confederate Fort Fisher or, at the very least, create enough damage that Union soldiers would be in a position to easily take the fort.

For his efforts that night, Ordinary Seaman James Sullivan of the U.S.S. Agawam received a Congressional Medal of Honor on May 12, 1865, aboard the U.S.S. Agawam as it was stationed off New Bern, North Carolina.

The only problem was that James Sullivan really wasn't James Sullivan at all. His real name was Peter Van Hoesen, who hailed from the Town of Bethlehem in New York.

I first became aware of Peter Van Hoesen when Rick Shanks, the senior vice commander of Ravena Unitas Memorial VFW Post 9594, sent me an email. He advised me that he had been working with the Medal of Honor Historical Society to replace the headstone of Peter Van Hoesen with one noting that Peter was a recipient of the Medal of Honor.

Rick passionately wanted to right a wrong that was done to Peter.

Peter Van Hoesen's story is one of youthful patriotism, of fear, and of redemption. It's a tale that has not been told in its entirety before, but one I hope to rectify with this article.

Peter Van Hoesen was the son of John Van Hoesen and his wife, Elizabeth Wademan, of the Town of Bethlehem. According to his Civil War Muster Roll abstract, he was born in Albany on January 24, 1831. He was 5 feet and 5 inches in height, with black hair, dark eyes, and a dark complexion. At the time he enlisted in the Civil War, he was a carpenter.

He was raised in the Town of Bethlehem with his sister, Elizabeth, who was two years younger, and his brother, Henry, who was four years younger, although I have not yet determined exactly where in the Town the family resided.

In the 1850 census, Peter's father was already aged 55, and Peter's wife was 47. A young child, Catharine Van Hoesen, aged 4, is listed before Peter and his siblings. I suspect that Catharine may be a second wife and Catharine, her daughter. It is also quite possible that young Catharine is their youngest child or even a grandchild. More research is definitely needed on the earlier days of the family.

It appears that the Van Hoesen family was relatively poor. There is no profession listed for John in the census, nor is there any indication that he owned any real estate. Peter, on the other hand, was already working as a farmer, most likely on someone else's farm. Only 12-year-old Henry had attended school in the previous twelve months.

I found the Van Hoesen family in the 1855 census, still in the Town of Bethlehem. Peter is no longer in the household, and I was unable to track down his location. By this time, Peter is 24 years old. He may have gone west or was simply working elsewhere. With the name Van Hoesen, one finds numerous spelling variations in all the official documents, which complicated tracking him in the censuses.

Peter married Nancy Acker in 1858 when she was just 18 years old. She was someone he would have known fairly well. She and her parents, Henry and Hannah Acker, are enumerated, with younger children, in the same neighborhood as the Van Hoesen household.

Nancy Van Hoesen, aged 20, appeared in the 1860 census, working as a servant in the household of farmer Stephen Baumer in Bethlehem Center. There is no sign of Peter, and again, I have been unable to locate him in the census. Nancy soon became pregnant, however. Her daughter, Hannah, was born in May 1861.

The national elections in the year 1860 were fractious, with passionate advocates on both sides of the contentious issue of the expansion of slavery to the western territories presenting their entrenched viewpoints.

The Republican platform was clear; they did not support slavery in the western territories and barely recognized the rights of the existing southern states rights to have slavery within their borders.

Abraham Lincoln, a Republican, won the national election that year, which set the southern states on edge. Their cotton-based economies were dependent on the institution of slavery and the cheap field labor it provided.

Before Lincoln could be sworn into office in March 1861, seven southern states, led by South Carolina, seceded from the United States of America to form the Confederacy. Mississippi, Florida, Alabama, Georgia, Louisiana, and Texas joined South Carolina in their defiance of Washington D.C. and the Republican policies of President-elect Abraham Lincoln.

The Civil War began in earnest when Confederate soldiers attacked Fort Sumter on April 12, 1861, a key federal fort on the Atlantic coast in South Carolina.

Peter enlisted in the 18th Infantry Regiment, NYV [New York Volunteers] on April 24, 1861, in Albany for a 2-year term, very likely looking for a steady income for his young family. Peter was mustered into Co. B as a private on May 17, 1861. He was paid $8.48 for the period April 24 to May 17, 1861.

The Regiment left New York State on June 19, 1861, arriving in Washington, D.C., on the 21st. The 18th joined the 2nd Brigade, 5th Division, Army of Northeastern Virginia on July 13th and began the march in search of Confederate forces.

There was a strong belief amongst the northern soldiers that the rebellious southern army would be crushed in their first engagement with northern troops. It was expected to be a short and decisive war. Spirits were high, and the troops, mostly fresh-faced young men, were eager for their first taste of battle.

The 18th encountered the enemy on Braddock Rd., at Fairfax Station, and at Blackburn's Ford between July 16th and 18th, with minimal casualties and only one death. The first true taste of war was experienced by the men of the 18th on July 21st at the First Battle of Bull Run, also called the First Manassas.

The First Battle of Bull Run has the distinction of being the first battle of the Civil War. The Union army fielded 18,000 poorly led and poorly trained troops against an equally untrained force of Confederate soldiers. Strategic errors on the side of the Union led to a resounding defeat on the battlefield.

As the Confederate Army advanced, Union soldiers panicked, broke ranks, and fled back towards Washington, D.C.

The Union Army suffered the loss of 2,708 soldiers - 481 killed in action, 1,011 wounded, and 1,216 missing. The Confederate Army's loss of 1,982 soldiers was slightly less - 387 killed in action, 1,582 wounded, and 13 missing. The 18th NYV had seen service that day as support for the artillery units on the field and had suffered no casualties.

The Union Army finally realized that defeating the south would not be as easy as they had originally thought.

Private Peter Van Hoesen was promoted to the rank of Corporal in October 1861.

The 18th regrouped in Alexandria, VA, and established winter quarters were near Fairfax Seminary, where the regiment was involved in the construction of Fort Ward over the winter.

It wasn't until late June 1862 that the men of the 18th were themselves tested in battle.

The Union Army of the Potomac had marched steadily toward the Confederate capital, Richmond, hoping to force a decisive battle and end the war. Initially, the Confederate Army was led by General Joseph E. Johnson, known as a relatively cautious battle commander. Wounded in the Battle of Seven Pines, Johnson was replaced with the far more aggressive Confederate General Robert E. Lee, who reorganized his troops and prepared for an offensive campaign.

Union Major General George B. McLellan was also well-known as a cautious commander. When faced with the tactical strength of Lee's Confederate troops, he moved his northern troops into defensive positions, and the Union Army began to retreat down the Virginia Peninsula. Lee's troops were hot on their trail.

Six major battles, known as the Seven Days Battles (or the First Battle of Cold Harbor), occurred over the period of June 25 to July 1, 1862, near Richmond, VA. The 18th Regiment participated in the battles at Gaines' Mills, Garnett's and Golding's Farms, Glendale, and Malvern Hill.

It was at Gaines' Mills, however, that the troops of the 18th Regiment experienced their first major casualties. Two officers were killed, along with 17 enlisted men. One officer and one enlisted man died of their wounds.

Over the course of the Seven Days Battles, an additional 3 officers and 58 enlisted men were wounded yet recovered from their injuries. Tellingly, however, 1 officer and 42 enlisted were missing at the end of the last battle.

There is no question that the men of the 18th were in the thick of battle and realized the mortality of their lives.

At the end of the Seven Days Battle, McClellan's army, which was in full retreat down the Virginia Peninsula, suffered 16,000 casualties. Lee's army, which had been on the offensive the whole time, lost over 20,000 men.

According to Rick Shanks, Peter Van Hoesen was demoted during the Peninsula Campaign for reasons unknown. He participated in one more skirmish at Burke's Station, VA, on August 28th before walking away from his regiment on September 6th, 1862, at Alexandria, VA.

We will likely never know the real reason Peter left his regiment. Was he afraid? Was he angry at his demotion? Was he embarrassed to serve with his fellow soldiers after his demotion? Was he simply missing his young wife and baby? Regardless, he walked home to Bethlehem.

Desertion was a hanging offense during the Civil War. Anyone could capture a deserter and hand him over to the authorities. Somehow, local authorities were advised that Peter had deserted. He was captured on July 2, 1863, in New Scotland, NY, not far from his hometown, and was taken to Albany. He escaped his detention three days later, on July 5th, and fled to New York City, where he could be lost amongst the throngs of people living there.

Nancy was pregnant with the couple's second child, Henry, who was born in December of that year.

Peter could have stayed in New York City for the duration of the war, waiting for the war to end. Instead, a chance meeting with James Sullivan, who had been drafted, changed the course of Peter's life. James was not interested in becoming a soldier and convinced Peter to assume his identity and enlist on his behalf.

Peter received $300 at his enlistment as James Sullivan, although it is unclear whether James paid him this money to assume his identity or whether this was bounty money paid at the time of enlistment. Regardless, this would have been welcome money for Nancy and the children back in Bethlehem.

Peter traveled to Connecticut, and on October 24, 1863, as James Sullivan enlisted in the 7th Regiment Connecticut Volunteer Infantry, who, with the 7th New Hampshire Volunteer Regiment, formed the 77th New England.

Peter stated in his pension records that his new regiment knew of his subterfuge and his real name, yet no one seemed to be bothered by it.

In April 1864, Peter was transferred to the Navy and was stationed on the U.S.S. Agawam. Was it his guilt for having deserted the 18th Regiment that led Peter to volunteer for the dangerous mission to sink the powder boat, the U.S.S. Louisiana? Had Peter merely found an environment and fellow sailors that simply inspired his patriotism? No records survive to tell the tale of why or how Peter came to volunteer for the mission.

Fort Fisher, NC, was a Confederate fort which protected the shipping lanes into Wilmington, NC, so vital for the Confederate war effort. British smugglers, known as blockade runners, would bring in important supplies for the Confederacy, including munitions, clothing, and food. Cotton and tobacco would be smuggled out to pay for these foreign goods.

The Union knew that the key to success was to choke off the flow of supplies so desperately needed by the Confederate Army. Fort Fisher's defenses needed to be neutralized. The problem was that the Fort was well-built, and a land assault was expected to be long and costly.

The U.S.S. Louisiana was built in 1861 and was a propeller-driven iron hull steamer. The plan was to strip her, load her hull with explosives, tow the powder-laden boat under cover of darkness as close to the walls of the fort as possible, and detonate her. Naval ordnance experts were not in favor of the idea.

The U.S.S. Wilderness towed the U.S.S. Louisiana into position, about 300 yards offshore from the walls of the fort, late in the evening of December 23rd. Captain Rhind from the U.S.S. Agawam and his volunteer crew, including Peter, were aboard the Louisiana.

Once the fuses and fires were lit, the volunteer crew boarded the small skiffs attached to the U.S.S. Louisiana and rowed back to the Wilderness, anchored a safe distance away.

In his report of the mission, Captain Rhind wrote, "When all was fairly done, we observed that the vessel would not tail inshore, and therefore let go another anchor with short scope. We then took to the boat and reached the Wilderness in safety at precisely midnight, slipped her anchor, and steamed out at full speed, reaching in less than an hour a point about 12 miles distant from the powder boat, when we hove to and ran our steam down."

"At precisely 1:40 a.m., the explosion took place, the shock being hardly felt, and four distinct reports heard. What result was occasioned near the vessel we can only estimate by the feeble fire of the forts the next day. My opinion is that owing to the want of confinement and insufficient fuzing of the mass, much of the powder was blown away before ignition and its effect lost."

The mission was a failure. Nonetheless, the volunteer crew was hailed as heroes and was awarded the Congressional Medal of Honor.

The Medal of Honor was first awarded during the Civil War. Initially, a medal bestowed upon Navy personnel, legislation was signed into law on July 12, 1862, to include the Army troops.

Of the 3,464 Medals of Honor awarded to date, just under half, 1,522, were awarded during the Civil War. Regardless, it was a high honor to be the recipient of this prestigious award.

Peter returned home to Bethlehem and resumed his life as Peter Van Hoesen. He and Nancy would have four more children: Garrett, born in 1865, who died as an infant, Helen Jane, born in 1867; Anna, born in 1872; and Peter, born in 1873.

Nancy died on April 17, 1875, from consumption and was buried in Mt. Pleasant Cemetery in South Bethlehem. Her two-year-old daughter, Anna, had died of the disease two months earlier, on February 20, 1875. Peter was left alone to raise his surviving children, 14-year-old Hannah, 8-year-old Helen Jane, and his two-year-old son, Peter.

On June 20, 1875, Peter was enumerated in the Town of Coeymans, living alone in the household of Ambrose Halsted and working as a farm laborer.

Peter married Charlotte Isabella, the daughter of Jacob and Margaret Mansfield, on September 6, 1875, at the Coeymans Dutch Reformed Church. The couple would have no children. Hannah and Helen Jane married and established households of their own. Young Peter Van Hoesen, however, was admitted to the Albany Orphan Asylum on May 8, 1879, at the tender age of 6 and was never heard from again.

On August 4, 1886, Peter Van Hoesen applied for an invalid's pension, which was approved. He made no secret, at the time, that his alias was James Sullivan.

Peter's name appears as one of the founding members of A.O. Bliss Post 305, Grand Army of the Republic in New Baltimore. Peter used his real name in the application, indicating that he had served in the Navy.

In the 1890 Veteran's Schedule, Peter appeared on the Soldiers and Seaman Schedule, stating that his disability began when he was shot in the head. He also stated that he was discharged from the Navy on April 27, 1865, after serving 1 year, 6 months, and 8 days. I have not discovered how nor when his injury occurred.

Peter lived a long life, outliving his second wife, Charlotte, who died in 1908. He moved back to the Town of Bethlehem after her death and eventually moved in with his eldest daughter, Hannah, her husband, George Snyder, and their large family.

Peter died on May 9, 1918, in his 87th year, and was laid to rest beside his second wife in the Coeyman's Hollow Cemetery.

His tombstone noted that he had served in the 7th Connecticut Volunteer Regiment. No notation was made that he had served in the 18th Regiment NYV, nor was there any mention of his Medal of Honor.

Further to the Act of February 6, 1907, Peter Van Hoesen was awarded a pension of $20 per month, effective April 18, 1907. He was listed as an Army Invalid, having served as Private James Sullivan in the 7th Connecticut Volunteer Regiment and also as an Ordinary Seaman aboard the U.S.S. Agawan. His pension was increased to $30 effective June 11, 1912, and $40 effective June 10, 1918.

Rick Shanks noted that the long arm of the government finally made the connection that James Sullivan was the Peter Van Hoesen who had deserted from the 18th Regiment NYV and stopped his pension payments.

On August 27, 2016, a new marker was installed beside Peter's old gravestone. It proudly indicated that he had served in both regiments and was a Medal of Honor recipient. A moving 30-minute ceremony followed the unveiling of the new gravestone. Kudos go out to Rick Shanks and the other members of the VFW Post 9595 from Ravena and the National Medal of Honor Society for their perseverance and dedication to this project.

Finally, Peter had received the due recognition he deserved.

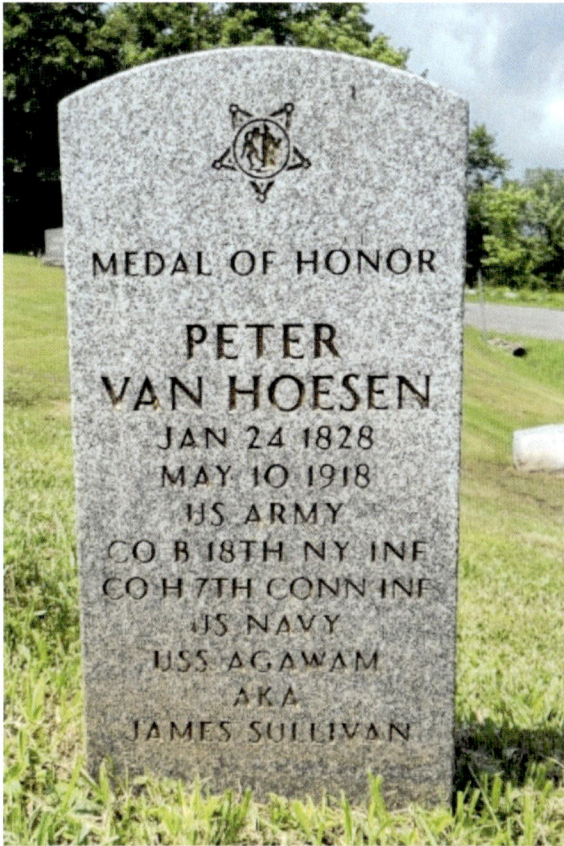

BREVET BRIGADIER GENERAL FREDERIC WILLIAM SWIFT; ARMY

January 30, 1831 (Mansfield Center, CT) – January 30, 1916 (Detroit, MI); 85 years old

Married Mary A. Bradford (1836-1872) on November 6, 1855

Children by Mary: Four daughters, Ann "Annie" K. Swift Burt (1859-1939), Louise B. Swift Robbins (1867-1906), Mary (1869-?), and Caroline "Carrie" B. (1870-1951). One son, Frederick W. Jr. (1865-1865).

Married Ella B. Hollbrook (1847-) on January 21, 1874, in Detroit, Michigan

Children by Ella: Two daughters, May R. Swift Dingwall (1874-1942) and Frederika W. (1891-1969). Two sons, Bradford H. (1877-1936) and Stanley H. (1878-1949).

Enlisted as a Captain on July 29, 1862, in Detroit, Michigan.

Captured on May 12, 1964, at the Battle of Spotsylvania Court House, Virginia, and held in Macon, Georgia.

Discharged on June 3, 1865.

Born to Dr. Earl (1784-1869) and Laura Ripley Swift (1792-1870). Brothers, Albert E. (1811-1864), Ralph (1822-1879), James D. (1825-1842), Henry F. (1829-1899), and Rowland (1834-1902). Sisters Harriet B. Swift Adams (1813-1899), Alathea H. Swift Newbury (1815-1884), Laura R. Swift Southworth (1818-1874), and Sarah F. Swift Adams (1823-1903).

Photo from FindAGrave.com

MEDAL OF HONOR CITATION

AWARDED FOR ACTIONS DURING: Civil War
BRANCH OF SERVICE: Army
UNIT: 17th Michigan Infantry
DATE OF ISSUE AND PRESENTATION: February 15, 1897 (34 years later)
AGE ON THE DAY OF THE EVENT: 31
CITATION:

The President of the United States of America, in the name of Congress, takes pleasure in presenting the Medal of Honor to Lieutenant Colonel Frederic William Swift, United States Army, for extraordinary heroism on 16 November 1863 while serving with the 17th Michigan Infantry, in action at Lenoire Station, Tennessee. Lieutenant Colonel Swift gallantly seized the colors and rallied the regiment after three Color Bearers had been shot and the regiment, having become demoralized, was in imminent danger of capture.

From the Detroit Free Press January 31, 1916

COL F.W. SWIFT DIES ON BIRTHDAY; ONCE POSTMASTER

Heart Trouble Takes Detroiter at 85; Was Civil War Veteran

Colonel Frederic William Swift, one-time postmaster of Detroit and a resident of the city for 69 years, died Sunday at his residence in the Garden Court Apartments at 870 Jefferson Avenue.

Sunday was Colonel Swift's eighty-fifth birthday. Until three weeks ago, he had been in fairly good health. Valvular heart trouble was the cause of death.

Colonel Swift was the Postmaster of Detroit from 1866 to 1874. This was almost immediately after he returned from the Civil War, in which he held the post of Colonel of the Seventeenth Michigan Infantry.

He was born in Mansfield, Connecticut, and came to Detroit when he was 16 years old. For many years, he was in the drug business in the city, being a senior member of the firm of Swift & Dodds. In later years, he was in the insurance business and, for several years, had been retired.

Colonel Swift was twice married, his second wife being Miss Ella Holbrook, a sister of Mrs. Franklin H. Walker.

He is survived by his widow, four daughters, and two sons. The daughters are Miss Caroline Swift, Mrs. Judson Burt, Mrs. Enos L. McMillan of Detroit, and Mrs. Har R. Dingwall of Walkerville. The sons are Bradford H. Swift of Fremont, Ohio, and Stanley H. Swift of Amsterdam, New York.

Colonel Swift was a member of the Loyal Legion and was the Recorder of the local branch at the time of his death.

The funeral services will be held Tuesday afternoon at 2 o'clock in the chapel of Elmwood Cemetery, where the interment will be made.

SECOND LIEUTENANT RALPH TALBOT; MARINE CORPS

January 6, 1897 (South Weymouth, MA) – October 25, 1918; 20 years old
Unmarried
Enlisted in September 1917

Born to Richard J. Sr. (1860-1915) and Mary A. O'Connell Talbot [born in Canada] (1863-1946). Three brothers, Henry E. (1886-1887), Arthur R. (1895-1903), John O. (1900-1981), Richard J. Jr. (1901-1904), and Harold A. (1903-1905). Three sisters, Jennie E. (1888-1900), Catherine G. (1889-1905), Alys L. Talbot Hall Kimmy (1891-1988), and Louise (1897-1902).

RALPH TALBOT
"DICK"

Class Pin Committee, chairman; Class Orator, Class Ode, Debate, Capt.; Track 1 2, 3, 4, Capt.; President of Union, School Paper 1, 2, 3; Year Book, Editor-in-chief, 4; Baseball 3, 4; Football 2, 3, 4; Class Basketball 1, 2, 3, 4.

We have before us a man young in years, but old in thought. He is the orator of his class and many are the novel orations that he has made in the class room. They say he is some ball player, especially in handing out alibis to his team mates. Wherever you see him, in the school corridor, on the athletic field or in the class room, he is always kicking something or somebody. He likes to talk and his fellow class mates believe that he will be a second Henry Clay. Dick, old boy, you should make your mark in the world, but you may feel assured that you have our best wishes for the prosperous years which must follow you.

Weymouth High School, Weymouth, Massachusetts, Class of 1915 yearbook

---

Ralph Talbot
South Weymouth, Mass.
"Ralph," "Dick"

Marshall, Debating Team, '16; Cross Country, '15; Fifteen, '16; Lit Board, '16; *News* Board, '16; Track Team, '16; KARUX, '16.

"The word impossible is not in my dictionary."

Ralph is one of the privileged few that have earned their diplomas in one year, and he has not limited himself to this task alone, although it is no trifling undertaking. Indeed he has shone on every newspaper board in school, he is one of our foremost debaters, is an excellent trackman, and he is an exceptional student. And modesty is his middle name!

Talbot hails from New England, and he is a New Englander to the backbone. But strange to say he is not going to Amhuhst, Dahtmouth or Hahvahd. He is going to Jale.

His success in school is due to three things; ambition, pluck, and earnest working, and we are confident that these same qualities will spell success for him in whatever enterprise he undertakes.

YALE

Ralph Talbot

Photo courtesy of Doug Smith, Archivist, Mercersburg Academy, Mercersburg, Pennsylvania.

Photo courtesy of Ancestry.com

Photo courtesy of Ancestry.com

MEDAL OF HONOR CITATION

AWARDED FOR ACTIONS DURING: World War I
BRANCH OF SERVICE: Marine Corps
UNIT: Airplane Squadron C, First Marine Aviation Force
CITATION:

The President of the United States of America, in the name of Congress, takes pride in presenting the Medal of Honor (Posthumously) to Second Lieutenant Ralph Talbot, United States Marine Corps, for exceptionally meritorious service and extraordinary heroism while attached to Squadron C, First Marine Aviation Force, in France. Second Lieutenant Talbot participated in numerous air raids into enemy territory. On 8 October 1918, while on such a raid, he was attacked by nine enemy scouts and, in the fight that followed, shot down an enemy plane. Also, on 14 October 1918, while on a raid over Pittham, Belgium, Second Lieutenant Talbot and another plane became detached from the formation on account of motor trouble and were attacked by 12 enemy scouts. During the severe fight that followed, his plane shot down one of the enemy scouts. His observer was shot through the elbow, and his gun jammed. Second Lieutenant Talbot maneuvered to gain time for his observer to clear the jam with one hand and then returned to the fight. The observer fought until shot twice, once in the stomach and once in the hip, and then collapsed, Second Lieutenant Talbot attacked the nearest enemy scout with his front guns and shot him down. With his observer unconscious and his motor failing, he dived to escape the balance of the enemy and crossed the German trenches at an altitude of 50 feet, landing at the nearest hospital to leave his observer and then returning to his aerodrome.

AUTHOR NOTES: The medal was sent to his mother on the day it was awarded, November 11, 1920. Both Lieutenant Talbot and his gunner, Gunnery Sergeant (later to be promoted to 1st Lieutenant) Robert Guy Robinson (pictured below), were awarded the Medal of Honor. Gunnery Sergeant Robinson survived the war and died on October 5, 1974, and is buried in Arlington National Cemetery, Section 46, Grave 390.

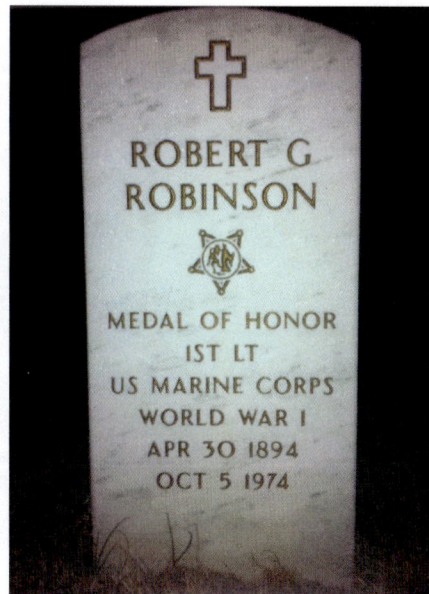

Seventeen days after the incident resulting in Lieutenant Talbot being awarded the Medal of Honor, his DH-4 crashed on takeoff during an engine test flight at Le Fresne Aerodrome in France. There was engine trouble; the machine failed on the takeoff, crashed into a high embankment, and instantly burst into flames. All efforts to extricate Lieutenant Talbot were in vain.

Riding with Lieutenant Talbot was Second Lieutenant Colgate W. Darden, Jr. He was in the observer's cockpit, was thrown clear of the wreck, and seriously injured. In WWI, he served with the French Army in 1916 and 1917 and later as a Lieutenant in the United States Marine Corps Air Service. After the war, he studied law, graduating from the University of Virginia at Charlottesville in 1922 and from Columbia University, New York City, in 1923. He was a member of the Virginia State House of Delegates from 1930 to 1933 and was elected as a Democrat to the Seventy-third and Seventy-fourth Congresses, March 4, 1933 to January 3, 1937. Reelected to the Seventy-sixth and

Seventy-seventh Congresses, serving from January 3, 1939, until his resignation on March 1, 1941, to become a candidate for Governor. He served as Governor of Virginia from January 21, 1942, to January 16, 1946, and as president of the University of Virginia at Charlottesville from June 23, 1947 to September 1, 1959. In 1955, he was a United States delegate to the Tenth General Assembly of the United Nations and, in 1960, accepted a presidential appointment to the Commission on National Goals. His last public office was in 1961 as chairman for the Commission on Goals for Higher Education in Norfolk, Virginia. Colgate Darden Jr. died at 84 years old in Norfolk, Virginia, and is buried in the family estate in Southampton, Virginia.

The honorary namesake of the destroyer U.S.S. Ralph Talbot (DD-390) in 1936. The *Ralph Talbot* (DD-390) was laid down on October 28, 1935, at the Boston Navy Yard and launched on October 31, 1936. The ship was sponsored by Mrs. Mary Talbot, mother of 2nd Lt Ralph Talbot, and then commissioned on October 14, 1937, with Lieutenant Commander Harry R. Thurber in command. The Talbot was anchored at Pearl Harbor on December 7, 1941, and served in the Pacific Theater during World War II, from the attack on Pearl Harbor through the battle of Okinawa, earning 14 battle stars for her service.

Ralph Talbot School and Ralph Talbot Street in Weymouth, Massachusetts.

An article published in The Patriot Ledger, Quincy, Massachusetts, in April 2017, titled 'Fascinating' new insight gained into Ralph Talbot. Used with permission.

WEYMOUTH - Eileen Dumont was happy to share what she knew about Ralph Talbot when a resident of a small Belgian town reached out to her several years ago for information about the World War I pilot and Medal of Honor recipient.

Paul Callens had briefly heard about Talbot's heroic actions in the skies above Pittem, Belgium, but he couldn't find much research on the U.S. Marine from Weymouth.

So Callens contacted the New England Historic Genealogical Society, which pointed him to Dumont, then a member of the Weymouth Historical Society.

Little did Dumont know that Callens' quest for information on Talbot would spur her to visit the Marine Corps archives in Quantico, Virginia, Mercersburg Academy in Pennsylvania, and ultimately join Callens in meeting members of the Talbot family in New Hampshire.

"(Callens') enthusiasm is infectious, and he is just so jolly – nobody could say no to him," Dumont said. "What I found is never-before-seen pictures and letters offering new insight into (Talbot). For anyone interested in history at all, it's very fascinating."

Dumont and Callens will present joint exhibits – she at Tufts Library in Weymouth and him in Pittem – on Thursday, May 25. They will highlight their findings on Talbot and his gunner, Robert Guy Robinson, who also received the Medal of Honor. Artwork by students from both Pittem and Weymouth's Ralph Talbot School will be displayed.

In the final days of the war, Talbot and Robinson were among the first Americans to fight alongside Royal Air Force squadrons over Belgium.

On Oct. 8, 1918, the two shot down one of nine enemy scouts that attacked them on a mission. Six days later, they became separated from their squadron over Pittem and were attacked by 12 enemy planes. Robinson was shot more than a dozen times, and the plane's motor failed, but they managed to shoot down one of the enemy planes. Talbot then flew a gravely wounded Robinson to a hospital.

Talbot was killed in a plane crash on October 25, 1918. Robinson survived his injuries and died at home in Michigan in 1974. Talbot was posthumously awarded the nation's highest military honor. He is one of five Weymouth men to earn the Medal of Honor.

Callens first heard about Talbot and Robinson during a Memorial Day event in Belgium, but he could find little information on the actions of the two American flyers. He later realized that the town's name was typically written "Pitthem" prior to the 1930s, which was changed to "Pittham" in many documents.

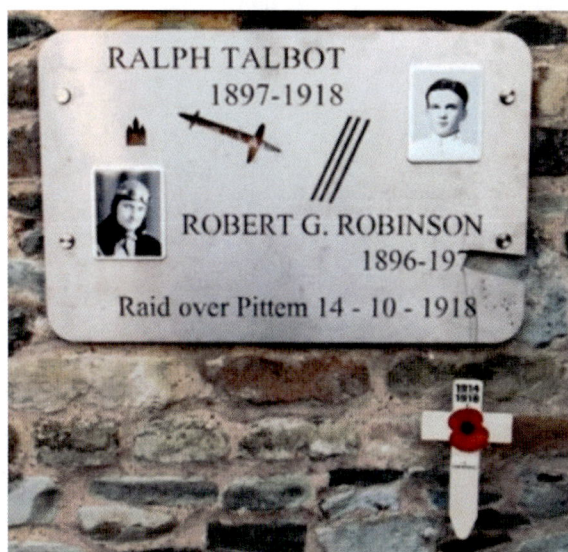

Dumont initially pointed Callens to old periodicals and provided him with details about Talbot's life as a Yale graduate, gifted orator, and aspiring poet, a young man who excelled in sports and academics. She even helped him locate Talbot's family members.

On Veterans Day in 2014, the town of Pittem put up a plaque on a church honoring Talbot and Robinson.

But Dumont's involvement didn't end there. In March of 2015, she traveled to Mercersburg Academy in Pennsylvania, a boarding school Talbot attended, and the Marine Corps archives in Quantico, Virginia, to locate Ralph Talbot's papers. She got to see and copy condolence letters, Talbot's school writings, and a scrapbook his mother had put together and donated.

"I met with different archivists, and it was really so interesting and so much fun," Dumont said. "Some people go to Vegas; I go to Quantico, Virginia."

Last summer, Callens and his family made the trek to America. Dumont joined them in touring Weymouth, seeing Talbot's grave in Mount Wollaston Cemetery, and visiting Ralph Talbot's nephew, Richard Talbot, and other extended family in New Hampshire.

"Meeting the family was wonderful," Dumont said. "They were really so pleased that people cared enough this long after the fact."

With the nation this month marking the centennial of its entrance into World War I, Dumont hopes people will take time to learn about a Weymouth native who earned the country's highest honor.

Photos of Lt Talbot's Medal of Honor were contributed by Owen Linlithgow Conner, Curatorial Section Chief, Uniforms & Heraldry, National Museum of the Marine Corps.

Front of Medal of Honor

Back of Medal of Honor.

The inscription reads

Awarded To Second Lieutenant Ralph Talbot
United States Marine Corps
Pittham, Belgium
October 14, 1918

Initially buried in Les Baraques Cemetery, Sangatte, Calais, France; Plot 45, Row B, Grave 43. His remains were repatriated and buried in Mount Wollaston Cemetery, 20 Sea Street, Quincy, Massachusetts; Old Section, Lot 22, Grave 9. Photos by the author.

SERGEANT EUGENE MORTIMER TINKHAM; ARMY

April 19, 1842 (Sprague, CT) – October 2, 1909 (Springfield, MA); 67 years old

Married Anna Jordan (1838-1910) on March 8, 1874, in Ephratah, New York

Enlisted on August 28, 1862, in Waterloo, New York.

Wounded on June 3, 1864, in Cold Harbor, Virginia.

Discharged on June 22, 1865, in Richmond, Virginia.

Born to Welcome E. (1805-1863) and Sarah L. King Tinkham (1814-1901). Four sisters, Susan E. (1835-1927), Sarah L. Tinkham Blakely (1838-1914), Martha L. Tinkham Berkshire (1841-1936), Alice C. (1846-1864). Three brothers, Albert F. (1849-1923), Edwin T. (1851-1929), and Frederick (1854-1864).

Photo courtesy of the Congressional Medal of Honor Society

MEDAL OF HONOR CITATION

AWARDED FOR ACTIONS DURING: Civil War
BRANCH OF SERVICE: Army
UNIT: Company H, 148th New York Infantry
DATE OF ISSUE AND PRESENTATION: April 5, 1898 (34 years later)
AGE ON THE DAY OF THE EVENT: 22
CITATION:

The President of the United States of America, in the name of Congress, takes pleasure in presenting the Medal of Honor to Corporal Eugene M. Tinkham, United States Army, for extraordinary heroism on 3 June 1864, while serving with Company H, 148th New York Infantry, in action at Cold Harbor, Virginia. Though himself wounded, Corporal Tinkham voluntarily left the rifle pits, crept out between the lines, and exposed to the severe fire of the enemy's guns at close range, brought within the lines two wounded and helpless comrades.

Subject: **Medal of honor.**

☞ Address: "Chief of the Record and Pension Office, War Department, Washington, D.C

502,995.

Record and Pension Office,

War Department,

Washington City,

April 5, 1898.

The Adjutant General,

    State of New York,

        Albany.

Sir:

    I have the honor to inform you that, by direction of the President and in accordance with the Act of Congress approved March 3, 1863, the Secretary of War has awarded a medal of honor to Eugene M. Tinkham, late corporal, Company H, 148th New York Infantry, for most distinguished gallantry in action at Cold Harbor, Virginia, June 3, 1864.

        Very respectfully,

        Colonel, U. S. Army,

        Chief, Record and Pension Office.

From the Norwich Bulletin October 4, 1909

Eugene M. Tinkham, one of Springfield's distinguished veterans of the Civil War, died at the Wesson Memorial Hospital, Springfield, at 10 o'clock Saturday morning from the effects of an operation in his 68th year. He had the honor of holding a government medal for bravery in the Battle of Cold Harbor on June 3, 1864. Since 1872, he had been a resident of Springfield, working at the armory for about twenty years and being twice elected to the Common Council on the Democratic ticket.

Mr. Tinkham was born on April 19, 1842, in the town of Franklin, which then bore the name of Sprague. At the age of ten, he went to work in the Allen Mills of his native town and worked there until he was 17 years old when he went to Lawrence, Massachusetts. He next worked at Marcellus, New York, and also lived in Ephratah, Auburn, and Waterloo, New York, and from the last place, on August 6, 1862, he enlisted in the 148th New York Infantry. He received his discharge at Richmond, Virginia, on June 22, 1865, after a notable service.

Mr. Tinkham became a member of the E.K. Wilcox Post, Grand Army of the Republic, in Springfield in 1883 and was its commander in 1890 and 1891. He was a prominent Odd Fellow and Mason. He had been a member of the Grace Methodist Church of Springfield since 1873. Mr. Tinkham was a man of quiet and modest nature who impressed acquaintances as having efficiency and high purpose.

He is survived by his wife, who was Anna Jordan and, whom he married in Ephratah, New York, on March 8,

1874; two brothers, Edwin T. Tinkham of Hanover and Albert F. Tinkham of Providence; and three sisters, Miss Susan E. Tinkham of Reading and Mrs. Sara Blakeley and Mrs. M.L. Brown of Providence. Burial will be in Hanover, Connecticut.

Buried in New Hanover Cemetery, 29 Potash Hill Road, Hanover, Connecticut. Photos by the author.

SERGEANT CHARLES HENRY TRACY; ARMY

October 3, 1833 (Jewett City, CT) – September 13, 1911 (West Somerville, MA); 77 years old
Married Mary E. Corbin (1834-1905) on December 27, 1853, in Upton, Massachusetts.
One daughter, Nellie A. (1872-1923).
One son, Oliver E. (1866-1933).
Enlisted on August 6, 1862, in Springfield, Massachusetts
Wounded on April 2, 1865. His right leg was amputated.
Discharged on July 4, 1865, in Chester, Pennsylvania, due to wounds received.

Born to Albert L. (1801-1878) and Harriet Birch Tracy (1803-1853). Three sisters, Mary L. (1828-1903), Susan A. Tracy Leavens (1840-1924), and Fanny S. (1846-1911). Two brothers, William C. (1839-1920) and Thomas (1842-?).

Tintype images of Charles H. Tracy from the Chicopee Archives Online. Public domain photo.

MEDAL OF HONOR CITATION

AWARDED FOR ACTIONS DURING: Civil War
BRANCH OF SERVICE: Army
UNIT: Company A, 37th Massachusetts Infantry
DATE OF ISSUE AND PRESENTATION: November 19, 1897 (33 years later)
AGE ON THE DAY OF THE EVENT: 31
CITATION:

The President of the United States of America, in the name of Congress, takes pleasure in presenting the Medal of Honor to Sergeant Charles H. Tracy, United States Army, for extraordinary heroism while serving with Company A, 37th Massachusetts Infantry. At the risk of his own life, at Spotsylvania, Virginia, 12 May 1864, Sergeant Tracy assisted in carrying to a place of safety a wounded and helpless officer. On 2 April 1865, at Petersburg, Virginia, he advanced with the pioneers and, under heavy fire, assisted in removing two lines of chevaux-de-frise [definition: a portable barrier of spikes, sword blades, etc. used to obstruct the passage of cavalry]; *was twice wounded but advanced to the third line, where he was again severely wounded, losing a leg.*

From The Boston Globe November 17, 1897

MEDAL OF HONOR FOR GALLANTRY
Charles H. Tracy of the Boston Custom House Gets One for Bravery Before Defenses of Petersburg.

A Washington dispatch yesterday contained the brief announcement that Charles H. Tracy, the one-legged watchman of the Boston custom house, had been awarded a Medal of Honor for bravery in action in the rebellion. Before the little army of custom house officials arrived at their desks yesterday, Mr. Tracy had departed for his home on Green Street, Charleston, as he is one of the night watchmen at "the old stone fort."

Mr. Tracy's daughter has been a long time at work establishing her father's rights to receive this distinguished honor, and when she read the news in yesterday's paper, she was delighted. Of course, Mr. Tracy was pleased, and it is safe to say there wasn't a happier home on top of Bunker Hill yesterday than the Tracy home on Greer Street.

On August 6, 1862, Mr. Tracy enlisted in the 37th Mass Infantry as a Private, his commander being Colonel Oliver Edwards. He served in Company A. On September 2 of that year, the 37th was mustered in as a regiment at Camp Briggs at Pittsfield. The regiment then proceeded on its way to Washington. a

He was mustered out on June 21, 1865. His first engagement was the Battle of Fredericksburg, and from that time to the close of his military, he served in 15 battles, as follows: Salem Heights, Marye's Heights, Gettysburg, Funkstown, Rappahannock Station, Mine Run, Wilderness, Spotsylvania, North Anna, Cold Harbor, Petersburg, Charleston, Winchester, Hatcher's Run, and Petersburg.

It was in the last-named battle Sergeant Tracy made his record for gallantry in action. Here, he lost his right leg, being wounded four times within 10 minutes.

The adjutant general's report for 1865 is the following account of the action which Mr. Tracy lost his leg: "The night of the 1st of April was occupied by the 6th Corps in preparation for a general assault on the enemy's lines below Petersburg. The brigades were formed in columns of attack, preceded by a band of pioneers and a heavy skirmish line. In our brigade, the pioneers were under the direction of Sergt Tracy, and the skirmish line was composed entirely of men detailed from the 37th, the 37th itself occupying the front line of the battle in the brigade.

"While cutting away the abattis in front of the enemy's forts, the pioneers suffered severely. Sergt Tracy was early disabled by a ball passing through his leg. He did not leave the field, but lying on his side, he still directed the movements of his men. While thus engaged, a second ball shattered his knee joint. Capt Robinson charged at the head of his skirmishers through abattis when he was wounded and had to be borne back. The colors of the 37th were the first in the division to wave over the rebel works."

From The Boston Globe September 15, 1911

BRAVE SOLDIER BURIED
Lieutenant Charles H. Tracy, a Medal of Honor Hero, Laid at Rest in Chicopee — Services There and in Somerville.

Lieutenant Charles H. Tracy of Somerville, who received a Congressional Medal of Honor for bravery at Petersburg, where he lost a leg, was buried this afternoon in the family lot in Fairview Cemetery, Chicopee. The services in that city were in charge of St John's Lodge of Odd Fellows and the 37th Massachusetts Regimental Association, in both societies of which he was a member.

Lieutenant Tracy was also an honored member of Abraham Lincoln Post 11 of Charlestown, and the services at his home in West Somerville held yesterday afternoon were in charge of the post, and the Grand Army ritual was impressively conducted by Commander Gibbs and other officers. A tribute to the memory of Lieutenant Tracy was paid by Reverend Dr. Ransom A. Greene, pastor of the First Universalist Church, Charlestown, who referred to the honorable record of his friend in the cause of his country and his sufferings in the hospital at City Point, Virginia when he was visited by President Lincoln and cared for by Clara Barton.

Floral tributes were received from the Department of Massachusetts, Woman's Relief Corps (W.R.C.), Mrs. Helen C. Mulford, past national aide, W. R. C., and by other friends of the family.

In addition to Abraham Lincoln Post and Corps of Charlestown, there were present at the ceremonies, representatives of the 37th Massachusetts Regimental Association, in which regiment he served, Department officers of the Woman's Relief Corps, Mrs. Florence Haynes national inspector W. R. C. Mrs. Sarah BL Fuller of the national executive board, Mrs. Maria W. Going and Mrs. Mary E. Knowles, past national officers W.R.C. and others.

The bravery of Lieutenant Tracy and his three years of army service was recognized by Governor Andrew and others of prominence, in addition to the members of Congress.

Lieutenant Tracy was born in Jewett City, Connecticut, on October 3, 1883, and was married in Upton, Massachusetts, on December 27, 1853, to Mary Elizabeth Corbin, who died six years ago. They lived in Chicopee from 1853 to 1891. He held a position in the Boston Customs House from 1890 to 1906. For many years, he had been a sufferer from his wound and, during the past five years, had been unable to walk unassisted but had been tenderly cared for by his daughter, Miss Nellie A. Tracy, who is officially connected with the department of Mass, W. R. C.

The other relatives are Reverend Thomas Tracy of Dehra Doon, U. P., of India, and William C. Tracy. of Chicopee, brothers; Mrs. W.H. Leavens of Connecticut, a sister: Oliver Edwards Tracy, a son, and Ralph Tracy, a grandson, both of Dorchester.

The home of Lieutenant Tracy had been one of unusual hospitality, and his valuable collection of war relics was often exhibited to friends. He had an inexhaustible fund of reminiscences and an entertaining way of relating a story. His cheerful manner and enthusiasm attracted many friends. Lieutenant Tracy was several years ago a member of the Department Council of Administration of the G.A.R. of Massachusetts and was well known throughout the state.

Buried in Fairview Cemetery, 60 Fanjoy Drive, Chicopee, Massachusetts; Oleander Path, Lot 26. Photo by the author.

SERGEANT HOWELL BURR TREAT; ARMY

March 31, 1833 (Hartland, CT) – July 21, 1912 (Painesville, OH); 80 years old
Married to Eliza J. "Jennie" Elias (1848-1911) on May 19, 1868.
Two sons, William B. (1872-1937) and Frederick E. (1879-1950).
Enlisted on August 5, 1862, in Painesville, Ohio.
Discharged on June 3, 1865.

Born to Howell (1793-1878) and Sally Beach Treat (1793-1833). Three brothers, Howell B. (1831-1832), William B. (1835-1860), and Edwin H. (1839-1923).

Photo courtesy of the Congressional Medal of Honor Society

MEDAL OF HONOR CITATION

AWARDED FOR ACTIONS DURING: Civil War
BRANCH OF SERVICE: Army
UNIT: Company I, 52nd Ohio Infantry
DATE OF ISSUE AND PRESENTATION: August 14, 1894 (30 years later)
AGE ON THE DAY OF THE EVENT: 31
CITATION:

The President of the United States of America, in the name of Congress, takes pleasure in presenting the Medal of Honor to Sergeant Howell B. Treat, United States Army, for extraordinary heroism on 11 May 1864, while serving with Company I, 52nd Ohio Infantry, in action at Buzzard's Roost, Georgia. Sergeant Treat risked his life in saving a wounded comrade.

PAINESVILLE (AP) – A Medal of Honor winner from the Korean War will honor a medal winner from the Civil War in special ceremonies today in Lake County.

Ron Rosser, 68, of Crooksville in southeastern Ohio, who received the Medal of Honor in 1952 from President Harry Truman, will lead the ceremonies dedicating the Medal of Honor plaque at Howell B. Treat's grave.

The ceremony at Evergreen Cemetery will mark the culmination of ceremonies that will include a Civil War reenactment, a parade, and a flyby of Air Force Reserve planes.

Treat fought with the 52nd Ohio Volunteer Infantry in the Civil War. He won the Medal of Honor for valor on May 11, 1863, during a battle with Confederate soldiers at Buzzards' Roost, George, just south of Chattanooga, Tennessee. The medal was awarded in 1894.

Treat returned to Painesville, northeast of Cleveland, after the war, raised a family, and died in 1912. His grave marker does not indicate his military honor.

The omission will be corrected with a bronze plaque. The oversight was found this year by Bonnie Walker, 47, while working on an internship to identify veterans at the cemetery.

Buried in Evergreen Cemetery, 501 Main Street, Painesville, Ohio; Division D, Lot 129. Photos from Brad Campbell. Used with permission.

HOWELL B TREAT
MEDAL OF HONOR
SGT CO I 52 OH INF
CIVIL WAR
MAR 31 1833   JUL 21 1912

SERGEANT ALLEN TUCKER; ARMY

April ?, 1837 * (Old Lyme, CT) – February 22, 1903 (New Haven, CT); 65 years old
Married to Amelia J. Bradley (1846-1897)
Married to Lucy A. Stevens (1852-1922) on September 11, 1898, in Hamden, Connecticut.
Two sons, George A. (1870-1928) and Leland T. (1876-1935).
One daughter, Carrie A. Tucker Smallman (1866-1917).
Enlisted on April 25, 1861, in Sprague, Connecticut

* The exact Date of Birth is unknown.
Born to Giles (1811-1870) and Lucy A. Havens Tucker (1810-?). Four sisters, Martha (1833-1892), Margaret (1840-?), Chloe (1841-?), and Ann M. (1853-1862). Three brothers, Frank (1845-1863), Samuel (1847-?), and James (1849-1917).

Photo courtesy of Ancestry.com

MEDAL OF HONOR CITATION

AWARDED FOR ACTIONS DURING: Civil War
BRANCH OF SERVICE: Army
UNIT: Company F, 10th Connecticut Infantry
DATE OF ISSUE AND PRESENTATION: May 12, 1865
AGE ON THE DAY OF THE EVENT: 27
CITATION:

The President of the United States of America, in the name of Congress, takes pleasure in presenting the Medal of Honor to Sergeant Allen Tucker, United States Army, for extraordinary heroism on 2 April 1865, while serving with Company F, 10th Connecticut Infantry, in action at Petersburg, Virginia, for gallantry as Color Bearer in the assault on Fort Gregg.

Buried in Evergreen Cemetery, 769 Ella T. Grasso Boulevard, New Haven, Connecticut; Grand Army of the Republic Plot, Grave 323 South. Photos by the author.

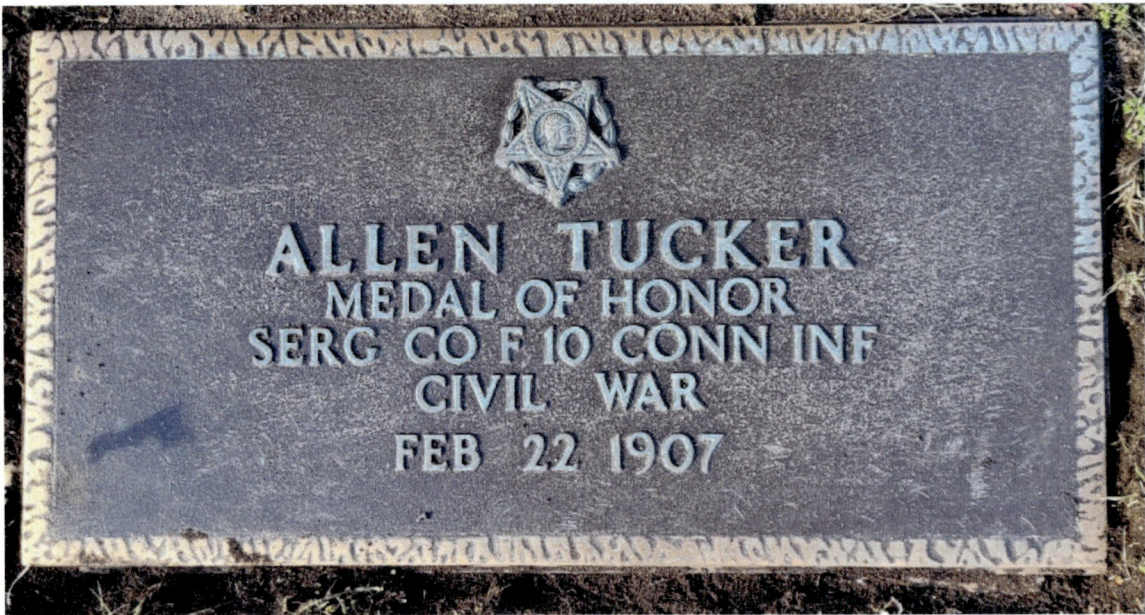

ALLEN TUCKER
MEDAL OF HONOR
SERG CO F 10 CONN INF
CIVIL WAR

FEB 22 1907

The year of death is incorrect. It should be 1903.

PRIVATE JOHN HENRY WEEKS; ARMY

March 15, 1845 (Hampton, CT) – March 10, 1911 (Milford, NY); 65 years old

Married Emma H. Wise (1854-1895) on February 26, 1869, in Douglas, Nebraska.

Married Adaline Chase (1848-1890) on February 3, 1886, in Hartwick, New York.

Married Laura Dingman (1860-1927) on November 4, 1891, in Sharon Springs, New York.

Children with Emma, Mark A. (1872-1950), Emma J. Weeks Ronan (1876-1978), Harriet E. Weeks Krupp (1878-1945), and Joanne V. Weeks Bowman (1879-1975.

Children Adeline, Horace C. (1886-1984), and Chester J. (1890-1984).

Children with Laura, John P. (1896-1955) and Elsie R. Weeks Doscher (1897-1990).

Enlisted on August 28, 1862, in Hartwick, New York.

Wounded on October 27, 1864, at Hatcher's Run, Virginia.

Discharged due to disability on May 27, 1865, from Campbell General Hospital in Washington, DC.

Born to Elisha J. (1814-1897) and Mary R. Tucker Weeks (1820-1862). Three sisters, Mary R. (1840-1891), Louise J. Weeks Heath (1843-1930), and Harriet E. Weeks Vibbard (1847-1919). Two brothers, Oliver E. (1841-1906), Hosea D. (1850-1931), and Andrew W. (1852-1934).

Photos courtesy of Great-Grandson John Stewart.

MEDAL OF HONOR CITATION

AWARDED FOR ACTIONS DURING: Civil War
BRANCH OF SERVICE: Army
UNIT: Company H, 152nd New York Infantry
DATE OF ISSUE: December 1, 1864
AGE ON THE DAY OF THE EVENT: 19
CITATION:

The President of the United States of America, in the name of Congress, takes pleasure in presenting the Medal of Honor to Private John Henry Weeks, United States Army, for extraordinary heroism on 12 May 1864, while serving with Company H, 152nd New York Infantry, in action at Spotsylvania, Virginia, for the capture of flag and Color Bearer using an empty cocked rifle while outnumbered by five or six.

<u>Presentation Date and Details</u>: December 6, 1864, by Major General George G. Meade, at a review of the 2nd Army Corps Headquarters, Peebles' House, near Petersburg, Virginia.

John Weeks' story as told by him and recorded in the book "Uncle Sam's Medal of Honor," collected and edited by Brevet Brigadier General Theo. F. Rodenbough.

"On the night of the 11th of May, 1864, we were relieved by the 5th Corps at Laurel Ridge (or Stony Ridge, I have forgotten which) after dark and moved out of the works, with instructions to move as silently as possible; not to allow our cups or bayonets to rattle or make any unnecessary noise. We marched all night through a cold rain until just before the break of day, on the morning of the 12th, we were halted in line of battle, with orders to 'in place rest.' The report had been in circulation during the night that we were going to relieve the 6th Corps in the Reserve, that we might get a chance to rest, as we had been under fire constantly for six days, and when we halted, we could see the light of campfires shining along the sky in our front, where we supposed were the 6th Corps. No sooner were we ordered to rest than I threw myself down in the mud and fell asleep. In a few minutes, I was awakened by the tramp of a horse coming on a lope. I raised up and saw an aide ride to General Hancock (who happened to be near our right) and give the verbal order to the general, as near as I can remember, as follows: — 'Gen. Meade's compliments and directs that you move your corps forward and occupy those works.'

"We were called to attention and ordered 'Forward, guide center, march!' Little did I think then what it would cost to obey that order, as I still thought it was the 6th Corps in our front.

"We were in the second line of battle, following close behind the first, till soon the Reb skirmishers commenced firing. Then, for the first, I began to realize that we had work before us. It was now getting quite light, but the fog prevented us from seeing far in our advance. We soon came to an open field with a gradual ascent to near the top, where there had been heavy timber, which had been felled with the tops toward us and the boughs sharpened; also, wire stretched through the tree tops. Still beyond this obstruction were the enemy's works, which consisted of a ditch, eight feet wide and nearly as deep, with a row of sharpened stakes set in front, the points about breast-high. Immediately in the rear of the ditch were the breastworks, which were formed of the dirt thrown up from the ditch, making the distance from the bottom of the ditch to the top of the works from twelve to fourteen feet without a chance of a foothold.

"As soon as we came to the edge of the open field, they opened on us with canister and musketry. The artillery had been massed at this point and all double-shotted with canister—thirty pieces if I remember right. Such a storm of iron and lead I never saw before or since. It did not seem possible for a man to live to reach the crest of the hill and pass the obstructions; but, as history tells, some did. But by the time we reached the ditch, there was no line of battle but a moving mass of yelling Yankees. We succeeded in wrenching the sharpened stakes from their places and used them in crossing the ditch and scaling the works. When I think now of all the difficult ties we had to overcome, with the flower of the rebel army behind such works pouring upon us a shower of lead, success seems impossible. It seemed to be an angle of their works where we made the charge, in the shape of the letter V. Our right was on the left wing of the angle so that when we got inside of the works, we could still see the enemy on the right wing opposing our men there from entering. It brought us in their rear. When we had sent our prisoners to the rear, we still advanced, but very slowly, on account of our broken ranks.

"I saw the enemy give way at this time on the right wing, and amongst the rest was a stand of colors and color-guard. These men fired their muskets in a volley and broke for the rear. They had to pass down our front to get out of the angle and would have succeeded, but I made up my mind, as soon as I saw them start, that I must have those colors. I had also fired my gun but had no time to reload. I ran up to the sergeant and snatched his colors from him, threw them on the ground and put my foot on them, cocked my empty gun, and told them the first one of them that moved out of his tracks I would shoot him down, and ordered them to throw down their guns and surrender. The sergeant said to them, 'Boys, they have got the colors, let us go with the colors,' so they threw down their guns and marched to the rear as my prisoners. When I got back to our line, Col. Curtiss told me to take them away, for we might get driven back at any moment.

"I recrossed the works and started for our rear when I met General Hancock and staff going to the front. As he passed, I saluted him. He returned the salute, and said, 'What have you got there?' I told him a stand of colors I had captured in the front. He then asked me if those were my prisoners. I told him they were. He looked at some of his staff and smiled (I thought at the time a little incredulously), for there were five or six lusty rebels, and I was at that time about eighteen years old.

Then he said, 'You deliver your prisoners to the provost marshal and write your Name, company, and regiment with the date of the occasion on a slip of paper, and pin it on your colors, and turn them into the adjutant of your regiment, which I did. I did not hear anything more about it till the following winter when, in Campbell Hospital, suffering from a wound received at the battle of Boydton Plank Road, on the left of Petersburg, I received a package. Upon opening it, I found it to be a Medal of Honor."

Buried in Hartwick Seminary Cemetery, 4773 NY-28, Cooperstown, New York. Photo from FindAGrave.com.

BREVET BRIGADIER GENERAL EDWARD WASHBURN WHITAKER; ARMY

June 15, 1841 (Killingly, CT) – July 30, 1922 (Washington, DC); 81 years old

Married Theodosia Davis (1848-1937) on June 7, 1865, in Washington, DC.

Three daughters, Clara B. Whitaker Chapline (1866-1957), Theodosia B. Whitaker Bell (1869-1947), and Grace D. Whitaker Seibold (1869-1947).

Enlisted on April 18, 1861 in Hartford, Connecticut.

One of 16 children born to George (1799-1870) and Mary Colegrove Whitaker (1806-1888). Eight brothers, George H. (1827-1909), Horace (1830-1910), Joseph (1831-1911), William (1833-1917), Daniel (1836-1863), Washington M. (1849-1895), Rozell J. (1850-1873), and Caleb A. (1853-1860). Seven sisters, Mary E. Whitaker Smith (1828-1918), Sarah C. Whitaker Brown (1832-1898), Bethiah A. Whitaker Pratt (1835-1930), Harriet Whitaker Hay (1838-1916), Adaline E. Whitaker James (1842-1936), Annah F. Whitaker Yoder (1844-1933), Emma J. (1846-1936). One grandson, First Lieutenant George Vaughn Seibold, was killed in a plane crash in France during World War I. His mother, Grace D. Seibold, formed the Gold Star Mothers to support mothers who had lost sons and daughters to war.

Member of the Connecticut Veterans Hall of Fame, Class of 2006.

Photo courtesy of the Library of Congress; photo LC-DIG-ppmsca-6880.

MEDAL OF HONOR CITATION

AWARDED FOR ACTIONS DURING: Civil War
BRANCH OF SERVICE: Army
UNIT: Company E, 1st Connecticut Infantry
DATE OF ISSUE AND PRESENTATION: April 2, 1898 (34 years later)
AGE ON THE DAY OF THE EVENT: 23
CITATION:

The President of the United States of America, in the name of Congress, takes pleasure in presenting the Medal of Honor to Captain Edward Washburn Whitaker, United States Army, for extraordinary heroism on 29 June 1864, while serving with Company E, 1st Connecticut Infantry, in action at Reams' Station, Virginia. While acting as an aide, Captain Whitaker voluntarily carried dispatches from the commanding general to General Meade, forcing his way with a single troop of Cavalry through an Infantry division of the enemy in the most distinguished manner, though he lost half his escort.

Location of the Medal: National Archives & Records Administration, Washington, DC

General Whitaker's Medal of Honor. The inscription on the back reads, "The Congress To Bvt Brig. Gen. Edward W. Whitaker, U.S. Vols, Reams' Station, June 29, 1864." Photos courtesy of the National Archives and Records Administration; Jane Fitzgerald, Archivist, Archival Operations, Washington, DC.

Edward Whitaker served as Brigadier General George Armstrong Custer's Chief of Staff, reaching the rank of Lieutenant Colonel. In this position, he bore the flag of truce at Appomattox, met with Lieutenant General James Longstreet, and made the negotiations which stopped the fighting. He was brevetted Brigadier General and, at age 23, became one of the youngest in the Civil War to hold the title of General. His brevet was recommended by Generals Ulysses S. Grant and William T. Sheridan "for gallantry and skill displayed in turning the enemy's left flank at Waynesboro, March 2, 1865, and for gallantry and uniform good conduct at the battle of Five Forks, April 1, 1865, and Appomattox Station, April 8, 1865, and throughout the entire campaign." He later was appointed Superintendent of the U.S. Capitol Building and still later by President Grant, Postmaster of Hartford, Connecticut.

From Beyer, W. F., & Keydel, O. F. (2000). Deeds of valor: How America's Civil War Heroes won The Congressional Medal of Honor. Smithmark Publishers.

A RIDE TO ALMOST CERTAIN DEATH

After its raid against the Danville and Southside Railway, the Third Cavalry Division, commanded by General James H. Wilson, on its return march to join the Army of the Potomac in front of Petersburg, found a large force of rebel infantry, cavalry, and artillery in position, barring its passage at Ream's Station, Virginia, within five miles of army headquarters.

Captain E. W. Whitaker, who was serving on General Wilson's staff, took in the whole position at a glance. Perceiving that it would be impracticable for this column, jaded and almost worn out by a week's incessant

476

marching, working, and fighting, to

force its way farther without assistance, he volunteered to take a squadron and charge through the rebel line and inform General Meade of the division's perilous straits and that help must be sent at once.

General Wilson accepted Captain Whitaker's offer and directed him to proceed immediately on his desperate mission. He was entirely ignorant of what had become of the Army of the Potomac, or where he should find it, or what perils he would encounter on the way. It looked as though he were starting on a ride to certain death.

Selecting Lieutenant Ford and forty troopers of the Third New York Cavalry, he explained to them the hazardous character of the undertaking and instructed them that whoever should survive should make his way as rapidly as possible to army headquarters and describe the position of the cavalry column he had left behind.

Not a man faltered, but the entire detachment dashed forward after their gallant leader, who, bearing to his left and striking the rebel right, broke through their line like a tornado and galloped on to headquarters, where he arrived at an early hour of morning with only eighteen of his gallant cavalrymen. They had cut through the enemy's line, which one of General Wilson's officers, after reconnoitering, had reported as "strong as a stone wall."

Captain Whitaker gave the necessary information and at once volunteered to guide the Sixth Corps to the rescue, but its movements were so dilatory that it did not arrive until long after the cavalry column, despairing of help, had made a great detour by which it eluded the enemy, extricated itself and rejoined the army several days later.

Captain Whitaker was highly commended by General Wilson, immediately promoted to the rank of Major, and received the Medal of Honor for his services in this notable charge.

From the Evening Star (Washington, DC) July 31, 1922

TO BURY CIVIL WAR HERO IN ARLINGTON, VA
Brigadier General Whitaker, Who Carried Truce Flag to Enemy, Passes Away

One of the outstanding heroes of the Civil War will be laid at rest among his comrades at 1 o'clock Wednesday when last rites for Brigadier General Edward Washburn Whitaker will be held in Arlington National Cemetery. The veteran died yesterday at his home, 756 Rock Creek Church Road, aged eighty-one. Arterial sclerosis was the cause.

Of his many brilliant achievements through the four years of fighting between the North and South, none was more noteworthy than when he bore a flag of truce through the Confederate lines near Appomattox Courthouse and convinced General Robert E. Lee that further resistance merely meant the further slaughter of Confederate troops. For this and other acts, he was awarded the Congressional Medal of Honor, the most coveted of American decorations.

Born in Killingly, Connecticut, in 1841, Whitaker was among the first to enlist when the call for men went out in 1861. He declined a commission and fought his way up until he was brevetted a brigadier general. He served in Connecticut and New York forces.

Since the Civil War, General Whitaker had made his home for the most part in Washington, his last post having been that of smoke inspector, and his labors active until a few months ago.

He is survived by his widow, Mrs. Thedosia Davis Whitaker; three daughters, Mrs. Charles T. Chapline, Mrs. Frank J. Bell, and Mrs. George G. Seibold, all of this city, as well as four sisters, Mrs. George L. James of Windsor, Connecticut; Mrs. Bertha Pratt, of Manchester Center, Connecticut; Mrs. Anne Yoder, of Lynchburg, Virginia, and Miss Emma Whitaker, of Poughkeepsie, New York.

General Whitaker was a member of Columbia Commandery, No. 2, Knights Templar; Columbia Chapter, No. 1, Royal Arch Masons: Lafayette Lodge, No. 100 Free And Accepted Mason, at Hartford, Connecticut, and of John A. Rawlings Post, Grand Army of the Republic; the Loyal Legion, and the Sons of the American Revolution.

The funeral service will be read at his late home.

GEN WHITAKER, UNION NOTE BEARER IN APPOMATTOX SURRENDER, DIES

Enlisted as Private at First Call of Lincoln

Burial in Arlington for Connecticut Grand Army of the Republic Founder

Brigadier General Edward W. Whitaker, eighty-one years old, the Union officer who, as courier, bore the message which halted the prepared Union charge at Appomattox and which resulted in the immediate, unconditional surrender of the Confederate forces, died at his residence, 756 Rock Creek Church Road, yesterday morning after an illness of more than two years. The Civil War veteran of eighty-two battles died from the effects of hardened arteries.

The funeral will be held at his late home on Wednesday at 1 o'clock. He will be buried at Arlington National Cemetery, his three sons-in-law and five grandsons acting as pallbearers. The sons-in-law are Charles T. Chapline, Frank J. Bell, and George G. Seibold. The grandsons are Edward G. Bell, F. Joseph A. Chapline, Frank J. Bell, Jr., Elmer T. Bell, and Louis E. Seibold.

He is survived by his wife, Theodosia Davis Whitaker, and three daughters, Mrs. Frank J. Bell. Mrs. Charles T. Chapline and Mrs. George G. Seibold, all of this city; and four sisters, Mrs. George L. James of Windsor, Connecticut; Mrs. Bethia Pratt of Manchester Center, Connecticut; Mrs. Anna Yoder of Lynchburg, Virginia, and Miss Emma J. Whitaker of New York.

Declines Commission.

Brig. Gen. Whitaker was one of the few surviving men who answered the first call of President Lincoln for volunteers in April 1861. He declined a commission and enrolled as a private, fighting his way up until he was breveted a Brigadier General.

He was at the surrender of Lee at Appomattox when Generals Gordon and Longstreet sent out a white flag of truce to General Custer, for whom General Whitaker was chief of staff. Being instructed by General Custer to advise the Confederate forces that he was not in sole command of the field. He entered the opposing lines and stated that it would be impossible to stop the prepared charge unless they gave an unconditional surrender. The Confederate forces accepted the message, thereby saving both forces many deaths.

At the conclusion of hostilities, General Whitaker came to Washington and took an active part in the improvement of the National Capital, serving as general superintendent of the board of public works. In 1874, he entered business for himself when there was a change in the form of government of the city. He was appointed as Postmaster at Hartford, Connecticut, by President Grant during his administration. Later, he served as smoke inspector in the health department of the city.

Organizer of Grand Army of the Republic

General Whitaker was a member of the Columbia Commandery. No. 2. of the Knights Templar, and Columbia Chapter, No. 1, of the Royal Arch Masons; also, a member of the La Fayette Lodge No. 100, F. A. A. M., at Hartford, Connecticut. He was the organizer of the first Grand Army of the Republic post in Connecticut, declining the position of provisional department commander when tendered to him. He was a member of the John A. Rawlings Post, Grand Army of the Republic, Loyal Legion, and Sons of the American Revolution.

On April 8, 1865, General Whitaker was awarded the Congressional Medal of Honor by President Lincoln for several acts of bravery.

The name of General Whitaker is known throughout the New England states, as well as Maryland and Virginia.

Reverend Dr. A. F. Anderson, assistant pastor of Calvary Baptist Church, will officiate at the religious service at 1 p.m. at his late residence. These services will be followed by services directed by the Columbia Commandery Knights Templar, also at the home, and military services at the grave.

Article from Military Images magazine article titled "Match His Record!" Text by Ronald S. Coddington, Military Images magazine; first two photos from the Buck Zaidel collection; all used with permission

Almost a half-century after the Civil War, an aged veteran wrote, "I will say to the whole world, match my old commander's record if you can!"

The writer, a former sergeant in the 1st Connecticut Cavalry, referred to the Lieutenant Colonel of his regiment, Edward Washburn Whitaker.

Born a farmer's son in Connecticut, Whitaker volunteered for the military just days after the fall of Fort Sumter. He enlisted as a corporal in the 1st Connecticut Infantry and fought at Bull Run, the first of 82 engagements credited to him. At the conclusion of the regiment's three-month term, Whitaker joined a battalion that grew into the 1st Connecticut Cavalry.

Over the next three-plus years, Whitaker rose in rank from First Sergeant to Lieutenant Colonel and Brevet Brigadier General. Along the way, he and his comrades battled rebel forces in the Shenandoah Valley, endured the brutal 1864 Overland Campaign, and bore witness to the triumph at Appomattox Court House on April 9, 1865.

Whitaker's leadership qualities caught the attention of senior commanders, who tapped him for various duties. As a Captain on Major General James H. Wilson's staff, Whitaker volunteered to lead about 40 troopers to break through enemy infantry that barred Wilson's main column from the rest of the army at Ream's Station, Va., on June 29, 1864. According to one source, Whitaker and his force hit the rebel line "like a tornado, and galloped on to headquarters, where he arrived at an early hour of morning with only eighteen of his gallant cavalrymen." Meanwhile, Wilson's column detoured around the Confederates and reconnected with the main army.

An appreciative Wilson promoted Whitaker to Major. In 1898, Whitaker received the Medal of Honor for his courage that June day.

Whitaker's most memorable war experience occurred at Appomattox. During the morning of April 9, Confederate Capt. Robert M. Sims approached the Union line bearing a white towel and a request from Lieutenant General James Longstreet for a truce. The request made its way to the commander in this sector of the line, Major General George Armstrong Custer. He sent Whitaker, who had risen to Custer's chief of staff, with Sims to Longstreet with a message that effectively arranged a temporary truce pending negotiations for the surrender of Gen. Robert E. Lee's army.

Whitaker came away with two trophies: the towel carried by Sims and the chair used by Lee during negotiations inside the McLean home. Whitaker cut the towel in two and gave half to his commander's wife, Elizabeth Bacon "Libby" Custer. This piece of the towel and the Lee chair eventually made its way to the Smithsonian Institution.

Whitaker went on to serve in government posts in Washington, D.C., and Hartford, Connecticut and remained active in veterans' affairs with the Grand Army of the Republic until his death in 1922 at age 81. His wife, Theodosia, and three daughters survived him. The old soldier's remains rest in Arlington National Cemetery.

QUARTERMASTER SERGEANT GEORGE CORNELIUS WILLIAMS; ARMY

December 9, 1839 (Gloucester, England) – November 14, 1926 (New London, CT); 86 years old
Married Anna "Annie" S. Raymond (1841-1920) on May 5, 1865 in New London, Connecticut
One son, George R. (1867-1909).
Enlisted on July 16, 1861, in New London, Connecticut.
Discharged on July 16, 1864.

Born to George [Mayor of New London, CT, and served in the Connecticut State Legislature] (1814-1902) and Comfort Byett Williams (1804-1893). Two sisters, Ellen Williams Getchell (1841-1927) and Jane A. Williams Hammond (1843-1926). One brother, Josiah C. (1848-1882).

From The Evening Post Annual, 1885, "Biographical Sketches."

MEDAL OF HONOR CITATION

AWARDED FOR ACTIONS DURING: Civil War
BRANCH OF SERVICE: Army
UNIT: 1st Battalion, 14th U.S. Infantry
DATE OF ISSUE AND PRESENTATION: August 28, 1897 (35 years later)
AGE ON THE DAY OF THE EVENT: 23
CITATION:

The President of the United States of America, in the name of Congress, takes pleasure in presenting the Medal of Honor to Quartermaster Sergeant George C. Williams, United States Army, for extraordinary heroism on 27 June 1862, while serving with 1st Battalion, 14th U.S. Infantry, in action at Gaines Mill, Virginia. While on duty with the wagon train as Quartermaster Sergeant, George Williams voluntarily left his place of safety in the rear, joined a company, and fought with distinguished gallantry through the action.

From the Genealogical and Biographical Record of New London County, Connecticut; 1905

George Cornelius Williams, eldest son of Honorable George, was born in Gloucester, England, and was only an infant when his parents came to America. He was educated in New London, but as he was taken out of school when only thirteen, his education was necessarily a limited one. He went into his father's bakery to learn the trade and was kept there until the war broke out. On July 16, 1861, he enlisted in Company F, 14th Connecticut Volunteer Infantry, under General Stone, the second man to enlist in that regiment. That company was known as the "fighting 14th" and, as such, earned a widespread reputation. Mr. Williams was detailed as Quartermaster's clerk and, in 1861, promoted to Quartermaster Sergeant. He was under fire in all the battles in which the regiment was engaged and an active participant in that at Gaines' Mills, where he was given a Medal of Honor for brilliant service, an honor recommended by two captains. Mr. Williams was one of the bravest men in line and was offered a commission as Second Lieutenant if he would remain in the regular service. He was mustered out on July 16, 1864, having never missed a day with his regiment.

Returning home when the war was over, Mr. Williams went into his father's business, and they built up what was truthfully known as one of the best in Connecticut. This continued to be his predominating interest until he retired. He is, at present, a trustee of the Mariner's Savings Bank. Fraternally, he belongs to Brainerd Lodge, Free and Accepted Masons, and religiously is an attendant upon the Second Congregational Church. In his politics, he is essentially independent but takes no active part in public affairs, although he has been school visitor and was once elected a Selectman. This latter office, he resigned.

George C. Williams was married on May 5, 1865, to Anna Sistare Raymond, born December 9, 1841, daughter of Edmond A. and Lucy (Coit) Raymond of New London. They have one son, George Raymond, born January 27, 1867.

Buried in Cedar Grove Cemetery, 638 Broad Street; New London, Connecticut; Section 14, Lot 1. Photos by the author.

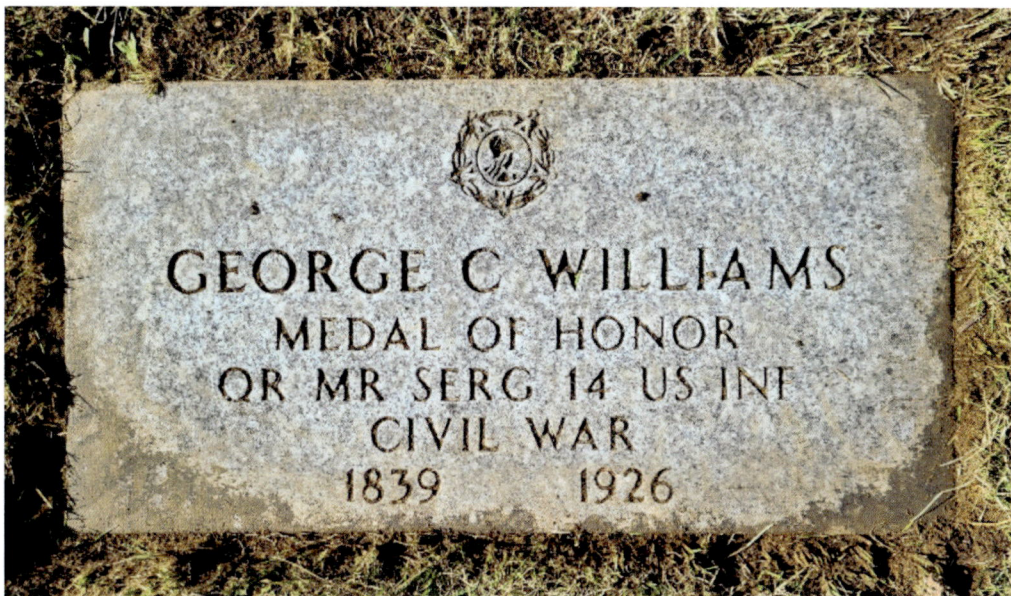

PRIVATE CHRISTOPHER WILLIAM WILSON, SR.; ARMY

February 14, 1846 (Dublin, Ireland) – September 12, 1916 (Sea Cliff, NY); 70 years old
Married Henrietta Hartwell (1849-1925) in 1868.
Three sons, George D. (1868-1944), Robert H. (1870-1934), and Christopher W., Jr. (1880-1942).
One daughter, Bessie D. Wilson Scofield (1876-1957).
Enlisted on July 5, 1861, in New York City.

Born to Joseph and Elizabeth Davis Wilson. No other information is known.

His family immigrated to Meriden and was living in today's downtown at the start of the Civil War in 1861. Enlisted in the Union Army infantry at Camp Scott in Staten Island as a private in Company F, 4th Regiment Excelsior Brigade.

Photo from Brooklyn Daily Eagle September 13, 1916

MEDAL OF HONOR CITATION

AWARDED FOR ACTIONS DURING: Civil War
BRANCH OF SERVICE: Army
UNIT: Company E, 73rd New York Infantry
DATE OF ISSUE AND PRESENTATION: December 30, 1898 (34 years later)
AGE ON THE DAY OF THE EVENT: 18
CITATION:

The President of the United States of America, in the name of Congress, takes pleasure in presenting the Medal of Honor to Private Christopher W. Wilson, United States Army, for extraordinary heroism on 12 May 1864, while serving with Company E, 73rd New York Infantry, in action at Spotsylvania, Virginia. Private Wilson took the flag from the wounded Color Bearer and carried it in the charge over the Confederate works, in which charge he also captured the colors of the 56th Virginia (Confederate States of America), bringing off both flags in safety.

Christopher W. Wilson, senior member of the firm of C.W. Wilson and Company, lumber dealers at the foot of Kent Street, and Vice President and Director of the Eastern District Hospital, died yesterday at his summer home in Sea Cliff, aged 71 years. Mr. Wilson was born in Ireland on February 14, 1846. He came to this country as a boy and, at the outbreak of the Civil War, enlisted as a Private in the Seventy-third Regiment, New York Volunteers. He was promoted rapidly for bravery and, at the close of the conflict, was acting-Major. Mr. Wilson was seriously wounded in the Battle of Williamsburg, Virginia, and later was awarded a Congressional medal. At the close of the war, he returned North and entered the Eastman Business College at Poughkeepsie. After completing his course there, he entered business in Brooklyn and had lived here up to the time of his death. He was connected with a great many business organizations and patriotic societies. He was a commander of the Loyal Legion of the United States, a member of the Third Army Corps Veteran Association, the New York Lumber Trades Association, the Business Men's and Manufacturers' Association, and the Hanover and Lincoln Clubs. He was also a Director of the Greenpoint National Bank and the New York Rubber Company. He is survived by his widow, Henrietta; three sons, George E., Robert H., and Christopher W. Jr., and one daughter, Mrs. Bessie W. Scofield, wife of Dr. Charles E. Scofield. Funeral services will be held tomorrow at 8:30 p.m. at his Brooklyn home, 331 Jefferson Avenue. Interment Friday morning in Evergreen Cemetery.

From The Times Union (Brooklyn, NY) September 14, 1916

The death of Christopher W. Wilson deprives the business world of Brooklyn of a fine and commanding figure, and although he had reached the Scriptural allotment of years and had not been a resident of the Eastern District for several years, his influence was still strong in its social and religious life, and his death will be deeply distressing to thousands. Mr. Wilson represented a type of Brooklyn businessman whose strict sense of honor and whose broad public spirit enriched the community. His great lumber yard is still one of the industrial assets of the Eastern District. His long activity in Christ Church, his participation in the club life of Williamsburg, and the intelligence and energy he displayed with respect to projects of public interest and value earned for him the high place he held in public esteem. He was a thorough American, although not of American birth, who bought his right to citizenship by a soldier's service under the Stars and Stripes.

From The Standard Union (Brooklyn, NY) September 15, 1916

Dr. Downey Delivers Eulogy at Funeral Services – Many Organizations Represented

The body of Christopher W. Wilson, head of an Eastern District lumber concern, was buried today at Evergreen Cemetery. Last night at his late home, 331 Jefferson Avenue, funeral services were conducted by the Rev. David G. Downey, D.D. book editor of the Methodist Episcopal Church. Delegations attended from the Hanover Club, New York Commandery of the Loyal Legion, Third Army Corps Veterans' Association, Marsh Lodge, Free and Accepted Masons; New York Lumber Trade Association, Lincoln Club, Commerce Club, Eastern District Hospital, Greenpoint National Bank, New York Rubber Company, Taylor Iron Works, and members of the Christ Episcopal Church. Dr. Downey, in his eulogy, spoke feelingly on the life of Mr. Wilson. He said that from the very time he was able to understand right from wrong, he had worked for the moral uplift of his fellow man. He said he loved his country and was at all times ready to serve it. "The good manner in which he lived preserved him, and although he had passed the three score and ten mark, he looked very young. All the time I knew him, I never heard him speak one cross word. He was always happy, and whenever he could be of service to his fellow man, he was never found lacking. In the death of Mr. Wilson, the borough, city, state, and country have lost an honorable and beloved citizen."

Buried in The Evergreens Cemetery, 1629 Bushwick Avenue, Brooklyn, New York; Tulip Grove Section, Lot 107.
Photos by author.

STAFF SERGEANT HOMER LEE WISE; ARMY

February 27, 1917 (Baton Rouge, LA) – April 22, 1974 (New Haven, CT); 57 years old

Married to Madolyn L. DiSesa (1913-2002) on August 11, 1945, in Stamford, Connecticut.

One son, Jeffrey L. (1949-1990).

Local address: 23 Tree Lane, Stamford, Connecticut.

Enlisted on September 10, 1941, at Jacksonville Army Air Field, Florida.

Army serial number 34150836.

Retired from the Army as a Master Sergeant in 1966.

Born to Edna P. Stephens Wise (1893-1942). His father is unknown. Three brothers, Edward (1922-1990), Leon (1926-2003), and Robert (1936-?). One sister, Gracie Wise Pipes (1930-2003).

Member of the Connecticut Veterans Hall of Fame, Class of 2009.

Photo courtesy of FindAGrave.com

MEDAL OF HONOR CITATION

AWARDED FOR ACTIONS DURING: World War II
BRANCH OF SERVICE: Army
UNIT: Company L, 142nd Infantry Regiment, 36th Infantry Division
GENERAL ORDERS: War Department, General Orders No. 90, December 8, 1944
AGE ON THE DAY OF THE EVENT: 27
CITATION:

The President of the United States of America, in the name of Congress, takes pleasure in presenting the Medal of Honor to Staff Sergeant Homer L. Wise, United States Army, for conspicuous gallantry and intrepidity in action above and beyond the call of duty on 14 June 1944, while serving with Company L, 142nd Infantry Regiment, 36th Infantry Division, in action at Magliano, Italy. While his platoon was pinned down by enemy small-arms fire from both flanks, Staff Sergeant Wise left his position of comparative safety and assisted in carrying one of his men, who had been seriously wounded and who lay in an exposed position, to a point where he could receive medical attention. The advance of the platoon was resumed but was again stopped by enemy frontal fire. A German officer and two enlisted men armed with automatic weapons threatened the right flank. Fearlessly exposing himself, he moved to a position from which he killed all three with his submachine gun. Returning to his squad, he obtained an M-1 rifle and several antitank grenades, then took up a position from which he delivered accurate fire on the enemy holding up the advance. As the battalion moved forward, it was again stopped by enemy frontal and flanking fire. He procured an automatic rifle and, advancing ahead of his men, neutralized an enemy machinegun with his fire. When the flanking fire became more intense, he ran to a nearby tank and, exposing himself on the turret, restored a jammed machinegun to operating efficiency and used it so effectively that the enemy fire from an adjacent ridge was materially reduced, thus permitting the battalion to occupy its objective.

Sergeant Homer L. Wise receives the Medal of Honor from Lieutenant General Alexander M. Patch, Commanding General Seventh Army, in Epinal, France, November 28, 1944, for heroism in Magalino, Italy, June 14, 1944. Photo courtesy of StamfordAdvocate.com.

Homer L. Wise Memorial Park, Chester and Bedford Streets, Stamford, Connecticut. Photo by the author.

Rt 137 (Washington Boulevard) from Broad Street to High Ridge Road in Stamford, Connecticut, was renamed Homer Lee Wise Memorial Highway in 2014. Photo by the author.

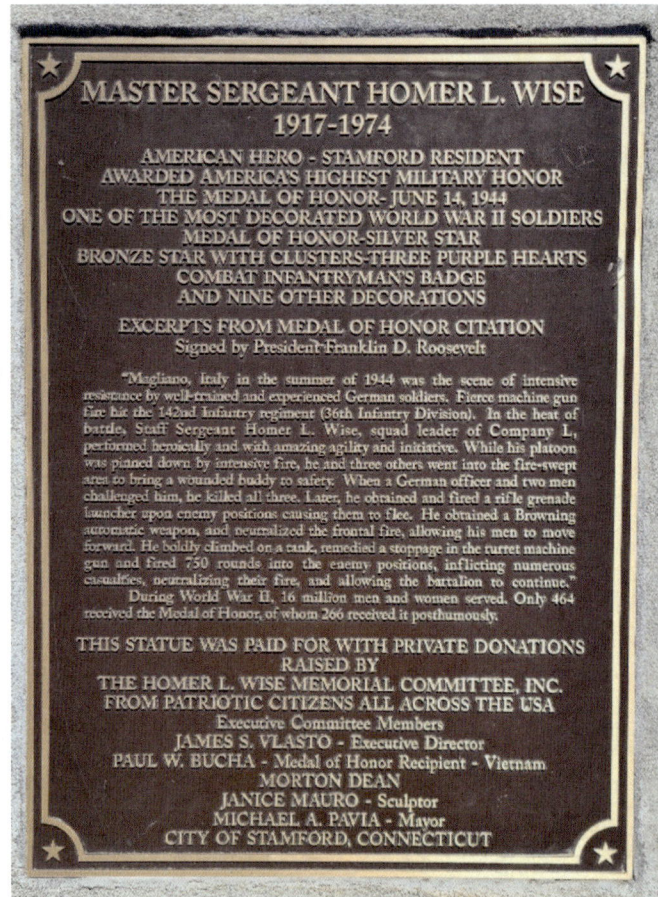

MASTER SERGEANT HOMER L. WISE
1917-1974
AMERICAN HERO - STAMFORD RESIDENT
AWARDED AMERICA'S HIGHEST MILITARY HONOR
THE MEDAL OF HONOR- JUNE 14, 1944
ONE OF THE MOST DECORATED WORLD WAR II SOLDIERS
MEDAL OF HONOR-SILVER STAR
BRONZE STAR WITH CLUSTERS-THREE PURPLE HEARTS
COMBAT INFANTRYMAN'S BADGE
AND NINE OTHER DECORATIONS

EXCERPTS FROM MEDAL OF HONOR CITATION
Signed by President Franklin D. Roosevelt

"Magliano, Italy in the summer of 1944 was the scene of intensive resistance by well-trained and experienced German soldiers. Fierce machine gun fire hit the 142nd Infantry regiment (36th Infantry Division). In the heat of battle, Staff Sergeant Homer L. Wise, squad leader of Company L, performed heroically and with amazing agility and initiative. While his platoon was pinned down by intensive fire, he and three others went into the fire-swept area to bring a wounded buddy to safety. When a German officer and two men challenged him, he killed all three. Later, he obtained and fired a rifle grenade launcher upon enemy positions causing them to flee. He obtained a Browning automatic weapon, and neutralized the frontal fire, allowing his men to move forward. He boldly climbed on a tank, remedied a stoppage in the turret machine gun and fired 750 rounds into the enemy positions, inflicting numerous casualties, neutralizing their fire, and allowing the battalion to continue."
During World War II, 16 million men and women served. Only 464 received the Medal of Honor, of whom 266 received it posthumously.

THIS STATUE WAS PAID FOR WITH PRIVATE DONATIONS
RAISED BY
THE HOMER L. WISE MEMORIAL COMMITTEE, INC.
FROM PATRIOTIC CITIZENS ALL ACROSS THE USA
Executive Committee Members
JAMES S. VLASTO - Executive Director
PAUL W. BUCHA - Medal of Honor Recipient - Vietnam
MORTON DEAN
JANICE MAURO - Sculptor
MICHAEL A. PAVIA - Mayor
CITY OF STAMFORD, CONNECTICUT

MASTER SERGEANT
HOMER L. WISE
MEDAL OF HONOR
JUNE 14, 1944
UNITED STATES ARMY

From The Redding Pilot (now defunct), June 17, 2010, by Janis Gibson

Redding artist and sculptor Janice Mauro has recently worked on a commissioned project that has a rare subject.

"During World War II, 16 million men and women served. Only 464 received the Medal of Honor, of whom 266 received it posthumously. That statistic alone compels us to honor this hero," said James Vlasto of Stamford at the September 2008 launch of a $150,000 fund-raising drive to erect a bronze statue of Master Sergeant Homer L. Wise (1917-1974). Sergeant Wise, who was raised in Baton Rouge. La., but married Stamford native Madolyn DiSesa and settled in that city after the war, was awarded the Medal of Honor for heroism in Magliano, Italy, on June 14, 1944.

Ms. Mauro has been commissioned to create the statue, which will be erected in the Homer L. Wise Memorial Park at Bedford and Chester Streets in Stamford.

"I was very honored to be selected to create this statue of Homer," said Ms. Mauro, "and even more so as I got to know more about the man." One of the most decorated infantrymen of World War II, Sergeant Wise also received the Silver Star, Bronze Star, three Purple Hearts, and 11 other decorations.

Creating maquettes (small samples) made of wax, Ms. Mauro presented the committee with a choice of three poses for the statute: standing, seated on a bench, or portrait bust. The standing pose was selected. She then created a 30-inch-high version, which can be seen on the website homerlwisememorial.org [**AUTHOR NOTE:** the website no longer exists as of late 2023], that gave detail to gesture and attitude. She is now completing the 6-foot, 5-inch version from which the bronze statue will be cast using the lost wax method.

Any sculpture in bronze is a complicated endeavor. "It takes an army of people to take a statue from concept to finished product," she said. "My job is to design it to show Homer's character, his inner strength, in his face, in his pose and gestures... he stands solidly, shoulders back, head to the side, his brows are knitted.

"If you look at Michelangelo's David," she continued, "he's looking at Goliath and wondering if he would survive; Homer was faced with a huge thing, and he made it. In creating a war piece, you want to show concern in his face that we would learn something.

"The emotion in his face is a large part of the stature; all figurative sculpture must have that. His feet are firmly planted, his head turning, what is going to happen next? What is the future? I want to show that through his gestures and expression," she said.

To help achieve the effect she was looking for, Ms. Mauro's husband, local wine expert Francois Saudeau, posed for her, moving under her direction to get the stance, posture, head turn, and other gestures just right. A friend who's a uniform collector loaned her a piece from his collection so she would be accurate in the details of Homer's jacket.

She is creating the statue in her home studio, called Goodwood Studio, which was constructed from a falling-down porch with 12 broken windows that was converted into a two-story art space when she and her husband moved to Redding eight years ago. Upstairs is a cathedral-ceilinged display space for her finished work, while downstairs is the concrete-floored working studio.

In addition to her bronze work, Ms. Mauro is a sculptor in traditional materials, including clay, terra cotta, and wax, and enjoys carving but prefers wood to the physical demands of stone. She also draws and occasionally paints, but sculpture is her first love.

Ms. Mauro has modeled heads for Nickelodeon's Rug Rats and has done puppet, hand, and mask modeling for productions by Julie Taymor, including The Lion King, Juan Darien, Fool's Fire, and Transposed Heads. She has also modeled marionettes for Eva Le Gallienne's Broadway production of Alice in Wonderland and served as studio adjunct for New York artist Richard McDermott Miller (1912-2004) for 30 years.

"I learned everything from Richard," she said. "I was a bronze chaser, patina person — applying the color chemically — green, black, brown. Homer will be chestnut brown; color is important."

She noted that there are many other people involved in a statue's creation other than the sculptor. The foundry, which does the physical casting, "is crucial," as is the work of the bronze chaser who removes the mold marks and makes sure the piece is as perfect as possible; she will be doing much of that work herself. The statue has to be mounted and installed on site, which is designed by a landscape architect. It should be ready in September (2010).

He received the high honor of being selected as one of six honorary pallbearers at the dedication of the Tomb of the Unknown Soldier at Arlington National Cemetery in 1958 under President Dwight D. Eisenhower. He retired from the U.S. Army in 1966 with the rank of master sergeant. He then worked in the Stamford area, where he was known locally for his humility regarding his heroic deeds and frequent individual kindness to neighbors and strangers.

Also the recipient of the Silver Star Medal, Bronze Star Medal with "V" device for valor, and three Purple Heart Medals.

From an unknown newspaper, likely in Louisiana. Found on Ancestry.com.

A sweet little lady 75 years old today can boast the distinction of being the grandmother of the first Baton Rouge serviceman to be awarded the Congressional Medal of Honor, the highest award given by the government to a member of the armed forces. The grandson is Staff Sergeant Homer L. Wise.

Mrs. Hattie Wise, who lives on RFD 4, a few miles from Camp Istrouma, was all aflutter Friday morning over her hero grandson's accomplishment, although she did not know of the award until. Some of her neighbors, who read the AP press release, told her.

A Mighty Fine Thing

"It was a mighty fine thing he did," Mrs. Wise said, and I am proud of my Homer."

The War Department in Washington announced Thursday that Sergeant Wise had been awarded the Medal of Honor for singlehandedly opposing a German advance with a machine gun, rifle, and grenades, thereby enabling his battalion to overwhelm the enemy and take the objective.

Homer's own parents are dead. His mother died since he entered the service in September 1941. The 27-year-old Baton Rougean has been overseas for two years.

Homer attended the Central school until the sixth grade when he had to go to work on the Wise's 91-acre farm. "When there's farming to be done, the children don't get much time for school," his grandmother said.

One of Mrs. Wise's neighbors, Mrs. Owen Brannon, said that Homer is a tall, dark-haired, nice-looking boy and that the people in that section were proud one of their fellows is to be presented the medal. "I can imagine that Homer would be pretty brave," Mrs. Brannon said. "He never got into any trouble when he was around here because the other kids just didn't pick on him."

Has Girl in Connecticut

It was suggested to Mrs. Wise that Homer might send his award back to her, but she said that he'd more likely send it to his girl. Homer met his "girl" when he was stationed in Connecticut, and her name is Miss Madolyn LeSesa, "He sends her his money," said Mrs. Wise, "cause he knows I don't need it, and they're saving it to be married with."

Homer has been stationed part of his time in Europe with his Uncle John, who is Mrs. Wise's son. In addition to Homer and John, Mrs. Wise writes letters to Charles and Henry Walker, her grandsons, who are the sons of Mrs. Livella Walker of Baton Rouge, and to the sons of another daughter, Mrs. Tina Shaffett of Doyle–LeRoy, J.D., Gene, and James.

Homer's brothers live with Mrs. Wise now and help her manage the small farm. Ed is 22, Leon just 18, and Robert is 8.

Mrs. Wise, her white hair rolled neatly into a bun, "was out taking care of the stock Friday morning when she heard about Homer's award. "Ed does most of the work," she confessed, "but I piddle around the place as best I can."

Will Write to Homer

Mrs. Wise says that now she must sit right down and write Homer a long letter telling him how proud she is. She's been worried about him anyway, for on October 22, he was wounded for the third time since shipping overseas. "It wasn't really serious, though," she added.

The action which heroized Homer occurred near Magliano, Italy, on June 14, 1944.

From The Town Talk (Alexandria, Louisiana) June 1, 1945

BATON ROUGE VET TOURING NATION WITH BOND SHOW

Jaycees to Sponsor "Here's Your Infantry" June 16

One of the most decorated and outstanding of this war's Doughboys, Technical Sergeant Homer Lee Wise of Baton Rouge, whose bride is the former Madolyn DiSesa of Stamford, Connecticut, appears in "Here's Your Infantry" now touring the United States for the 7th War Loan. The show will be here on June 16 under the sponsorship of the Junior Chamber of Commerce.

Decorated with the Medal of Honor, the nation's highest military award, for a series of conspicuously gallant acts in combat against the Germans in Italy on June 14, 1944, the big Louisiana infantryman takes part in a realistic battle demonstration that shows how your heroic Doughboys fight in Europe and the Pacific.

The thrice-wounded sergeant also won the Silver Star for gallantry, the Bronze Star Medal for heroism, and the Combat Infantryman Badge for exemplary conduct in action against the enemy. He wears the Purple Heart with two Oak Leaf Clusters for his three wounds, the Good Conduct Medal, the American Defense Ribbon, and the European Theater Ribbon with four battle stars.

His top-ranking ribbon, designating a holder of the Medal of Honor, has five white stars on a blue background.

Will Sell More Bonds

Commenting on the war bond tour of "Here's Your Infantry," battle-experienced Sergeant Wise says: "Sure, let's show America how the infantry fights. "Here's Your Infantry" will probably sell more war bonds than anything else could. This is the way we had to fight over there. And every real front-line infantryman is a hero, don't forget, whether he was decorated or not."

Composed of battle veterans from all our combat fronts, 25 "Here's Your Infantry" teams are presented for the tour by Army Ground Forces and the Treasury Department. The 25 teams stage the outdoor sham attack with flame-throwers, mortars, blanks-firing machine guns, rifles, bazookas, and explosives.

They trained at the Infantry School, Fort Benning, Georgia, where Sergeant Wise is permanently stationed.

The heroic Louisiana Infantryman used four Infantry weapons when he won the Medal of Honor. Leading his squad of riflemen in the attack against the Germans near Magliano, he dashed forward under fire and killed with his .45-caliber submachinegun three of the enemy trying to set up an automatic weapon to fire against his squad's unprotected flank.

Again, he fired 15 rifle grenades from an exposed position against Germans concealed and firing in a gully. When the grenades were used up, and the enemy was dead or fleeing, he pursued them, shooting his submachinegun from the hip. Later, he stood up in a hail of enemy fire while firing an automatic rifle against enemy machine guns aiming at his squad, and knocked out the German gun.

When his squad fought forward, it again was pinned down by German machinegun fire. Then Sergeant Wise leaped on an American tank that was under fire and sent 750 bullets from its machinegun against the German positions. His squad and company fought ahead and took their objective. That was part of one day's fighting by the sergeant.

Regarding his combat in the 36th Infantry Division in Italy and France during his 22 months overseas, Sergeant Wise looked back on his intrepid fighting actions and smiled. He said: "I guess I just never slowed up. From the night we hit them at Salerno to the day I left combat near Strasbourg, I tried to give the enemy hell."

Now 28 years old, the battle veteran was a service station manager in Louisiana and Texas for the De Luxe Oil Company before entering the Army in 1941. His grandmother is Mrs. Hattie Wise, Route 4, Baton Rouge. He was married in Stamford, where his wife lived at 19 First Street, last February 19 after returning to this country in January.

Sergeant Wise won the Silver Star in Italy on January 7, 1944, for a reconnaissance mission under fire on the icy slopes of a mountain. The day after the invasion of Southern France, he won the Bronze Star on August 16, 1944, for capturing with six other Doughboys, a German motor park, and 32 prisoners.

Last year was a busy one for Sergeant Wise. He not only earned his three decorations for heroism but also was wounded three times and fought in four campaigns.

Buried in Saint John's Cemetery, 25 Camp Avenue, Darien, Connecticut; Zone 4, Lot 9, Grave 1. Photos by the author.

HOMER L WISE
MEDAL OF HONOR
1ST SGT US ARMY
WORLD WAR II
FEB 27 1917   APR 22 1974

PRIVATE FIRST CLASS FRANK PETER WITEK; MARINE CORPS

December 10, 1921 (Derby, CT) – August 3, 1944; 22 years old
Unmarried
Enlisted on January 20, 1942.
Serial number 353244.

Born to Jacob D. (1866-1939) and Honorada "Nora" S. Jedlos Witek (1892-1962) [both parents were born in Poland]. Four sisters, Stephanie M. Witek Mulsoff (1911-2008), Constantine "Connie" (1919-1989), Genevieve S. (1923-1986), and Jean Witek Christy (1923-2006). Three brothers, John J. (1913-1983), Joseph M. (1915-1952), Stanley P. (1916-1990).

The family moved from Derby, Connecticut, to Chicago when he was 9. He graduated high school there and went to work as a laborer at the Standard Transformer Company.

Photo courtesy of the U.S. Marine Corps. Public domain.

MEDAL OF HONOR CITATION

AWARDED FOR ACTIONS DURING: World War II
BRANCH OF SERVICE: Marine Corps
UNIT: 1st Battalion, 3rd Marine Division
AGE ON THE DAY OF THE EVENT: 22
CITATION:

The President of the United States of America, in the name of Congress, takes pride in presenting the Medal of Honor (Posthumously) to Private First Class Frank Peter Witek, United States Marine Corps Reserve, for conspicuous gallantry and intrepidity at the risk of his life above and beyond the call of duty while serving with the First

Battalion, Ninth Marines, Third Marine Division, during the Battle of Finegayen at Guam, Marianas, on 3 August 1944. When his rifle platoon was halted by heavy surprise fire from well-camouflaged enemy positions, Private First Class Witek daringly remained standing to fire a full magazine from his automatic at point-blank range into a depression housing Japanese troops, killing eight of the enemy and enabling the greater part of his platoon to take cover. During his platoon's withdrawal for consolidation of lines, he remained to safeguard a severely wounded comrade, courageously returning the enemy's fire until the arrival of stretcher-bearers and then covering the evacuation by sustained fire as he moved backward toward his own lines. With his platoon again pinned down by a hostile machinegun, Private First Class Witek, on his own initiative, moved forward boldly to the reinforcing tanks and infantry, alternately throwing hand grenades and firing as he advanced to within five to ten yards of the enemy position, and destroying the hostile machinegun emplacement and an additional eight Japanese before he himself was struck down by an enemy rifleman. His valiant and inspiring action effectively reduced the enemy's firepower, thereby enabling his platoon to attain its objective, and reflects the highest credit upon Private First Class Witek and the United States Naval Service. He gallantly gave his life for his country.

Presentation date and details: May 20, 1945, by General Alexander A. Vandegrift, Marine Corps Commander, at a public ceremony in Soldiers' Field, Chicago, Illinois.

Photo courtesy of the Chicago Tribune May 21, 1945

Witek Memorial Park, Stillbelt Lane, Derby, Connecticut, is named for him. The park was dedicated in a ceremony on May 29, 1999. Photos with this description were taken by the author.

Medal of Honor Recipient PFC Frank P. Witek Memorial Park is a 144-acre park on the east side of the city on property that was formerly a reservoir. It was one of the earliest settled areas of the city, dating back to the 1600s. In 1859, the burgeoning Borough of Derby on the west side of town needed a stable water supply, and the Birmingham Water Company bought the land in the area, which was mostly meadows and farmland. They dammed the brooks in the area to create the reservoirs, which they continued to own and utilize until selling it to the City in 1997. On May 29, 1999, the city dedicated the park in honor of PFC Witek. In addition to two beautiful ponds, the complex also contains trails for walking and hiking. On September 16, 2006, the City officially opened two new soccer fields on part of the property.

In 2011, bronze plaques in the park honoring Witek were stolen. His brother Leonard said, "Didn't you read what it was for? What the honor is? A person got killed for this, and you're taking it away?" The monuments in the pictures that follow are replacements for the stolen plaques, which were never recovered.

This Park and Land is Dedicated
To the Memory of

Frank P. Witek

Private First Class
United States Marine Corps Reserve

Born in the City of Derby, Connecticut 10 December 1921
Killed in Action on the Island of Guam 3 August 1944
Posthumously Awarded

The Medal of Honor

20 May 1945
Dedicated by the Citizens of Derby
Marc J. Garofalo, Mayor
29 May 1999
Semper Fidelis

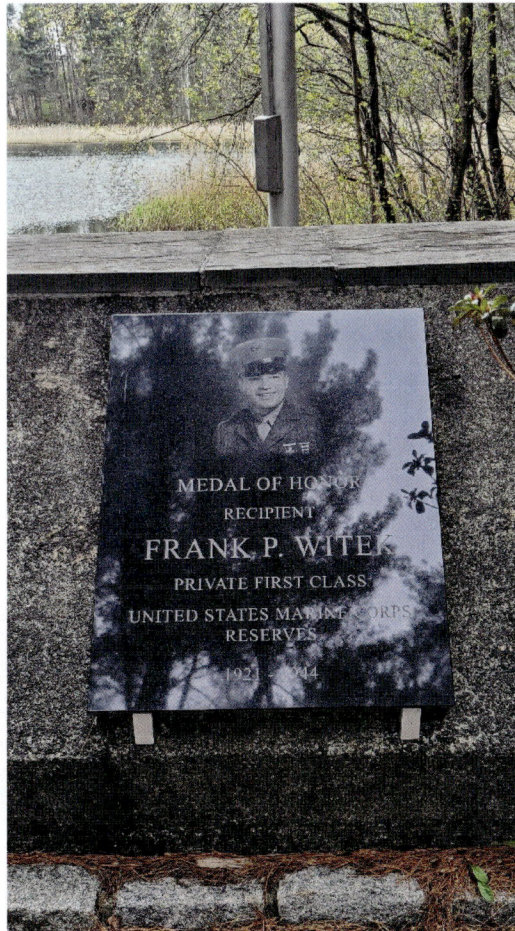

MEDAL OF HONOR
RECIPIENT
FRANK P. WITEK
PRIVATE FIRST CLASS
UNITED STATES MARINE CORPS
RESERVES
1921   1944

CITATION

Private First Class Frank P. Witek
United States Marine Corps Reserve

For conspicuous gallantry and intrepidity at the risk of his life above and beyond the call of duty while serving with the First Battalion, Ninth Marines, Third Marine Division, during the Battle of Finegayan at Guam, Marianas, on 3 August 1944. When his rifle platoon was halted by heavy surprise fire from well camouflaged enemy positions, Private First Class Witek daringly remained standing to fire a full magazine from his automatic weapon point-blank range into a depression housing Japanese troops, killing eight of the enemy and enabling the greater part of his platoon to take cover. During his platoon's withdrawal for consolidation of lines, he remained to safeguard a severely wounded comrade, courageously returning the enemy's fire until the arrival of stretcher bearers and then covering the evacuation by sustained fire as he moved backward toward his own lines. With his platoon again pinned down by a hostile machine-gun, Private First Class Witek, on his own initiative, moved forward boldly ahead of the reinforcing tanks and infantry, alternately throwing hand grenades and firing as he advanced to within five to ten yards of the enemy position, destroying the hostile machine-gun emplacement and an additional eight Japanese before he, himself, was struck down by an enemy rifleman. His valiant and inspiring action effectively reduced the enemy's firepower, thereby enabling his platoon to attain its objective, and reflects the highest credit upon Private First Class Witek and the United States Naval Service. He gallantly gave his life for his country.

Franklin D. Roosevelt
President of the United States

The U.S.S. Witek (DD/EDD-848) was a Gearing-class destroyer named for him. It was decommissioned in 1968.

U.S.S. Witek (DD/EDD-848); photo courtesy of Navsource.org

From the Quad-City Times (Davenport, Iowa) May 31, 1976

GUAM HERO REMEMBERED

Medal Of Honor Winner Buried At RI Arsenal [note: RI = Rock Island]

The "bold" and "daring" heroics of a good-natured 22-year-old Marine who gave his life for his country on Guam in World War II will be recounted in services today at the Rock Island National Cemetery.

Private First Class Frank Peter Witek was killed Aug. 8, 1944, "in the line of duty in the Battle of Finegayen at Guam, Marianas Islands."

He is the only congressional Medal of Honor recipient among the more than 9,800 persons buried in the cemetery on Arsenal Island.

Relatives said it was the decision of Witek's mother to have him buried in the Rock Island Cemetery because it was the nearest national cemetery to Chicago, where the family lived then.

In the services at 10:45 a.m. today, Capt. Donald L. Dickerson, Moline, U.S. Marine Corps, will read a citation summarizing Witek's achievements.

Interviewed by telephone, a sister of Witek, Mrs. Harold Christy of Chicago, recalled Frank as "the type who would do almost anything for his friends."

He was, she said, "very handsome" and "extremely neat" but, according to friends, "He didn't like to polish his rifle."

He was about 5-11 in height with a slender build, "but not thin." He had brown hair and brown eyes. He was "very proud" of the Marine Corps.

He attended Crane Tech High School, Chicago, "a couple of years." He had, Mrs. Christy said, a "very good mind," but after the attack on Pearl Harbor, he could not wait to enlist.

With much reluctance but with considerable insistence from the son, his mother signed papers so he could join the Marines shortly after the Pearl Harbor attack.

Friends, Mrs. Christy recalled, said that on the day he was killed, he had remarked, "This is going to be my last day."'

Witek, she said, "was not belligerent at all. He was extremely kind and good-hearted, and he was always telling Mom not to worry."

A destroyer was named the U.S.S. Witek after him. It was commissioned on April 2, 1945, and decommissioned Sept. 16, 1968. A camp and a baseball field on Guam also were named in his honor.

Meantime, a new white marble marker with a Medal of Honor emblem and gold lettering has been placed at Witek's grave, according to Claude E. Arnold, superintendent of the national cemetery.

The citation says Witek is honored "for conspicuous gallantry and intrepidity at the risk of his life above and beyond the call of duty while serving at Guam."

Witek, according to the citation, "daringly remained standing to fire a full magazine from his automatic (weapon) at point-blank range into a depression housing Japanese troops when his rifle platoon was halted by heavy surprise fire from well-camouflaged enemy positions, killing eight of the enemy and enabling the greater part of his platoon to take cover."

During his platoon's withdrawal for consolidation of lines, Witek "remained to safeguard a severely wounded comrade, courageously returning the enemy's fire until the arrival of stretcher bearers, and then covering the evacuation by sustained fire as
he moved backward toward his own lines."

With his platoon again "pinned down by hostile machine gun," Witek, on his initiative, "moved forward boldly to the reinforcing tanks and infantry, alternately throwing hand grenades and firing as he advanced to within five to 10 yards of the enemy position," and destroying the hostile machine gun emplacement and an additional eight Japanese before he himself was struck down by an enemy rifleman."

The citation concludes that Witek's "valiant and inspiring action effectively reduced the enemy's firepower, thereby enabling his platoon to attain its objective, and reflects the highest credit upon (him) and the United States Naval Service. He gallantly gave his life for his country."

He was born December 10, 1921, in Derby, Connecticut, a city of about 13,000 near New Haven. Distant cousins of his still reside there.

He entered the military service on January 20, 1942. His parents are deceased. The father, Jacob, died while the family lived in Connecticut. They later moved to Chicago.

Witek's body was returned to the United States for burial on January 19, 1949.

Military sources said Witek was one of two Marine Medal of Honor winners in the Battle of Guam. The other was then Capt. Louis H. Wilson Jr., who now is a General in command of the Marine Corps.

Besides Mrs. Christy, two brothers, another sister, and two nieces of Witek are expected to attend the ceremonies.

The brothers are John J. and C. Paul, and the sister is Mrs. Stanley (Stephanie) Musolff, all of Chicago. The nieces are Linda and Susan, daughters of Mrs. Christy.

Another brother, Stanley, lives in Madeira Beach, Florida, and will not be
able to attend.

CAPTAIN * ERI DAVIDSON WOODBURY; ARMY

* Brevet promotion to Captain.

May 30, 1837 (Francistown, NH) – April 14, 1928 (Cheshire, CT); 90 years old

Married Ann A. Jarvis (1849-1877) on July 8, 1873, in Cheshire, Connecticut.

Two sons, Roger A. (1875-1958) and Sanford J. (1876-1946).

Remarried Emma McChesney (1859-1933).

One adopted daughter, Rose E. (1904-1986).

Enlisted on February 9, 1865, in St. Johnsbury, Vermont.

Wounded on April 8, 1865, at Appomattox Court House, Virginia.

Discharged on June 21, 1865.

Born to William H. (1808-1881) and Hannah Davidson Woodbury (1812-1849). Three brothers, Adoniram J. (1833-1877), Samuel S. (1839-1907), and Roger [Civil War veteran wounded at Petersburg] (1841-1903). Four sisters, Sallie D. Woodbury Scott (1835-1899), Hannah R. (1843-1849), Mary Ann H. (1845-1847), and Rebecca (1847-1847).

Photo (left) courtesy of the National Park Service. Photo (right) courtesy of FindAGrave.com.

MEDAL OF HONOR CITATION

AWARDED FOR ACTIONS DURING: Civil War

BRANCH OF SERVICE: Army

UNIT: Company E, 1st Vermont Cavalry

DATE OF ISSUE AND PRESENTATION: October 26, 1864

AGE ON THE DAY OF THE EVENT: 27

CITATION:

The President of the United States of America, in the name of Congress, takes pleasure in presenting the Medal of Honor to Sergeant Eri Davidson Woodbury, United States Army, for extraordinary heroism on 19 October 1864, while serving with Company E, 1st Vermont Cavalry, in action at Cedar Creek, Virginia. During the regiment's charge, when the enemy was in retreat, Sergeant Woodbury encountered four Confederate infantrymen retreating. He drew his saber and ordered them to surrender, overcoming by his determined actions their willingness to further resist. They surrendered to him together with their rifles and the 12th North Carolina (Confederate States of America) regimental flag.

<u>Location of the Medal</u>: Cheshire Historical Society, 43 Church Drive, Cheshire, Connecticut.

Photos by the author with thanks to the Cheshire Historical Society.

This photo above is attached to the back of the frame, holding the medal. The medal, in its case, is secured, and the back is unable to be read, thus the picture. The inscription on the medal reads, "The Congress to Sergeant Eri D. Woodbury, E, 1st Vt. Cav Vols, Cedar Creek, VA, Oct 19, 1865."

Eri Woodbury's Medal of Honor. Photo by the author.

From the "Biographical sketches of the Class of 1863, Dartmouth College" published by the Class of 1903.

Eri Woodbury was a descendant of "The Old Planters," John and William Woodbury, who came from England in 1628 and settled in Beverly, Massachusetts. In the words of the historian of the family, "few enterprises of great pith and moment were set on foot in the colony except a Woodbury was of the party." Eri graduated from Dartmouth in the Class of 1863. Before graduation, he had taught school for the winters in New Hampshire, Massachusetts, and for a short time in Vermont. Although he had thus early chosen for his life work the quiet life of a teacher, nevertheless soon after graduation, impelled by the same patriotic feelings that had animated his Revolutionary ancestors, he rushed to his country's defense and enlisted as a Private in Company E, First Vermont Cavalry, of which Company his classmate, Oliver T. Cushman, was then Captain. He participated in every action of the Cavalry Corps under Sheridan from that time until the end of the war. In the Battle of the Wilderness, his horse was shot under him. He was promoted From Private to First Sergeant on July 1, 1864, and made Acting First Sergeant. In August, his Division, the Third Cavalry, was sent with Sheridan into the Shenandoah Valley. In all the engagements of that campaign, the First Vermont was conspicuous. On October 19, 1864, in the Battle of Cedar Creek, to which Sheridan made his famous "twenty-mile ride," Sergeant Woodbury was in command of his company, and General George A. Custer was commanding the Division. In the fight, Woodbury captured the battle flag of the Twelfth North Carolina Infantry and, two days later, with others who had taken flags, was sent to Washington with General Custer to turn over to the War Department the captured colors. For this exploit, he received twenty days' furlough, the Medal in Bronze from Congress, and, from Governor Smith of Vermont, a commission as Second Lieutenant in Company E. He was at once transferred to the command of Company B, and soon afterward, while still in command, was placed in the Adjutant's office as Acting Adjutant. Though urged to accept an Adjutant's commission, he preferred to remain with his company. In March 1865, he was promoted to First Lieutenant and shortly afterward Captain by Brevet "For gallant and meritorious service in the Field." Two horses were shot under him while on a charge with his regiment at the Battle of Five Forks. He was there made a prisoner but succeeded in making his escape before his captors took him from the field. In the Battle of Appomattox Station, Virginia, the evening before Lee's surrender, in a charge led by the gallant Custer, Woodbury was struck by a fragment from a shell which knocked him from his horse, passed through his left arm near the shoulder, across the breast, cutting open the jacket and shirt without scratching the skin, then took off half of the right band. Captain Woodbury was mustered out with his regiment on June 21, 1865. At the close of the war, bearing with him a hero's scars of battle, he again took up the teacher's occupation and went to Cheshire, Connecticut, as a classical teacher in The Cheshire Military Academy. Five years later, he became Head Master. In 1874, he moved to Denver, Colorado, but two years later, he returned to the Academy as Vice Principal. In 1892, he went to Florida to give personal attention to fruit growing, in which he had been engaged for ten years. But after a little more than a year's absence, he was induced by the Trustees to return and resume his place as Vice Principal, and in June 1896, he was elected Principal. So that, with two short breaks, he has occupied various positions in the same institution for thirty-eight years (1903). The Academy, corporate name "Episcopal Academy of Connecticut," is one of the most famous in New England. It was founded by Bishop Seabury in 1794 and has educated many of our most distinguished men. Mr. Woodbury's long service has left a distinct impress for good upon the school. He was long its classical teacher, is a master of discipline, yet with the power to inspire the affectionate regard of his pupils. In politics, he is an ardent Republican. In college, he was a member of the Delta Kappa Epsilon fraternity and of the Phi Beta Kappa. He was married July 8, 1873, to Ann Augusta Jarvis of Cheshire, who died April 12, 1877, leaving two children, Roger Atwater, born in Denver, January 10, 1875, and Sanford Jarvis, born in the same city, August 30, 1876. Professor Woodbury has given all of his sons a good education but did not send any of them to Dartmouth. His elder son is an Amherst (Massachusetts) Agricultural College man and is a successful horticulturist and pomologist in Florida, where he and his father have a valuable farm and are doing a large and profitable business in raising fruits for northern markets. This son has a daughter who is six years old. The other two sons are successful and well-to-do farmers in Cheshire, Conn. The young son is not married. After the service, Eri Woodbury was the headmaster of the Episcopal Academy in Cheshire from 1896 to 1903. It's now called the Cheshire Academy.

From Beyer, W. F., & Keydel, O. F. (2000). Deeds of valor: How America's Civil War Heroes won The Congressional Medal of Honor. Smithmark Publishers.

The following tell of interesting episodes centering around the colors, Federal and Confederate, at the long-drawn-out and bloody battle of Cedar Creek.

Early in the engagement, the standard of the Fifteenth New Jersey Infantry had been captured by the enemy. The loss became quickly known among the Union troops, and several unsuccessful attempts to recapture the flag were made. Corporal John Walsh of Company D, Fifth New York Cavalry, during one of the subsequent fierce charges, had the good fortune to succeed where so many others had failed. During the heat of a hand-to-hand struggle, he noticed a Confederate color-bearer carrying a flag which he at once recognized as the one taken from the New Jersey boys. With a sudden rush, he made for the rebel guard, overpowered him, and wrenched the trophy from him. All of this was done on the spur of the moment and so quickly that the Confederate color guard and his comrades hardly realized what had happened until it was all over and the daring corporal with his precious prize was back within the Union lines.

It was an impressive scene when, after the battle, the New Jersey regiment was called out on parade and, in the presence of General Sherman, received back its colors at the hands of Corporal Walsh.

The last decisive charge was made in the afternoon between three and four o'clock. It was by far the bloodiest of the entire battle and put the individual bravery of the Union soldier to its highest test. The conduct of Private Martin Wambsgan of Company D, Ninetieth New York Infantry, furnishes a good illustration. While on the advance, the color-bearer of his regiment was killed – shot through the head. He fell forward on his face and landed squarely on the flag, which was riddled with bullet holes, while the staff had been shot in two.

When this occurred, Private Wambsgan was only a few feet away from the unfortunate flag-bearer. With one leap, he was at his side, pulled the colors from under him, and, yelling as loudly as he possibly could, waved the flag over his head. Then he ran to the front of his regiment, where he took post during the remainder of the fight, holding the colors aloft, the piece of pole and his arm serving as a flag-staff. At the time the color-bearer was killed, and the colors went down, the regiment showed signs of wavering, but Private Wambsgan's quick action renewed the energy
and courage of the men and contributed materially to the success of the charge.

During the same charge, when the enemy was already in full retreat, Sergeant Eri D. Woodbury of Company E, First Vermont Cavalry, encountered four Confederate infantrymen retreating toward a small knoll. He drew his saber and ordered them to
surrender. The rebels hesitated but did not raise their rifles. The actions of one made Woodbury suspicious, and scanning him more closely, he perceived that he was trailing behind him a flag rolled on his staff.

"Give up that flag!" Woodbury demanded.

Naturally, the Confederate objected, but the determination of the Union cavalryman soon convinced him that resistance would be folly, and reluctantly, he handed over his colors. The brave sergeant then rode proudly back to his regiment, where he handed over his prisoners and captured colors and received the commendation of his superior officers.

CONGRESSIONAL MEDAL OF HONOR
SERGEANT ERI DAVIDSON WOODBURY
FIRST VERMONT CAVALRY
OCT. 19, 1864
CIVIL WAR

The Medal of Honor Plaza and "Living Classroom"
Dedicated May 26, 1996

Alfred G. Adinolfi, U.S. Air Force, Chairman and Town Councilman

S. Kenneth Baril, U.S. Air Force   Henry E. Carson, U.S. Army
Harold Mosher, U.S. Army   Lori Rusnack, Parks and Recreation Commissioner
John White, U.S. Navy   Thomas Williams, U.S. Air Force

Robert Ceccolini, Parks and Recreation Director   Kevin Simmons, Parks and Recreation Staff
Sandra Mouris, Mayor   Monument Design: Jerry Lodynsky

The Medal of Honor Living Classroom plaque

The Medal of Honor Living Classroom monument

Buried in St. Peter's Episcopal Cemetery, 59 Main Street, Cheshire, Connecticut; Section B, Lot 37, Grave 3. Photos by the author.

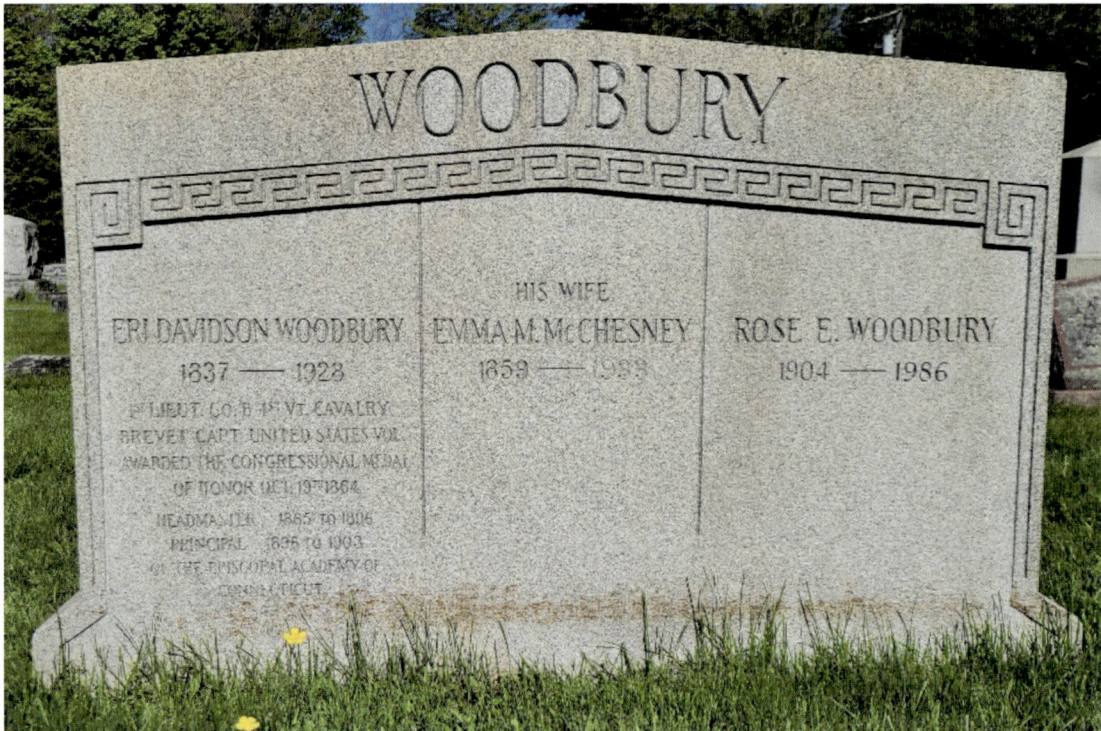

PRIVATE ROBERT WRIGHT; ARMY

1830 (Armagh, Ireland) – October 22, 1885 (Paterson, NJ); 55 years old
Married to Maria (1842-1919)
Three sons, John K. (1863-?), Robert R. (1873-?), and Joseph (1880-?).
Three daughters, Mary (1865-?), Ellen (1867-?), and Emma J. (1875-?).
Enlisted on April 13, 1861 in Woodstock, Connecticut.
Mustered out on May 22, 1863, in Albany, New York.

Parent and sibling information are unknown.

MEDAL OF HONOR CITATION

AWARDED FOR ACTIONS DURING: Civil War
BRANCH OF SERVICE: Army
UNIT: Company G, 14th U.S. Infantry
DATE OF ISSUE: November 25, 1869 (5 years later)
AGE ON THE DAY OF THE EVENT: 34
CITATION:

The President of the United States of America, in the name of Congress, takes pleasure in presenting the Medal of Honor to Private Robert Wright, United States Army, for gallantry in action on 1 October 1864, while serving with Company G, 14th U.S. Infantry, in action at Chapel House Farm, Virginia.

From The Morning Call (Paterson, New Jersey) October 23, 1885

SUDDEN DEATH

Was It Opium? Robert Wright, of Beech Street, Dies in a Very Suspicious Manner

Thirty-one years ago, Robert Wright left Armagh, Ireland, and came to this country to make his fortune. At the breaking out of the war, he enlisted in the Union Army and served faithfully until the close, when he was honorably mustered out. Coming to Paterson, he, after some years, was variously employed. He started to work at the Rolling Mill and has been employed there since. His long and faithful service was rewarded by the firm with considerable respect, which has been exhibited during the last few years, by allowing him certain 'liberties' which are not enjoyed by the other employees. For instance, he was allowed to go out of the mill during working hours and go and come pretty much just as he felt like doing. More recently, however, he has abused these privileges by continually going out and getting whisky to such an extent that it was noticeable and caused his wife considerable alarm lest he should lose his work. It is asserted, though, that these occasions were infrequent, as he would teetotal for a year or so at a stretch and then go on a big spree, during which, while not actually absenting himself from the works, he would be continually running out for a horn, and so keeping himself in a prolonged muddle, without losing his employment. This was the easier, as his work was neither laborious nor constant but consisted chiefly in giving out the oil and being around the place somewhat in the capacity of a day watchman. On Saturday last, the employees of the works were paid off, and Wright soon after began to drink but, as usual, went to work at the beginning of the week and worked alone until Wednesday, when Mr. John Cooke, Jr., noticing that the man was sick, told him that he had better go home and lie down. At this, Mr. Wright quit work but did not arrive home until about seven o'clock that night, decidedly under the influence of liquor. The deceased, when he reached home, handed his wife a bottle containing about a gill of whisky, at the same time requesting her to send out for another gill, promising that if she would do so, that he would not go out again. As Mrs. Wright preferred that he should he should stay home, she did get another gill of whisky so that her husband drank two gills of whisky after coming home. The house occupied by the Wrights is a two-story frame with a basement and was built by Mr. Wright as a member of the Celtic Building and Loan Association. The basement, which is floored, is used as a kitchen, but the walls are unplastered and of hard stone; leading from it to the rooms above is the ladder contrivance in place of a stair, the steps being wide apart and very dangerous, so much so that any but a nimble person would be liable to make a miss-step and be dashed down against the projecting corners of the stone wall. It was into this basement that the deceased went when he came home, and it was here that he spent the evening. For many years, Wright has complained of terrible pain in his heart, and on occasions when the pain would become unbearable, he would ask his wife to place her ear against his breast and listen to the working of his heart at the same time, saying, "I am sure this will take me off, sudden, someday." Mrs. Wright described the action of the heart by saying that "when he would draw a breath a 'fizzing' noise was made, and when he expelled the air, it would 'gurgle' as though there was a hole in the windpipe" the deceased on such occasions saying, "Oh, this is killing me."

As previously described, Wright came home last Wednesday night and drank two gills of whisky, sitting in the basement until quite late, his wife meanwhile frequently coming in and out to keep him company. As the hours grew towards morning, she bestirred herself as to how she should get him upstairs, but eventually had to abandon the idea: as he was simply helpless, and his weight (200 lbs.) and the awkward stair prevented her from attempting such a feat. Accordingly, she fetched a roll of carpets for him to lie on and a pillow for his head, thinking that it would be far safer for him to lie there till morning than to attempt the risk of getting him up the dangerous stairway. During the evening, he complained of "the old pain," and his wife had frequently given him hot coffee to soothe and quiet him; but, as the attacks were frequent and hitherto had resulted harmlessly, she never thought of any special danger, and hence, felt no alarm, About three o'clock in the morning, she noticed that her husband had grown worse, and calling her daughter, Minnie, told her to get upstairs and waken a Mr. Falls, a tenant occupying the top floor. When Mr. Falls saw the sick man, he went for Dr. O'Grady, who in a little time was on hand, and promptly assured the family that the man was beyond his skill, being, in fact, dead. The above is the statement of Mrs. Wright, an intelligent, middle-aged woman of perhaps forty-five or six. She indignantly denies that she gave him laudanum or anything else save the hot coffee during the evening. The lady is the mother of eight children, three by her first husband and five by Mr. Wright, the latter being small and helpless. The woman is paralyzed with grief and is certainly honest and thorough in her sorrow, though evidently dazed at the suddenness of her loss. The deceased was a member of the "Redmen" but belonged to no other benevolent organization. The house is but partially paid for so that the five little children, together with the awful suddenness of the death, makes the event one of peculiar sadness.

The statement Doctor O'Grady places the affair in altogether a different light and presents the case as one of fatal carelessness by an overdose of laudanum. The doctor says that when he arrived, he noticed that the man was frothing at the mouth, apparently dying from the effects of an overdose of poison. He did all that was to be done, but it was too late. The doctor left and notified Coroner Hopson, who proceeded to the house and began to investigate the cause. He inquired of Mrs. Wright what she had given her husband, and she replied that she had given him nothing but coffee and was totally unconscious of what had caused his death. Just before this, however, she admitted to Dr. O'Grady that she had given her husband's dose of laudanum to quiet him. The doctor inquired how large a dose she had given
him, whereupon the woman replied: 'Oh, I don't know, I did not measure it; I just poured it out in a cup and gave it to him." The doctor called for the bottle and found that it still contained about an ounce of laudanum.

Mrs. Wright, in reply to further questioning, admitted that she had given her husband about as much as there was in the bottle, which was really enough to kill two men. The Coroner, after learning the above facts, considered an investigation necessary and accordingly empaneled a jury and ordered Drs. Grady and Myers to hold an autopsy, which was done at 10:30 yesterday morning. The result of their examination proved beyond a doubt that the deceased had come to his death through an overdose of laudanum but removed the contents of the stomach for analysis. The jury viewed the body during the afternoon, and the inquest will be held at the Coroner's office on Monday night.

From The Morning Call (Paterson, New Jersey) November 7, 1885

As was expected, the coroner's jury in the case of Robert Wright disagreed when they decided to render a verdict. The majority, as well as the minority, were fully convinced that Wright died from an overdose of opium. Five of the jurors were of the opinion that no one was responsible for his death, while three argued that Mrs. Wright was criminally responsible for the death of her husband.

From The Morning Call (Paterson, New Jersey) November 21, 1885

TOO OLD A WARRIOR
TO CLAIM THE BENEFITS OF ACQUACKANONK TRIBE OF RED MEN

New System of Indexing the County Records. Proving to be a Great Benefit to Property Owners

The sad and sudden death of the brave soldier, Robert Wright, is no doubt fresh in the memory of the readers of the Call. There were few men in Paterson who had more warm friends than Robert, and those of his comrades who served with him on the battlefield speak of him as a soldier and one who, in the thickest of the fight, was always anxious for the welfare of his companions in arms. It is now nearly a month since his remains were deposited in their last resting place, and strange to say, there is
still a dispute as to the payment of the funeral expenses. It seems that on the day following his death, some member of Acquackanonk Tribe No. 56 of the Order of Red Men of this city waited upon the wife of the deceased and advised her to give her husband a decent burial; that the society would pay the expenses. Mrs. Wright did as requested, and ordered a handsome burial outfit for her beloved husband. It now turns out that Tribe No. 56 refuses to pay any part of the expenses on the grounds that the deceased had made false representations as to his age when he joined the order. Immediately after his death, the Red Men investigated not only the cause of his death but ascertained from his family his exact age and found that his age was something over fifty-five years. They then examined the books and discovered that he was only a member of the Tribe only about four years. According to the by-laws of the society, no person over forty-five years of age can become a member. Notwithstanding the fact that Mr. Wright has paid up his dues regularly ever since he joined, his helpless family is now not only debarred from receiving any assistance, but they are obliged to pay the funeral expenses, which amount to over one hundred dollars. Yesterday afternoon, a reporter of the Call interviewed Mrs. Wright as to the stories which were afloat as to the proposal of the society to pay the bill to which the members partly contributed for. The almost broken-hearted widow was inclined not to speak of the matter, saying that there was enough said already in the newspapers about her and her little family's misfortune and that any further publicity about the sad ending of her husband would but add another pang to her misery. She said, however, that the action of the Tribe was a surprise to her but that she still had hopes that the order would at least pay the funeral expenses, as he was always attentive to the meetings and took particular pride in speaking the praises of the benevolence of that organization. Among the effects found in Mr. Wright's letter-box was the following, which speaks for itself:

War Department,
ADJUTANT GENERAL'S OFFICE
Washington, Nov 29, 1869.

Sir:

Herewith I enclose the Medal of Honor which has been awarded you by the Secretary of War, under the resolution of Congress, approved July 12, 1862, "To provide for the presentation of Medals of Honor to the enlisted men of the army and volunteer forces who have distinguished or may distinguish themselves in battle during the present rebellion.

Please acknowledge its receipt.

Very respectfully, your obedient servant,
E. D. Townsend,
Adjutant General.

Private Robert Wright, Battery B, 2nd Artillery, late Private Company G, 1st Battalion, 14th Infantry, care of Commanding Officer Battery B, 2nd Artillery, Alcatraz, California.

Buried in Cedar Lawn Cemetery; 200 McLean Boulevard, Paterson, New Jersey; Section 13, Block A, Grave 419.
Photo by the author.

Made in the USA
Monee, IL
21 August 2024

b5cd8545-2396-4877-bad1-14b3148c0ed6R03